Cloud Computing using Salesforce

Build and customize applications for
your business using the Salesforce Platform

2nd Edition

Dr. Ashwini Kumar Raj

Saifullah Saifi

bpb

www.bpbonline.com

Second Revised and Updated Edition 2025

First Edition 2021

Copyright © BPB Publications, India

ISBN: 978-93-65894-592

To View Complete
BPB Publications Catalogue
Scan the QR Code:

Dedicated to

My wife Mamita
my children Ashmita and Aryan
for bearing my consistent absence in
their life while I was engrossed in writing this book
— *Dr. Ashwini Kumar Raj*

My family, especially Ammi, for
their never-ending blessings
— *Saifullah Saifi*

About the Authors

- **Dr. Ashwini Kumar Raj:** Some people are born to teach as it's in their DNA - a desire to teach what they know with a larger audience, and Ashwini exemplifies the same. He has tenacious commitment and passion for training/teaching.

  Having a decade of industry exposure, he has grown with a multi-faceted career in delivery, operation, program management, and academics. He has provided leadership and technology vision for the Academics and Delivery to the organization. He is an award winner for Delivery Monitoring and professional achievements at the organization level. He has managed many projects with implementation of Project Management practices and Six Sigma quality standards across the globe by putting his footprints in Malaysia, China, South Africa, Srilanka, Indonesia, Nigeria, and Vietnam.

  Dr Ashwini is certified on various technologies on Salesforce, Microsoft, Oracle, Cisco, Prince 2, ITIL, Six Sigma, and PMI. He is a PMI authorized coach. He is also an Amazon Best selling author.

  Currently Dr Ashwini owns a IT consulting company to build digital enterprises using Salesforce, AWS, SAP and ADM practices.

- **Saifullah Saifi:** Hope for the best, prepare for the worst. Based on this principle, Saifullah makes things happen.

  Saifullah Saifi is a passionate salesforce developer having seven years of experience in the IT Industry. In his early professional career, he started writing a blog to inspire many to learn Salesforce.

  Some of his inspiring works are the most watched and loved among Salesforce beginners. Saifullah is a proud alumnus of Aligarh Muslim University, having an MCA degree. He is currently working as a Sr Salesforce Developer with one of the top five companies and is passionate about his work. He loves teaching, writing, and giving training.

About the Reviewers

❖ **Dr. Ashish Mulajkar** is an assistant professor at MIT Academy of Engineering, Alandi, Pune. He did his MTech in embedded systems in 2014 and PhD in VLSI Design in 2022. He specializes in embedded systems, VLSI Design, IoT, and has 15 years of teaching and a year of industry experience.

His areas of interest include Embedded Systems, VLSI Design, microwave engineering, digital communication, and IoT. He has also taught several courses and authored various publications.

❖ **Darshan Chhajed** is a seasoned Salesforce professional with over 12 years of industry experience, having worked with leading multinational companies across various domains. He currently serves as a Salesforce Technical Architect at Cloudwerx and holds the prestigious Salesforce Certified Application Architect credential, along with 12+ Salesforce certifications.

Passionate about knowledge sharing and mentorship, Darshan has trained over 20 batches of fresh graduates, empowering them with hands-on Salesforce expertise. His commitment to teaching and community engagement continues to make a meaningful impact in the Salesforce ecosystem.

❖ **Rob Cowell** is a Salesforce DevOps Advocate at Gearset, the leading provider of Salesforce DevOps solutions. With a strong background as a Salesforce Developer and Application Architect, he helps teams navigate the complexities of DevOps in the Salesforce ecosystem, providing practical guidance on best practices, tooling, and automation.

As an active member of the Salesforce community, Rob is passionate about knowledge-sharing and mentorship. He regularly contributes through speaking engagements, blog posts, and community forums, offering insights that empower teams to build robust, scalable, and efficient DevOps processes. His experience spans the full software development lifecycle, from source control and CI/CD automation to release management and compliance.

Rob is also the author of Salesforce DevOps for Architects, where he distills years of experience into a comprehensive guide for technical leaders looking to implement modern DevOps practices. His work focuses on helping organizations embrace automation, continuous delivery, and iterative improvements to achieve higher-quality deployments and faster innovation.

He is a firm advocate for community-driven learning and enjoys engaging with fellow architects and developers to push the boundaries of what's possible in Salesforce DevOps.

❖ **Santosh Chitalkar** is a Salesforce Architect with over 13 years of hands-on experience in the CRM ecosystem, primarily focused on the finance and banking domain. His core expertise includes system integrations, Sales Cloud, Financial Services Cloud (FSC), and Experience Cloud. Throughout his career, he has led numerous enterprise-scale implementations, helping organizations drive digital transformation and customer success through Salesforce.

Passionate about knowledge sharing, Santosh actively mentors freshers and early-career professionals, guiding them as they embark on their Salesforce journeys. As a dedicated reader and reviewer, he offers practical insights into Salesforce literature to help others grow their understanding and skills within the platform.

Acknowledgements

I acknowledge everybody who was a part of my learning process. There is no one I dare to forget to mention but if I gratefully remember:

Ram Chandra Raj and Jamuna Raj – My parents, who started the journey of my learning.

Mamita – My loving wife for having the patience with me, for having taken yet another challenge which decreases the amount of time I can spend with her, to see me grow as an author.

Ashmita and Aryan - my children who sacrificed their personal time with me without knowing what I am doing. I hope that one day, my children can read this book and understand why I spent so much time in front of my computer. Manish Verma and Sudeep Verma to guide me in starting my Salesforce journey. Amarendra Kumar, Vinay Verma, and Nitin Paranjpe for their mentorship to grow in Salesforce Ecosystem.

Kamal Mansharamani, Shiv Sharma, and Atul Singhal for their support to continue my writing work while I perform my job.

All my friends who continued their friendship in spite of many differences, all colleagues, both seniors and juniors, who encouraged me to learn every day, and customers who helped me grow professionally.

All partners who supported and have grown with me, and all mentors who always guided me to reach my goal.

All mentees who respected me and taught me how to coach in a better way.

Salesforce Trailhead, and the Trailblazer community for making my writing job easier.

There are many more people I could thank, but time, space, and modesty compel me to stop here.

— *Dr. Ashwini Kumar Raj*

First of all, I thank the Almighty. There are a few people I want to thank for the ongoing support they have given me during the writing of this book. First and foremost, I would like to thank my family - Ammi, Abbu, Sana, Afsar, Aman, Salma, Tahura, Najm, and Lubna for their support and love. I would like to thank my friends Luqman, Qamar, Mubashshir, Daud, and Wasim for putting up with me while I was spending many weekends and evenings on writing—I could have never completed this book without their support.

I would also thank my uncles and aunts for their never-ending blessing.

This book would not have happened if I had not had the support from my mentors Atul Rai, Ashwini Raj, and friends like Danish, Surbhi, Raghav, and Karan Soni.

I acknowledge the reviewers for their role in this book.

— *Saifullah Saifi*

Preface

The world is revolving around new era of technology. Everything and everyone are talking about Cloud, Machine Learning, and Artificial Intelligence. Salesforce is also making an impact in this era. Salesforce is not only a company or a CRM, it is also a software, a platform, and a technology, which has the largest share in today's sales service and marketing industry.

This book is written for all Salesforce learners who want to contribute, learn, and earn from this ecosystem. We will cover CRM, Cloud Computing using Salesforce, how to use Salesforce, how to be a Salesforce admin, Salesforce Developer, or Salesforce Business Analyst. This book will also focus on Salesforce Cloud, its tools, how to customize hem, how to use the platform, and how to do coding in Salesforce. This book is a complete solution for a salesforce developer and admin to show how to design, develop and deploy.

Salesforce also recognized the Salesforce Trailblazer with the certification such as PD1(Platform Developer 1) and Admin. This book will also focus on a different certification. There is no book so far that can give you a manual or guide so that you can use most of Salesforce and strengthen your skills. This book is written keeping that in mind and will not only help learners to gain knowledge on Salesforce but also prepare them well for the three certifications.

Wishing you all the best, and hoping this book will definitely help you to become a certified Salesforce Admin and a Salesforce Developer.

Over the 24 chapters in this book, you will learn the following:

Chapter 1 - Introduction to Cloud Computing - Introduces basics of Cloud Computing.

Chapter 2 - Introduction to Salesforce - Discusses the fundamentals of Salesforce.

Chapter 3 - Introducing Salesforce Lightning and Salesforce Data ModelingI- Introduces the Salesforce Lightning interface.

Chapter 4 - Introducing Salesforce Customer Relationship Management - Focuses on Customer Relationship Management.

Chapter 5 - Organizational Setup - Discusses the basic of Organization set up.

Chapter 6 - Designing Applications on Salesforce - Describes designing applications on Force.com platform.

Chapter 7 - Implementing Business Processes - Introduces the salesforce business process tools and features such as Validation rule, Approval Process and different type of Lightning Flows.

Chapter 8 - Data Management - Discusses Data Management.

Chapter 9 - Report and Dashboard- Describes Data analytics using reports and Dashboards.

Chapter 10 - Security - Discusses Security and Access.

Chapter 11 - Introducing Chatter for Collaboration - Describes Collaboration using the Salesforce Chatter.

Chapter 12 - Introducing Mobile Administration - Discusses Mobile Application

Chapter 13 - Programming with APEX - Introduces Apex as Salesforce Programming language, which is also based on object-oriented programming.

Chapter 14 - SOQL and SOSL - Discusses the Salesforce query and search language with their feature and limitation known as SOQL and SOSL.

Chapter 15 - Data Manipulation Language Essentials - Introduces DML statements used in Apex and its limitations.

Chapter 16 - Trigger Essentials - Revolves around a very useful and complex automation technique based on event such as creation or updation of data known as Trigger.

Chapter 17 - Creating Visualforce Page - Discusses about the custom UI in salesforce using the Visualforce page.

Chapter 18 - Basic of Lightning Web Component - Introduces widely used most elegant framework of Salesforce UI known as LWC or lightning web component

Chapter 19 - More Customization and Less Coding - Discusses choosing the best too, coding or automation tool, for different types of problems.

Chapter 20 - Testing Essentials - Describes how testing is done in Salesforce, and how to write test class and best practice.

Chapter 21 - Apex Handler and Using Apex Class - Introduces some Apex features such as Async Apex. Future, Batchable, Scheduler, Integration , e-mail service, Web services, and also discusses web-to-case or web-to-lead.

Chapter 22 - Debugging and Deployment - Describes how to debug the project and module, how to deploy a project from testing to live org. How to install application from App Exchange.

Chapter 23 - Certificaton Exam Guide Paper 1 - Acts as the certification guide

Chapter 24 - Certificaton Exam Sample Paper 2 - Provides a sample question paper for three certifications

Code Bundle and Coloured Images

Please follow the link to download the
Code Bundle and the *Coloured Images* of the book:

https://rebrand.ly/5c345c

The code bundle for the book is also hosted on GitHub at
https://github.com/bpbpublications/Cloud-Computing-using-Salesforce-2nd-Edition.
In case there's an update to the code, it will be updated on the existing GitHub repository.

We have code bundles from our rich catalogue of books and videos available at
https://github.com/bpbpublications. Check them out!

Errata

We take immense pride in our work at BPB Publications and follow best practices to ensure the accuracy of our content to provide with an indulging reading experience to our subscribers. Our readers are our mirrors, and we use their inputs to reflect and improve upon human errors, if any, that may have occurred during the publishing processes involved. To let us maintain the quality and help us reach out to any readers who might be having difficulties due to any unforeseen errors, please write to us at :

errata@bpbonline.com

Your support, suggestions and feedbacks are highly appreciated by the BPB Publications' Family.

Piracy

If you come across any illegal copies of our works in any form on the internet, we would be grateful if you would provide us with the location address or website name. Please contact us at business@bpbonline.com with a link to the material.

If you are interested in becoming an author

If there is a topic that you have expertise in, and you are interested in either writing or contributing to a book, please visit www.bpbonline.com. We have worked with thousands of developers and tech professionals, just like you, to help them share their insights with the global tech community. You can make a general application, apply for a specific hot topic that we are recruiting an author for, or submit your own idea.

Reviews

Please leave a review. Once you have read and used this book, why not leave a review on the site that you purchased it from? Potential readers can then see and use your unbiased opinion to make purchase decisions. We at BPB can understand what you think about our products, and our authors can see your feedback on their book. Thank you!

For more information about BPB, please visit www.bpbonline.com.

Join our Discord space

Join our Discord workspace for latest updates, offers, tech happenings around the world, new releases, and sessions with the authors:

https://discord.bpbonline.com

Table of Contents

CHAPTER 1
Introduction to Cloud Computing

Introduction

Cloud is somewhere at the other end of your internet connection – a place where you can access apps and services, and where your data can be stored securely. Cloud computing is a buzz-word today in most industries. It is a model that enables consumers to hire computing resources as per their requirements. Through Cloud computing, the resources over the internet can be used from anywhere in the globe without managing them.

Structure

In this chapter, we will discuss the following topics:

- Introduction to Cloud
- Understanding Cloud computing
- History of Cloud computing

Objectives

After studying this unit, you would be able to understand the concept of Cloud. We will also discuss the history, models, and services of Cloud computing. You will be able to understand the advantages and disadvantages of Cloud computing as well. You will also be able to understand various technologies involved in Cloud computing.

Introduction to Cloud

The Cloud is unique because of the following three reasons:

- Very negligible effort is required in maintaining or managing it.
- No need to worry about its capacity as it is almost infinite in size.
- Cloud-based applications and services can be accessed from anywhere. The only need is to have a device and internet connection.

Cloud signifies moving to the Cloud, running in the Cloud, storing in the Cloud, and accessing from the Cloud.

Understanding Cloud computing

Cloud computing as defined by **US National Institute of Standards and Technology (NIST)**– *Cloud computing is a model for enabling ubiquitous, convenient, on-demand network access to a shared pool of configurable computing resources that can be rapidly provisioned and released with minimal management effort or service provider interaction.*

Cloud computing refers to internet-based computing, which involves shared resources, software, and information provided by computers and mobile devices. The following figure explores this in detail:

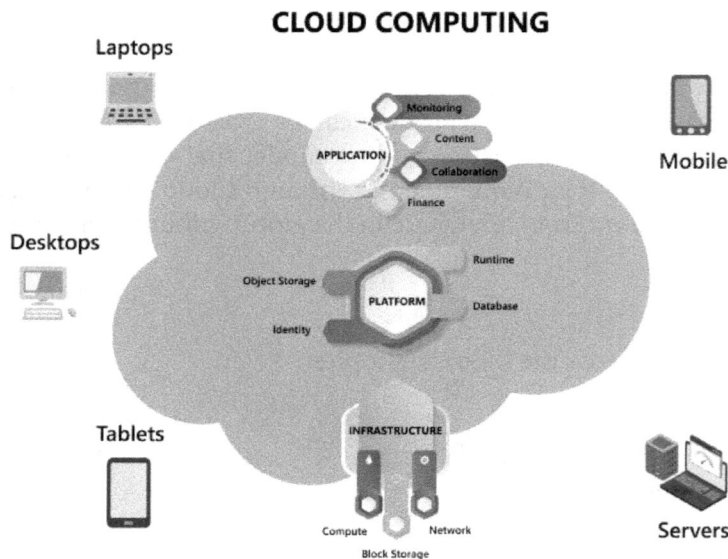

Figure 1.1: Cloud computing

Most organizations spend millions of dollars on purchasing the right software and hardware for their organization. These include not only computers and laptops, but also software and software licenses for their employees. For every new employee, a new software license must be purchased. This is expensive for any organization, whether big or small.

Many companies provide software services that an organization needs for its business processes. By connecting these companies through the internet and using their services, an organization can access all the software needed for running its business. This web-based service is called **Cloud computing**. This allows a remote machine of the Cloud-based services provider to run several business processes of a client's business. The services provided by the provider can be as simple as an ordinary word processing or more complex CRM software.

Cloud computing is one of the greatest developments in technology in recent years. Cloud computing creates virtual space and applications that can be used and shared by consumers, no matter where they are. An organization pays a subscription amount to the Cloud computing service provider and customization to access the Cloud services. To access the Cloud services is as simple as logging on to the internet.

Cloud computing refers to accessing, configuring, and manipulating the applications online. It offers applications, online data storage, and infrastructure services.

History of Cloud computing

The internet had its base in the 1960s. but in the early 1990s, it had much relevance for businesses. Over the years, internet connections went very fast and more reliable. This gave birth to a new type of company called an **Application Service Provider** (**ASP**). However, at the end of 1990s, salesforce.com introduced its multi-tenant application, which was specifically designed for the following purposes:

- To run in the Cloud
- To be accessed over the internet using a web browser
- To be used by large number of customers simultaneously at a lower cost

Cloud computing models and services

Many services and models are working behind the scenes, making the Cloud computing feasible and accessible to end-users. The following are the working models for Cloud computing:

- Deployment models
- Service models

Deployment model

The deployment model defines the type of access to the Cloud. There are four types of access to the Cloud: public, private. hybrid, and community. Let us discuss them briefly.

Public Cloud

The public Cloud allows systems and services to be easily accessible to the public. In the public Cloud, the user has no control over the resources. The public Cloud provides benefits, such as low cost and pay per usage. Public Cloud may lead to less security because of its openness.

Private Cloud

The private Cloud allows the services to be accessible within an organization. As it is private in nature, it offers increased security. Services on the private Cloud can be accessed only within the premises. In a private Cloud, service providers offer the Cloud infrastructure exclusively to a particular organization or business. This Cloud infrastructure is not provided to others. There are two types of Cloud in the private Cloud:

- **On-premises private Cloud**: This type of Cloud is hosted and maintained internally by the same company/organization.
- **Externally hosted private Cloud**: This type of Cloud is hosted and maintained externally by the third party.

Community Cloud

The community Cloud allows services to be accessible by a group of organizations. It is based on a multi-tenant architecture. The multi-tenant architecture refers to a set of resources provided over the Cloud, which can be accessed by several users across the organization. In this case, all applications run in a single logical environment. It is faster, more secure, more available, and is automatically upgraded and maintained. All patches, upgrades, updates, security, and disaster recovery improvements are made available to all customers at once.

The meaning of single tenancy architecture is that each customer is given a dedicated software stack, and each layer in its stack needs to be configured, monitored, and secured.

Hybrid Cloud

The hybrid Cloud is a mixture of a private and public Cloud. However, in this case, the critical activities are performed using a private Cloud, while the non-critical activities are performed using the public Cloud. The following figure represents the hybrid Cloud:

Figure 1.2: Hybrid Cloud

A hybrid Cloud is a combination of the number of different types of Clouds. However, the Cloud can allow data and applications to be moved from one Cloud to another. Hybrid Cloud is a combination of public Cloud, private Cloud, and community Cloud. In this case, the API is used as an interface between the public and private Clouds.

Service models

Servers, storage, network, operating system, and database are essential things to run an organization successfully. Before Cloud computing technologies, every industry needed infrastructure, platform, and software, due to which, the organizations had to make huge investments. Once Cloud computing technology evolved, all these services became available in the form of a service called **Cloud**. Now, there is no need of installation, maintenance, or upgrades. All these services are maintained by third parties called **service providers**.

Service models are the models on which Cloud computing is based. The service models can be categorized into three basic service models listed as follows:

- **Infrastructure as a Service (IaaS)**
- **Platform as a Service (PaaS)**
- **Software as a Service (SaaS)**

These three services are called **pillars of Cloud computing**. The following figure depicts the three service models of Cloud computing:

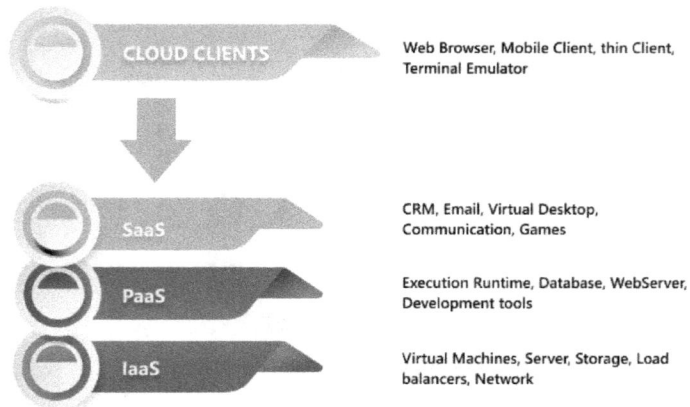

Figure 1.3: Service models of Cloud computing

Software as a Service

In this case, the software applications are managed by the Cloud services provider and can be accessed by organizations simply through a browser. The browser loads all applications of the service provider. Client businesses need not worry about licensing or server costs. Through SaaS, all software is distributed over the Cloud. There is no need to install software that are readily available over the internet. SaaS is a substantial Cloud service provided to all types of organizations without any risk of software. SaaS supports **service-oriented architecture** (**SOA**) and web services. The following figure explains the SaaS model:

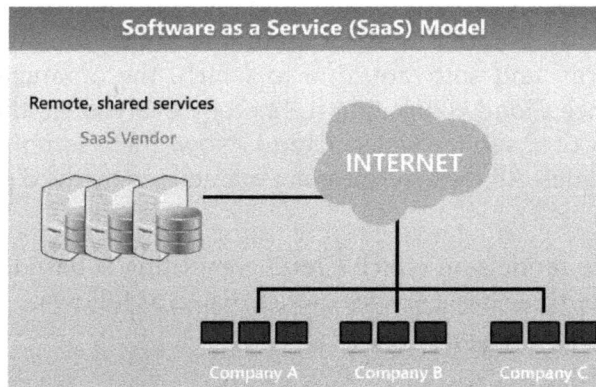

Figure 1.4: The SaaS model

The advantages of SaaS services are:

- Easy administration
- Automatic updates
- Patch management
- Same version for all users

The top Cloud providers of SaaS are:

- Abiquo
- Accelops
- Akamai
- App Dynamics
- Apprenda
- Cloud9
- Cloud Switch
- CloudTran
- Cumulux
- MegaWare

Platform as a Service

In this case, dedicated software platforms are managed by the Cloud service provider to run and develop business applications of the organization. This platform supports the creation of web applications online. There is no need for any additional software on the local computer.

PaaS means the providers offer hardware, storage, network services, and even the operating system over the Cloud. Without the platform, the application has no meaning as we need a platform to develop the apps. PaaS has many advantages, such as operating system features that can be changed and upgraded frequently by the IaaS Cloud service provider. The following figure illustrates the services offered by PaaS:

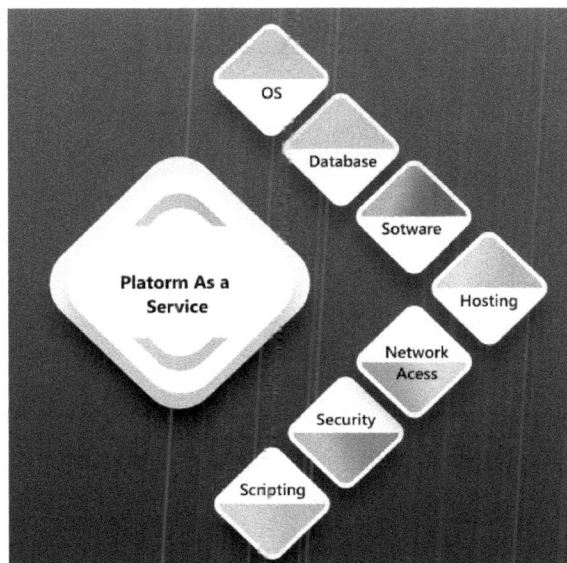

Figure 1.5: PaaS

It is like a rental service where the organization must pay to service providers on subscription. Without PaaS, every organization must arrange their own hardware, storage, network services, an operating system, adding up to the company's cost. So, using PaaS applications are built on a platform.

The main aim of the PaaS Cloud is to provide an environment for developing various applications. All tools that are required for development are provided by the PaaS service providers only.

When using PaaS features, there is no need to:

- Update the software at all
- Maintain databases
- Have a host
- Have an external support
- Possess tools for application design and development.

The following figure explains the features of PaaS.

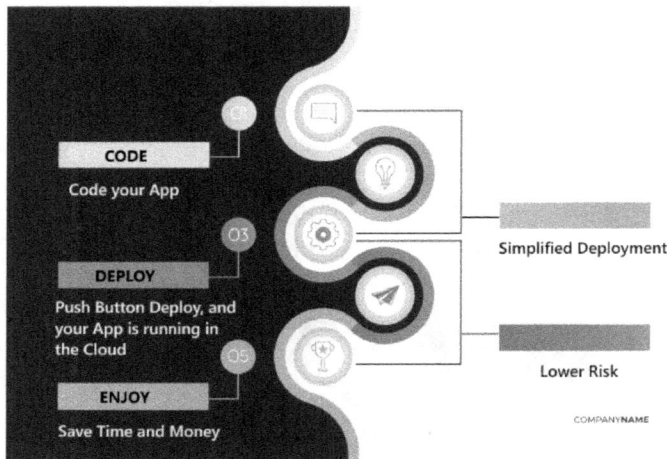

Figure 1.6: IaaS

The advantages of PaaS are as follows:

- Provides security to the data
- Provides backup to the database
- Provides customized features
- Provides a tool for faster application development without any development skill
- Requires very low maintenance cost

The top Cloud providers of PaaS are as follows:

- Amazon Web Services

- Salesforce.com
- Appistry – CloudQ Platform
- App Scale
- CA technologies

Infrastructure as a Service

IaaS means that the Cloud service providers will provide infrastructure, such as servers, storage, and hosting services, to the consumers. Servers and storage are basic services provided by any Cloud service provider. IaaS is the most advanced form of Cloud computing. In IaaS, the virtual servers are purchased by the organization along with software and hardware from the service provider on a pay-per-use basis. The following figure depicts the features of IaaS:

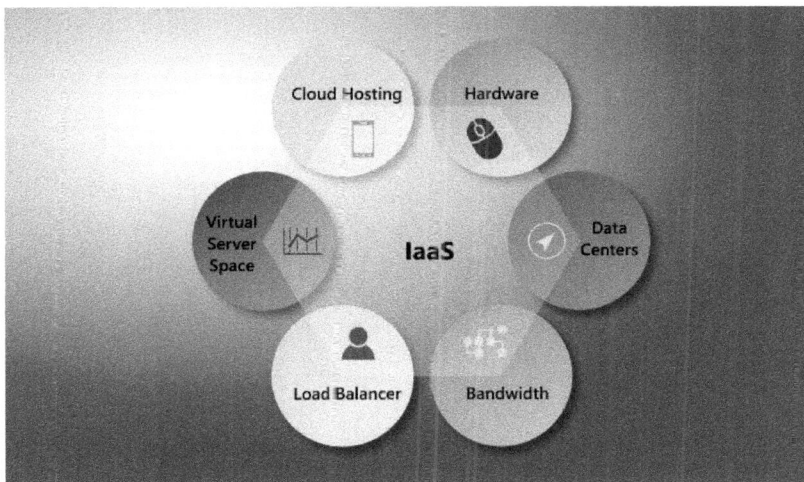

Figure 1.7: Features of IaaS

Choosing the right IaaS provider is crucial for any organization. Many Cloud service providers offer maximum size servers at low charges. Servers as well as storage will be collectively provided by IaaS providers.

The top Cloud providers of IaaS are as follows:

- Amazon Web Services
- AT&T
- Bluelock
- Cloudscaling
- DATAPIPE

Characteristics of Cloud computing

It is important to carefully select a Cloud service provider for any organization. The following characteristics must be taken into considerations while deciding the provider:

- On-demand self-service
- Broad network access
- Resource pooling
- Rapid elasticity
- Measured service
- Multi-tenant architecture

The following figure depicts various characteristics of Cloud:

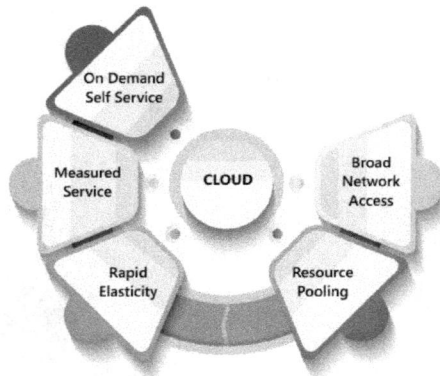

Figure 1.8: Characteristics of Cloud computing

Here are six essential characteristics of Cloud computing:

- **On-demand self-service**: On-demand self-service, such as network, server, e-mail, and mobile application are in-built in the services.
- **Broad network access**: The services can be accessed from a variety of devices, such as personal computer, laptop, tablet, and mobile phone.
- **Resource pooling**: The resources of the provider are pooled to serve multiple consumers with different physical and virtual resources dynamically. It dynamically assigns and reassigns the resources according to consumer's needs.
- **Rapid elasticity**: Cloud computing providers can provide scalable services. The user can get computing capabilities automatically as per demand.
- **Measured service**: User always gets as he demands and pays as per use.
- **Multi-tenant architecture**: A single instance of a software application serves multiple users. A set of resources can be accessed by many users across the organization with a set of permissions.

Advantages of Cloud computing

Cloud computing has many advantages. A few of them are mentioned as follows:

- Cloud computing drastically reduces the cost of hiring developers and support people.
- A user of Cloud computing services can use the processing power of the Cloud that it is a part of. So, it never falls short on processing power.
- There is no need to keep space for giant servers in the organization as Cloud computing removes the need to buy hardware. Thus, plenty of space is saved by the organization.

Disadvantages of Cloud computing

While Cloud computing has many advantages, it does have a few disadvantages as well. A few are mentioned as follows:

- It may not always be easy to fulfill the company's requirements by the Cloud computing service provider.
- Some company data may be too confidential to be stored on the Cloud.
- Few companies may find the pay-per-use model tough to handle.

Cloud computing technologies

There are few technologies working behind the Cloud computing platforms making Cloud computing reliable, usable, and flexible. These technologies are as follows:

- Virtualization
- SOA
- Grid computing
- Utility computing

Let us discuss these technologies briefly.

Virtualization

Virtualization is a technique that allows us to share a single physical instance of any resource among multiple organizations. It assigns a logical name to a physical resource and provides a pointer to that physical resource when demanded. The following figure depicts the working of virtualization:

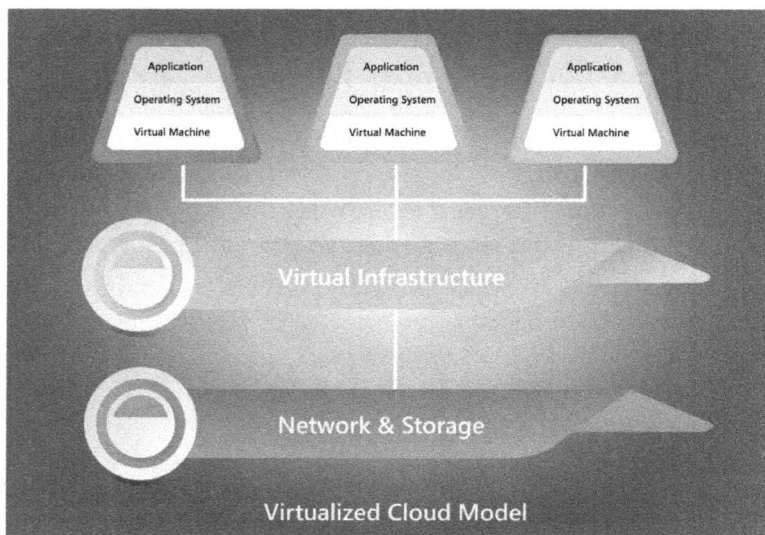

Figure 1.9: Virtualization

Service-oriented architecture

SOA helps to use applications as a service for any other application. These applications can be regardless of the type of technology, product, or vendor. Due to this, it is possible to exchange the data between applications of different vendors without any additional programming effort. The following figure represents the architecture of SOA:

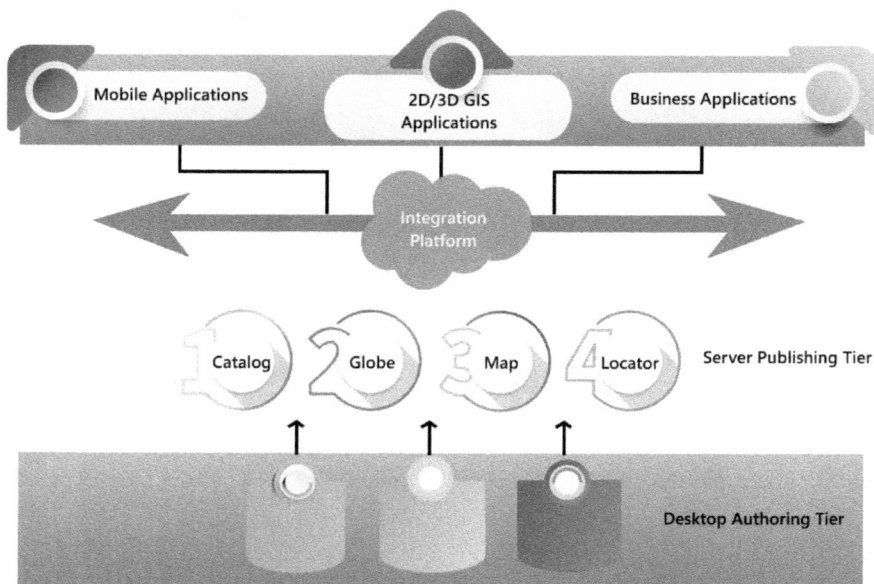

Figure 1.10: The SOA

Grid computing

Grid computing is a type of distributed computing in which a set of computers are connected for a common purpose. These computer resources are geographically dispersed and heterogeneous.

Grid computing breaks up a complex task into smaller pieces. These small pieces are distributed to CPUs that are available within the grid.

Utility computing

Utility computing is based on the pay-per-use model. It offers resources on-demand as a metered service. Some examples of utility computing are Cloud computing, managed IT services, and grid computing.

Cloud computing architecture

The Cloud computing architecture consists of many components that are loosely coupled. The Cloud architecture can broadly be divided into two parts:

- **Front end**: Fat client, thin client, mobile device
- **Back end**: Server, storage

Each end (front end and back end) is connected through a network, usually via the internet. The following figure illustrates the graphical view of Cloud computing architecture:

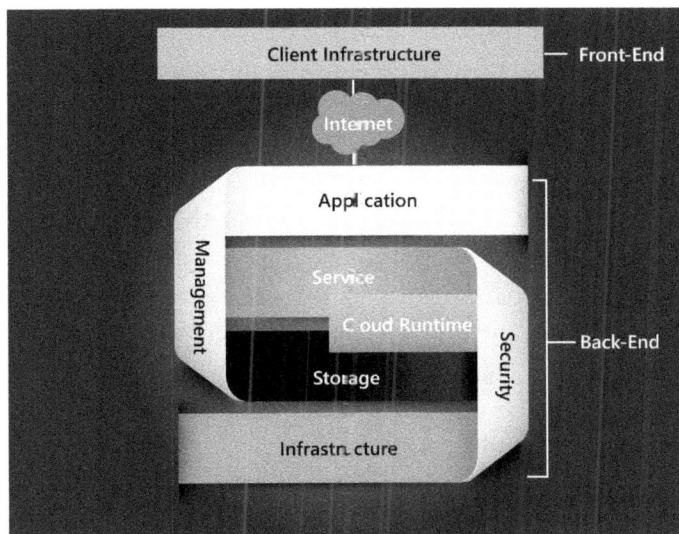

Figure 1.11: Cloud computing architecture

Front end and back end

The front end of Cloud computing architecture is the client part. This consists of the interfaces and applications that are required to access the Cloud computing platforms, for example, the web browser.

The back end of Cloud computing architecture refers to the Cloud itself. It consists of all resources required to provide the services to the customers. It comprises of huge data storage, servers, virtual machines, services, deployment models, security mechanism, to name a few.

It is the responsibility of the back end of Cloud computing to provide a built-in security mechanism, protocols, and traffic control mechanism.

The server maintains certain protocols that are known as **middleware**. The middleware helps the connected devices to communicate with each other.

Cloud infrastructure components

Cloud infrastructure consists of many components. These include servers, storage, network, software, and platform virtualization. Let us discuss a few important components:

- **Hypervisor**: The hypervisor is a firmware or low-level program that acts as a Virtual Machine Manager. It allows sharing a single physical instance of Cloud resources between several users.
- **Management software**: Management software helps to configure and maintain the infrastructure.
- **Deployment software**: Deployment software helps to deploy and integrate the applications on the Cloud.
- **Network**: The network is one of the key components of Cloud infrastructure. It allows us to connect and access Cloud services over the internet. It is also possible to deliver networks as a utility over the internet, that is, the user can customize the network route and protocol.
- **Server**: The server helps to compute resource sharing and offers other services, such as resource allocation and de-allocation, security, and monitoring resources.
- **Storage**: Cloud uses a distributed file system for storage purposes. If one of the storage resources fails for any reason, the same can be extracted from another one. This makes Cloud computing more reliable.
- **Infrastructural constraints**: While we discussed the benefits of Cloud computing, there are certain constraints as well. Few infrastructural constraints are discussed as follows:
  - o **Transparency**: Virtualization is the key to expose the resources in the Cloud environment. However, it is not possible to fulfill the demand with a single

resource or server. Therefore, there must be transparency in resources, load balancing so that we can scale them on demand.

o **Scalability**: Scaling up an application delivery solution is not as easy as scaling up an application. It involves configuration overhead and even re-architecting the network. Therefore, the application delivery solution is essential to be scalable, which will need the virtual infrastructure that can be provisioned and de-provisioned easily.

o **Intelligent monitoring**: Achieving scalability and transparency, the application solution delivery is required to be capable of intelligent monitoring.

o **Security**: The mega datacenter in the Cloud should be securely architected. Also, the control node, an entry point in the mega datacenter, needs to be secure.

Application development

The rapid growth of distributed computing creates new approaches for IT people to develop new programming within an organization. This provides technologies that enable organizations to re-engineer their businesses.

Mainframe dominated the mid-20th century. In the late 20th century, client-server systems evolved in association with advances in desktop computing, new storage technologies, improved network communications, and enhanced database technology.

The widespread of networks, and especially the connected networks, like the internet, has imposed a new shift of computing happens. Now the resources to be used are widespread. The application components are to be reused by many applications. There is a need to use resources on demand. Therefore, the pay-per-use model was created with Cloud computing.

The following figure describes the evolution of computing models:

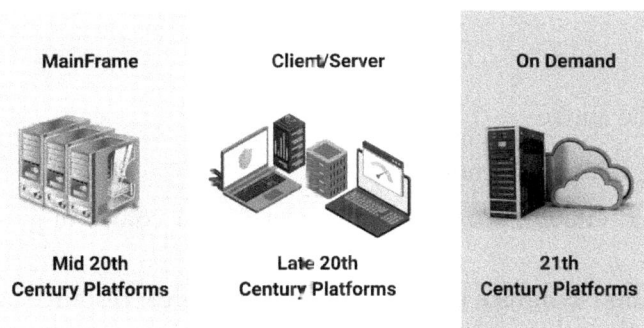

Figure: 1.12: Application development model

Conclusion

While the book focuses more on Salesforce, this chapter gives insight into Cloud computing. Cloud computing allows applications to run in the Cloud, to be accessed over the internet using a web browser, and can be used by many consumers simultaneously at a low cost. There are various deployment models, such as private Cloud, public Cloud, hybrid Cloud, and community Cloud. There are different service models, such as IaaS, PaaS, and SaaS. Understanding the basics of Cloud computing is necessary before jumping to the main topic, that is, Salesforce. In the next chapter, you will be introduced to Salesforce's data modeling and lightning feature.

Questions

1. **What is the public Cloud?**
   a. A Cloud formation that can be seen across the globe
   b. A Cloud service that can only be accessed from a publicly shared computer
   c. A multi-tenant Cloud environment accessed over the internet
   d. A Cloud environment owned, operated, and controlled by a public company

2. **What is a hybrid Cloud?**
   a. A blend of public and private Cloud services with orchestration between them
   b. A Cloud service deployed across multiple offices or locations
   c. A blend of private Cloud and legacy on-premises hardware
   d. None of the above

3. **Which of the following acronyms refers to a software distribution model in which a Cloud provider manages and hosts an app that users access via the internet?**
   a. IaaS
   b. PaaS
   c. SaaS
   d. None of the above

4. **Point out the wrong statement:**
   a. Abstraction enables the key benefits of Cloud computing: shared, ubiquitous access
   b. Virtualization assigns a logical name for a physical resource and then provides a pointer to that physical resource when a request is made

c. All Cloud computing applications combine their resources into pools that can be assigned on demand to users

d. All of the mentioned

5. **Which of the following type of virtualization is also characteristic of Cloud computing?**

   a. Storage

   b. Application

   c. CPU

   d. All of the above

6. **Which of the following is not a characteristic of Cloud computing?**

   a. Resource pooling

   b. Rapid elasticity

   c. Measured services

   d. None of the above

7. **Which of the following is not a deployment model of Cloud computing?**

   a. Private Cloud

   b. Shared Cloud

   c. Public Cloud

   d. Hybrid Cloud

8. **Which of the following is a feature of PaaS?**

   a. Provides backup to our database

   b. Provides high security to our data

   c. Provides customer choice features

   d. All of the above

9. **Which of the following is a disadvantage of Cloud computing?**

   a. The data for a few companies may be too confidential to be kept on the Cloud

   b. There is no need to keep space, for instance, on the company premises for big servers

   c. The organization that avails of Cloud computing can use the processing power of the entire network

   d. Cloud computing reduces the cost of hiring software engineers significantly

10. **Which of the following is true?**

    a. A hypervisor is a firmware or low-level program that acts as a Virtual Machine Manager

    b. Deployment software helps to deploy and integrate the application on the Cloud

    c. Grid computing refers to distributed computing in which a group of computers from multiple locations are connected with each other to achieve the common objective

    d. All of the above

Answers

1. c
2. a
3. c
4. c
5. d
6. d
7. b
8. d
9. a
10. d

Join our Discord space

Join our Discord workspace for latest updates, offers, tech happenings around the world, new releases, and sessions with the authors:

https://discord.bpbonline.com

CHAPTER 2
Introduction to Salesforce

Introduction

Salesforce innovation is one of the main and incredibly niche technologies in IT enterprises. According to Forbes magazine, about 55% of ventures foresee that distributed computing will empower a new plan of action in the next three years. Salesforce gives diverse venture distributed computing applications to any or all sizes of enterprises and organizations. Through *Salesforce.com*, a large number of job opportunities are created for Salesforce Engineer and Salesforce Administrator.

Salesforce applications are given on a membership basis fundamentally through direct deals and in a roundabout way through accomplices.

Structure

In this chapter, we will discuss the following topics:

- History of Salesforce
- Introducing Salesforce
- Choosing Salesforce
- Salesforce architecture
- Multitenant architecture

- Metadata-driven development model
- APIs
- Apex
- Custom user interface
- Mobile access
- AppExchange

Objectives

After studying this unit, you will be introduced to Salesforce. You will also be able to understand the history of Salesforce. We will discuss the Salesforce architecture. The Salesforce Lightning platform will be introduced. The various benefits that it offers will also be discussed.

History of Salesforce

Salesforce.com was set up in 1999 by *Marc Benioff* and *Parker Harris*. Salesforce is an American-based Cloud computing company that provides **Software as a Service (SaaS)** solution for the organizations. Salesforce is not only a software, but also gives complete Cloud-based **customer relationship management** (**CRM**) applications through the internet and a browser.

In June 2004, *Salesforce.com* organization was first recorded in an initial public offering.

After five years, the organization was available for open market after they brought the US $110 million up in the New York Stock Exchange. As time passed, the number of financial specialists increased and an opportunity arrived when the speculators needed to contribute, yet there was barely any room available at Salesforce.

In the year 2008, Salesforce was added to the New York stock trade after the government took over *Freddie Mac* and *Fannie Mae Inc.*

Salesforce headquarters is in San Francisco, USA, with its central territorial command in Morges, Switzerland, India, and Tokyo. Their key workplaces are in New York, London, Sydney, Dublin, Hyderabad, San Mateo, and California.

In 2008, Salesforce, with the assistance of an AMD processor, relocated to *Dell* on Linux from *Sun Fire E25k*. Later in the year 2012, Salesforce reported assembling a datacenter in the United Kingdom for European clients' information.

In the year 2013, Salesforce consented to a nine years arrangement with *Oracle* in which Salesforce will utilize *Oracle Linux, Oracle Exadata, Oracle Database,* and the *Java* platform in their future administrations.

In the year 2014, Salesforce reached the annual revenue of $5 billion milestone, faster than any other enterprise software company. Salesforce Tower London also opened.

In the year 2015, *Fortune* recognized Salesforce as one of the Top 10 Best Companies to Work For and also one of the World's Most Admired Software Companies. At *Dreamforce*, Salesforce announced its new Lightning Experience, a completely new CRM experience.

In the year 2016, Salesforce launches *Einstein*, the first comprehensive **artificial intelligence (AI)** technology for CRM, making AI accessible to every company and business user.

In the year 2017, the company achieves net-zero greenhouse gas emissions and begins delivering a carbon-neutral Cloud. Revenue grows to $10.548 billion for the fiscal year ending January 31, 2018, up 25% on the previous year.

In the year 2018, the company acquires *MuleSoft* to help power Salesforce's integration capabilities. Fortune names Salesforce #1 on the 100 Best Companies to Work For list.

In the year 2019, Salesforce acquires *Tableau*, bringing the world's #1 CRM and #1 analytics platform together to supercharge customers' digital transformations.

In the year 2020, Salesforce launched a number of products and resources to help companies navigate the pandemic, including:

- **Salesforce care**: A set of free rapid response solutions, companies can stay connected to employees, customers, and partners during the pandemic.
- **Work.com**: A suite of expert advice, content, data, and new products to help companies around the globe reopen their businesses and communities, then get back to growth.
- **Vaccine Cloud:** To help public health authorities, healthcare providers, and nonprofits quickly scale vaccine operations, from recipient registration and scheduling to inventory management and public health outreach.

In the year 2021, Salesforce completed the acquisition of *Slack*, sharing a vision for Slack-driven Digital HQ.

In the year 2022, at the 20th annual Dreamforce, Salesforce announced Customer Data Cloud, a hyperscale real-time data platform that now powers the Einstein 1 platform.

In the year 2023, Salesforce introduces the next generation of Einstein AI, Einstein GPT, the world's first generative AI for CRM.

Introducing Salesforce

Salesforce.com is SaaS, which recommends that the user need not install software or servers to keep up. The *Salesforce.com* user should sign up for an account, and once signed, they, in a split second, will utilize the product to maintain their business. *Salesforce.com* offers a thirty-day trial, and since there is no agreement, you will have the option to drop whenever and leave if it does not fit your business. The *salesforce.com* accedes through a browser. At first, *salesforce.com* started as a CRM product, however, over the years it has emerged as a Cloud-based platform.

From an elevated level, *salesforce.com* comprises of numerous items, like Sales Cloud, Service Cloud, Community Cloud, Content, Ideas, Analytics, Chatter, Einstein processing, and so on. Software developers will extend the platform by creating applications on the *Force.com* platform using salesforce.com's programming language, *Apex. Salesforce.com* is on the *Fortune* 500 list. The following important features make Salesforce unique:

- *Salesforce.com* is a Cloud computing company.
- It has a pre-engineered application
- It saves cash and time.
- *Salesforce.com* provides reports and Dashboards that help user's to run their reports and Dashboards.
- The trends can be analyzed.
- The forecast can be seen.
- It has outlook integration, email templates, and an inbuilt record search and might produce new leads, accounts, contacts, and opportunities.

Salesforce is presently ranked among the 100 best corporations on the planet.

Salesforce began as a SaaS-based CRM organization. As of now, it gives different software solutions and a platform for users and developers to create and distribute custom software. The following figure shows the capacity of Salesforce in the present technically knowledgeable world. From technical mammoths, like *Facebook* and *Google* to your call center, use Salesforce services and products to unwind their issues.

The following figure depicts the applications of Salesforce:

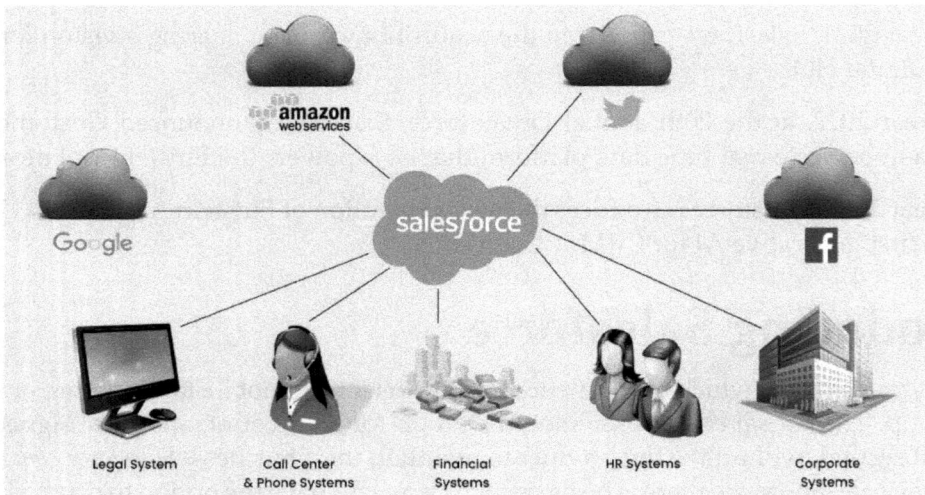

Figure 2.1: Applications of Salesforce

Salesforce can help in connecting with your customers in a whole new way. It can help build more meaningful and lasting relationships with the customers, even better understand their needs, identify new opportunities to help, address any problems faster, and deploy customer-focused apps lightning fast. As per Salesforce, with a single view of every customer interaction, you can sell, service, and market like never before.

Choosing Salesforce

Salesforce provides the quickest path from a new idea to an app. You would now be able to build your app using Salesforce tools instead of building the infrastructure and tools by yourself. This can save you years and millions of dollars, as you can visualize through the following figure:

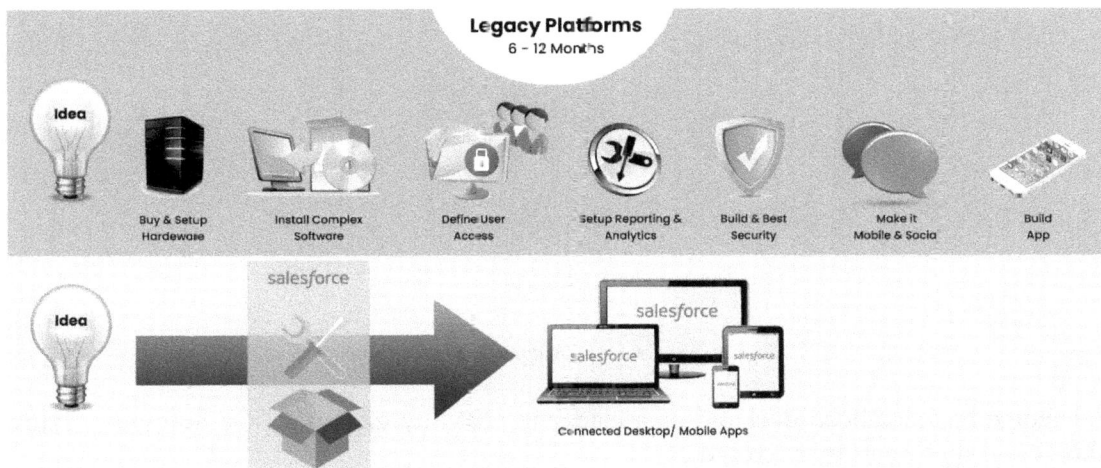

Figure 2.2: Salesforce tools

Salesforce customers mostly say that it is unique for the following major reasons:

- **Fast**: Traditional CRM software can take more than a year to develop and deploy. However, Salesforce takes months or even weeks.
- **Easy**: Salesforce can be used with ease.
- **Effective**: As it is easier to use, it can be customized to meet business needs effectively.

Salesforce is in the Cloud, so your group can utilize it from anyplace with access to the Web. Salesforce is versatile in your business development. Salesforce flawlessly incorporates outsider applications like Gmail, accounting programming, and so forth. Salesforce is reasonable, thinking about its immense assortment of abilities. Indeed, even small companies can utilize Salesforce.

As per Salesforce, on average, customers using Salesforce CRM have seen the following trend:

- 38% faster decision-making
- 25% increase in revenue
- 35% jump in customer satisfaction

In the year 2023, Salesforce (NYSE: CRM), the #1 AI CRM, has been recognized as a leader by *Gartner Magic Quadrant™* for Salesforce Automation Platforms for the 17th consecutive year. The following figure showcases the Magic Quadrant report by Gartner:

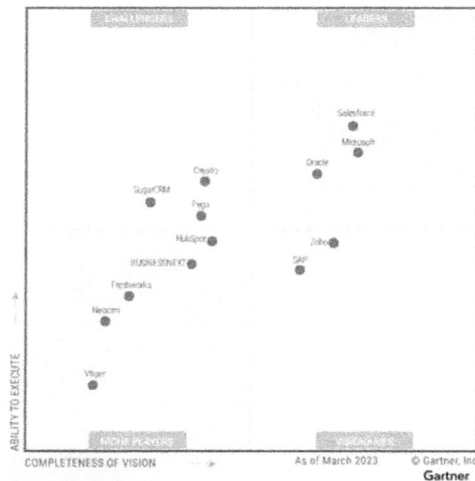

Figure 2.3: Gartner's Magic Quadrant report

Salesforce has also been declared as a leader in CRM by g2crowd. The following figure showcases the report by g2crowd:

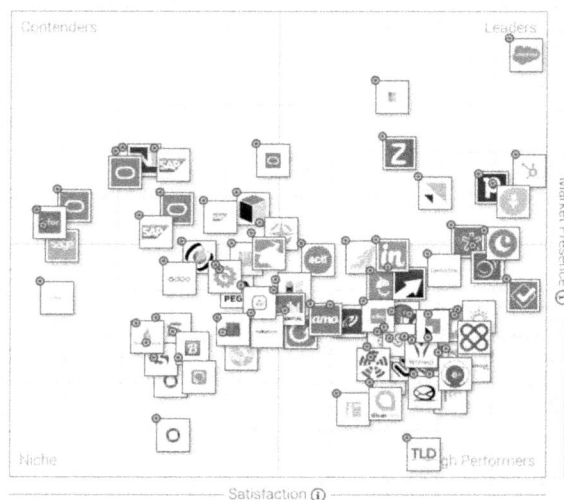

Figure 2.4: Salesforce as per go2crowd
(Source: https://www.g2crowd.com/categories/crm)

International Data Corporation (IDC) has ranked Salesforce as the #1 CRM provider in its 2024 Worldwide Semiannual Software Tracker®. This is the 11th consecutive time Salesforce has earned the top spot. The following figure represents the IDC report of 2024:

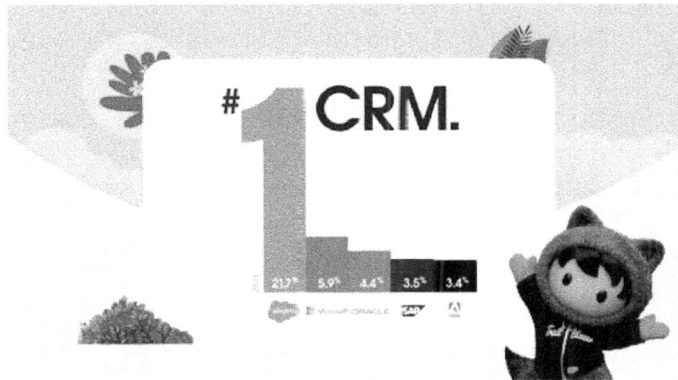

Figure 2.5: CRM market share
Source: https://www.salesforce.com/news/stories/idc-crm-market-share-ranking-2024/

Salesforce architecture

At this point, you might have comprehended how powerful the Salesforce application is.

To see the Salesforce capacities, it is imperative to comprehend the architecture of Salesforce.

Before we start discussing the Salesforce architecture, it is important to understand a few key terminologies of Salesforce architecture, as shown in the following figure:

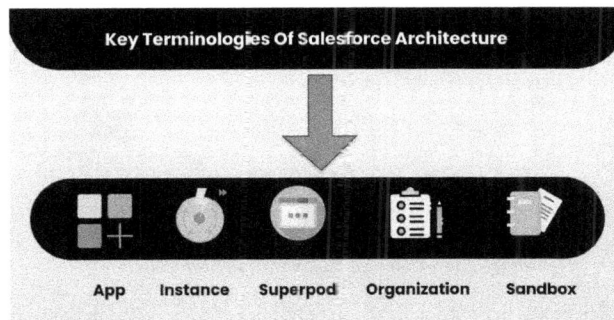

Figure: 2.6: Key terminologies of Salesforce

The key terminologies in Salesforce architecture are discussed as follows:

- **App**: All metadata components like objects, Visualforce pages, classes, and so forth are independent of the application. An application helps to bunch things visually. Though internally metadata has nothing to do with the application, however, you will have the option to have a comparative tab, VF page, and so on in different applications.

- **Instance**: An instance of Salesforce is that the explicit configuration that you simply see after you log into Salesforce. Salesforce instance is truly showing server details for specific Salesforce organization on that it remains. It is doable for several Salesforce instances living on one server. The instance was created supported the placement of the user. It will be modified based on the region from wherever you log in.

- **Superpod**: Superpod is the arrangement of frameworks and stack balancers, as well as outgoing intermediary servers, system and capability foundations, mail servers, SAN texture, and varied alternative framework supporting different instances.

- **Organization (Org)**: The Salesforce Org is a single consumer of the Salesforce application. Every trial that starts on *salesforce.com* or developer.force.com produces another organization. An Org is flexible and has clear security and sharing setting. The user interface look and feel, custom fields, triggers, custom articles, on standard salesforce.com are entirely versatile.

- **Sandbox**: Whenever a sandbox is made, Salesforce copies the metadata (data about data) from your production Org to the sandbox Org. By doing, therefore, the multiple copies of the production Org are crated in separate environments.

- There are four kinds of sandboxes available in Salesforce:
  - Developer sandbox
  - Developer pro
  - Full sandbox
  - Partial copy

The Salesforce architecture is a series of layers sitting on top of each other. The following figure depicts the architecture of Salesforce:

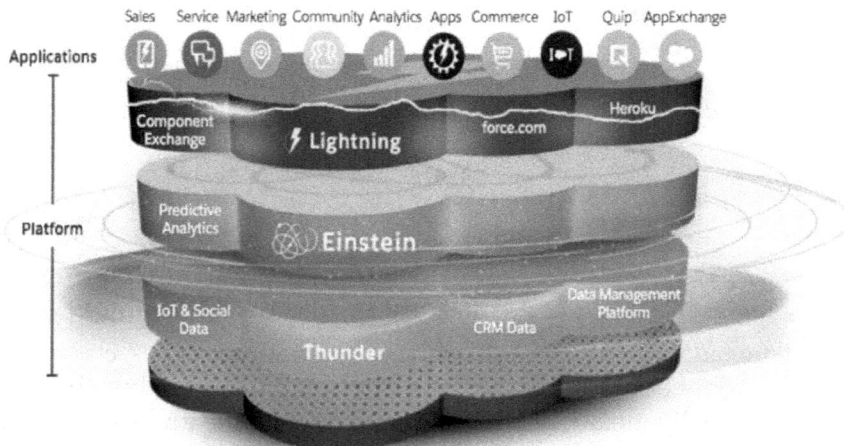

Figure 2.7: Salesforce architecture

The various layers in Salesforce architecture are explained as follows:

- **Sales Cloud**: The Sales Cloud is a CRM which empowers to manage the three pillars of any organization: Marketing, sales, and service. It very well may be utilized for both **business to consumer** (**B2C**) and business-to-**business** (**B2B**) clients.

- **Service Cloud:** The Service Cloud is a service platform for the customer service and support team. It gives features like tracking cases, lightning service console, telephony integration, and analytics. These just not cause your agents to take care of client issues quicker, yet in addition, offers your clients access to responses through knowledge solutions. Utilizing these answers, the clients can take care of issues all alone.

- **Marketing Cloud**: The Marketing Cloud gives one of the world's most powerful digital marketing platform. The advertisers in your association can utilize it to oversee customer journey, email, mobile, social media, Web personalization, content creation, content administration, and data analytics.

- **Community Cloud**: It is the social platform for your organization to interface and encourages correspondence among your employees, partners, and even the clients. This platform can be utilized to exchange information in real-time. Now it is names as experience Cloud.

- **Analytics Cloud**: The Analytics Cloud gives a **business intelligence** (**BI**) platform for the organizations to work with enormous information records. You can make diagrams, graphs and other pictorial portrayals of information. It is, as a matter of course, streamlined for mobile access. It can, without much of a stretch, be integrated with other Salesforce Clouds. Now it is known as CRM analytics.

- App Cloud: App Cloud can be utilized to create custom applications that will run on the Salesforce platform. It gives an assortment of development tools that can be used to make custom applications. It integrates social, mobile, and Cloud, such that it lets developers center around code, not infrastructure. Empowering developers to focus on code rather than infrastructure was the original promise of **Platform as a Service** (**PaaS**). Through the App Cloud, Salesforce is connecting across its CRM, mobile tools, and core developer platform to deliver a unified PaaS. A few of the tools in the App Cloud are:

  o **Force.com:** It permits developers and admins to create applications into the main *Salesforce.com* application. It provides a platform on which the developer can build various apps.

  o AppExchange: The applications build using *Force.com* are made available in an online application marketplace called **AppExchange**.

  o **Heroku:** Lets you deploy, run, and manage applications written in open languages and frameworks, such as Java, *Python, Ruby, Node.js, Scala,* and

PHP. You can easily deploy your code with a single command using developer tools like Git, GitHub, etc.

o **Salesforce** Thunder: This is the most scalable event processing engine in the world. It is designed to analyze billions of connected events and take personalized actions. Now Salesforce offers Hyperforce as an infrastructure model for the Salesforce CRM platform, while Salesforce Lightning is the core infrastructure of Salesforce. Hyperforce was introduced in 2020 to improve the platform's performance, security, scalability, and flexibility.

o **Salesforce Sandbox**: This permits developers to check ideas in a very isolated and safe development environment.

• **Commerce Cloud**: The commerce Cloud empowers the organizations to give consistent client experiences and services independent of your client's location, whether online or in-store. It gives client data integration with the goal that the consumers can have a superior encounter. It gives a positive connecting with client experience.

• **IoT Cloud:** IoT is the glue that connects the world of connected devices with the world of CRM. Salesforce IoT makes it easier to connect events from devices to the relevant data in Salesforce and use all of this information to trigger the right action. The platform is built to take in the huge volumes of data that are generated by websites, applications, devices, partners, and customers.

• **Einstein**: Salesforce Einstein is a layer within the Salesforce platform that infuses features and capabilities of AI across all Salesforce Clouds. Einstein takes care of the data modeling and infrastructure needed to embed and scale predictive models throughout your Salesforce workflows. You can immediately reap the benefits of Einstein with AI algorithms built natively into your Salesforce apps or leverage intelligent APIs to customize Einstein according to your use-case. Salesforce Einstein Platform offers two APIs that can be leveraged for image recognition and language processing:

o **Einstein vision**: It is a part of the Salesforce Einstein technology suite which has Classifiers to solve an array of specialized image-recognition.

o **Einstein language**: It enables to leverage the power of natural language processing to analyze the intent of the customer in the body of the text. This would help to understand the requirements of the customer and help them with what they need.

• **Lightning**: The new Lightning Experience is built on the Salesforce App Coud that combines the new Lightning Design System, Lightning Components, and Lightning App Builder to enable to quickly and easily create modern enterprise apps. It gives the user interface a seamless experience across all your devices.

Introducing the Lightning platform

Salesforce's Lightning platform is a platform for developing and deploying next-generation Cloud apps. As there are no servers or software to buy or manage, you can completely focus only on building apps that include built-in mobile and social functionality, business processes, and reporting. Your apps run on a secure and proven service that scales, tunes, and backs up data automatically.

Using the Lightning platform

It is very important to understand the various benefits of using Salesforce. The following features of Salesforce make it unique and proven as a leader among its competitors:

- **Proven**: More than 100,000 companies have trusted the Lightning platform, including many industry leaders across verticals. They have built approx. 220,000 apps that run in world-class data centers with backup, failover disaster-recovery, and an uptime record exceeding 99.9%. The real-time system performance data can be seen at *trust.salesforce.com*.

- **Agile**: One of the benefits of the Lightning platform is that it requires nominal coding. Your apps can be assembled in building-block fashion using the library of components and visual tools. The development can be streamlined with sandbox environments, and using APIs; the applications can be integrated.

- **Social**: You can work effectively with your colleagues using your secure social network. The Lightning platform includes pre-built components for feeds, conversations, updates, profiles, and file sharing. All components are available through REST APIs, which can be easily integrated into any custom app.

- **Mobile**: Your business can be run from your phone using the Salesforce mobile app. Your mobile apps can be built powered by a secure Cloud database, with rock-solid APIs. Even the mobile-optimized browser apps can be built using a UI framework and HTML5 to support any device with one codebase. Lightning platform is having what is needed to deliver apps on mobile devices securely.

Benefits of the Lightning platform app

When you think for Lightning platform apps, following two huge benefits start to come into focus:

- **Data-centric apps**: The Salesforce Lightning platform revolves around a database. So, it permits the composition of data-centric applications. A data-centric application is an application that depends on organized and steady data. These data-centric applications are accessible wherever, whether in desktop databases like Microsoft Access or in large systems running on **Relational Database Management Systems (RDBMS)** like Oracle or SQL Server The data-centric applications make it simple to get to access, control, and manage data. Then again, applications that are built around unstructured information, similar to plain content documents or HTML files, do not give such adaptability.

While it is consistently not expected to have a data-centric application to monitor something besides contacts, photographs, or music, organizations of all sizes continually need to inquiry and aggregate their tremendous measures of data to settle on quick business decisions. Along these lines, the data-centric nature of the Lightning platform builds and host business applications.

- **Collaborative apps**: It is one of the benefits of the Lightning platform is that multiple users can access it at the same time. So, it allows us to write collaborative apps. A collaborative app is an application that has data and services that are shared by multiple users in different locations. Traditional software those are installed on a single machine, like a PC and is hard to access from a distance. However, the collaborative apps on the platform can be accessed from all over the globe with only a Web browser. This makes it easy to work together on activities, like selling a product, managing a project, or even hiring an employee.

In addition to easy access over a Web browser, several built-in platforms features also facilitate group collaboration, such as:

o The security and sharing model of the platform can be used to control a user's access to different data finely.

o The salesforce flows can be used to automatically update data, assign tasks, or send email alerts when certain predefined events occur.

o The approval processes can be used to set up a sequence of steps necessary for a record to be approved.

These features provide a framework for sharing apps across groups, divisions, and an entire organization without relinquishing administrative control over sensitive data.

Multitenant architecture

In a multitenant architecture, all users share the same infrastructure and the same version of the Lightning platform. As opposed to the single-tenant architecture, for example, client-server enterprise applications or email servers, multitenant architecture release updates consequently and all the while for all users. So, nobody needs to stress over purchasing and keeping up their hardware, and software, or to ensure that the application is refreshed with the most recent fix. The following figure explains how a multitenant architecture works:

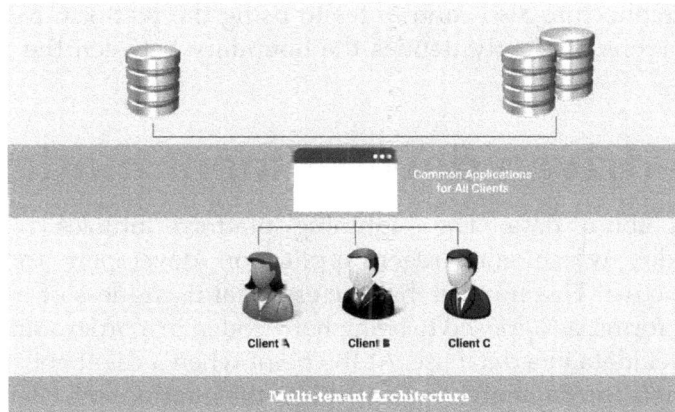

Figure 2.8: *Multi-tenant architecture*

Other than the Lightning platform, many popular, consumer-based applications also use a multitenant architecture, like Gmail, eBay, etc. Multitenant architecture gives lots of benefits to these applications, like low-cost, quick deployment, and openness to rapid innovation. The following figure illustrates an example of a multitenant architect:

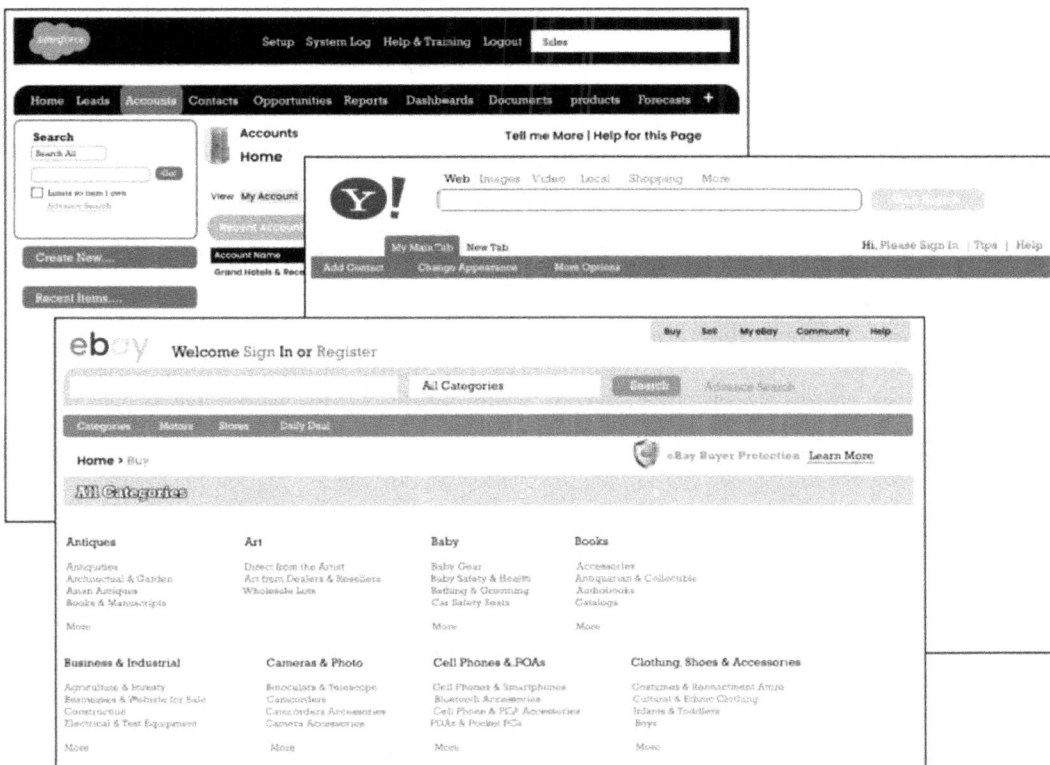

Figure 2.9: *Examples of multi-tenant architecture*

The multitenant architecture also contributes to using the platform for how developers create new applications. It clearly defines the boundary between the platform and the applications.

Metadata-driven development model

Metadata is data about data. The Lightning platform utilizes a metadata-driven advancement model, which encourages application developers to turn out to be increasingly productive. This implies that the essential usefulness of an application like the tabs, links, and forms, as opposed to being hard-coded in a programming language are characterized as metadata in a database. At the point when a client gets to an application, the application's meta information is rendered into the interface the client encounters.

As a result of metadata-driven development, the Lightning platform application developers work at a significantly more elevated level of deliberation. The developers are not stressed over low-level system subtleties that the platform handles consequently. Lightning platform developers can likewise use advanced features that the platform gives as default.

Redoing your application's metadata may sound awkward, yet the stage's UI makes it simple. Any individual who knows about utilizing a Web program can rapidly be gainful, regardless of whether the person does not have the foggiest idea about any programming dialects.

The metadata-driven development works the very same model for how Web programs work. A Web page creator initially characterizes the page as HTML, which is itself a sort of metadata. Instead of hard-coding the meaning of a Web page in a freestyle programming language. At the point when a client requests a page, the Web program renders the page utilizing the metadata gave in the HTML tags.

So, the Lightning platform rearranges the work of building an application and inevitably expands a developer's overall productivity. The Lightning platform gives approaches to further advanced developers to add custom functionality to the applications you build.

APIs

While the metadata-driven development model of the platform permits application developers to rapidly and effectively build a lot of functionalities that are provided by the platform, in some cases, application developers might need to adjust the real data in an application and may utilize third-party services. They can, without much of a stretch, utilize various APIs to coordinate with the platform. The set of APIs incorporates Lightning platform SOAP API and REST API, the bulk API, streaming API, metadata API, and so forth. These APIs can be called from a wide assortment of customer side dialects. Readymade toolkits are likewise accessible to facilitate the integration.

The APIs give powerful and open approaches to programmatically get to the data and capacities of any application running on the platform. The APIs permit developers to access manipulate applications from any server, utilizing any programming language that supports Web services, like PHP, Java, C#, and so on.

Apex

Salesforce not just conveyed the world's first Cloud computing platform, but also, presented the world's first Cloud computing programming language, Apex. The syntax of Apex is like Java. Apex is explicitly intended for building business applications to manage data and processes for the Lightning platform. It gives an exceptionally powerful and productive way to create logic and functionality. It permits developers to concentrate just on the components explicit to their application while leaving the rest to the Lightning platform.

Custom user interface

In any business application, an incredible UI is necessary that it is powerful, easy to use, and suited for the required users, tasks, and the devices the application serves. Visualforce is a finished framework for making such UIs, encouraging any sort of interface design and collaboration to be fabricated. The Visualforce UIs can be expanded the standard Lightning platform look and feel, or even supplant it with a totally one-of-a-kind style. The Visualforce mark-up is eventually rendered into HTML. So, the creators can, without much of a stretch, use Visualforce tags along with standard HTML tags, JavaScript, Flash, and so forth that can be executed inside an HTML page on the platform.

Mobile access

In the recent past, the essential purposes of Internet access have been moved from work areas and workstations to cell phones and tablets. So, the applications that do not give mobile access to basic information will immediately get obsolete. Salesforce application can be utilized to convey your Lightning platform customizations to the mobile users.

Downloadable versions of the Salesforce application can be installed from AppExchange on mobile devices and utilize the native functionality of the device. At the point when clients sign in using a mobile, they can access and update their information through an interface exceptionally designed formable device. It permits you to work with the vast majority of the standard Sales objects, Service objects, and all custom objects.

For this, the administrators do not need to make exceptional arrangements for mobile users to get to their organizational information.

Salesforce mobile app is supported on Apple iPhones and iPads as well as Android phones.

AppExchange

AppExchange is the last bit of innovation that separates the Lightning platform from other platforms. The AppExchange is a Web directory where applications based on the Lightning platform are accessible to Salesforce customers to peruse, review, and install. Developers can build up their applications and submit them on the AppExchange directory if they need to impart them to the community.

To fully appreciate the benefits of the AppExchange, visit **https://appexchange.salesforce. com.** Hundreds of innovative and exciting apps are available there.

Conclusion

The chapter introduced Salesforce to the readers. It is very important to understand various terminologies, like Apps, Org, Instance, etc., of Salesforce architecture. We were also briefed about various instances. The Lightning platform is introduced and is proven to be agile, social, and mobile. The Lightning platform is data-centric and collaborative. The multitenant architecture allows users to use the same version of the infrastructure. The metadata-driven development model makes the developers more productive.

In the next chapter, you will be introduced to Salesforce's Data modeling and Lightning features.

Questions

1. **The first Cloud computing language is?**
   a. Java
   b. C
   c. Apex
   d. Python

2. **Which component of Salesforce architecture lets you deploy, run, and manage applications written in open languages and frameworks.**
   a. IOT
   b. Heroku
   c. Einstein
   d. Thunder

3. **CRM helps any organization in which of the following?**
   a. Faster decision-making
   b. Increase in revenue

c. Jump in customer satisfaction.

d. All of the above

4. **Which feature of Salesforce allows developers and admins to create applications into the main Salesforce.com application?**

a. Force.com

b. App Exchange

c. App Cloud

d. All of the above

5. **Which is the social platform for your organization to connect and facilitate communication among your employees, partners, and even the customers?**

a. Sales Cloud

b. Service Cloud

c. Community Cloud

d. Marketing Cloud

6. **Which of the following provides powerful, open ways to programmatically access the data and capabilities of any app running on the platform?**

a. Apex

b. API

c. IOT

d. Thunder

7. **The data about data is?**

a. API

b. Meta Data

c. App Cloud

d. Force.com

8. **The Multitenant architecture of Salesforce means?**

a. All users share the same infrastructure and version of the Lightning platform

b. The APIs provide powerfully, and open ways to programmatically access the data and capabilities of any app running on the platform App Cloud

c. It requires nominal coding

d. The Salesforce Administrators do not have to create special configurations for mobile users to access their organization's data

9. The Web directory where apps built on the Lightning platform are available to Salesforce customers to browse, preview, and install is?

    a. App Cloud

    b. Multitenant

    c. Sandbox

    d. App Exchange

10. Which of the following provides BI platform for the organizations to work with large data files?

    a. App Cloud

    b. Community Cloud

    c. Analytics Cloud

    d. Service Cloud

Answers

1. c
2. b
3. a
4. a
5. c
6. b
7. b
8. a
9. d
10. c

Join our Discord space

Join our Discord workspace for latest updates, offers, tech happenings around the world, new releases, and sessions with the authors:

https://discord.bpbonline.com

CHAPTER 3
Introducing Salesforce Lightning and Salesforce Data Modeling

Introduction

As you have gone through in the previous chapter, Salesforce's Lightning platform is a platform for developing and deploying next-generation Cloud apps. Lightning Experience is a new generation productive user interface designed to build rich enterprise experiences and custom applications.

As per Salesforce, the Lightning Experience is a modern, productive user experience designed to help your sales team close more deals and sell faster and smarter.

The support team can close cases faster using various Lightning components tools.

Structure

In this chapter, we will discuss the following topics:

- Salesforce Lightning interface
- Salesforce Lightning editions
- Creating a Salesforce developer account
- Lightning Experience navigation menu
- Data modeling of Salesforce

Objectives

By the end of this chapter, you will understand various Salesforce Lightning editions and will be introduced to the Salesforce Lightning interface. You will also learn about its various benefits and learn about data modeling for Salesforce. You will be introduced to the basics of objects, fields, field types, and object relationships.

Salesforce Lightning interface

The augmentation in mobile usage is influencing how people work in every field. Sales representatives are now using mobiles to get potential customers, socially connect with their customers, and get the details of customer offices. So, Salesforce has synced the desktop Lightning Experience with mobile Salesforce1.

The new Lightning interface offers the following benefits:

- Navigate from one page to another.
- Switch between various apps using the built-in navigation bar.
- Take notes with the notes tool. This includes autosave and rich text capabilities.
- Find records with powerful search capabilities. This includes viewing recent records and top search results.

Salesforce Lightning editions

With the introduction of the Lightning editions, Salesforce has established them to be more customizable, have more capabilities, and add value to its customers. The initial focus in designing Lightning Experience was to improve the core sales features that are used by salespeople every day.

Sales Cloud Lightning editions

Sales Cloud is a Cloud-based **Artificial Intelligence Customer Relationship Management (AI CRM)** product from Salesforce that enables businesses to grow and serve their customers better. It has features such as customization, top-notch security, detailed reporting and analytics, and a mobile app that works seamlessly. These features make Sales Cloud the world's #1 AI CRM.

With Sales Cloud, powered by Einstein 1, you can sell faster, smarter, and more efficiently. Sales Cloud empowers sellers, sales leaders, sales operations, and even partners with data from any source and built-in trusted AI. It engages buyers, improves productivity, closes deals faster, and grows revenue with sales software on the most complete platform for sales.

It caters to companies of all sizes, both small and large enterprises.

Small businesses are perfect for Salesforce Essentials. It can be ready to use after a few steps and is designed for businesses with simple workflows.

Medium-sized businesses are perfect for any professional edition. More customizations and improved collaboration tools make the professional edition an ideal solution for customers who want to take their business to the next level with a growing team.

Business customers are best for enterprise or unlimited editions. The biggest customers with complex workflows can be accommodated for them. The various editions of Salesforce Sales Cloud are mentioned as follows:

Figure 3.1: *Sales Cloud editions*

Note: **Salesforce Sales Cloud edition prices may change from time to time.**

Service Cloud Lightning editions

Salesforce's Service Cloud helps organizations to streamline the customer service process. This will help the organization to close a case faster. Service agents can connect with customers through the agent console. Service Cloud includes case management, **Computer Telephony Integration (CTI)**, Service Cloud console, knowledge base, Salesforce communities, Salesforce Private AppExchange, reports, and Dashboards with many other analytics features.

You can transform how service teams deliver value across every customer touchpoint with Service Cloud built on the Einstein 1 platform. You can increase customer satisfaction, deflect more cases, and maximize efficiency with a complete platform powered by AI and data from self-service and contact centers to the field.

Based on the Salesforce customer success metrics 2023, here is what sets Service Cloud apart:

- **30% deflection**: Salesforce customers deflected 30% of cases via self-service.
- **32% higher customer satisfaction**: Salesforce customers saw a 32% increase in customer satisfaction, customer effort, or **Net Promoter Score (NPS)** Score.

- **29% faster case resolution with AI**: Salesforce customers resolved cases 29% faster due to investment in AI.
- **31% higher agent productivity**: Salesforce customers saw a 31% improvement in agent productivity.

The various editions of Salesforce Service Cloud are mentioned as follows:

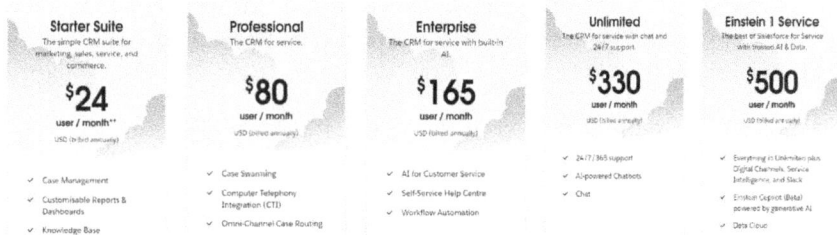

Figure 3.2: Sales Cloud editions

Note: **Salesforce Service Cloud edition prices may change from time to time.**

Salesforce Lightning platform

Salesforce's Lightning platform is a powerful Cloud development solution that not only offers speed and ease of point-and-click app building, but the flexibility of programmatic development and built-in enterprise services as well. Apps that are mobile, intelligent, and connected can easily be built on right out of the box functionality. Since the Einstein 1 platform is built API-first, it is easy to unlock data from the back-office systems and give the team all the information they need in a single place. The Lightning platform's leading multitenant, metadata-based Cloud infrastructure gives the apps the same scalability and security that is trusted by more than 100,000 customers to run their businesses.

As per the IDC White Paper 2018, the Lightning platform gives the following benefits:

- 57% faster IT app development life cycle.
- 5.8 times more business.
- 545% of 5-year ROI.

The following figure depicts different types of platform licenses of Salesforce:

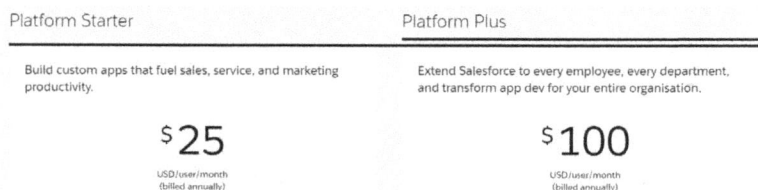

Figure 3.3: Sales Cloud editions

Note: **Salesforce Lightning Platform edition prices may change from time to time.**

Creating a Salesforce developer account

It is recommended that you use a Salesforce developer account to start using Salesforce and practice it. You can use the Salesforce developer account to practice the examples covered in this book. The Salesforce developer account is completely free and can be used to practice the topics you want to learn.

To create a new Salesforce developer account, refer to the following steps:

1. Type the UR **https://developer.salesforce.com/signup** in your browser.
2. Fill in the details in the Sign-up page as mentioned in the following figure:

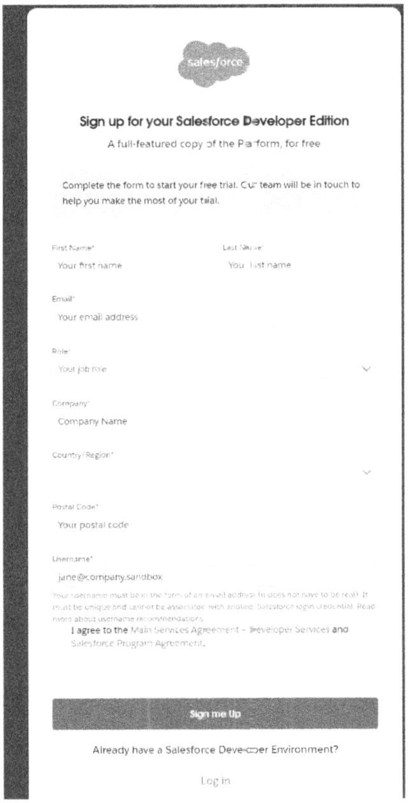

Figure 3.4: Developer edition Sign up form

3. Accept the main service agreement checkbox and click on the **Sign me up** button
4. You will get an e-mail from *Salesforce.com* to verify your account.
5. Click on **Verify Account**.
6. Once you verify successfully, you are ready to use Salesforce.

Logging in to a Salesforce account

Perform the following steps to log in to a Salesforce account:

1. Type the URL in any browser: **https://login.salesforce.com**

Figure 3.5: Log in to Salesforce account

2. Fill in the **Username** and **Password**.
3. Click on **Log In** to log in to your Salesforce account.

Lightning Experience navigation menu

The first screen you get after logging-in is the home screen. Here is a figure of the home screen:

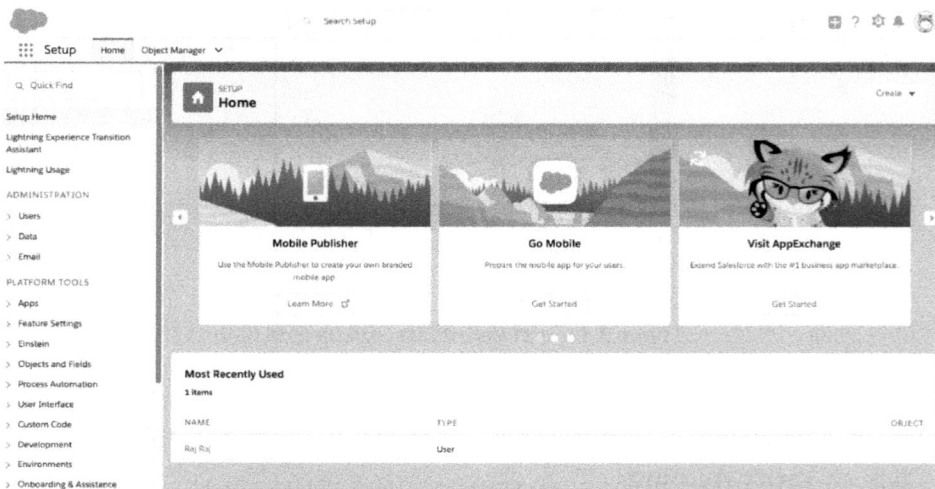

Figure 3.6: Salesforce home screen

1. Go to **App Launcher** (On the top-left corner of the page), as shown in the following figure:

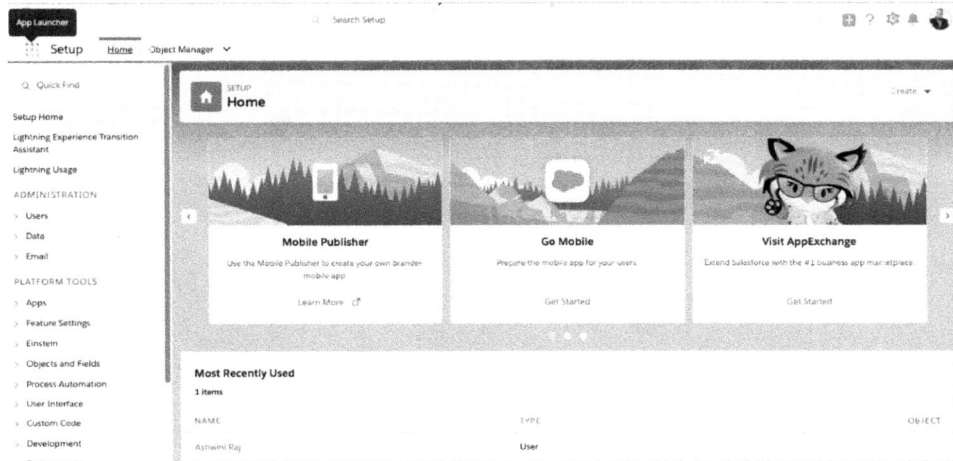

Figure 3.7: App Launcher

2. Select the **Sales** app from the list of apps as shown in the following figure:

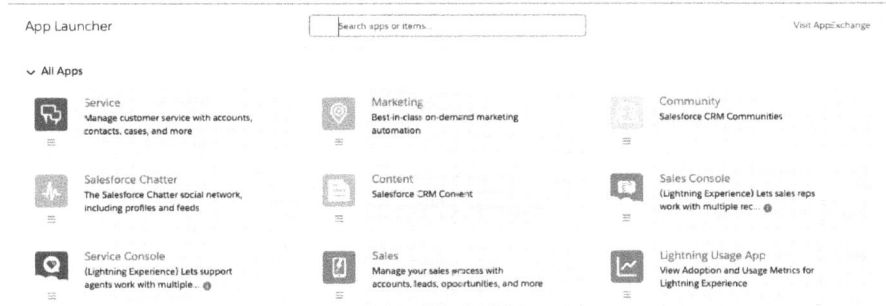

Figure 3.8: Using Sales app

The screen will look as shown in the following figure:

Figure 3.9: The 1st screen of the Sales app

In the Lightning Experience, users can see the tabs on top of the screen, shown as follows:

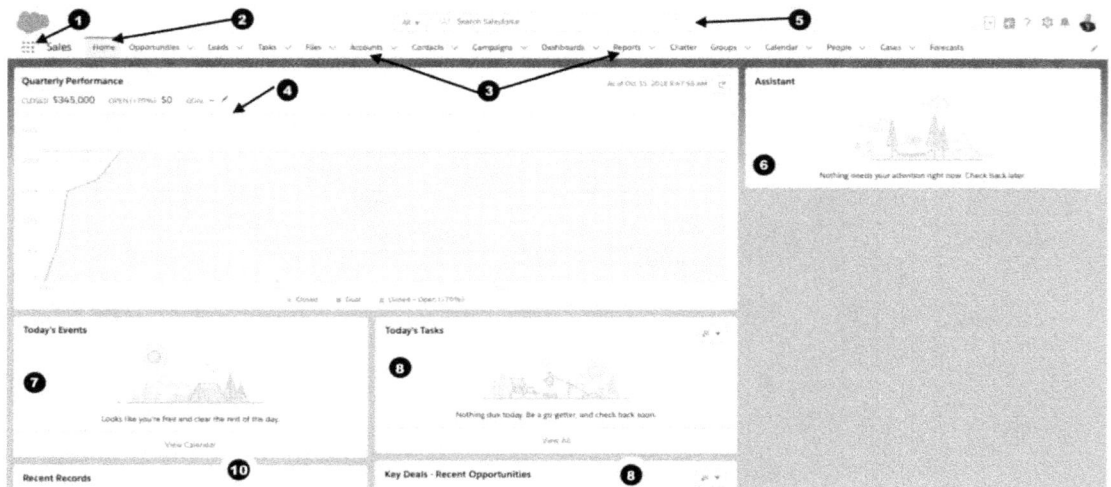

Figure 3.10: Options in the Sales app

In the figure, we see will the following:

- App Launcher
- Selected app
- Tabs in selected app
- Quarterly Performance
- Global search
- Assistance enabled with artificial intelligence
- Today's Event
- Today's Task
- Recent Opportunities
- Recent Records

The **Home** tab is generally set as the opening page for users when they first log in to the application.

The users of Salesforce can access the information and data that is most relevant to them quickly. The home page of Salesforce CRM Lightning Experiences is a great way to view sales performance, top deals, tasks, and events, to name a few.

Global Search

Global Search finds what you are looking for intelligently. The Global Search box is available at the top of every page in Lightning Experience. When you click and start typing on the Global Search box, you see a drop-down of all related data, as shown in the following figure:

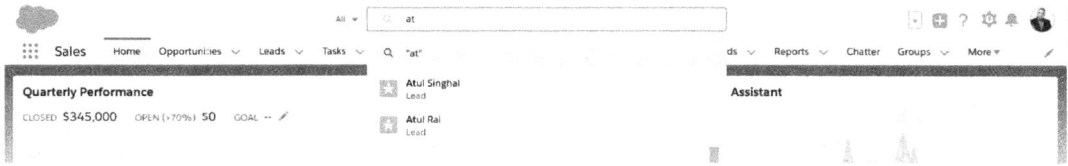

Figure 3.11: Global Search

Switching between Lightning Experience and Salesforce Classic

If you want to switch to the old interface, that is, Classic, you can use Switcher.

Every time you switch between the Classic or Lightning interface, the Switcher remembers the user experience as their new default preference. So, if a particular user switches from Lightning Experience to Classic, it is now their default user experience until they switch back to Salesforce Lightning.

To switch from the Lightning interface to Classic, you can perform the following two steps:

1. Click on the user profile.
2. Select **Switch to Salesforce Classic** as displayed in the following figure:

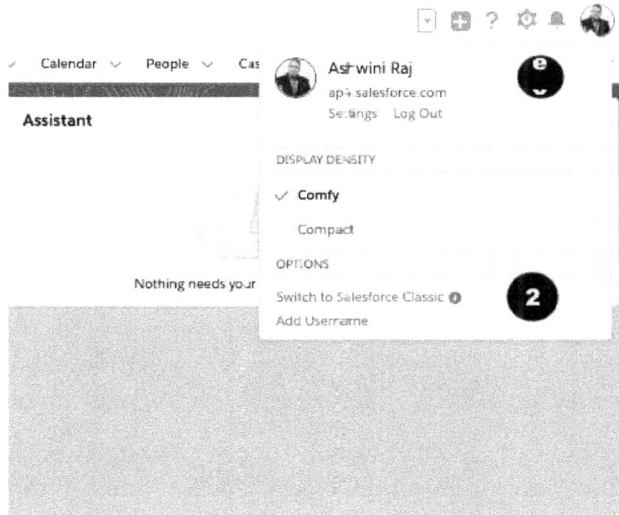

Figure 3.12: Salesforce Switcher

Now, the interface looks like:

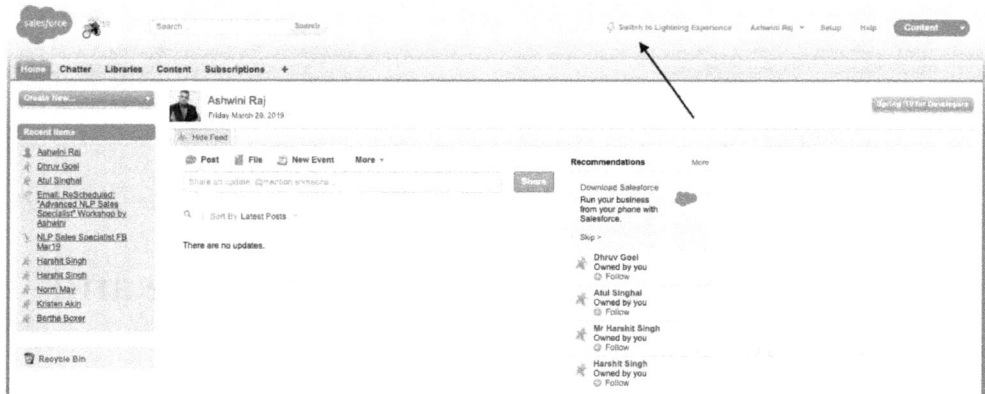

Figure 3.13: *Classic interface*

You can switch back to the Lightning interface by clicking on the **Switch to Lightning Interface** option as the arrow marked in *Figure 3.13*.

As the Lightning interface is the latest, in all of the remaining chapter of the book, we will work on Lightning interface only.

Data modeling in Salesforce

Data modeling is a methodology that models database tables in a way that is comprehensible to humans. In Salesforce, database tables are referred to as objects, columns as fields, and rows as records. Salesforce data model is nothing but a collection of objects and fields in an app.

Objects

Objects are the key elements of Salesforce. As mentioned earlier, objects are the database tables. They provide structure for storing data and are incorporated into the interface. This helps users to interact with the data. Objects are containers for the information. They also give special functionality required in the app. For example, when the custom object is created, the platform automatically builds things like the page layout for user interface.

Salesforce supports various types of objects, such as standard objects, custom objects, external objects, platform events, and BigObjects. The two most common types of objects are as follows:

- **Standard objects**: They are included with Salesforce by default. For example: Account, contact, lead, and opportunity.

- **Custom objects**: They are objects created to store information that is specific to the organization. Once custom objects and records for these objects are created, the reports and Dashboards based on the record data in your custom object can be created. Custom objects are identified by **a __c** suffix.

Note: **We will learn how to create custom objects in** *Chapter 6, Designing Applications on Salesforce.*

Difference between standard and custom objects

The following table describes the differences between standard and custom objects:

Standard object	Custom object
Cannot be deleted	Can be deleted
Cannot change the Grant Access Using Hierarchies sharing access	Can change the Grant Access Using Hierarchies sharing access
Cannot be truncated	Can be truncated
It is possible to create custom fields on standard objects	Custom objects contain some standard fields, for example, name, created by, last modified by, and so on

Table 3.1: Differences between standard and custom object

External objects

External objects are similar to custom objects. They allow you to map data stored outside your Salesforce organization.

Each external object trusts on an external data source definition such as Salesforce Connect or OData to connect with the external system's data. The following figure depicts how Salesforce is connected with external repositories:

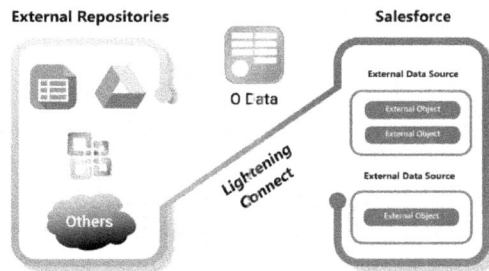

Figure: 3.14: Salesforce External object

In each external object, the fields of the object are mapped to a data table and columns on the external system. External objects are usually identified by **a __x** suffix.

Fields

Every standard and custom object has fields attached to it. The following table will help to understand it better:

Field type	Remarks
Identity	• Number of characters are15. • Case-sensitive field. • Automatically generated for every record. • You can find a record's ID in its URL.
System	Read-only fields Provides information about a record from the system, like when the record was created or when it was last changed.
Name	Distinguishes between records. Can be used as a text or auto-numbered.
Custom	Fields you create on standard or custom objects.

Table 3.2: Salesforce field types

For every Salesforce object; identity, system, and name fields are standard. In Salesforce, each standard object comes with a set of predefined, standard fields. Standard objects can be customized by adding relevant custom fields. Custom fields can also be added to custom objects.

There are two types of fields:
- Standard fields
- Custom fields

Standard fields

Standard fields are predefined fields that are included within the Salesforce application. These fields can neither be edited nor deleted, but non-required standard fields can be removed from page layouts whenever needed. Both standard and custom objects contain a few common standard fields such as **Name**, **CreateDate**, **LastModifiedDate**, and **Owner** fields.

Custom fields

Custom fields are unique to your business needs. These fields can be created and deleted. Creating custom fields helps in storing the information that is necessary for your organization. Custom fields are identified by **a __c** suffix.

Every field has a data type. A data type of a field indicates what kind of information the field can store.

There are various data types, such as **ID**, **String**, **Boolean**, and **Double**.

Different field types

The following table describes various types of fields and their description:

Field type	Description
Address	A compound data type. It contains address field data.
AnyType	A polymorphic data type. It returns a String, Boolean, currency, int, Double, Picklist, reference, percent, ID, Date, date-time, URL, or email data depending on the kind of field.
Calculated	It is defined by a formula.
Combobox	It includes a set of enumerated values. It allows the user to specify a value, not on the list.
Currency	Currency values.
DataCategoryGroupReference	It gives reference to a data category group or a unique category name.
Email	An e-mail address.
Encryptedstring	It contains any combination of letters, numbers, or symbols that are stored in an encrypted form. It can contain a maximum length of up to 175 characters.
ID	A primary key field for the object.
Location	A compound data type. It contains latitude and longitude values for geolocation fields.
Masterrecord	When records are merged, the ID of the record that is saved.
Multipicklist	Multi-select picklists. It includes a set of enumerated values from which multiple values can be selected.
Percent	A percentage of values.
Phone	A phone number value. It can include alphabetic characters. Client applications are responsible for phone number formatting.
Picklist	They include a set of enumerated values from which one value can be selected.
Reference	Cross-references to a different object.

Field type	Description
Textarea	A string that is displayed as a multiline text field.
URL	URL values. This is commonly displayed as hyperlinks.

Table: 3.3: Field types

Note: **We will learn how to create custom fields in** *Chapter 6, Chapter 6, Designing* **Applications on Salesforce.**

Object relationship

In Salesforce, an object can be associated with another object. Object relationships are a special type of field that connects two objects. The relationship types determine how they take care of record sharing, data deletion capability, and required fields in page layouts.

For example, for an account, a sales representative probably has been in touch with many people like an IT manager or business head. Storing this contact information for this account is important. Thus, it makes sense that there should be a relationship between the account object and the contact object.

In the account record in Salesforce, there is a section for contacts on the related tab. The button in contacts can be used to add a contact to an account quickly.

The following figure describes how the account and contact objects are related:

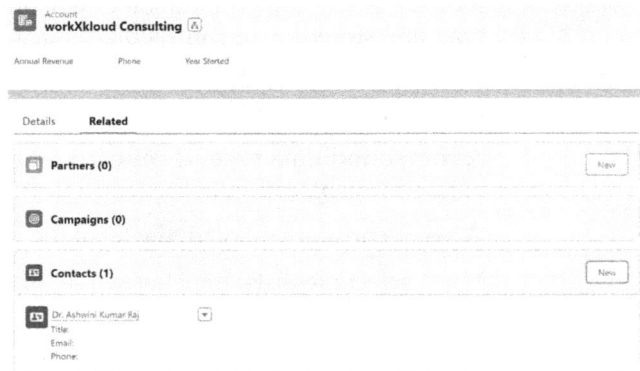

Figure 3.15: Relationship between objects

The account and contact object relationship is an example of a standard relationship in Salesforce. You can also build custom relationships between two or more custom objects.

Salesforce provides the following types of relationships:
- Master-detail relationship

- Lookup relationship
- Self-relationship
- External lookup relationship
- Indirect lookup relationship
- Many-to-many relationship (junction object)
- Hierarchical relationship

Master-detail relationship

A master-detail relationship is a strongly coupled relationship between Salesforce objects. In this type of relationship, visibility and sharing are a concern, and the parent record controls the behavior of the child record. It means that the security setting of a parent object by default applies to the child object too. If a master record gets deleted, then the child records associated with it are also deleted.

For example, in a recruitment application, every Position should have one or more Interviewers associated. An Interviewer record should always be associated with at least a Position record. If a Position is deleted, the associated Interviewer data should also be deleted.

In this case, there exists a master-detail relationship between Position and Interviewer objects. The following figure gives a visual representation of the master-detail relationship between Interviewer and Position objects:

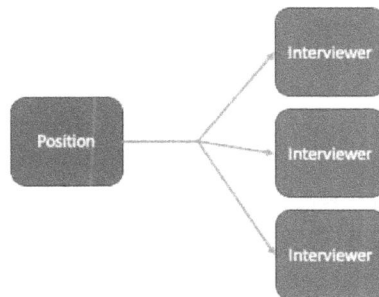

Figure: 3.16: Master-detail relationship

In the master-detail relationship, a unique type of field is created on the master object, called roll-up summary. A roll-up summary field allows us to calculate values from child records linked to a parent record.

Lookup relationship

A lookup relationship links two objects so that you can **look up** one object from the related items on another object. It can be one-to-one or one-to-many. It is a loosely coupled relationship between Salesforce objects. In this case, even if a parent record gets deleted, the child records remain. Both the parent and child have their security controls as well as sharing settings.

The standard objects account to contact are having a lookup relationship. The standard objects account to contact have a one-to-many relationship as a single account can have many related contacts. The following figure depicts how the lookup relationship is established between contact and account objects:

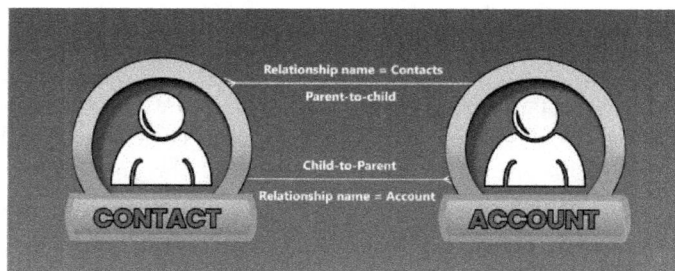

Figure: 3.17: *Lookup relationship*

Difference between master-detail and lookup relationships

The following table depicts the difference between master-detail and lookup relationships:

Master-detail relationship	Lookup relationship
Strongly coupled.	Loosely coupled.
Parent record is always required to create a child record.	Parent record is not required while creating a child record.
The Master-detail field is always required on the page layout of the detailed record.	Lookup fields are not required on the page layout of the detail record.
Standard object records cannot act like a child.	A standard object record can be on the detail side of a custom object in a lookup relationship.
The parent controls the record ownership of child records. The owner field is not available on the detail record in master-detail relationship queues. Sharing rules and manual sharing is not possible for detail records as it requires the owner field.	Record ownership of child records is not controlled by the parent by default.
Impossible to have a child record without a parent.	Possible

Master-detail relationship	Lookup relationship
Maximum two master details on an object.	Maximum 40 lookups on an object.
A roll-up summary field can be created.	A roll-up summary field cannot be created.
Cascade delete.	No cascade delete.

Table 3.4: *Difference between master-detail and lookup relationship*

Self-relationship

Self-relationship is a special type of lookup relationship. Lookup relationships can be used to create self-relationship among objects. There can be a maximum of 40 self-lookups; for example, a campaign can have a parent campaign.

External lookup relationship

Two individual lookups can be created on an external object apart from the standard lookup relationship:

- External lookup relationship
- Indirect lookup relationship

An external lookup relationship allows one to link an external object to a parent external object whose data is stored in an external data source. In simple words, it allows linking two external objects.

Indirect lookup relationship

With an indirect lookup relationship, an external object can be linked to a standard or custom object. An indirect lookup to an object can only be created with a unique external ID field on the parent object that is used to match the records in this relationship. While creating an indirect lookup relationship field on an external object, it is required to specify the child object field and the parent object field to match and associate records in the relationship.

For example, the orders from SAP can be linked with accounts, and in doing so, generate a related list on the accounts page.

Many-to-many relationship

The many-to-many relationship in Salesforce allows one to link a child record to multiple parents. For example, a lead can be attached to many campaigns, and a campaign can have many leads. The many-to-many relationship is shown in the following figure:

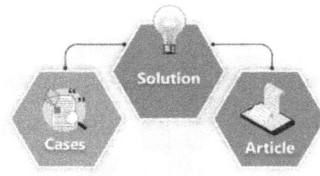

Figure 3.18: *Many-to-many relationship*

Let us assume we have two objects, called cases and article, and it is required to relate these two objects in such a manner that one article is linked to many cases, and one case can have multiple articles. In this case, there is a need to use a many-to-many relationship. The many-to-many relationship is made with the help of a third object called junction object. In this case, a third object named solution is created with two master-detail relationships with solution – case and solution – article.

Hierarchical relationship

In Salesforce, this type of relationship exists only with the user object. In this case, a hierarchy of users is created in the organization. For example, a sales representative can have his sales manager, and the sales manager may have a senior manager, and so on until the CEO or CIO level.

When developing an approval process, a custom hierarchical relationship field on the user object enables one to specify the next person up in a hierarchy. This is useful if the standard manager field is not appropriate for the given approval process that you are developing. A custom hierarchy of approvers can be created using a custom hierarchical relationship field and use that field to designate a specific **higher-up** for each user in the hierarchy. Then, the approval process can be set up to use the value in that field to determine who is the next approver for a given step.

The best example is the manager field on a user object, as shown in the following figure:

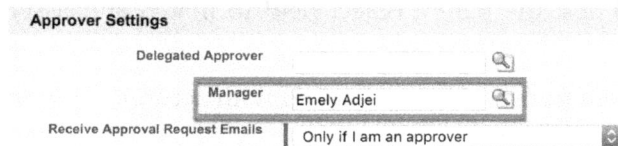

Figure 3.19: *Hierarchical relationship*

Conclusion

This chapter introduces the Lightning interface of Salesforce. It also gave insight into the data modeling of Salesforce. The various parts of data modeling are objects, fields, records, and so on. You also learned about the two types of objects, which are standard and custom objects. Salesforce creates standard objects by default. Custom objects are created depending on the requirements of the organization. The objects are related to each other through object relationships. It is very important to understand these before we start using it. The next chapter will focus on Salesforce CRM.

Questions

1. **Which of the following is not a Salesforce Sales Cloud edition?**

    a. Starter suit

    b. UnLimited

    c. UnProfessional

    d. Enterprise

2. **As per the IDC report, the Lightning Platform gives what?**

    a. Faster IT app development life cycle

    b. More Business

    c. More ROI

    d. All of the above

3. **Which of the following is not a feature of Service Cloud?**

    a. Knowledge base

    b. Service Cloud console

    c. Campaign management

    d. CTI

4. **Which of the following is not a type of relationship in Salesforce?**

    a. Master-detail relationship

    b. Hierarchical relationship

    c. Self-relationship

    d. Direct lookup Relationship

5. **Which of the following provides structure for storing data and are incorporated into the interface, so that users can interact with the data?**

    a. Relationship

    b. Objeco

    c. Essential Edition

    d. App Cloud

6. **Which of the followings is not true about custom object?**

    a. Custom object can be deleted.

    b. Custom object cannot be truncated.

    c. Custom object can change the Grant Access Using Hierarchies sharing access.

    d. None of the above.

7. **Which of the followings is not the difference between master-details and lookup relationship?**

    a. The master-details relationship is strongly coupled, whereas the lookup relationship is loosely coupled.

    b. In the case of the master-detail relationship, it is impossible to have a child record without a parent. However, it is possible in case of lookup relationship.

    c. There can be maximum two master details on an object possible; however, unlimited lookup on an object is feasible.

    d. None of the above.

8. **In a situation, a campaign is attached to many leads, and one lead may have more than one campaign. Which type of relation is depicted?**

    a. Many-to-many relationships

    b. One-to-one relationship

    c. Many-to-one relationship

    d. One-to-many relationships

9. **A maximum how many lookups on an object can be created:**

    a. 30

    b. 20

    c. 40

    d. 60

10. **Which object relationship allows us to link an external object to a standard or custom object?**

    a. Self-relationship

    b. External relationship

    c. Direct lookup relationship

    d. Indirect lookup relationship

Answers

1. c
2. d
3. c
4. d
5. b
6. b
7. c
8. a
9. c
10. d

References

1. *Salesforce Sales Cloud license pricing:* **https://www.salesforce.com/in/sales/pricing/**

2. *Salesforce Service Cloud license Pricing:* **https://www.salesforce.com/in/service/pricing/**

3. *Salesforce Platform license pricing:* **https://www.salesforce.com/in/editions-pricing/platform/**

Join our Discord space

Join our Discord workspace for latest updates, offers, tech happenings around the world, new releases, and sessions with the authors:

https://discord.bpbonline.com

## CHAPTER 4

Introducing Salesforce Customer Relationship Management

Introduction

In this chapter, we will learn about **Customer relationship management** (**CRM**) is, a data-driven software solution that improves the way people interact and do business with their customers. CRM systems help to manage and maintain customer relationships, track sales, marketing, and pipeline, and deliver actionable data. CRM makes sure the data is visible to various stakeholders within the organization. It helps businesses gain insights into the behavior of their customers and modify their business operations to make sure that customers are served in the best possible way.

Structure

In this chapter, you will learn the following topics:

- Introducing Sales Cloud
- Campaign management
- Lead management
- Activity management
- Account management
- Contact management

- Product and price book management
- Opportunity management
- Quote management

Objectives

After studying this chapter, you will understand the basics of Salesforce CRM. You will be introduced to Sales Cloud, in which you will learn to do campaign management, lead management, account and contact management, opportunity management, product and price book management, and quote management.

Introducing Sales Cloud

Sales Cloud is a product from Salesforce, which is designed to automate the sales processes of the organization. It helps not only in managing the customers in a simple and faster way but also increases the sales reps' productivity. It includes features such as campaign, lead, account, contact, opportunity, quote, report, and dashboard. Sales Cloud can help an organization to close deals faster using inbuilt functionalities.

Sales Cloud helps you to maintain a robust sales pipeline, from quotation to contract management, on the Cloud. The productivity accomplished by implementing Sales Cloud in your organization will allow your sales reps to focus on managing good relationships with existing customers. It will help them bring new business as well. Your sales team will work more competently while your marketing executives are provided with the actual information for making more informed and quicker business decisions.

Sales Cloud also helps align the marketing, inside sales, and sales teams so they can work together in an organized manner to win more deals, bring in new customers, and retain existing customers. There are some advantages to implement the Sales Cloud are as follows:

- Improve lead conversion rate.
- Close more deals with the help of Einstein.
- Align territories and quotas to business strategy.
- Get a 360-degree view of your customer.
- Standardize quoting and contracting management capability.
- Accelerate productivity with Salesforce1 mobile app.
- Automate business processes by using lightning flows and approval processes.
- Make insightful decisions with the help of reports and Dashboards.

Campaign management

A campaign is an awareness or branding program that a company runs to promote its products or business.

With campaigns, marketers analyze how many leads they are generating, how much pipeline they are building, and how many deals they are closing as a result of marketing activities.

With campaigns, you can also group your marketing programs into hierarchies for greater visibility into the results of a large group of campaigns.

An organization can run campaigns through various channels like advertisement, seminar, trade show, banner, and bulk e-mail. Through a campaign, an organization can generate prospects (a person or another organization who is interested in your product or services).

Salesforce allows the marketing team to capture their campaign plan, manage, execute, and track it within Salesforce. It is pretty easy to capture new prospects directly from your corporate website's Contact Us form into Salesforce. Even the prospects can be captured easily from the GoToWebinar register attendees for an event to Salesforce. Once the prospects are captured, you can easily associate those prospects with a campaign to track and view how successful the marketing effort was. This helps in calculating the **return on investment** (ROI) for the campaign.

To create a campaign, you can perform the following steps:

1. From the **Campaigns** tab, click on **New**, as shown in the following figure:

Figure 4.1: Creating a campaign

2. Enter a name for the campaign.
3. Select a campaign type such as conference, webinar, and tradeshow.
4. Select a **Status** for the campaign.
5. Select **Start Date**, **End Date**, and so on.
6. For now, enter an estimate for budgeted cost and expected revenue.
7. Enter a description.
8. Click on **Save**, as shown in the following figure:

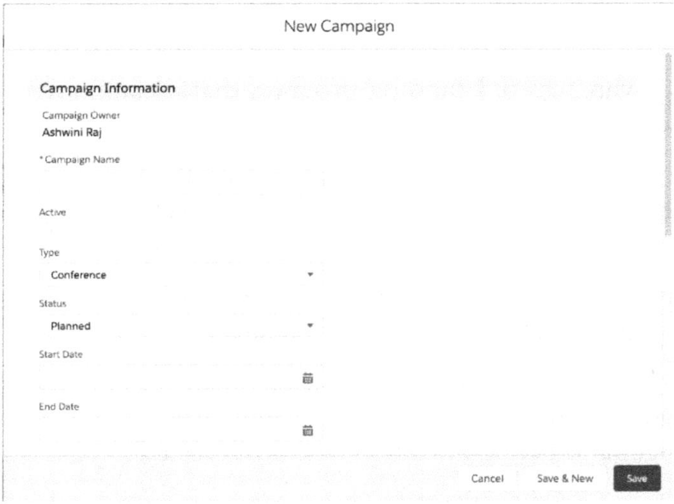

Figure 4.2: Filling details in a new campaign

Note: **You should have a marketing user profile to create a campaign. Your admin can give you that permission if you do not already have it. To check whether you have the Marketing User option in your user profile, follow these steps:**

1. **Click on Setup and enter Users in the Quick Find box.**

2. **Click on Users and then your username.**

3. **Look for the Marketing User checkbox on the user detail page. If the box is not checked, edit the record and select the checkbox.**

Campaign hierarchy

By using the Parent Campaign field on the campaigns, you can relate your campaigns to each other in a hierarchy. With a hierarchy, you can group your campaigns into categories that suit your business.

There are many different ways in which hierarchies can be applied to a business's marketing practices. A common approach is to use the hierarchy to group campaigns by marketing strategy. While the hierarchy can have as many levels as you want, a minimum of three levels is well-suited for many companies. The top level may represent the overall strategic focus such as selling a new product or building brand awareness. The second level may represent the different aspects of that focus, such as the product launch, getting feedback from purchasers, or upselling previous customers. Finally, the third level may include individual marketing efforts, for example, an e-mail, an online ad, or conducting demo.

Assuming we create a campaign named **Sell New Product**, the campaign hierarchy will be like the following figure:

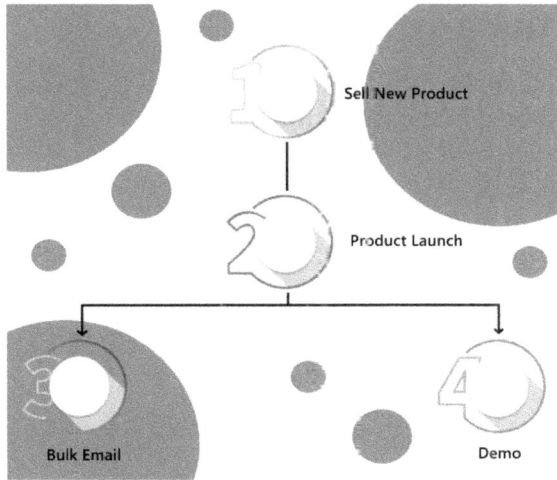

Figure 4.3: *Campaign hierarchy*

To create a new campaign named **Product Launch**, you can select the **Sell New Product** campaign from the **Parent Campaign** option:

Figure 4.4: *Selecting Parent Campaign*

Adding data to campaign

You can add relevant data to the campaign. The activities performed on the campaign can be recorded as well as shown in the following figure:

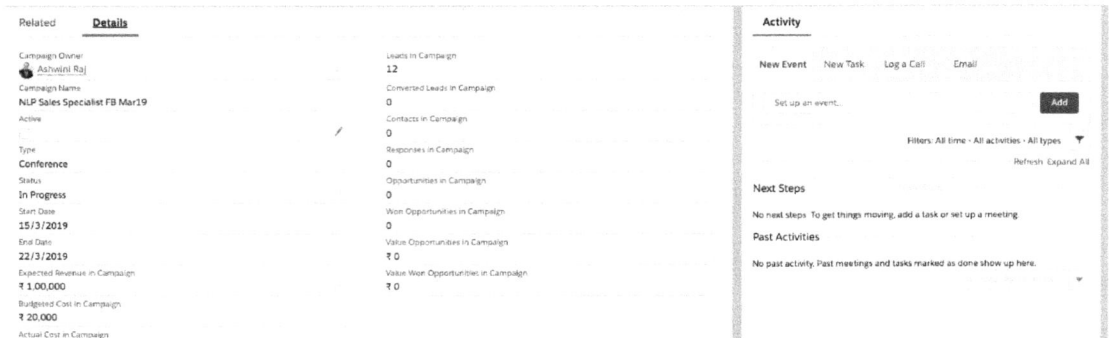

Figure 4.5: Adding data to campaign

Adding prospects to the campaigns

Leads, contacts, and person accounts can be added to the campaign created by you. This can be done in the following ways:

- Adding leads:
  - Using the record detail page.
  - By clicking on **Add Leads** from a campaign's **Campaign Member** related list.
- Adding contacts:
  - Using the record detail page.
  - From an account by clicking on **Add Contacts** in the campaign.
- Adding members
  - By clicking on **Manage Campaign Members** from the dropdown menu on the **Campaign Members** related list.
  - From the contacts related list on an account detail page.

The following figure shows the Campaign Members added to a campaign:

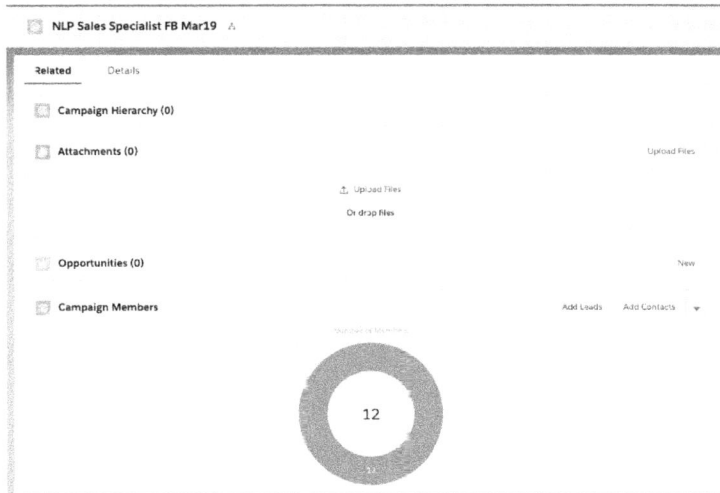

Figure 4.6: Adding contact to campaign member

Lead management

Lead is the prospects that are interested in purchasing your product or something your organization is selling. Lead generation is the center of the relationship between sales and marketing of an organization. Lead management has a few steps such as capturing a lead, qualifying it, nurturing it, and then pursuing it. The following figure depicts the lead management process:

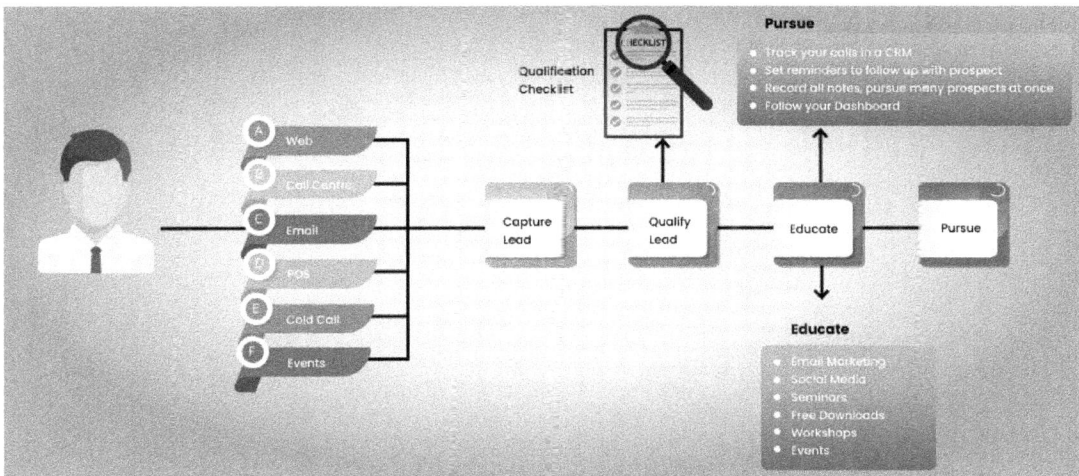

Figure 4.7: Lead management

The lead can be captured through different methods such as referrals, cold calls, the website's contact page, trade fair, etc.

Once the lead is captured, it has to be qualified based on certain criteria. Here are some questions that may help you in evaluating the lead:

- Does the lead have sufficient money to afford your product or service?
- Who is the decision-maker to buy your product or service?
- What is the timeframe to buy your product or service?

Once the lead is qualified, it is allocated to the sales person, and goes through the sales cycle.

Creating a new lead

To create a lead manually, perform the following steps:

1. From the Leads tab, click on New, as shown in the following figure:

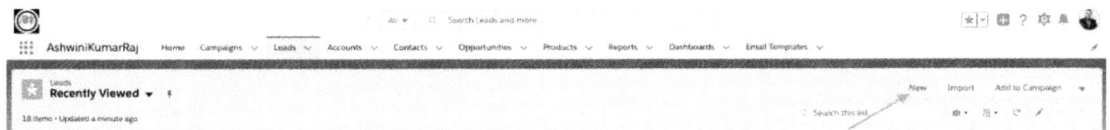

Figure 4.8: Adding a lead

2. Enter the information such as Last Name, Company Name, and Lead Status:

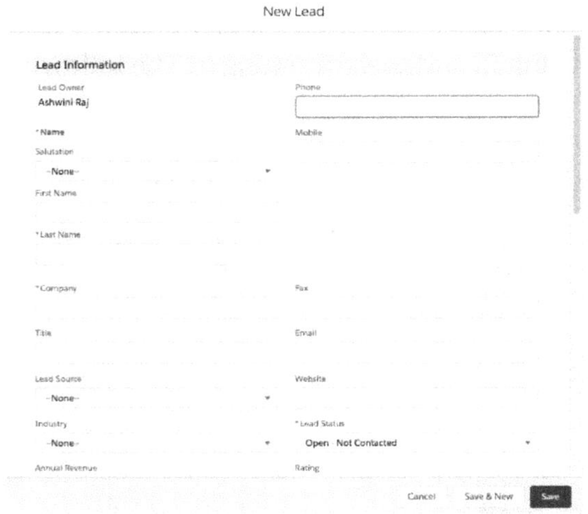

Figure 4.9: Adding details to lead

3. Click on **Save**.

Configuring Web-to-Lead

Apart from the manual process, leads can also be added to Salesforce through an automatic process such as a Web-to-Lead form that collects leads from your business website.

The Web-to-Lead forms are embedded in the company website to gather all the leads.

You can perform the following steps to configure Web-to-Lead:

1. Click on the Setup icon on top right.
2. Choose **Setup** as shown in the following figure:

Figure 4.10: Accessing set up

3. Type `Web-To-Lead` in the Quick Find box.
4. Choose **Web-To-Lead**.
5. Now, select the **Create Web-to-Lead Form**, as shown here:

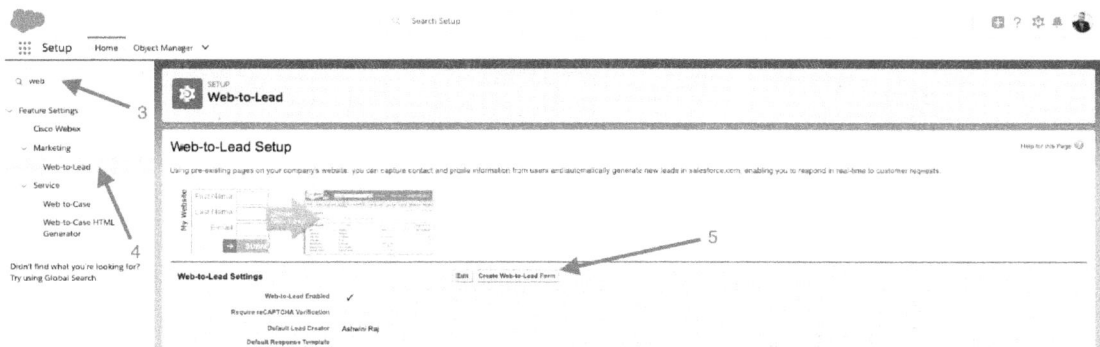

Figure 4.11: Creating Web-to-Lead

6. In the Web-to-Lead setup page, select the fields from **Available Fields** that should appear in the Web-to-Lead form. You may like to use **Add**, **Delete**, **Up**, and **Down** buttons.
7. Enter the **Return URL** (Typically a Thank you page).
8. Deselect on **Include ReCAPTCHA in HTML**.
9. Click on **Generate** to generate the HTML code:

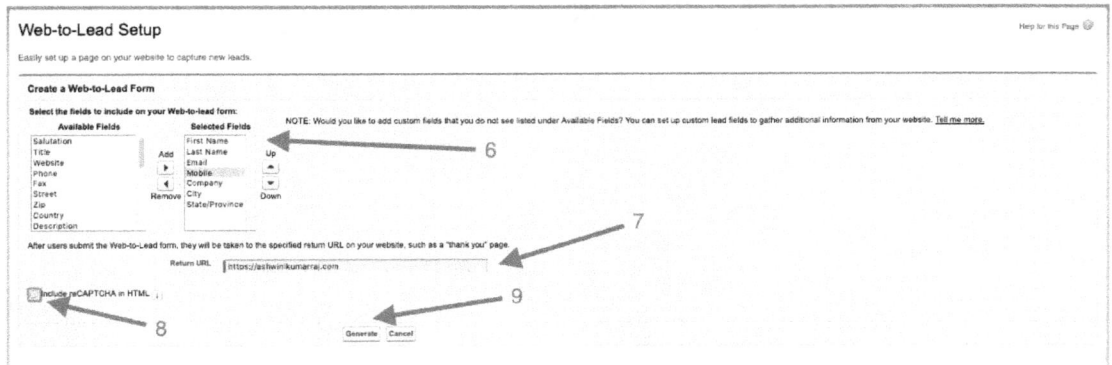

Figure 4.12: Creating Web-to-Lead

10. The HTML code will be generated as follows:

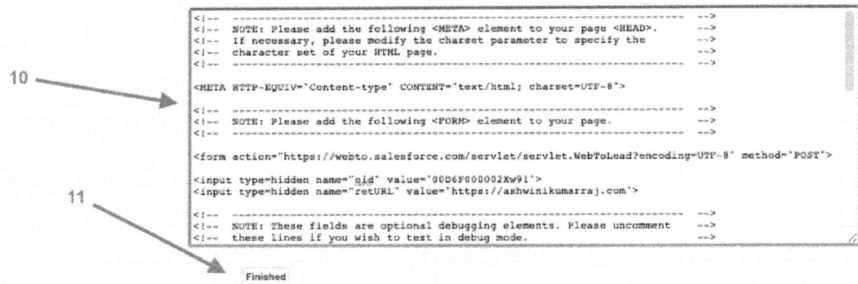

Figure 4.13: Web-to-Lead HRML code

11. Copy the HTML code and click Finished.

12. Paste the code on the website page, for example, the Contact Us page.

13. To experience the functionality, copy and paste the code on any editor like Notepad and then save it with a **.html** extension. (For example: **WebToLead.html**)

14. Now, open the HTML file and fill in the details. The screen will look as follows:

Figure 4.14: Web-to-Lead form

15. Click on **Submit**.
16. Now, in Salesforce, check the availability of a lead by clicking on Leads and Today's Lead view:

The lead entered by the lead form is available in Salesforce.

Editing a lead

You can edit a lead by opening it, clicking on the drop-down, and selecting Edit , s shown in the following figure:

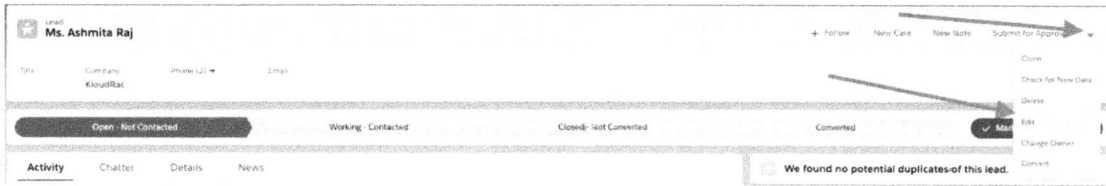

Figure 4.15: Editing a lead

Adding lead to a campaign

To add a lead to an active campaign, you can perform the following steps:

1. Select **Campaign History** from the drop-down list:

Figure 4.16: Selecting a campaign

2. Select **Add to Campaign**, as shown in the following figure:

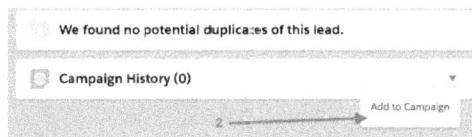

Figure 4.17: Adding to the campaign

3. Choose the campaign you want the lead to be added from the list, as shown in *Figure 4.18*:

Choose a Campaign

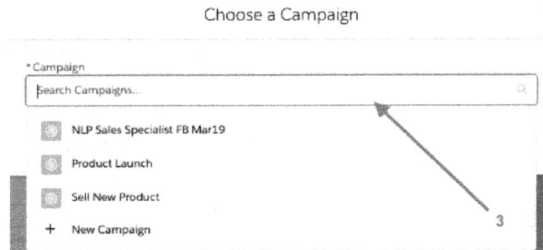

Figure 4.18: Choosing a campaign to add

4. Click on **Save**.

Adding activities to the lead

You can record activities done on the lead. These include tasks like events and e-mails.

Follow these steps to add a task to the lead:

1. Select the lead (For example, Ashmita Raj)
2. Choose **New Task**.
3. Select **Subject, Due Date**, and so on
4. Click on **Save**, as shown in the following figure:

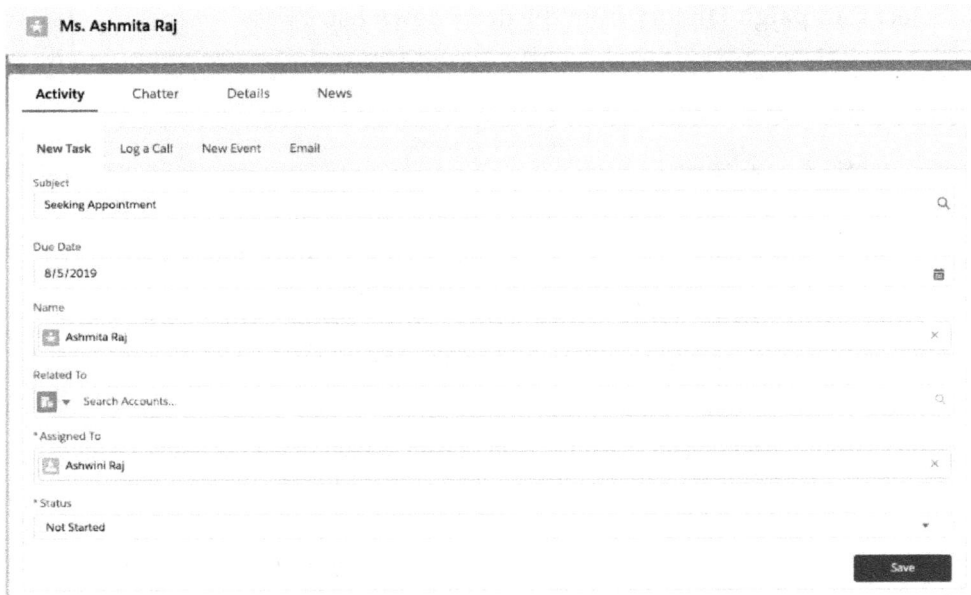

Figure 4.19: Adding activities to a lead

Similarly, you can log a call, new event, and send an email as well.

Changing the status of lead

As you work on the leads, the lead progresses towards the prospect. There are different status of the leads, which are as follows:

- **Open**: Not Contacted
- **Working**: Contacted
- **Closed**: Not Converted
- **Closed**: Converted

You can change the status of the lead in two different ways:

1. Editing the lead:

Figure 4.20: Changing status through editing a lead

2. Changing the lead status from the lead page shown in the following figure:

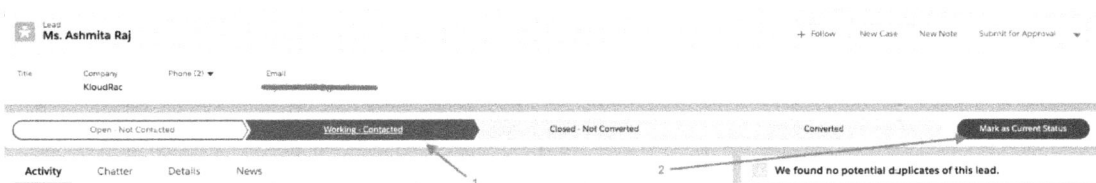

Figure 4.21: Changing status from lead page

Activity management

Activities are the events and tasks that the sales representatives manage in Salesforce. Events and tasks are the backbones of sales productivity. Lightning Experience helps the sales representatives get prepared for any meeting and know which task is the highest priority. It is easy to track meetings and tasks together in lists and reports to keep record of all your leads, contacts, opportunities, accounts, and campaigns. Activity management allows you to see your activity as well as the activities of the people below you in the role hierarchy in Salesforce.

Adding task

The sales representatives can keep the to-do list in Salesforce and stay on top of your deals and accounts.

Tasks can be easily related to leads, contacts, campaigns, contracts, and objects.

Salesforce gives options to create and update tasks, pre-filtered task lists, and task notification options.

To add a task to a lead, follow these steps:

1. Open the lead.
2. Under **Activity** click on **New Task**.
3. Fill the **Subject**, **Due date**, and so on.
4. You can assign the task to somebody under **Name**. By default, the lead owner name is mentioned.
5. Click on **Save** once it is done, as shown in the following figure:

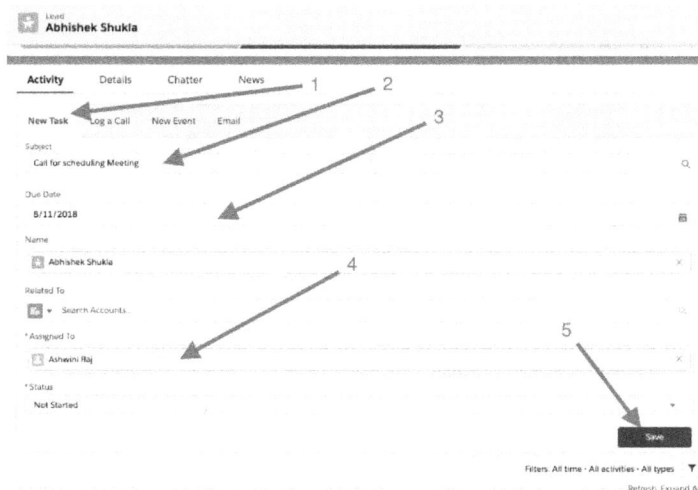

Figure 4.22: Adding a task to a lead

You can see the Activity list on the lead, as shown in the following figure:

Figure 4.23: Activities on a lead

Adding an event

With Salesforce it is easy to track, create, and update meetings and invitation responses in different locations depending on how you work and what meetings are relevant at a given moment.

Similar to the task, an event can be added to the lead as well, as shown in the following figure:

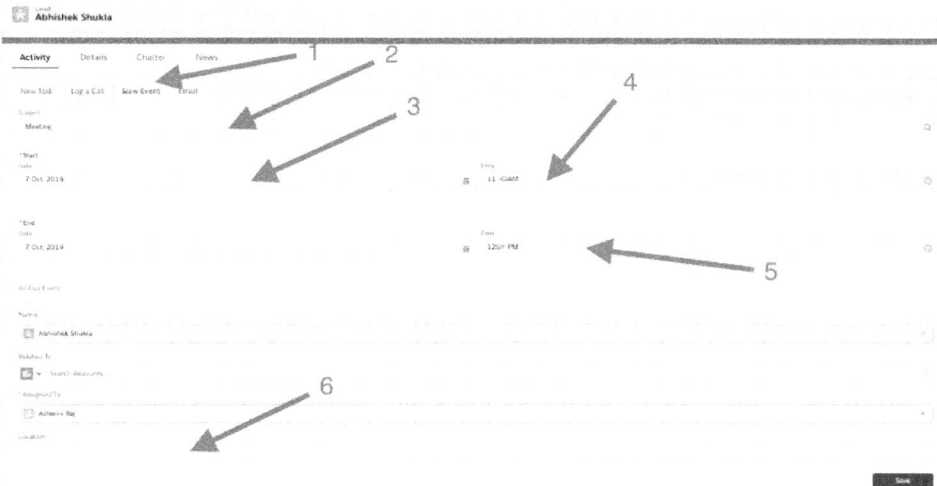

Figure 4.24: Adding a vent

Sending an e-mail

An e-mail can also be sent to a lead in Salesforce. It not only sends e-mails from the organization, but also adds it as an activity:

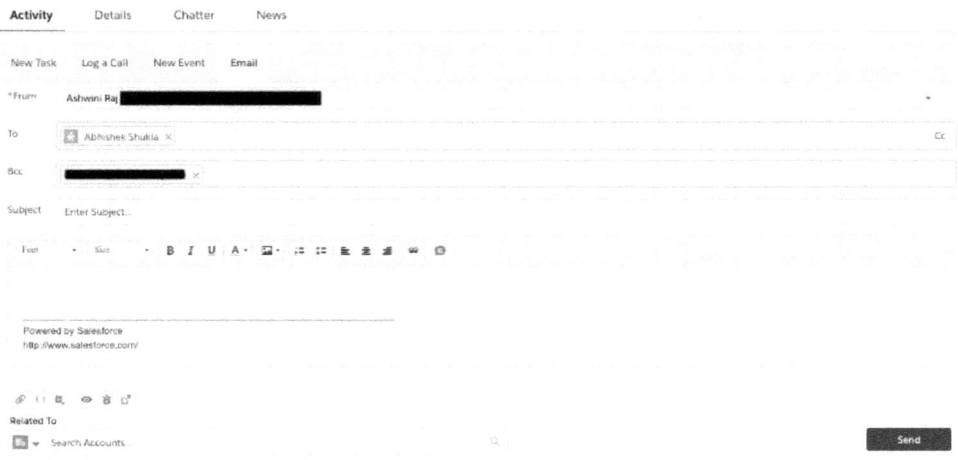

Figure 4.25: Sending email

Note: **There is a limit on sending e-mails from the organization. The Enterprise edition can send up to 5000 e-mails per day.**

Converting a lead

Converting a lead to opportunity takes place when a lead is qualified. When a lead is converted to opportunity, it appears on the forecasting reports in Salesforce.

Lead conversion will create an account, contact, and, optionally, an opportunity in case of a business. However, in the case of an individual consumer, a person account and opportunity are created. During lead conversion, the opportunity amount field on opportunity remains blank, which is shown as follows:

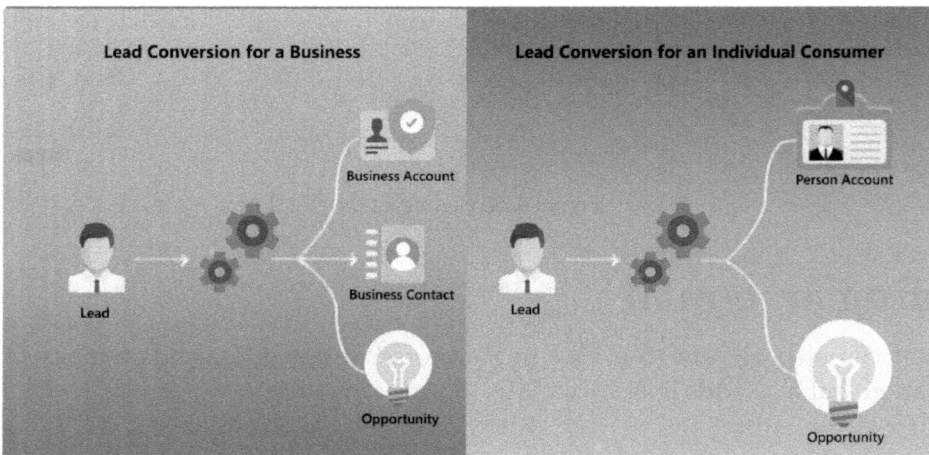

Figure 4.26: Lead conversion process

To convert a lead, perform the following steps:

1. To convert a lead, click on the Converted button and then select Converted status on the Lead page as shown in the following figure:

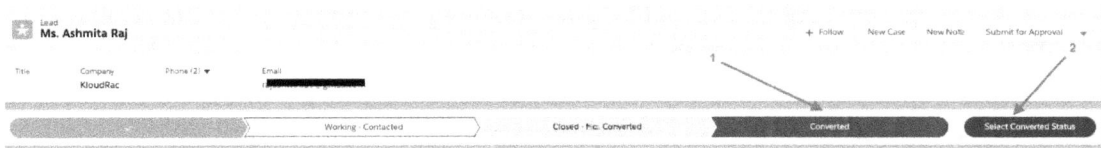

Figure 4.27: Converting a lead

2. Observe the next window.
3. Account is created with company name.
4. Contact is created with lead first name and last name.
5. Opportunity is created with company name and a "-."
6. Please note, creation of opportunity is optional.
7. Please fill the **Opportunity Name** and click on **Convert**:

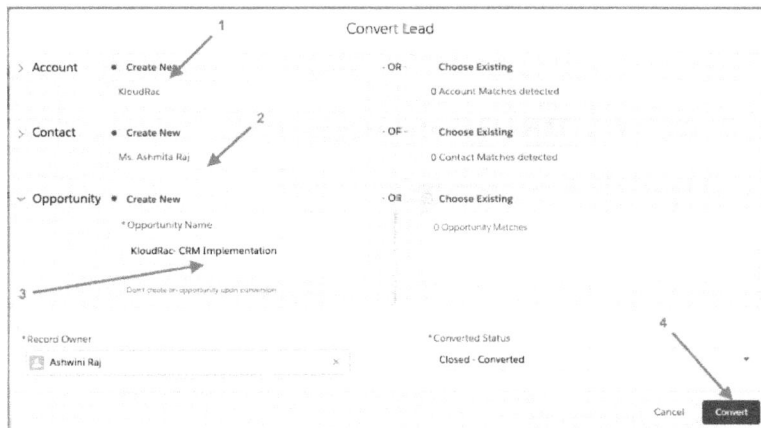

Figure 4.28: Converting a lead

Account management

An account represents the customer, partner, or competitor of an organization. To get insight into the business, it is important to understand with whom the business is being done. The information about customers is stored using accounts and contacts. Accounts are companies that you are doing business with, and contacts are the people who work for them. An account allows you to store and have a 360-degree view of customer data.

As per the survey done by *Gartner*, 65% of a company's business comes from existing customers, and it costs them five times more to attract a new customer than to keep an existing one satisfied. Increasing customer retention rates by 5% increases profits by 25% to 95%, according to research done by *Frederick Reichheld* of *Bain & Company*.

This indicates how important it is to maintain a good relationship with existing customers and, at the same time, follow-up with customers' engagement to grow the relationship and increase revenue on an ongoing basis.

Types of accounts

If you are doing business with a single person, like a solo contractor or an individual consumer, you use a special account type called a person account.

There are two different types of accounts in Salesforce which are as follows:

- **Business account (B2B)**: When products or services are sold to another organization, it is called business-to-business. In Salesforce, the companies that are sold to are business accounts. For every Salesforce organization, the business account is enabled by default.
- **Person account (B2C)**: When products or services are sold to an individual, it is called business-to-person. This account stores customer (Individual) information in Salesforce.

Creating a new business account

There are two ways to create a business account. They are:

- Lead conversion
- Manually adding an account

The former has already been discussed when we converted lead.

To add an account manually, please perform the following steps:

1. Click on the **Accounts** tab.
2. Click on **New**, as shown in the following figure:

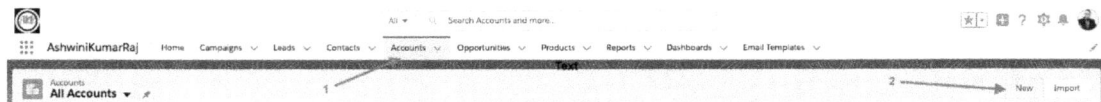

Figure 4.29: Creating a new account

3. Enter the account's name.
4. Enter all the information about the account.
5. Click on **Save**, as shown in the following figure:

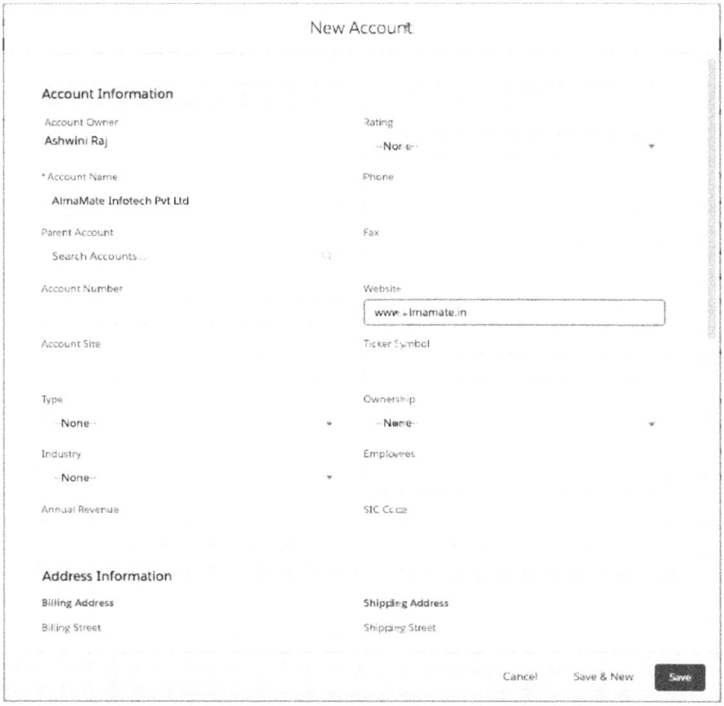

Figure 4.30: *Saving a new account*

Contact management

One of the most important things to know about a company are their employees and a method to reach them. In Salesforce, the people who work at your accounts are called contacts.

You will find the existing contacts by clicking on the Contacts tab and locating them in the Recent Contacts list or selecting a view and clicking on Go.

Like an account record, a contact record can have its related lists of information such as cases that each contact has filed, meetings you have had, or logs of calls to that contact.

Product and price book management

Products are the physical products or services sold to customers. Sales representatives can use the products to generate sales quotes, contracts, or orders. The service representatives can also use products to create customer service cases.

Once you have listed all the products in Salesforce, you can associate it with multiple price books at different prices. Price books are used for selling products at different prices based on the geography or based on the agreement with a customer.

Salesforce.com defines price book as a list of products and their associated prices. Each product and its price is called a price book entry. When you combine price books and products, you can see the various products along with the prices of your company. This helps in providing the payment and delivery cycle of the products, which are required to give companies a proper lifecycle prediction.

PricebookEntry is a junction object that is associated with a product in a price book. What it means is that multiple price books can be added to one product. There are two main prices in price books: standard price and list price. They are depicted as follows:

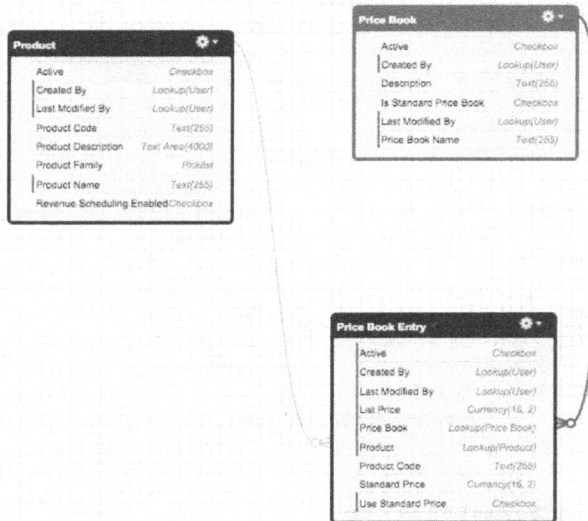

Figure 4.31: Relationship between product and price book

Standard prices are the prices fixed by the manufacturer which cannot be changed.

List price is the selling price of a product. The sales representatives may sell the same product with different prices to customers based on geography or any other criteria.

Adding a new product

Perform the following steps to add a new product:

1. Go to the **Product** tab.
2. Click on the **New** button as shown in the following figure:

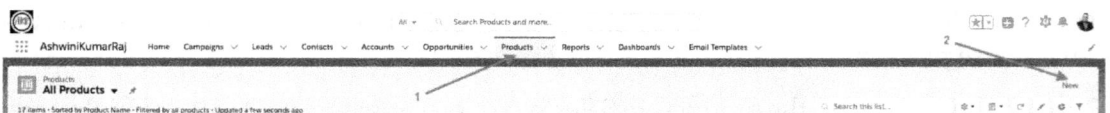

Figure 4.32: Adding a new product

3. Enter the **Product Name** and other details.

4. Check **Active** if you want to make it active immediately.

5. Once you are done, click on **Save** to save the record, as shown in the following figure:

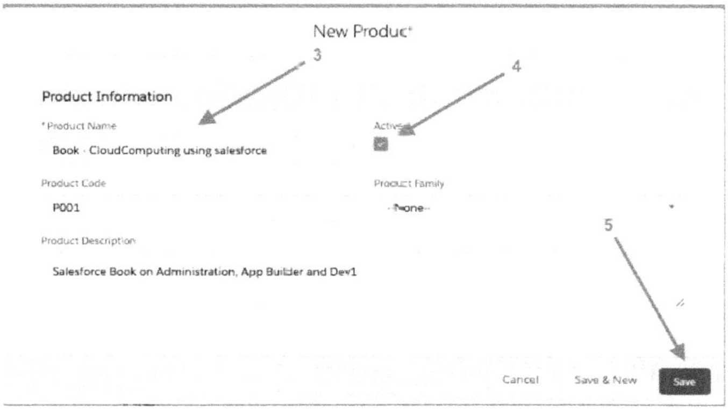

Figure 4 33: Saving a new product

Perform the preceding steps (one to three) to enter as many products into Salesforce as you want.

Adding standard price to a product

Once the product is added to Salesforce, the next step is to add a standard price to it. Standard prices are prices fixed by the manufacturer, which cannot be changed.

To add the price book, perform the following steps:

1. Select the product for which you want to add price book from the Product tab.

2. From the details page, navigate to the **Related** list.

3. Click on the **Add Standard Price** button available under the **Price Books** related list, as shown in the following figure:

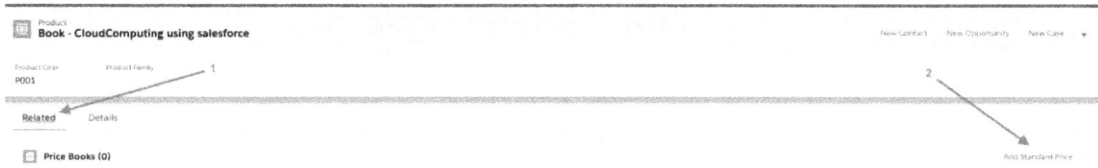

Figure 4.34: Adding price to a product

4. On the new window, enter the standard price into the **List Price** box.

5. Once you are done, click on the **Save** button:

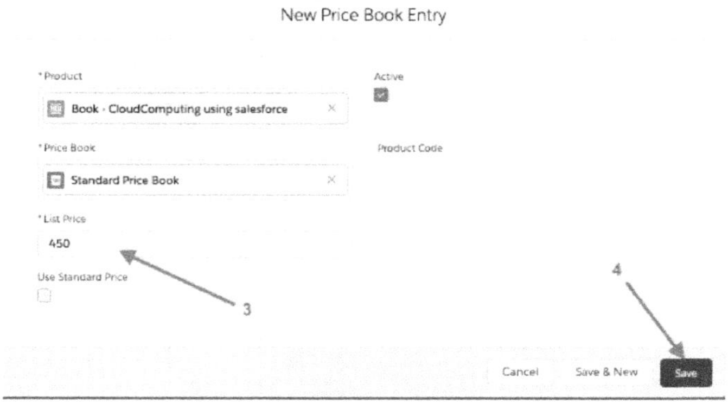

Figure 4.35: Adding a new price book

Note: **One product can have only one standard price. Standard Price Book is by default available in all instances of Salesforce.**

Creating a price book

Price books are used for selling products at different prices based on geography or based on the agreement with a customer. The following two types of price books exist in Salesforce:

- The standard price book is a price book that contains all products and their standard prices.
- A custom price book allows us to offer products to distinctive groups of customers at different list prices.

Follow these steps to create a new price book:

1. Choose **New** from the **Price Books** tab:

Figure 4.36: Creating a new price book

2. Fill the details and choose **Save** to save when you are done:

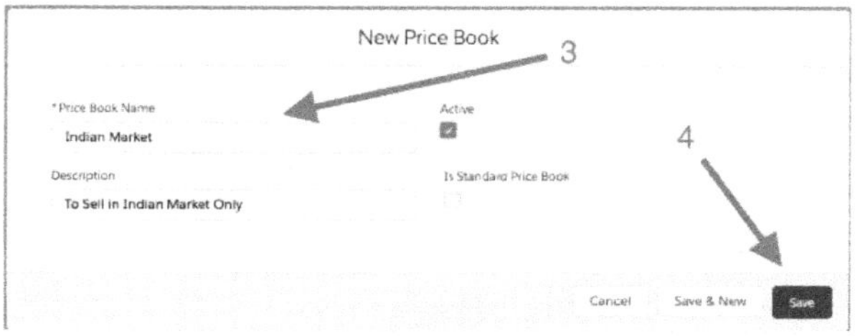

Figure 4.37: Saving a price book

Associating a product with the price book

Once both products and price books are defined, the next step would be to associate both of them, using the price book entry object. You can do so through the product page or from the price book page.

You can perform the following steps to associate a price book with a product:

1. Choose the product you have created from the Product tab, as shown in the following figure:

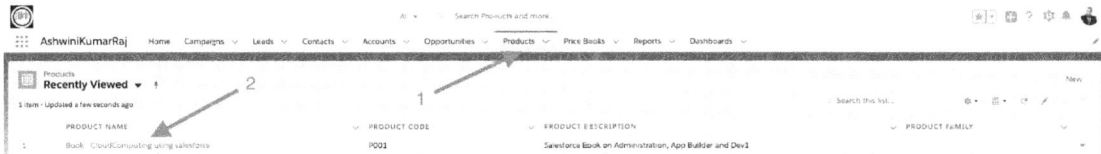

Figure 4.38: Associating a product with a price book

2. Go to the **Related** list and select **Add To Price Book**. A new window will open.
3. In the new window, select the **Price Book** you have created.
4. Choose the current and click on **Next**:

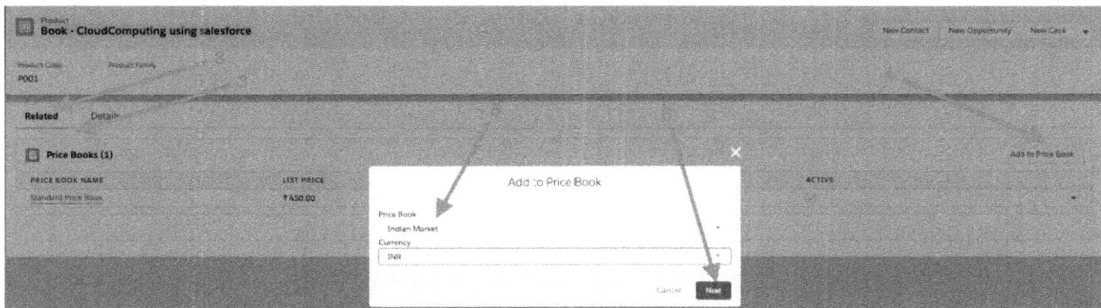

Figure 4.39: Associating a product with a price book

5. On the next screen, you can see that **List Price** is automatically populated from the standard price. You may like to change the **List Price** from 450 to 400.
6. Once you are done, click on the **Save** button:

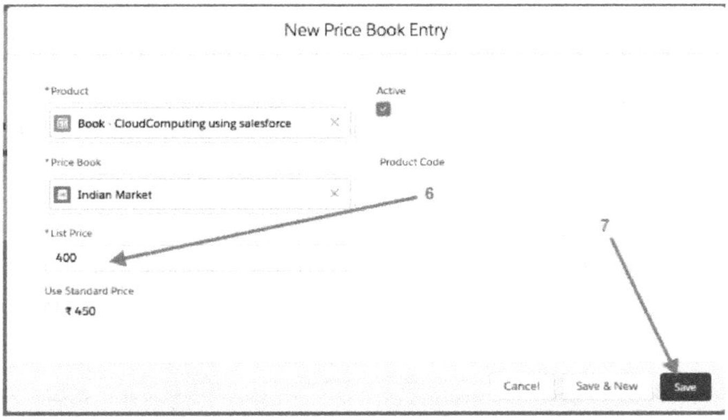

Figure 4.40: Associating a product with a price book

Similarly, you can create another price book for the US market and associate it with the same product.

Creating a product family

Using product family, the products can be categorized for the organization. If you sell both books and stationaries, you can create two picklists under product family and associate products accordingly.

If your organization uses forecasting, the users can have a different quota for book sales and stationaries sales. Users can also view forecasts for various opportunities with book products which are separate from opportunities that include stationaries products.

You can perform the following steps to create a product family for your organization:

1. Select **Setup** from the setup icon on the right-hand upper corner.
2. Select **Object Manager**, as shown in the following figure:

Figure 4.41: Accessing object manager

3. Scroll down to select Product:

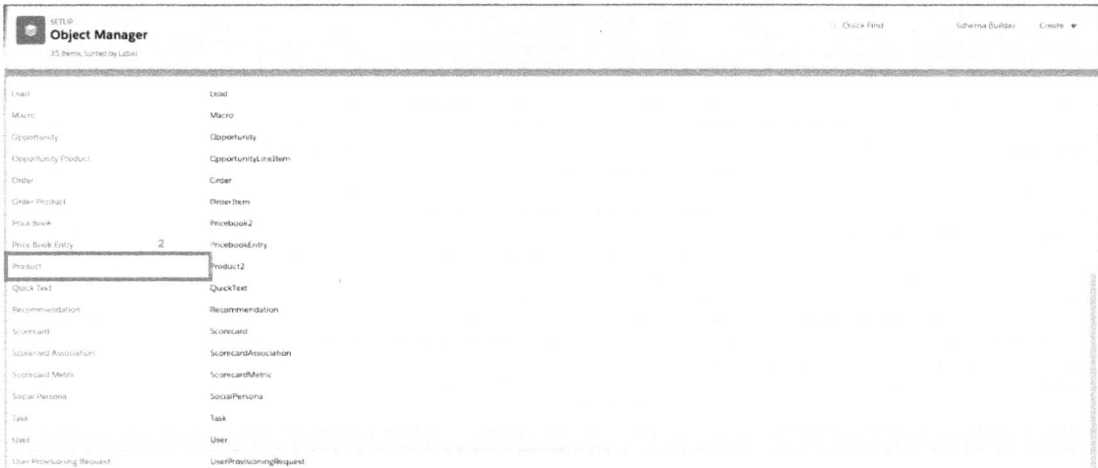

Figure 4.42: Selecting product object to configure

4. Under **Fields and Relationship**, choose **Product Family**:

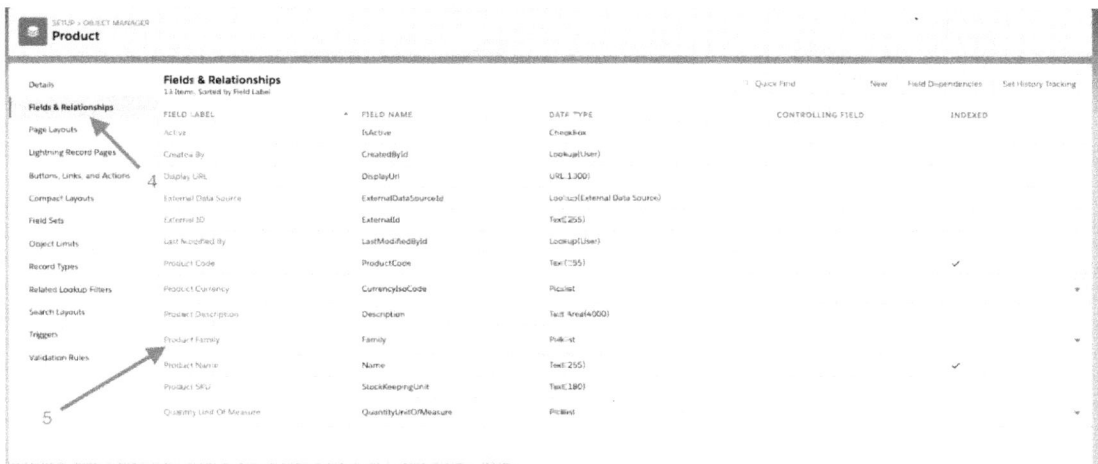

Figure 4.43: Using fields and relationships

5. Under **Product Family Picklist Values**, click on **New**:

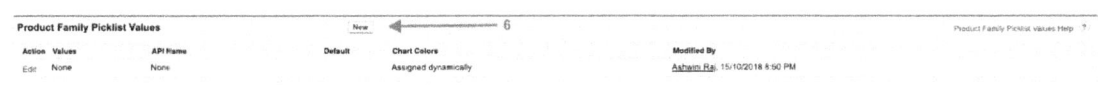

Figure 4.44: Create a new value

6. In the **Product Family** field, enter the values.

7. Click **Save** once it is done:

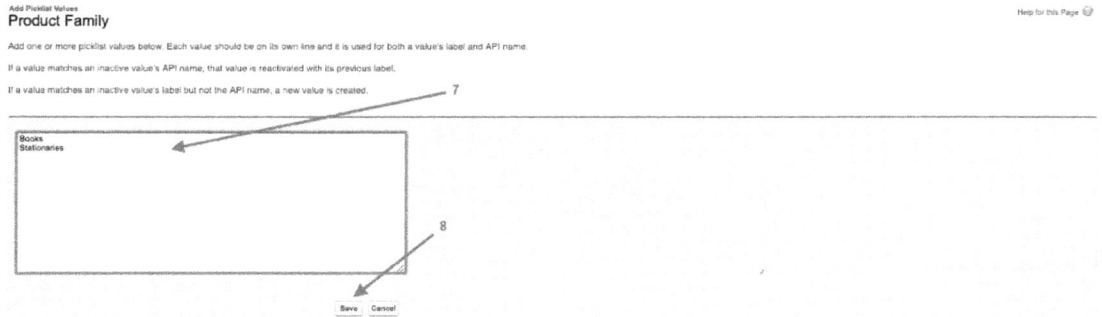

Figure 4.45: Adding new values to the list

Once the product family is created, the product can be associated with it while adding a new product or editing the existing product.

To associate an existing product with the product family, perform the following steps:

1. Select the product you want to edit from the **Product** tab, as show in the following figure:

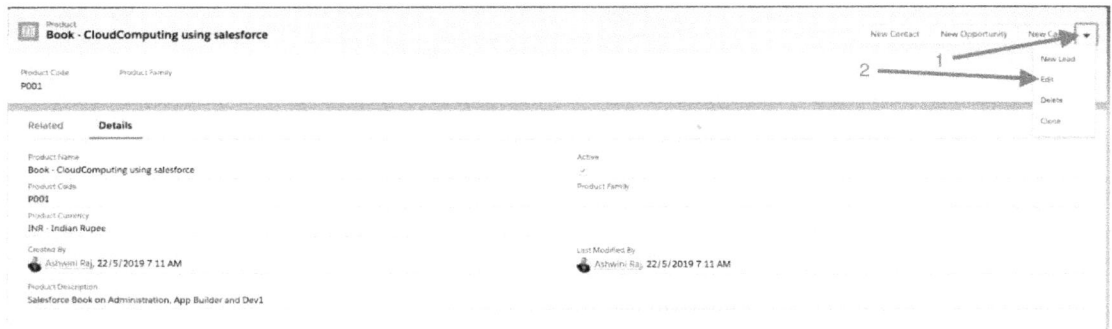

Figure 4.46: Associating a product with the product family

2. Now, select the product family from **Product Family** picklist:

3. Click on **Save** once it is done:

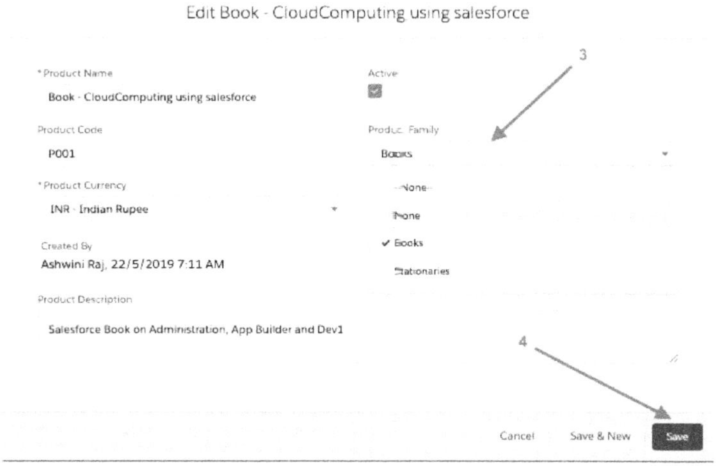

Edit Book - CloudComputing using salesforce

Figure 4.47: Associating a product with the product family

Opportunity management

Once the time and effort are spent by the marketing team to build the pipeline and qualify leads, the next phase is to close the deals. However, to get deals up to the finish line, it needs a winning strategy—something we call opportunity management. As the adage goes, an opportunity is a deal you have the opportunity to close.

Here are a few main reasons why opportunity management matters for any organization:

- It helps the sales representatives take the right steps to close a deal each time.
- It gives management a better view of the pipeline.
- It keeps deals moving forward toward closure.

Visualizing success with Path and Kanban

In the Salesforce Lightning Interface, Path is a simple tool with powerful features. The Path shows at what stage the record is in the sales process. It is a quick indicator that helps to visualize where you are and where you are heading to. The following figure illustrates the Path of an opportunity:

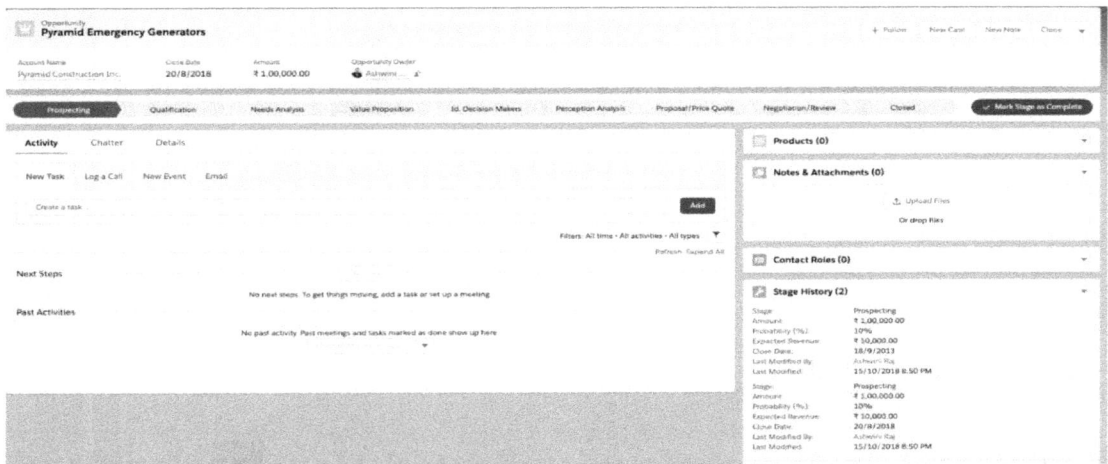

Figure 4.48: Path of an opportunity

Each step on the Path helps to understand the critical activities.

Using Path, the status of the record can be updated, as shown in the following figure, by clicking on Mark Status as Complete. Click the step on the path, then click on Mark Current Status:

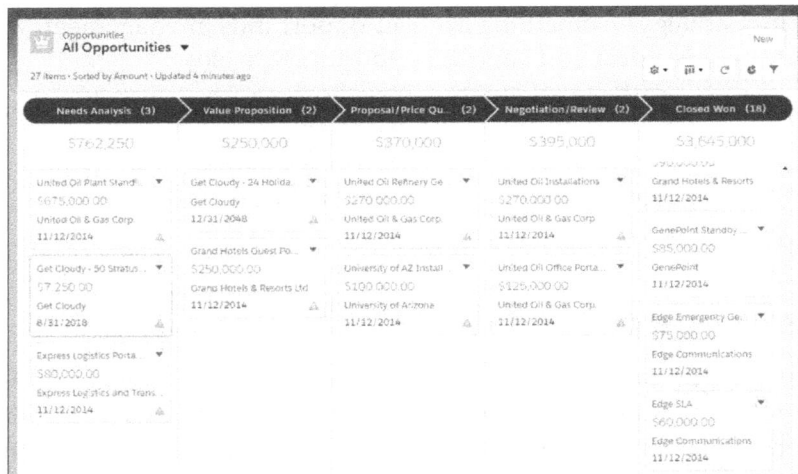

Figure 4.49: Updating the latest stage on a Path

The Kanban view is a powerful tool that helps to manage work efficiently.

Moving an opportunity to the next stage

In Kanban, the opportunities are organized by stage. Each column in Kanban represents one stage.

Perform the following steps to move an opportunity to the next stage:

1. Click a deal in the leftmost column.
2. Drag the deals into a different stage while holding down the mouse.
3. Release the mouse button when done.

The following figure depicts the Kanban view of the opportunities:

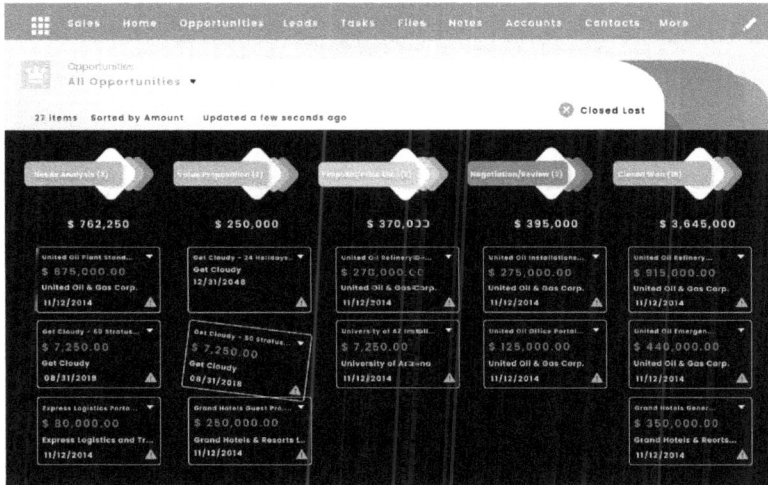

Figure 4.50: Kanban view

View a chart

To view data in the list view in the form of a chart or graph, click on Show Charts(1). To quickly see the most business done by account, select Pipeline by Account. To know which stages the deals are in, select Pipeline by Stage. For more details, just hover the mouse over the section of the chart. The following figure shows the way a chart can be created from the Kanban:

Figure 4.51: Creating chart from Kanban

Now, choose the type of chart you want to display as per the following figure:

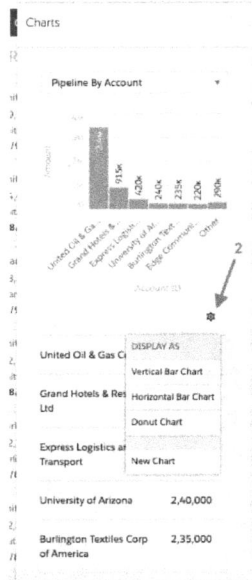

Figure 4.52: Chart from a Kanban

Creating a new opportunity

An opportunity can be added in the following different ways:

- Through Lead Conversion
- Adding on the Opportunity tab
- Adding on the Accounts detailed page

Creating a new opportunity through Lead Conversion was already discussed. Here, we will discuss how to add an opportunity in the Opportunity tab. Perform the following steps to do so:

1. Choose the **New on Opportunity** tab, as shown in the following figure:

Figure 4.53: Creating a new opportiunity

2. Fill the fields such as **Opportunity Name**, and **Amount**.

3. Select the option such as **Account Name**, **Close Date**, and **Stage**:

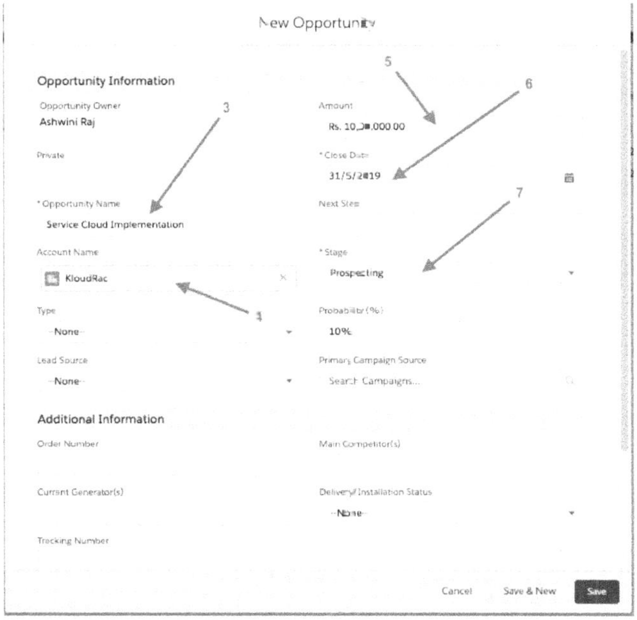

Figure 4.54: Filling details on a new opportunity

4. Click on **Save** to save the opportunity.

Note: The various options of stages and the relationship with probabilities are shown in the following figure:

Stage Name	Type	Probability	Forecast Category
Prospecting	Open	10%	Pipeline
Qualification	Open	10%	Pipeline
Needs Analysis	Open	20%	Pipeline
Value Proposition	Open	50%	Pipeline
Id. Decision Makers	Open	60%	Pipeline
Perception Analysis	Open	70%	Pipeline
Proposal/Price Quote	Open	75%	Pipeline
Negotiation/Review	Open	90%	Pipeline
Closed Won	Closed/Won	100%	Closed
Closed Lost	Closed/Lost	0%	Omitted

Figure 4.55: Probabilities on opportunity stages

Adding product to opportunity

You can track what is selling and in what quantity by adding products to opportunities. Then make sure that you maintain accurate records by updating the quantities and prices of the products.

Perform the following steps to add a product to an opportunity:

1. Open the opportunity to which the product to be added (by clicking on the opportunity name in the **Opportunity** tab).

2. From the **Products** related list, click on the button on the right side and select the **Choose Price Book** option:

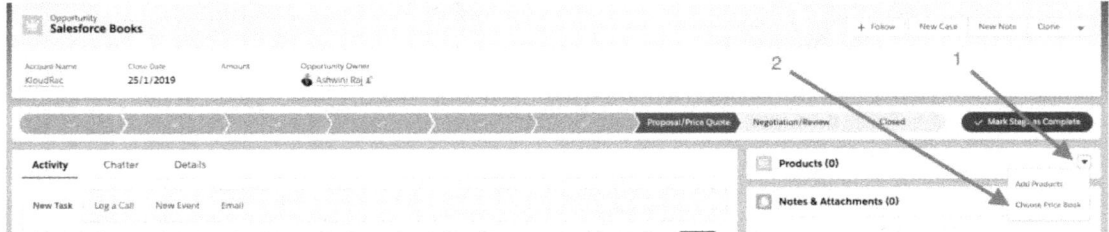

Figure 4.56: Adding a product to an opportunity

3. Select the **Price Book** from the picklist.

4. Click on **Save** when done:

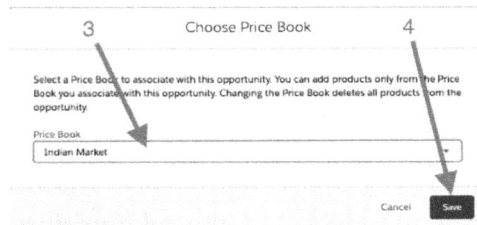

Figure 4.57: Choosing a price book for an opportunity

5. The next step is to add products from the price book to opportunity. To add this, from the Products-related list, select the **Add Products** option:

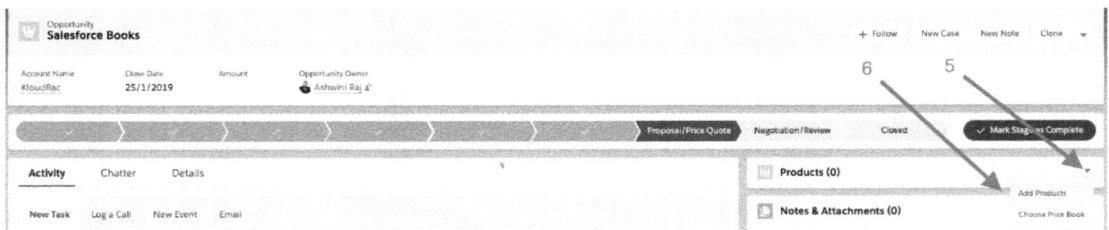

Figure 4.58: Adding a product

6. Select the checkbox to add products. You may like to use the search box option to find a product. You can use multiple products too.

7. Once done, click on the **Next** button:

Figure 4.59: Adding a product

8. Now enter the values to various attributes such as **QUANTITY, SALES PRICE,** and **DATE**:

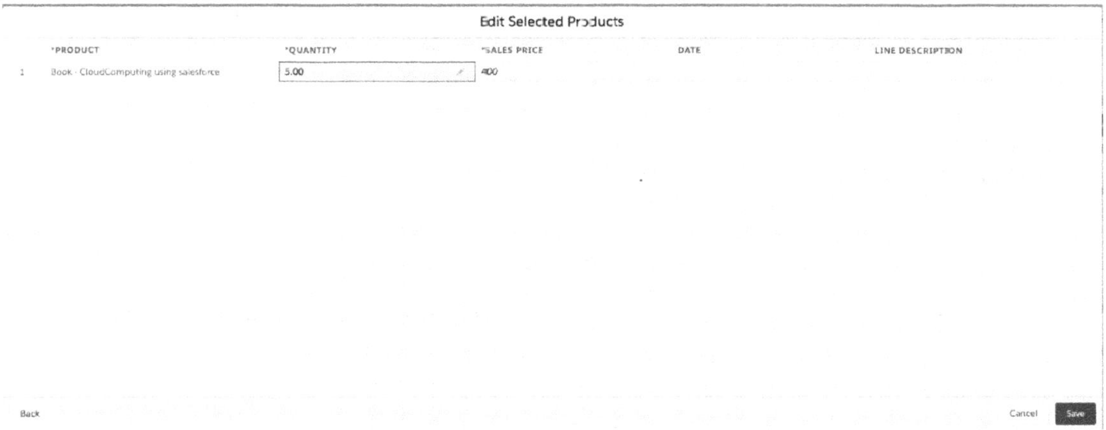

Figure 4.60: Filing the values to add product

9. Once done, click on **Save** to save the record.

Quote management

The term quote designates a formal offer for products or services with set prices.

As your sales representatives work on their deals, they need to share quotes to customers. Quotes show your customers the prices of the products or services your company offers.

Your representatives have the flexibility to create multiple quotes that show different combinations of products, discounts, and quantities. This helps your customers to compare prices.

You can create multiple quotes linked to an opportunity, but only one of them can be synced with the opportunity. The products that are associated with that quote and opportunity are synchronized with each other. The following figure depicts how a quote is required in a sales cycle:

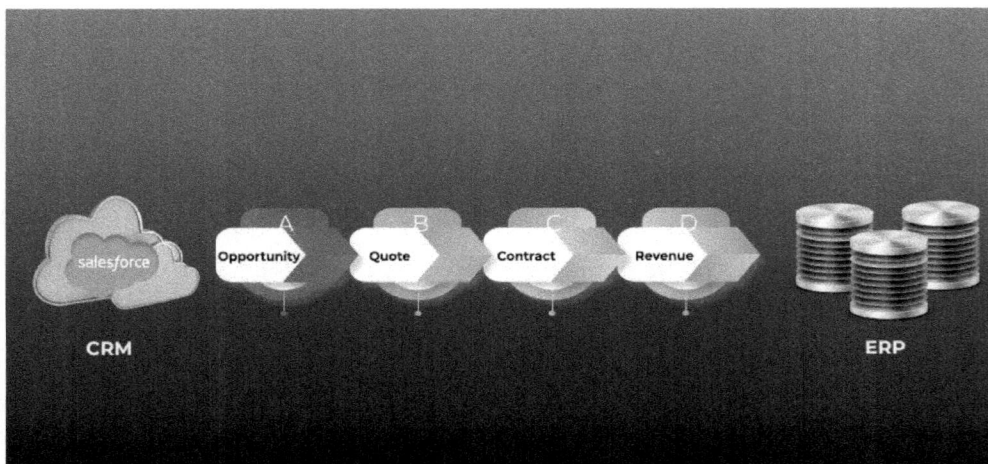

Figure 4.61: Quote management

Enabling quotes

In Salesforce, by default, quotes are not enabled. However, the system administrator can perform the following steps in Lightning Experience to enable it:

1. From Setup, type **quote** in the quick find box, then select **Quotes Settings**.
2. Select **Enable** to enable Quote, as shown in the following figure:

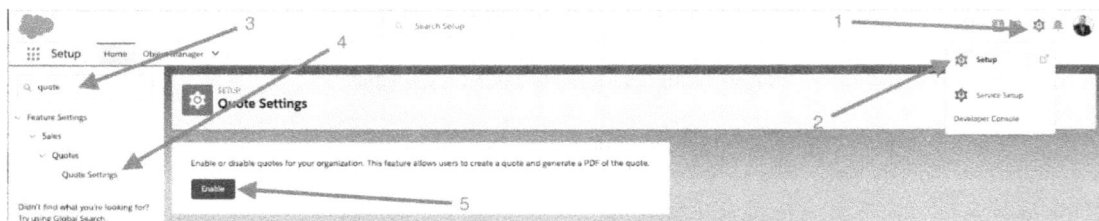

Figure 4.62: Enabling quote

3. On the next screen, make sure to add a quote to the related list to opportunity page layouts:
4. Once you are done, click on the **Save** button:

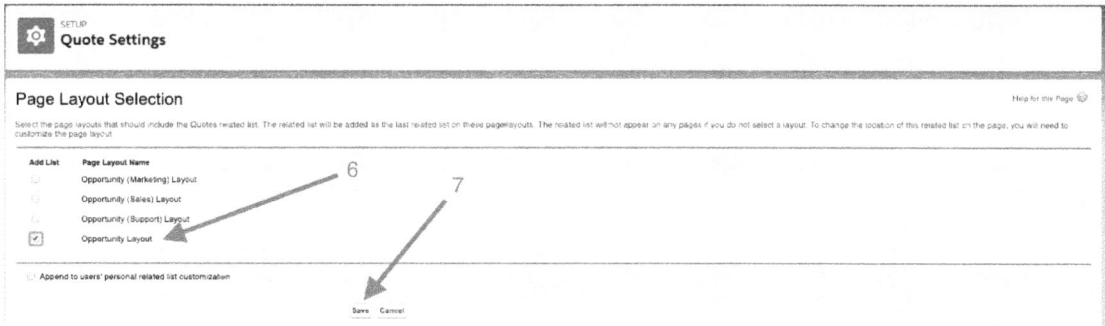

Figure 4.63: Enabling quote

Creating a new quote

The quote can be created from an opportunity. Perform the following steps to create a new quote:

1. From **Select List View**, select **All Opportunities**.

2. Under **Opportunity Name**, select the opportunity for which you want to create a quote.

3. In the **Quotes** section (at the bottom of the page), click on **Quotes**.

4. Click on **New Quote** as shown in the following figure:

Figure 4.64: Creating a new quote

5. Enter details such as **Quote Name**, **Expiration date**, and other details:

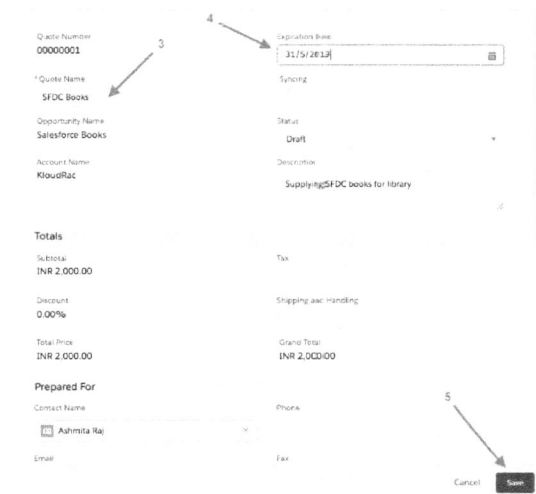

Figure 4.65: Creating a new quote

6. Click on **Save** once you are done.

You may observe that the Quote has been created as shown in the following figure:

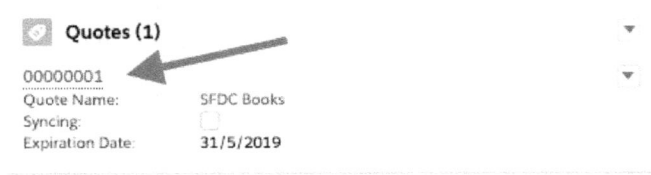

Figure 4.66: Quote is created

Editing the quote

Now, open the quote and make some changes using the following steps:

1. Click on either Quote number or Name to open the Quotes, as shown in the following figure:

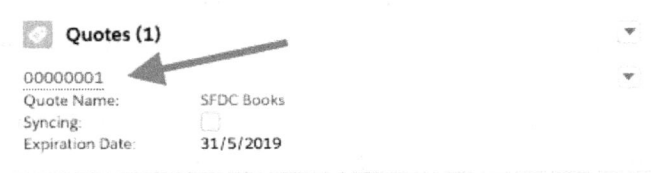

Figure 4.67: Editing a quote

2. In the **Quote Line Items** section, click on **Edit Products**:

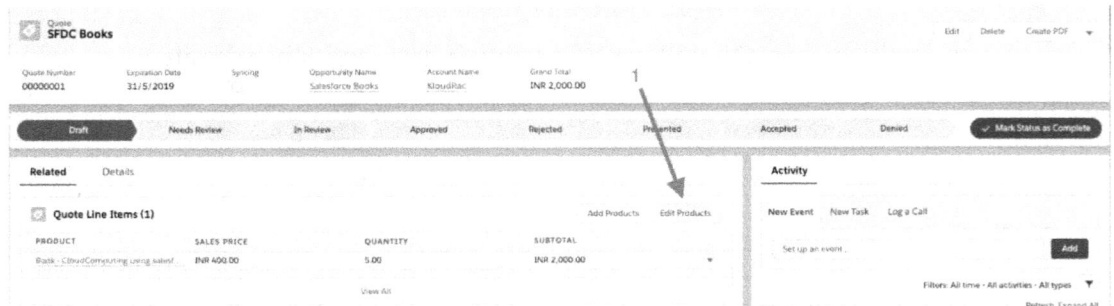

Figure 4.68: Editing products in a quote

3. For the Product Book **Cloud Computing using the Salesforce**, you may like to add a discount:

Edit All Quote Line Items

	*PRODUCT	LIST PRICE	*SALES PRICE	*QUANTITY	DISCOUNT	
1	Book CloudComputing using salesforce	INR 400.00	INR 400.00	5.00	10.00%	

2

3

Cancel Save

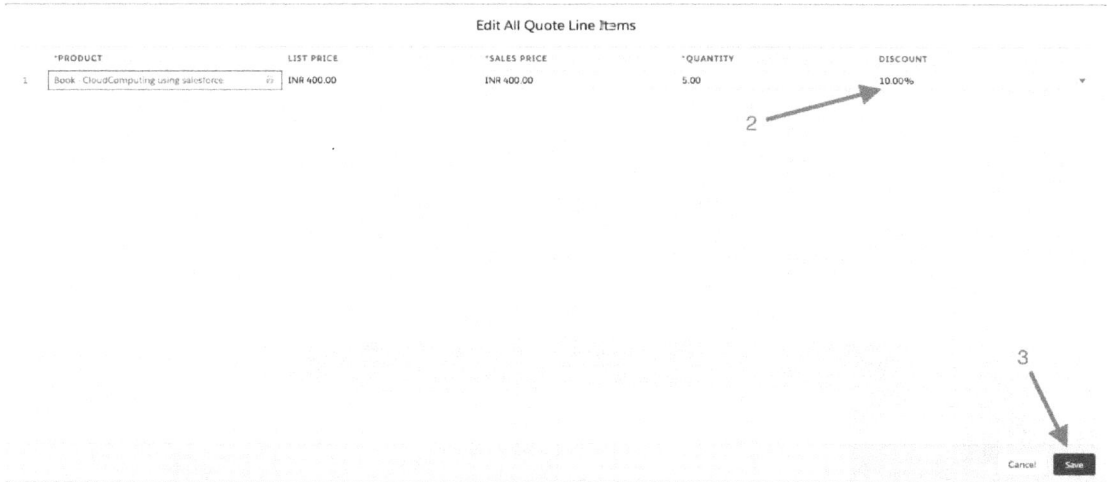

Figure 4.69: Adding discount in a quote

4. Click on **Save** once it is done.

Opening a quote

You can open the quote in two different ways:

- From the Quote section of the **Opportunity** tab

Note: This has already been discussed in the previous section.

- From the **Quote** item:
  - ○ Click on ⠿ to open the App Launcher and select **Quote**.
  - ○ From the **Select List View**, select **All Quotes**.
  - ○ Under **Quote Name**, click on the name of quote that you want to open.

Generating a quote to PDF

If you want to send a quotation to your customer from Salesforce itself, you can generate a quote in a PDF format and send it to your customer. To create a quote in the PDF format, perform the following steps:

1. Open the quote using any of the preceding methods.
2. Click on the **Create PDF** button to generate a quote PDF, as shown in the following figure:

Figure 4.70: Creating a quote PDF

3. In the PDF preview, click on **Save to Quote**:

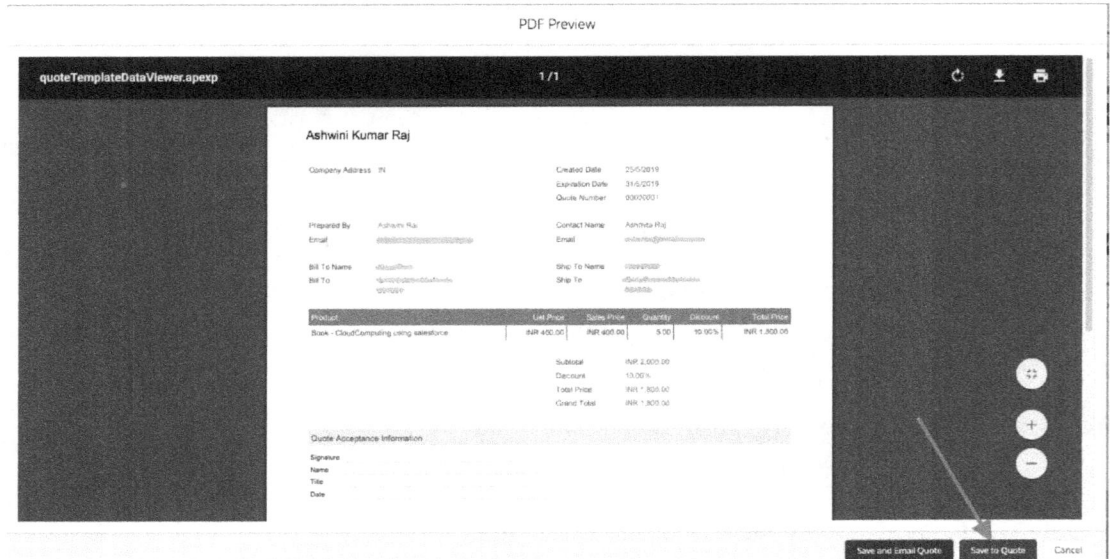

Figure 4.71: A generated quote PDF

4. Observe the **.pdf** file is uploaded under the **Notes & Attachments** section:

Figure 4.72: Quote PDF attached

E-mailing the quote to the customer

It is also possible to send a copy of the quote PDF to the customer for approval directly from Salesforce itself. To do so, perform the following steps:

1. Open the Quote you want to send it to your customer.
2. On the right side, click on the **Action** button and choose **Email Quote**, as shown in the following figure:

Figure 4.73: Emailing a quote

3. On a new window. Fill the e-mail subject, content, and so on.

4. Once you are done, click on the **Send** button:

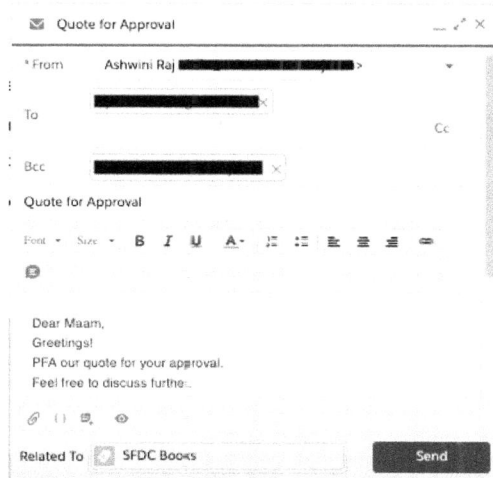

Figure 4.74: Emailing a quote

5. Observe the activity log added. shown in the following figure :

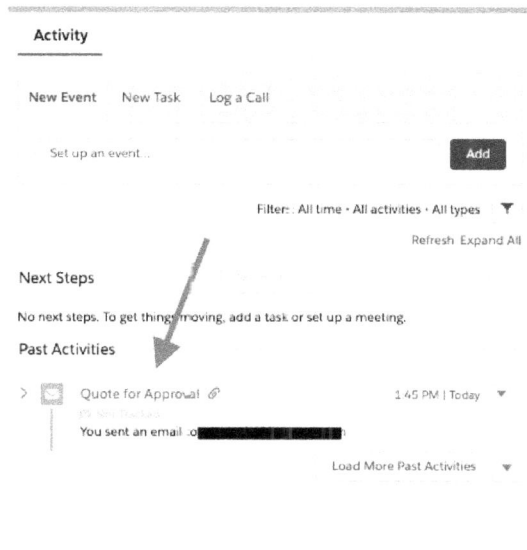

Figure 4.75: Emailing a quote

Conclusion

In this chapter, we introduced Salesforce CRM and covered a detailed explanation of the sales lifecycle. We started with campaign management and discussed lead management, account management, and contact management. We also covered key concepts of product, price book and learned how to create and manage quotes.

In the next chapter, we will discuss how to do the organization setup.

Questions

1. **CloudyGlobal is organizing a trade show. The marketing and sales users would like to have more visibility into the lead and contact who participated in the trade show. How would an administrator build this?**

   a. Create a cross-object formula field to display campaign member record details on a contact or a lead record.

   b. Create a custom object to track the contact and lead.

   c. Request the leads to send their confirmation via an e-mail.

   d. Associate the contact or lead with a campaign when they register for the trade show.

2. **CloudyGlobal needs to enable the Web-to-Lead option in its Salesforce org. However, the admin is concerned about the leads that contain spam. Which of the following options depicts the best possible solution to prevent receiving spam?**

   a. Create an auto-response rule for lead.

   b. Create a blacklist rule.

   c. Require reCAPTCHA verification.

   d. Create validation rules on the Lead object.

3. **The prospects who are interested in purchasing your product are called what?**

   a. Campaign

   b. Lead

   c. Account

   d. Opportunity

4. **When converting a lead to account, the administrator can set up field mapping from the lead field to which objects? (Choose any three)**

   a. Opportunity

   b. Case

   c. Contact

   d. Account

5. **Which feature of Lightning Experience Sales Cloud allows the Sales representatives to view a visual summary of their opportunities by the sales stage?**

   a. Opportunity Manager

   b. Opportunity Workspace

   c. Sales path

   d. Opportunity Kanban

6. **Prince has added a lead to his Salesforce Org. Now, he found that the lead belongs from the company already exists in the system. How can Prince create contact from the information capture in the lead?**

   a. Create a report based on lead and use the information in the report to create the contact.

   b. Create a contact with formula fields and fetch the lead information.

   c. Create a workflow rule on the lead object.

   d. Convert the lead using the convert button.

7. **Which of the following is not true?**

   a. One product can have only one standard price. Create a contact with formula fields to fetch the lead information.

   b. It is possible to send a copy of the quote PDF to the customer for approval directly from Salesforce.

   c. Multiple quotes can be created on the same opportunity.

   d. None of the above.

8. **Which of these allows us to offer products to distinctive groups of customers at different list prices?**

   a. Standard Pricebook

   b. Custom Pricebook

   c. Opportunity

   d. Product family

9. **Which of the following is true regarding Web-to-Lead? (Choose any three.)**

   a. Standard and custom fields need to be captured online can be selected.

   b. Data entered in the web form is validated before it is sent to Salesforce.

c. There is a limit of 100 leads that can be captured per day.

d. The default lead creator for when generated leads can be specified.

10. **Your organization wants to sell its product at different prices to different types of customers. How can this be set up?**

a. Create multiple records in the standard price book for each product.

b. Create a price book for each customer type.

c. A workflow can be used to update the opportunity line item price based on the customer type.

d. The discount field on opportunity line item can be filled in for each customer.

Answers

1. d
2. c
3. b
4. a, c, d
5. d
6. d
7. d
8. b
9. a, b, d
10. b

Join our Discord space

Join our Discord workspace for latest updates, offers, tech happenings around the world, new releases, and sessions with the authors:

https://discord.bpbonline.com

CHAPTER 5
Organizational Setup

Introduction

In the previous chapter, we learned how to create a developer account. Now, it is time to move ahead. We need to do some basic setup for our organization. This includes company profile settings, currency setup, and fiscal year setup.

Structure

In this chapter, we will discuss the following topics:

- Setting up company information
- Viewing the licenses
- Understanding the concept of currency setup
- Setting up the fiscal year

Objectives

After studying this unit, you will learn how to access company information, what type of licenses are being used, which types of currencies are enabled, how to enable multiple currencies, personal currency, and corporate currency, and how to set up the fiscal year for the organization.

Setting up company information

Company information contains all the basic information about your company, such as a local address, fax number, and phone number.

Once the company purchases the Salesforce organization, the company has to set up the company profile.

Perform the following steps to set up various company information in your organization:

1. Click on the gear icon at the top of the page and launch the setup, as shown in the following figure:

Figure 5.1: Launching set up

2. On the left-hand side, you will see the Quick Find box.
3. Type **Company Information** there, as shown in the following figure:

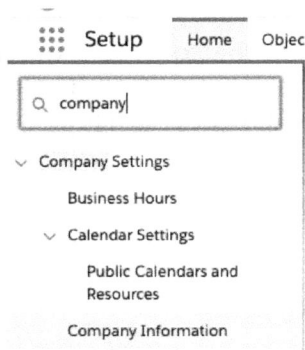

Figure 5.2: Setting up company information

The **Company Information** page contains the company address, company contact details, corporate currency, organization default time zone, language, and locale setting. You can also use it to find details about licenses, such as the licenses available, used, and remaining. At any time, the system administrator can update the company information in Salesforce. To do so, you need to click on **Edit** and update the details:

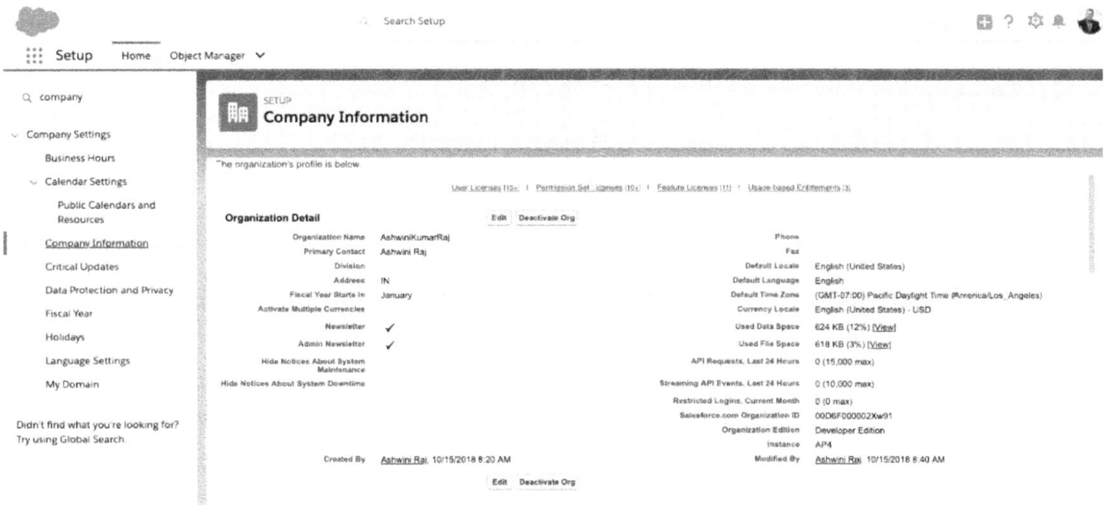

Figure 5.3: Updating organization details

Viewing the licenses

The Company Information page also displays all the user licenses, permission set licenses, feature licenses, and usage-based entitlements you have purchased for your organization. On the Company Information detail page, the user can find the information about these licenses, which are as follows:

- **User licenses**: A user license permits a user to use the distinctive functionality of Salesforce. It additionally figures out which profiles and permission sets are accessible to the user. Each user must have precisely one user license. You dole out user permissions for data access through a profile and alternatively, at least one permission sets.

- **Permission set licenses**: You can assign permission sets to the users so that they can have access to specific features and functions. Users can assign any number of permission-set licenses.

- **Feature licenses**: A feature license qualifies a user to access an extra feature excluded with their user license, for example, marketing or *Work.com*. Organisations can be assigned with any number of feature licenses.

- **Usage-based entitlement:** For functionality that is subject to usage limits, you can see the current usage and limits in this section. For example, the permitted number of month-to-month logins to a partner community or as far as the limit for *Data. com* list users.

Understanding the concept of currency setup

Understanding the value of deals is a top priority for any organization.

Multi-currency is one of Salesforce's advanced features, as the platform allows you to control which currencies are available to the system. You can indicate which currency standards your organization uses, and individual users can apply explicit currencies to their settings depending on where they do business.

After enabling it, sales representatives can enter the amount in the opportunity field in their local currency. Organizations can also use multiple currencies in the forecasts, reports, quotes, and other currency fields.

By default, Salesforce organizations use only one currency. If you set the required currencies in your company settings, all currency values in the records will be displayed in that currency.

Perform the following steps to enable and apply multiple currencies in your organization:

1. Click on the gear icon ⚙ at the top of the page and launch setup.
2. Search for Company Information in the Quick Find box, then select **Company Information**.
3. Click on **Edit**.
4. Check **Activate Multiple Currencies**.

Once the multiple currencies are enabled, you also:

- Activate additional currencies.
- Need to ensure users have correct personal currencies.
- Make sure that while creating records, users use the correct currency.

Active currency

Once a multicurrency feature is activated in the organization, currencies can be activated or deactivated.

Perform the following steps:

1. Click on the gear icon ⚙ at the top of the page and launch setup.
2. Search for `Company Information` in the Quick Find box, then select **Company Information**.
3. Click on the **Currency Setup** button. The Active Currencies and Inactive Currencies will be listed out.

The following figure represents various active currencies in the Salesforce organization:

Active Currencies		New Edit Rates Change Corporate					
Action	Currency Code	Currency Name	Corporate	Conversion Rate	Decimal Places	Last Modified By	
Edit | Deactivate	EUR	Euro		1.000000	2	Admin User, 1/26/2017 9:46 AM	
Edit | Deactivate	GBP	British Pound		0.656010	2	Admin User, 1/26/2017 9:46 AM	
Edit | Deactivate	JPY	Japanese Yen		100.000000	2	Admin User, 1/26/2017 9:46 AM	
Edit | Deactivate	SGD	Singapore Dollar		1.375320	2	Admin User, 1/26/2017 9:46 AM	
Edit | Deactivate	USD	U.S. Dollar	✓	1.000000	2	Admin User, 1/26/2017 9:46 AM	

Inactive Currencies		Edit Rates				
Action	Currency Code	Currency Name	Conversion Rate	Decimal Places	Last Modified By	
Edit | Activate	ARS	Argentine Peso	3.931500	2	Admin User, 1/26/2017 9:46 AM	
Edit | Activate	BRL	Brazilian Real	1.586500	2	Admin User, 1/26/2017 9:46 AM	

Figure 5.4: Active currencies

4. From the list of inactive currencies, click on Activate next to the currency to activate a currency.

5. To deactivate the list of active currencies, click on **Deactivate** and then **OK**.

Deactivating a currency does not modify the amounts in items that use that currency. The users will no longer be able to enter new amounts in the inactive currency Additionally, deactivating a currency that is set as a user's personal currency automatically resets the user's currency to the company currency.

Note: **The corporate currency cannot be deactivated.**

Adding a new currency

The administrator can add a new currency to the organization. This can be completed by performing the following steps:

1. Click on **New** in the **Active Currencies** window.

2. Select **Currency Type**. Currencies are alphabetized using their ISO currency codes.

3. Mention the **Conversion Rate** and **Decimal Places**.

4. Click on **Save**:

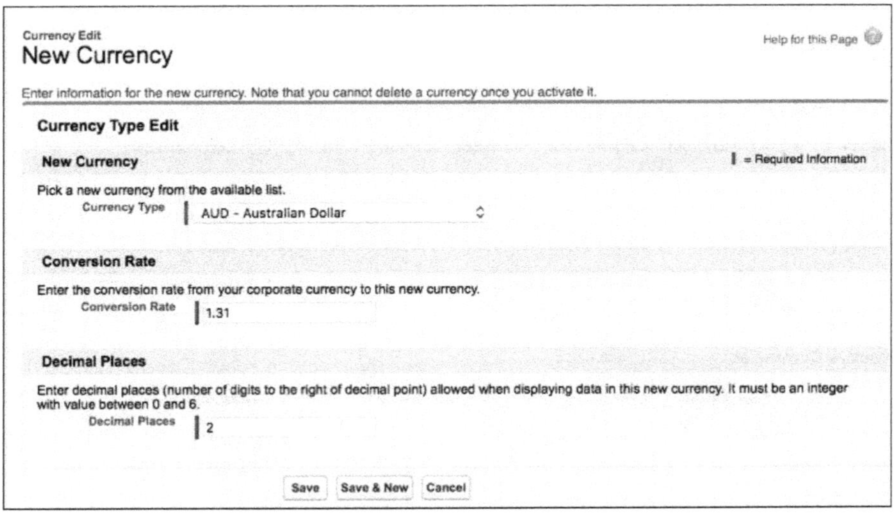

Figure 5.5: Adding new currency

Setting up a corporate currency

The administrator can set up the corporate currency, which reflects the currency of the corporate headquarters. The administrator can also maintain the list of active currencies and their conversion rates relative to the corporate currency.

Perform the following steps:

1. From setup, enter Company Information and choose Company Information.
2. In the **Active Currencies** list, select **Change Corporate**.
3. Select your new corporate currency from the dropdown, as shown in the following figure:

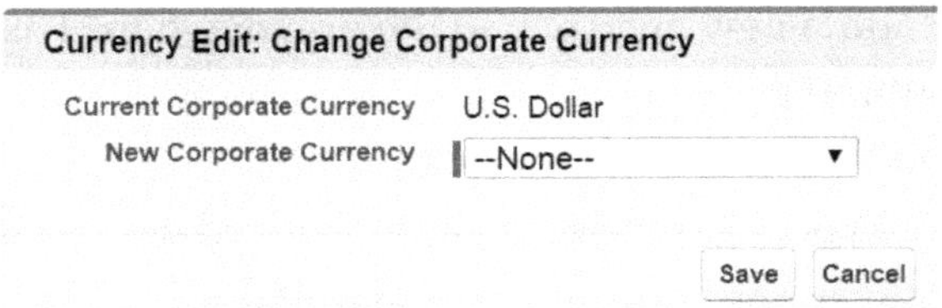

Figure 5.6: Setting up corporate currency

4. Click on **Save**.

Note: **Only currencies that are active in your organization will be available.**

Add personal currencies

Once multicurrency is enabled in the Org, currencies are activated, and conversion rates may be altered. Users may also add personal currencies to their profiles.

Follow these steps to add a personal currency to your Org:

1. Click on your profile image at the top of the page and click on **Settings**, as shown in the following figure:

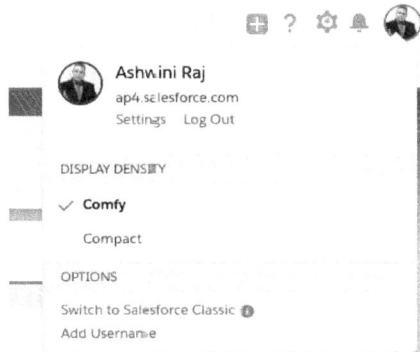

Figure 5.7: Adding personal currencies

2. Enter **Language** in the Quick Find, then select **Language & Time Zone**.
3. Update the **Currency** field and click on **Save**.

Setting up the fiscal year

A fiscal year is a period utilized to compute yearly financial summaries in the organizations. The system administrator can set the fiscal year for the organization. The fiscal year data is utilized in reporting and forecasting.

Salesforce uses two types of fiscal years. They are as follows:

* Standard fiscal year
* Custom fiscal year

Standard fiscal year

The standard fiscal years follow the Gregorian calendar but can start on the first day of any month of the year.

Salesforce uses the Gregorian calendar as a standard fiscal year calendar by default.

However, every organization may not start its fiscal year from the same point.

So, they need to change the fiscal year start month.

For example, in the USA, the fiscal year starts on 1st October and ends on 30th September. However, in India, it starts on 1st April and ends on 31st March.

If your fiscal year follows the Gregorian calendar but does not start in January, you can define a standard fiscal year with a different starting month.

To set up the standard fiscal year for your organization, perform the following steps:

1. From setup, enter the fiscal year and choose **Fiscal Year.**
2. Select the **Standard Fiscal Year** option, as shown in the following figure:

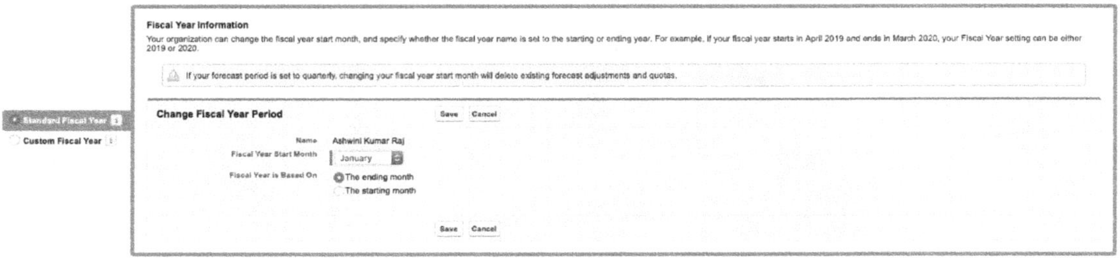

Figure 5.8: Changing fiscal year

3. Select the start month for the fiscal year.
4. Select whether the fiscal year is defined based on the start or end of the month.
5. Click on **Save**.

Custom fiscal year

For a few companies, the standard fiscal year does not fulfill their requirement. They break down their fiscal years, quarters, and so on into custom fiscal periods based on their financial planning requirements. Salesforce gives the flexibility to define these periods using custom fiscal years. For example, you can create a 13-week quarter represented by three periods of four, four, and five weeks.

If you use a common fiscal year structure, such as a 4-4-5 or a 13-period structure, you can rapidly define a fiscal year. Just specify a start date and choose an included template. A template can easily be modified to suit the business.

The custom fiscal periods can be named based on your standards. For example, a fiscal period could be called *P2* or *February*.

To set up the custom fiscal year for your organization, follow these steps:

1. From setup, enter the fiscal year and choose **Fiscal Year**.
2. Select the **Custom Fiscal Year** option.
3. Select the checkbox next to the statement **Yes, I understand the implications the custom fiscal year feature has on my organization, and I want to enable it**.

4. Click on **Enable Custom Fiscal Years**.
5. Click on **OK**.

Before enabling custom fiscal years, be cautious about the following points:

- Enabling custom fiscal years is irreversible. Once enabled, it cannot be reverted to standard fiscal years.
- Fiscal year definitions are not automatically created. They have to be defined each year.
- Defining custom fiscal years impacts your forecasts, reports, and quotas.
- Fiscal period columns cannot be used in an opportunity with the product or an opportunity with schedule reports.

Conclusion

In this chapter, we covered basic organizational setup. We got to know various company information, such as viewing license types and the currencies being used. We also learned to set up multiple currencies, personal currency, corporate currency, and adding new currency to the organization. We also learned to set up a fiscal year for the organization. There are two types of fiscal year: Standard fiscal year and custom fiscal year.

In the next chapter, we will develop apps using Salesforce.

Questions

1. **How would an administrator see how many remaining Salesforce licenses are available? Choose two.**

   a. Security Controls | Licenses

   b. Limits | Licenses

   c. Manage Users | Licenses

   d. Company information page

   e. System Overview page

2. **What is the period used for calculating annual financial statements in the organizations called?**

   a. Fiscal year

   b. Annual year

   c. Golden year

   d. Statement Year

3. **Which currency is used as the basis for all currency conversion rates when the multiple currencies feature is enabled in the organization?**

   a. Corporate currency

   b. Record currency

   c. Active currency

   d. Personal currency

4. **Which of the following are true for a fiscal year in Salesforce?**

   a. Used for an organization's financial planning.

   b. Impacts forecasts, quotas, and reports.

   c. Standard fiscal years follow the Gregorian.

   d. All of the above.

5. **Which of the following is true?**

   a. Enabling custom fiscal years is irreversible.

   b. The corporate currency can be deactivated.

   c. Multi-currency cannot be enabled in Salesforce.

   d. All of the above.

Answers

1. d, e
2. a
3. a
4. d
5. a

Join our Discord space

Join our Discord workspace for latest updates, offers, tech happenings around the world, new releases, and sessions with the authors:

https://discord.bpbonline.com

CHAPTER 6
Designing Applications on Salesforce

Introduction

So far, we have learned to use the core CRM functionality of Salesforce. In this chapter, we are going to learn how to develop customized applications using the Salesforce platform. The topic is divided into two chapters, some of which we will be covering in this chapter, to make this broad topic more manageable. In this chapter, we will focus on building an application on Salesforce platform. Before we jump into the application building, we need to understand a few application design questions, which are as follows:

- Who are your stakeholders and business partners?
- What are the business requirements?
- Who will use the application?
- What do you want to be able to report on?
- How will people learn to use the application?

These questions and their answers are vital to effectively designing applications for Salesforce.

Structure

In this chapter, we will discuss the following topics:

- Application building blocks
- Sample recruitment application
- Building data model
- Building user interface

Objectives

After studying this unit, you will learn the application building blocks. We will also discuss the data model and building the user interface of an application.

Application building blocks

A typical application design consists of the following:

- User interface
- Business logic
- Data model

The application building blocks comprise two significant parts: Declarative (low code / no code) and programmatic (pro code).

While the declarative part gives simplicity and speed, the programmatic part gives control and adaptability.

The following figure depicts the various application building blocks in both declarative and programmatic approaches:

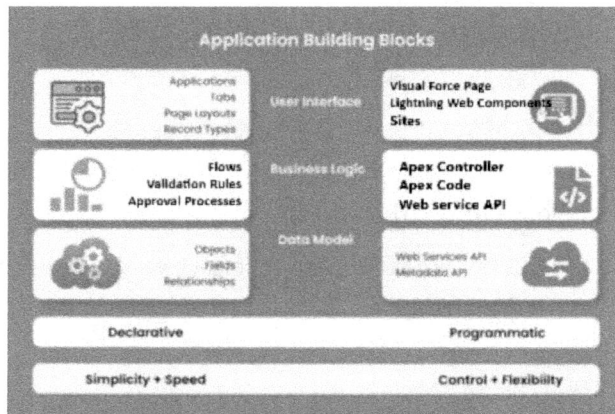

Figure 6.1: Application building blocks

In the next section, we will look at implementing some of these building blocks to create a sample application.

Sample recruitment application

In this chapter, we are going to build a customized application – recruitment application. Let us understand the requirement.

The requirements of the app are:

- Track positions in all phases of the procedure, from those that are available to those that have been filled or dropped.
- Track the candidates who apply for the position, including the status of their application (regardless of whether they have had a telephone screen, are booked for interviews, have been dismissed or employed, or have passed on an offer that was introduced).
- Track the posting of jobs on external websites, for example, *Monster.com* or *Naukri. com*, and so on.
- Allow employees to post surveys for candidates whom they have interviewed.
- Provide security for the recruiting information so it is not erroneously seen, altered, or erased by representatives who shouldn't have access.
- Automatically inform the recruiters about the subsequent stages that ought to be taken when a choice has been made about a candidate.
- Automatically inform all the employees regarding new openings that have been posted.
- Make sure that a new position opening has an official endorsement before it gets active.
- Include reports that give users the recruitment status.
- Allow recruiters to outline the locations of all candidates who are applying for a job to all the more likely comprehend relocation cost.
- Make it simple to perform a few related tasks immediately, such as dismissing multiple applications.
- Automatically post open positions on the website.

The following are the users of the application:

- **Recruiters**: Number of positions are open by department.
- Department-wise number of positions are open.
- **Hiring managers**: The qualifications of all candidates who have applied for a given position.
- **Recruiting managers**: The recruiting patterns of the new hires.

The structure of the recruitment application is as follows:

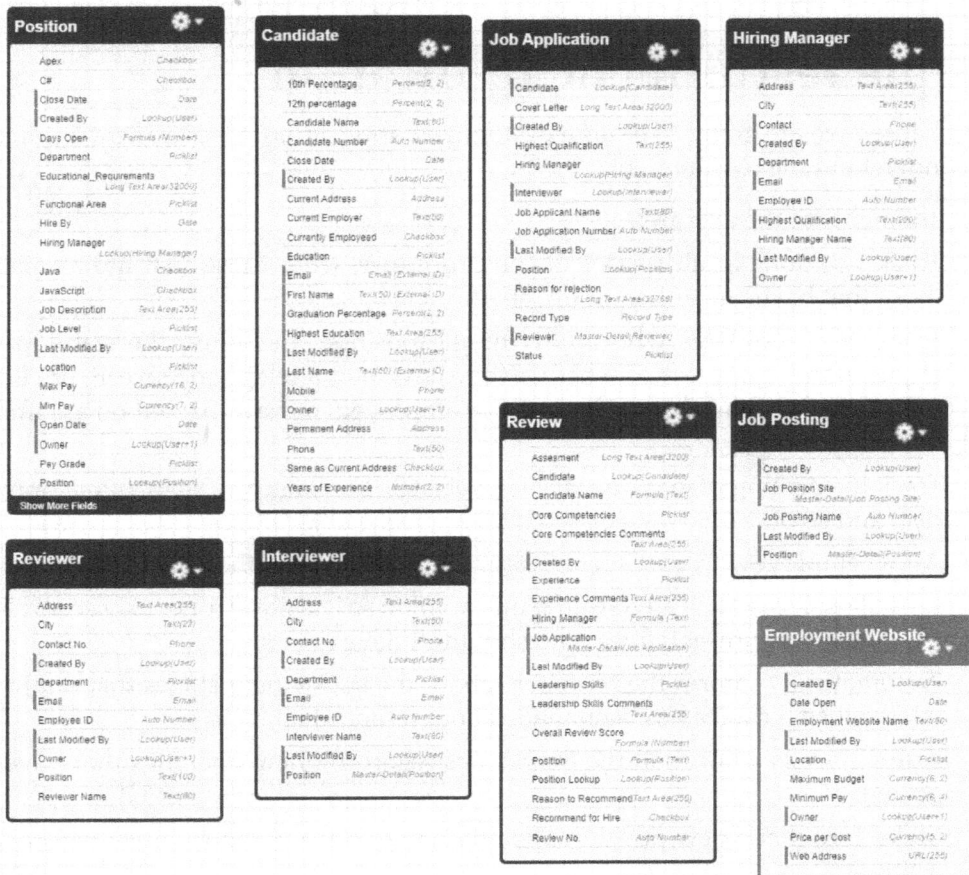

Figure 6.2: Recruitment apps structure

As discussed earlier, we are going to build the following:

- Data model
    o Objects
    o Fields
- Object relationships
- User interface
    o Application
    o Tabs
    o Page layouts
    o Record Types

- Business logic
  - o Flows
  - o Validation rules
  - o Approval processes

We will continue learning the building data model in this chapter. The rest of the topics will be discussed in the next chapter.

Building data model

Data modelling is a mechanism to model what database tables look like in a way that makes sense to humans. In Salesforce, database tables are treated as objects, columns as fields, and rows as records. So, in Salesforce, the data model is the collection of objects and fields in an app.

Custom object

Custom objects are the main part of any application. Custom objects provide a structure for storing data and give power to the interface elements for users to interact with the data.

Creating a custom object

Let us take a scenario for a recruitment application.

Scenario: Currently, the organization is using spreadsheets to track new positions. This is an inefficient process that is very difficult to manage. To improve this process and make it more efficient, the administrator has decided to create a custom object to track positions. All internal communication and activity relating to a position should be tracked on this object. In addition, the users should be able to run reports on these.

The tasks is to create a custom position object.

Solution: Follow the below steps to create a custom object named Position.

1. Click the gear icon ⚙ at the top of the page and launch **Setup**.
2. Click the **Object Manager** tab.

The following figure describes how to access **Object Manager**:

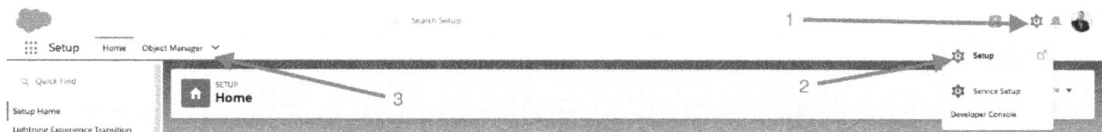

Figure 6.3: Accessing object manager

3. Click **Create** and then **Custom Object** in the top right corner:

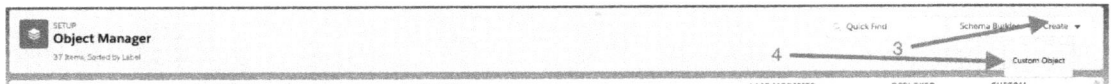

Figure 6.4: Creating custom object

4. For labels, enter **Position**. Notice that the **Object Name** and **Record Name** fields auto-fill.

5. For **Plural Label**, enter **Positions**.

The following figure shows how to create a custom object:

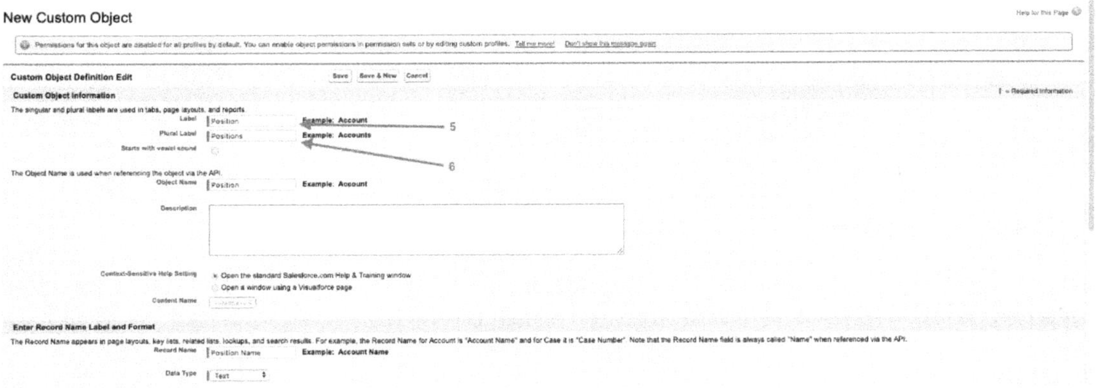

Figure 6.5: Creating new custom object

6. Check the box for **Launch New Custom** tab Wizard after saving this custom object.

7. Click **Save**.

8. Select your desired **Tab Style** and click **Next**, **Next**, and **Save**.

Observe that a custom object named Position has also been created. A tab with the same name is also there.

Create a custom field

Let us understand the following scenario:

Scenario: With a new custom object created, we have to create fields to track data regarding Position.

The tasks are as follows:

- Add custom fields to position and candidate object.
- Create dependent picklists.

Solution:

Task one: Let us add some custom fields to the position custom object we created.

The field name, type, values, and remarks are mentioned in the following table:

Custom field level	Custom field type	Values	Remarks
Date closed	Date/Time		
Date opened	Date/Time		
Status	Pick list	New, Open, Closed	Mandatory field
Sub status	Pick list	Pending, not approved, approved, filled, cancelled	
Department	Pick list	Engineering, IT, Finance, Support, Sales	
Location	Pick list	*San Francisco, CA, New York, NY, Atlanta, GA, London, England, New Delhi*	
Duration	Number	Length 2, Decimal 0	
Job description	Text area	Required, Checked	
Legacy position number	Text	Length 20	Set this field as the unique record identifier from an external system
Max pay	Currency	Length 20	
Min pay	Currency	Length 7	
Education	Text area		
Responsibility	Text area		
Skills required	Text area		
Start date	DATE		
Type	Picklist	Full time, part-time, temporary	
Pay grade	Picklist	C-100, C-200, C-300, C-400, IT-100, IT-200, IT-300, IT-400, ACT-100, ACT-200, ACT-300, ACT-400, ENG-100, ENG-200, ENG-300, ENG-400, S-100, S-200, S-300, S-400	

Table 6.1: Field details of Position object

With the following steps, we are going to create a custom field named **Status**:

1. From **Setup**, go to **Object Manager**. Then, search for **Position** object that was created earlier.

The following figure shows how to access **Position** object:

Figure 6.6: Accessing position object

2. Click on **Fields & Relationships** from the sidebar. Notice that there are already some fields there.

3. Click on **New** in the top right.

The following figure reflects creating a new field:

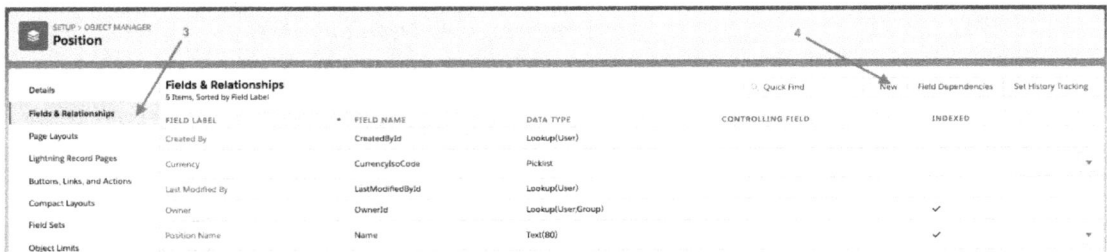

Figure 6.7: Create a new field

4. Select the data type as **Picklist** and click **Next**.
5. Fill out the **Field Label** as **Status**.
6. From **Values**, select the options button **Enter values, with each value separated by a new line**.
7. Enter values as **New**, **Open**, and **Closed** each on separate lines.
8. Check the option Always require a value in this field to save a record in the **Required** checkbox. This will make this field mandatory:

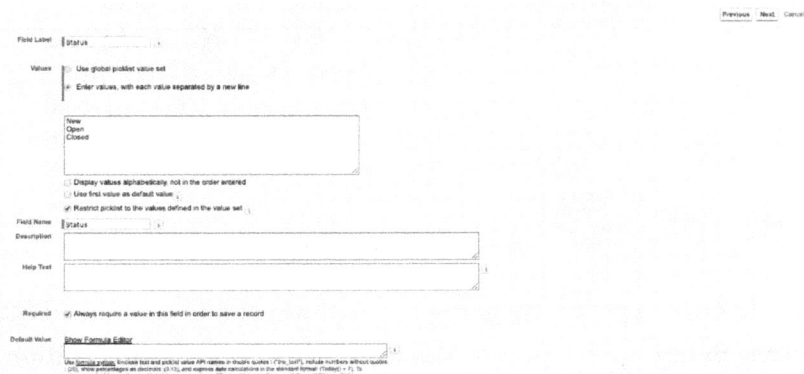

Figure 6.8: Creating a mandatory field

9. Click **Next** two times and then save.

Now, you will be able to see the new **Status** field in the list of **Position** fields. In the **Field Name** column, notice that it says **Status__c**. The "__c" part. It is a simple way to tell that a particular field is a custom field.

Similarly, the other fields can be created for Position objects.

Task two: Create dependentPick Lists. (Controlling field: Department, Dependant field: Pay grade)

A dependent field works in a relationship with a controlling field to channel its values. The value in the controlling field influences the values accessible in the dependent field.

Note: **Custom picklist fields can either be controlling or dependent. However, a standard picklist field can only be controlling.**

The following table depicts various data types and whether these can be the controlling and dependent field or not:

Data type	Controlling field	Dependent field
Standard Picklist	Yes	No
Custom Picklist	Yes	Yes
Multi-Select picklist	No	Yes
Checkbox	Yes	No

Table 6.2: Controlling and dependent fields

Perform the following steps to create dependent picklist:

1. From **Fields & Relationships**, select **Field Dependencies**, as shown in the following figure:

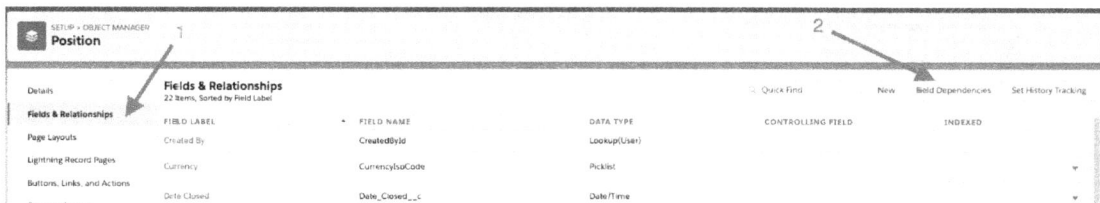

Figure 6.9: Field dependencies

2. Click **New**, to create new dependent picklist:

Figure 6.10: Creating new dependent field

3. Choose **Department** for **Controlling Field** and **Pay Grade** for **Dependent Field**.

4. Click on **Continue**, as shown in the following figure:

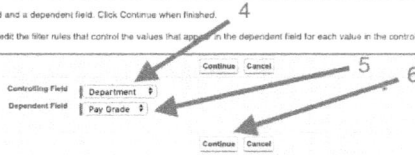

Figure 6.11: Creating field dependencies

5. Edit the field dependencies based on the following table. You need to select values and click on **Include Values**. The field dependencies are:

Sales	IT	Finance	Engineering	Support
C-100	IT-100	ACT-100	ENG-100	S-100
C-200	IT-200	1CT-200	ENG-200	S-200
C-300	IT-300	ACT-300	ENG-300	S-300
C-400	IT-400	ACT-400	ENG-400	S-400

Table 6.3: Values to be included

The following figure depicts how to include the values of dependent field:

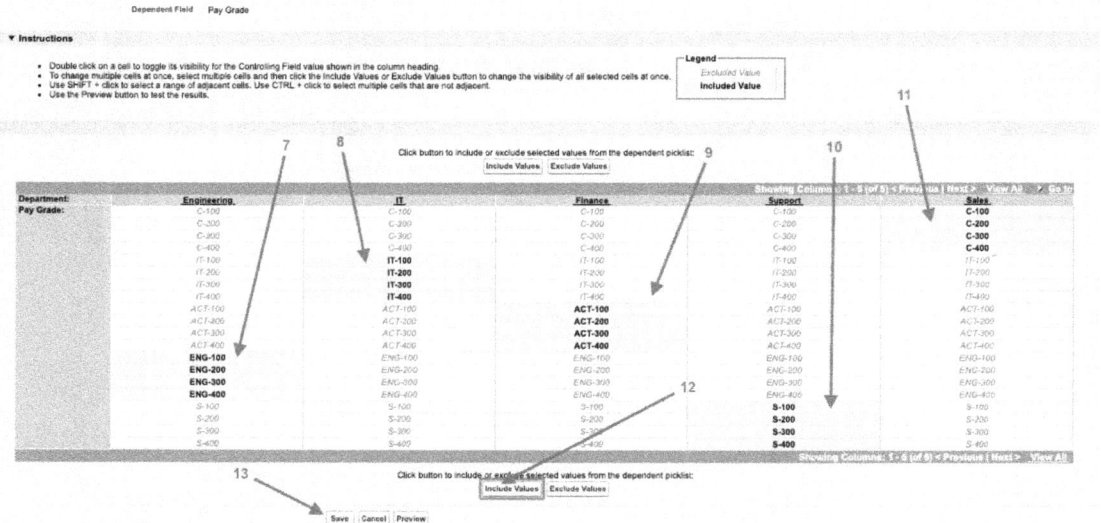

Figure 6.12: Including dependent values

6. Click on **Save** once done.

Create depended Pick Lists (Controlling field: Status, Dependent field: Sub-status), through the following steps:

1. From **Fields & Relationships**, select **Field Dependencies** and then **New**.
2. Select **Status** as **Controlling Field** and **Sub Status** as **Dependent Field**, then click **Continue**.
3. Insert the values.
4. Click **Save** once it is done.
5. Click on **OK** when a pop-up message displays stating **1 controlling values have no dependent values included. Save, anyway?**

Object relationship

As we have discussed earlier, object relationship links two objects in two different ways:

- Parent-to-child
- One-to-many

Object relationship is of the following two main types:

- Lookup
- Master-detail

There exist two special types of object relationships:

- Self-position
- Many-to-many

Creating a look-up relationship

Take a look at the following scenario:

Scenario: It is needed to see which job applications are related to each position. Additionally, the company needs to see which hiring managers are related to each position.

The following figure depicts the look-up relationship between position and hiring manager:

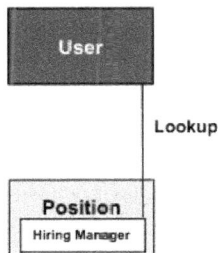

Figure 6.13: Look up relationship between position and hiring manager

The tasks are as follows:

- Create a Look-up relationship between Job Application and Position object
- Create a Look-up relationship between Position and Hiring Manager object

Solution:

Task one: Create a look-up relationship between job application and position object through the following steps:

1. Click the gear icon ⚙ at the top of the page and launch **Setup**.
2. Click the **Object Manager** tab.
3. Select the **Job Application** object.
4. From **Fields & Relationships**, click **New**.
5. Select **Data Type** as **Lookup Relationship** and click **Next**.
6. Select **Related to** as **Position** and click **Next**.
7. Select **Field Label** and **Field Name** as **Position** and click **Next**.
8. Accept the defaults to Field-Level security and click **Next**.
9. Accept the default to add the reference field to **Page Layouts** and click **Next**.
10. Accept the default to add **Custom Related Lists** and click **Save**.

Task two: Similarly, create look-up the relationship between position and hiring manager.

Creating a master-detail relationship

Let us understand this topic with a scenario:

Scenario: Every position should have one or more interviewers associated with it. An interviewer record should always be associated with a position record. If a given position is deleted, then the associated Interviewer data should also be deleted.

The tasks are as follows:

- Create a master-detail relationship between the interviewer and position.
- Create a master-detail relationship between the job application and reviewer.

Solution:

Task one: Create a master-detail relationships between Interviewer and Position through the following steps:

1. Click the gear icon ⚙ at the top of the page and launch **Setup**.
2. Click the **Object Manager** tab.
3. Select the **Interviewer** object.
4. From **Fields & Relationships**, click **New**.

5. Select **Data Type** as **Master-Child Relationship** and click **Next**.
6. Select **Related to** as **Position** and click **Next**.
7. Select **Field Label** and **Field Name** as **Position** and click **Next**.
8. Accept the defaults to Field-Level security and click **Next**.
9. Accept the default to add the reference field to **Page Layouts** and click **Next**.
10. Accept the default to add **Custom Related Lists** and click **Save**.

Task two: Similarly, create a master-detail relationship between Job Application and Reviewer.

Creating self-relationship

Understand the following scenario:

Scenario: When members of the HR team are looking at a position in their recruiting app, she would like each recruiter to be able to identify other open positions that require similar skills or have similar job descriptions. This will allow recruiters to determine appropriate roles for candidates more easily.

Solution:

Task one: The task is to create a self-relationship with the position object:

1. Click the gear icon ⚙ at the top of the page and launch **Setup**.
2. Click the **Object Manager** tab.
3. Click on **Position**.
4. Click **Fields & Relationships**, then **New**.
5. Select **Look-up Relationship** as the **Data Type**.
6. Click on **Next**.
7. In the **Related To** picklist, select **Position**.
8. Click on **Next**.
9. Change the **Field Label** to **Related Position**.
10. Click on the **Next** three times.
11. Change the **Related List Label** to **Related Position**.
12. Click on **Save**.

Create a junction object

When structuring a many-to-many relationship, a junction object is utilized to associate the two objects with relating with one another. A junction object is a custom object with two relationships.

While making a junction object, think about the following:

- Name the object with a mark that shows its motivation.
- Use the auto-number information type.

Let us understand the following scenario to understand more about a junction object:

Scenario: The company will have many positions advertised on the various job posting sites. The company wants to be able to connect and manage records within Salesforce.

The tasks are as follows:

- Create a new custom junction object.
- Create the master-detail relationships of Job Posting with Position and Job Posting Site.

Solution:

Task one: Create a new custom junction object through the following steps:

1. Click the gear icon ⚙ at the top of the page and launch **Setup**.
2. Click the **Object Manager** tab.
3. Select **Custom Object** from **Create**.
4. Enter the following details:
   a. **Label**: Job posting
   b. **Plural label:** Job postings
   c. **Data type:** Auto number
   d. **Display format:** JOBPOSTING-{0000}
   e. **Starting number:** 1
5. Click **Save** once it is done.

Task two: Create the master-detail relationships of Job Posting with Position and Job Posting Site through the following steps:

1. Click the gear icon at the top of the page and launch **Setup**.
2. Click the **Object Manager** tab.
3. Select **Job Posting** and then **Fields & relationships**.
4. Click **New** and select the following details:
   a. **Data type**: Master-Detail Relationship, click **Next**
   b. **Related to**: Job Posting Site, click **Next**
   c. **Field label:** Job_Posting_Site, click **Next**

d. Accept the default and click **Next** twice

e. Accept the default and click **Save & New**

f. **Data Type**: Master-Detail Relationship, click **Next** again

g. **Related To**: Position, click **Next**

h. **Field Label**: Position, click **Next**

i. Accept the default and click **Next** twice

j. Accept the default and click **Save**

Building user interface

This section consists of building user interface for the applications. The user interface includes tabs, page layouts, and Record Types, etc. Through these user interface components, the users interact with the application. In this section, we will create a Lightning app, tabs for the app, page layout, record page, compact layout, Record Types.

Creating Lightning apps

In Salesforce, an application is a mix of tabs, processes, and services related to business work. A Salesforce application is a group of tabs that fill-in as a unit to give functionality.

The next goal is to create a custom app for our recruitment process. Let us create an app named RecruitForce. To do so, perform the following steps:

1. Click the gear icon at the top of the page and launch Setup.

2. Type **App** in Quick Finder and select **App Manager** (Alternatively, you can navigate **Platform Tools – App Manager**).

3. Click on **New Lightning App**. On a new screen, you need to enter the following app details and branding information:

    a. **App name**: App name appears in the navigation bar, so users can easily identify the app name they are currently using. In our case, enter RecruitForce.

    b. **Developer name**: This will be auto-populated based on app name. Let us keep as it is.

    c. **Description**: We can keep a meaningful description of the custom app here.

    d. **App branding**: We can optionally add an image to our custom app. The file size of a custom app image must be smaller than 5MB.

The following figure reflects creating a new app called **RecruitForce**:

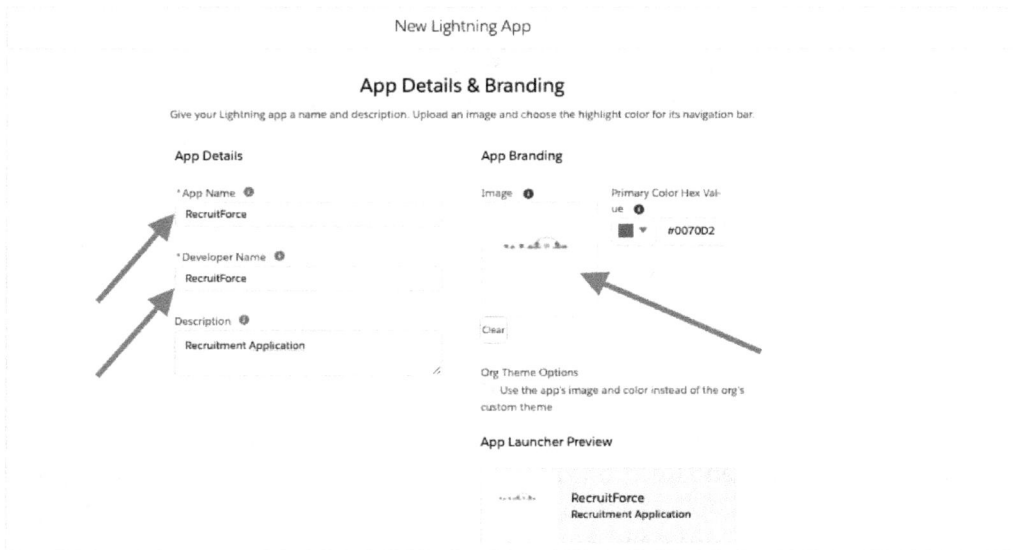

Figure 6.14: Creating a new app

4. Once done, click on **Next**.

5. Let us keep **App Options** as it is and click **Next**.

6. In the next screen for **Utility Items**, we may not like to add an item for the time being. Click on **Next**.

7. In the next screen, let us select a few navigation items for our app. To do so, move the tabs from the **Available Items** tabs pane to the **Selected Items** tabs pane. You can also rearrange the order of the items.

    The following figure shows how to add navigation items to an app:

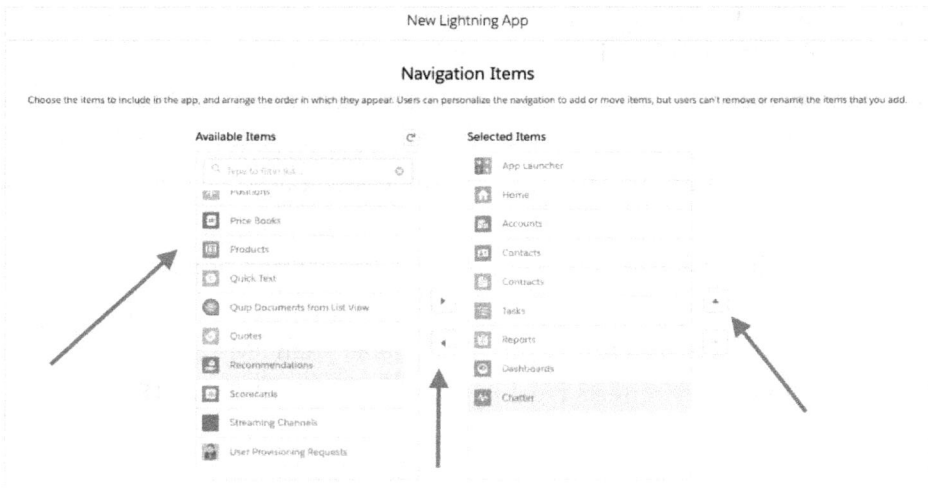

Figure 6.15: Adding navigation items

8. Click on **Next** once done.

9. The final step is to assign the app to user Profiles. Assigning user Profiles will help the users to access the app. To do so, move the Profiles from the **Available Profiles** pane to the **Selected Profiles** pane.

10. Once done, click **Save** and **Finish**.

11. The app, RecruitForce, is ready to be used. To access the app, navigate to app launcher ⠿ and select **RecruitForce** app.

The following figure depicts how to select an app from app launcher;

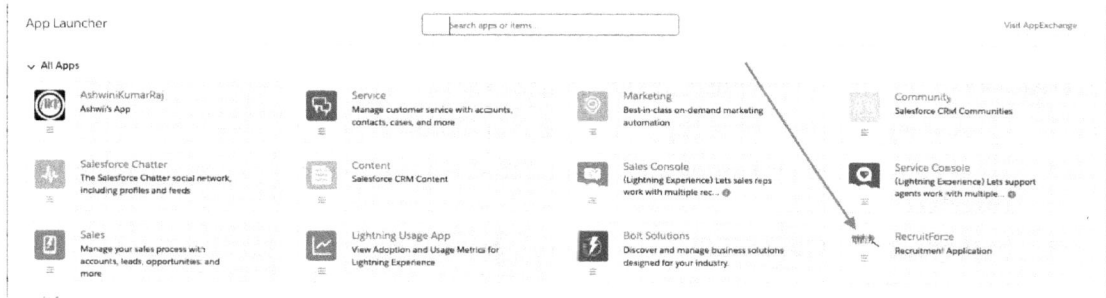

Figure 6.16: Selecting an app from the app launcher

The screen should look similar to the following figure:

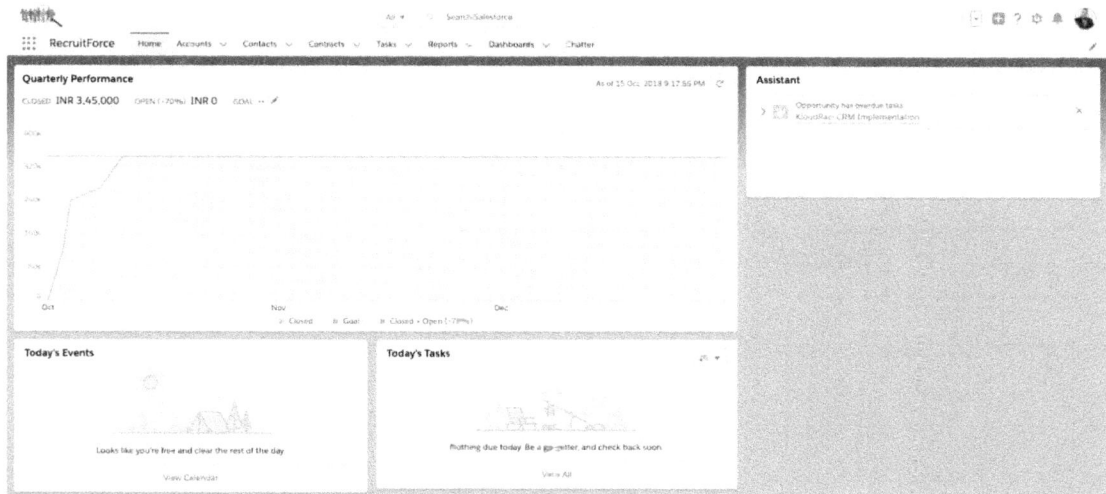

Figure 6.17: Home screen of RecruitForce app

Creating tabs for apps

In the Lightning platform, clicking tabs is how you explore an application. Each tab in the application fills in as the beginning stage for viewing and entering data for a specific object. At this point, when we make custom objects for an application, we can likewise make custom tabs that look and carry on like standard objects. Let us discuss a situation to create tabs for the RecruitForce application:

Situation: The HR group of RecruitForce needs to put candidates into open positions in the organization. They might want their recruiters to have a rich UI that causes them to coordinate the right candidate with the right job all the more rapidly.

The task is as follows: Create a new tab named **Reviews**.

Solution:

Task one: Create tab reviews.

To create a tab (Reviews), perform the following steps:

1. Click the gear icon at the top of the page and launch Setup.
2. Type **Tabs** in Quick Finder and select **Tabs** (Alternatively, you can navigate **User Interface** – tab)
3. In the **Custom Object Tabs** section, click **New**.
4. From the **Object** picklist, select **Review**
5. Click 🔍 in **Tab Style** and select the style you want.
6. Click **Next**.

    The following figure shows how to create a custom tab:

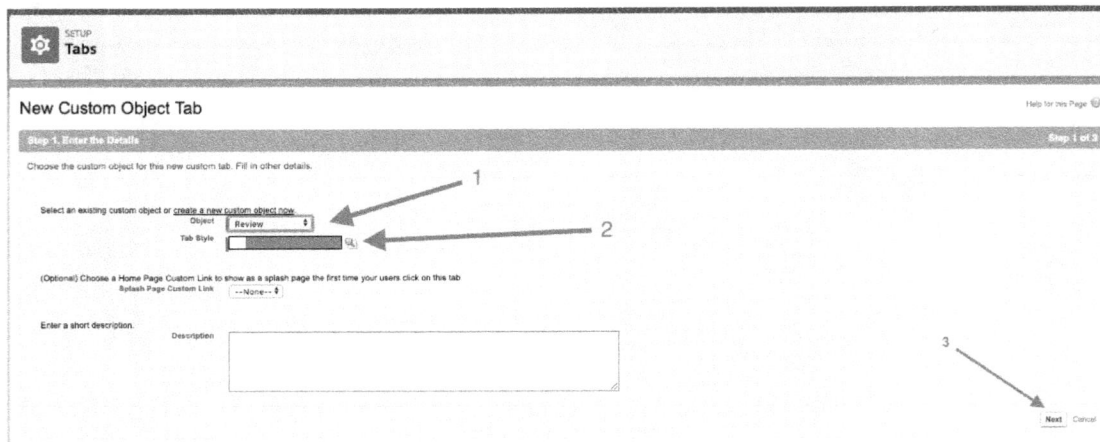

Figure 6.18: Creating a custom tab

7. Leave the Profile as is and click **Next**.
8. In the **Add to Custom Apps** section, do the following:
    a. Deselect **Include** tab.
    b. Select the **Append** tab to users' existing personal customizations.

9. Click **Save**.

Now that we have created a tab, we need to associate the tab with the recruitment app. To do so, perform the following steps:

1. From Setup, enter `App Manager` in the Quick Find box, then select **App Manager**.
2. Click **Next** to the RecruitForce and select **Edit**.
3. Click **Navigation Items**.
4. From the **Available Items** list, hold control/command and select **Job Application** and **Positions**, then click ˙ to add the tabs to the **Selected Items** list.
5. In the **Selected Items** section, rearrange the tabs by clicking on each and using the up or down arrows to put the tabs in order.
6. Click **Save**, then click **Back**.

Similarly, we can create tabs for other custom objects we created and associated with the app.

Creating a customized page layout

A page layout determines the fields, related lists, sections, and buttons when users view or edit a record. You may like to modify an object's default page layout or create a new one. Let us discuss the following scenario to create a page layout for the candidate:

Scenario: Giving the HR team of RecruitForce easier access to the records they need. They need to match the right candidates with the right jobs. Now, customize the review page layout to help the team easily access information from the interviewing process.

The tasks are as follows:

- **Task one**: Create a new section for core competencies on the page layout.
- **Task two**: Create a new section for leadership skills.
- **Task three**: Create a new section for experience.
- **Task four**: Create a new section for recommendation.

Solution:

Task one: Create a new section for core competencies on the page layout:

1. From Setup, click **Object Manager** and then **Review**.
2. Click on **Page Layouts**.
3. Click ˙ next to **Review Layout** and select **Edit**.

   The following figure shows how to create a new page layout for an object:

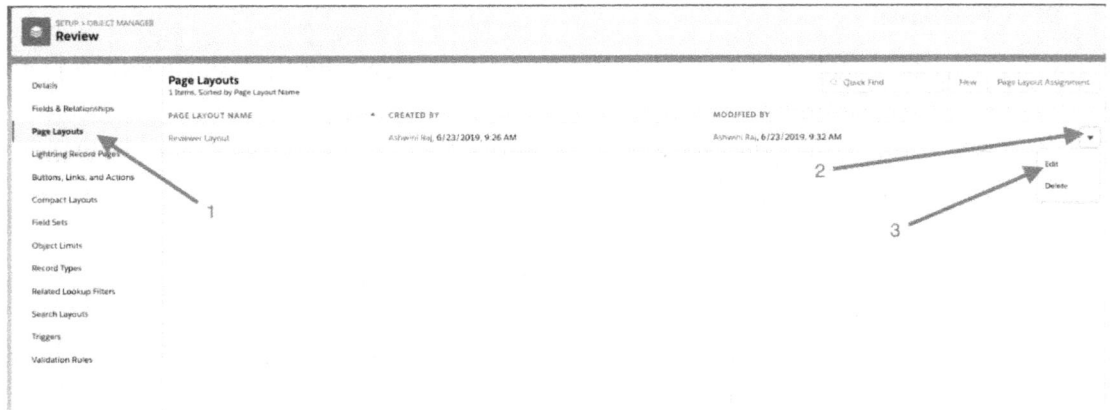

Figure 6.19: Creating a new page layout

4. Add a new section to the page layout by dragging the section from the palette to fall below the **Information** section.

5. Fill in the following section properties:

   a. For **Section Name**, enter `Core Competencies`.

   b. For **Layout**, select **1-Column**.

6. Click on **OK**.

   The following figure shows how to add a field to a layout:

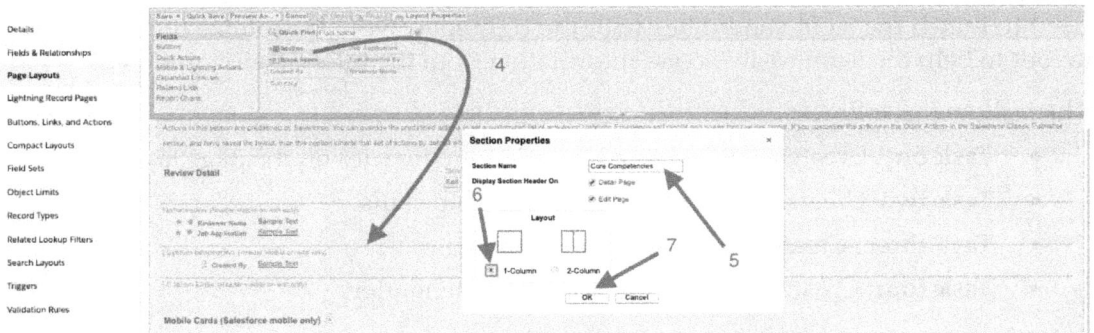

Figure 6.20: Adding a field to a layout

7. Drag the **Core Competencies** and **Core Competencies Comments** fields from the **Information** section into the **Core Competencies** section.

Task two: Create a new section for leadership skills through the following steps:

1. Drag **Section** from the palette to fall below the **Core Competencies** section.

2. For **Section Name**, enter **Leadership Skills**.

3. Under **Layout**, select **1-Column**.

4. Click **OK**.

5. Drag the **Leadership Skills** and **Leadership Skills Comments** fields from the **Information** section into the **Leadership Skills** section.

Task three: Create a new section named **Experience** through the following steps:

1. Drag **Section** from the palette to fall below the **Leadership Skills** section.

2. For **Section Name**, enter **Experiences**.

3. Under **Layout**, select **1-Column**.

4. Click on **OK**.

5. Drag the **Experience** and **Experience Comments** fields from the **Information** section into the **Experience** section.

Task four: Create a new section for **Recommendation** through the following steps:

1. Drag **Section** from the palette to below the **Experience** section.

2. For **Section Name**, enter **Recommendation**.

3. Under **Layout**, select **1-Column**.

4. Click on **OK**.

5. Drag the **Recommend for Hire** and **Reason Recommended** fields from the **Information** section into the **Recommendation** section.

6. Select the **Core Competencies** field, then hold down *Ctrl* or *Command* and select the **Leadership Skills** and **Experience** fields as well.

7. Hover over one of the highlighted fields and click the gear icon ✎ edit them all.

8. For **Field Properties**, select **Required** for all three fields.

9. Click on **OK**.

10. Click on **Save**.

Creating Lightning record pages

Using the Lightning App Builder, a customized view for each object's records can be given. The Lightning App Builder permits to add, reorder, and remove components on a Lightning record page. To make Lightning record pages for a candidate object, perform the following steps:

1. Click the gear icon at the top of the page and launch Setup.

2. Click the **Object Manager** tab.

3. Select **Candidate** and then **Lightning Record Pages**

The following figure shows how to create a Record Page:

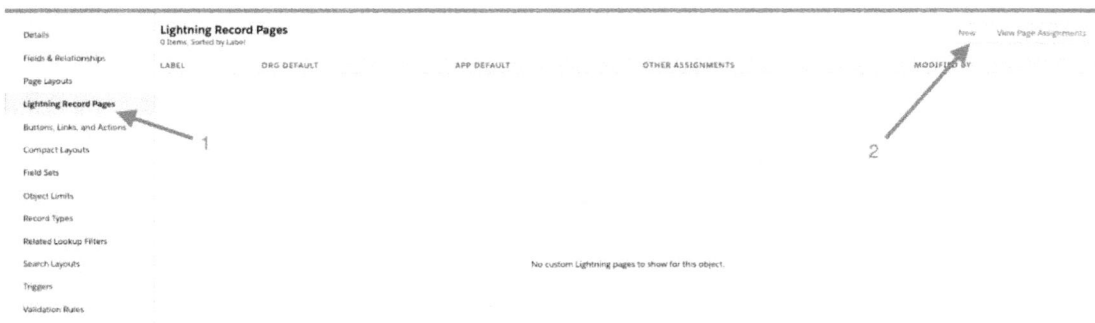

Figure 6.21: Creating Record Page

4. Select **Record Page** on the left side and, then click **Next**:

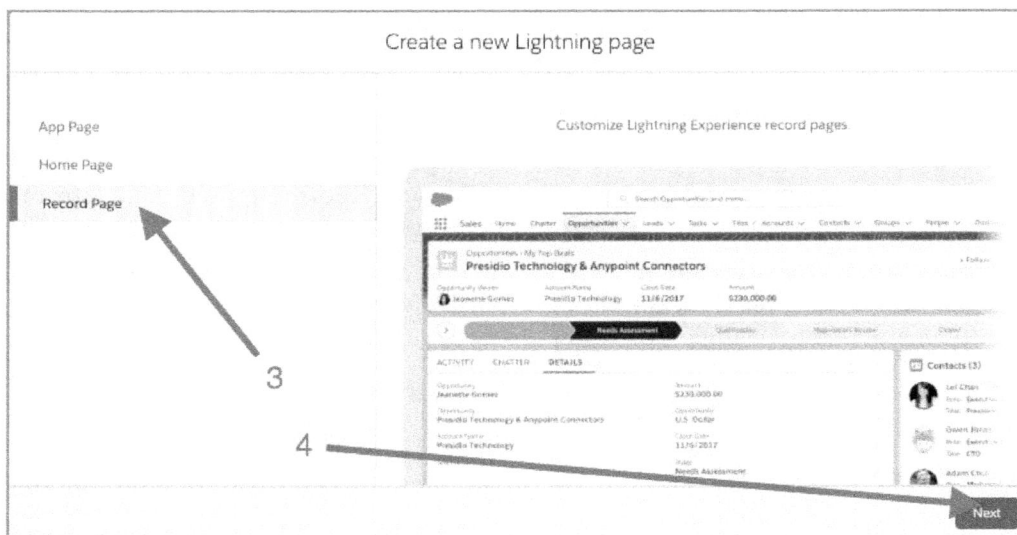

Figure 6.22: Creating record page

5. Give a label and choose the **Object** (Candidate in this case). Click on **Next**.

6. The next step is to select a page template. For the current scenario, select the **Header** and two equal region template.

7. Click **Finish** once done.

8. In the Lightning App Builder, add, edit, or remove components to customize the page's layout:

9. Click **Save** once it is done.

10. Click on **Activation** to activate the page.

11. The next step is to assign the page as the default record page, or you can assign it to specific apps, as per your requirement. For the current situation, select **Assign this page as the default record page**, as shown in the following figure:

Figure 6.23: *Assigning the record page to an app*

12. Now select the app (**RecruitForce**) and, then click **Next:**

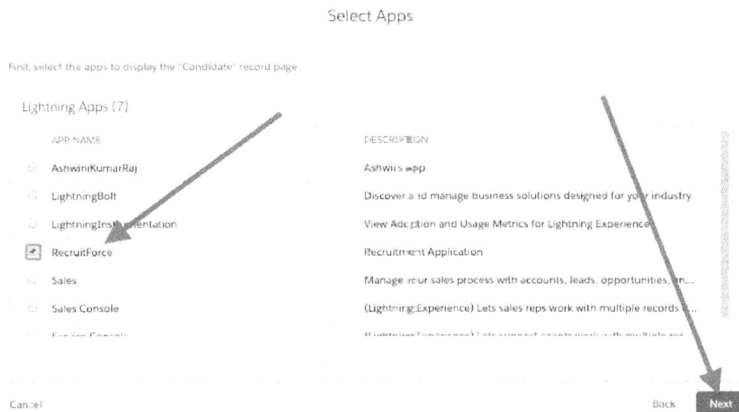

Figure 6.24: *Selecting the app for the record page*

13. On the next page, keep default **Form Factor** and click **Next**.
14. Select **Record Type** as **Master** and click **Next**.
15. Select the Profile as **System Administrator** and click **Next**.
16. Finally, click on **Save**.

Creating a custom compact layout

The compact layout of Salesforce, controls which fields to appear in the Highlights Panel component on the Record Page.

Let us create a custom compact layout that includes more than just the candidate's name through performing the following steps:

1. Click the gear icon at page and launch Setup.
2. Click the object **Manager** tab and then **Candidate** object
3. Click **Compact Layouts**, then click **New** and fill in the details:
   a. **Label**: Include Candidate Name
   b. **Selected fields**: Candidate Number, First Name, Last Name

   The following figure shows how to create a Compact Layout for an object:

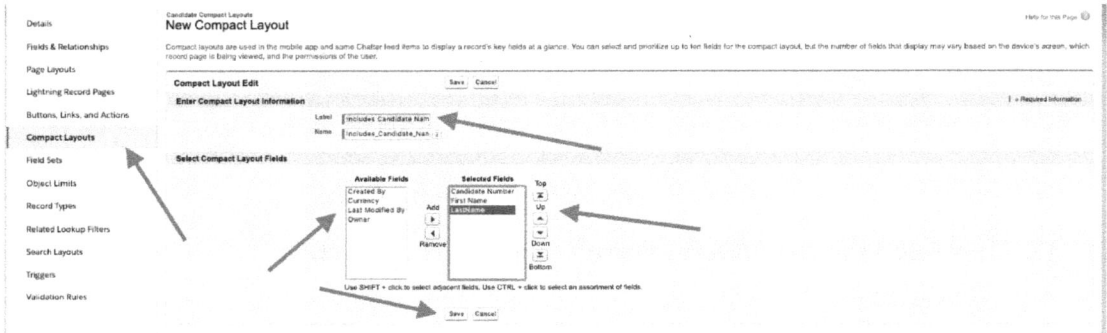

Figure 6.25: Creating a Compact Layout for an object

4. Click on **Save**.
5. Click the **Compact Layout Assignment**, then **Edit Assignment**.
6. Set the New Compact Layout you just created as the first compact layout.
7. Click **Save**.

Creating Record Types

Record Types determine which features are available on page layouts, including fields, locations, and properties.

Scenario: It is required that the hiring managers at RecruitForce be able to create new positions only for their own departments. For example, she wants technical hiring managers to create positions only for their IT and engineering departments.

Task: We can do this with a custom Record Type. The Record Type you create here limits the picklist choices available to hiring managers. The tasks are as follows:

- **Task one**: Create profiles.
- **Task two:** Create Record Types.
- **Task three**: Add the Record Type field to the Position page layout.

Solution:

Task one: Create Profiles:

1. From Setup, enter **Profiles** in the Quick Find box and select **Profiles**. (Alternatively, you can choose to navigate **Users – Profiles**)

2. From the list of Profiles, select **Standard User**.

3. Click **Clone** next to Standard User.

4. For **Profile Name**, enter `Recruiter Technical`.

5. Click on **Save**.

6. On the Recruiter: Technical Profile page, click on **Clone**.

7. For **Profile Name**, enter `Recruiter Non-Technical`.

8. Click on **Save**.

Task two: Create Record Types

In this task, we are going to create two Record Types:

- Technical position
- Non-technical position

Technical position

Perform the following steps:

1. From Setup, click **Object Manager**.

2. Click **Position**, then **Record Types**.

3. Click **New** and fill in the details shown in the following table:

Field	Value
Existing Record Type	Master
Record Type label	Technical position
Description	Use this Record Type (Technical Position) for technical positions only.
Active	Select

Table 6.4: Record Type fields for the technical position

4. Deselect the checkbox next to **Enable for Profile** and select these Profiles:

   a. **Recruiter**: Technical

   b. System administrator

5. Click **Next** and then **Save**.

6. Under **Picklists Available for Editing**, click **Edit** next to **Department**.

7. Remove all but **IT and Engineering** from the **Selected Values** column.

8. Click on **Save**.

Non-technical position

Perform the following steps:

1. Navigate to **Setup** | **Object Manager** | **Position** | **Record Types**.

2. Click **New** and fill the details provided in the following table:

Field	Value
Existing Record Type	Master
Record Type label	Non-technical position
Description	Use this Record Type for non-technical positions only.
Active	Select

Table: 6.5: Record Type fields for non-technical position

3. Ensure the checkbox next to **Enable for Profile** is deselected, then select the following Profiles:

    a. **Recruiter**: Non-technical

    b. System Administrator

4. Click on **Next**, then **Save**.

5. Under **Picklists Available for Editing**, click **Edit** next to **Department**.

6. Keep **Finance**, **Support**, and **Sales** in the **Selected Values** column.

7. Click on **Save**.

Task three: Add the **Record Type** field to the **Position** page layout, through the following steps:

1. Navigate to **Setup** | **Object Manager** | **Position** | **Page Layouts**.

2. Click ˙ next to **Position Layout** and select **Edit**.

3. Drag the **Record Type** field from the palette into the Information section and drop it just below the **Department** field.

4. Click on **Save**.

To test the functionality, perform the following steps:

1. Go to app launcher and select RectuitForce app.

2. Click on **Position Tab** and click **New**.

3. You can see a new window with two Record Types as seen in the following figure:

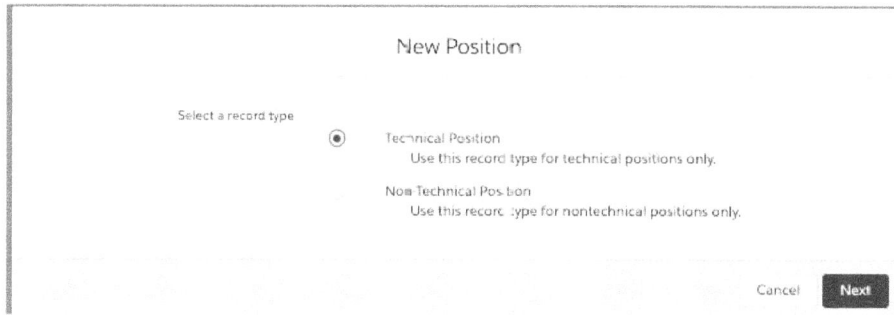

Figure 6.26: Showcasing two Record Types

Conclusion

In this chapter, we got introduced to designing custom applications using the Force.com platform. We discussed the application building blocks like data model, user interface, and business logic. The data model includes custom objects, custom fields, and object relationships. The user interface of an application consists of tabs, page layouts, record pages, and so on. In this chapter, we learned how to create data models elements and user interface elements.

In the next chapter, we will learn how to implement business logic to the application.

Questions

1. **The application design of Salesforce consists of:**
   a. User interface
   b. Business logic
   c. Data model
   d. All of the above

2. **Objects, fields, and relationships are part of which application design of Salesforce?**
   a. User interface
   b. Business logic
   c. Data model
   d. All of the above

3. **To create a field for an object named Customer, which path will you follow?**
   a. Object Manager | Customer | Fields
   b. Object Manager | Customer | Relationship

    c. Object Manager | Customer | Fields and Relationship

    d. None of the above

4. **Building user interface consists of what?**

    a. Applications

    b. Page layouts

    c. Record Types

    d. All of the above

5. **Which of the following determines the fields, related lists, sections, and buttons when users view or edit a record?**

    a. Applications

    b. Page layouts

    c. Record Types

    d. All of the above

Answers

    1. d

    2. c

    3. c

    4. d

    5. b

Join our Discord space

Join our Discord workspace for latest updates, offers, tech happenings around the world, new releases, and sessions with the authors:

https://discord.bpbonline.com

CHAPTER 7
Implementing Business Processes

Introduction

This chapter will focus on how you can configure validation rules and approve processes to automate, improve quality, and generate high-value processes within the organization. We will also learn how to write a formula field and about roll-up summary field. Lastly, we will learn different types and uses of Lightning Flow.

Structure

In this chapter, we will discuss the following topics:

- Creating a cross-object formula
- Creating formula field
- Roll-up summary field
- Approval process
- Lightning Flow
- Flow Builder

Objectives

After studying this unit, you will learn to use formulas and roll-up summary fields. You will also learn how to automate the approval process and perform operations using Lightning Flow.

Creating a cross-object formula

The cross-object formula is a special formula field that is used to display data from the parent object. It helps prevent data duplication or redundancy, for example, if the value is stored in the parent object, we can just create a formula field on child objects that will populate the value automatically. The user does not have to enter the data more than once. If we have a lookup relationship, then we can use the formula field in the child object.

However, if we have a master-detail, then we have one extra option to create a roll-up summary field on the parent object. Using a roll-up summary, we can count the number of child records, and the average value of child, total, maximum, or minimum of child record also.

Creating a formula field

The steps for creating a formula field are easy; the formula field can use fields from the same object or parent objects. Suppose we have an object Job Application, which is a child object of Position. This means Position is the parent and Job Application is a child, so that we can create a formula field on Job Application, and we can use fields of Job Application and Position in this formula field.

In the formula field, we can use multiple functions that Salesforce has provided as logical functions like **AND**, **OR**, **IF**, **NOT**, **ISBLANK** mathematical functions like **ABS**, **MAX**, **MIN**, **SQRT**, text function, date-time functions, and so on. We can also use operators like **&, +, -, ||, &&, ==, >=,<>** and so on.

You can search the formula field function and operator in the Salesforce doc.

Let us create a formula field; we will do the following steps:
1. Go to Setup, click **Object Manager**.
2. Choose or search **Job Application**.
3. Click on **Fields & relationship**.
4. Click on **New** (We performed these steps each time we created fields).

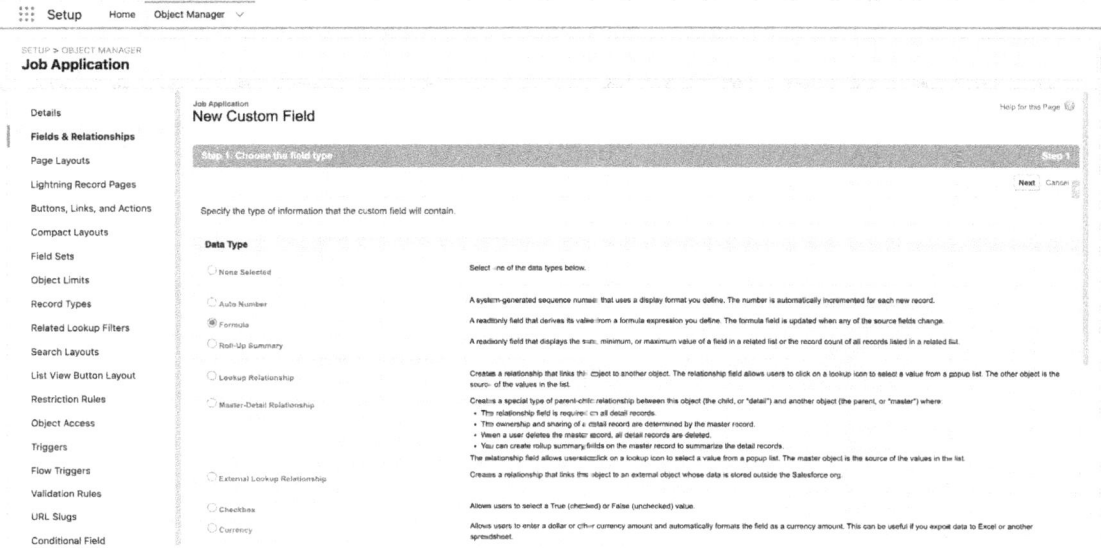

Figure 7.1: Creating formula field

5. Choose the formula field option and click **Next**.

6. Type the name of the field and choose the type of formula field as we want the Position name in the formula field. So, the name is text and we will choose **Text**. Then, click **Next**.

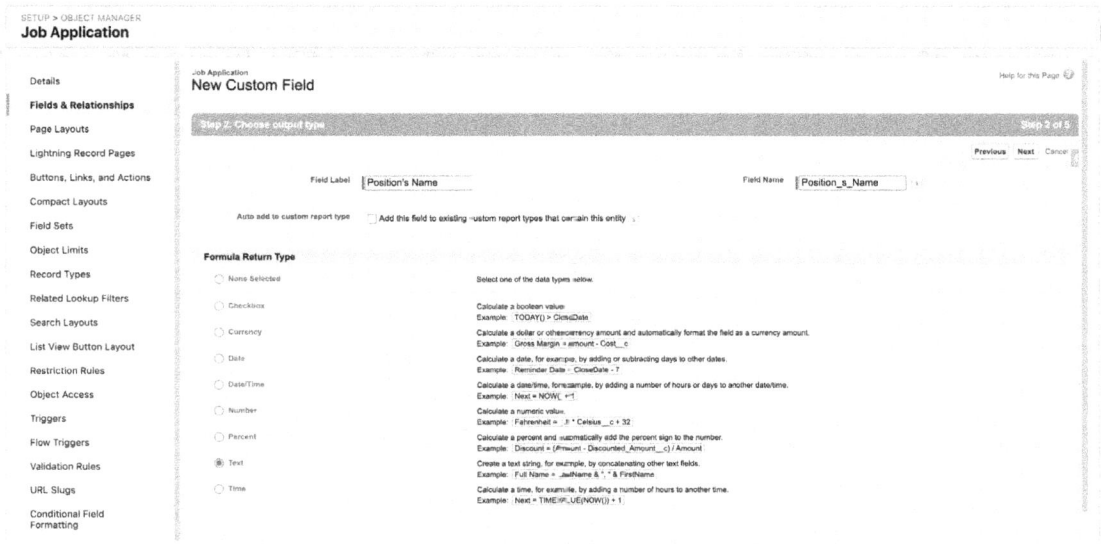

Figure 7.2: Formula field name

7. This is the main formula editor and here, you can see all the functions on the right.

8. You will see a button named **Insert Field**. Similarly, the **Insert Operator** option is also there.

9. Click on **Insert Field**, and you will see a popup of all fields from the Job Application. You will also see all the lookup objects related to the Job Application and their related fields. As you can see in *Figure 7.3*, we click on **Position** and choose the name of the Position:

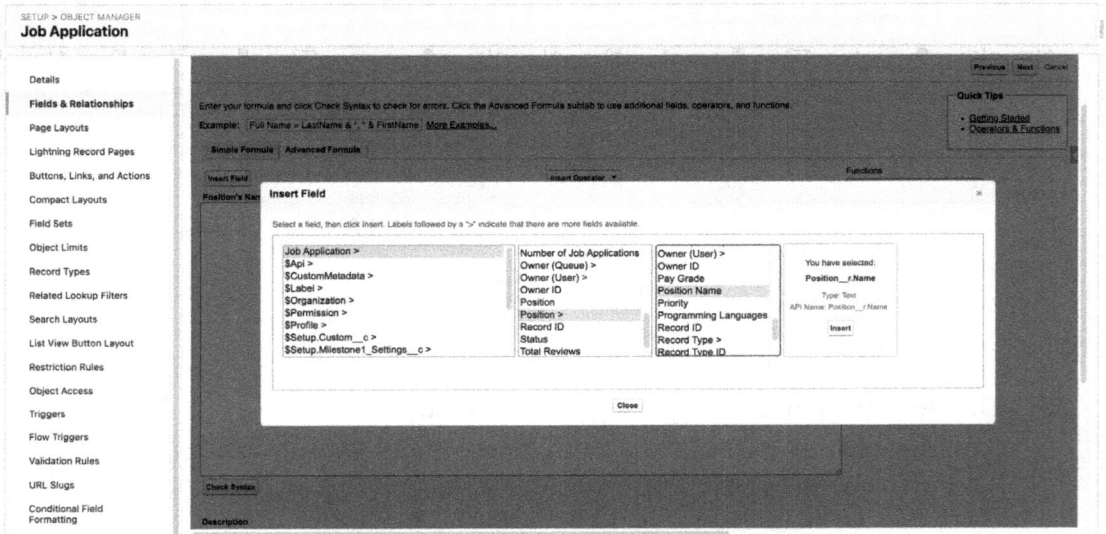

Figure 7.3: Formula insert field

10. Click on **Insert**.

11. Your formula is ready. Click on syntax checker, and if your formula is correct, you will see the green text otherwise it will be red.

12. Click on **Next** and save it your formula field. It is now is ready. You will see on your Job Application. The Position name will be auto displayed on UI.

The following figure depicts the creation of formula fields:

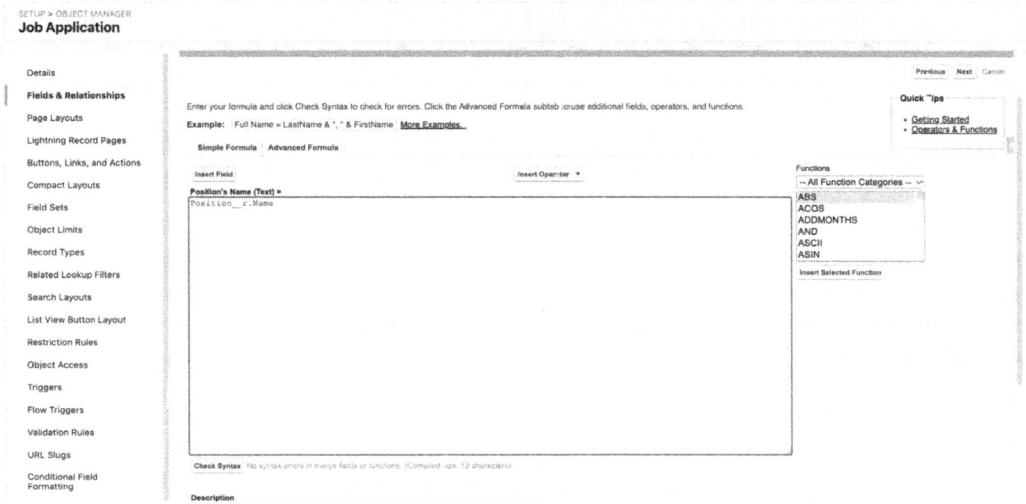

Figure 7.4: Formula field syntax

Some examples of formula fields

Job Application has multiple reviews scores, like technical, logical, analysis score. We want average score from all, so, we can create a formula field like average review score.

```
(technical_score__c + logical_score__c + Analysis_score__c) / 3
```

We have a candidate object as the parent object of the Job Application; the candidate has a first name and last name, and we can create a formula field if we want the name of the candidate in a Job Application:

```
First_Name__c & " " & Last_Name__c
```

Suppose we have a field named **Review Score** on **Job Application** object.

We want to see the qualification based on **Average_Review_Score__c** out of 5, like if someone has a score less than 3, they are is unqualified, and if the score is greater than 3.75, then they are qualified. If the score is > 4.75, then highly qualified. So, we can create a formula field like the following:

```
IF( Average_Review_Score__c < 3, "Not Qualified", IF(
Average_Review_Score__c <3.75, "Minimally Qualified", IF(
Average_Review_Score__c < 4.75, "Qualified", "Highly Qualified") ) )
```

Roll-up summary field

One of the best features is a master-detail relationship between objects in Salesforce.

Master details give us the option to count the number of child records associated with the parent record, the maximum value of a given field across all child records that have the same parent, and the sum of a particular field of the child object.

Suppose we have an object Position, and Job Application is a child using a master-detail object, we can create a roll-up summary field on Parent, i.e., Position to count no of Job Applications for particular to a single Position. Similarly, if we have a score field on the Job Application, so we can find out the highest score for a particular Position using roll-up summary field.

The steps are as follows:

1. Go to Setup, click on **Object Manager**, choose **Position** object.
2. Click on **Fields & Relationships** and click **New**.
3. Choose roll-up summary field options when you see Data Type choices.

Note: **You will see this option only when if you have any child object for this object using master-detail.**

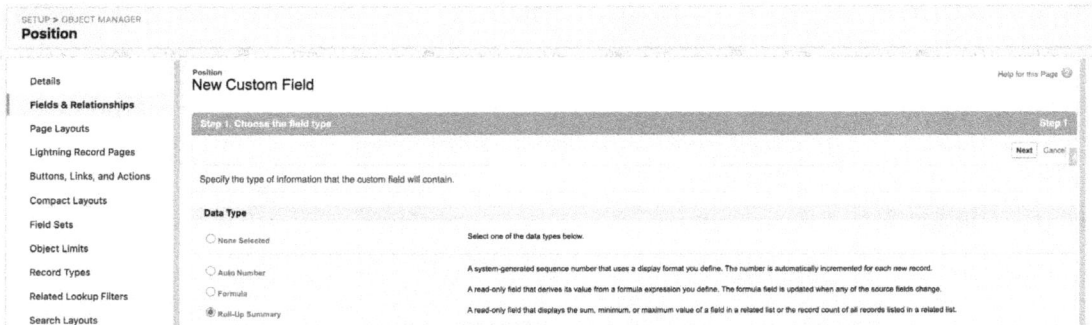

Figure 7.5: Roll-up formula field

4. Click **Next**. You will see the options to choose the child objects.
5. You will see four methods: **COUNT, SUM, MAX** and **MIN**.
6. The count will give you the count of the child object.
7. Click on **COUNT** and click **Next**. Then click on **Save**.

The following figure depicts the creation of roll-up formula field:

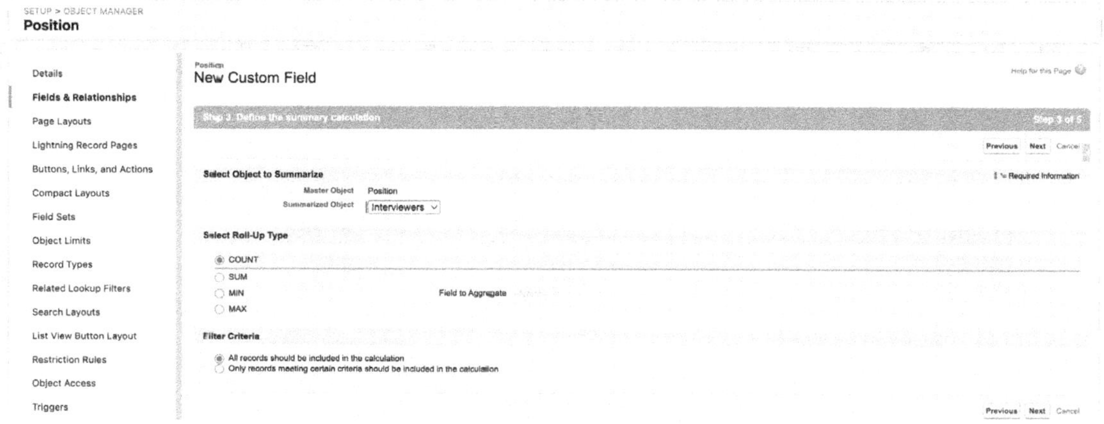

Figure 7.6: Roll-up Formula COUNT field

If we want to sum the maximum or a minimum of a particular field of the child object, we can click any of the three. You will see fields option that you want to select, and it will give you SUM or MAX or MIN, accordingly.

The following figure depicts the usage of various formula:

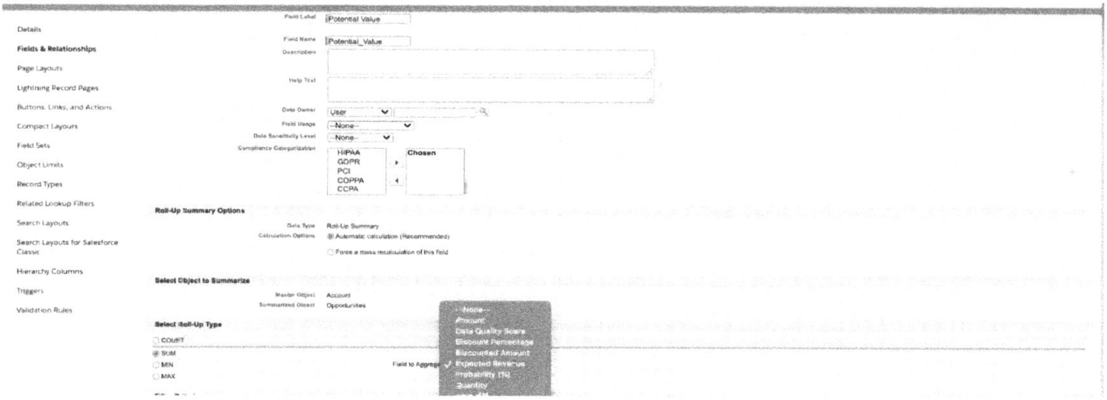

Figure 7.7: Roll-up formula SUM field

Data validation rules

A validation rule is a great feature that is used to prevent a user from making any data mistakes; whenever the user fills the data, and some field is blank or based on some condition, we need specific validation that we can customize using validation rule.

We can create a validation rule on one or more standard or custom fields. We can activate and deactivate the validation rule. When the validation rule is active, and data has some issue, then it will show an error, and data will not be saved.

Note: Whatever validation we want to put, we check just the opposite in the validation rule. For example, if we are saying this field should not be blank, we will check *isblank* for that field.

Let u take an example to understand this validation rule. Suppose we have an object Position, and two fields. One is status as a picklist with values (created, started & closed), and the second field is Hiring Manager as a lookup of the User object.

So, we want a validation. When the Position is started, the hiring manager should not be blank.

So, for that we will write a validation rule, in which we will check the status as started and we will also check if hiring manager field is blank or not. If it is blank, we will show an error.

You can refer to the following steps:

1. Go to Setup, choose object Position from the object manager.
2. Click on **Validation rule**, and click **New**.
3. Type the rule name.
4. You can see an active checkbox to activate or deactivate.
5. This is just like a formula editor so we can use fields and formulas from here and type the validation code in this editor.
6. We need to check the status, so we choose **ISPICKVAL** from **Function**:

   `ISPICKVAL( Status__c , "Started")  && ISBLANK( Hiring_Manager__c )`

   Here, you can see we are checking the status as created, and the hiring manager is blank.
7. We can click on the syntax checker to check the formula.
8. In the error message field, we will write the message we want to show to the user.
9. Error location gives us the option to choose where we need to show the error.
10. Click on **Save**; our validation rule is ready.

The following figure depicts the steps required to create a validation rule:

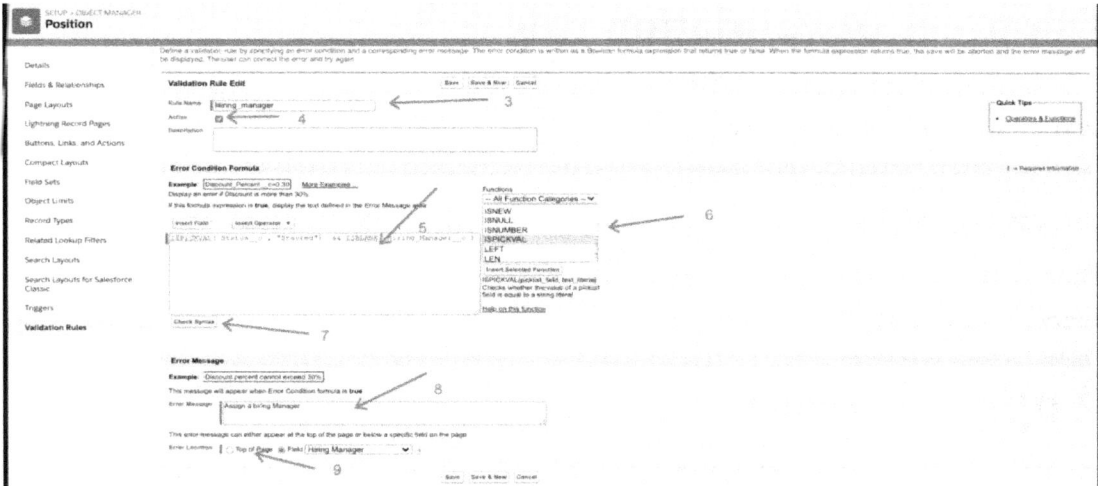

Figure 7.8: *Validation rule example*

We can test this validation and it will show the error. As you can see in the following figure, the status is started, but Hiring Manage is blank. So, when we click on **Save**, it gives the error as **Assign a hiring Manager**:

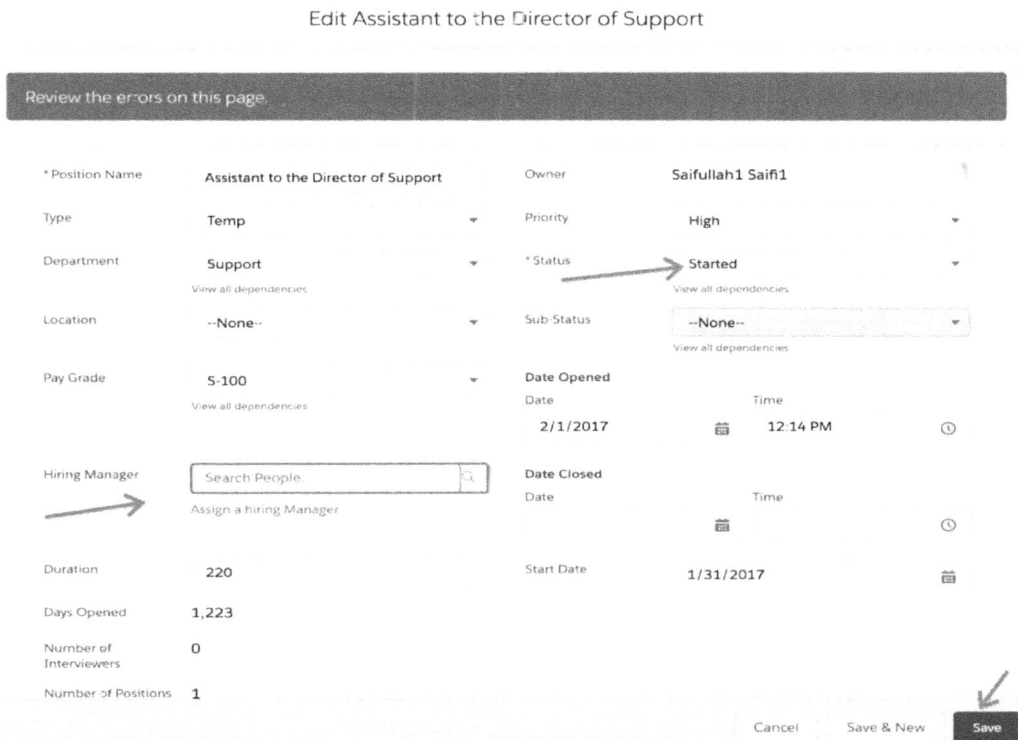

Figure 7.9: *Validation rule testing*

Examples of validation rule

If we want to put a validation, the close date should be greater than the start date:

`Start_Date__c > Close_date__c`

Phone number should be in this format: **(989) 769-9028**

`NOT((REGEX( Phone ,'\\([7-9]{1}[0-9]{2}\\) [0-9]{3}-[0-9]{4}')))`

The city field of contact should be the same as `Account.billingCity`

`Account.BillingCity <> City__c`

Approval process

Do you remember when you sent an email for a leave? Your manager approves it, or it is sent to a higher manager for the next approval. Similarly, as in the sales process, everything is about quality, integrity, and business processes. So, in some cases, for any records or object, we need such type of approvals. Salesforce has a tool named approval process in which, based on condition, we can automate sending an approval request to the related manager, and they can see the records and field value and then approve or reject it. We can create multiple condition-based steps and a multi-level approval process. There will be a button on that object detail page to initiate the submission process.

Approval processes play an integral part of any business. We need to pre-plan it carefully before creation.

To create an approval process, refer to the following steps:

1. Go to Setup, search **Approval Process**, click on it.
2. Choose the object, and create approval process:

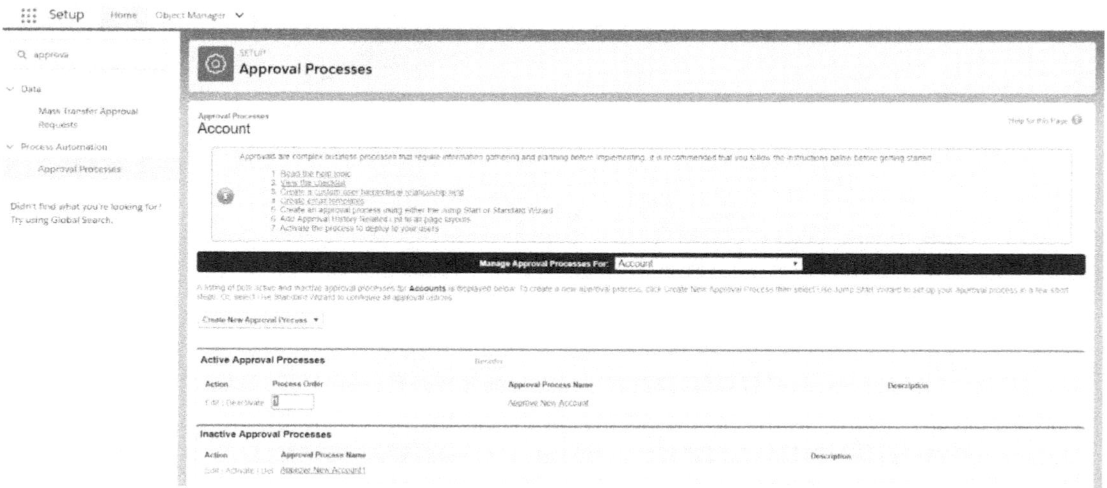

Figure 7.10: Creating approval process

We have created one approval process. The approval process will look like the following:

1. In the top section, you can see the name criteria option to activate/deactivate or delete:

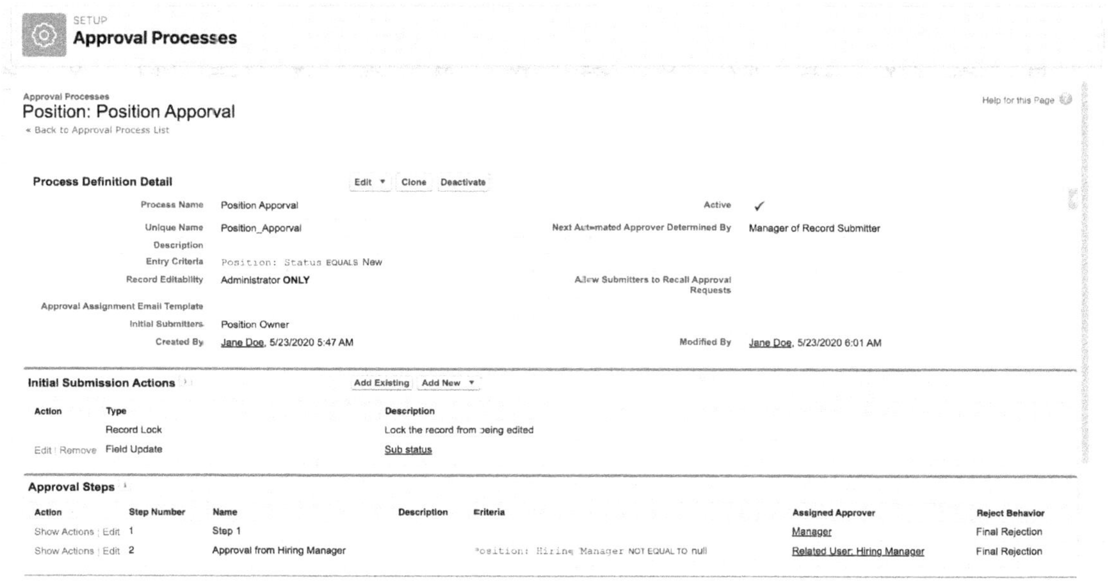

Figure 7.11: Approval process UI

2. This is the section in which all approved steps will be added. When it will be submitted, who can approve it or what will be the next steps, etc. can be defined here:

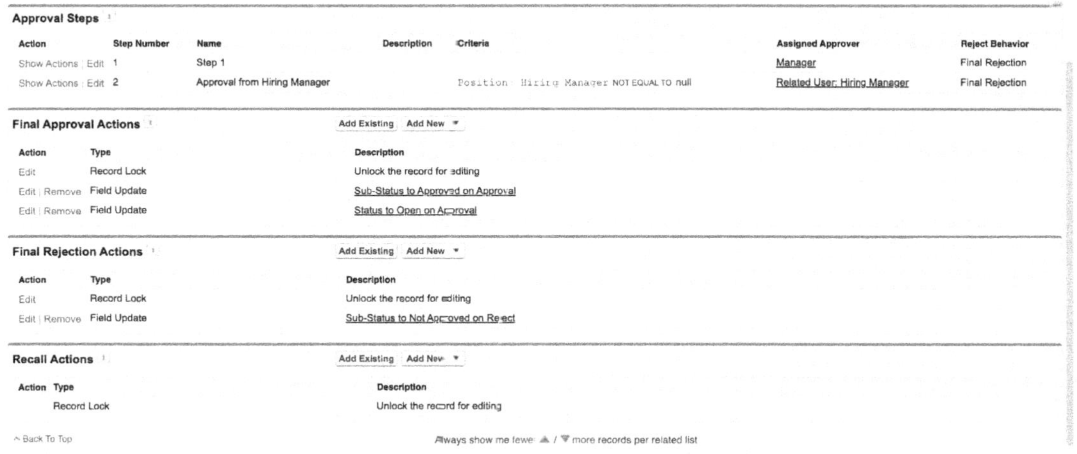

Figure 7.12: Approval process basic

Approval process example

Whenever a Position is created, we will send an approval request to the manager and the hiring manger to approve this Position of status. When a creator submits this approval, the Position status is new, and the sub status will change to pending. One automatic email will be sent to the manager and hiring manager, and the record will be locked. They can see the records and approve or reject this Position. When it is approved, the Position will be open; otherwise, it will be closed and rejected.

Solution: Refer to the following steps:

1. Search approval process in setup, choose an object, and click on **Create New Approval Process**. We choose the Jumpstart wizard option, as it is easy:

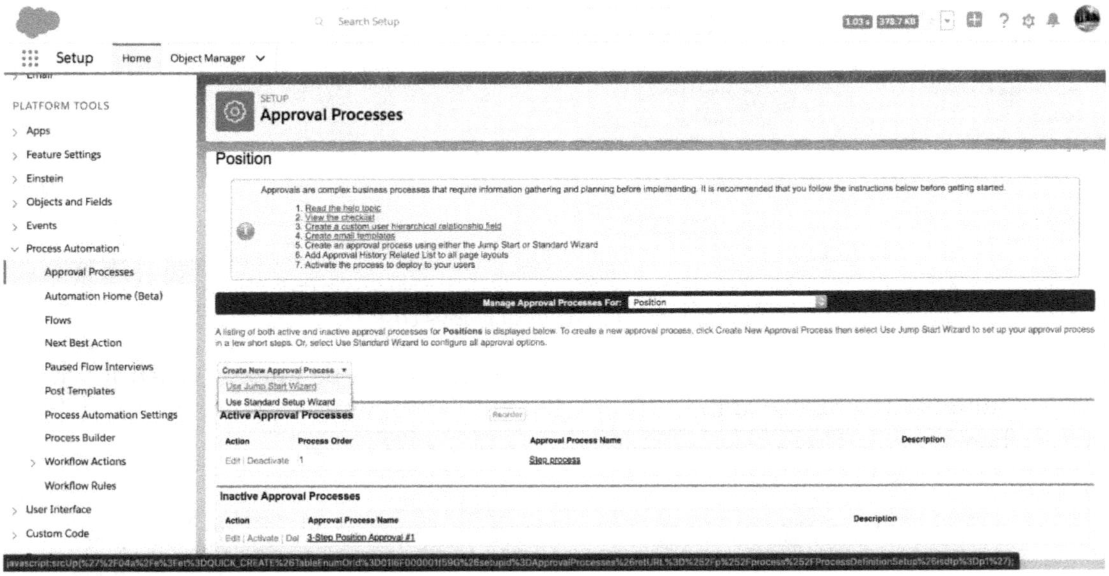

Figure 7.13: Create new approval process

2. Type the name of approval process and enter the entry criteria for approval, so when Position is created, the status will be new. We will choose the approver as manager of the creator:

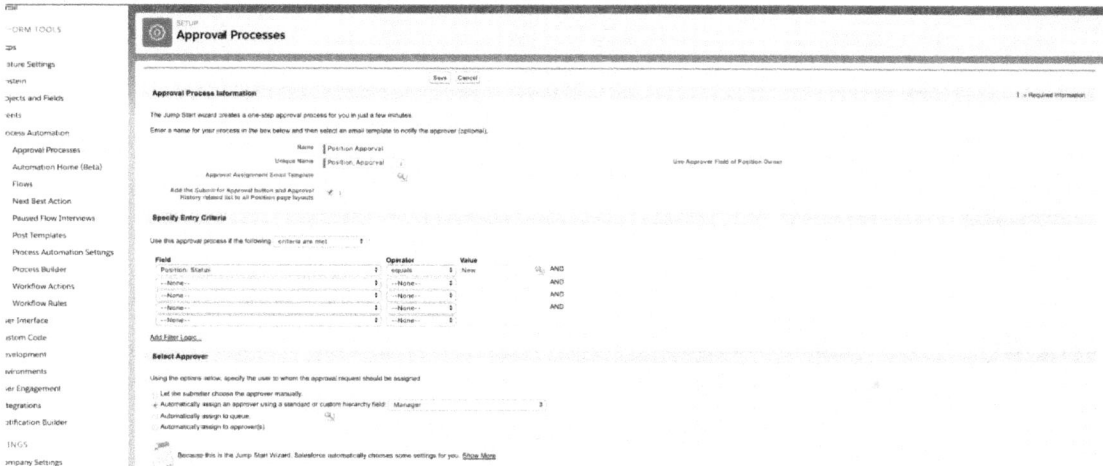

Figure 7.14: Approval process conditions

3. When we click on **Save**, the approval process is ready to use, but we will activate once all approval steps and actions are added:

Figure 7.15: Approval process example

4. We will update the Position sub status to pending, as pending for approval, when the user submits the record for approval (this is a simple field update action). You can create a field update action and set the value pending in the sub status:

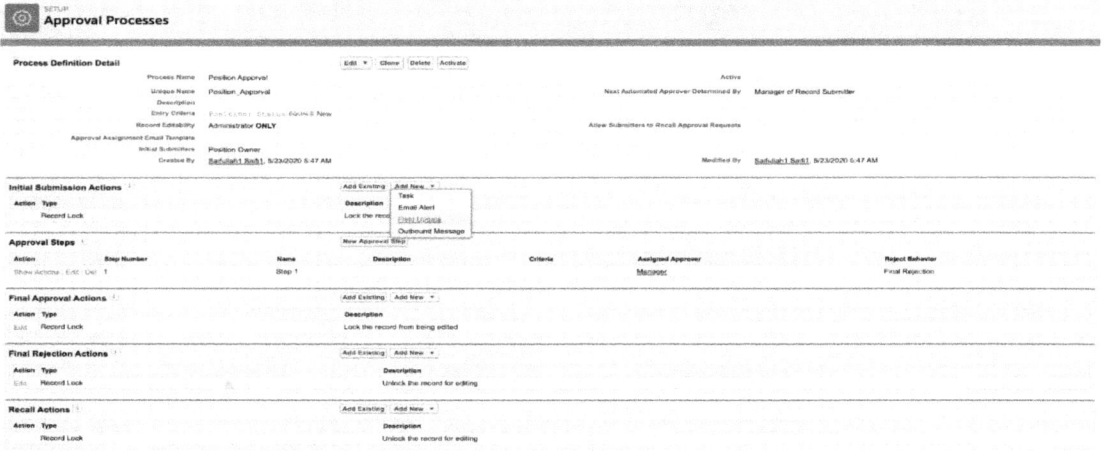

Figure 7.16: Update field in approval process

5. We also need approval from the hiring manager, so we will create a second approval step. Click on New Approval Step,and type the name of the step. Click on **Next**:

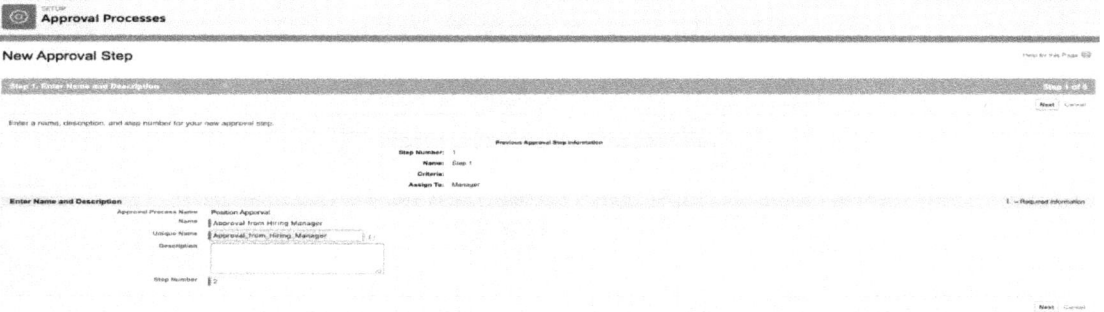

Figure 7.17: New Approval Step 1

6. 2nd window is criteria and we will check the hiring manger is not blank. Click on **Next**:

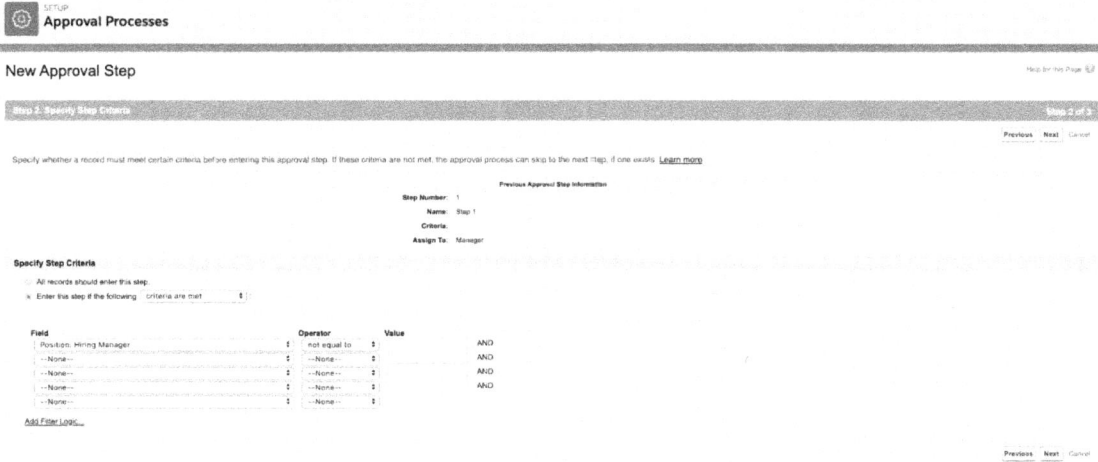

Figure 7.18: New Approval Step 2

7. We will choose the approver as the hiring manager and will click on **Save**. The second step is ready. We have also locked the record from being edited, as you can see in the figure:

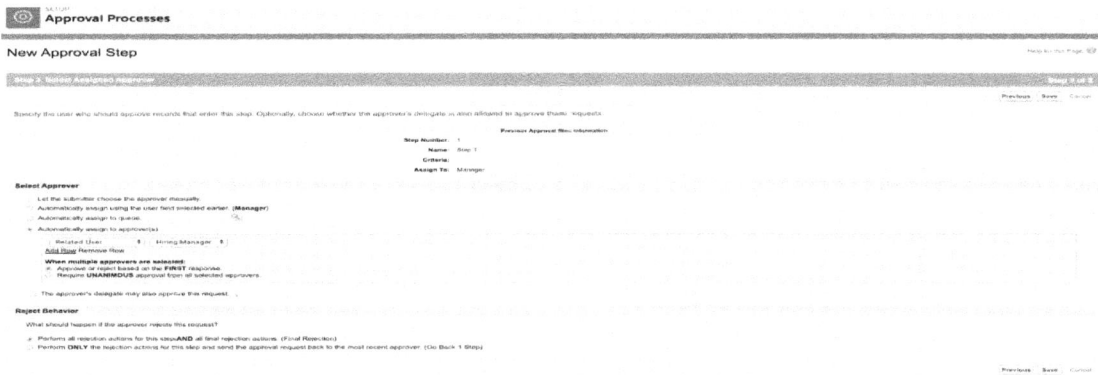

Figure 7.19: New approval process step 3

Now, we are adding some field updates and unlocking the record when a record will be approved or rejected. When it is approved, the Position status will be open with approved sub-status, and it will be closed with rejected sub status:

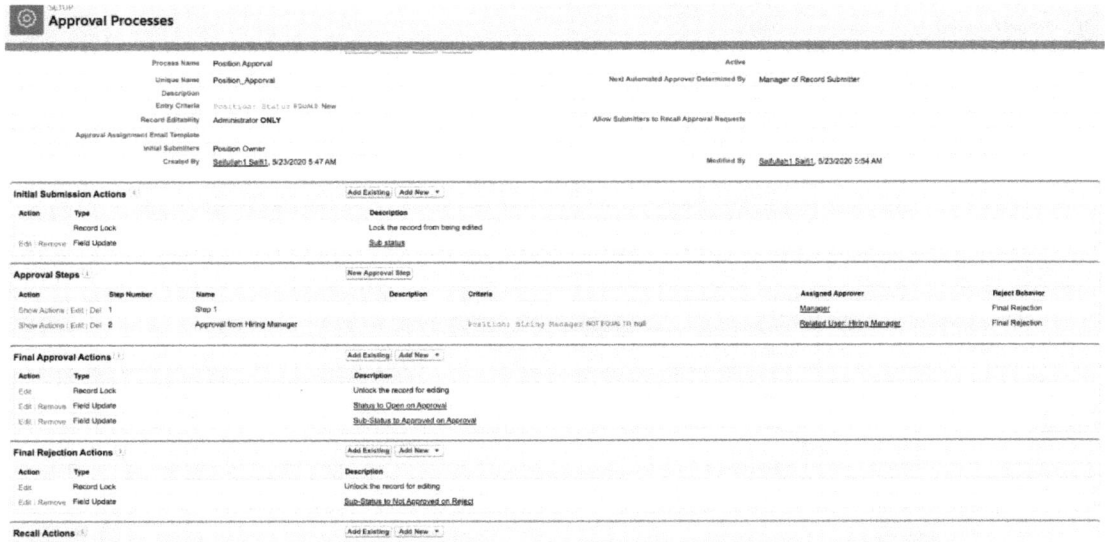

Figure 7.20: Approval process example 2

Activate the approval process. Now, it is ready for the test. Create a new Position and click on **Submit for Approval**:

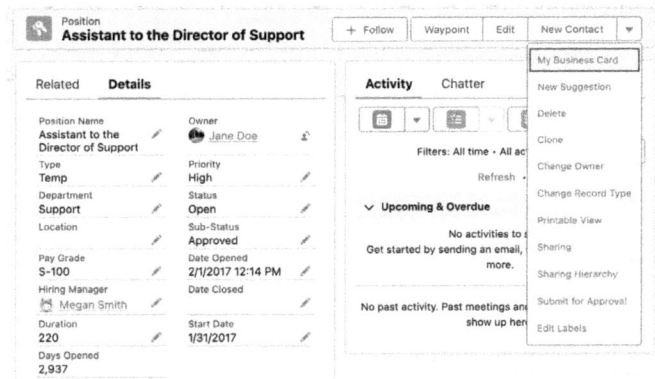

Figure 7.21 Submitting for approval

Put the comment while submitting it:

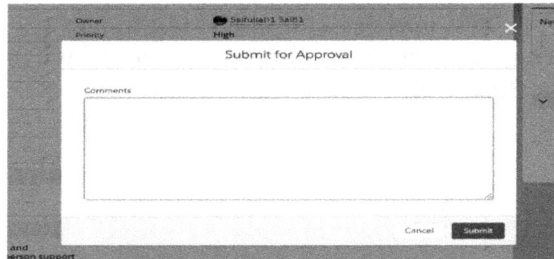

Figure 7.22: Putting comments for approval process

You can see the approval history in the related list of Position records. Manager can see Approve or Reject button on record page related list; they can make a decision to approve or reject and click the button:

Related   Details

Position History (5)

Date	Field	User	Original Value	New Value	
5/23/2020 6:05 AM	Record locked.	Saifullah1 Saifi1			▾
5/23/2020 6:04 AM	Status	Saifullah1 Saifi1	Closed	New	▾
5/23/2020 6:04 AM	Record locked.	Saifullah1 Saifi1			▾
5/23/2020 6:04 AM	Status	Saifullah1 Saifi1	New	Closed	▾
5/23/2020 6:03 AM	Record locked.	Saifullah1 Saifi1			▾

View All

Job Applications (0)   New

Interviewers (0)   New

Job Postings (0)   New

Approval History (4)   Approve Reject ▾

Step Name	Date	Status	Assigned To	
sabse end me	5/23/2020 6:05 AM	Pending	Saifullah1 Saifi1	▾
Approval Request Submitted	5/23/2020 6:05 AM	Submitted	Saifullah1 Saifi1	▾
sabse end me	5/23/2020 6:04 AM	Approved	Saifullah1 Saifi1	▾
Approval Request Submitted	5/23/2020 6:03 AM	Submitted	Saifullah1 Saifi1	▾

View All

Figure 7.23: Approval history

Now, if the record is approved, you can see the values are updated as Open and Approved:

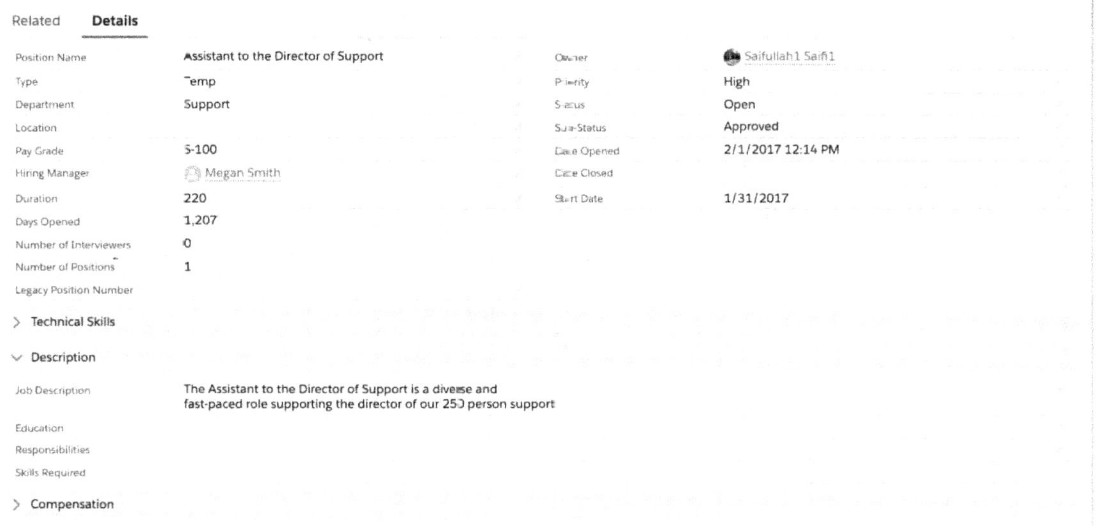

Related   **Details**

Position Name	Assistant to the Director of Support	Owner	Saifullah1 Saifi1
Type	Temp	Priority	High
Department	Support	Status	Open
Location		Sub-Status	Approved
Pay Grade	5-100	Date Opened	2/1/2017 12:14 PM
Hiring Manager	Megan Smith	Date Closed	
Duration	220	Start Date	1/31/2017
Days Opened	1,207		
Number of Interviewers	0		
Number of Positions	1		
Legacy Position Number			

> Technical Skills

∨ Description

Job Description   The Assistant to the Director of Support is a diverse and fast-paced role supporting the director of our 250 person support

Education
Responsibilities
Skills Required

> Compensation

Figure 7.24: Status of approval process

Lightning Flow

Salesforce Lightning Flow empowers you to build complex business solutions using clicks, not code. Salesforce Flows are an automation tool provided by Salesforce that can be used to perform various tasks, such as sending an email, posting a Chatter, sending custom notifications, etc. It is a tool that can be used to collect data and also to perform some actions. It helps us to create multiple forms and screens without doing any code. It can be used to capture data or automate some processes in the background. As an admin, Flows is going to be your best friend because you will be able to handle the majority of complex business requirements without the help of a Salesforce developer.

Types of flow

There are many types of Flow, some of most used types are as follows:

- **Screen Flow**: With Screen Flow, you can create a custom **user interface** (**UI**) and guide users through a business process that can be launched from Lightning Pages, Experience Cloud (previously known as Community Cloud), quick actions and more.

- **Record-Triggered Flow**: Record-Triggered Flow launches when a record is created, updated, or deleted. So far, we have used Apex triggers for this automation, some of which can now be done using flows.

- **Scheduled-Triggered Flow**: This Flow launches at the specified time and frequency for each record in a batch. Traditionally, we have met this kind of requirement by using Apex batch jobs.

- **Platform Event Flow**: Platform event Flow launches when a platform event message is received. For example, you can pump the data from an external system in Platform Events and then use Flows to split and save the records in different objects.

- **Auto-Launched Flow**: Auto Launches Flow execute when it is called by Apex or Flow, invoked by Apex, Process Builder or even REST API.

- You can go to Setup and search **Flow**, click it, and click **New**:

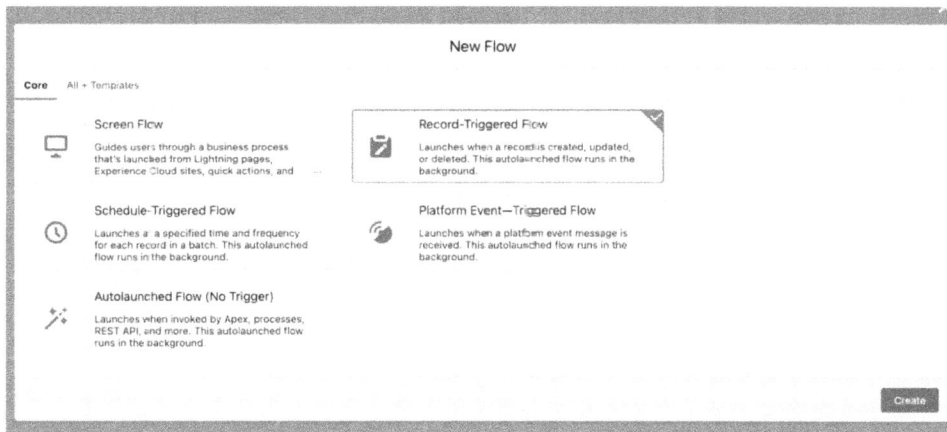

Figure 7.25: Creating a new Flow

Components of Salesforce Lightning Flow

There are 3 main *building blocks* of any flow. Elements are the individual building blocks of the Flow. These perform logical actions such as assignments, decisions, or loops. There are also data elements that will query the database or commit record changes.

Connectors determine which element leads to which. Winter '21 enables Auto-Layout, and connects the Elements together automatically.

Resources are the individual variables of data that are to be used in a Flow – these can be strings of text, numbers, records, formulae, or collections.

Now, let us see all components of Flow in detail:

- **Interaction**: Elements that interact with users or other areas of Salesforce are:
  - ○ **Screen**: Displays information or collects information from the user.
  - ○ **Action**: Interacts with other features, such as Apex, or pre-existing actions like Send Email.
  - ○ **SubFlow:** Interacts with another Flow.
- **Logic**: Elements that allow Flows to run dynamically based on data in variables are:
  - ○ **Assignment**: Assigns values to variables.
  - ○ **Decision**: Creates two paths based on given conditions.
  - ○ **Loop**: Iterates over a collection of records to perform operations on each.
- **Data elements**: Elements that execute **Data Manipulation Language** (**DML**) statements and push and pull data between the database and the Flow:
  - ○ **Create records**: Creates records based on values gathered through Flow.

o **Update records**: Updates records based on values collected from Flow.

o **Get records**: Fetches one or more records and stores the required values for later use.

o **Delete records**: Deletes designated records within Flow.

Examples of Salesforce Lightning Flow

Example 1: We will learn how to capture candidate records using Flow, through the following steps:

1. Go to **Setup** and, search **Flows**, click on **New Flow**. In this, we will create three-screens: one for the welcome, a second for taking input from candidate, and a third for thank you a message:

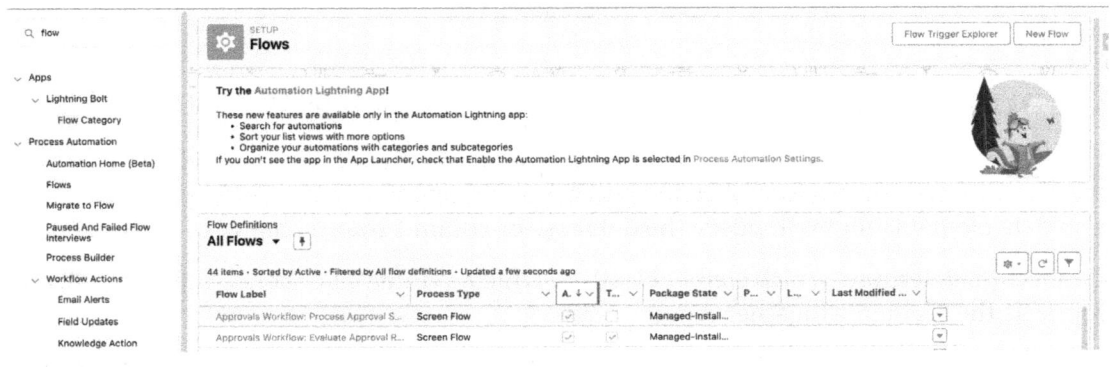

Figure 7.26: Flow setup

2. Choose **Screen Flow** and click on **Continue**:

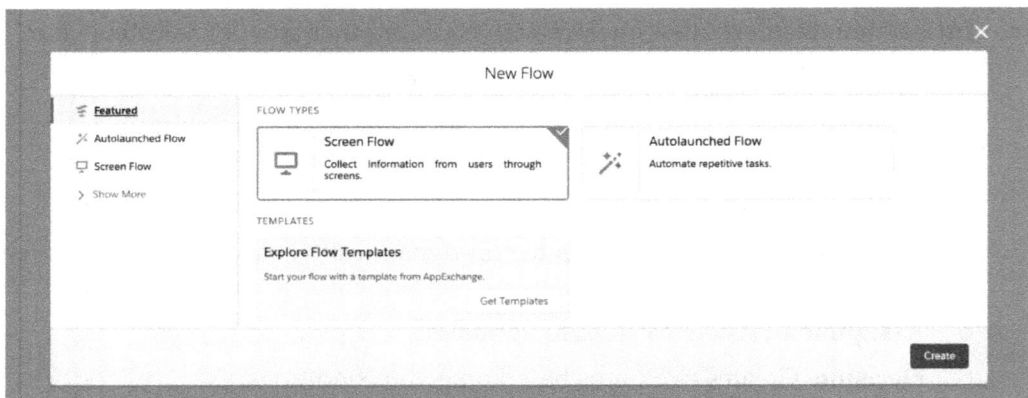

Figure 7.27: Screen Flow

3. In the canvas section, you will see **Start** and **End**, when we will click on + you will see screen option click on **Screen**.

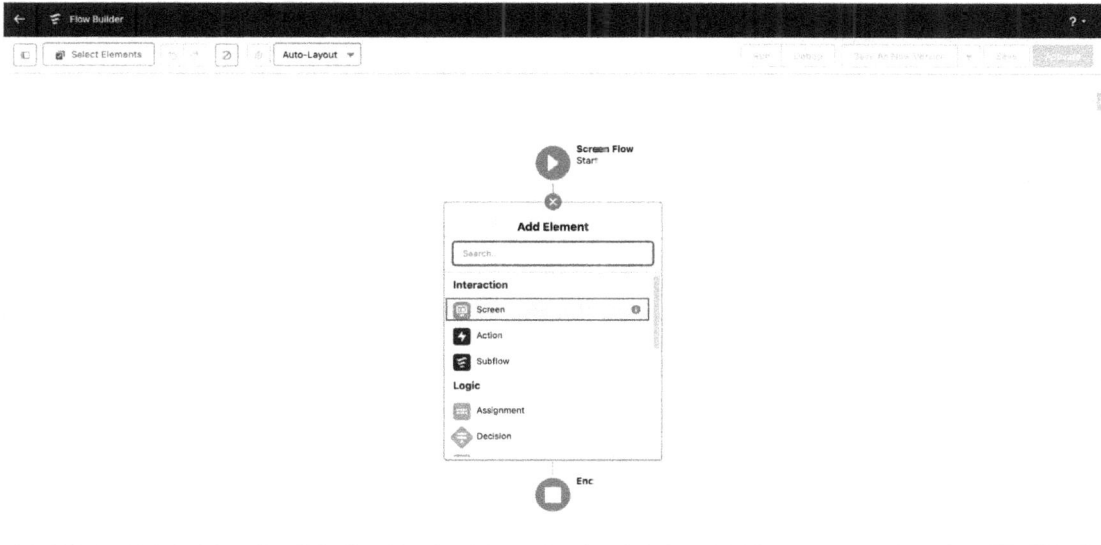

Figure 7.28: Flow Builder I

4. Put the label of screen **Display 1** and click on **Done**:

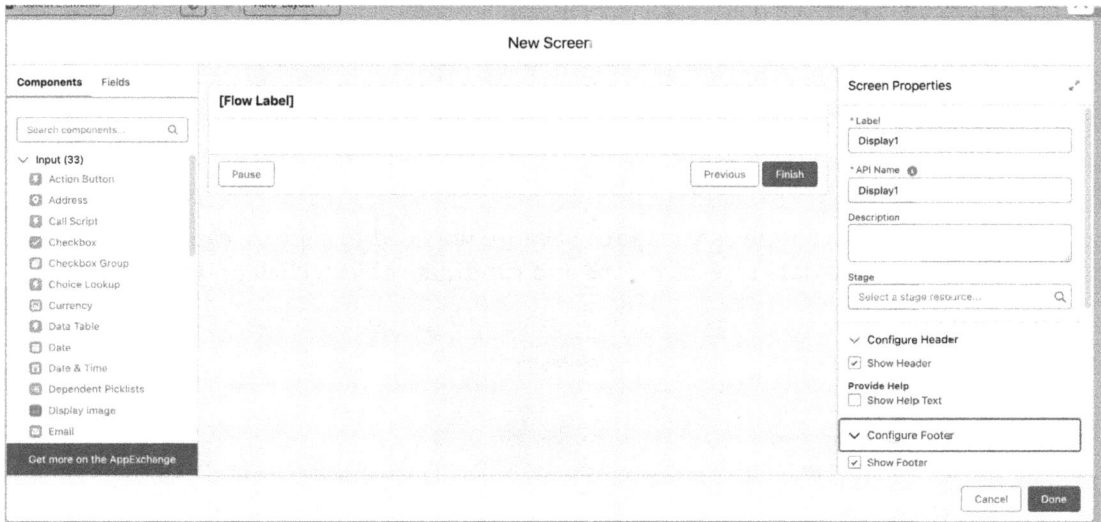

Figure 7.29: Flow Screen Label window

5. Add welcome text on the screen, and choose the color or font size click on **Done**:

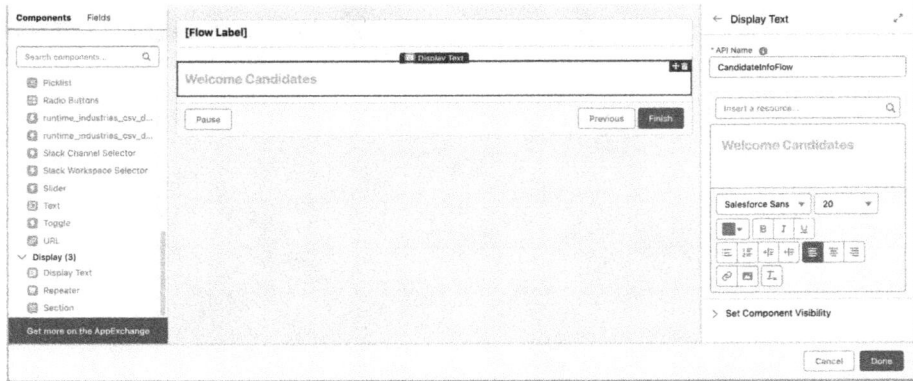

Figure 7.30: *Flow Screen Label window*

6.   The display is ready, now start the second section, and choose **New Resource**:

Figure 7.31: *Resource and Toolbar*

7.   Choose resource type as **Variable** because we need to capture candidate info. So, we will choose data type as record and candidate object, click on **Done**:

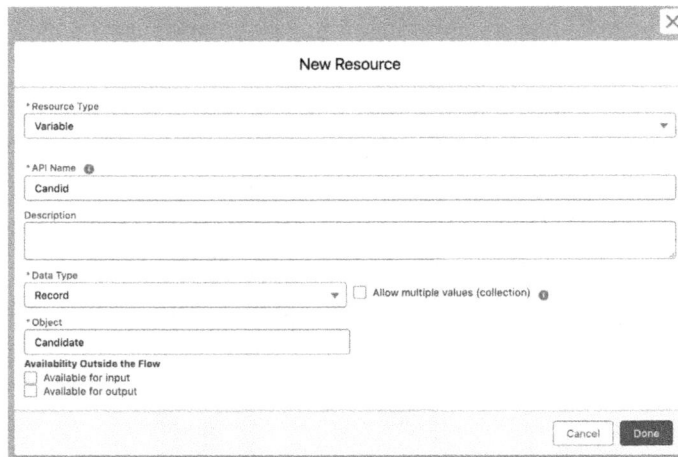

Figure 7.32: *Flow Resource*

8. We are adding a **Display Text**, just to show some text, like **Please enter all required information**. As you can see in the following figure, we can control the size, font type, color of that display text:

9. Now, we will add a text box to take input. We can drag and drop the text, label it and design it. We have now added 4 text boxs to capture 4 fields of the candidate, as first name, last name, city, and country:

Figure 7.33: Flow default value

10. We will create the 3rd section and add a message as thank you, as shown in the following figure:

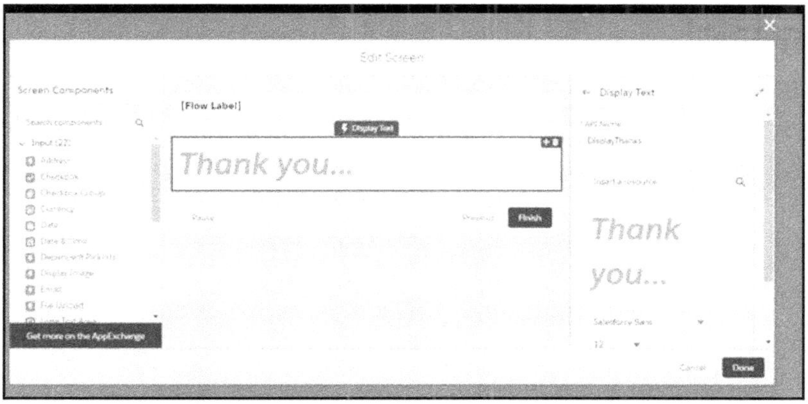

Figure 7.34: Flow Screen II

11. We can join every screen by click and dragging the arrow, like which screen will be started and what is next screen. The welcome message, then the Candidate Info form will be displayed:

12. We will join the last screen and will click on **Save**.

13. Put the name of Flow and click **Save**.

14. Flow is ready we can run and preview it:

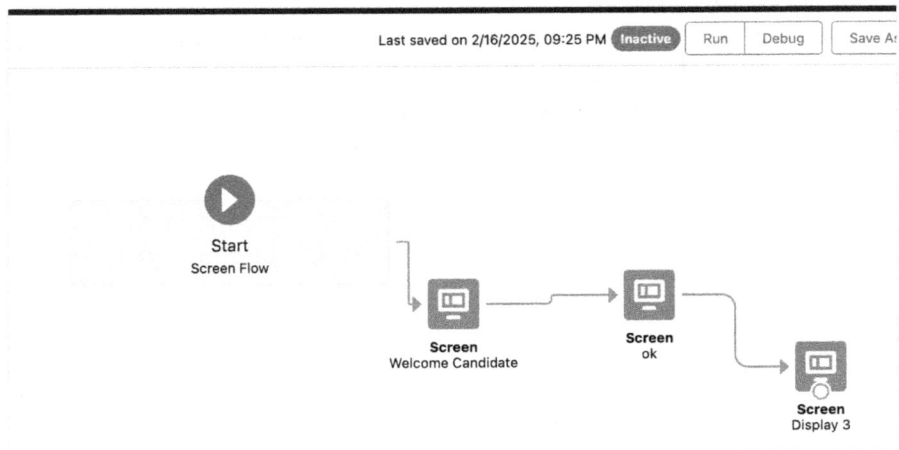

Figure 7.35: Preview and activate

15. Before making it to live, we can debug it and activate and deactivate it accordingly. Click on **Run**. You will see the following first screen:

Figure 7.36: Flow Screen

16. The next screen will look like the following:

Figure 7.37: Flow Preview

17. We have added validation on the form to check the value. It should not be blank, as shown in the following figure:

test1

Please enter all required info?

* First Name

Complete this field.

* Last Name

Complete this field.

* City

Complete this field.

Previous   Next

Figure 7.38: Erro checking Flow

18. The third screen will give you the Thank you message, as shown in the following figure:

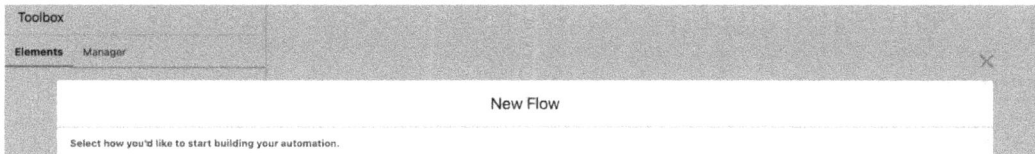

Toolbox

Elements   Manager

New Flow

Select how you'd like to start building your automation.

Figure 7.39: Last page Flow

Example 2: When an applicant submits his Job Application, we want to send a mail to the hiring manager about that specific application.

This is an example of record triggered Flow, in which whenever an object is created, we want to do some action like create another object, send an email, call an Api, etc. When you will click **New Flow** from Flow setup, you will see a screen, which is as follows :

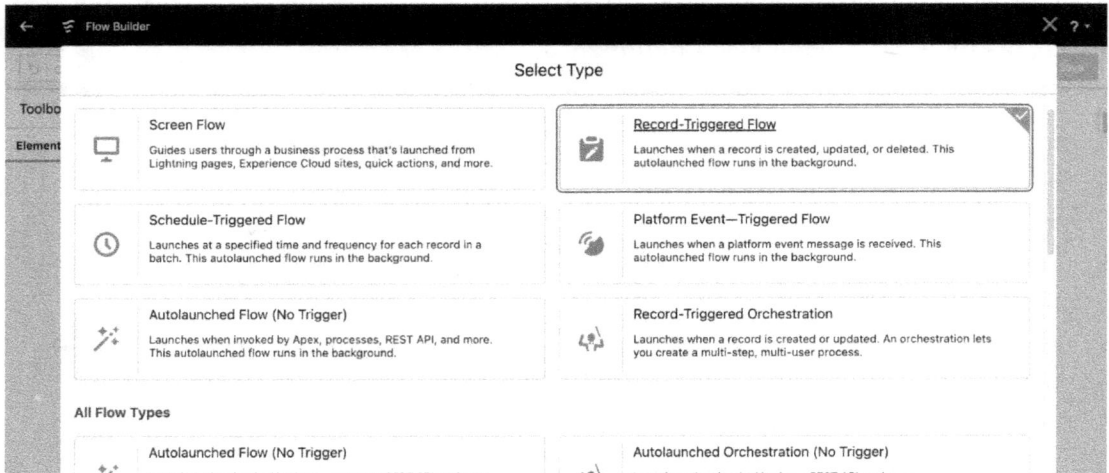

Figure 7.40: Flow scratch

You can choose existing salesforce-provided templates, but for learning purposes, we will choose start from scratch option. Then, you will see the following screen where we have to choose the type of Flows:

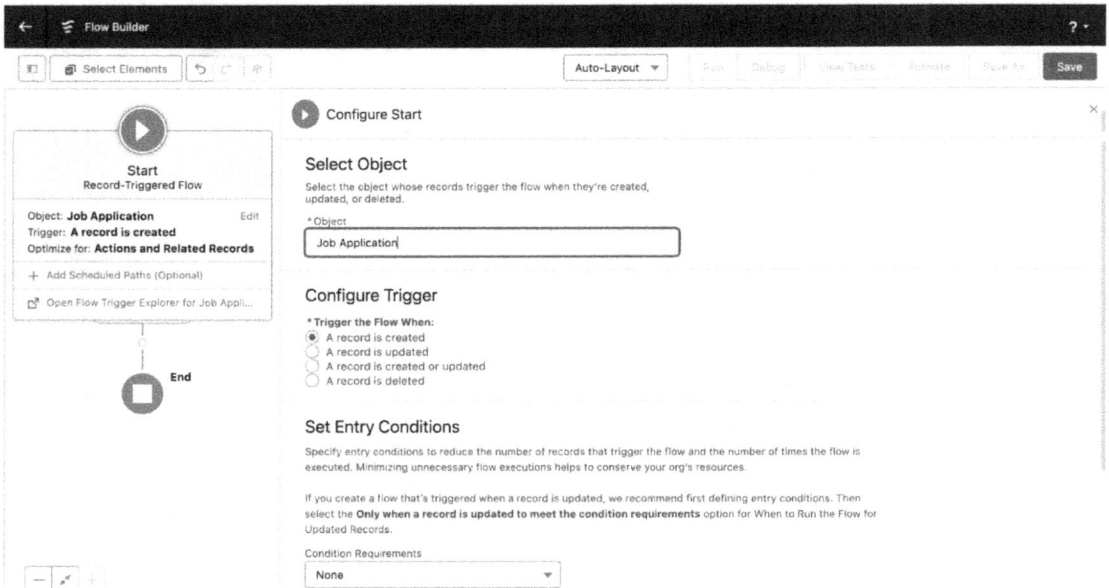

Figure 7.41: Record Triggered Flow

After choosing Record-Triggered Flow, we will see following screen. According to our problem, we will choose the object Job Application. In this same screen, we will decide when to run this Flow, like when a record is created or it is updated or deleted:

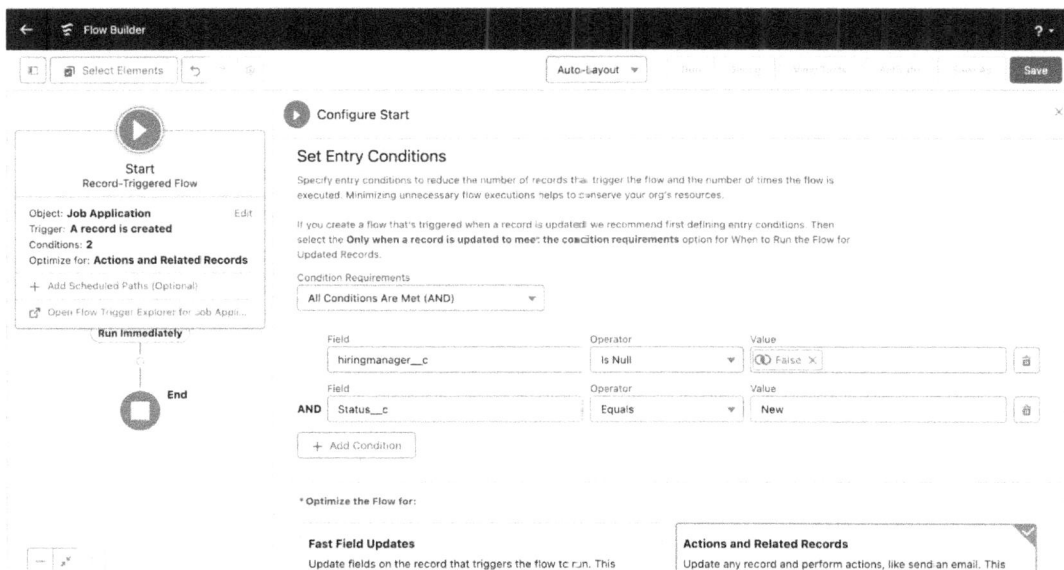

Figure 7.42: Flow choice of object and event

Then, we will choose the entry condition which will decide when this Flow run, so that it can filter and run only when needed. Here, we are checking if the hiring manager field is not blank and the status is new then only this Flow will run:

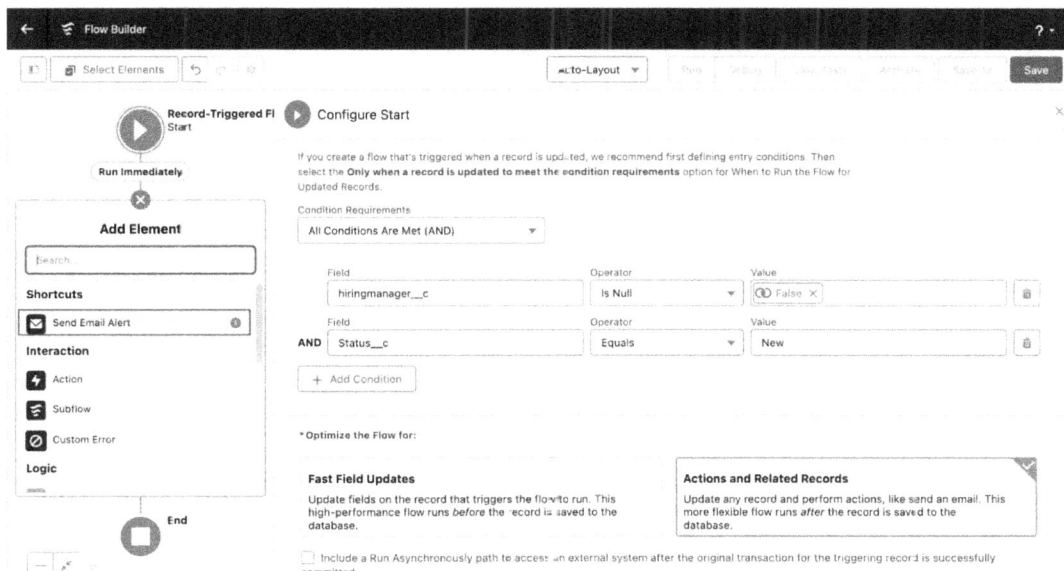

Figure 7.43: Flow entry condition

Now, we are deciding what action needs to be taken, either we need to update the fields or do some action, as we have to send an email. So, we will choose **Action & Related Records**:

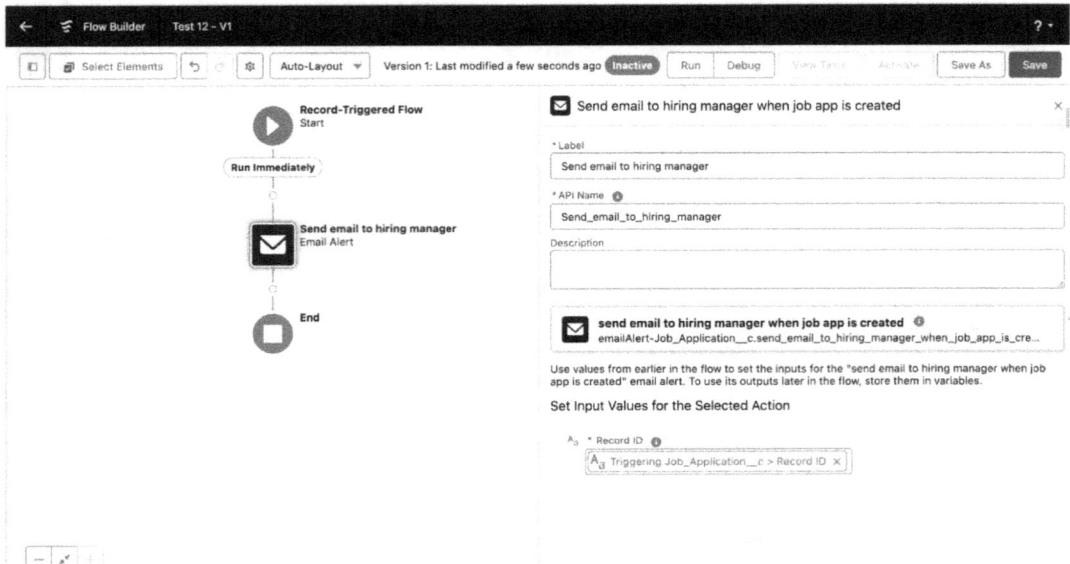

Figure 7.44: Flow Action and add elements

Now, we will click on **Add Elements** and search for send Email Alert and click on it. A window will open in the right panel, and it will show us to enter the label. You can create an email alert here or choose an existing email alert. We will pass the record ID of the Job Application to send an email:

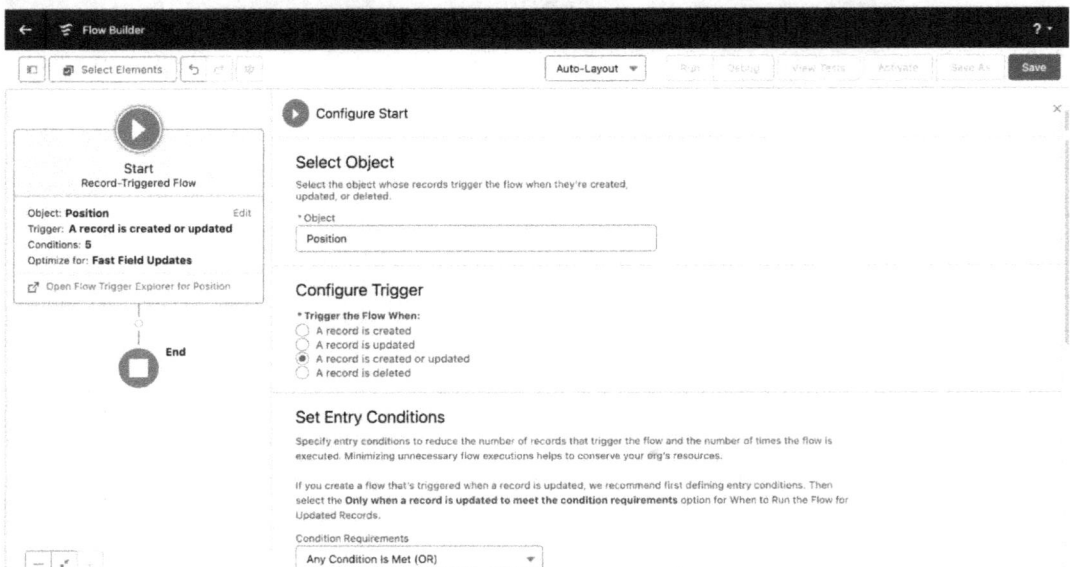

Figure 7.45: Flow Email action

Now, you can save the Flow and activate it. You can create a Job Application and test if an email has been sent to Hiring manager.

Example 3: In the Position object, we have a pay grade picklist. Whenever users choose Pay Grade as ACT-100, IT-100, ENG-100, S-100, then we will auto-populate min wage as $600 to $750.

In this example, we are creating a record-trigger Flow, and will do the action of fast field updates. In the following screen, we are choosing the Position object and checking the events, and setting the condition of pay grade as described in problem:

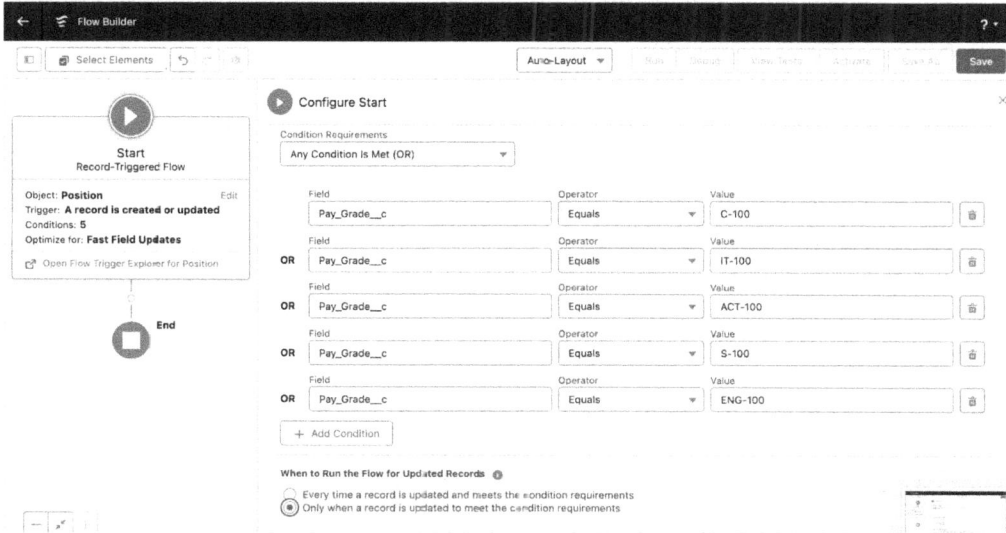

Figure 7.46: Record Triggered Flow

You can see the entry condition for the pay grade:

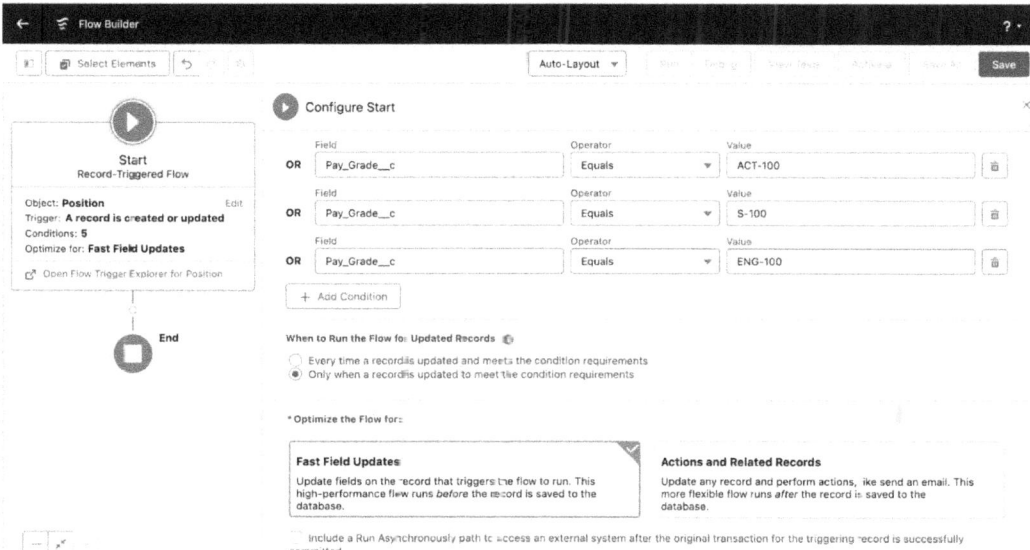

Figure 7.47: Entry Condition

Now, we will choose the action as **Fast Field Update**:

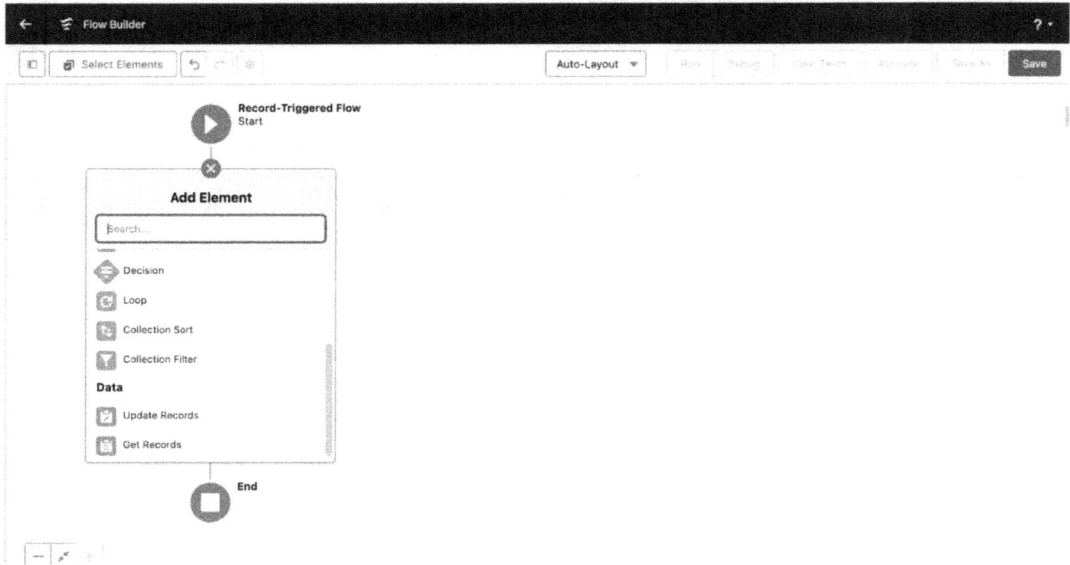

Figure 7.48: Flow action

Click on **Add Element** and choose **Update Records**, as shown in the following figure:

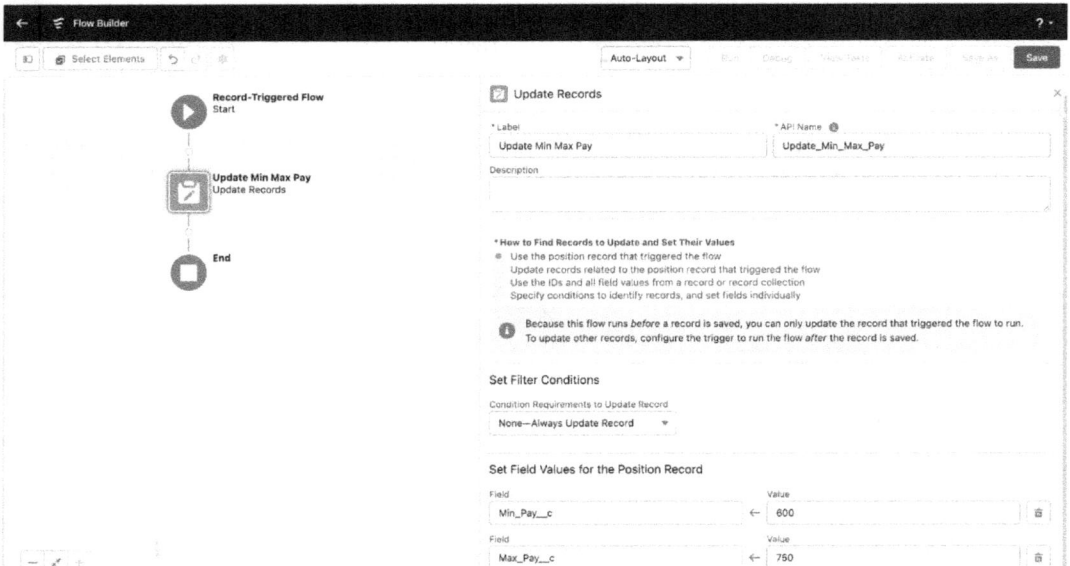

Figure 7.49: Flow Update records

Put the label name and assign the field value on min pay and max pay field:

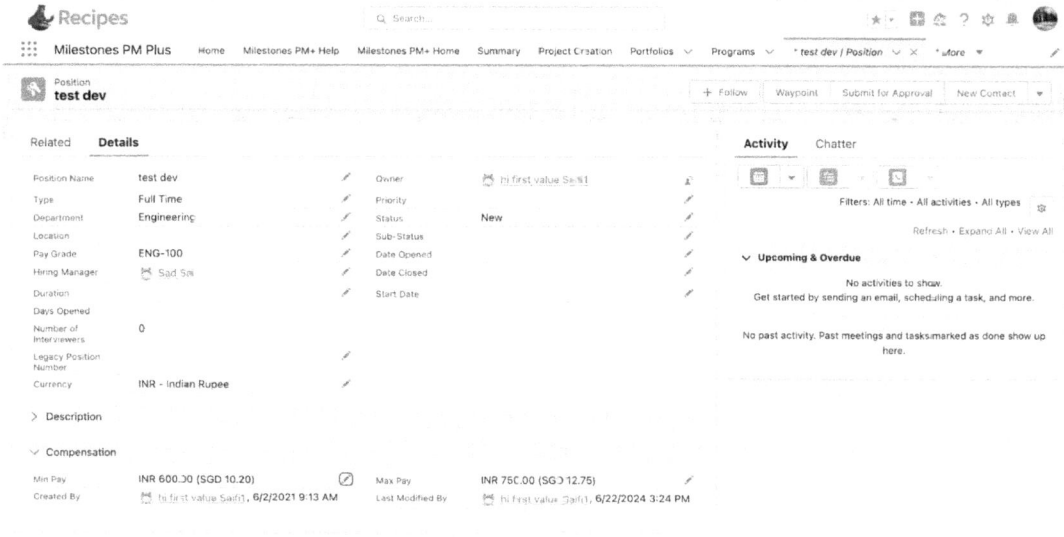

Figure 7.50: Flow field update

Click on **Save** and activate it. Now, you can create a Position record, and put the pay grade and save it, you will see the min pay and max pay populated:

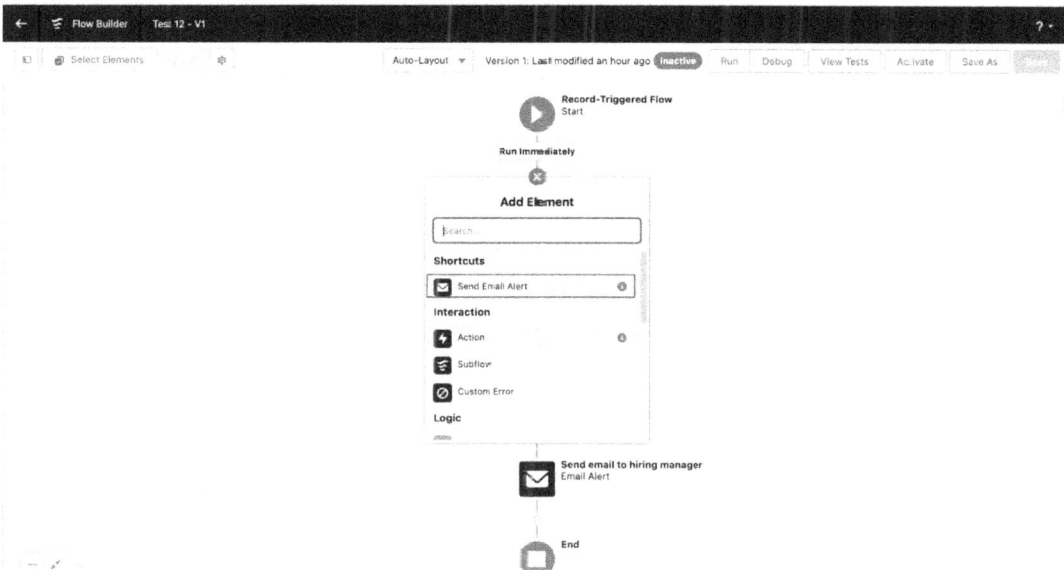

Figure 7.51: Record testing for Flow

Example 4: When an applicant submits his Job Application, we want to create one task for the owner to conduct an interview or call the candidate. In this case, we will use our first Flow and add more actions.

In this example, we will create an object as Flow action, so we will add the element and choose **Create Records**:

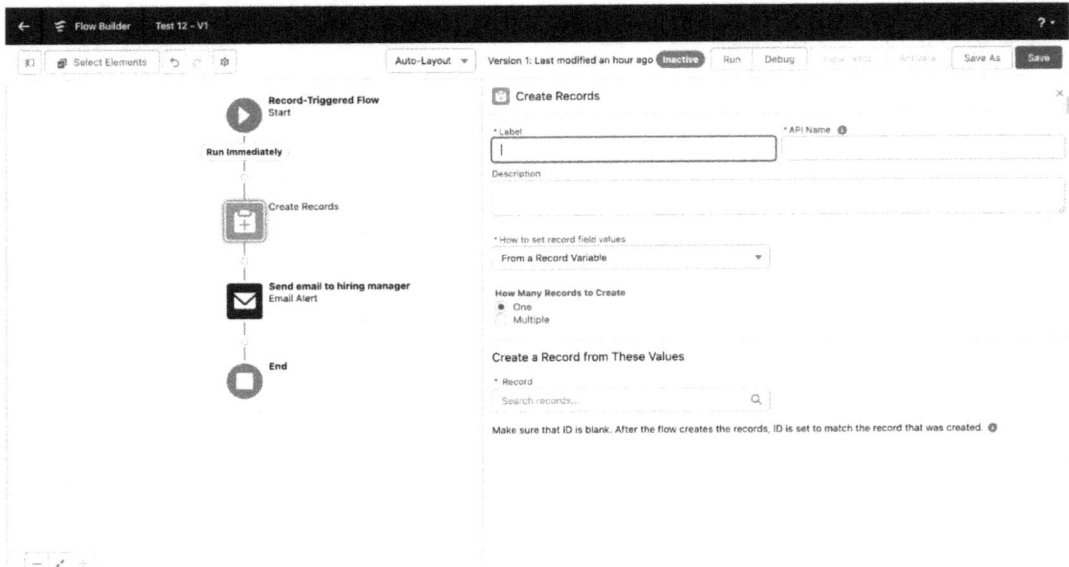

Figure 7.52: Record Triggered Flow

In this create record, we will put the label and choose the record variable, and we will create one records:

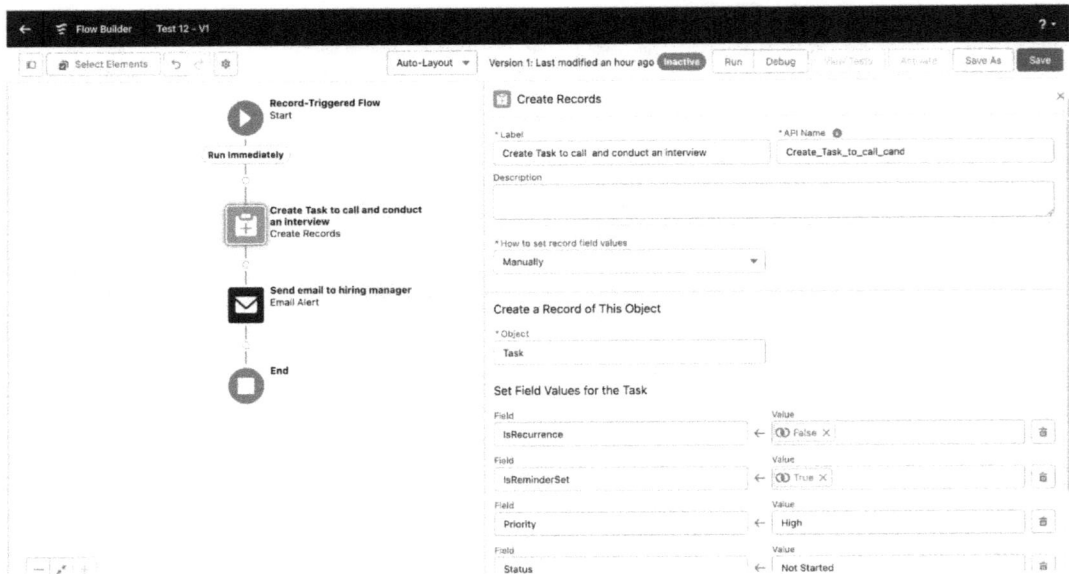

Figure 7.53: Flow create record

Choose the **Object Task** and assign the values in required field, we will create some new resources to assign values:

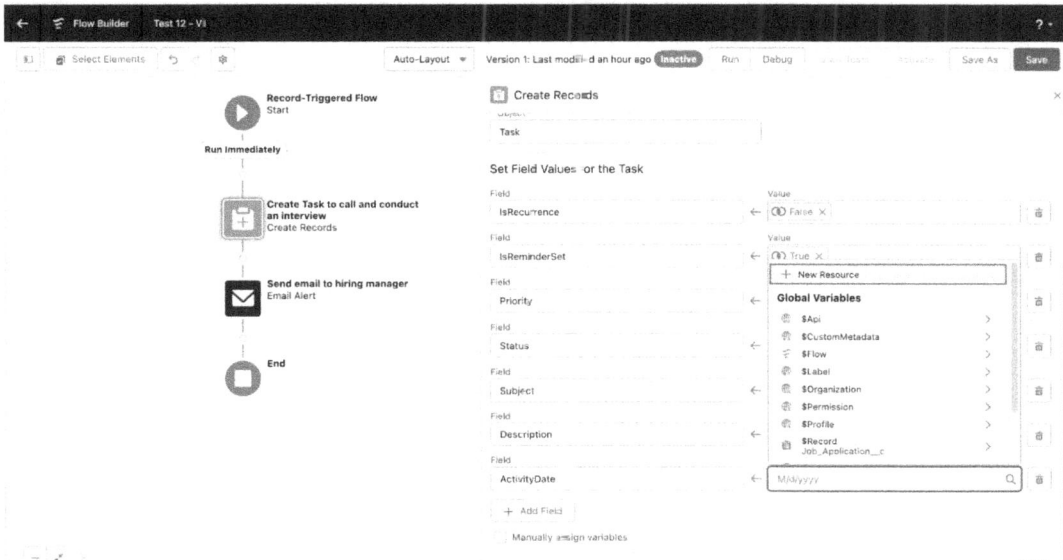

Figure 7.54: Flow Task fields

For Activity date, we will use new resource, as shown in the following figure:

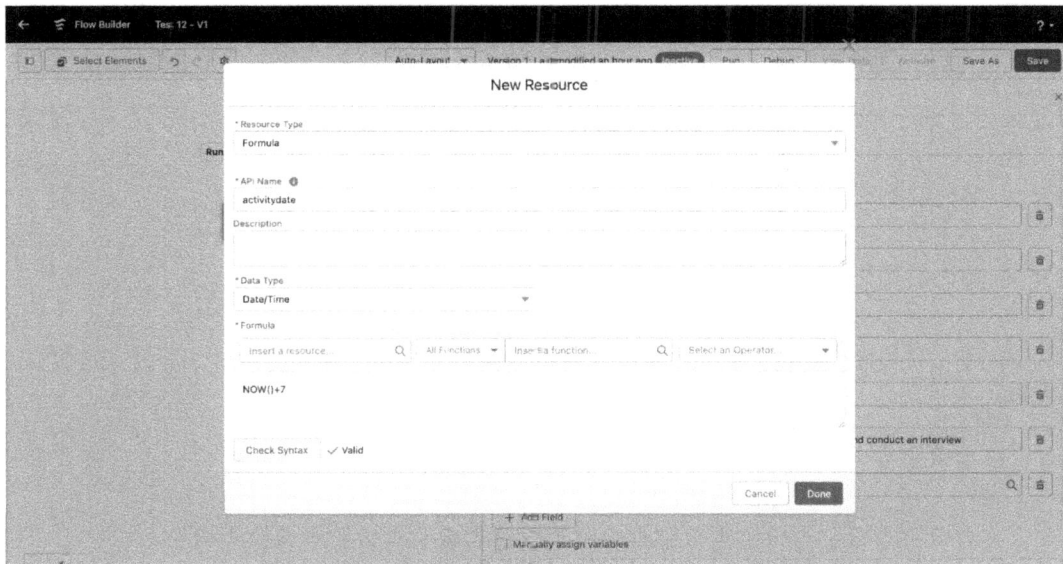

Figure 7.55: Flow Field assignment

We will create a variable choose resource type as formula, and datetime for data type and in the formula, it will be seven days later than today. We will check syntax and click **Done**:

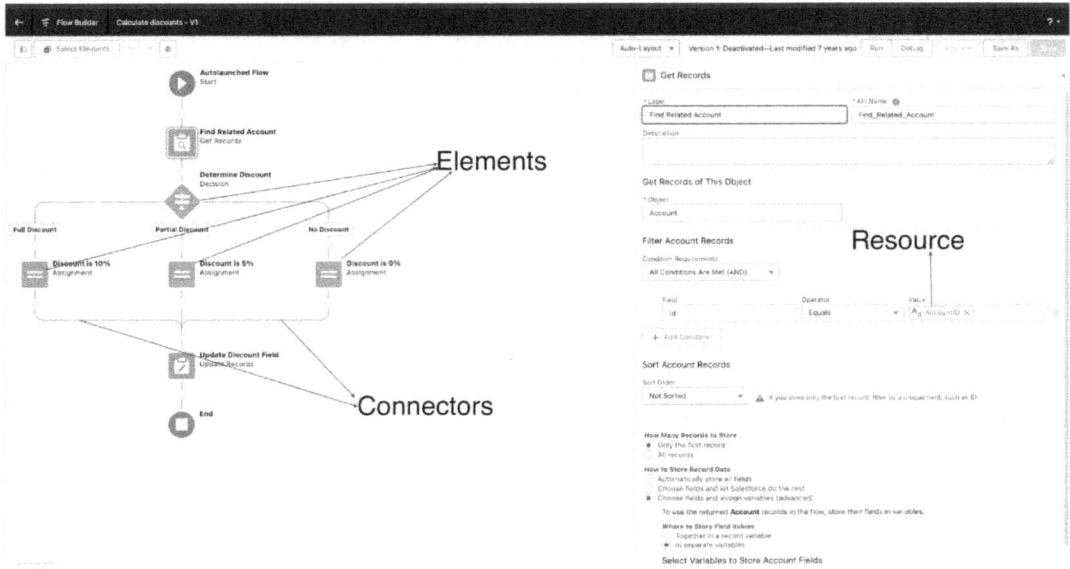

Figure 7.56: Flow resource variable

For the reminder date, we will do the following:

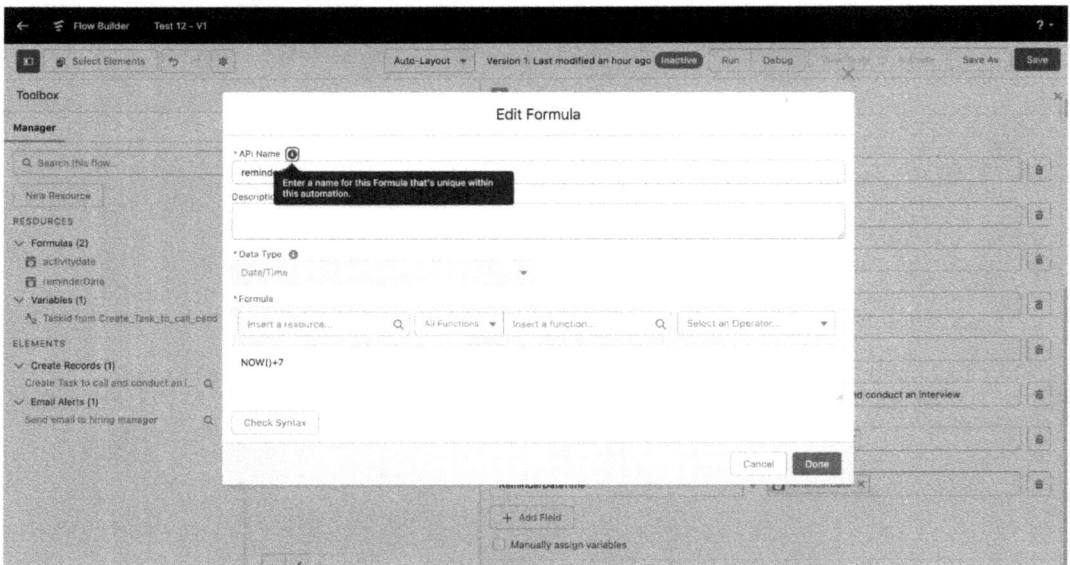

Figure 7.57: Flow resource formula type

You can see all the existing resources in the left bar:

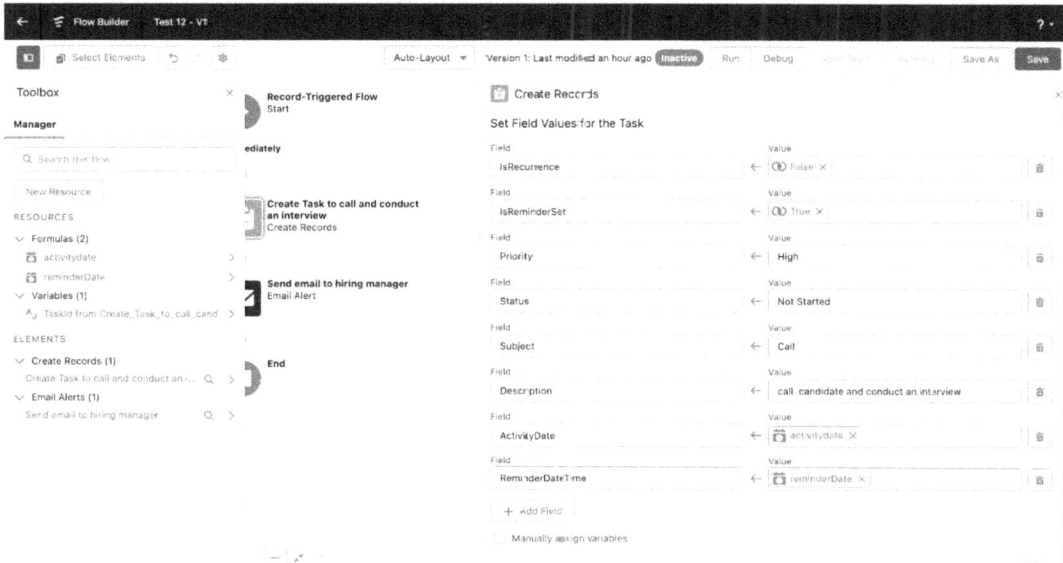

Figure 7.58: Flow sample

You can click **Save** and activate it.

Flow Builder

Let us talk about Flow Builder and their parts:

- **Toolbox**: The toolbox lists the elements and resources that you have built into your Flow. You can also create resources such as variables, formulas, and choices to use in your Flow.

- **Canvas**: The canvas is the working area, where you build a Flow by adding elements. Adding elements to the canvas creates a visual diagram of the Flow.

- **Button bar**: Button bar provides the information like: is the Flow active, when it was last saved, does Flow have some errors and options to save activate and debug:

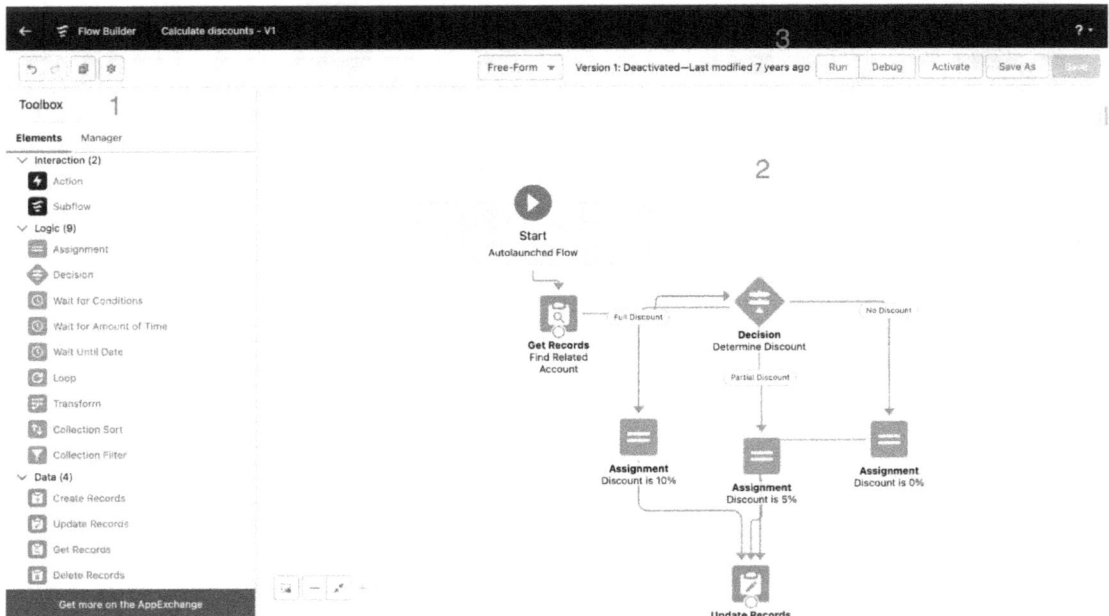

Figure 7.59: Flow Builder Screen

Flows use three building blocks: elements, connectors, and resources:

- Elements are nodes on the canvas that make things happen. To add an element to the canvas, hover over **Add Element** and click **Add Element**.

- Connectors are lines on the canvas that define the path the Flow takes when it runs. They tell the Flow which element to execute next.

- Resources are containers that do not appear on the canvas, but are referenced by the Flow's elements. Each resource contains a value or a formula that resolves to a value. For example, your Flow can search for an account's ID, store that ID in a variable, and later use that variable to tell the Flow which account to update.

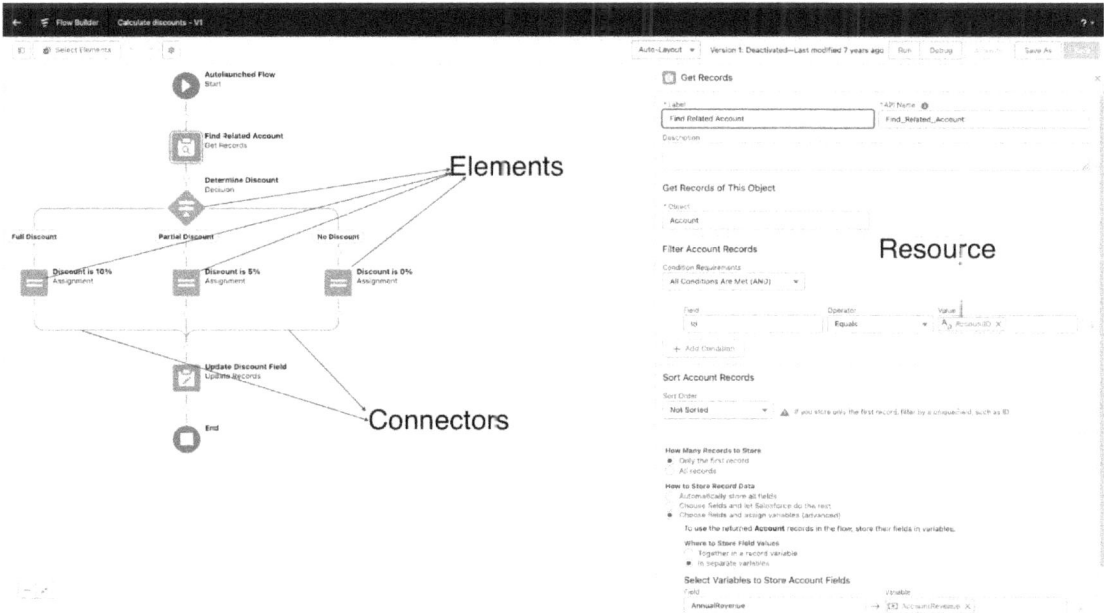

Figure 7.60: Record Triggered Flow

Conclusion

In this chapter, we learned how we could create cross object formula field and roll-up summary field. We have created some formula fields and roll-up summary fields as well. We also covered multiple business automation tools like Salesforce Lightning Flow which can be used to update some fields or to send an email or task creation. We learned about the approval process, which can automate the approval concept. We discussed Salesforce Lightning Flow with one example to show that we can create one input form without any code. In the previous chapter, we covered the validation rule with some examples. In the next chapter, we will discuss data management.

Questions

1. **Which among the following true about approval process?**

    a. A delegated approver can reassign approval requests.

    b. An approval action defines the result of record approval or rejection.

    c. An assignment rule defines the approver for each process step.

    d. The approval history related list can be used to track the process.

2. **Choose the elements of approval process?**

   a. Name and description to distinguish it from other approval processes.

   b. Entry criteria if you only want records with certain attributes to be included

   c. Any number of steps that determine the sequence of actions to take when a record matches the criteria.

   d. Each step can have up to 80 actions, 10 of each type: email alerts, field updates, tasks, and outbound messages.

3. **Choose the correct options for Roll-Up Summary fields.**

   a. Since roll-up summary fields are not displayed on edit pages, you can use them in validation rules but not as the error location for your validation.

   b. Validation errors can be displayed when saving either the detail or master record.

   c. Once created, you cannot change the detail object selected or delete any field referenced in your roll-up summary definition.

   d. Advanced currency management does not affect roll-up summary fields.

   e. Automatically derived fields, such as current date or current user, are allowed in a roll-up summary field.

4. **Choose two decision points for a roll-up summary field.**

   a. A roll-up summary can be performed on formulating fields, but if their formulate contains an #error results, it may affect the summary.

   b. Roll-up cannot be performed on formula fields.

   c. Roll-up summary fields do not cause validation rules on the parent object unless that object is edited separately.

   d. Roll-up cannot be performed on formula fields that use cross-object reference or on-the-fly-calculation, such as Now().

5. **When creating a Lightning Flow, which action requires a formula as the rule criteria?**

   a. Checking if the record was modified today.

   b. Checking if the value in a field has changed.

   c. Checking if the current user's profile is System Administrator.

   d. Checking if the status of a record is new.

6. **Choose the right option about Lightning Flow.**

   a. We can use Apex methods with the @InvocableMethod annotation.

   b. Both server-side can be considered in the Order of Execution.

    c. You can use Apex to implement the Process. Plugin interface.

    d. It can be embedded directly into Visualforce pages.

7. **Choose the wrong option about Validation Rules.**

    a. Validation formulas can reference campaign statistic fields, including statistics for individual campaigns and campaign hierarchies.

    b. If validation rules exist for activities and you create an activity during lead conversion, the lead converts, but a task isn't created.

    c. When defining validation rules, you can set the error location to Top of Page or Field.

    d. A validation formula must always start with a condition, an IF statement, to define the kind of data being filtered.

8. **We need to update a field on an Account when an Opportunity Stage is changed to Closed Lost. (choose 2).**

    a. WorkFlow Rule

    b. Lightning Flow

    c. Assignment Rule

Answers

1. b, d
2. a, b
3. a, c, d
4. a, c
5. a
6. c, d
7. a, d
8. a, c

Join our Discord space

Join our Discord workspace for latest updates, offers, tech happenings around the world, new releases, and sessions with the authors:

https://discord.bpbonline.com

CHAPTER 8
Data Management

Introduction

Customer relationship management (CRM) is not useful if the information cannot be trusted. The expansion of collectible client data makes it simple to have a deep understanding of leads and clients. However, it additionally expands the potential for poorly migrated and for the most part, low-quality information. If the organization is huge, data management and governance become crucial. This includes importing and exporting data in different forms.

Structure

In this chapter, we will discuss the following topics:

- Importance of data management
- Introducing Data Import
- Introduction to Data Export

Objectives

After studying this chapter, you will learn the importance of data management. You will also be introduced to the methods of Data Import and Data Export, like Data Import Wizard, Data Export Wizard ,and Data Loader.

Importance of data management

The genuine benefit of setting up strong data management is not just taking care of issues – it is forestalling them as well. This remains constant for Salesforce administrators at organizations of any scale and inside any industry.

For instance, a non-profit administrator, utilizing its free licenses, need strong donor contact records, and great data management causing them to be positive about observing where cash is rolling in from, and where it is spent.

For the enterprise administrator team, with a huge number of records, great data management keeps their data dependable while keeping dangerous mistakes from escaping everyone's notice. For alleged lone wolf administrators, in the case of contracting or working in-house, legitimate data management causes them to keep steady over everything. However, it likewise encourages them to train others in their organization not to make issues on the mishap.

Introducing Data Import

External data from different sources can undoubtedly be brought into Salesforce. Supported data sources include any program that saves data in the comma-delimited text format, for example, `.csv`.

Salesforce offers two main methods to import data:

- **Data Import Wizard:** It lets you import data in standard objects, for example, leads, accounts, contacts, and so on, just as the data in custom objects. It has a limitation of importing up to 50,000 records one after another. It gives a straightforward interface to indicate data sources, field mappings in the import document with the field names in Salesforce.
- **Data Loader**: It is an application that can import up to 5,000,000 records one after another, of any data type. It may work either through the command line or UI.

While both the preceding methods have advantages, the following guidelines will help in deciding on different situations:

- **Use the Data Import Wizard when**:
  - Less than 50,000 records are to be imported.
  - The wizard supports the objects to be imported.
  - Automation of the process is not required.
- **Use Data Loader when**:
  - The requirement is to import 50,000 to 5 million records.
  - The objects that are not supported by Data Import Wizard to be imported.
  - Regular data loads are to be scheduled.

Importing data using Data Import Wizard

Let us assume that we have a **.csv** file containing lead data collected through partner referral. First, we need to clean up the data to be imported.

Perform the following steps to import data using the Data Import Wizard:

1. From Setup, click the gear icon at the top of the page and launch Setup.
2. Search Data Import Wizard from the Quick Find box.

The following figure depicts the step-by-step method to launch the Data Import Wizard:

Figure 8.1: Launching Data Import wizard

3. Click **Launch Wizard**.
4. Select the required tab:

   a. **Standard objects**: To import accounts and contacts, leads, solutions, or campaign members.

   b. **Custom objects**: To import custom objects.

5. Click **Standard Objects** since we are going to import lead data. Then select **Leads**.
6. Specify whether new records to Salesforce are to be added or updated or records to be added and updated simultaneously. If a record exists, it will be updated. If not, it will be added. In our case, we need to choose **Add New Records.**, as mentioned in the following figure:

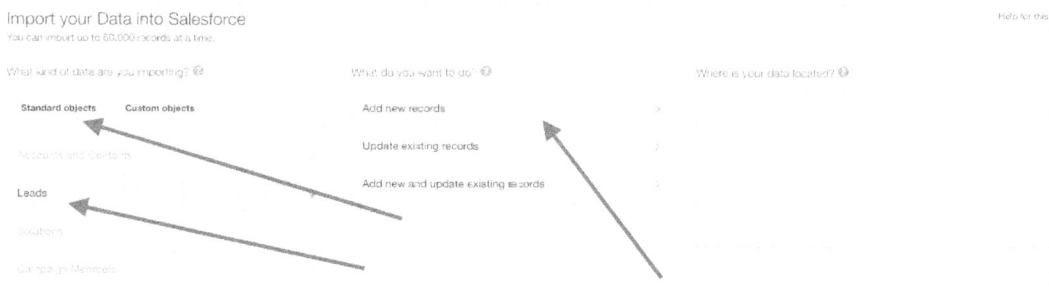

Figure 8.2: Adding new record using the Data Import Wizard

7. Specify matching and other criteria like "Match Contact by," "Match Account by," etc., as per your requirement. You may like to hover over the question marks to know more about each option.

8. Under **Where is your data located** select the CSV type you want to import.

    The following figure shows the option to import the `.csv` file:

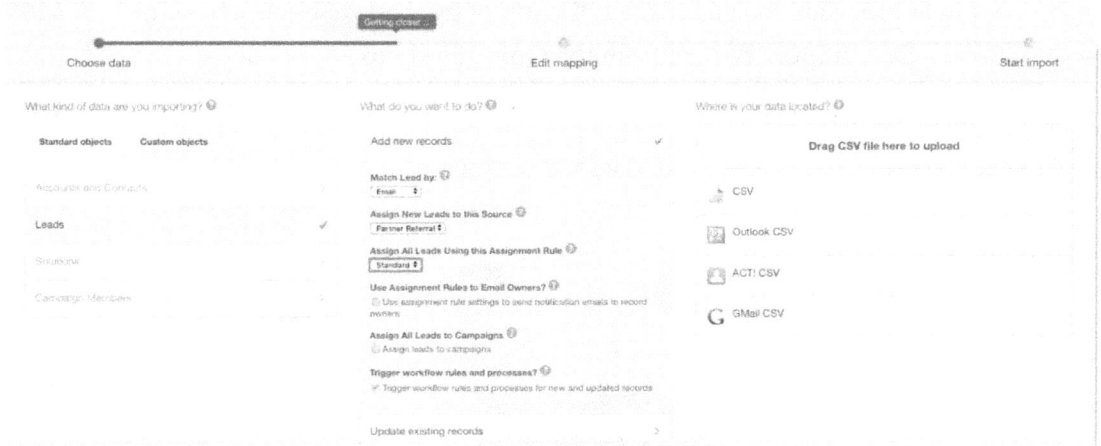

Figure 8.3: Locating the csv file to import

The data file can be mentioned by either dragging the CSV to the upload area or by clicking the CSV and then navigating to the folder containing the file and selecting the file.

9. Click **Next** once it is done.

The Data Import Wizard maps as many data fields as possible to standard Salesforce data fields. However, in a few cases, if Salesforce is not able to map automatically, it is required to be done manually. Unmapped fields are never imported into Salesforce. Now, it needs to map the data fields of the `.csv` file to the Salesforce data fields:

1. Check the list of mapped data fields and look for any unmapped fields.

2. Click **Map** to the left of each unmapped field.

3. In the **Map Your Field** dialog box, choose which Salesforce fields needs to be mapped to and click **Map**.

4. Click **Next**.

5. Now review the import information on the Review page.

6. Click **Start Import**.

7. Check import status.

Note: The user will receive a status email when the import is completed. Campaigns, Opportunities, Contracts, Documents, Assets, and Cases cannot be imported using the Data Import wizard.

Introduction to Data Export

Data from Salesforce can, without much of a stretch, be exported either manually or on an automatic schedule. The data is exported as a CSV file. Salesforce's Data Export tools give a good strategy to get a copy of your Salesforce data, either for backup or for bringing it an alternate system.

Salesforce permits two different ways of exporting data. They are:

- **Data Export Wizard:** It permits the export of data manually once in 7 days or 29 days. Data can also be exported automatically at weekly or monthly intervals. It can be accessed through the Setup menu and is an in-browser wizard.

- **Data Loader:** It is a client application that must be installed independently. It tends to be worked through the UI or the command line. The command-line option is helpful when it is required to automate the export process or use APIs to integrate with another framework.

Using the Data Export Wizard

You can perform the following steps to export data using the wizard:

1. From Setup, click the gear icon ⚙ at the top of the page and launch Setup.
2. Search Data Export from the Quick Find box.
3. Click **Export Now** or **Schedule Export**, depending on whether the data needs to be exported now or to be scheduled for the future:

   a. **The Export Now**: It prepares the files to export immediately. This option is available only if sufficient time has passed since the last export.

   b. **The Schedule Export**: It permits the export process to be scheduled for weekly or monthly intervals.

   In this example, click on **Export Now**, as shown in the following figure:

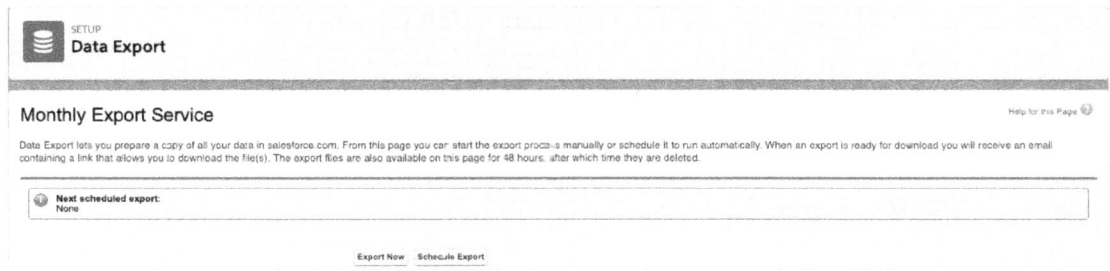

> SETUP
> **Data Export**
>
> Monthly Export Service   Help for this Page
>
> Data Export lets you prepare a copy of all your data in salesforce.com. From this page you can start the export process manually or schedule it to run automatically. When an export is ready for download you will receive an email containing a link that allows you to download the file(s). The export files are also available on this page for 48 hours, after which time they are deleted.
>
> ⓘ **Next scheduled export:**
> None
>
>   Export Now   Schedule Export

Figure 8.4: Data Export

4. Select the necessary encoding for the export document:

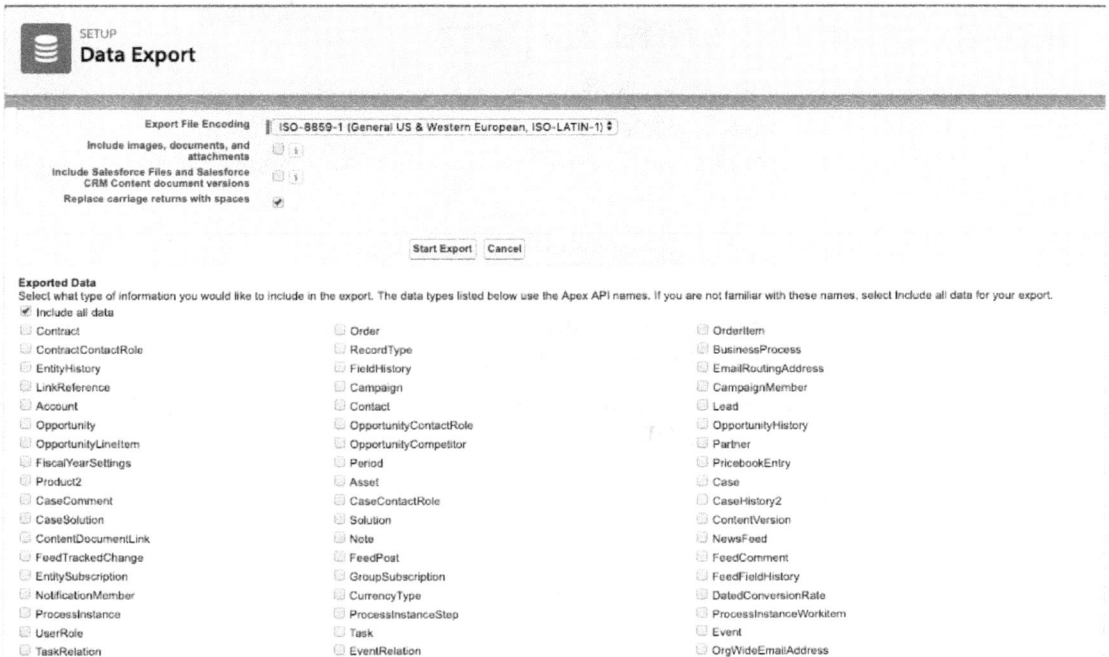

Figure 8.5: *Options in Data Export*

If pictures, reports, and attachments are to be included for your data, select the suitable option.

5. Under **Exported Data**, select the kinds of data to be included for the export. It is prescribed to choose to **Include all data** in case you're inexperienced with the terminology utilized for a portion of the types of data.

6 Click **Start Export**.

Salesforce makes an archive of CSV file zip and sends emails on status. Large exports are separated into various documents. Follow the link in the email or click **Data Export** to download the Zip file. Zip files are erased 48 hours after the email is sent.

Note: **If you are scheduling your export, select the frequency, start and end dates, and time of day for your scheduled export.**

Using Data Loader

Data Loader is a client application utilized for bulk import or export of data. It tends to be utilized for different operations like addition, updation, deletion, or export of Salesforce records. When data is imported by utilizing Data Loader, it reads, extracts, and loads data from a database connection or CSV files. When exporting data, it makes a CSV file.

Data Loader provides the following features:

- A wizard interface with easy-to-use and interactive use.
- Support for large files of up to 5 million records.
- An alternate **Command-Line Interface (CLI)** for automated batch operations This is for only Windows users.
- Drag-and-drop field mapping facility.
- Support for both standard and custom objects.
- Detailed log file creation facility.
- An in-built CSV file viewer.

Data Loader can be used in two different ways:

- **Using User Interface:** In this case, the configuration parameters and CSV files are utilized for import and export. The fields mappings that map the field names in the file with the field names in Salesforce need to be determined.
- **Using command-line (Only for Windows):** In this cause, the configuration parameters, data sources, field mappings, and activities need to be mentioned in the file. This empowers to set up Data Loader for automated processing.

Exporting data with the Data Loader

Let us take an example of the need to extract accounts data using the Data Loader:

1. Downloading Data Loader:

   a. From Setup, enter **Data Loader** in the Quick Find box.

   b. Click **Download the Data Loader for Windows** or **Mac**.

   c. The corresponding help on installation is also available there.

2. Open Data Loader and log in to the correct org:

   a. Open the Data Loader application.

   b. Click **Export**, as shown in the following figure:

Figure 8.6: Data Loader

   c. Select **Password Authentication**.

   d. Enter your Username, Password, use **https://login.salesforce.com** for the Salesforce Login URL, then click **Log in**.

   e. Once verified, click **Next**.

The following figure displays the authentication required to log in to Salesforce from Data Loader:

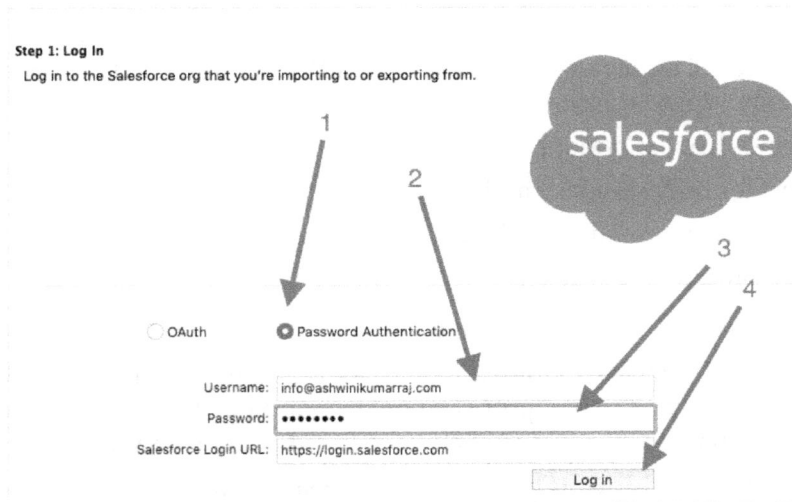

Figure 8.7: Login to Salesforce from Data Loader

The next step is to select the Account object, rename the file to be extracted, and save it to your desktop.

Note: All file name defaults to extract.csv. The remaining files prevent losing or overwriting them.

Select **Data Objects**, from the **Select Salesforce Object** list, select **Account (Account)**.

3. In the **Choose a target for extraction** text box, enter **Accounts exctract.csv**.

4. Click **Browse**.

5. Select the desired folder, click **Save**, then click **Next**.

6. Now, in edit your Query window, create the necessary **Salesforce Object Query Language** (**SOQL**) query.

7. Choose the following query fields:

    a. ID

    b. Name

    c. Phone

The query looks like the following:

Select Id, Name, Phone FROM Account

The following figure shows the query editor to be used to edit the query:

Figure 8.8: Displaying the query for editing

8. Click **Finish**, then click **Yes**.

The terminal window appears, reporting the number of successful extractions.

Similarly, Data Loader can also be used to update data.

Conclusion

In this chapter, we discussed data management. Data management includes Data Import and export. Through using Data Import, data from different sources can be brought into Salesforce. Similarly, by Data Export, data from Salesforce can be exported to different formats. Data Import can happen through Wizard or Data Loader. In the next chapter, we will discuss reports and Dashboards.

Questions

1. **You are building an application that requires you to import up to five million records at a time of any data type. Which method of Data Import will you follow?**
   a. Data Import Wizard
   b. Data Loader
   c. All of the above
   d. None of the above

2. As a responsible Salesforce administrator, it is important to perform data management. Data Export is one of the activities within data management. Which of the following is correct for Data Export and backup?
   a. Exports will always be completed within 5 hours.
   b. Large exports are broken up into multiple files.
   c. Formula and roll-up summaries are always excluded from exports.
   d. The Schedule Export option allows you to schedule the export process daily.

3. What are some differences between using the Data Import Wizard and Data Loader? Choose 3 answers.
   a. Both Data Import Wizard and Data Loader can be accessed by all users.
   b. The Data Import Wizard can only loa0d standard objects, but the Data Loader can load custom objects.
   c. Mappings can be saved with Data Loader but not with the Import Wizard.
   d. Triggering Workflow rules is optional when using the Import Wizard but not with data Loader.
   e. Data Import Wizard cannot export records but Data Loader can.

4. The Salesforce administrator would like a backup of account, contact, and opportunity data to be automatically run and stored on a local company server each week. What is the best way to accomplish this?
   a. Use Salesforce Data Export service.
   b. Write a custom program that accesses the Salesforce API.
   c. Use the CLI of Data Loader and schedule a weekly job on the local server.
   d. Use the Data Export Wizard and schedule a weekly run.

5. When using the "Data Export" page in Setup, which file type is used to export the back up of Salesforce data on a weekly or monthly basis?
   a. SFDC
   b. DOC
   c. HTML
   d. CSV

Answers

1. b
2. b, c
3. c, d, e
4. c
5. d

CHAPTER 9
Report and Dashboard

Introduction

Reports and Dashboards are powerful tools in Salesforce that allow businesses to harness the full potential of their data. They offer actionable insights, helping organizations make data-driven decisions with ease. In Salesforce, these tools are designed to be intuitive yet flexible, catering to users of all experience levels.

In this chapter, we will explore the fundamental concepts of reports and Dashboards, how they are structured, and how to leverage them for maximum impact. Salesforce Reports are essentially lists or summaries of data presented in an organized and easy-to-understand manner. Dashboards, on the other hand, provide a visual representation of report data, offering real-time snapshots of key metrics through graphs, charts, and tables.

Structure

In this chapter, we will discuss the following topics:

- Introduction to Reports and Dashboards
- Data visualization using Dashboard
- Dynamic Dashboard

Objectives

After studying this unit, you should be able to understand the importance of reports and Dashboards. You will learn different report types like Tabular, summery, matrix reports, etc. You will also understand how to export report data and data visualization using Dashboards. In this chapter, you will learn to create a Dashboards, add various components to the Dashboards, and make dynamic Dashboards too.

Introduction to Reports and Dashboards

A report is a list of records that meets the criteria defined by the user. To get the data required, records can be filtered, grouped, and calculated. Reports can even be displayed graphically in the form of a chart.

The report would be the solution for the following types of requirements from business:

- Which products are sold most?
- Who are my highest value prospects?
- Which marketing campaigns give maximum ROI?
- How satisfied are my customers?

For this sort of advanced analysis, the report would be useful.

Each report is stored in a folder. Report folders decide how reports are accessed, and who can see, edit, or manage them. Folders can be hidden, shared, and public. Access to the contents of the folder can be controlled depending on roles, permissions, public groups, and license types. A folder containing reports can be made accessible to the whole organization or made private so that only the owner has access to it.

The Dashboards is a visual portrayal of key metrics and trends for records in the organization. For every Dashboards component, there is a single report as a source. Nonetheless, the same report can be utilized as a source in numerous Dashboards components on a single Dashboards. Different Dashboards components can be made on a single Dashboards page.

Like reports, Dashboardss are likewise stored in folders, which control who approaches it. Access to a folder offers access to its Dashboards. Be that as it may, to see the Dashboards components, access to the underlying reports is required too.

Report types

A report type is similar to a predetermined template that makes reporting simpler. It defined which fields and records are accessible to utilize while creating a report. This depends on the relationships between two objects, for example, a primary object and its related objects. For example, with the 'Contacts and Accounts' report type, 'Contacts' is the primary object, and 'Accounts' is the related object. Reports show only those records that meet the criteria referenced in the report type.

The following figure represents a venn diagram of outer join report type in Salesforce:

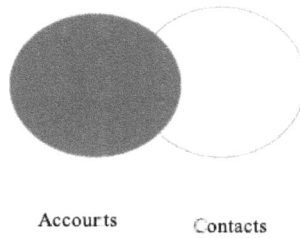

Accounts   Contacts

Figure 9.1: Venn diagram for Report types

Before building a report, it is most important to choose the right report type. When a report type is chosen, the records and fields are picked up, which will be available in report.

There are two different kinds of report types as follows:

- Standard report types
- Custom report types

Standard report types

Standard report types are accessible for building reports on standard and custom objects and their related objects. At the point when another custom field is made, it is automatically added to standard report types.

Follow the following steps to access standard report available:

1. Click on **Report** tab and select **New Report**.

2. Select **Lead** (Left Hand Side) in **Choose Report Type** and select **Leads with converted lead information** from the right-hand side, as shown in the following figure:

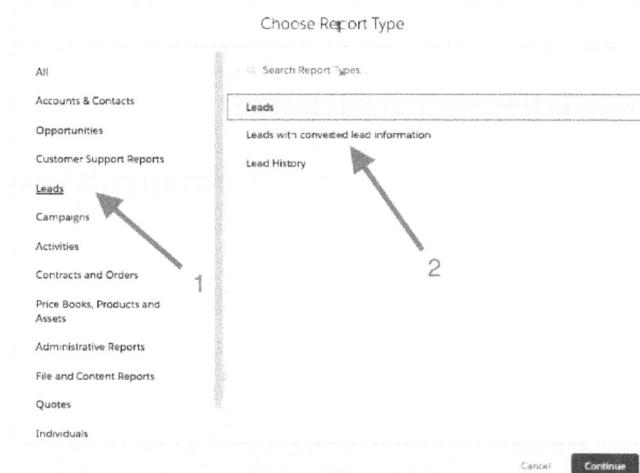

Figure 9.2: Choosing report type

Note: **The standard report types cannot be edited.**

Custom report types

Custom report types allow building the report framework in the report wizard. Through this, users can create custom reports.

While creating custom report types, the following points need to be kept in mind:

- Select combinations of related objects with or without relationships.
- Select which fields can be used as columns in reports.
- Add fields that are related through lookup.

Salesforce provides a simple wizard for defining custom report type. Let us create a report type to list all the accounts that have at least one order record.

Perform the following steps to create a Report Type name Accounts with Order:

1. Click the gear icon ⚙ at the top of the page and launch setup.
2. Enter **Report Types** in the Quick Find box, then select **Report Types**. (Alternatively, you can follow **Feature Settings** | **Analytics** | **Reports & Dashboards** | **Report Types**).
3. Click New Custom Report Type.
4. Select the **Primary Object** for your custom report type. Accounts object in this case.
5. Enter the **Report Type Label** and the **Report Type Name**.
6. Enter a description for your custom report type. (Up to 255 characters long).
7. Select the category in which you want to store this custom report type.
8. Select a **Deployment Status**.
9. Click **Next** to proceed:

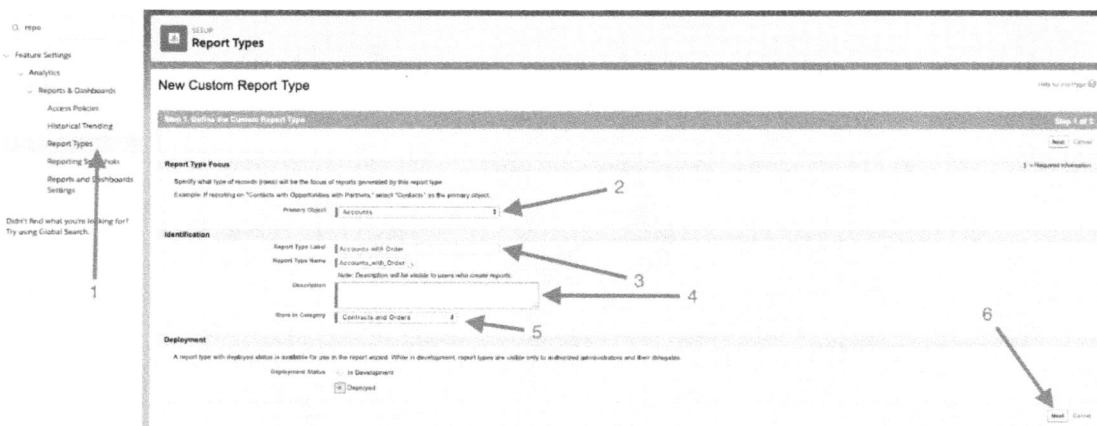

Figure 9.3: Create a new custom report type

10. In the next screen, click on **Click to create another object**:

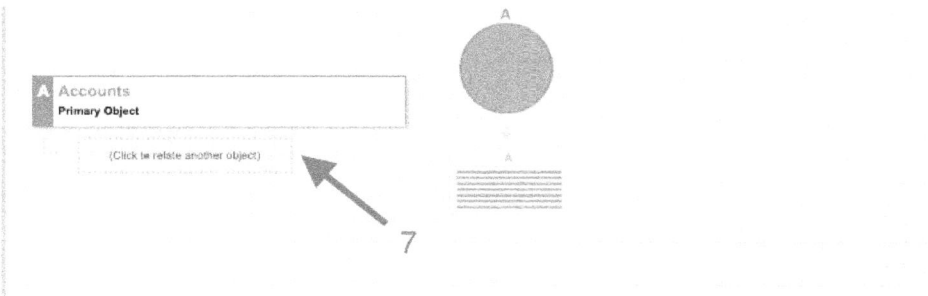

Figure 9.4: Adding object to report type

11. Select **Order**.

12. In A to B Relationship, select **Each A record must have at least one related B record.**, as shown in the following figure:

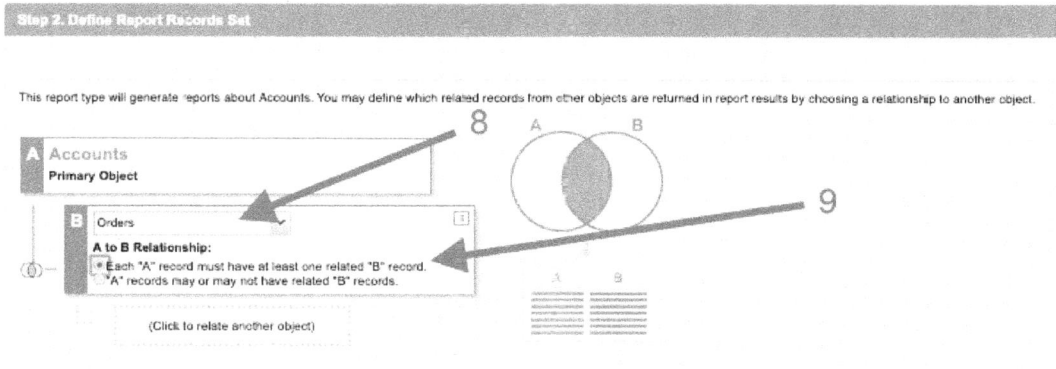

Figure 9.5: Establishing relationshop in report type

13. Click on **Save** once done.

Every report type has a primary object relationship. The object relationship makes sense of which records of the objects the report type consolidates. Every object relationship refers to a primary object and at least one related object. If you determine only a primary object with no related object, the report type incorporates just records for that primary objective. If a related object is included, by then, the report type joins the primary object with or without the related object. If the related object is incorporated, the object relationship can be arranged in the following two unique ways:

Primary object with related object: Records returned by this sort of object relationship are just those where the primary object has at least one related item record.

The following figure depicts the relationship between a primary object with a related object:

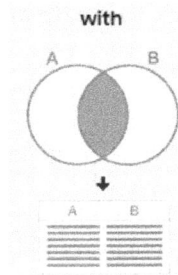

Figure 9.6: *Relationship between objects – Primary with related*

Primary object with or without a related object: In this type os object relationship, records returned are only where the primary object may or may not have a related object record.

The following picture depicts the relationship between a primary object with or without a related object:

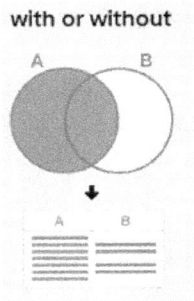

Figure 9.7: *Relationshi between objects – Primary with or without related*

There can be a maximum of four related objects, and every object can have the "with" or "with or without" distinction.

Format reports

Salesforce allows the creation of reports on different predefined formats. Four different report formats can be used as follows:

- Tabular
- Summary
- Matrix
- Joined

Tabular reports

The easiest and fastest way to make a report is the Tabular report. This is similar to a spreadsheet, consisting of a set of fields in columns with matching records in a row.

Let us create a Tabular report on the Opportunity object. Perform the following steps to create a Tabular report:

1. On the **Reports** tab, click on **New Report**.
2. Choose Opportunities from Report Type and click **Continue**.

The Lightning Report Builder will demonstrate the following screen. The report builder is a visual editor for building reports. It lets you work with report fields and filters and shows you a preview of your report with only a portion of the data:

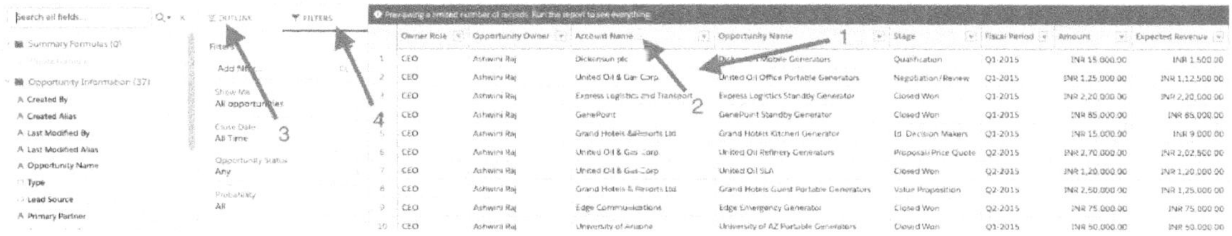

Figure 9.8: Tabular report

Let us discuss various panes available in the report, which are as follows:

- The **Preview** [1] displays a dynamic preview of data that makes it easy to customize the report.
- The **Fields** pane [2] displays the fields from the selected report type. Fields can be searched using the Quick Find box and dragged to add them to your report.
- The **Outline** pane [3] allows us to add, delete columns with as simple as through drag and drop mechanism. It also allows us to add Summary Formula Columns and Bucket Columns in the **Outline** pane.
- The **Filters** pane [4] allows us to set the view, time frame, and custom filters to limit the data shown in a report.

Now, let us set the scope of the report using the standard filters. Follow these steps to add filter to the report:

1. Click the **Filters** pane.
2. Click **Close Date** and set the date field range to **All-Time** and click **Apply**:

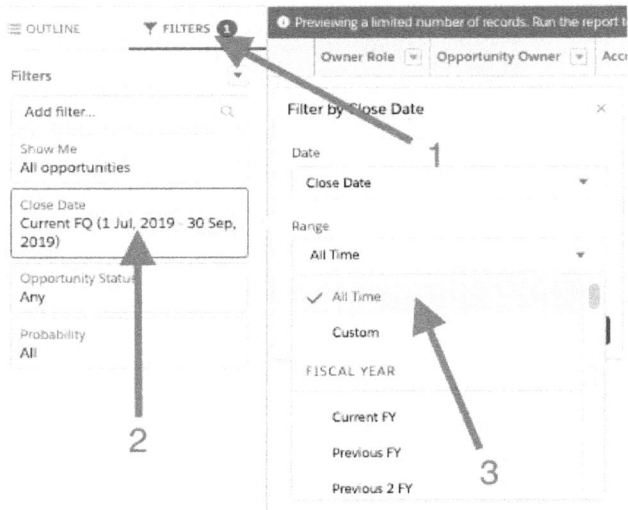

Figure 9.9: Applying filters into the report

3. Click on **Opportunity Status** and change to **Open**, and click **Apply**.

4. Click on the arrow next to any column and select the options based on the actions, like **Sort Ascending**, **Sort Descending** or **Remove Column**, and so on to be performed:

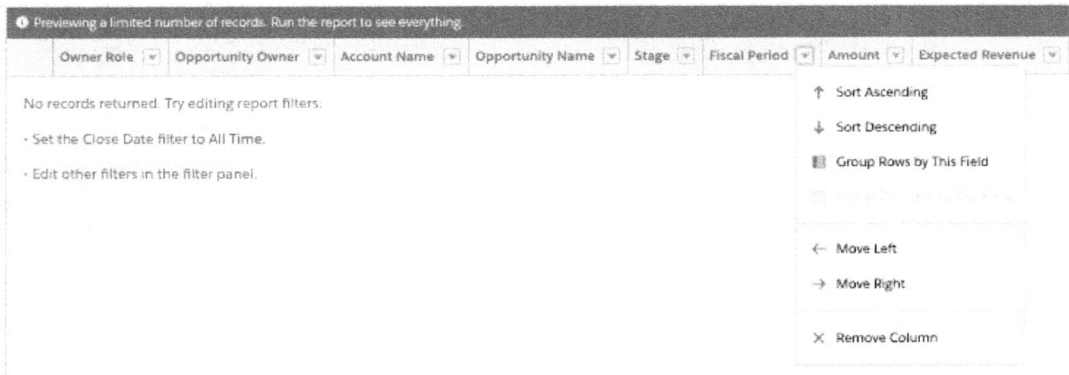

Figure 9.10: Sorting the field in report

5. Let us keep the following columns:

   Account Name, Opportunity Name, Stage, Amount, Expected Revenue, Probability (%), Fiscal Period, and Close date.

6. Click **Save**.

7. Name your report, Open Opportunities All Time.

8. Enter the description and save the report in the **Public Reports** folder.

9. Click **Run**.

The report should look like the following screenshot:

	Account Name ▾	Opportunity Name ▾	Stage ▾	Amount ▾	Expected Revenue ▾	Probability (%) ▾	Close Date ▾
		REPORT: OPPORTUNITIES **Opportunity All Time**					
		Total Records 16					
1	Dickenson plc	Dickenson Mobile Generators	Qualification	INR 15,000.00	INR 1,500.00	10%	24/8/2018
2	United Oil & Gas Corp.	United Oil Office Portable Generators	Negotiation/Review	INR 1,25,000.00	INR 1,12,500.00	90%	12/8/2018
3	Grand Hotels & Resorts Ltd	Grand Hotels Kitchen Generator	Id. Decision Makers	INR 15,000.00	INR 9,000.00	60%	3/7/2018
4	United Oil & Gas Corp.	United Oil Refinery Generators	Proposal/Price Quote	INR 2,70,000.00	INR 2,02,500.00	75%	26/9/2018
5	Grand Hotels & Resorts Ltd	Grand Hotels Guest Portable Generators	Value Proposition	INR 2,50,000.00	INR 1,25,000.00	50%	11/10/2018
6	Pyramid Construction Inc.	Pyramid Emergency Generators	Prospecting	INR 1,00,000.00	INR 10,000.00	10%	20/8/2018
7	Express Logistics and Transport	Express Logistics Portable Truck Generators	Value Proposition	INR 80,000.00	INR 40,000.00	50%	6/7/2018
8	GenePoint	GenePoint Lab Generators	Id. Decision Makers	INR 60,000.00	INR 36,000.00	60%	5/10/2018
9	United Oil & Gas Corp.	United Oil Installations	Negotiation/Review	INR 2,70,000.00	INR 2,43,000.00	90%	8/8/2018
10	University of Arizona	University of AZ Installations	Proposal/Price Quote	INR 1,00,000.00	INR 75,000.00	75%	9/7/2018
11	Express Logistics and Transport	Express Logistics SLA	Perception Analysis	INR 1,20,000.00	INR 84,000.00	70%	7/7/2018
12	United Oil & Gas Corp.	United Oil Plant Standby Generators	Needs Analysis	INR 6,75,000.00	INR 1,35,000.00	20%	5/9/2018
13	Edge Communications	Edge Emergency Generator	Id. Decision Makers	INR 35,000.00	INR 21,000.00	60%	17/10/2018
14	KloudRac	Salesforce Books	Proposal/Price Quote	INR 2,000.00	INR 1,500.00	75%	25/1/2019
15	KloudRac	KloudRac- CRM Implementation	Prospecting			10%	30/6/2019
16	KloudRac	Service Cloud Implementation	Prospecting	INR 10,00,000.00	INR 1,00,000.00	10%	31/5/2019

Figure 9.11: Viewing the report

Filter the report

The filter can be applied to the report as per the required criteria. There could be up to 20 filters added to a report directly in the Filters pane. This can be done either by using the Add button or by dragging in fields from the Preview pane. In addition to this, filter logic like **and**, **or**, **and not** operators can also be used. The following filter types can be used in a report:

- **Standard filter**: These filters are applied by default to most objects. For example: Show me, All Times, Last Month, and so on.
- **Field filter**: These filters are available for reports, workflow rules, and list views. For each filter, field, operator, and value can be set.
- **Filter logic**: These filters add Boolean conditions to control how field filters are evaluated. At least one field filter must be added before applying any filtering logic.
- **Cross filter**: These filters filter a report by the child object using WITH or WITHOUT conditions. Even subfilters can be added to filter by fields on the child object.
- **Row limit**: These filters restrict the number of rows for a report.

The operators used in filters are like the verbs in a sentence. Operators specify how to filter criteria relate to one another. Find the following operators used in a report:

Operator	Uses
Equals	Used for an exact match. For example, "Created equals today."
less than	Used for results that are less than the value entered.
greater than	Used when the required results that exceed the value entered.
less or equal	Used for results that match or less than the value entered.
greater or equal	Used for results that match or exceed the value entered.
not equal to	Used for results that do not have the value entered. This operator is beneficial for eliminating any empty fields.
Contains	Used for fields that include the search string, but sometimes also include other information. This is not case-sensitive.
does not contain	Used to eliminate records that do not contain the value entered. This is not case-sensitive.
starts with	Used when the value starts with is known, but not the exact value. This is a narrower search compared to "contains."
Includes	Used to choose a multi-select picklist as the selected field. This is useful to find records that include one or more of the values entered.
Excludes	Used to choose a multi-select picklist as the selected field. This is useful to find records that do not contain any values that match the ones entered.
Between	Used for Dashboards filters only. It is useful to filter on ranges of values. For each range, the filter returns results that are between the Minimum and Maximum values.
Within	Used when you create list views based on a Geolocation custom field. It shows results that are within the specified radius from a fixed latitude and longitude.

Table 9.1: Filter logics

The following filter logic can be applied to the report:

Operator	Definition
AND	Finds records that match both values.
OR	Finds records that match any one value.
NOT	Finds records that exclude values.

Table 9.2: Filter options

Use Cross-Object filters

Cross-Object filters permit to extend the report types to objects related to the original object characterized in the report type. Cross filters help to calibrate the outcomes, without composing code or utilizing formula. Some use of Cross-Object filters is Opportunities without activities in the previous 30 days, Contacts without accounts, Accounts with no opportunities.

Let us make a report that shows Contacts and Accounts, where the contacts are related to opportunities that are Closed Won.

Follow these steps to create a Cross-Object filter to a report:

1. Click **New Report** on **Reports** tab.
2. Select the **Contacts & Accounts** report type and click **Continue**.
3. Click **Filters**, then click the More Actions arrow and select **Add Cross Filter**:

Figure 9.12: Adding Cross filters

4. Select a parent object from the **Show Me** drop-down list. Select **Contacts**.
5. Choose with as the operator.
6. Select a child object from the **Secondary Object** drop-down or search by its name. The drop-down list contains all eligible child objects of your selected parent object. Select **Opportunities** and click **Apply**

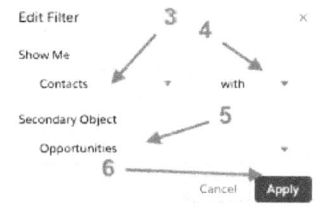

Figure 9.13: Adding filters in cross filters

Now, let us add sub filters:

1. Click on Add Opportunities Filters.
2. Select **Stage** as a field for subfilter.
3. Select equals operator.
4. Choose **Closed Won** under value(s)
5. Click **Apply to** apply the sub filter, as shown in the following figure:

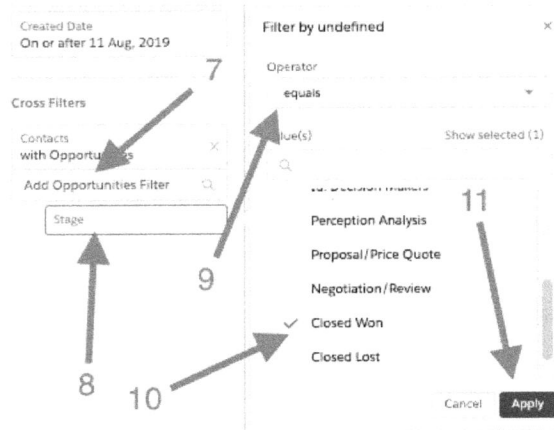

Figure 9.14: Applying filters

6. Click **Save**.
7. Give a name to the report.
8. Click **Save**.

Summary reports

Summary reports are like Tabular reports, yet also permit you to group columns of data, see subtotals, and make charts. Summary reports give us a lot more alternatives for arranging the data and are incredible for use in Dashboards. This kind of report is utilized to show groupings of rows of data.

Let us assume the administrator has received a requirement to make a custom report that would show just those accounts that do not have related contacts, and the outcome must be grouped by account type.

Let us perform the following steps to create a summary report:

1. Click the **New Report** button from **Reports** tab.
2. Select the Accounts report type and then click on **Continue**.
3. In the filters section, go to **Add | Cross Filter**.

The next step is to select a parent object from the drop-down list. In this case:

1. Select the **Account** object.
2. Then, choose without.
3. Then, select a child object from the drop-down list. Select **Contacts** in this case.

To make this report as a summary report, need to group rows. In this case, apply grouping based on Type through the following steps:

1. Click on **Outline**.

2. Under **GROUP ROWS**, from Add group picklist, select **Type**.

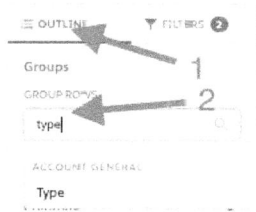

Figure 9.15: Creating summery

3. Click **Save**.
4. Name your report, Open Opportunities All Time.
5. Enter the description and save the report in the **Public Reports** folder.
6. Click **Run**.

Matrix reports

These types of reports allow grouping records by row and column. These reports are the most complicated ones.

For instance, the requirement is to get totals of revenue or quantity of products sold; then the matrix report is useful.

Let us assume that there is a requirement to know revenue trends, month over month.

Let us start by creating the basic report. In this step, we will create a matrix report showing sales by type for each month:

1. From the **Reports** tab, click on the **New Report** button.
2. Select the Opportunities report type and then, click on **Continue**.
3. Click on **FILTERS**, then select apply these standard filters:
4. For the **Show Me** standard filter, select **All Opportunities** and then click **Done**.
5. In the **Opportunity Status** standard filter, select **Closed Won** and click on **Apply**.
6. In the **Date Field** standard filter, select **Close Date**.
7. In Range, select Current FY.
8. Click on **Apply**.
9. To summarize the report by Sum of Amount, click on **More Actions** drop-down arrow on the **Amount** column. Now, click **Summarize** and select **Sum**.
10. To change the report format to the matrix, first group rows by Close Month and columns by type.
11. Click on **Outline** to start grouping.
12. In **GROUP ROWS**, from the **Add group** picklist, select **Close Month**.

13. In **GROUP COLUMNS**, from the **Add group** picklist, select **Type**.

14. Save the report once done.

15. Click **Run Report** to run it.

Joined report

A **joined report** is a type of report that allows you to combine data from multiple objects or report types into a single view. It is particularly useful when objects are not directly related in a parent-child hierarchy.

Adding a Bucket field to report

A bucket field is a very powerful functionality used in the Salesforce report to easily categorize values for a field in a report without a custom formula field at the object level. When a bucket field is created, multiple categories are defined into groups depending on the record values. If it is required to categorize multiple numbers of values of a field into one category, then we create Bucket fields.

Bucket fields are available only in Tabular, Summary, and Matrix reports. Joined Reports does not support Bucket fields.

Perform the following steps to create a bucket field:

1. Click the **New Report** button from the **Reports** tab.

2. Select the Accounts report type and select the Contacts & Accounts report type and click **Continue**.

3. In the Filter section, change Show to All Accounts. Change the Date Field Range to All Time.

4. Under Outline, in the Column section, click on Remove All Columns to clear the report without any columns.

5. Under Column, Add Account Name and Account Owner.

6. Under Column, add Bucket field.

7. Set Field to Type.

8. In Bucket Field Name, entre "Core."

9. Click on the **Add Bucket** button and type in **Customer**.

10. Click **Apply**.

Exporting report data

Salesforce allows exporting report details in.CSV or XLS formats. Follow the following steps to export a report into CSV file:

1. Click the **Reports** tab.
2. Click the report to be exported.
3. Click the arrow ⏷ next to **Edit**.
4. Click **Export**.
5. Click **Details Only** and select the following options:
    a. Format: Comma Delimited **.csv**
    b. Encoding: ISO-8859-1 (General US & Western European, ISO-LATIN-1)
6. Click **Export**.

To open the exported file, locate the file on your computer and open it.

Note: **The export will not have formatting, groupings, or subtotals.**

Report chart

A report chart allows you to place a single chart right at the top of your report. This helps in viewing the chart along with the report.

Follow the following steps to create a report chart:

1. From the **Reports** tab, click the report you made earlier to open it.
2. Click on **Add Chart** button:

Figure 9.16: Adding Chart to report

3. The chart can be shown and hidden by clicking the chart icon (🔆).

Data visualization using Lightning Dashboard

The Dashboard is only a graphical portrayal of a report. It shows data from the source as a graphical part. Salesforce, on a single Dashboards page payout, presents multiple reports, one next to the other, utilizing Dashboards components. Dashboard components accompany an assortment of tables, metrics, chart types, and gauges. It very well may be customized how data is grouped, summed up, and displayed for each component. The components give a snapshot of performance pointers for the organization. The various types of components and their usage are discussed in the following table:

Component type	When to use it
☰ ▮▮ ≣ ▯▯ ⟋ ◔ ▽ ⬚	Use a chart when data to be shown graphically. A variety of chart types can be chosen.
⏲	A gauge can be used when a single value to be shown within a range of custom values.
123	A metric can be used when one key value to display.
▦ ≣	A table to be shown to represent data in column form.

Table 9.3: Componets of a Dashboards

The drag-and-drop Dashboards builder is an intuitive interface for building Dashboardss from various reports made in Salesforce. The relationship between Dashboard, Report, and Report Types is portrayed in the following figure:

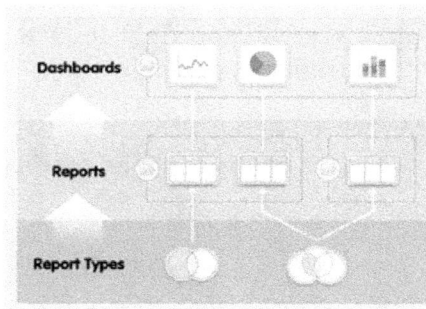

Figure 9.17: Relationship between Report and Dashboard

A Dashboards does the following work:

- Displays data from single or multiple custom source reports.
- Has users who determine what data is visible.
- Can be scheduled to be refreshed.
- Can be scheduled to be emailed automatically.

Creating a Dashboard

Now that you have understood about the Dashboard, let us create a Dashboards on the Sales pipeline. First of all, the source report for the Dashboard to be created. Let us make a simple Leads report through the following steps:

1. Click the **Reports** tab, **New Report**.
2. Select **Leads** as the report type. Click **Continue**.

3. Click **FILTERS** and apply below standard filters:

4. For the Show Me standard filter, select **All Leads**. Click **Apply**.

5. For the **Date Field** standard filter, select **Create Date**. For **Range**, select **All Time**. Click **Apply**.

6. From **OUTLINE** and group rows by **Lead Source**.

7. From the **Add group** lookup, select **Lead Source**.

8. Ensure that these columns are included in your report: Lead Owner, First Name, Last Name, Account, Email.

9. Click **Save**.

10. Name the report **Leads by Source**.

11. Click **Run**.

Now that the report is createt, let us create a Dashboards and visualize data through the following steps:

1. From the **Dashboards** tab, click **New Dashboard**.

2. Name your Dashboards Leads by Source Dashboard.

3. Click **Create**.

4. To insert a component, click + **Component**.

5. From **Select Report**, choose the Leads to report you created earlier, Lead by Source, and click **Select**. From **Add Component**, select the donut chart, as shown in the following figure:

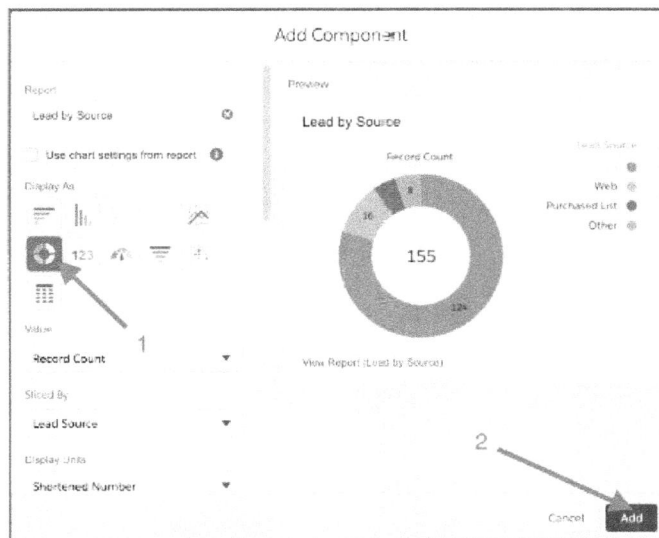

Figure 9.18: Adding component to Dashboards

6. Click **Add**. Then, your new component appears on the Dashboard.

7. The Dashboards component can be resized by clicking on it, then dragging the corners and sides.

8. Click **Save** and then click **Done**. Your Dashboard should look similar to the following screenshot:

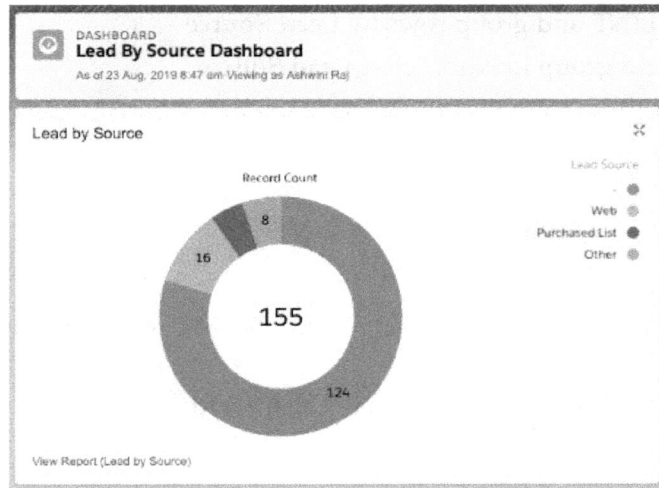

Figure 9.19: Viewing Dashboard

Adding more components to the Dashboard

Let us add another component to this Dashboard, through the following steps:

1. First, create a summary report.
2. From **Dashboard** tab, select the **Lead By Source Dashboard** Dashboards.
3. Click **Edit**.
4. Click **+Component** to add components:

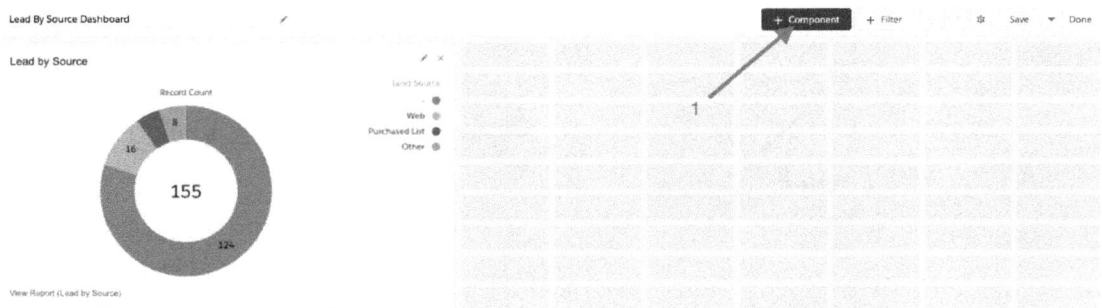

Figure 9.20: Adding component to Dashboard

5. Select the Summary report created and then, click on **Select**.
6. Select **Gauge** and click on **Add**:

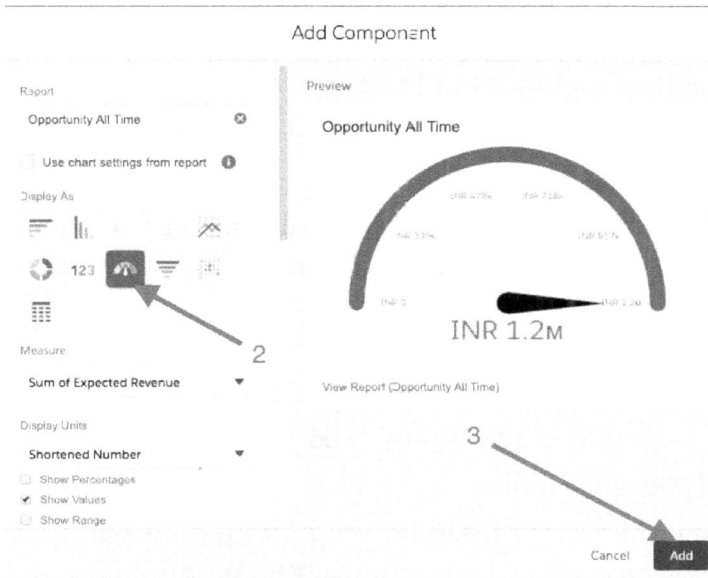

Figure 9.21: Adding component

7. Click **Save** and **Done**.

Now, the Dashboard should look similar to the following screenshot:

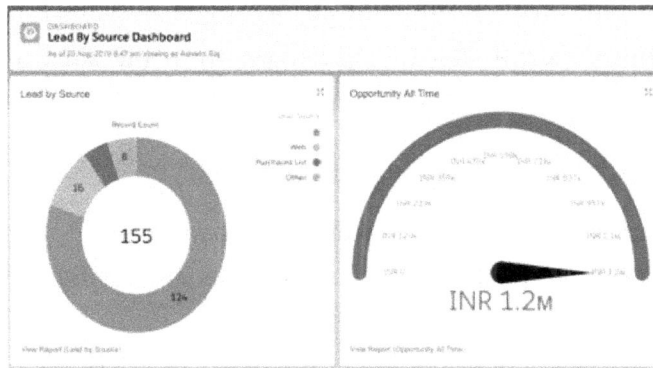

Figure 9.22: Viewing Dashboards

Dynamic Dashboards

Dynamic Dashboardss are special sorts of Dashboard which empower every user to see the data they approach. With a dynamic Dashboards, data permeability can be controlled without making a different Dashboards for each degree of information to get to. Dynamic Dashboard can be made from the summary and matrix report. With dynamic Dashboardss, every user can see the data they have access to. This does not require making separate Dashboards for every user. This implies that a single Dashboards can be utilized for multiple users because the signed-in users dependent on their security and sharing settings see the Dashboards data they should see.

Note the following restrictions:

- Dynamic Dashboardss cannot be saved to personal folders.
- Dynamic Dashboardss cannot be scheduled. They must be refreshed manually.
- Dynamic Dashboard can be created only for Enterprise, Performance, Unlimited, and Developer edition.
- Dynamic Dashboard has the limitation of:
  o 5 dynamic Dashboards for Enterprise Edition.
  o 10 for Unlimited and Performance Edition.
  o 3 for Developer Edition.

Let us use an example where the business group comprises of one sales head, four-Team Leads, and 30 salespeople. The sales repersentative should just observe their data. Team Lead should see data just for the salespeople they oversee, and the sales head should see data over the whole group. In this situation, the administrator commonly would need to make 35 distinct Dashboardss—one for everyone. The admin likewise needs to make various folders to manage access rights.

However, the admin can create dynamic Dashboardss and store them in a single folder.

Team Leads with the View My Team's Dashboards or View All Data permission can preview the Dashboard from the perspective of users under them in the role hierarchy.

Create a dynamic Dashboard

Perform the following steps to create a dynamic Dashboard:

1. From the **Dashboards** tab, create a new Dashboards or Edit the existing one by clicking on **Edit** button:

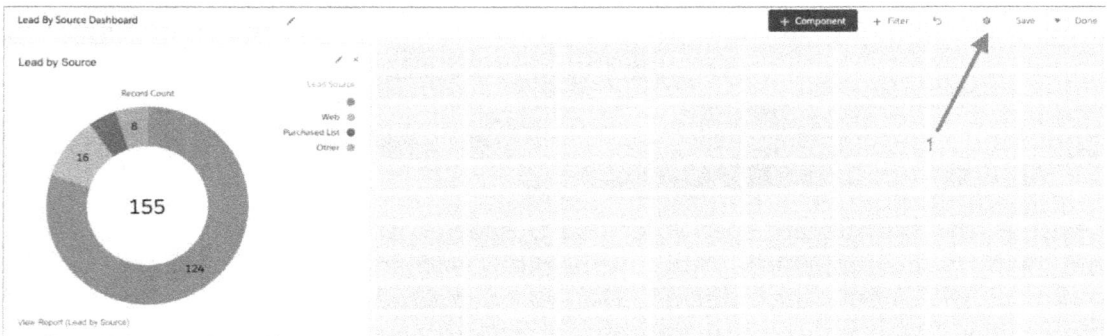

Figure 9.23: Creating dynamic Dashboard

2. Open the **Properties** menu by clicking ⁝ :

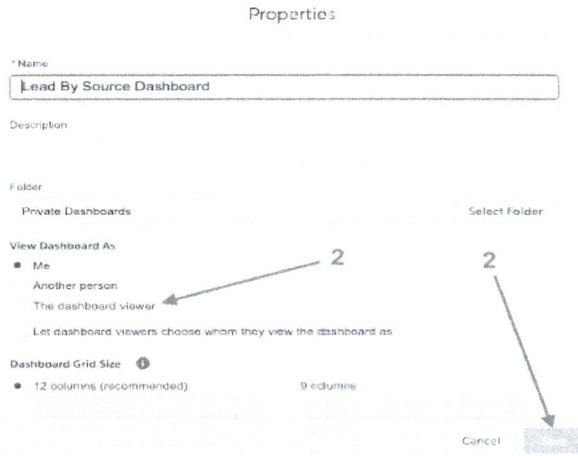

Figure 9.24: Creating dynamic Dashboard

3. Under **View Dashboard As**, select who people view the Dashboard as the following:

   Me: In this case, the users see data in the Dashboard as per their access to data.

   a. **Another individual**: In this case, the users see information in the Dashboard as indicated by the data available to whom specified.

   b. **The Dashboards watcher**: In this case, the users see data as indicated by their access to data. These sorts of Dashboardss are additionally called dynamic Dashboards.

4. Optionally, select **Let Dashboards viewers choose whom they view the Dashboard as** to let a user with appropriate permissions choose who they want the dashibaord to be viewed. With the View My Team's Dashboards permission, the user can view the Dashboard as himself or herself or as anyone beneath them in the role hierarchy. With the View All Data permission, the user can view the Dashboard as anyone.

5. Click **Save** once it is done.

6. Again, click **Save** from the Dashboard Builder.

When people open this Dashboard, they see data as the person that is specified.

Conclusion

In this chapter, we discussed reports and Dashboard. A report is a list of records that meet the criteria defined by the user. A report displays data in rows and column formats. There could be two report types: Standard report type sand Custom report types. There could be different report formats like Tabular, Summary, Matrix, and Joined.

The Dashboard is a graphical representation of a report. It shows data from the source as a graphical component. You can add a few components to a Dashboards.

In the next chapter, we will discuss the security features of Salesforce.

Questions

1. **What is correct about the refreshing Dashboardss? Choose 2 answers.**

   a. A Dashboards can be scheduled to refresh hourly, weekly or monthly.

   b. After a scheduled Dashboards refresh, it can be sent via email automatically to a group of users.

   c. A user can refresh the Dashboard as and when required by clicking the refresh button.

   d. A Dashboards is refreshed each time it is displayed.

2. **Which of the following best defines a report type?**

   a. An option to export an existing report.

   b. A definition of objects and fields which can be utilized to create a report.

   c. A mechanism of grouping together similar reports.

   d. A predefined list of fields from an object.

3. **The administrator of Cloudy analyses has made a joined report to show accounts with open cases. A sales repersentative would like to view this data on his Dashboard in Lightning Experience. How can the administrator fulfill this requirement?**

   a. Make a summary report that displays the same data and add it as a data source to a Dashboards component.

   b. Make a Tabular report that shows the same data and add it as a data source to a Dashboards component.

   c. Make a matrix report that shows the same data and add it as a data source to a Dashboards component.

   d. Make a joined report using a lightning report builder, add a chart to the joined report, and then add the report as a data source to a Dashboards component.

4. **The Sales manager of Cloudy Analyze would like to get a report of opportunities grouped by Sales stage. What type of report would fulfill this requirement?**

   a. Summary

   b. Matrix

   c. Tabular

   d. Two Column

5. **What report format can never be used when making reports with field groupings?**

   a. Summary

   b. Matrix

   c. Tabular

   d. Joined

6. **When are Dashboardss refreshed?**

   a. When a user clicks the 'Refresh' button.

   b. The Dashboards refresh frequency can be set per Dashboard.

   c. Every time someone accesses the home page of Salesforce Org.

   d. Every Day

Answers

1. a, b
2. b
3. d
4. a
5. c
6. a, b

Join our Discord space

Join our Discord workspace for latest updates, offers, tech happenings around the world, new releases, and sessions with the authors:

https://discord.bpbonline.com

CHAPTER 10
Security

Introduction

We use innovation in our lives throughout the day. Thus, cybercrime is at the forefront of everybody's thoughts. In 2015, Verizon's Data Breach Investigation Report assessed that the yearly expense of worldwide cybercrime is approximately $100 billion.

The cybercrime danger is more mind-boggling than at any time in recent memory. It is exceptionally critical for security groups to forestall, distinguish, break down, and react to dangers. Criminals are moving their strategies from innovative assaults to focused attacks on workers by controlling social practices. The organization's employees are currently the greatest security danger. They make the most straightforward open doors for programmers. Presently, a day, each individual affects security, paying little attention to their title or capacity.

Just a single representative can set off a chain of occasions that may bargain with the organization's information. Along these lines, Cybercrime is more about individuals than technology.

In this chapter, we will discuss some essential practices that each representative can receive to help the organization progressively secure.

Structure

In this chapter, we will discuss the following topics:

- Basic security
- Decide the right Salesforce security settings
- Control access to the organization
- Whitelisting rusted IP ranges for the org
- Manage object permissions
- Profiles
- Permission sets
- Field-level security
- Control access to records
- Organization-wide sharing
- Role hierarchy
- Sharing rules
- Viewing setup and audit trail

Objectives

After studying this unit, you will learn the basic security requirements of any organization. You will learn to understand the right security settings. You will also learn various features like data security, multitenancy platform, two-factor authentication, IP restriction, and limiting users. You will be able to know how to monitor events, maintain data security, control access organization through managing users, setting password policy and field level security setting, etc. You will also learn to set control access records, set **Org-wide Defaults (OWD)**, create sharing rules, and set up audit trails.

Basic security

Intruders exploit normal human behaviors. Criminals have learned that they can exploit human emotions and reactions to steal credentials and infiltrate your network, hence they target the following types of emotions:

- Fear
- Trust
- Morality
- Rewards
- Conformity
- Curiosity

The following essential methods are utilized by cybercriminals to go after our humanity and get what they need:

- **Phishing and malware**: This technique is utilized to entice users to download software planned to harm or control a device or network.

- **Social engineering**: In this procedure, social designing is utilized to manipulate individuals into taking action or uncovering confidential data.

- **Exploiting public presence**: Openly accessible data is utilized to help plan a social building assault, break a password login, or make a focused-on phishing email.

- **Eavesdropping**: In this case, the criminals attempt to listen to private conversations secretly.

- **Installing rogue devices**: This method Installs remote switches or USB thumb drives where they can give a hacker's access to a protected network.

Decide the right Salesforce security settings

Protecting the data is the responsibility of both Salesforce and users. The security includes empowering Salesforce to assist users by carrying out their responsibilities effectively.

Security is the establishment of all services by Salesforce. The security schemes, according to the need of the organization, can be constructed.

To protect the business, Salesforce keeps numerous layers of security work together. The hierarchical information is not just shielded from unapproved access from outside the organization; additionally, it is kept protected from unseemly utilization by internal users.

The administrator can monitor the users, ensuring the correct users can work with the correct data.

The following figure depicts how security is managed in Salesforce:

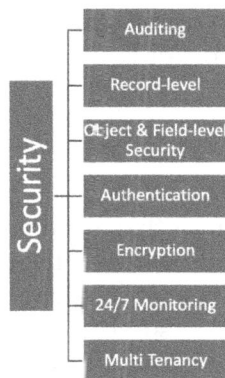

Figure 10 1: *Security options*

The administrator can activate features built into the platform to make the organization as secure as possible.

We will discuss each security layer in detail.

Multitenancy platform

Salesforce is a multitenant platform that utilizes a single pool of resources to offer support to a wide range of clients. Salesforce shields individual organization's information from different organizations by utilizing a unique identifier related to every user session. At the point when an individual signs into the organization, the subsequent requests are related to your organization utilizing this identifier.

Salesforce utilizes the most cutting-edge innovation for web security accessible in this day and age. At the point when the application is accessed using a browser, **Transport Layer Security (TLS)** ensures the data utilizes both server authentication and great encryption. It guarantees that the information is protected, secure, and accessible just to registered users in your organization.

Moreover, Salesforce is facilitated in secure server conditions that utilization firewalls and other trend-setting innovations to keep obstruction or access from outside interlopers.

Two-factor authentication

One incredible approach to make sure about the Salesforce organization is to require a second level of authentication when users sign in. Users can react to a notice from the Salesforce Authenticator mobile application or enter a code they get from their phone. Along these lines, the user's account can be ensured regardless of whether the user's credentials are undermined.

In Salesforce, it is simpler to set up two-factor authentication through Salesforce Authenticator. To limit the burden on users, two-factor authentication can be set up only for certain profiles, as for administrators or users who approach sensitive information, for example, account details, and so on.

IP restriction

The logins can be limited to the IP address that belongs to the organization's **virtual private network (VPN)**. Anyone who attempts to log in to Salesforce from outside the assigned scope of addresses will be denied access to it. Along these lines, a malevolent user who steals login credentials using some other sort of assault, despite everything, cannot utilize them outside of your corporate system. You can set up trusted IP address ranges for the whole organization or for explicit users.

Deactivate ex-users

The users who no longer work for the company can be deactivated. Along with these lines, individuals who left the organization cannot access to Salesforce org.

Limit what users can do

In *Salesforce*, a few layers of access and control are figured out to decide *who sees what* and *who can do what*.

You can limit access to particular sorts of resources dependent on the level of security associated with the authentication (login) technique for the user's present session.

Audit trail

Audit trail helps with characterizing a strategy to retain field history information. This feature assists with complying with data retention and audit capability. The setup audit trail tracks the recent setup changes that administrators have made to the org. Audit history can be helpful in an organization with multiple administrators.

Trigger automatic actions on security events

Transaction security policies assess activities utilizing events you determine. For every policy, the real-time activities, sending a notification, forcing two-factor authentication, or picking a session to end and so on, can be characterized in Salesforce.

Transaction security is a piece of Salesforce shield, a bundle of incredible and valuable add-on security features.

Monitor events in your organization

Event monitoring permits access to event log files to track user activity and feature adoption and investigate issues. Any data analysis tool can likewise be integrated with the data log.

Event monitoring is a piece of Salesforce shield, a bundle of ground-breaking and valuable add-on security features.

Data security

The security of the Salesforce Org is influenced by the data set picked for the users.

When the data model is structured, the data on which the users will work should be planned.

For instance, if we take our recruiting app to oversee candidates where the confidential data like social security number, salary, and candidate reviews to be stored. These might be available just to certain sorts of users. It is critical to make sure about the delicate information for recruiters, hiring managers, and interviewers.

It's pretty easy to relegate various data in sets of users in Salesforce due to its adaptable, layered sharing model. Security and convenience can be adjusted to diminish the danger of stolen or abused information.

The Salesforce platform makes it simple to determine which users can view, create, edit, or delete any field or record in the application. The control access to your entire organization, a particular object, a particular field, or even an individual record can be given to a user or a group of users. Security controls can be given at various levels. The correct level of data access to a large number of users without indicating permissions for every user exclusively can be given.

Levels of data access

Access to data can be controlled for any users for the entire organization or a particular field, object, or even an individual record:

- **Organization**: For your entire organization, a list of authorized users, set password policies, and limit logins to specific hours and locations can be managed.

- **Objects**: By setting permissions on a particular type of object, a group of users can be prevented from viewing, creating, editing, or deleting any records of that object.

- **Fields**: Even if the user has access to the object, access to certain fields can be prohibited. You can limit access to specific fields, regardless of whether a user accesses the object. For instance, the salary field in a position object can be made invisible to interviewers, but visible to hiring managers and recruiters.

- **Records**: A specific user can be permitted to see an object. However, view access to individual object records can be limited. For instance, an interviewer can see and edit their reviews, yet not the reviews of different interviewers. Record-level access can be overseen in the following four ways:

- **Organization-wide defaults** (**OWD**): Indicates the default level of access users have. It is utilized to secure the data to the most prohibitive level, and afterward utilizes the other record-level security and sharing tools to offer access to different users specifically.

- **Role hierarchies**: It gives access to users higher in the hierarchy to all records possessed by the users beneath them. Role hierarchies will not have to facilitate your organization chart decisively. On the other hand, possibly, every role in the hierarchy represents a level of information access to that the users need.

- Sharing rules are automatic special cases to the OWDs for specific groups of users to get access to the records not owned by them. Like role hierarchies significance, sharing rules are simply used to give additional users access to records.

- Manual sharing permits owners of specific records to share them with different users. Even though manual sharing is not automated like organization-wide sharing settings, role hierarchies, or sharing rules, it very well may be valuable in certain circumstances when a recruiter going on leave needs to briefly dole out responsibility for a request for job application to some other recruiter.

- **Audit system use**: The auditing feature of Salesforce gives significant data to diagnosing potential security issues. It is prompted that somebody in the organization should audit consistently to identify potential maltreatment.

- **Login history**: The attempts for logins can be viewed for both successful and failed for the last six months.

- **Record modification fields**: All the fields and objects store the name of the user who created and last modified the record. This gives basic auditing information to the administrators.

- **Field history tracking**: Auditing to automatically track changes can be turned on for any individual.

- **Setup audit trail**: Every time any modifications are done to the organization's configuration, the setup audit trail logs about it.

Control access to the organization

To make sure that only employees of the organization who meet certain criteria can log in to Salesforce, managing authorized users, setting password policies, and limiting when and where users can log in, and so on can be configured:

- **Manage users**: In Salesforce, each user is identified by a username, password, and profile. Along with other settings, the profile decides what tasks users can perform, what data they can see, and what actions they can take on the data.

- **Creating a user**: Creating a user in Salesforce is as simple as just entering a username, first name, last name, alias, and E-mail, and selecting a role, license, and profile.

  Salesforce auto-generates a password and informs new users. Once the users log in, they can add or change their personal information. Perform the following steps to create a new user:

  1. Click on the gear icon ⚙ at the top of the page and launch Setup.

  2. Use the Quick Find box to find Users and select Users.

  3. Click on **New User**:

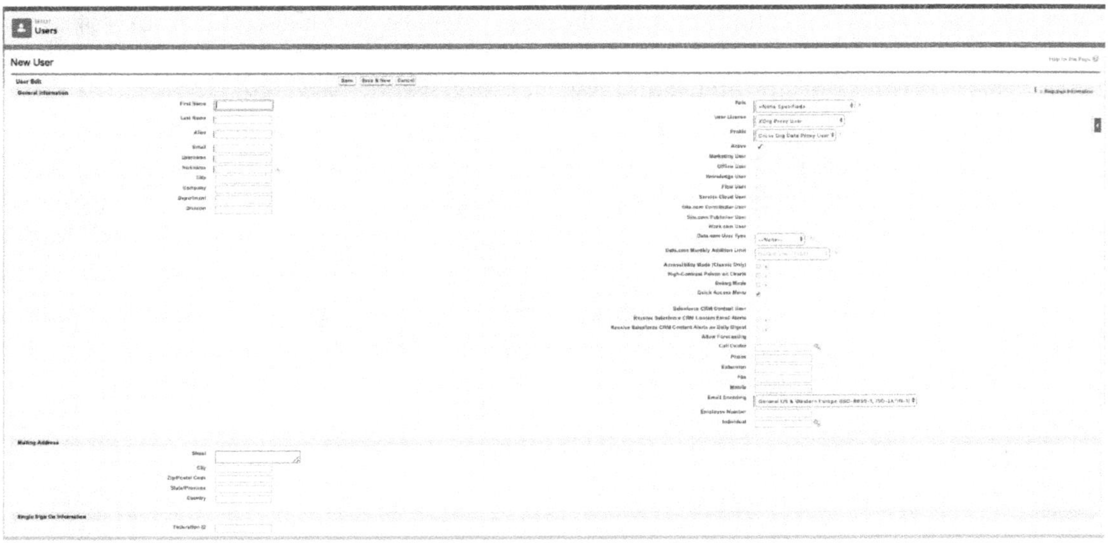

Figure 10.2: Creating new user

4. Enter the user's first name, last name, e-mail address, and so on.

5. Enter a unique username in the form of an e-mail address. By default, the username is the same as the e-mail address.

6. Select the license type this user will have. The license will determine which profiles will be available for the user.

7. Select the profile for the user. This specifies the user's minimum permissions and access settings.

8 Select the option to generate a new password and notify the user.

8. Click on **Save** once it is done.

- **Deactivating a user**: In Salesforce, a user can never be deleted but can be deactivated. Deactivated users lose accessibility to all records. However, the data of those users can be allocated to other users. Perform the following steps to deactivate a user:

  1. Click on the gear icon ⚙ at the top of the page and launch Setup.

  2. Use the Quick Find box to find Users and select Users.

  3. Click on **Edit** next to the name of the user you want to deactivate.

  4. Uncheck the **Active** checkbox and click on **Save**.

- **Setting a password policy**: The Salesforce Org can be configured in different ways to ensure that the users' passwords are strong and secure:

- **Password policies**: The login policies such as indicating an amount of time before all users passwords expire and the degree of complexity required for passwords, and so on can be set.

- **User password expiration**: "Password Never Expires" permission can be set for particular users, and Expiry the password for all users can be set.
- **User password resets**: Reset the password for specific users that can be configured.
- **Login attempts and lockout periods**: The person's access can be unlocked if the user is locked due to too many failed login attempts.

    Follow these steps to set the password policy:

    1. Click on the gear icon ⚙ at the top of the page and launch Setup.

    2. Use the Quick Find box to find **Password Policies**:

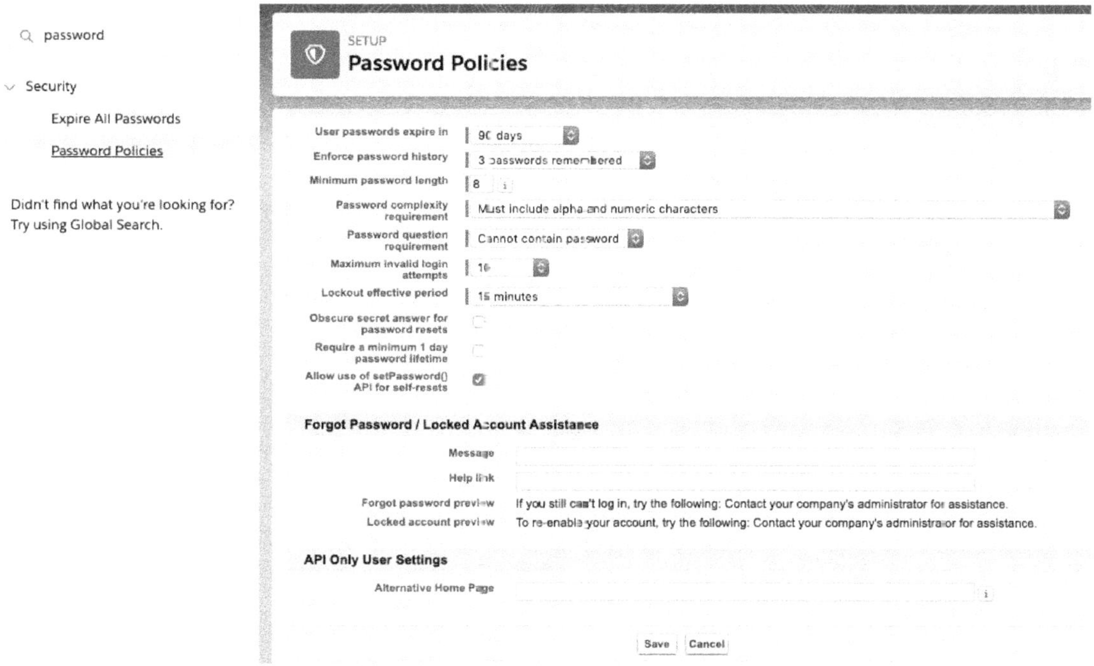

Figure 10.3: Setting password policy

3. Customize the following password settings:

    a. Duration of the password

    b. Complexity of the password

    c. Validity of the password

    d. No of times someone try to log in with invalid credentials before being locked out

4. Select what to do about forgotten passwords and locked accounts.

5. Click on **Save**.

Whitelisting trusted IP ranges for the Org

When the user first-time logs in to Salesforce, the IP address is cached in the browser. The next time, when the user logs in from a different IP address, the user is asked to verify their identity by entering a verification code. This verification step can be bypassed for trusted IP ranges. Perform the following steps to bypass the verification process when the users are in office:

1. Click on the gear icon ⚙ at the top of the page and launch Setup.

2. Use the Quick Find box to find **Network Access**, then select **Network Access**.

3. Click on **New**:

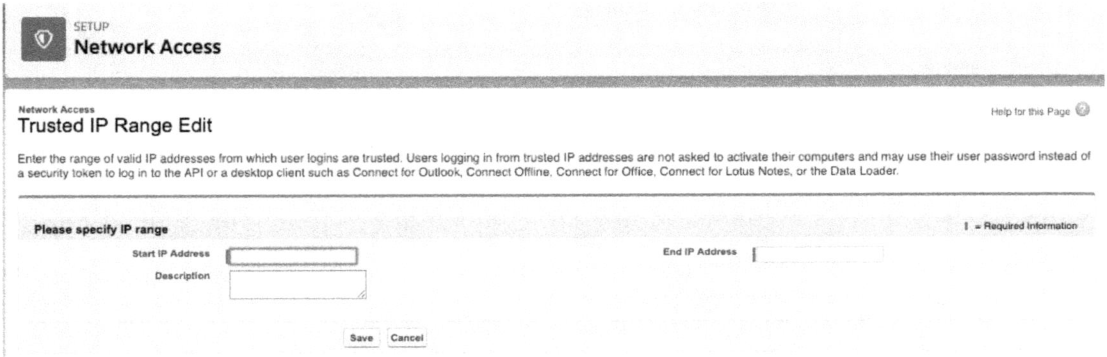

Figure 10.4: Specifying IP range

4. Enter the start and endpoint of the range of trusted IP addresses.

5. Click on **Save** when done.

Restricting login access by IP address using profiles

Salesforce does not provide any restriction for login access from any location. By default, the users can log in from any IP address. The profiles of the users can be restricted from where they log in. For instance, a few users should not be able to log in if they are using an IP address outside of the office. Perform the following steps to do so:

1. Click on the gear icon ⚙ at the top of the page and launch Setup.

2. Use the Quick Find box to find Profiles, then select **Profiles**.

3. Select a profile and click on its name.

4. Click on IP Ranges. If you do not have an Enhanced Profile Interface enabled, scroll down to the Login IP Range related list.

5. Click on **New**.

6. Enter the start and endpoint of the range of trusted IP addresses:

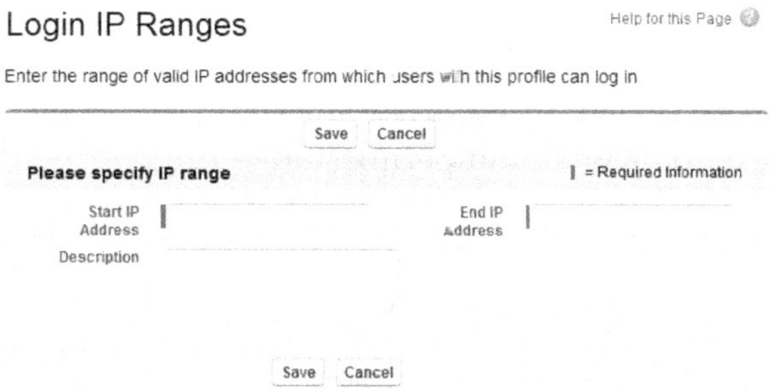

Figure 10.5: Specifying IP range to profile

7. Click on **Save** when done.

Now with this, all users with this profile who are outside the trusted range will not be able to log in to Salesforce. When this profile IP ranges are used, no verification codes are required.

Restricting login access by time

Access time for each profile can be specified when users can log in. For instance, if it is necessary that recruiters can access the candidate's data only from nine to six on weekdays, they can be restricted. Follow these steps to do so:

1. Click on the gear icon ⚙ at the top of the page and launch Setup.
2. Use the Quick Find box to find Profiles, then select **Profiles**.
3. Click on the profile you want to change.
4. Under Login Hours, click on **Edit**.
5. Set the days and hours when users with this profile can log in:
   a. To allow users to log in at any time, click on Clear all times.
   b. To prohibit users from using the system, set the start and end times to the same value:

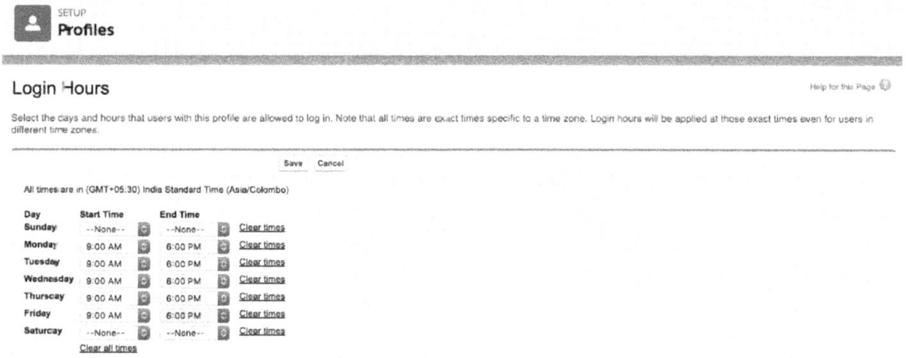

Figure 10.6: Specifying login hours to a profile

Manage object permissions

The simplest way is to control data access is to set permissions on the object. The permission on an object can be set with profiles and permission sets.

A user can have one profile and many permission sets. Note the following object permissions:

- A user's profile chooses the objects they can access and activities such as create, edit, or delete they can do with any object.
- Permission sets allow extra permissions and access settings to a user.
- The combination of profiles and permission sets gives you a lot of adaptability in determining object-level access.

The necessary permissions for every one of the four sorts of clients of the RecruitForce application can be seen in the following table:

Role	Position	Candidate	Job application	Review
Recruiter	Read Create Edit	Read Create Edit	Read Create Edit	Read Create Edit
Hiring Manager	Read Create Edit*	Read* (No SSN)	Read Edit (No lookup fields)	Read Create Edit
Interviewer	Read (No min/max pay)	Read * (No SSN)	Read *	Read ** Create Edit **
Standard Employee	Read (No min/max pay)			

Table: 10.1: Object permissions

* Only for those records that are associated with a position to which the hiring manager or interviewer has been assigned.

** Only for those records that the interviewer owns.

Profiles

Profiles are one of the approaches to customize the general permission of a Salesforce user. In Salesforce, profiles are utilized to choose data security by granting object-level permissions and field-level security. This decides which fields should be appeared to which specific users. Profiles have certain rules or settings that we can set to give or limit a lot of user permissions.

Each user has a single profile that controls the data and features that user approaches. A profile is an assortment of settings and permissions. Profile settings make sense of which data the user can access, and permissions make sense of what moves the users can make on that data. To know about the Profile and Permissions, look at the following points:

- The settings made in a user's profile decide whether he will be able to view a particular app, tab, field, and so on.
- The permissions in a profile of a user decide whether he will be able to create or edit records of a given type, customize the app, and so on.
- Even though profiles usually match with a user's job role, profiles can be created, which makes sense in Salesforce Org.
- A profile can be assigned to numerous users, yet a single user can have just one profile in turn.

There are two types of profiles in Salesforce, which are as follows:

- **Standard**: These are the profiles that accompany standard **Customer Relationship Management** (**CRM**) when a new Salesforce organization is taken. A standard profile cannot be deleted.
- **Custom**: These are the profiles that are created by cloning the Salesforce standard profiles.

The significant differences among standard and custom profiles depend on permissions and settings, administrative permissions, general user permissions, object-level permissions, and so on. The Password Never Expires setting can never be applied to the standard profile. A custom profile cannot be deleted when users are not assigned to it.

Standard profiles

The Salesforce platform include a set of standard profiles. Some examples are as follows:

- Read-only
- Standard user
- Marketing user
- System administrator

Every standard profile incorporates a default set of permissions for the standard objects accessible on the platform. For instance, a standard user can create and edit records, while a read-only user can view records but not make or edit them. The system administrator profile has the most extensive access to data and the best capacity to configure Salesforce. The system administrator profile additionally incorporates two special permissions, for example, **View All Data** and **Modify All Data**. These permissions abrogate all other sharing settings on the Org. The list of all standard and custom profiles can be viewed in **Setup**.

The object permissions on a standard profile cannot be edited. However, it can be cloned for a new profile. For instance, in the RecruitForce app, it may be necessary to create three new profiles-recruiters, interviewers, and hiring managers. Each profile can be configured to provide the specific type of data accessibility required for a particular role. The permissions sets can be utilized to grant additional permissions required.

Managing profiles

The profile overview page provides an entry point for all of the settings and permissions for all profiles:

- **Viewing profiles**: The following steps will help you view all listed profiles in the Org:

    1. Click on the gear icon ⚙ at the top of the page and launch **Setup**.

    2. Use the Quick Find box to find Profiles, then select **Profiles**:

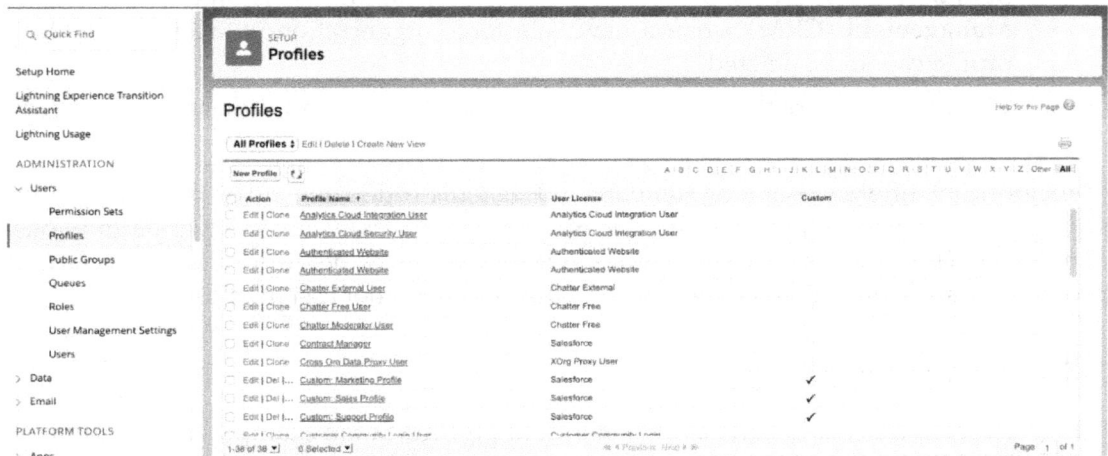

Figure 10.7: Managing profiles

- **Creating a profile**: The easiest way to create a profile is to clone an existing profile and then edit it.

    Salesforce has an upgraded profile UI that makes it simpler to discover a profile and change its settings. Perform the following steps to enable it:

    1. Click on the gear icon ⚙ at the top of the page and launch **Setup**.

    2. Use the Quick Find box to find **User Management Settings**.

    3. Enable **Enhanced Profile User Interface**, as shown in the following figure:

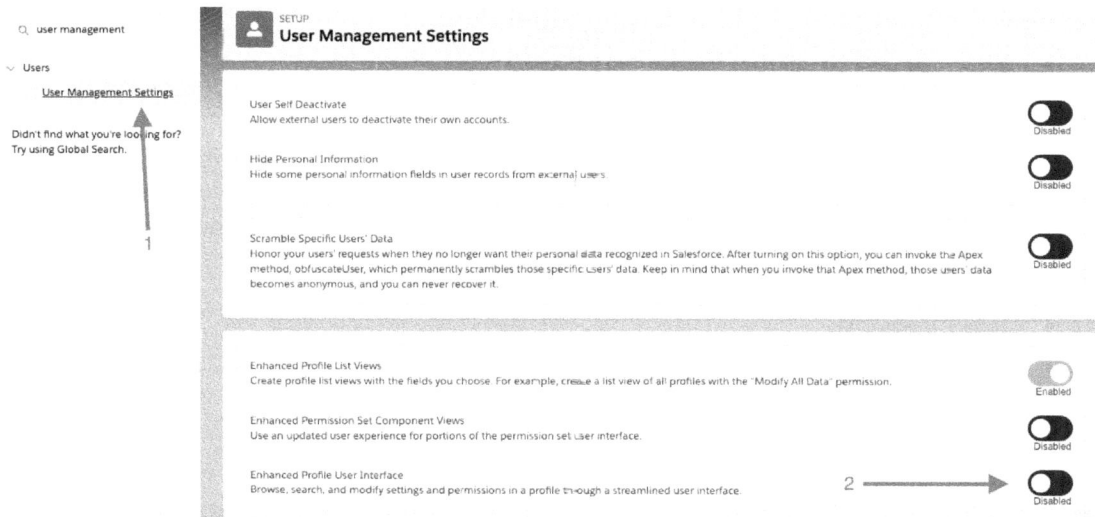

Figure 10.8: *Creating profile*

4. In Setup, in the Quick Find box, search for Profiles and select **Profiles**.

5. Click on **Clone** next to a profile similar to the one you want to create.

6. Give a name to the new profile.

7. Click on **Save** once it is done.

- **Assigning a profile**: Once the profile is created, it can be assigned to the users.

    1. Find users in the Quick Find box in Setup.

    2. Select a user to whom profile to be assigned and click on **Edit** next to it.

    3. From the Profile drop-down, select the profile you just set up and save.

Permission sets

A permission set is an assortment of permissions and settings that give users access to different functions. The permissions sets expand users' useful access without changing their profiles.

Salesforce grants to assign only one profile to a user. Anyway, sometimes, it is required to allot more than one profile to users subject to the business requirements. Through the permission set, a group of settings and permissions can be allowed to the users that allows them to get to various applications and functions, notwithstanding the profile.

Permission sets make it simple for administrators to concede access to the different applications and custom objects in the organization, and to remove access when it is no more required.

Users can have just one profile and yet have multiple different sets.

Permission sets are used for the following two purposes:
- Grant access to applications or custom objects.
- Grant permissions to particular fields.

If a user has permission in their base profile, it cannot be removed by assigning a permission set to that user. Permission can simply incorporate permission. To remove a permission, it must be removed from the user's base profile, and any permission sets the user may have.

The following settings are available under permission sets:
- Assigned apps
- Object settings
- Tab settings
- Record type settings
- App permissions

Managing permission sets

The starting point for the permissions in a permission set is the permission set's overview page. Follow these steps to open a permission set overview page:

1. Click on the gear icon ⚙ at the top of the page and launch Setup.
2. Use the Quick Find box to find permission sets.
3. Select the permission set to view.

Permissions and settings are organized into system settings, application settings, object permissions, and field permissions in every permission set. There are two permissions.

- **Custom permission**: In this case, permission can be granted to access custom processes and apps to users.
- **System permissions**: In this case, permissions can be defined to perform actions that apply to apps, such as Password Never Expires.

Creating a permission set

To grant additional permissions to a particular user above its profile, create a permission set. With this activity, there is no need to modify the existing profile or create a new profile.

To create a permission set, perform the following steps:

1. Click on the gear icon ⚙ at the top of the page and launch Setup.
2. Use the Quick Find box to find permission sets.
3. Click on **Clone** next to the permission set you to want to copy (Else a new permission set can be created).
4. Enter a label and a description.

5. If this is a new permission set, select a user license option:

   a. Select – **None**- if you want to assign this permission set to multiple users with different licenses.

   b. Select the user license, if only users with one type of license will use this permission set, select that user license:

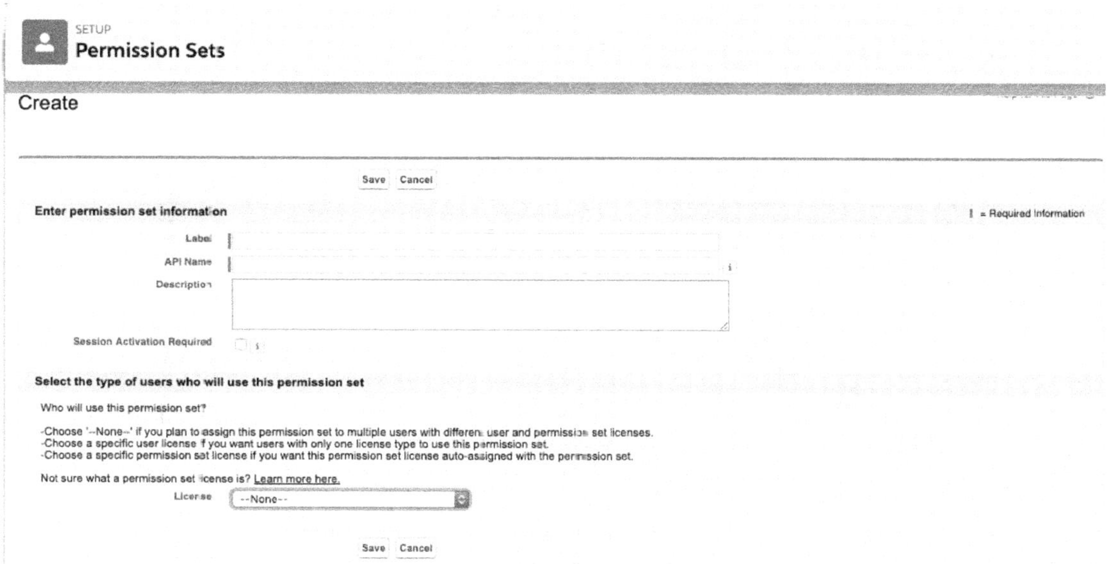

SETUP
Permission Sets

Create

Save   Cancel

Enter permission set information | = Required Information

Label
API Name
Description

Session Activation Required

Select the type of users who will use this permission set

Who will use this permission set?

-Choose '--None--' if you plan to assign this permission set to multiple users with different user and permission set licenses.
-Choose a specific user license if you want users with only one license type to use this permission set.
-Choose a specific permission set license if you want this permission set license auto-assigned with the permission set.

Not sure what a permission set license is? Learn more here.

License   [--None--]

Save   Cancel

Figure 10.9: Permission sets

6. Click on **Save** once it is done. This will take you to the permission set overview page.

7. In the permission set toolbar, click on **Manage Assignments**, then click on **Add Assignments**.

8. Select the users to assign to this permission set and click on **Assign**.

9. Review the messages on the Assignment Summary page. If any user was not assigned, the Message column tells you why.

10. Click on **Done** to return to a list of the users assigned to the permission set.

Field-level security

In the wake of controlling object-level access, characterizing field-level security for sensitive fields is the second level security that can be allotted. Occasionally, it is required to access an object; however, you must limit their access to individual fields of that object.

The field-level security settings control whether a user can see, alter, and delete the value for a particular field on an article. These settings permit to ensure sensitive fields without hiding the object.

Page layouts simply control the visibility of fields on detail and edit pages. Yet, the field-level security controls the visibility of fields in any piece of the application, including list view, related lists, search result, and reports.

Field settings can be applied in the following three different ways:

- Modifying object
- Modifying profile
- Modifying Field Accessibility

Field access by modifying object

Let us assume that there is a need to have a process created to auto-set the rating for lead objects based on a few fields. For this, we need to set the Rating field on the Lead object to be read-only for all users.

Perform the following steps to achieve this:

1. Click on the gear icon ✿ at the top of the page and launch Setup.
2. In **Object Manager** and choose **Lead**.
3. From **Detail** section, choose **Fields & Relationships**.
4. Click on the **Rating** field.
5. The next step is to click on the **Set Field-Level Security** button:

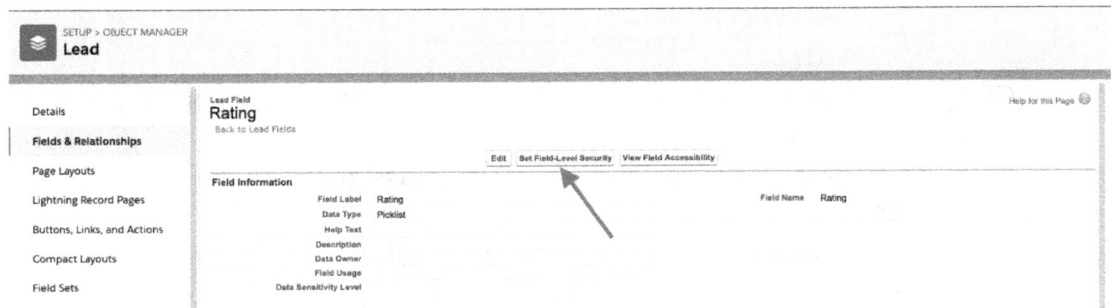

Figure 10.10: Field level security

It will redirect you to a new page where you can set the field-level security through the following steps:

1. Select **Visible** and **Read-Only** for all profiles other than that of the System Administrator. For **System Administrator**, select only **Visible**, as shown in the following figure:

Field-Level Security for Profile	☑ Visible	☑ Read-Only
Analytics Cloud Integration User	☑	☑
Analytics Cloud Security User	☑	☑
Contract Manager	☑	☑
Custom: Marketing Profile	☑	☑
Custom: Sales Profile	☑	☑
Custom: Support Profile	☑	☑
Gold Partner User	☑	☑
Marketing User	☑	☑
Partner Community Login User	☑	☑
Partner Community User	☑	☑
Read Only	☑	☑
Recruiter Non-Technical	☑	☑
Recruiter Technical	☑	☑
Silver Partner User	☑	☑
Solution Manager	☑	☑
Standard User	☑	☑
System Administrator	☑	◯

Figure 10.11: Field level security to profiles

2. Click on **Save** once it is done.

Restrict field access by modifying the profile

The field-level setting can also be performed on the profile. Perform the following steps to solve the other business requirement using profile settings:

1. Click on the gear icon ⚙ at the top of the page and launch Setup.
2. Search for Profiles in the quick find box and select **Profiles**.
3. Select **System Administrator**.
4. Under the **Apps** section, click on **Object Settings**:

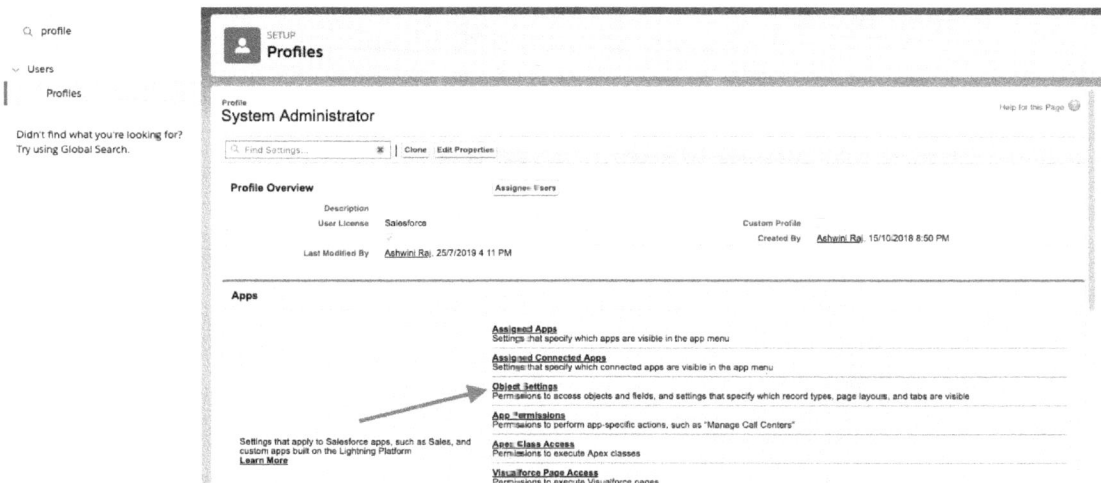

Figure 10.12: Managing field permission through app setting

5. Click on Leads from the list.

6. The next step is to click on **Edit** and navigate to the **Field Permission** section.

7. You can set the Field-Level Security for Lead object fields.

Restricting field access by modifying Field Accessibility

The following steps will help you solve the previous business requirement using Field Accessibility:

1. Click on the gear icon ⚙ at the top of the page and launch Setup.

2. Search for Field Accessibility in the quick find box. (Alternatively, you can follow path **Security | Field Accessibility**)

3. Click on **Lead** object.

This will redirect to a new page where you can select **View by Fields** or **View by Profiles**:

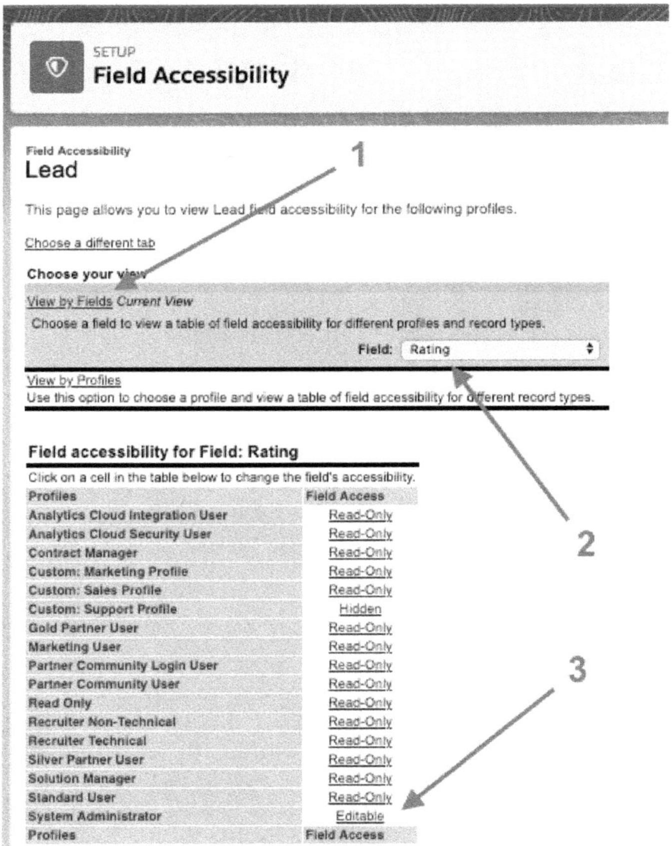

Figure 10.13: Field Accessibility

4. Select **View by Fields** in this case.

5. Select the field **Rating**.

6. Click on the editable link for System Administrator.

7. Now, the **Lead Settings** for **Lead Field** page will be opened. Here you can edit the field | level security.

8. Click on **Save** once it is done.

Control access to records

In Salesforce, mostly, beyond the access restriction for the objects and fields, it is required to restrict access to certain records of an object. This needs setting up of access restriction for a user based on the values in the records.

One of the features of Salesforce is the ownership of every record. Each record on the object has a field that denotes the ownership for the record. A user who needs access to this record turns out to be the part of the profile, which is the same as the profile of the owner of that record. Let us discuss the same in detail.

You can allow a specific set of users to view specific fields of a specific object, be that as it may, can similarly restrict the individual records they're allowed to view.

Record access to makes sense of which records can be viewed by users and which objects can be edited.

For example, you make a profile called Recruiter to give recruiters the object-level permissions. You need to confine them to delete recruiting-related objects. Allowing recruiters permission to make, read, or edit recruiting objects does not mean recruiters can read and edit each record in the recruiting object.

> **Note: The permissions on a record are assessed based on the combination of object-level, field-level, and record-level permissions.**
>
> **When object-level permissions conflict with record-level permissions, the most restrictive settings are applied.**

It infers that even a profile is allowed with create, read, and edit permissions on an object if the record-level permissions for an individual record are increasingly prohibitive. These are the guidelines that characterize what can be accessed.

The record-level access can be controlled in four distinct manners. They are mentioned in order of increasing access. The organization-wide defaults are utilized to secure the data to the most restrictive level and afterward utilize the other record-level security to grant access to chosen users:

- **Organization-wide defaults**: It is the default level of access any users can have in the organization.

- **Role hierarchies**: It ensures that the users at a higher level can access to the same records as their subordinates.
- **Sharing rules:** These are exceptions to OWDs for a particular group of users, to give them access to records that are nor owned by them.
- **Manual sharing**: It allows record owners to assign read and edit permissions to users who might not have access to the record:

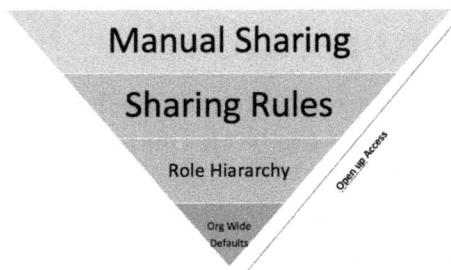

Figure 10.14: Control access records

Organization-wide sharing

OWD reflects the standard degree of access that the most restricted users should have. The OWD can be used to make sure about the data. Afterward, other record-level security and sharing tools (role hierarchies, sharing rules, and manual sharing) can be utilized to open up the data to users who need it.

The object permissions decide the baseline level for accessing the records of an object. OWD updates the permissions for the records that are not owned by users. Organization-wide sharing settings can be indicated independently for each object. OWD can never allow users more access than they have based on their object permission.

The following questions will help to determine the OWD needed for the app:

- Who is the most restricted user of the object?
- Is there going to be any situation that the user should not be allowed to view the object?
- Is there going to be any situation that the user should not be allowed to edit the object?

The following figure describes different types of **Organisation Wide Default (OWD)** accesses:

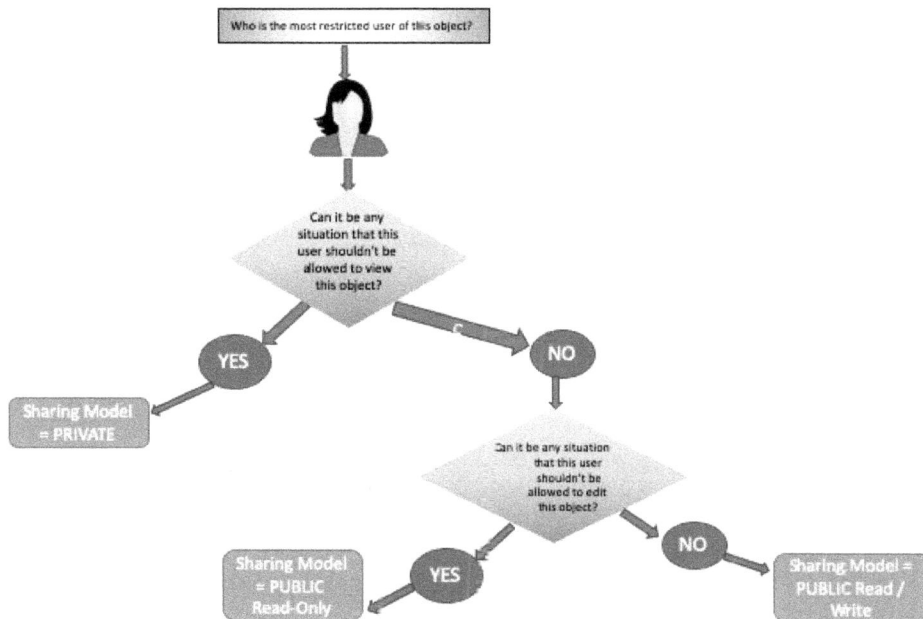

Figure 10.15: CWD accesses

The following table depicts the various types of OWD access available:

OWD access	Description
Private	The owner and the users above in the role hierarchy can view, edit, and report on the records.
Public Read Only	All users can view the records, but only the owner and the users above the role hierarchy can edit those.
Public Read/Write	All users can view, edit, and report on all records.
Public Read/Write/ Transfer	All users can view, edit, transfer, and report on all records. This is available only for the case and lead objects.
Controlled by Parent	The parent controls access to the child object's records.
Public Full Access	In this case, all users can view, edit, transfer, and report on all records. This is available for campaigns.

Table 10.2: OWD access

Setting your organization-wide sharing defaults

Use OWD to specify the baseline level of access that the most restricted user should have, through the following steps:

1. Click on the gear icon ⚙ at the top of the page and launch Setup.

2. Search for **Sharing Settings** in the quick find box. Alternatively, you can follow path **Security | Sharing Settings**:

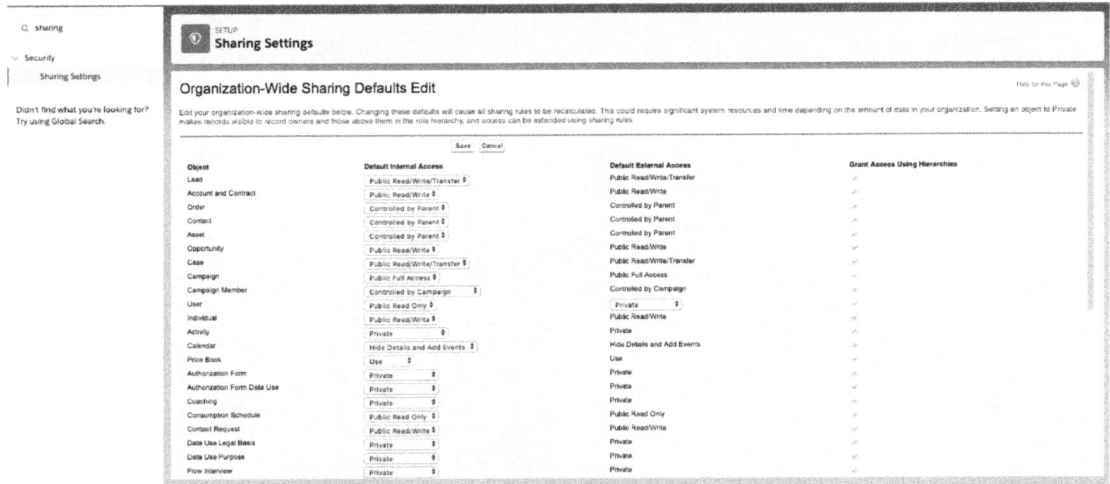

Figure 10.16: Default sharing in OWD

Click on **Edit** in the OWD area:

3. For each object, select the default access you want to give everyone.
4. To disable automatic access using the hierarchies, uncheck **Grant Access**.
5. Click on **Save** once it is done.

The role hierarchy consequently grants access to records for the users above the record owner in the role hierarchy through **Grant Access Using Hierarchies**. Making an object Private makes the records visible only to record owners and users above them in the role hierarchy. For standard objects, it is by default chosen, and for custom objects, it has to be selected explicitly.

Regardless of whether **Grant Access Using Hierarchies** is deselected, users with **View All** and **Modify All** object permissions and the **View All Data** and **Modify All Data** permissions can access records even not owned by them.

Role hierarchy

Salesforce allows you to control record access using roles. This means that you can utilize it to control record-level access in Salesforce. The roles may or may not be exactly aligned with the organization hierarchy. It is recommended that you make sure that each user is assigned a role when first added to the system.

A role hierarchy works with sharing settings to determine the levels of access users have to the Salesforce data. Users can access the data of all the users directly below them in the role hierarchy.

Users such as the **Chief Executive Officer (CEO)** and **Managing Director (MD)**, who need to view a lot of data, appear at the top of the role hierarchy.

Note that the role hierarchies not necessarily have to match the org chart.

Each role in the hierarchy just reflects a level of data access, which are described as follows:

- A manager can always access the data his or her employees own, regardless of the OWD settings.
- Users who need to access the same types of records can be grouped together:

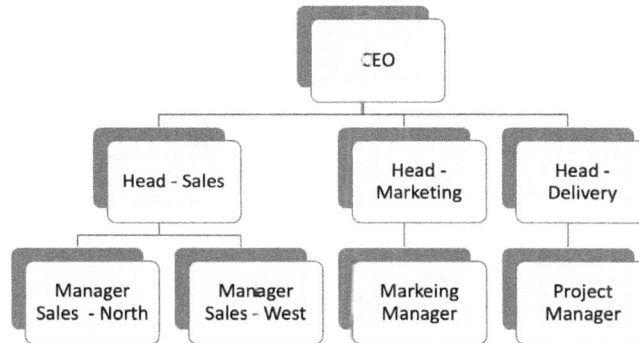

Figure 10.17: Example of role hierarchy

In the preceding image, the CEO can see all the organization records, as he is at the top of the role hierarchy. Similarly, the Sales Head and Marketing Head cannot see each other's records even though both are at the same level. While the Sales head can access the Sales Manager West and North records, the Marketing Head can access the marketing manager records. The Sales Manager West, Sales Manager North, and the Marketing Manager can see only their records as these roles are lower in the role hierarchy.

Depending on the sharing settings of the organization, roles can control the level of visibility of Salesforce data. Users at any role level can view, edit, and report the data owned by or shared with users below them in the role hierarchy.

Defining a role hierarchy

Creating a role hierarchy in Salesforce is very easy when you know what the hierarchy should look like. It is always a good practice to start with your company's organization chart and then consolidate different job titles into single roles wherever required.

Perform the following steps to create a role hierarchy:

1. Click on the gear icon ⚙ at the top of the page and launch **Setup**.
2. Search for **Roles** in the quick find box. (Alternatively, you can navigate to **Users | Roles**):

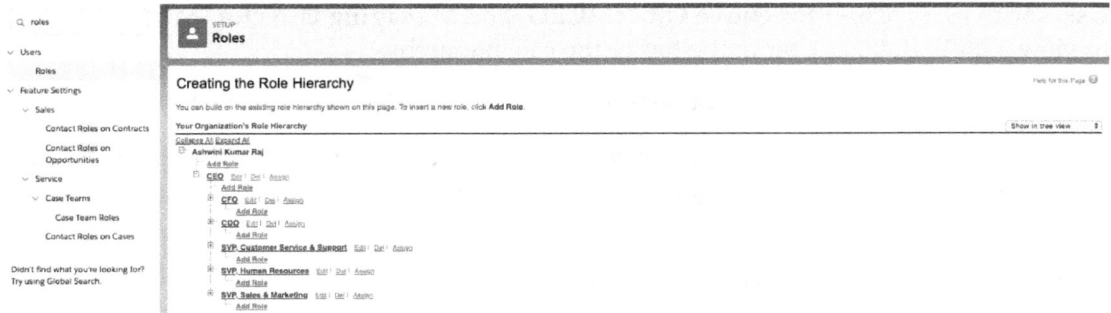

Figure 10.18: Defining role hierarchy

The default view for this page is the tree view, as mentioned in the drop-down list on the right side of the Role Hierarchy title bar.

When for the first time, a role hierarchy is defined, the tree view displays a single placeholder node with the name of the organization. From here, we need to add the name just under the company name. Click on **Add Role**. Perform the following steps to create the role hierarchy for your organization:

1. In the **Label** text box, enter the **CEO**.
2. The **Role Name** text box auto-populates with the CEO.
3. This role reports to the text box, click on the lookup icon 🔍 and click on **Select** next to the name of your org.

   With this step, we are indicating that the CEO role is a top-level position in the role hierarchy and does not report to anyone.
4. In the **Role Name** as displayed on the reports text box, enter the **CEO**.
5. Click on **Save** once it is done.

The next step is to assign an appropriate user to the role:

1. Click on **CEO**.
2. On the CEO role detail page, click on **Assign Users to Role**.

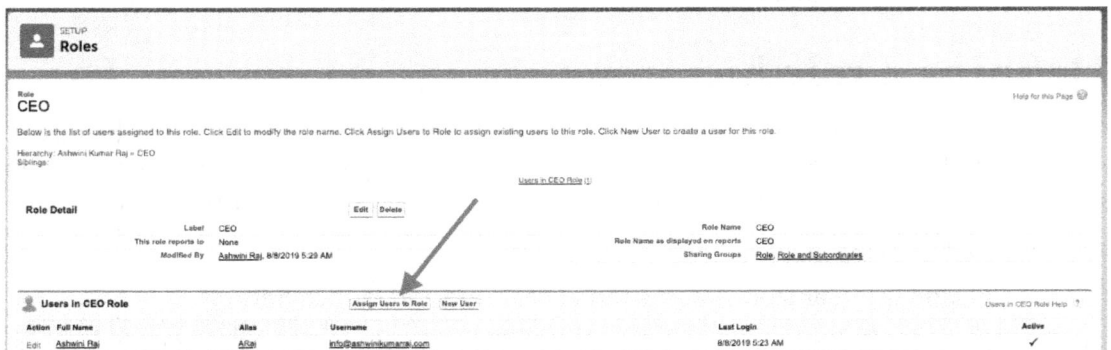

Figure 10.19: Assigning user to a role

3. In the **Available Users** drop-down list, select **All Unassigned**.

4. Choose a user from the list and click on **Add** to move her to the Selected Users for the CEO list, then save.

Through the preceding steps, you can create the rest of the roles and assign users to these.

Sharing rules

The OWD sharing settings provide a baseline level of access for every object. To open record-level access for a group of users, role sharing rules can be utilized. If the organization-wide sharing defaults of either Private or Public Read Only, you can open access back up for a few users with sharing rules. This enables creating automatic exceptions to the organization-wide sharing settings for some users.

Before deciding the sharing rules, ask the following questions to yourself:

- Which records to be shared?
- With which users to be shared?
- What kind of access to be shared?

Let us take the instance of the RecruitForce recruiting application; it is critical to share each position, candidate, job application, and review with each recruiter. Since recruiters are part of either the recruiting manager or recruiter roles in the hierarchy, a sharing rule can be utilized to share those objects to the recruiting manager role and its subordinates.

The following are sharing rules can be defined for RecruitForce recruiting application:

Object	Rule Label	Owned by	Share with	Access Level
Review	Edit Reviews	Entire Organization	Recruiters and Hiring Managers	Read/Write
Candidate	Edit Candidates	Entire Organization	The role and subordinates of the Recruiting Manager	Read/Write
Position	Edit Positions	The role and subordinates of the Recruiting Manager	The role and subordinates of the Recruiting Manager	Read/Write

Table 10.3: Sharing rule for objects

Salesforce has the following different types of sharing rules:

- **Criteria-based sharing rule**: This sharing rule is used to share the records based on the values of fields in the record. A maximum of 50 criteria-based sharing rules per object can be possible here.
- **Owner-based sharing rule**: This sharing rule is used to share the records based on the record owners.

- **Manual sharing**: In this case, a sharing button can be enabled when the OWD is set to Private or Public Read Only. Using this, the record owner, or users who are at a higher level in the role hierarchy, will be able to share records with other users.
- **Apex managed sharing**: In any complex business requirement scenario, to share the record access with users for a few hours or days only, Apex-managed sharing can be used.

Defining a public group

Before creating a sharing rule, it is important to set up the required public group. A public group is a collection of roles, users, groups that have a common function. For instance, users with the Recruiter profile and users in the Team Lead -Developer role both need to review job applications.

When defining a sharing rule, a public group makes the rule easier to create.

As per the mentioned example, we need to implement two objects that need a public group for their sharing rules: Job Application and Review. We can make these objects in a single group because of the Review object. Now, with this, it inherits the sharing settings applied to the Job Application object. Since both recruiters and hiring managers need to read and update permission to job applications and reviews, we need to create a public group called **Reviewers** that includes both recruiters and hiring managers.

You can refer to the following steps to do so:
1. Click on the gear icon ⚙ at the top of the page and launch **Setup**.
2. Search for Public Groups in quick find box. (Otherwise, you can navigate to **Users | Public Groups**)
3. Click on **New**.
4. Name the label as **Reviewers**.

The Group Name textbox, when clicked on it, populates automatically:
1. In the Search drop-down list, choose **Roles**.
2. In the **Available Members** list, select **SW Dev Manager**, **Director Product Management**, and **Director QA**.
3. Click on **Add**.
4. Again, in the Search drop-down list, choose **Role and Subordinates** this time.
5. In the **Available Members** list, select the **Recruiting Manager**, click on **Add**, and save.

Defining a sharing rule

A sharing rule can be characterized by a single public group, role, or role plus subordinates.

There is already one default public group that includes every user in your organization. To define a sharing rule, refer to the following steps:

1. Click on the gear icon ⚙ at the top of the page and launch **Setup**.
2. Search for **Sharing Settings** in quick find box. (Alternatively, you can navigate to **Security | Sharing Settings**).
3. Choose **Job Application** in the **Manage sharing** settings for the drop-down list.
4. In the **Job Application Sharing Rules** area, click on **New** and give your rule the label **Review Records**.
5. The **Rule Name** text box populates automatically when you click on it.
6. For the rule type, select the option based on record owner.
7. Select which records to be shared, select **Public Groups**, then choose **Entire Organization**.
8. Select users to share with, select **Public Groups**, then choose **Reviewers**.
9. Select the level of access for the users, select **Read/Write**.
10. Click on **Save** once it is done.

Viewing setup and audit trail

The **setup audit trail** feature of Salesforce helps you to track recent changes made to your organization closely. It records all updating concerning the administration, customization, security, sharing, data management, development, and so on, in the Salesforce org.

This is very useful for an organization that has multiple administrators.

You can check audit trail for the following types of changes:

- Administration
- Customization
- Security and Sharing
- Data management
- Development
- Using application

To view the audit history, perform the following steps:

1. Click on the gear icon ⚙ at the top of the page and launch Setup.
2. Search for **View Setup Audit Trail** in quick find box. (Alternatively, you can navigate to **Security | Public Groups**).
3. Click on **Download** to download the organization's full setup history for the past 180 days.

Note:

- After 180 days, setup entity records are deleted.
- The history shows the 20 most recent setup changes made to the org.

Conclusion

Cybercrimes are growing day by day, managing security for the organization is crucial. In this chapter, we covered the most important part of any organization – Security. To manage security for the organization, it is important to understand the rights security settings in salesforce. In this chapter we learnt that the administrator of the organization can activate various features such as authentication, monitoring tool, object, record and Field level security, and so on, can be enabled. We have also understood that control access to the organization can be configured through managing users, setting password policies, setting IP restrictions, creating role hierarchy, and so on. We have used setup audit trail which can be useful is keeping track of set up changes. In the next chapter, we will discuss Chatter – a collaboration tool.

Questions

1. **In the private sharing model, will a manager be able to edit account records owned by a user below them in the role hierarchy?**

    a. Only if 'Grant Access Using Hierarchies' setting is checked.

    b. Only if a sharing rule has been created.

    c. No, users on higher roles are only able to view records owned by users below them in the role hierarchy.

    d. Yes, access is granted by default to users in a higher role for standard objects.

2. **Which of the following are organizational-level security access controls? Choose 3 answers.**

    a. Permission sets

    b. Trusted IP range

    c. Password policies

    d. Two-Factor Authentications

    e. Platform encryption

3. **Raj is being moved from a service support role to a sales role in the same company. What changes would a Salesforce Administrator do to ensure Harold's user account would have the necessary permissions? Would he be able to view the information required for his new role in his new department? Choose 2 options.**

a. Use an old sales user record and replace the details with Raj's information.

b. Change the profile in the user settings.

c. Change the role in the user settings.

d. Create a new user record for Raj.

4. **What do profiles control access to? Choose 3 answers.**

a. Whether a user can manually share records.

b. Which Record Types are available to users.

c. Whether the user can see data of other users.

d. Which Apes classes and Visualforce pages users can access.

e. Which fields are ready only.

5. **What feature can a Salesforce Administrator use to control record sharing? Choose 3 answers.**

a. Sharing Rules

b. Role Hierarchy

c. Organization-wide default settings

d. Permission sets

e. Profiles

6. **Raj and Saif are Sales users and share the same custom profiles. The sales profile allows create and edit contacts but not delete. The sales manager would like Saif to be able to create and edit contact records. However, Raj should also be able to delete contacts. How can the administrator configure this most efficiently?**

a. Two sales cannot have different permissions on the Contact object.

b. Create a permission set and assign it to the users accordingly.

c. Create a new custom profile for Raj.

d. Set up the role hierarchy to meet this requirement.

7. **An administrator is setting up a new organization for a company with over 300 employees that will require setup of several roles and profiles. Which statement regarding profiles and roles is correct?**

a. A profile controls what records a user can see in the application..

b. The profile hierarchy determines record access in a read-only sharing model

c. The role hierarchy determines record access in a private data sharing model.

d. A role determines what parts of the application the user can access.

8. **What gives access for users higher in the hierarchy to all records owned by users below them in the hierarchy?**

    a. Role Hierarchy

    b. Sharing rules

    c. OWDs

    d. Manual sharing

9. **In a private sharing model, if the administrator needs to make some exceptions to give access to records, what features can you use?**

    a. Accsounts Team

    b. Manual Sharing

    c. Sharing Exception Rules

    d. Sharing Rules

10. **Find out which is/are true statements?**

    a. The permissions on a record are evaluated according to a combination of object-level, field-level, and record-level permissions.

    b. When object-level permissions conflict with record-level permissions, the most restrictive settings are considered.

    c. Record access determines which users can view records and which objects can be edited.

    d. Both a and b

    e. All of the above

Answers

1. d
2. b, c, d
3. b, c
4. b, d, e
5. a, b, c
6. b
7. c
8. a
9. a, b, d
10. e

## CHAPTER 11

Introducing Chatter for Collaboration

Introduction

In this chapter, we will learn about Chatter in Salesforce as a great tool to provide the functionality to collaborate with many people in the organization. By using Chatter, one can easily connect with their co-workers and share the required information accordingly. We learn how Chatter helps to securely connect, collaborate, and share files, data, and expertise in real-time. It is easy to create groups like sales groups or operation groups to connect with your co-workers by inviting them, and one can also share comments and images with others' feeds.

Structure

In this chapter, we will discuss the following topics:

- Enabling Chatter
- Working with Post
- Using a poll
- Using a question
- Introduction groups
- Enabling Chatter e-mail notifications

Objectives

After studying this unit, you will learn how to enable Chatter in your Salesforce org. You will be able to create, share, and edit a post. You will learn to create a poll, use questions and group. You will also learn how to enble email notifications too.

Enabling Chatter

By default, the Chatter header is enabled in Salesforce org. To make sure, follow the following steps:

- Go to Setup.
- Search for **Chatter** and select **Chatter Settings**.
- Make sure to **Enable** the **Turn on Chatter** and **Global Search** features. We have given you a head start—your users may auto-follow a few people or records by default and your search box is in the header:

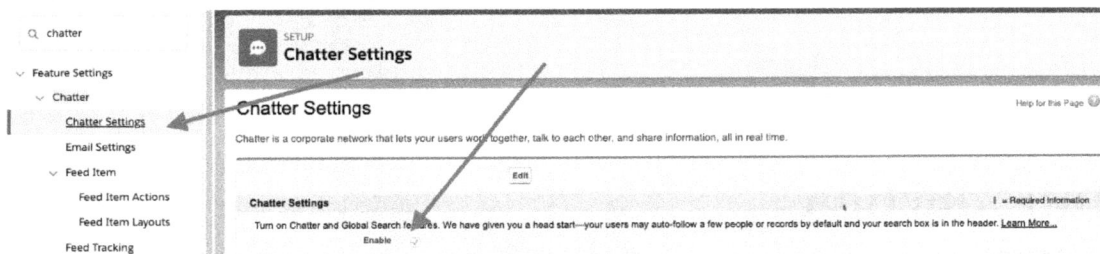

Figure 11.1: Enabling Chatter

Working with a post

The most useful feature of Chatter is probably the publisher. It can be used to add content to any Chatter feed. With a Post, the required data can be shared. You also tag a person and reply to a post.

Creating a post

Perform the following steps to add a post:

1. Click on the **Chatter** tab.
2. Select **Post**.
3. Type the required information to be shared.
4. Use the rich text editor to do the following:
   a. Add styles, lists, images, links, code snippets, emojis, and mentions to the post.

    b. Link to a record, like an Account, Opportunity, Case—even another user with the link-to-records feature.

    c. Attach up to ten files to a post or question, by using the paperclip icon.

    d. Add searchable terms with HashTag (#).

5. Click on **Share** once done, as shown in the following figure:

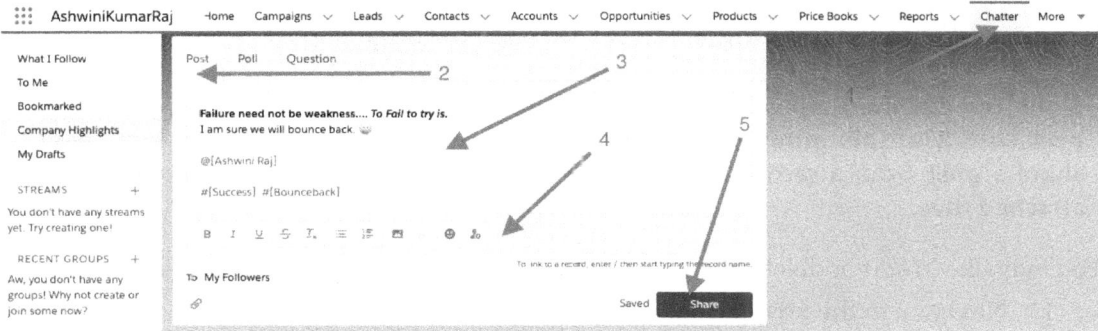

Figure 11.2: Creating a post and tagging a perosn

When a post is added to your profile feed, anyone who has access to your profile can see your post, and your followers are notified about your activity.

Sharing a post

A post can be shared from the post itself. You can refer to the following steps to share a post:

1. Go to the Chatter post and click on the **Share** icon ⤴ Share to share the post:

    a. Select **Share with Group** to share the post with a group.

    b. Select **Share with Followers** to share the post on your profile page so that your followers can see it.

    c. Select **Copy Link** to copy a link:

Figure 11.3: Sharing with group or followers

2. In the editor, you can add the remarks you want to publish with the shared post.

3. Click on **Share**.

In case you have shared the post with your followers, the added remarks, along with the original post, are posted to your profile. These also appear in What I follow feed. The users with access to your profile will be able to see the shared post in your profile page. However, only the people who follow you are notified about the post.

In case you have shared in a group, the added remarks, along with the original post, are posted to the specified group.

You can click on the **View Original Post** link to see the original post.

> **Note: You can share a post with all your followers and a group. However, you cannot post with Multiple groups in one action. You can comment on a post. You cannot share a post from a record feed and cannot share the original posts comments or attached files.**

You may like to edit or delete or even put a bookmark to a post. Follow the following steps:

1.   Navigate to the post.
2.   Click on its Actions menu icon ▾ , as shown in the following figure:

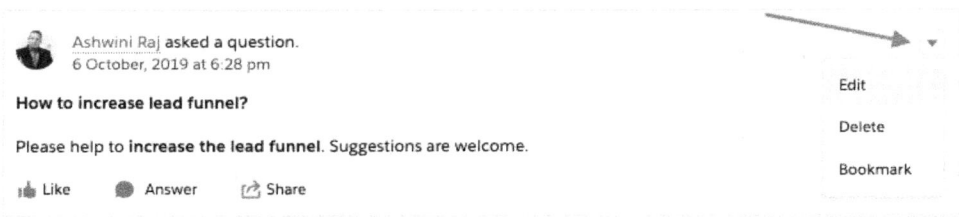

Figure 11.4: Editig the post

3.   Select **Edit**, **Delete** or **Bookmark** as required.

You may like to follow people, groups, and even records. The people and things that you follow have their feeds. You will get notifications about the feed activity when you follow the feed in the form of an e-mail and through in-app notifications.

> **Note: You can follow up to 500 people and things. You follow a few things by default, like your manager and team, and so on.**

You can also follow someone from their profile page or follow a record from its home page, as shown in the following figure:

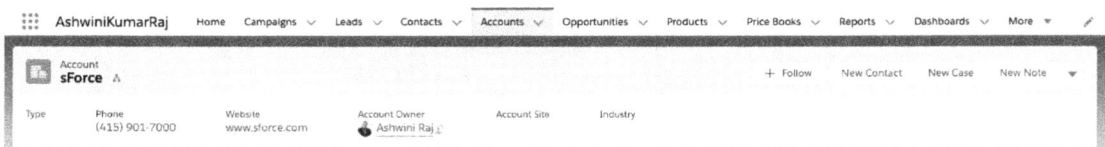

Figure 11.5: Following someone

Mentioning an individual or a group

To mention someone, enter the @ symbol and mention the name. A list of suggested matches opens, and you choose a name from the list:

Figure 11.6: Mentioning a person or a group

The group also can be mentioned through an @ symbol. Group mentions are a good way to share relevant information (in the form of a post) from one feed to another.

If a few group members do not have access to the mentioned group, they cannot see the shared content in their group feed.

The records can be linked in your posts using a similar mechanism. Instead of the @ symbol, enter a forward slash (/) and type the record name. A selection of matching records will pop up:

Figure 11.7: Tagging a group

Using a poll

Chatter offers a feature called poll for gathering opinions from the users. When a poll is created, anyone who has access to your profile can see and participate in the poll.

To access poll follow the following steps:

1. Select **Poll** on the **Chatter** tab.

2. In the **Question** field, enter the poll to be conducted.

3. Enter the options to be provided for the poll. Click **Add new choice** if required.

4. To publish your poll, click on **Ask**:

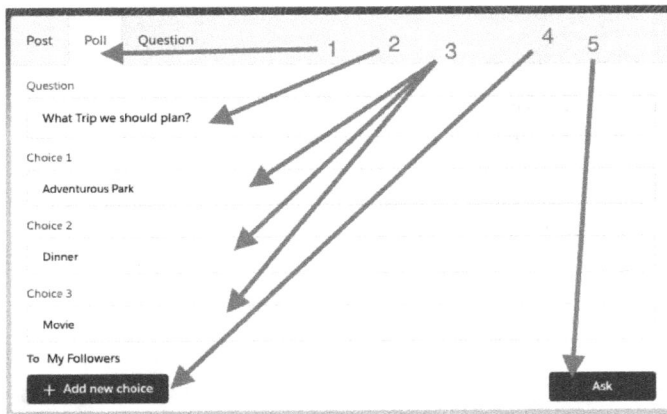

Figure 11.8: Using poll

To participate in the poll, choose an option, and click on **Vote**. After the vote, the current results are shown. On clicking **View Result**, you can see how the vote is going.

Using a question

Using a question is the best way to appeal to the group of people to get the right answer. You can just post the question and optionally add details as well. It can be formatted as per your wish. You can perform the following steps to add a question:

1. On **Chatter** tab, click on **Question**.

2. Enter the **Question** the question to be asked.

3. Enter the details about the question:

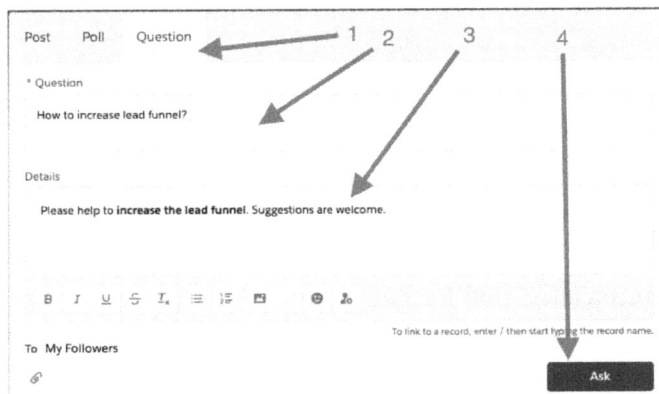

Figure 11.9: Using question

4. Click on **Ask** once done.

Now, the question is ready to be answered by anyone with access to the feed.

Like polls, your followers can access the answer questions that you posted to your profile page or the Chatter tab. The visibility of the best answer can be raised by selecting it as best. The best answer is marked to the top of all answers.

Introducing groups

Group is one of the important collaboration mechanism in Chatter.

You can organize a group around a department or project and add all relevant user participants to it. Groups help users to build and share the knowledge that is important to getting the job done and keeping everyone aligned.

Members of the group use the group feed to exchange information, make a decision, and ask doubts (in the form of question) and answer the questions.

Type of groups

Salesforce provides the following four different group types for different purposes:

- **Public groups**: These are visible to all employees. Anyone in the company can join a public group, and then post, comment to it.
- **Private groups**: These are visible to members only. Users must request to join a private group and become member of the group. Only the members of the group can post comments. Users who are not members of the group can see the group's picture and description, but not the group feeds.
- **Unlisted groups**: These allow invitation-only, and the members do not appear in list views or search results. The unlisted group is hidden from everyone except the members of the group. Only the group's owner and managers can invite users to join an unlisted group.
- **Broadcast only**: These groups are used for making announcements. Only the owner and managers of this group can post to it. Group members can comment on those posts.

Creating groups

To create a group, you can refer to the following steps:

1. Click on the **Groups** tab. Alternatively, if you don't see it, open the App Launcher, search for Groups, and click on it.
2. Click on **New** to open the new group window, as shown in the following figure:

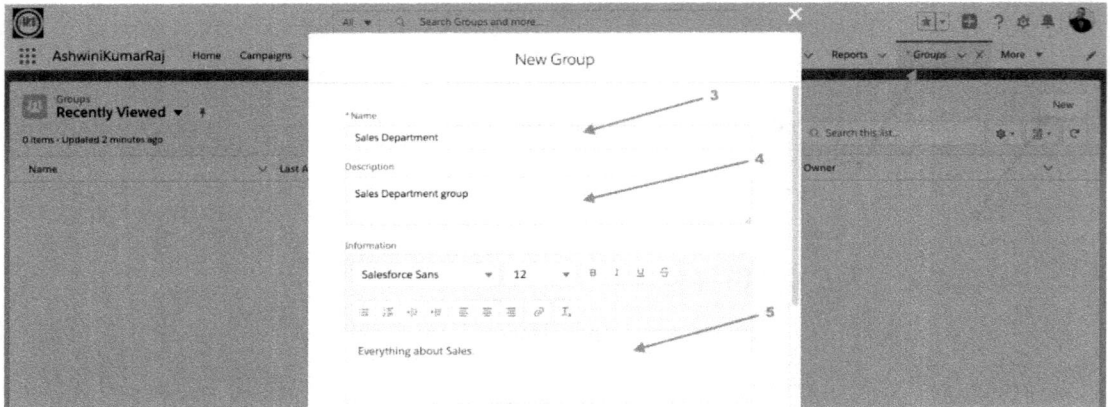

Figure 11.10: Creating group

3. Enter information about your group:

    a. **Name**: Enter the name of group. In this case, Sales Department.

    b. **Description**: Describe the group.

    c. **Information**: Provide the group details that you want to share, and format your details using rich text editor controls.

    d. **Access Type**: Public:

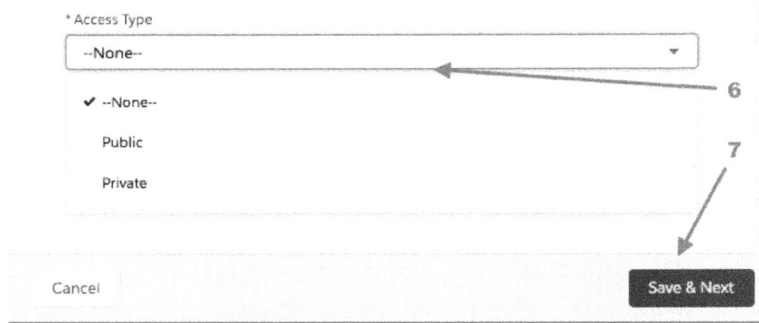

Figure 11.11: Selecting access type

4. Click on **Save & Next**.

5. Upload the image of the group you want to and click on **Next**:

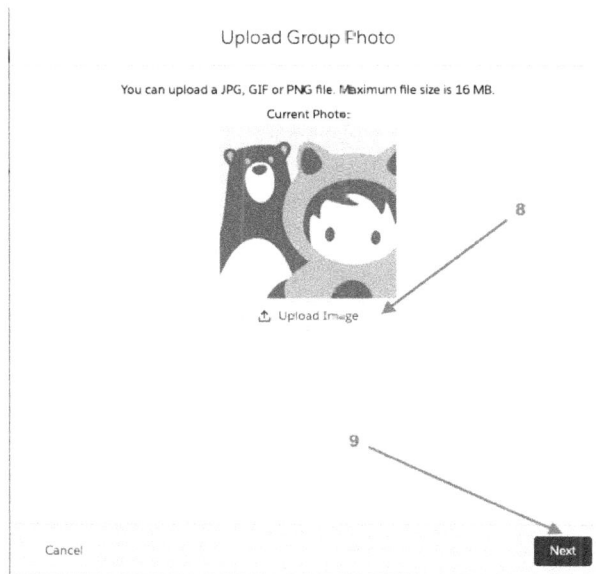

Figure 11.12: Uploading image

6. Add the members into the group by clicking on the **Add** button near the user:

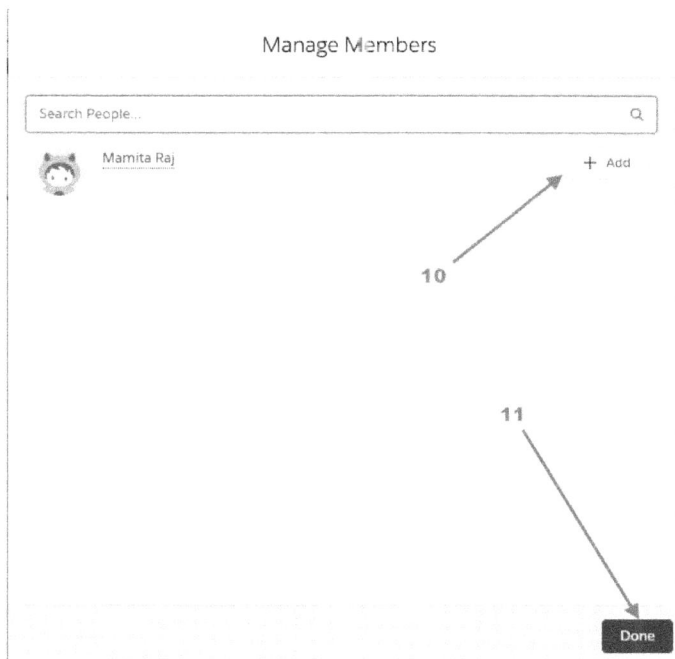

Figure 11.13: Managing members

7. Click on **Done** once it is done.

Your group is created. The group will be displayed as follows:

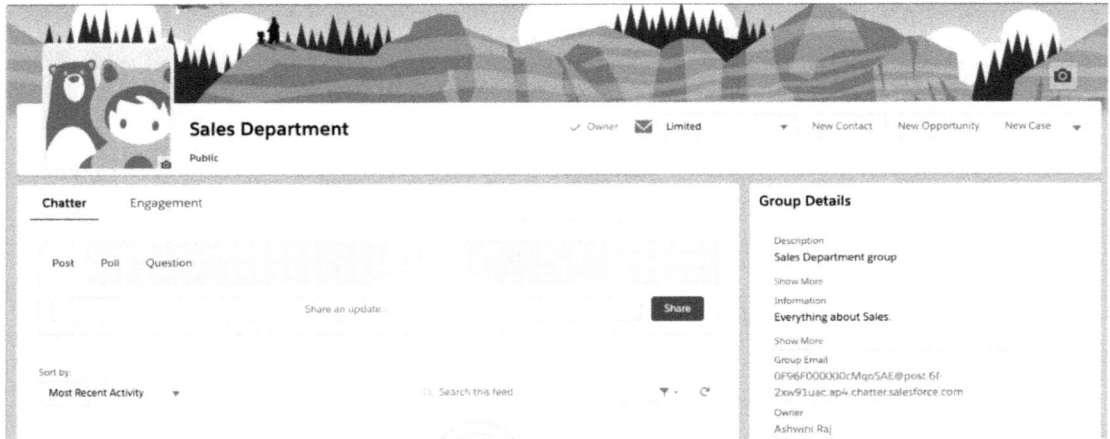

Figure 11.14: Viewing a group

Similarly, a private group can be created.

Enabling unlisted groups

By default, the unlisted group is not enabled in Salesforce. To enable the unlisted group, follow these steps:

1. Enter **Chatter Settings** in the Quick Find box in Setup and click on **Chatter Settings**:

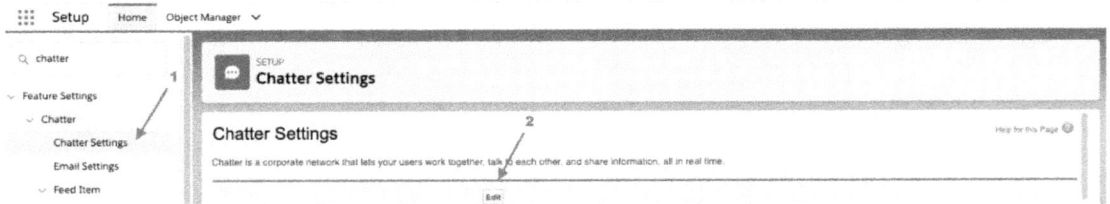

Figure 11.15: Enabling unlisted group

2. Click on **Edit**.

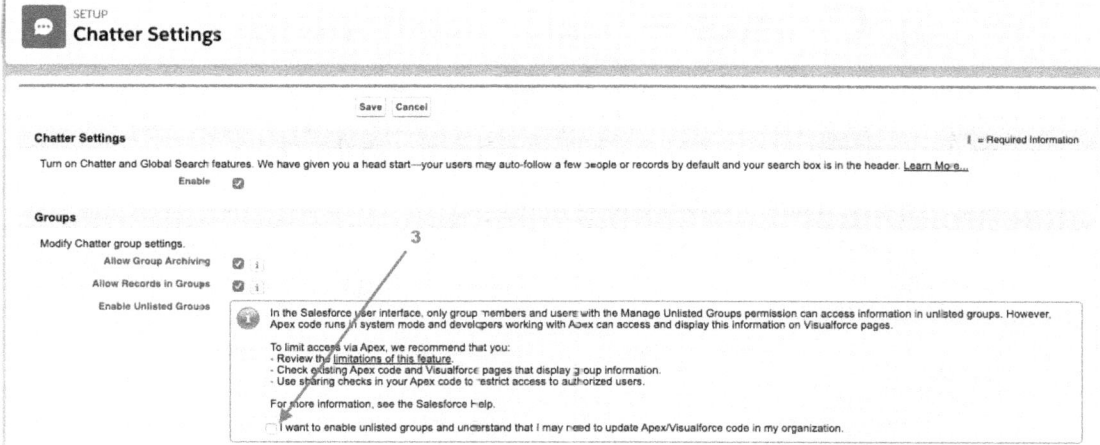

Figure 11.16: Editing Chatter setting

3. Check **I want to enable unlisted groups and understand that I may need to update Apex/Visualforce code in my organization** to enable it.

4. Click on **Save** once it is done.

Monitor engagement

To monitor the group membership and activity, the group offers the **Engagement** tab. The following figure shows Membership

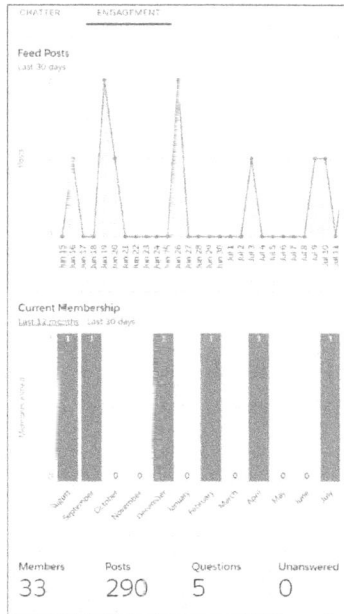

Figure 11.17: Monitoring engagement

Enabling Chatter e-mail notifications

When the e-mail notifications for Chatter is enabled, the users receive e-mail notifications about new posts, comments, and other changes. The users can keep the default notifications that are set up, or they can override the default settings with their own.

Follow these steps to enable Chatter e-mail notifications:

1. Search e-mail settings in the set up Quick Find box and select **Email Settings**. Alternatively, you can follow the path **Feature Settings** | **Chatter** | **Email Settings** as shown in the following figure:

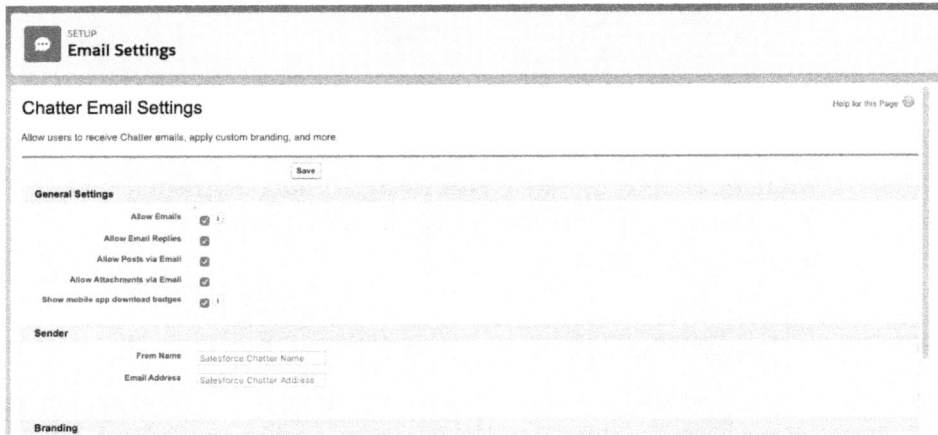

Figure 11.18: Enabling e-mail notification

2. Select the following:

    a. **Allow Emails**: It turns on the Chatter e-mail notifications for all your users.

    b. **Allow Email Replies**: It allows users to post their replies to e-mail notifications in Chatter.

    c. **Allow Posts via Email**: It allows users to post to groups through e-mail.

    d. **Allow Attachments via Email**: It allows users to include attachments when they use e-mail to post to a group.

    e. **Show mobile app download badges**: It adds App Store and Google Play badges for the Salesforce app to all Chatter email notifications from the internal org.

3. Under **Sender**, fill the name and email address for your org's Chatter e-mail account.

4. Under Branding, upload the image, for example, company logo (150 x 150 pixels or less), and a footer that contains your company address.

5. Click on **Save** once it is done.

Conclusion

In this chapter, we covered the Chatter collaboration tool in Salesforce. Chatter helps to securely connect, collaborate, share files, and data in real-time. We learned that you can create posts, questions, and polls. Different types of groups such as public, private, unlisted groups can be created to share data. You can also monitor the group through engagement. The e-mail notifications for Chatter can be enabled to receive e-mail notifications about new posts, comments, and other changes.

In the next chapter, we will learn mobile administration.

Questions

1. **Which of the following are features included in Chatter? Choose 3 answers.**

   a. Selected record data can be added to posts automatically.

   b. Posts can be shared to your Chatter profile or groups that you are a member of.

   c. Topics can be selected and added to a post.

   d. A Poll can be used within a Chatter post.

2. **What is true regarding editing Feed Posts and Comments? Choose 2 options.**

   a. Record owners can always edit any post on records they own.

   b. The ability for users to edit their feed post is enabled by default.

   c. The edit option is not available on posts with file attachments.

   d. Administrators can edit any posts.

3. **After a question has been asked in Chatter Questions, the best answer can be selected. What is true regarding the best answer? Choose 2 answers.**

   a. Only one answer can be selected as the best answer.

   b. A copy of the best answer appears at the top the list of answers with a checkmark.

   c. Once set the best answer cannot be changed.

   d. Only the person that asked the question can select the best answer.

4. **A user would like to send a question as a private message to another user in Salesforce. Which of the following locations can be used to start a message and send it to the user? Choose 2 answers.**

   a. Home Tab

   b. Receiver's profile

   c. Sender's profile

   d. Chatter tab

5. **A user would no longer like to receive updates about a certain post in his feed. What feature should he use?**

   a. Hide post

   b. Mute post

   c. Unsubscribe post

   d. Remove post

Answers

1. b, c, d
2. b, d
3. a, b
4. b, d
5. b

Join our Discord space

Join our Discord workspace for latest updates, offers, tech happenings around the world, new releases, and sessions with the authors:

https://discord.bpbonline.com

CHAPTER 12
Introducing Mobile Administration

Introduction

We are in the middle of a mobile upheaval. Mobile use is at an untouched high. A large portion of us invest as much time in our mobile devices as we do before our PCs. Portable innovation has changed how we live, learn, shop, and remain associated. According to an ongoing study, consumers spend around 4 four hours per day on their phone.

In this chapter, we will learn about Salesforce's mobile application, which takes profitability, personalization, and speed to the next level. Salesforce has carried the intensity of Lightning to the Salesforce mobile application. Consistently, nearly 2 million users maintain their business from their mobile utilizing the Salesforce mobile application.

Mobile administration is one of the important jobs of a Salesforce administrator.

Structure

In this chapter, we will discuss the following topics:

- Salesforce mobile application
- Overview of the Salesforce Authenticator application
- Overview of the Salesforce mobile application

Objectives

After studying this unit, you should be able to learn about the Saleforce mobile application and its features. You will also learn to install and log in to the Salesforce mobile application. You will learn about the Salesforce Authenticator application and how to enable offline access for the mobile application.

Salesforce mobile application

The Salesforce application is an enterprise-class mobile application that furnishes users with instant access to the organization's CRM data from a mobile or tablet. The following are scarcely any advantages of the Salesforce mobile app:

- **Incorporated with each Salesforce license:** It is free with each license of Salesforce.
- **Cross-platform:** It runs on both Android and iOS platforms.
- **Plug-and-play:** It does not require any set up to be done. The users simply need to download it from the Play Store or App Store and begin using it.
- **Offline abilities**: Cell signals will not influence mobile users.
- **Not only an application but also a platform**: The Salesforce platform fuels the application. So, it is exceptionally customizable.

A SalesforceA mobile application accompanies different features. The following are the activities that a Salesforce admin can perform through the SalesforceA mobile application:

- Get the present status of the system
- Create another user
- Edit a user account
- Reset password of a user
- Check login history of the users
- Unlock or deactivate user account
- Add and delete permissions
- Reassigning licenses to the users

Installing the Salesforce mobile application

SalesforceA mobile application can be downloaded from the Play Store or App Store. The following devices support it:

- Android phone or tablet with OS 4.4 or higher
- Apple iPhone, iPad, and iPod Touch with iOS 8.0 or higher

Logging in to the Salesforce mobile application

Follow the following steps to login into the SalesforceA mobile application:

1. Click on the Salesforce mobile app icon on your device.
2. Enter your login credentials and verification code.
3. Allow the Salesforce application to access your Salesforce basic information.
4. Enter the Passcode.

It will redirect to the application home page.

Now, start administrating your Salesforce organization on the go.

Overview of the Salesforce Authenticator application

The Salesforce Authenticator application allows us to generate a time-based token. It helps to implement two-factor authentications for your account.

Installing the Salesforce Authenticator mobile application

The Salesforce Authenticator mobile application can be downloaded from the Play Store or Appstore. It is supported by the following devices:

- Android phone or tablet with OS 4.2 or higher
- Apple iPhone and iPod Touch with iOS 7.0 or higher

Overview of the Salesforce mobile application

Salesforce1 is a mobile application for users to access, create, update, and delete records from anywhere. It also allows users to view reports and Dashboards.

Features of the Salesforce mobile application

There are many features of the Salesforce1 mobile application. A few features are as follows:

- Send push notifications.
- Submit a record for approval.
- Get insights into accounts and opportunities.

- Access a list view and related list.
- Access custom objects and apps through the navigation menu.
- Access reports, Dashboards, and charts.
- Access Visualforce pages and components in the navigation menu.
- Access Salesforce files.

Installing the Salesforce mobile application

You can download the Salesforce1 mobile application from the App Store or Play Store. The following devices support it:

- Android phone or tablet with OS 4.4 or higher
- Apple iPhone and iPod Touch with iOS 9.2 or higher

Enabling Salesforce for a mobile browser

Perform the following steps to enable Salesforce1 for a mobile browser:

1. Click the gear icon ⚙ at the top of the page and launch Setup.
2. Search for apps and then follow the path **Apps** | **Mobile Apps** | **Salesforce** | **Salesforce Settings**.
3. Select the **Enable the Salesforce1 mobile browser** app checkbox:

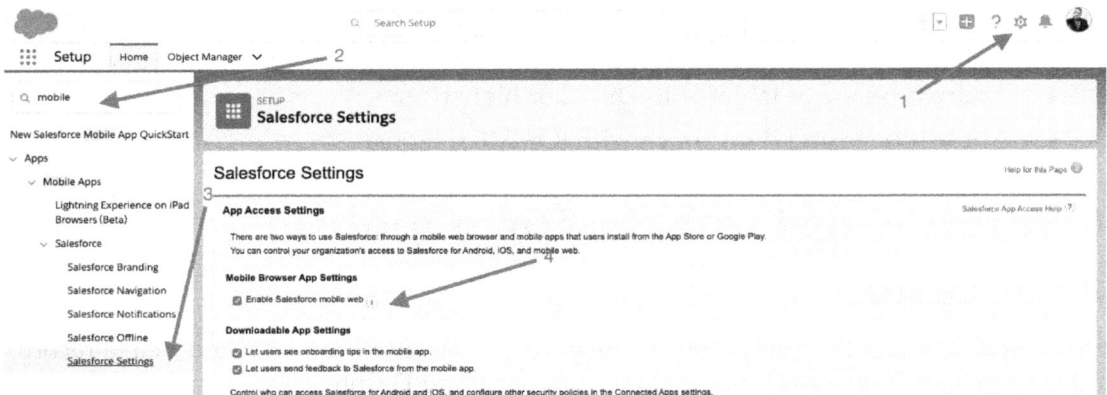

Figure 12.1: Installing the Saleforce mobile browser

4. Click on **Save** once done.

Granting Salesforce access to users

If you are looking for a way to automatically redirect your user to the Salesforce1 mobile browser app when they login to Salesforce from a supported mobile browser, perform the following steps:

1. Click the gear icon ⚙ at the top of the page and launch Setup.
2. Edit your user record.
3. Make sure the **Mobile User** option is checked.
4. If you turn this option off, your mobile browser will be directed to the full Salesforce site instead.
5. Click on **Save** once done.

Logging in to a Salesforce application

Perform the following steps to log in to a Salesforce1 mobile application:

1. Click on the Salesforce mobile app icon on the mobile device.
2. Enter your login credentials and code.
3. Allow the Salesforce application to access your Salesforce basic information.
4. Enter the passcode to access the Salesforce1 application.
5. You will be redirected to the application home page.

Enabling offline access for Salesforce application

You can safeguard Salesforce1 users against the whims of mobile connectivity. This allows to enable two levels of offline access:

1. Enable caching for frequently accessed records so that users can view data when offline.
2. Enable the option through which users could create, edit, and delete records even when they are offline.

Perform the following steps to enable Salesforce offline access for your Salesforce organization:

1. Click the gear icon ⚙ at the top of the page and launch Setup.
2. Follow the path **Apps** | **Mobile Apps** | **Salesforce Offline**.
3. Navigate to the **Offline Settings**.
4. Make sure to enable caching in Salesforce for Android and iOS.
5. Enable offline create, edit, and delete in Salesforce for Android and iOS are checked:

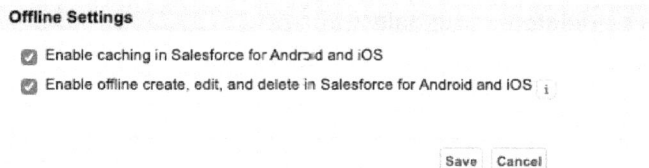

Offline Settings

☑ Enable caching in Salesforce for Android and iOS

☑ Enable offline create, edit, and delete in Salesforce for Android and iOS ℹ

Save   Cancel

Figure 12.2: Enabling offline feature

6. Click **Save** once it is done.

Conclusion

In this chapter, we covered the mobile application feature of Salesforce. We understood that Salesforce has carried the intensity of Lightning to not only the web application but also to the Salesforce mobile application. We learned the many advantages of the Salesforce mobile app. The SalesforceA mobile application, Salesforce Authenticator application, and Salesforce1 Mobile application can be downloaded from both the Play Store and App Store. We also came to know that the Salesforce1 mobile application can also be enabled for offline usage. In the next chapter, we are going to learn the programming way to develop an application using Apex.

Questions

1. **Which of the following are features included in Chatter? Choose 3 answers.**
   a. Selected record data can be added to posts automatically.
   b. Posts can be shared to your Chatter profile or groups that you are a member of.
   c. Topics can be selected and added to a post.
   d. A Poll can be used within a Chatter post.

2. **As an administrator, what are you able to do using the Salesforce app? Choose 3 answers.**
   a. Delete user records.
   b. Update certain user details fields.
   c. Unlock a user.
   d. Create custom object records.
   e. Freeze a user.

3. **Which of the following are true regarding creating user management using the SalesforceA app? Choose 3 answers.**
   a. A user license can be reassigned using the Salesforce app.
   b. Permission sets can be assigned to users using the Salesforce app.
   c. Users can be deleted using Salesfore app.
   d. It is possible to create new users using Salesforce app.

4. **Which of the following is true when a user converts a lead using the Salesforce app?**

    a. Lead conversion is not available on a group or Professional Edition.

    b. A new contract should be associated with an existing account.

    c. Duplicate records can be created.

    d. Lead sources from existing contacts must be kept during conversion.

5. **For which objects can a user create new records in the Salesforce mobile app? Choose 2 answers.**

    a. Opportunities

    b. Reports

    c. Cases

    d. Dashboards

Answers

1. b, c, d
2. b, c, e
3. a, b, d
4. c
5. a, c

Join our Discord space

Join our Discord workspace for latest updates, offers, tech happenings around the world, new releases, and sessions with the authors:

https://discord.bpbonline.com

## CHAPTER 13

Programming with APEX

Introduction

In this chapter, we learn about a new language named Apex, developed by Salesforce developed similar to Java, which helps us add or update the data of Salesforce. We will also learn about Apex as an **object-oriented programming (OOP)** language which adopts common OOP concepts such as classes, objects, interfaces, and inheritance.

Structure

In this chapter, we will discuss the following topics:

- Introduction to Apex
- Apex language features
- First line of code in Apex
- Comments
- Data types in Apex
- Operators
- Condition statements
- Iteration
- Apex classes

- Object-oriented programming concepts
- Use of Apex class in Salesforce

Objectives

After studying this unit, you should be able to understand the fundamentals of Apex as a programming language. We will also learn Apex datatypes and variables, as well as datatype, sObject and collections, like list, set, and map. Further in this chapter, we will learn about conditional logic using statements such as the if-then-else structure, and control iteration using for and while loops. All of these will be supported by examples of using Apex on the Salesforce platform.

Introduction to Apex

For the last two decades, programming has been the heart of Information Technology. It is a method of achieving a customizable task or productive work with a line of code. At first, Salesforce was a customer relationship management or **Software as a Service (SaaS)**, but after 2008, it became popular as a **Platform as a Service (PaaS)**. Here, the programming began in Salesforce.

Salesforce developed a new language called **Apex**, which is similar to Java, and can be used to write logic programmatically and interact with Salesforce data. We will discuss more on OOP later in this chapter in the section *OOP* **concepts**.

As a language, Apex has the following features:

- It is saved on the Cloud, and compiled and executed on the Cloud.
- There is no need to upgrade it. Code is stored as metadata in the platform; Apex is automatically upgraded as part of Salesforce releases.
- It is strongly typed. Apex checks the reference while compiling.
- It is not a general-purpose language. It is developed only for the Salesforce-based multitenant platform.
- It is database integrated, so it is an indirect communication with the database using queries and **Data Manipulation Language** (DML).
- Apex provides access to the database for transactions as per the **Atomicity Consistency Isolation Durability** (ACID) standard. This means that it allows us to roll back any operations.
- The syntax is very similar to Java C#, and Apex is very easy to learn if you want to start as beginner.
- Easy-to-write debug and test. Apex has built-in support for unit test creation, execution, and code coverage.

- **Versioned**: Custom Apex code can be saved against different versions of the API. It is best to use the most recent version of Apex.

- **Cloud-based language**: Due to it's multitenant environment and to avoid monopoly in resource access, It is bound within Governor limits. We will learn about governor limit in *Chapter 19, More Customization and Less Coding*.

Apex language features

Like other OOP languages, Apex supports the following constructs:

- Classes, interfaces, properties, and collections (including arrays).
- Object and array notation.
- Expressions, variables, and constants.
- Conditional statements (if, else if).
- Control flow statements (for loops and while loops).

In addition to the common functionality of other OOP languages, Apex supports the following features:

- Salesforce Cloud-based development.
- Triggers that work similarly to triggers in database systems.
- Database syntax, such as **Salesforce Object Query Language** (**SOQL**), DML, that allow you to make direct database calls and query languages to query and search data.
- Transactions and rollbacks.
- The global access modifier which can be accessed in all applications and namespaces.
- Case-insensitivity.
- Bound by Governor limits.

First line of code in Apex

This is the first line of code in Apex. Take a look at the following format and sample:

```
System.debug('Hey! You are new in Apex');
```

Now, let us see how we can run this code in Salesforce. The following steps will help you in the same:

1. Log in to your Salesforce Developer Org.
2. On the top, right-click the settings button ⚙ .
3. Click on Developer Console, as shown in the following figure:

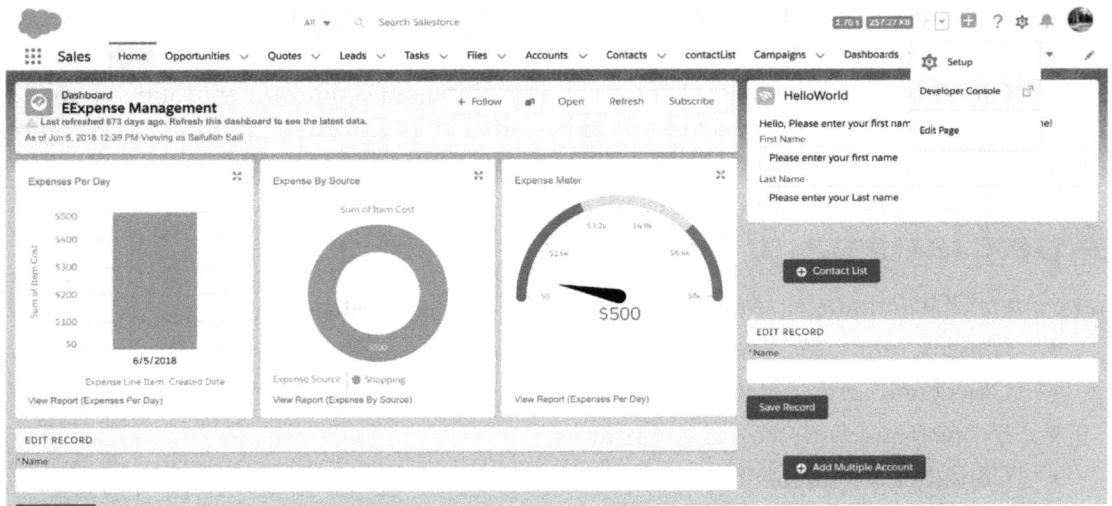

Figure 13.1: Setup

4. In the developer console, click on **Debug** and select **Open Execute Anonymous Window**. You can also use the shortcut key (*Ctrl + E*) or (*Command +E*) to open it, as shown in the following figure:

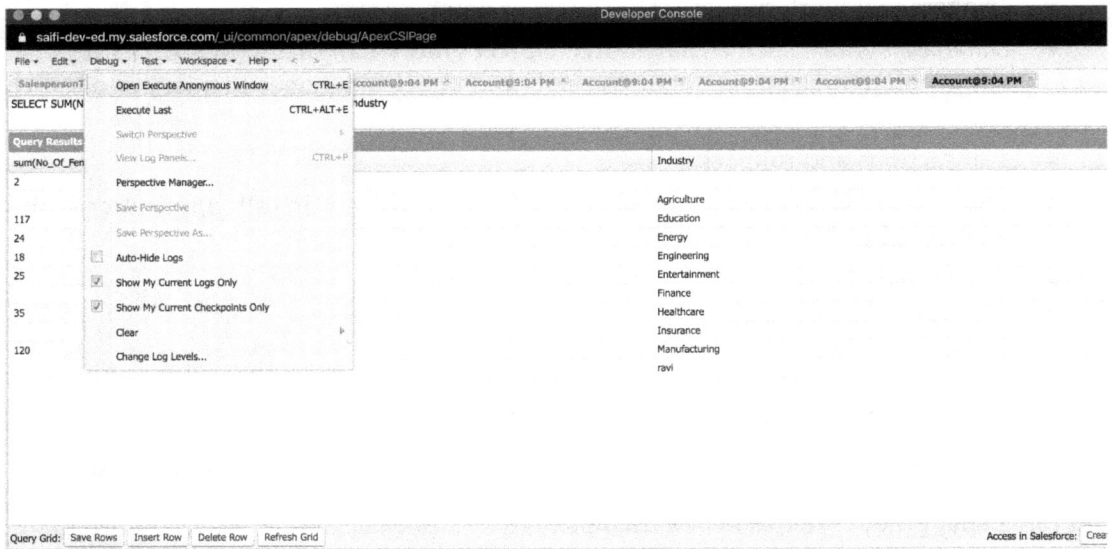

Figure 13.2: Developer console

Now, the execute anonymous window will allow us to create and run code for the examples in this chapter, as shown in the following figure:

Figure 13.3: Anonymous window

5. Click on Open log, which will help you check the output and flow. Copy and paste this code **System.debug('Hey! You are new in Apex');** into this window and click on **Execute**, as shown in the following figure:

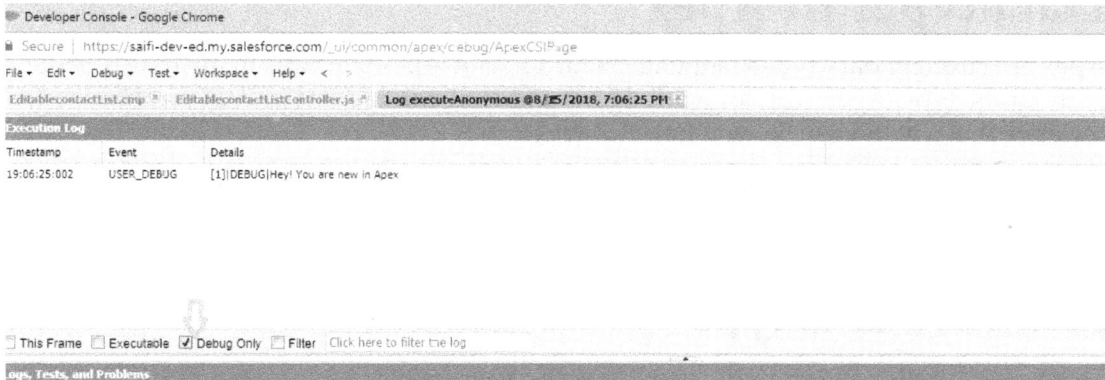

Figure 13.4: Debug log

6. Click on **Debug Only**, and you will see the first output of your program.

Note: **From now on, you will write the code in the Anonymous Window of the developer console and will execute it for practice.**

We will write our codes and do practices in our developer org, For actual live org, it's recommended to avoid using code on developer console unless necessary.

7. If you want to print something or check the output, you should write **System. debug()** in Apex.

Note: In Apex, if we use //, this means it is a comment used to understand the code by developer.

Comments

Comments are lines of text that you add to your code to describe what it does. The two types of comments are:

- **Single-line comment:** It is as follows:

```
//this is a single line
```

- **Multi-line comment:** It is as follows:

```
 /* in between multi line comment*/
/* smsmsms
Msmmsms
*/
```

Data types in Apex

Apex is a strongly data-typed language, which means Apex supports many data types but without the type, Apex will not work. For example, if you are saying *a=8*, you have to tell the apex that a is Integer. So, you have to write:

```
Integer a=8;
```

Apex has various data types such as collection, primitive data types, and sObject.

Primitive data type

These are the following primitive data types in Apex:

- Variable and constant
- Integer/double/decimal/long
- Boolean
- BlobString / ID
- Date, Time and Datetime

Variable and constant

A variable is a value provider and storage holder that stores a value throughout the code. For any value, you will use some name that is a variable. If Integer *a=8*, a variable has a value 8, and if we want to change the value, we can change it. *a=5*; If you declare a variable and you have not initialized it, the value of that variable is null.

Apex constants are variables that are not changed after initialization; for that purpose, we will use the final integer, which is:

```
Final Integer a=8;
```

Integer, double, decimal or long

The types of numbers are:

- **Integer**: A 32-bit number that does not include a decimal point.
- **Long**: A 64-bit number that does not include a decimal point.
- **Double**: A 64-bit number that includes a decimal point.
- **Decimal**: A number that includes a decimal point, we can set the scale for number of digit after deicmal.

These data types will be used to store numbers such as integers, decimals, and so on.

For example, try the following code:

```
Integer a=9;
system.debug('value of a is '+a);
a=a+1; // a+=1; or a++;
System.debug('the value of a after increment >>'+a);
```

In the preceding code, we define a variable **Integer** **a** and set value **9**. This means whenever we write **a** after that line, it will give us **9**. If we run this code, it will give **9** in line 2 and 3. If we add 1 in **a**, these are three ways to add 1 in **a. when you debug line 4** 10 will the output:

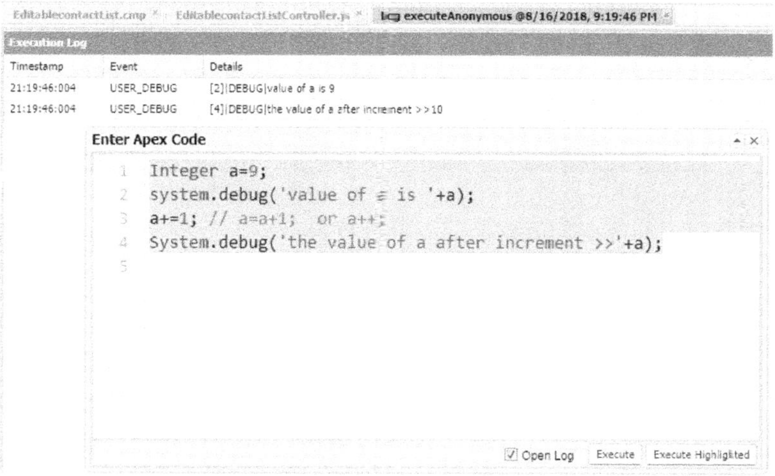

Figure 13.5: Code Sample for variable

Similarly, we can set decimal or double like **Double b=9.8;** or **Decimal c=1.23;**. We can convert an integer to a decimal or decimal to an integer easily through the following:

```
Integer num=8;
Double dbl= Double.valueOf(num);
System.debug(dbl);
Decimal dcm= Decimal.valueOf(num);
System.debug(dcm);
Decimal x=8.76;
Integer y=Integer.valueOf(x);
System.debug(y);
```

Try to run that code in your org, you will see the value as 8.0, 8.0, and 8.

Boolean

This data type contains true/false values used for a logical condition or checkbox field of the Salesforce object. Syntax will be as follows:

```
Boolean fl=true;
```

You can see in the user object that the active field has the Boolean datatype (checkbox).

ID

The ID data type is used to store Salesforce ID, which means record ID such as account ID and user ID, as shown in the following figure:

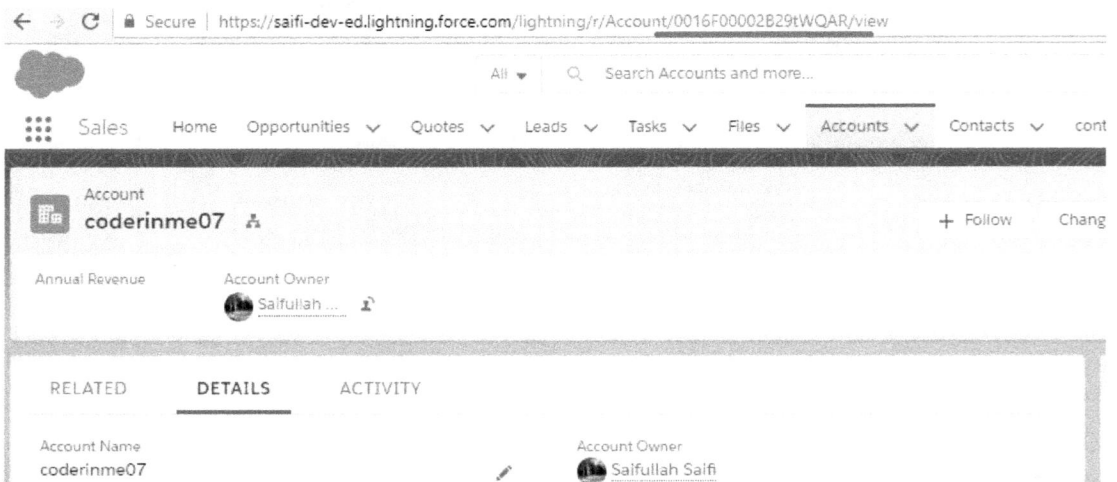

Figure 13.6: ID in URL

String

String is a very popular data type that can store any data such as text, textarea, number, and ID. It will also store everything within ' ', for example:

```
string str= 'my first string';
string a='9';
string accId='0016F00002B29tWQAR';
```

> **Note: In Apex, every hardcoded value and string data should be enclosed with single quotes (") as a string.**

The string data type is useful in Apex. We can add, split, find, replace, and remove using string-related methods. Try the following code:

```
String str= 'Account name Coderinme has Account Id ';
String accId='0016F00002B29tWQAR';
str=str+accId;
String var='this is added with >' + str;
system.debug(var);
```

The **+** operator acts as a concatenation operator.

The output will be:

```
this is added with >Account name Coderinme has Account Id 0016F00002B29tWQAR:
```

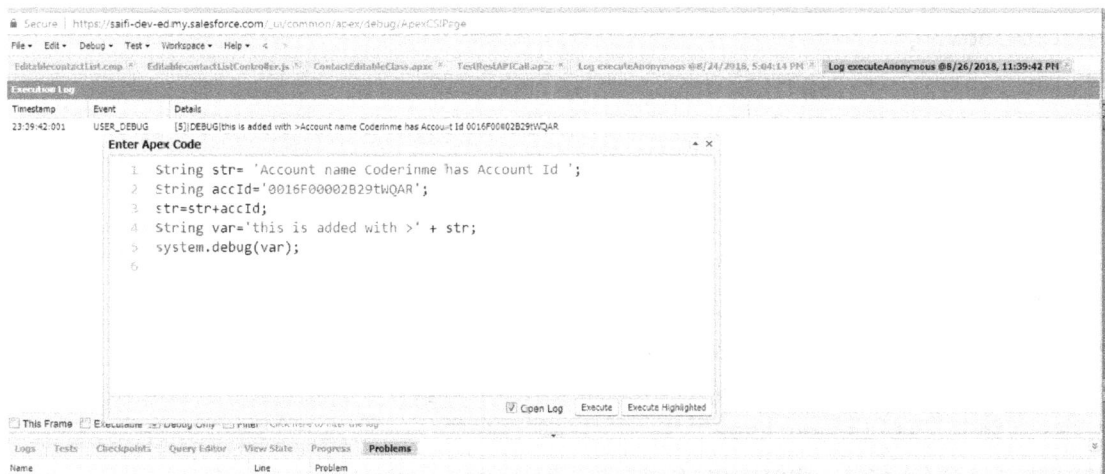

Figure 13.7: String Concat

Suppose **String name='John Deo'**, then we can remove **Deo** from it:

```
String Name='John Deo';
```

```
Name.remove('Deo'); // now name is John
```

We can replace some word/letters of a string as follows:

```
Name='John Deo';
Name.replace('John', 'Jane'); // now name is Jane Deo
Number of letter , character in the string
Name='John Deo';
Integer strLen = Name.length(); // strLen is 8
```

We have hundreds of methods for strings, such as **find()**, **left()**, and **right()**.

If we want to convert something to string, you can use the following code:

```
String.valueOf(variable):
Integer num=1919;
String numStr = String.valueOf(num);
```

You can practice some methods used for a string on the anonymous window:

```
string str='now it is you know';
string revStr = str. reverse();
//reverse() is used to reverse the string
//revStr = 'wonk uoy si ti won'
string lft = str.left(4);
// this is used to find leftmost n number of characters of string
// lft='now '
string rgStr= str.right(4)
// this is used to find rightmost n number of characters of string
//rgStr= 'know'
string stRef = lft.trim() ;
//is used to remove unwanted space in the beginning or end of the string
// now lft is 'now'
string subst= str.substring(4) ;
 // it will take new string from n index to last
// substr = 'it is you know'
string subst1= str.substring(0,4) ;
// new string which will take from frst index to 4 index
// substr1='now i'
```

You can debug every variable to check the value on the developer console.

Date, Time and DateTime

When you need to use dates and times in Salesforce, you can choose from a Date, Time or DateTime type. You know that when you create a new **Date** field or **Datetime** for an object,. For example, opportunity object, **CloseDate** is of **Date** type, and **CreatedDate** or **LastModifiedDate** is of **Datetime** type.

Time is a data type only to store time-value hours, minutes, seconds, and milliseconds.

Here are some examples of these various data and time types in Apex:

```
Date dat1 = Date.newInstance(2018,3,18); // 18th March
Date todDate = system.today();           // today Date like 26th July 2018
Datetime dtime1= Datetime.newInstance(2018,03,18,20,18,30);
 // dtime1 is 08:18 pm and 30 sec On 18th March 2018
Datetime nwTime= system.now();           // time and date of now like 11:50
pm of 26th July 2018
Time tm= Time.newInstance(1,15,20,0);    // 01:15:20 am
```

There are various methods used for **Date**. We will use some of them, which as as follows:

- We want to add three days into a **Date**:
  ```
  Date dt1 = Date.newInstance(2018, 2, 17);
  Date dt2 = dt1.addDays(3); //Now dt2 is 20/02/2018
  ```
- We want to add months and years also:
  ```
  Date dt1 = Date.newInstance(2018, 2, 17);
  Date dt2 = dt1.addMonths(2); //Now dt2 is 20/04/2018
  Date dt2 = dt1.addYears(4); //Now dt3 is 20/02/2022
  ```
- We want to find a day, year or month of a given **date**:
  ```
  Date gvnDate = Date.newInstance(2016, 10, 17);
  Integer dyDate= gvnDate.day(); // 17
  Integer mnthDate= gvnDate.month(); // 10 i.e. october
  Integer yrDate= gvnDate.year(); // 2016
  ```
- We want to find the number of days between two dates or a number of months:
  ```
  Date gvnDate = Date.newInstance(2016, 10, 17);
  Date nxtDate = Date.newInstance(2016, 10, 27);
  Integer countDays= gvnDate.daysBetween(nxtDate); //10
  ```
  If we run this code in the developer console, the output will be as follows:

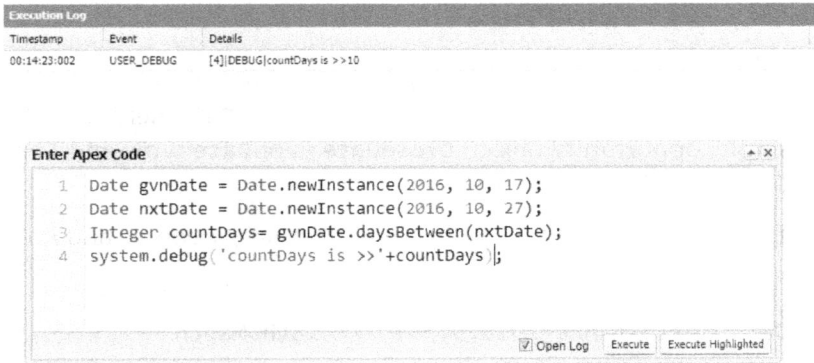

Figure 13.8: Date sample code

```
Date gvnDate = Date.newInstance(2016, 10, 17);
Date nxtDate = Date.newInstance(2017, 01, 27);
Integer countMnths= gvnDate.monthsBetween(nxtDate); //3
```

- **Date.today()**: It is the current date in the current user's time zone.
- **toStartOfMonth()**: Returns the first of the month for the **Date**:
```
Date gvnDate = Date.newInstance(2016, 10, 17);
Date nwDt= gvnDate.toStartOfMonth(); // 01/10/2017
```
- **toStartOfWeek()**: Returns the start of the week for the **Date**:
```
Date gvnDate = Date.newInstance(2016, 10, 21);
Date nwDt= gvnDate. toStartOfWeek(); // 17/10/2017 Monday start
```
- **Date.valueOf()**: Changes the string date value to **Date** type.
  The String should use the standard date format **yyyy-MM-dd HH:mm:ss**:
```
String dtVal='2009-10-26 11:24:43';
Date dat1= Date.valueOf(dtVal);
```

Note: There are various methods used for Datetime

Some are similar to **Date** such as **addDays()**, **addMonths()**, **addYears()**, **day()**, **month()**, **year()**.Others are as follows:

```
Datetime dtime1= Datetime.newInstance(2018,03,18,2,2,2);
Datetime dt1= dtime1.addHours(2); // 18th March 2018 04:02:02
Datetime dt2= dtime1.addMinutes(12); // 18th March 2018 02:14:02
Datetime dt3= dtime1.addSeconds(10); // 18th March 2018 04:02:12
Integer hours= dt1.Hour(); // 4
Integer mins= dt1.Minute(); // 2
```

```
Integer scnds= dt3.Second(); // 12
Date dt= dt1.Date(); // 18/03/2018
Time tm= dt1.Time(); // 04:02:02
```

There are various methods used for time. Some are similar to **Datetime addMinutes()**, **addHours()**, **addSeconds()**, **Hour()**, **Minute()**, **Second()**.

sObject

sObject is a Salesforce object. It has the following types:

- Standard object such as Account/Lead
- Custom object such as Salary__c
- Custom setting, metadata, label, and so on
- Collection (List/Set/Map) of objects
- User-defined Apex classes
- System-supplied Apex classes

sObject datatype

All Salesforce standard and custom objects are known as **sObject,** and we can directly use them in Apex, which is the beauty of Apex.

Since Apex is tightly integrated with the database, you can access Salesforce records and their fields directly from Apex. Every record in Salesforce is natively represented as an **sObject** in Apex.

Here are some common **sObject** type names in Apex used for standard objects:

- Account
- Contact
- Lead
- Opportunity

If you have added custom objects in your organization, use the API names of the custom objects in Apex. For example, a custom object called **Salary** corresponds to the **Salary__c** **sObject** in Apex.

Note: **In Apex, every sObject will be used by its API name:**

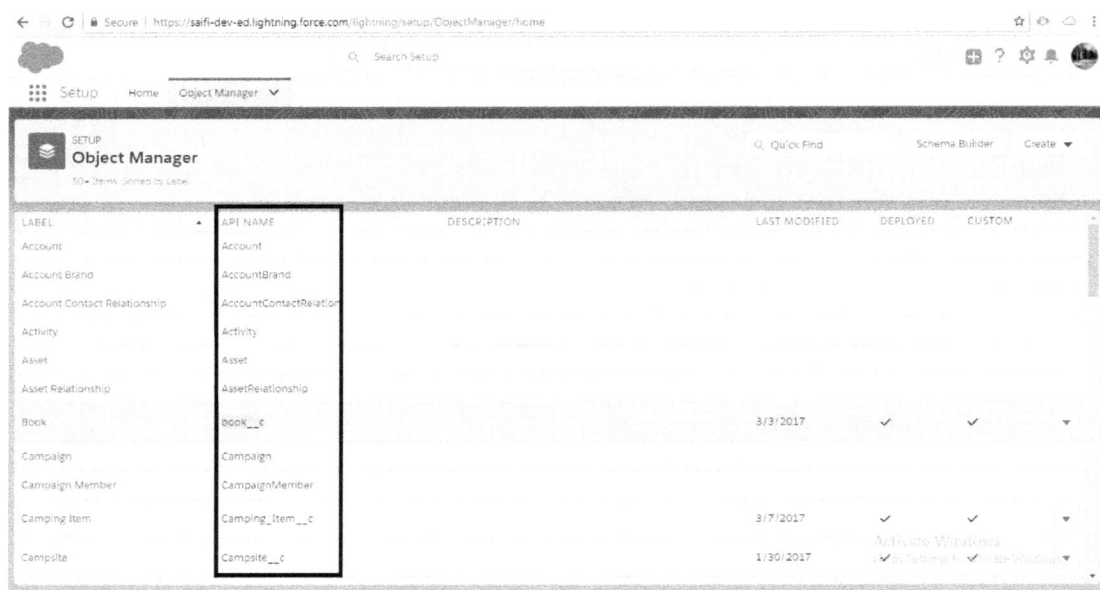

Figure 13.9: Api name for object

Creating sObject variables in Apex

To create **sObject**, you need to declare a variable and assign it to an **sObject** instance like:

```
Account acc= new Account();
Salary__c sal= new Salary__c();
```

The names of **sObjects** correspond to the API names of the corresponding standard or custom objects. Similarly, the names of **sObject** fields correspond to the API names of the corresponding fields.

> Note: **For custom objects and custom fields, the API name always ends with the __c suffix. For custom relationship fields, the API name ends with the __r suffix.**

For example:

- A custom object with a label of merchandise has an API name of Merchandise__c.
- A custom field with a description label has an API name of Description__c.
- A custom relationship field with a label of Items has an API name of Items__r.

Let us check the following code:

```
Account acc = new Account();
acc.Name = 'Coder in Me';        // line 2
//another way
```

```
Account acc = new Account( Name = 'Coder In Me');    //line 4
```

In the preceding code, you can see that we have created a new instance of an **Account** and named this instance as **acc** variable. This **acc** variable contains every thing related to the **Account** object, means every field, validation rule, and so on.

Now, in the second line, we assign this account name as **Coder in Me**. There is another way to initialize it, like in the fourth line. The same thing can be done for custom object:

```
Salary__c sal = new Salary__c();
sal.Type = 'Temporary';          // line 2
//another way
Salary__c acc = new Salary__c (Type = 'Temporary'); //line 4
```

Collection

As the word suggests, the collection is a set or group of similar types of data or things. For example, a student is a single instance, but a group of students is a collection or class.

In Salesforce, Apex has three types of collection:

- List
- Set
- Map

List

List is a collection of elements in an ordered way like an array. List has the following features:

- It can store duplicate elements.
- It is indexed.
- Useful because SOQL* always returns List.
- Due to the Governor limit, we can use list to execute any DML* operation on up to 10000 records in a single time.
- We can iterate each element of list easily.
- It can contain any data type, such as integer, double, string, date, list, and set.
- We can also have lists of sObjects, lists of other collections (List<List<Integer>>) and list of custom Apex types/classes.

The syntax for List will be as follows:

```
List<Integer> intList = new List<Integer>();
intList.add(1);
intList.add(5);
```

```
intList.add(5);
system.debug('First List of Integer >>> '+intList);
List<Integer> intList1 = new List<Integer>{1,3,4};
system.debug('Second List of Integer >>> '+intList1);
```

In the preceding code, you can see that the intList variable is a list of integer, which means we can add any integer in this list (not sum, added into group) like we added 1, then 5, and 5 in **intList**. Therefore, now, **intList = (1, 5, 5)**.

Similarly, another way to add an integer in the list is similar to how we added it into **intList1**. Check the developer console and debug, as shown in the following figure:

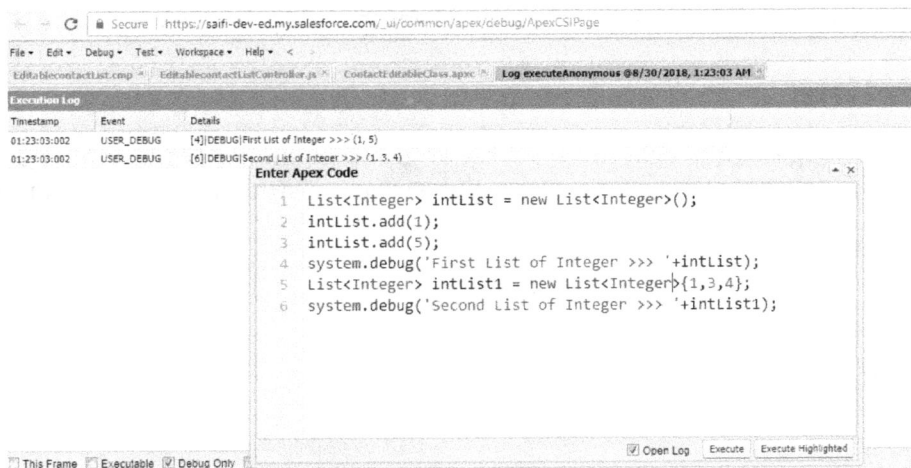

Figure 13.10: List sample code

We can also use some methods of list for different purposes which are as follows:

- **add()** method is used to add an element in the list
- **size()** used to find out the number of elements in a list
- **sort()** used to sort the list in ascending order
- **addAll()** used to add a whole list or set into another list

We will use the preceding methods while doing the practice questions in this chapter:

- **SOQL**: Salesforce Object Query Language (We will learn about it in the next Chapter)
- **DML**: Insert, update, Delete, Upsert, Undelete (later)

Set

Set is a collection of unique elements in an unordered way. A set has the following features:

- It cannot store duplicate elements
- It is not indexed, but behind the set, there is a logic of Hashing Map concept. You can check more detail at the following link: **https://www.geeksforgeeks.org/hashing-in-java/**
- We can find any element in the set without iteration
- We can iterate each element of List easily
- It can contain any data type such as integer, double, string, date, list, and set

The syntax for set will be as follows:

```
Set<Integer> intSet = new Set <Integer>();
intSet.add(1);
intSet.add(5);
system.debug('First set of Integer >>> '+ intSet);
Set <Integer> intSet1 = new Set <Integer>{1,3,4};
system.debug('Second Set of Integer >>> '+ intSet1);
```

In the preceding code, you can see that the **intSet** variable is a set of Integer, which means we can add any integer in this set(not sum, added in to group) like we added 1, then 5 in intSet. So now, **intSet = (1, 5)**.

However, if we add 5 again in the set, it will not be added because 5 is already there, no duplicate value will be accepted (it will not give any error but will store unique only).

Similarly, another way to add an integer in a set is like the way we added into **intSet**. Check the following image for the developer console and the use of **system.debug**:

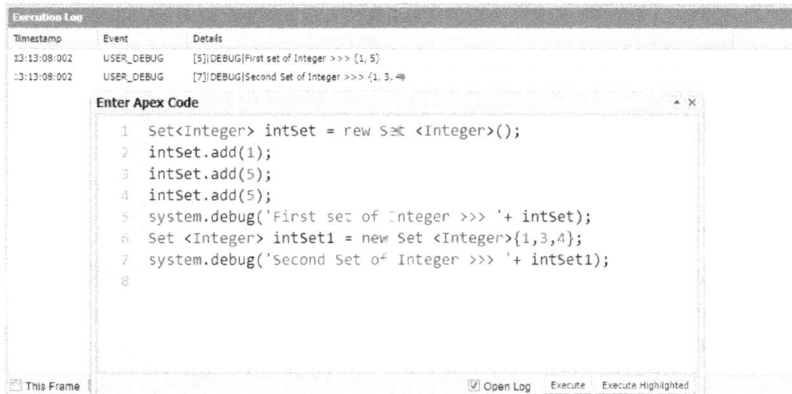

Figure 13.11: Set sample code

We can also use the following methods of **Set** for a different purpose:

- **add()** method is used to add an element in the set

- **size()** used to find out the number of elements in a set
- **contains()** used to find the element in a set
- **addAll()** used to add a whole **List** or set into another **Set**

We will use the preceding methods while doing the practice questions in this chapter.

Map

Map is one of the most popular data types in every programming language due to its features. With map, we can optimize our code and relate two different or similar things in a way that a developer can reduce the size, storage, and line of code.

The map is just a pair of keys and values. At one side, we put a unique value (integer, sObject, and so on) as a key and put other datatypes (list, integer, sObject) as a value so that whenever we need to find a value, we can search it using a key. The following table is a representation of the map:

Key	Value
1	One
Account	Contact

Table 13.1: Map structure

Syntax for Map is as follows:

```
Map<Key,value> mapVariableName= new Map<Key,Value>()
//code
Map<Integer,String> keyMap=new Map<Integer,String>();
keyMap.put(1, 'One');
keyMap.put(10, 'Ten');
system.debug(keyMap);
system.debug(keyMap.get(1));
system.debug(keyMap.get(10));
```

In the preceding code, we initialized a map of integers and strings. This means the key will be an integer and the value will be a string for this **keyMap**. Now, we want to fill this map, so let us use the **put()** method.

In this method, the first value is an integer followed by a string value. After the debugging, we can have **keyMap= {1=One, 10=Ten}**. To find which value is key 1 or key 10 is storing, we used the **get()** method. In the get method, we passed the key value.

When we execute it, we will get the following output:

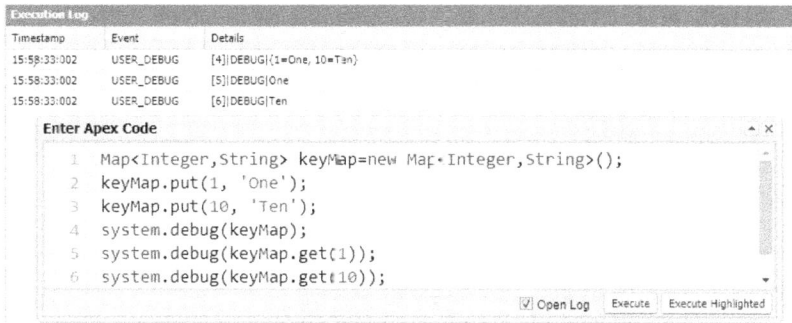

Figure 13.12: Map sample code

Note: Key will always be unique. The put() an d get() methods will be used to fill and find the value using a key.

Some popular methods are used for map other than get and put which are as follows:

- **ContainsKey()**: It is used to check whether that key exists in map
- **Size()**: It is used to find the size or number of keys in map
- **Values()**: This will return a list of all the values stored in map

We will use these methods while doing the practice questions in the chapter.

Note: There is no limit on the size of the collection but there is a general Governor limit and heap-size issues.

Operators

The following are the operators:

- + - * Mathematical operator is used to add, subtract or multiply.
- = assignment operator used to assign. For example, integer a=2; now a is 2.
- ! negation operator is used to negate the value.
- == condition operator checks equal.
- != condition operator checks not equal
- && AND operator used is to combine two or more conditions.
- | | OR operator is used to check either 2 or more conditions.
- < greater than , less than operator.
- ++ is used to increase any number by 1.
- -- is used to decrease any number by 1.

Here, we will write syntax on how to use operators in Apex:

```
integer a=2;
a++;// value will increase so a was 2 now a will be 3
system .debug(a);
a--; // decrease by 1 so a was 3 now a will be 2
system.debug(a);
```

The output will be 3, and then 2:

- **Pre-Increment** : ++a means value is increased first and then assigned.
  e.g. integer a=2; x = ++a;   , so the x will be 3 and a will be 3
- **Post-Increment** : a++ means value is assigned first and then increased.
  e.g. integer a=2; x = a++;   , so the x will be 2 and a will be 3

Condition statements

Similar to other programming languages, we use decision-making statements like IF, ELSE IF, ELSE for condition checking.

If we want to check the value or make some decisions based on a certain condition, we can use IF, ELSE IF, ELSE.

Here, we will write syntax on how to use condition statements in Apex:

```
IF(-- Condition ---){
  Execution statement
}
Else IF(---if above condition fails then new condition--){
   Execution statement
}
Else{
 Execution statement
}
```

Let us do some coding.

Check the following code, you can see a is 2. Now, we are checking whether a is 2 or not because the condition is true. Therefore, it will print **yes a is 2**:

```
Integer a=2;
if(a==2){
  system.debug('yes a is 2');
```

```
}
//Example 2
Integer a=2;
if(a==1)
    system.debug('yes a is 1');
else
    system.debug('a is 2');
```

Here, else will execute because a==1 condition failed, so it took the else part and it will print else part *a is 2*.

We can use && , | | or ! operator in statements like:

```
if(b>4 && b<8) // if b is between 4 and 8
if(flag == true || b>7) // if flag is true or b > 7
if(!flag) // if flag is false
```

Iteration

If we want to execute a certain code or statement more than once, then for multiple executions we use loop or iteration. In Apex, for this purpose, we have the following statements:

- For loop
- While or do while

For loop

One of the most popular iteration statement is for loop. We can use the for loop statement in multiple ways.

Please check the following syntax:

```
for(from where to where or how much time){
}
```

For example, we want to print all elements of list 1 by 1:

```
List<Integer> intList = new List<Integer>{1,2,3,5,6,1};
For(Integer i=0; i< intList.size(); i++){
    System.debug(intList[i]);
}
```

In the preceding code, **i=0** is an initial statement from where this loop will start. **i< intList. size()** is the condition where loop will end or exit. The last syntax **i++** is increment like here **i** is increase by 1.

We can see the results in the following figure after execution:

Timestamp	Event	Details
17:13:02:002	USER_DEBUG	[3]|DEBUG|1
17:13:02:002	USER_DEBUG	[3]|DEBUG|2
17:13:02:002	USER_DEBUG	[3]|DEBUG|3
17:13:02:002	USER_DEBUG	[3]|DEBUG|5
17:13:02:002	USER_DEBUG	[3]|DEBUG|6
17:13:02:002	USER_DEBUG	[3]|DEBUG|1

Figure 13.13: For loop

Similarly, we know **intList.size()** will give several elements in **intList**, but you know, as an array, the first index starts from 0, so the 1st element will be at 0, and 2nd element will be at 1 index, and so on. That is why the preceding loop is going from 0 index up to the last element. Also, **intList[0]** is the value of the first element (at 0 index). Similarly, **intList[2]** means the value of the third element, which is at the second index. Therefore, **intList[i]** has the value of *(i-1)*th element at ith index.

While

While will execute the code inside loop multiple times until the condition that is given in While statements fails.

The syntax is as follows:

```
While(condition){
    statement
}
```

Let us take an example:

```
Integer i=0;
while (i<4){
  System.debug('Ok'+i);
  i++;
}
```

As you can see in the preceding code system, debug will give the output until the while condition fails, which means if **i>=4**, then it will stop.

In the beginning, **i** is 0. So, if the while statement is true, it will print **ok0**, then **i** will be increased by 1. Again, while will check the condition **i<4**, and if that is true, it will again print **ok1** and so on. For example, ok0, ok1, ok2, and ok3, but after that i=4, so the while condition will fail and the loop will stop, with no execution in the loop after that, as shown in the following figure:

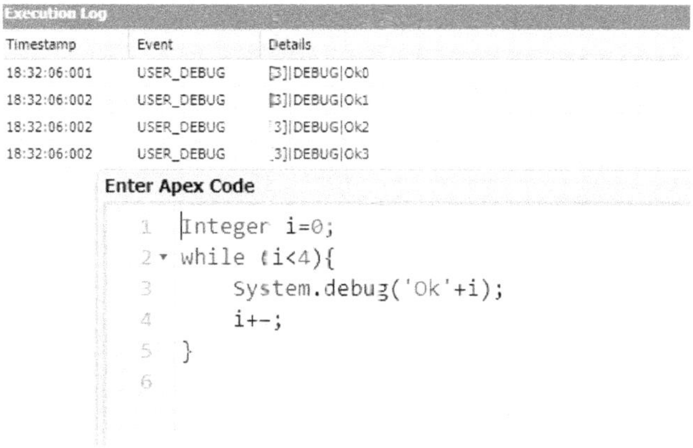

Execution Log

Timestamp	Event	Details
18:32:06:001	USER_DEBUG	[3]|DEBUG|Ok0
18:32:06:002	USER_DEBUG	[3]|DEBUG|Ok1
18:32:06:002	USER_DEBUG	[3]|DEBUG|Ok2
18:32:06:002	USER_DEBUG	[3]|DEBUG|Ok3

Enter Apex Code

```
1  Integer i=0;
2  while (i<4){
3      System.debug('Ok'+i);
4      i+-;
5  }
6
```

Figure 13.14: While loop

Let us check the following code:

```
List<Integer> intList = new List<Integer>{1,2,3,5,6,1};
Integer i=0;
while (i<intList.size()){
  System.debug(intList[i]);
  i++;
}
```

The output will be as follows:

Execution Log

Timestamp	Event	Details
20:58:10:004	USER_DEBUG	[4]|DEBUG|1
20:58:10:004	USER_DEBUG	[4]|DEBUG|2
20:58:10:004	USER_DEBUG	[4]|DEBUG|3
20:58:10:004	USER_DEBUG	[4]|DEBUG|5
20:58:10:004	USER_DEBUG	[4]|DEBUG|6
20:58:10:004	USER_DEBUG	[4]|DEBUG|1

This Frame Executable ✔ Debug Only Filter Click here to filter the log

Figure 13.15: While statement

Do while is similar to while but in while no statement can be executed before the while condition. In do while for the first time, statement will be executed, and then the while condition will be checked from the second time as shown in the following code:

```
do{
// statement
}while(condition)
//Example
Integer num=0;
do{
system.debug(num);
num++;
}while(num<4); // here num will print once then while will check condition
```

Apex classes

Let us check the following figure:

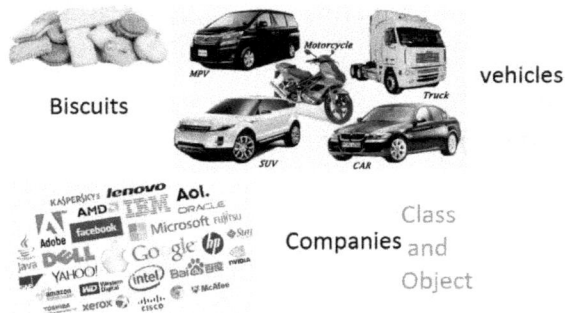

Figure 13.16: Object

In the preceding figure, each vehicle, company, and biscuit is called a class. Anything from this class, either from vehicles or companies or biscuits, say MPV or Google, or Oreo is said to be an object. This means that a collection of similar things that have common attributes or properties have a class for them, and anything in that class will be called an object. If codeine is a company mentioned in a list of properties of the companies then **codeine** is an object for the **companies** class.

Object-oriented programming concepts

In OOP, a class is structure of all those variables and methods which has similar attributes.

After defining the class, we can create as many instances as we need, for example, an object. For sObject, such as an account, it is a class in OOP, and we use it:

```
Account acc=new Account();
```

Here, **acc** will act as an object. We can use any field(Attributes) of the account in the **acc** object. For example, if we call **acc.Name='Saif Pvt Ltd'**, this means acc is an account with the name Saif Pvt Ltd. Let us take a look at the following figure containing a class company which has some properties:

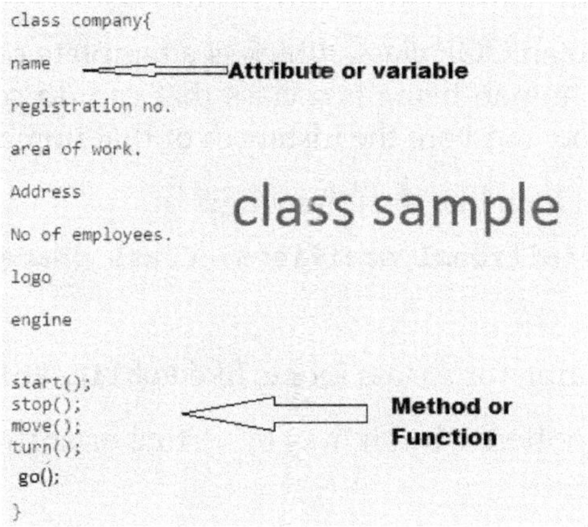

Figure 13.17: Class sample code

Now, if we create an object, it will look like this:

```
Company cmp = New Company();
```

If we want to use some property of the company:

```
cmp.name='BPB Publication';
```

If we want to use all the functions or methods, use the following code:

```
cmp.start();
```

Constructor

Every class has a specific method or function that can be executed automatically if we call the class. That is known as a constructor. This means that for the preceding class **Company**, a constructor was there, which was executed when we created an instance **cmp** for **Company**. A crucial aspect of a constructor is that their name is the same as their class name, and we do not need to write one line of code to call the default constructor. We can manually define the constructor if we want some extra customization like initializing some variables:

```
Public Class Company{
    Public string Name; // property
Public Company(String Name){
    This.Name = Name;
```

```
}
```

We will create an instance like the following:

```
Company cmp = new Company('BPB Publication');
```

Apex class

An Apex class is similar to an OOP class, which is a template or blueprint with state and behavior. For example, a human being is a class that can do certain things or has some good and bad qualities. You and I are the instances of that human being.

The Apex class syntax will look like the following:

<Access Modifier> <definitional modifiers> Class <Name Of Class> {
}

Access modifier is a definition for a class scope, like **Public**, **Private**, and so on.

A definitional modifier is optional, but it may be virtual or abstract.

For example:

```
Public Class Company{
    Public string Name; // property
Public integer registrationNo;
Public Boolean isOpen;
Public company(){
// this is constructor
Public string country='India';
}
Public void hire(){
// a method used to hire staffs
-----statement---
}
}
```

Here, you can see the company is a class with some properties such as **Name registrtionNumber** and **isOpen** . After that, we will see there is a method with **Name** company that is constructor; it will automatically call when we create an object of company, and that object will have the country name India like:

```
Company cmp= New Company(); cmp.Name='I am company';
```

Now, you can understand that **cmp** is defined as **I am company** and **country** as **India** country was already initialized and defined in the constructor and value was India, so when we created the instance (Object) **cmp** of class company, the constructor was already executed.

You can see there is a method **hire()**, it is using void as this method does not return a value. We will discuss the method as next topic.

We can write an Apex class in Salesforce in the following ways:

- Using the developer console.
- Using setup and quick find search.
- Use of Salesforce-approved **Integrated Development Environment** (**IDE**) like Visual Studio Code.

Using the developer console

The steps to use the developer console are:

1. Open the developer console.
2. Go to File. Click on that and you can see the New in the dropdown.
3. You can see Apex Class, just click on that.

   You will see a screen like the following figure:

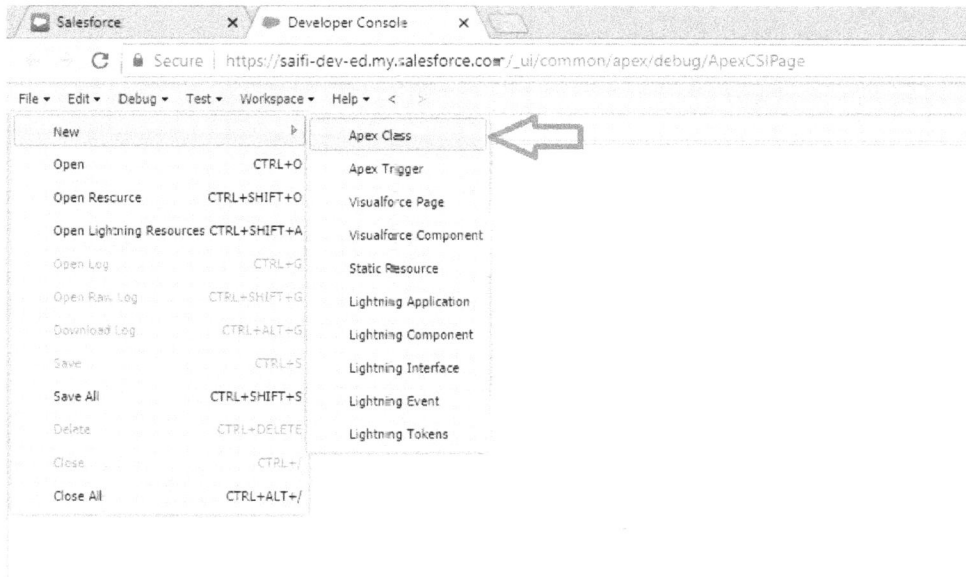

Figure 13.18: Apex class in developer console

4. Now, you have to write the name of the class, then click on OK, as shown in the following figure:

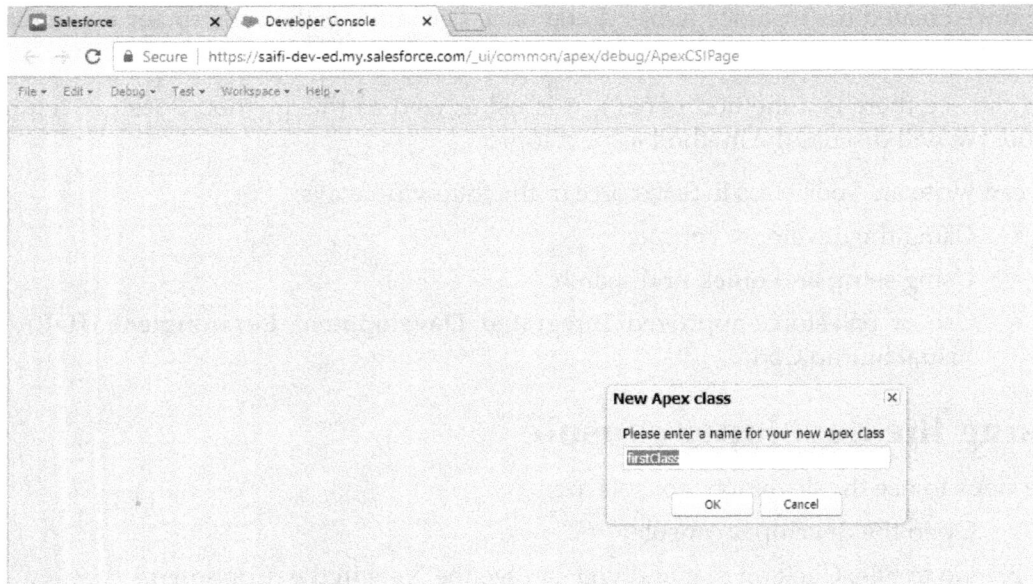

Figure 13.19: Apex class name

5. Now, you have a class where you can write into it:

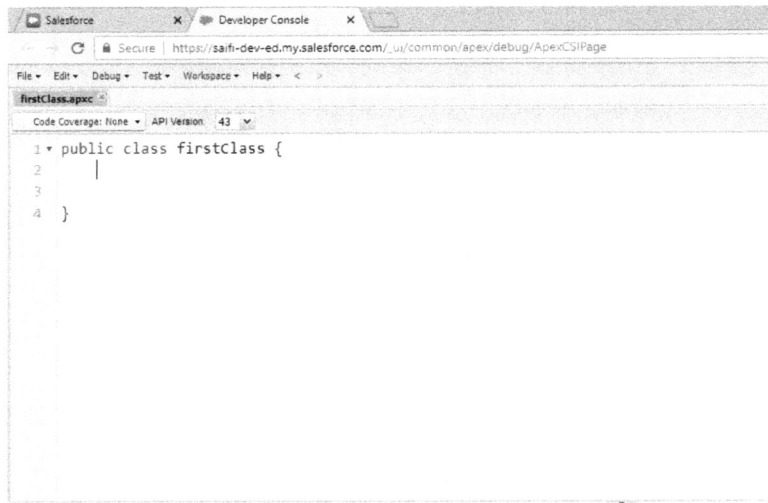

Figure 13.20: Apex class

Using the setup and quick find search

You can create a class with the following steps as well:

1. Click on the Setup in Salesforce, and then in the quick find, type Apex class. You will see Apex classes.

2. Click on that, and you will see all the Apex classes created in your Org. Now, click on the New button and create the class, as shown in the following figure:

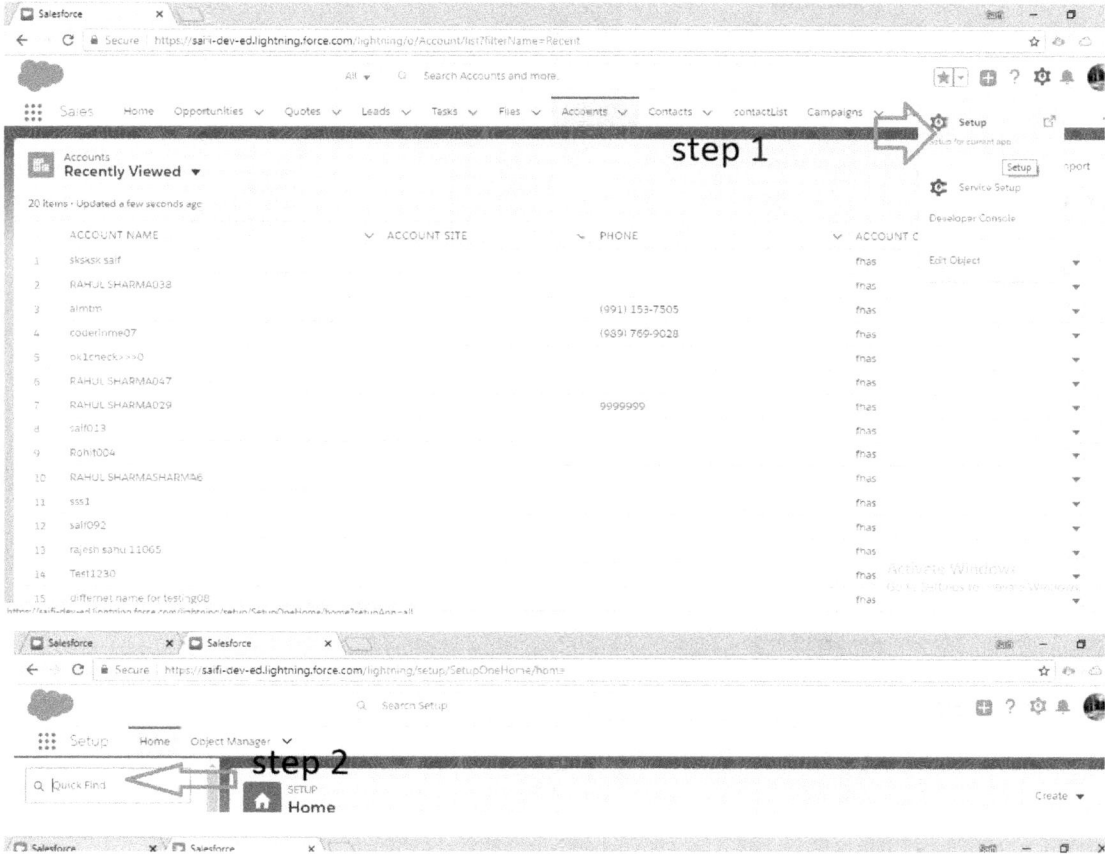

Figure 13.21: Setup

Take a look at the next figure:

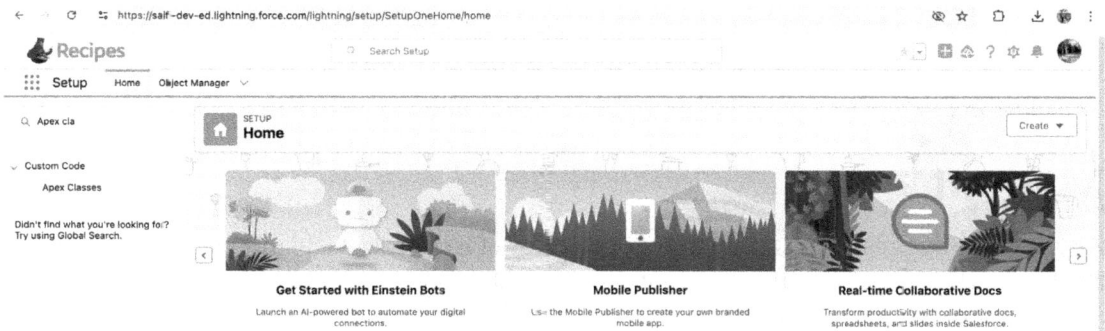

Figure 13.22: Apex class from Setup

The next step is shown in the following figure:

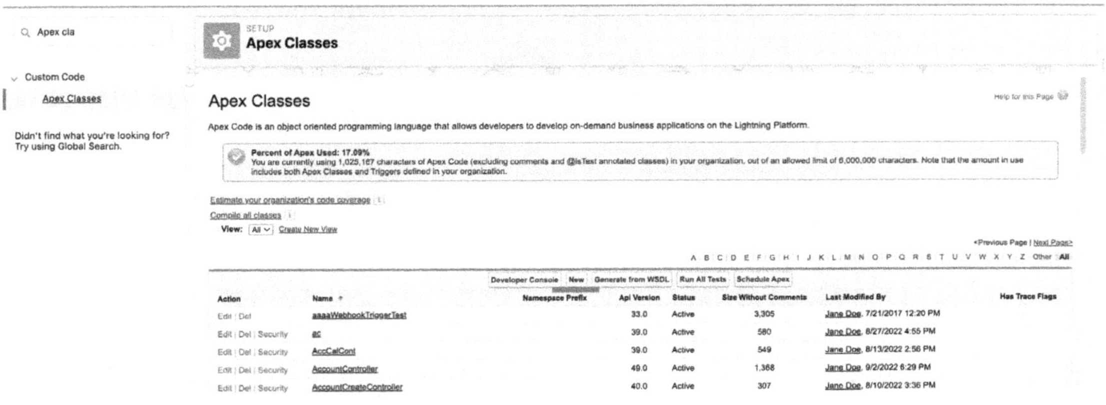

Figure 13.23: Apex class list view

The next step is shown as follows:

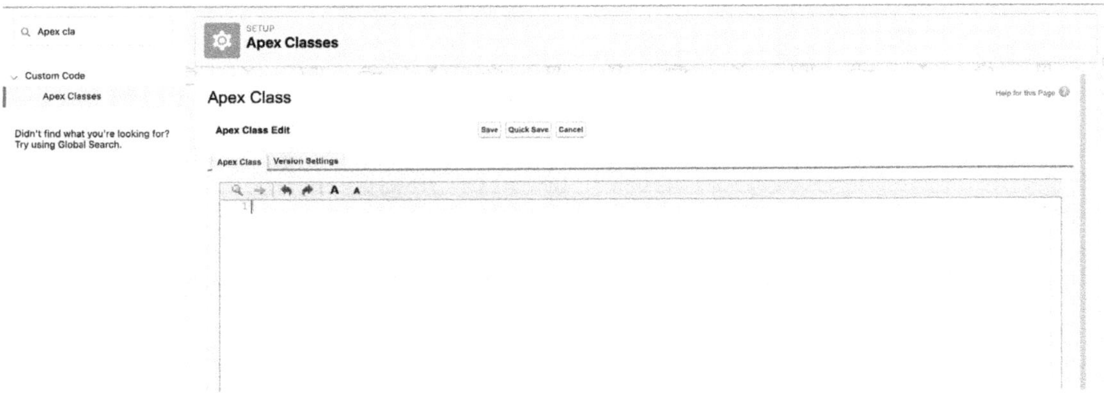

Figure 13.24: Apex class new form

Using the IDE

We will discuss this in *Chapter 18, Basics of Lightning Web Components* on how to use IDE for salesforce.

Method

As the name suggests, it is a function or behavior of a class. If we want to call some specific type of work or function, then we define a function. Suppose we want to add two numbers, so we will define the add method that will add two numbers and return the sum. Now, if we want to add two numbers, we can just call the method and get the results as many times as We want, as shown in the following code:

```
Public class firstClass{
    Public Integer add(Integer num1, Integer num2){
        Integer sum= num1+num2;
        return sum;
    }
}
// above was class and method now we will create an instance or object
```

Just copy the preceding code in your class **firstClass**.

If you want to test it, just copy the following code in the anonymous window:

```
firstClass f1= new firstClass();
Integer result = f1.add(23,32);
System.debug(result);
// it will call the method and result will be 55
```

Now, you know how to call the class and method.

You can check the following figure to see use of class and object:

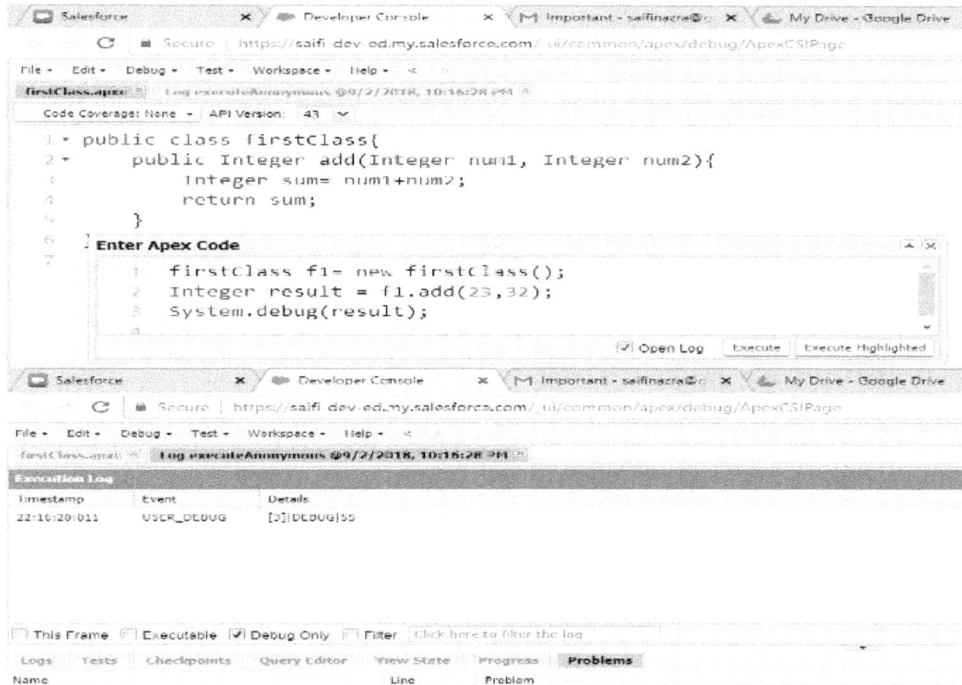

Figure 13.25: Class and object in develepor console

Use of Apex class in Salesforce

You might have heard about **Model View Controller (MVC)**. Mostly software development, particularly web application has three components, which are architectural patterns based on a logical design. They are as follows:

- The model is like a database in Salesforce. It means how you will design the structure of the f database using *o*bject and *f*ields.

- The view is a **user interface** (**UI**) or a design screen such as a record page, detail page, Lightning page and **Visualforce** (**VF**) page in Salesforce.

- The controller is the bridge between the view and the model. It is also used to apply business logic. Anything we do in code for some business logic is controller. There are two types of controller, such as:

   o **Without code-based controller**: Workflow, Process Builder.

   o **Class-based controller**: Standard controller, trigger, and so on.

In conclusion, the Apex class will be used as a C of MVC or as a controller.

In the Apex class, we will code the business logic.

The Apex class will be used as:

- **Custom controller**: Used for VF page .
- **Controller extension**: Used for VF page.
- **Batch class**: Executes some code as batch of size n. if you have 1000 record, it will use Batchable apex to run 5 times with batch of size 200.
- **Scheduler class**: Schedules a logical Batch Class at a certain time*.
- **Web services and callouts**: REST and SOAP-based call to connect an external system.
- **E-mail service**: When an e-mail comes, this class will update or insert some records in SFDC.
- **Helper class for trigger**: Used to help trigger. We will learn this in *Chapter 16, Trigger Essentials)*.
- **Utility class**: Stores common methods for Org.
- **Test class**: All Apex will be tested using their test classes.

We will discuss the above in detail in *Chapters 20, Testing Essentials*, and *Chapter 21, Apex Handler and Using Apex Class*.

Apex as business purpose or database processor language

As we all know, Apex is not general-purpose. It was designed to build or develop complex logic that cannot be achieved by Workflow, Process Builder, or Flow.

It will help you with the following conditions:

- If we want a custom roll-up summary, there is no lookup.
- If we want to update the first child record of a parent if the second child is updated or created.
- If we want to send a mass email based on some complex calculation.
- If we want to design a custom UI, Apex will be the controller. If anyone sends a mail on your help page, it will automatically create a record.
- If we want to connect and communicate with some external application.
- If you want to update or delete multiple records on a single click.
- If you want to create some custom quotations or invoices.

These are only a few examples; we can do many things like that according to customer needs.

We will use the lightning component, Lightning page for design. We will also use a trigger to update or do work on some deletion, insertion, and updation of record.

We will use DML for record processing. We can do this in the following ways:

- To create one record, we will write insert.
- To change something in the record, we will write an update.
- We will use upsert if we are not sure if we need to update or insert.
- Delete commands will delete the records.
- Undelete commands will restore the deleted records.
- We will use SOQl and SOSL to query the records from the object.

Conclusion

In this chapter, we learned about Apex as a programming language. We also covered the OOP concept using Apex. We discussed how Apex is useful in Salesforce.

In the next chapter, we will discuss SOQL and SOSL which includes how you can serach data in Salesforce using Salesforce object query and search language, we will also learn syntax and feature with limitation of these languages.

Questions

1. **Let us take one example of a code. You will see the following output:**

```
List<Integer> intList = new List<Integer>{1,3,4,1,5,6,7,9,3,4,5};
Set<Integer> intSet = new Set <Integer>();
intSet.addAll(intList);
system.debug('size of List is >>> '+ intList.size());
system.debug('size of set is >>> '+ intSet.size());
```

2. **Tell me the output of the following code:**

```
Map<Integer,String> keyMap=new Map<Integer,String>();
keyMap.put(1, 'One');
keyMap.put(1, 'Two');
keyMap.put(10, 'Ten');
keyMap.put(3,'Three1');
system.debug(keyMap);
system.debug(keyMap.get(1));
system.debug(keyMap.get(10));
system.debug(keyMap.get(3));
system.debug(keyMap.size());
```

3. **Tell me the output of the following code:**

```
Integer b=8;
if(b<4)
   system.debug('b is less than 4');
else if(b>4)
   system.debug('b is greater than 4');
else
   system.debug('b is equal to 4');answers
```

Note: Run all the code in the developer console and test the output.

4. **Convert double 8.9 into a string.**
5. **Create a variable birthdate and set it to your date of birth using the date new instance.**

6. Create a variable hourbeforeteTime and set it to now -1 hour using DateTime new instance.

7. Add 2 hours 3 days and 20 minutes into time 12 pm 1st August 2018.

8. Take three strings. In first string, store firstName, in second-string store LastName, and the third string is Name, which will combine first two strings.

9. Make a list of *any suitable type* in which we will store the following:

    34 , 56, 77, 96, 47, 81, 72

    Now, after adding it, print the sum of all even numbers.

10. `System.debug(sum);` From 1 to 50, add an all-natural number and then all prime numbers in one list:

    a. Print the size of the list

    b. Add this list to the set and print the size of set.

11. Create a new class MathsClass. Make two function Subtract() and Product(), which will take two inputs and return the subtraction and multiplication.

12. In a single record, a user selects multiple values from a multi-select picklist. How are the selected values represented in Apex?

    a. As a string, with each value separated by a comma B.

    b. As a set, with each value as an element in the set.

    c. As a string, with each value separated by a semicolon.

    d. As a list, with each value as an element in the list previous.

13. .Which statement would a developer use when creating test data for products and price books?

    a. Id pricebookId = Test.getStandardPricebookId();

    b. Pricebook pb = new Pricebook();

    c. IsTest(SeeAllData = false);

    d. List objList = Test.loadData(Account.sObjectType, 'myResource');

14. Which method from DescribeSObjectResult can check whether the user can create the object using Apex?

    a. The isInsertable() method

    b. The isCreatable() method

    c. The hasAccess() method

    d. The canCreate() method

Answers

1. The answer is as follows

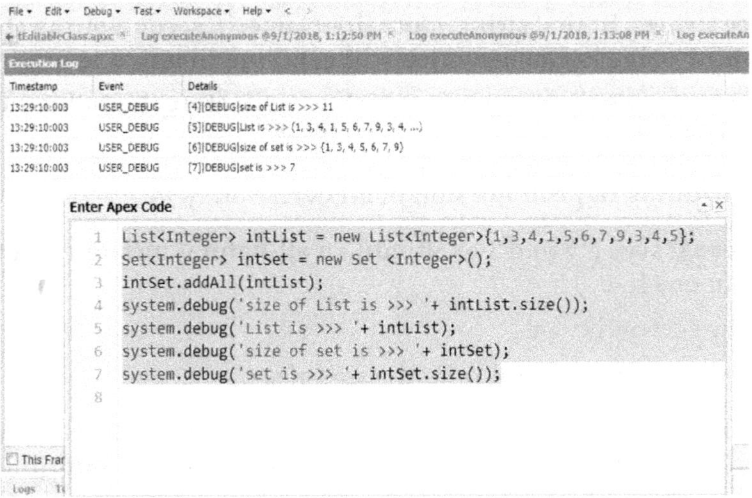

Figure 13.26: List add method

2. The answer is as follows

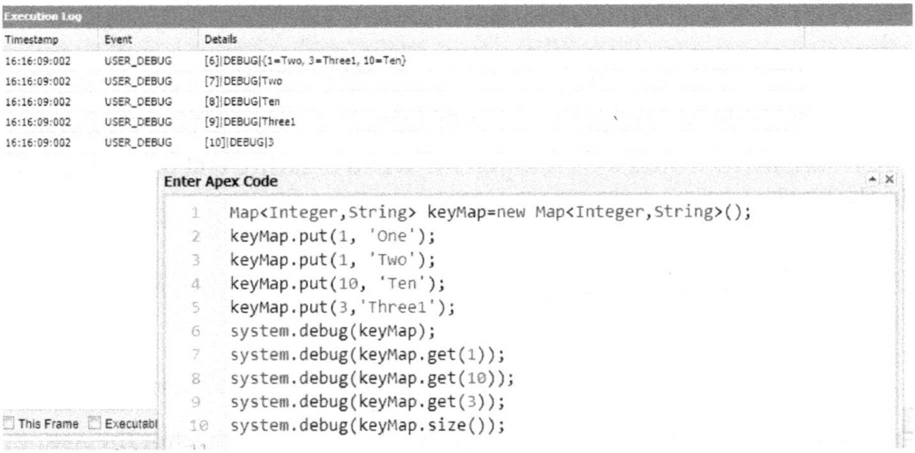

Figure 13.27: Map method

3. b is greater than 4.

4. ```
Double db=8.9;
String str=String.valueOf(db);
```

5. ```
Date birthDate=Date.newInstance(1992,10,05);
```

6. ```
Datetime hourbeforeteTime=Datetime.newInstance(2018,08,16,22,08,00);
hourbeforeteTime = hourbeforeteTime.addHours(-1);
```

   or

   ```
Datetime hourbeforeteTime=system.Now().addHours(-1);
```

7. ```
Datetime dt=Datetime.newInstance(2018,08,01,12,00,00);
dt=dt.addHours(2);
dt=dt.addDays(3).addMinutes(20);
```

8. ```
string firstName= ' Saifullah';
string lastName= ' Saifi';
string Name = firstName + lastName;
system.debug(Name);
```

9. ```
List<Integer> numList=new List<Integer>{334 , 56, 77, 96, 47, 81, 72};
Integer sum = 0;
for(Decimal nm: numList){
if(Math.mod(nm,2)){
sum+=nm;
}
}
```

10. ```
List<Integer> numberList= new List<Integer>();
// all natural Number from 1 to 50
for(Integer i=1; i<=50; i++){
  numberList.add(i);
}
//prime number from 1 to 50
List<Integer> primeList= new List<Integer{2, 3, 5, 7, 11, 13, 17, 19,
23, 29, 31, 37, 41, 43, 47};
// adding it into single list
numberList.addAll(primeList);
system.debug('size of list of natural and prime is >>>'+numberList.
size());
// set of numberList
set<Integer> numberSet= new set<Integer>();
numberSet.addAll(numberList);
```
```

11. The answer is as follows:

```
public class MathsClass {
    public Integer subtract(Integer a, Integer b) {
        return a - b;
    }
    public Integer prduct(Integer a, Integer b) {
        Integer prod = a * b;
        return prod;
    }
}

/*
in The developer console
*/
MathsClass m1= new MathsClass();
system.debug(m1.subtract(12,4)); //8
system.debug(m1.prduct(5,4)); //20
```

Figure 13.28: Class and methods

12. c

13. a

14. b

Join our Discord space

Join our Discord workspace for latest updates, offers, tech happenings around the world, new releases, and sessions with the authors:

https://discord.bpbonline.com

CHAPTER 14
SOQL and SOSL

Introduction

Salesforce Object Query Language (SOQL) and **Salesforce Object Search Language (SOSL)** are query languages used to fetch or find the data from the Salesforce table or object. A SOQL query is quite similar to SQL or **procedural language (PL)** /SQL extensions to the structured query language such as `SELECT FROM WHERE`. SOSL is more like a programmatic way with text-based search logic. You will understand the use of SOQL or SOSL; according to the field, how many objects, what type of text, or data.

Structure

In this chapter, we will discuss the following topics:

- SOQL and SOSL
- SOQL with Date
- SOQL with related objects
- SOQL and SOSL in Apex
- Limitation of Salesforce for SOQL and SOSL

Objectives

After studying this chapter, you will learn how to use SOQL and SOSL in Apex. You will also learn the different uses of SOQL and Dynamic SOQL. Lastly, you will understand how to fetch data from parent to child and child to parent.

SOQL and SOSL

In the previous chapters, you saw the UI interface for the object and detail page, list view, and so on. Now, if we want to use some records or data through Apex, or do modifications in any **Salesforce Object (sObject)** records for certain conditions, we use the SOQL and SOSL to search or find the data in Salesforce Org.

Using SOQL

If we want to know in which field and object the data is, then we will use SOQL in the following situations:

- If we want to retrieve records or data from a single object or two or more related objects (Lookup, master-detail) child-parent objects.
- If we want to count the number of records for certain conditions or find the minimum, maximum, or sum an average of one field data.
- If we want the data sorted from the query itself.
- When we want data from any datatype field, such as a checkbox and a date.

Using SOSL

SOSL is used when we are unsure in which field of one or multiple objects is the data in. We will use SOSL in the following scenarios:

- When we want to extract data for a specific text we know exists within a field. This is because SOSL can tokenize multiple terms within a field and build a search index from this.
- SOSL searches are faster and can return more relevant results due to indexing.
- Helpful to extract data from multiple objects and fields so efficiently that we do not need to think if objects are related or not.
- Extract data from multiple languages like Chinese, Japanese, Korean, or Thai.

Note: **SOSL does not support big objects.**

Best practice for performance

To increase the efficiency of queries and searches, we will implement some best practices.

SOQL and SOSL can work to filter data; for example, we can make a query for a specific term or search for it. For searching partial matching text where we use contains or LIKE, SOSL is fast. Suppose we have an account name: R & D Ryan Book Store, and we want to search it using the keyword Ryan so SOQL and SOSL both can do that, but SOSL is faster because of its indexing from terms-based tokens.

We need to extract only the necessary fields in the query because more fields mean more data storage and logical permutation.

Salesforce has several limitations, which are known as governor limits, which we will discuss in *Chapter 19, More Customization and Less Coding.*

Therefore, we will discuss an increased number of records that can be searched.

Syntax of SOQL

Here is the syntax of SOQL:

```
SELECT id FROM ACCOUNT
We will use [] for SOQL in Apex:
[SELECT id FROM Account]
```

We can test or develop SOQL on the query editor of the Developer Console, anonymous window, and Workbench query tool through the following steps:

1. Go to the **Developer Console**.
2. Check the bottom section of the Developer Console and you will see the query editor as shown in the following figure:

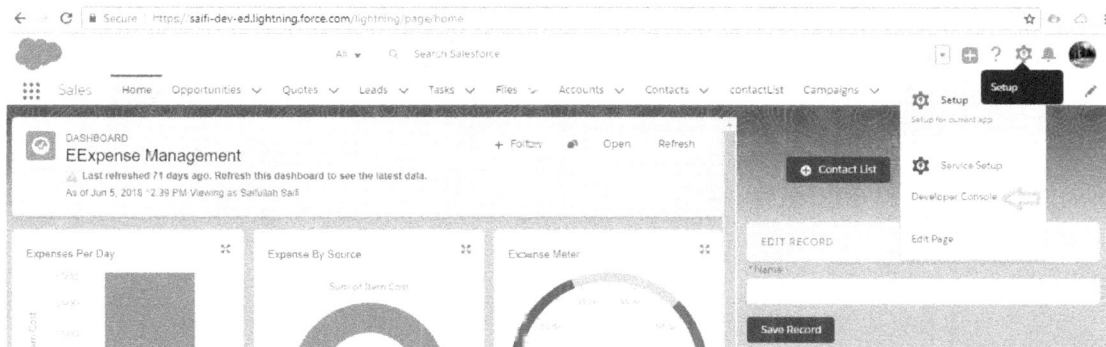

Figure 14.1: Setup to Developer Console

3. In the query editor, we can directly write the query, as shown in the following figure:

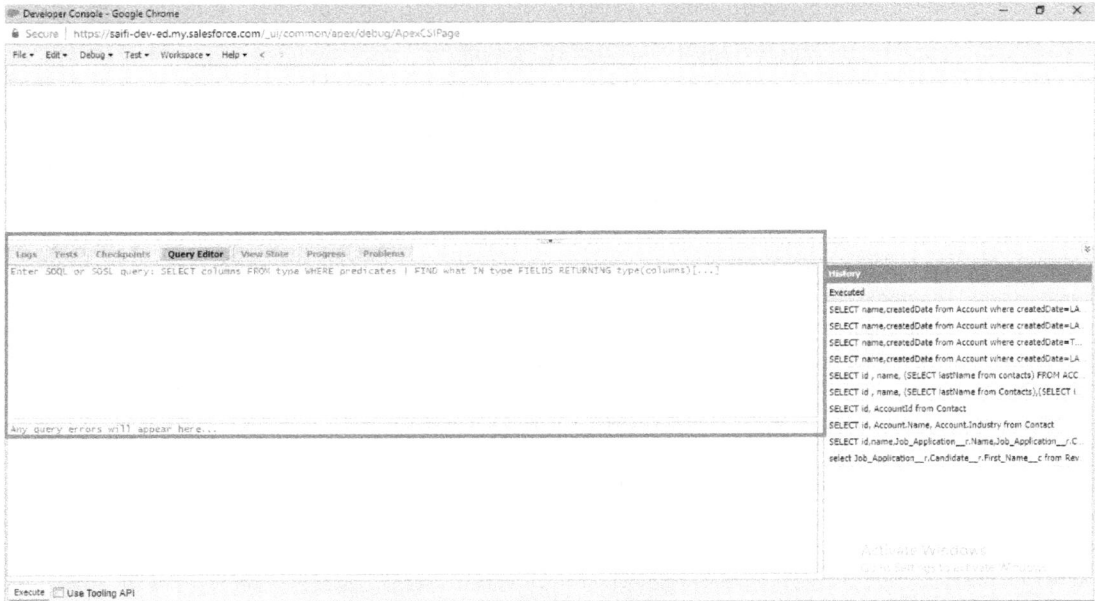

Figure 14.2: Developer Console query editor

4. We can write and execute the query as shown in the following figure:

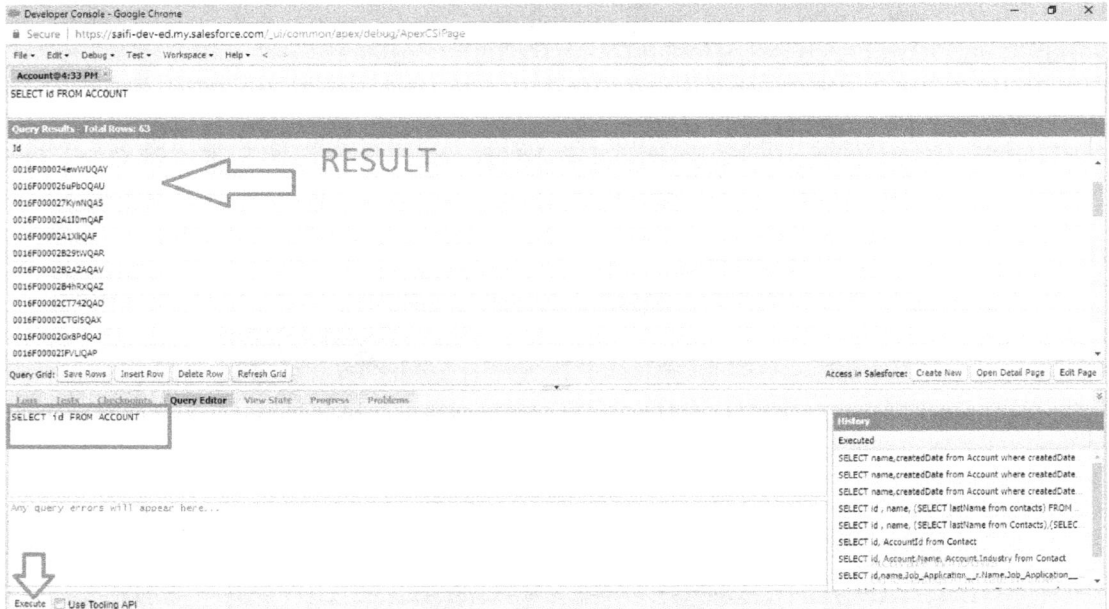

Figure 14.3: First query in query editor

5. We can write SOQL in an anonymous window and debug it, as shown in *Figure 14.4*:

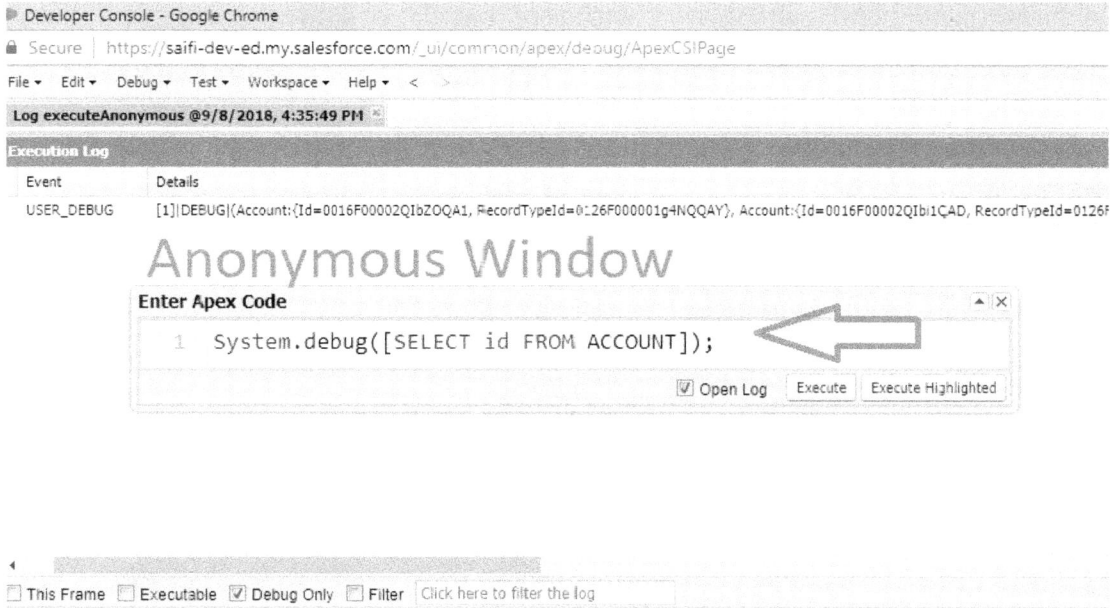

Figure 14.4: Query in anonymous window

6. We can also make the query using Workbench as shown in the following figure, the URL of the Workbench is **https://workbench.developerforce.com**:

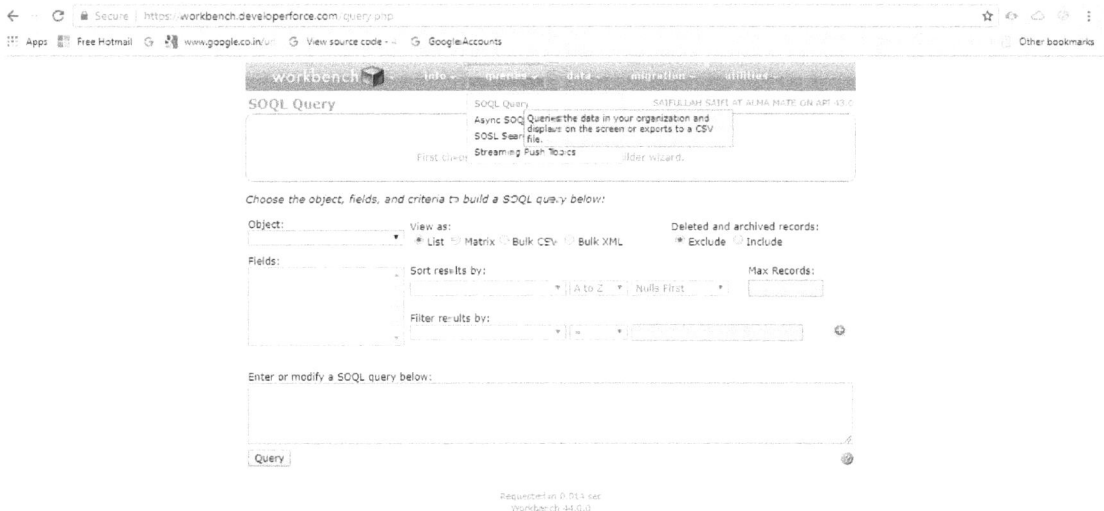

Figure 14.5: Query at Workbench

Note: For practice, we will write the SOQL in the query editor from now on.

In the SOQL query, we will use the API name of the fields of **sObject**.

If we want to retrieve all the names of the account, then we will perform the following command:

```
SELECT Name FROM Account
```

The result will look like this:

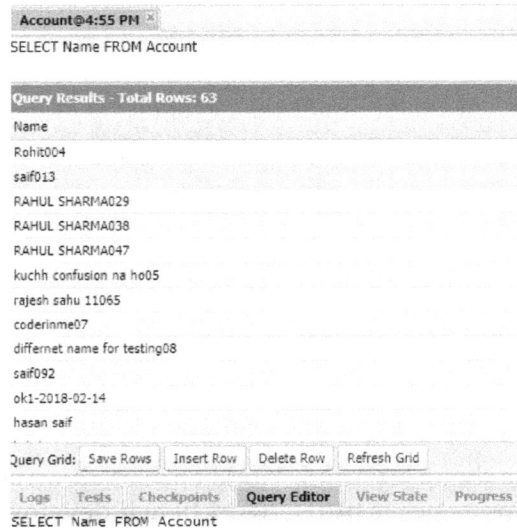

Figure 14.6: Query result

Use of the WHERE clause

It is used to filter some records based on conditions. Suppose you have multiple accounts in an Org, and you want to limit the records returned to only those that fulfill a certain condition, you can add this condition inside the **WHERE** clause.

Note: Comparisons on strings are case-insensitive.

Let us see the following examples:

- Only the account whose name is **saif013** then we will do the following:

  ```
  SELECT id, Name FROM ACCOUNT WHERE Name='saif013'
  ```

  Let us see the results in the following figure:

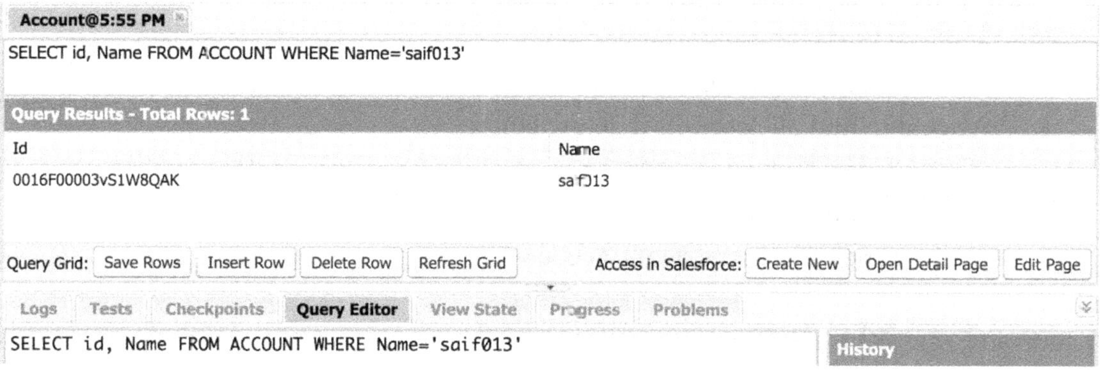

Account@5:55 PM ⊠	
SELECT id, Name FROM ACCOUNT WHERE Name='saif013'	

Query Results - Total Rows: 1

Id	Name
0016F00003vS1W8QAK	saf013

Query Grid: [Save Rows] [Insert Row] [Delete Row] [Refresh Grid]   Access in Salesforce: [Create New] [Open Detail Page] [Edit Page]

Logs   Tests   Checkpoints   **Query Editor**   View State   Progress   Problems   ⩔

SELECT id, Name FROM ACCOUNT WHERE Name='saif013'   [History]

Figure 14.7: Query and result

- We want to find only those accounts that are from the energy industry then we will do the following:

  SELECT Name,Industry FROM Account WHERE Industry='Energy'

- Let us say we want to find only those accounts that are from the energy industry, and the gender is male. Then we will do the following:

  SELECT Name ,Industry FROM Account WHERE Industry = 'Energy' AND Gender__c='MALE'

- We want to find all opportunities whose probability is greater than 50, then we will do the following:

  SELECT Name, Probability FROM Opportunity WHERE Probability >= 50

Use of AND and OR in SOQL

The AND and OR operators are used when we want to filter some records based on one or more filter criteria, such as:

- We want to find all accounts that are male and from the energy industry then:

  SELECT Name ,Industry FROM Account WHERE Industry = 'Energy' AND Gender__c='MALE'

- We want to find all those accounts that are either from the energy or the education industry (any one of two) then:

  SELECT Name ,Industry FROM Account WHERE Industry = 'Energy' OR Industry= 'Education'

- We can combine these two according to our filter condition then:

  SELECT Name, Industry FROM Account WHERE (Industry = 'Energy' AND Gender__c='MALE') OR (Industry= 'Education' AND Gender__c='FEMALE')

  This means we want a girl from the education department or boys from the energy department.

Use of = and <>

The equal and not equal operator will be used to match exact text:

- We want to find all accounts that are female:

  `SELECT Name ,Industry FROM Account WHERE Gender__c='FEMALE'`

- We want to find all accounts that are not male:

  `SELECT Name ,Industry FROM Account WHERE Gender__c<>'MALE'`

Use of LIMIT

The limit is used to bound records or specify the number of records you want from queries. For example:

- If we only need ten accounts from query then:

  `SELECT Name from Account LIMIT 10`

- Only one record of **Opportunity** of stage **Closed Won** then:

  `SELECT Name from Opportunity WHERE stageName='Closed Won' LIMIT 1`

Note **We use limit at the end of the query.**

Use of ORDER BY

If we want to search the records in a sorted way; then, we can use **ORDER BY <fieldname>** or **ORDER BY <FIELDNAME> DESC** or **ORDER BY <FIELDNAME> ASC** in the following ways:

- We want the name of the account in the alphabetical order then:

  `SELECT Name FROM Account ORDER BY Name`

- We want only ten Opportunities that are recently Closed-Won then:

  `SELECT Name from Opportunity WHERE stageName='Closed Won' ORDER BY LastModifiedDate DESC LIMIT 10`

ORDER BY always sorts record in an ascending order, so if you want the latest or last records in alphabetical order, then we will use **ORDER BY LastModifiedDate DESC** or **ORDER BY Name DESC**.

Note: **By default ORDER BY and ORDER BY <fieldname> ASC is the same.**

Use of LIKE

When we are not sure about the name, know it contains that word, or is at the beginning of the end, then we use **LIKE** and **%** keywords in the following ways:

- We want to find the account whose name contains **saif** then:

  `SELECT id FROM ACCOUNT WHERE Name LIKE '%saif%'`

- We want to find the account whose name starts with **saif** then:

  `SELECT id FROM ACCOUNT WHERE Name LIKE 'saif%'`

- We want to find the account whose name ends with **saif** then:

  `SELECT id FROM ACCOUNT WHERE Name LIKE '%saif'`

- We want to find the account whose name doesn't contain **saif** then:

  `SELECT id FROM ACCOUNT WHERE NOT (Name LIKE '%saif%')`

Use of IN

When we have two or more values to search for a single field, we use **IN** despite =, we use the following code:

`SELECT id FROM ACCOUNT WHERE Name IN ( saif','raj','surbhi')`

SOQL in Apex

Like other languages, C#, PHP, JAVA, etc, use SQL to get records from the database. We can also retrieve data from databases using SCQL in Apex. In Apex, we write SOQL within [], and it always returns the list of any objects in the following way:

`List<Account> accList = [SELECT id FROM Account];`

`List<Opportunity> OppList=[ SELECT Name from Opportunity WHERE stageName='Closed Won'];`

The preceding type of query can return 1 record in list or empty list, or list of records based on the condition it matches the record.

In Apex, when we use SOQL, we can use the result of SOQL and manipulate it according to our needs.

We want to update the name of every account with the year 2018 which was created in 2017 then:

`List<Account> accList=[SELECT Name FROM Account WHERE CreatedDate=THIS_YEAR];`

`For(Account acc: accList){`

` acc.Name= acc.Name+'2018';`

`}`

`Update accList;`

Use of variable in SOQL

We use Apex for dynamic things; hence, we normally use the hardcoded value in SOQL.

We will need to use a variable in SOQL. We will use to identify the variable. Let us look at the following example:

- ```
  String var= 'saif';
  List<Account> accList =[SELECT Name from Account WHERE Name=:var];
  ```
- ```
  Set<String> nameSet=new Set<String>{'saif', 'varsha', 'Atul'};
  List<Account> accList =[SELECT Name from Account WHERE Name IN:nameSet];
  ```

Inner query

The following query returns account IDs if an associated opportunity is **Won**:

```
SELECT Id, Name FROM Account WHERE Id IN (SELECT AccountId FROM Opportunity
WHERE StageName = 'Closed Won')
```

Let us understand the preceding code. In this SOQL statement, we used a keyword **IN and a subquery**. However, this is not so simple. First, break the code into two parts; the last part(subquery) will give you all the **AccountId** of closed Won Opportunity. This means the query within () will give us the list of opportunities with **AccountId**.

Let us check the result in the following figure:

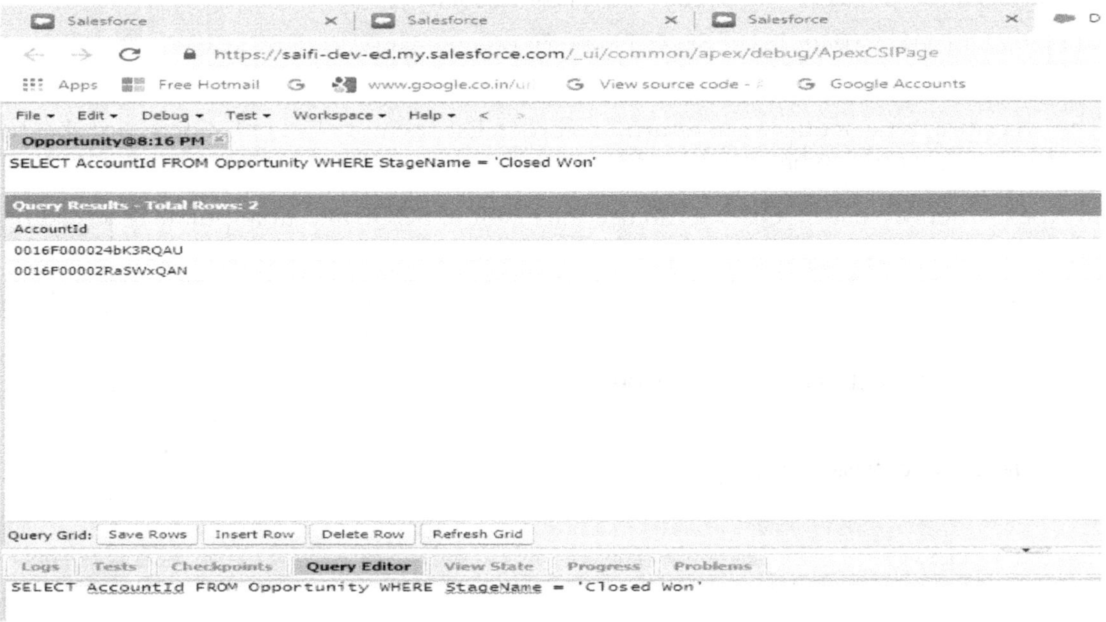

Figure 14.8: Opportunity query

Now the main code will run on **Account**, and **Id** will be searched in the subquery. We are using the result of one query into another:

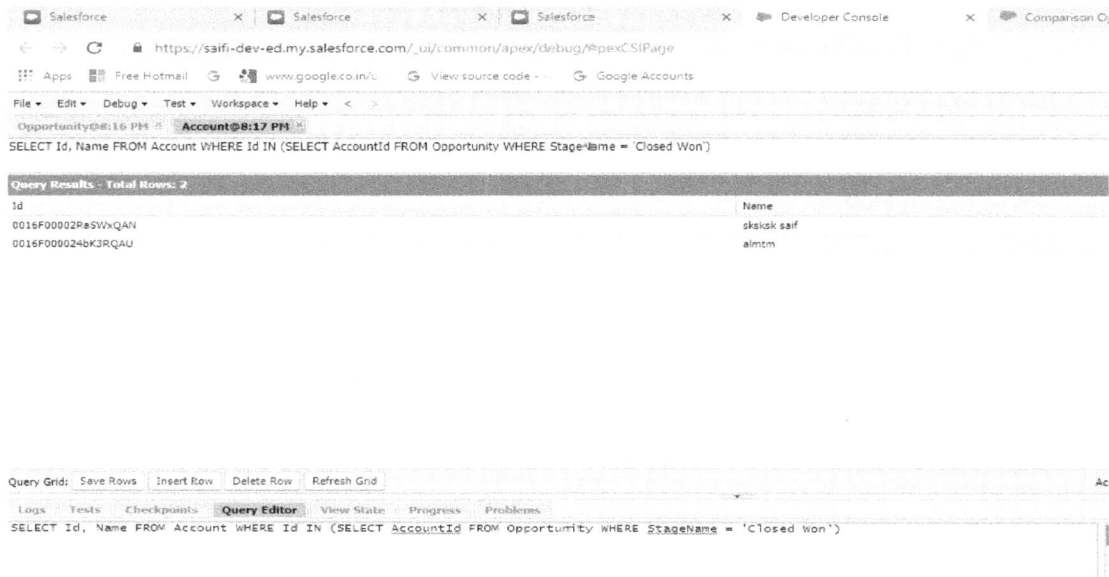

Figure 14.9: Inner query

SOQL with Date

Salesforce is an easy to use technology with several inbuilt tools like Apex, and it seems that Apex and SOQL are quite interesting, but the most amazing fact about SOQL is that it works with Date beautifully. SOQL has hundreds of keywords related to **Date** from **TODAY**, **TOMORROW** to **NEXT_YEAR**. Let us try the following query:

```
SELECT Id, Name FROM Account WHERE lastModifiedDate=TODAY
SELECT Id, Name FROM Account WHERE createdDate=LAST_YEAR
```

The output is shown in the following figure:

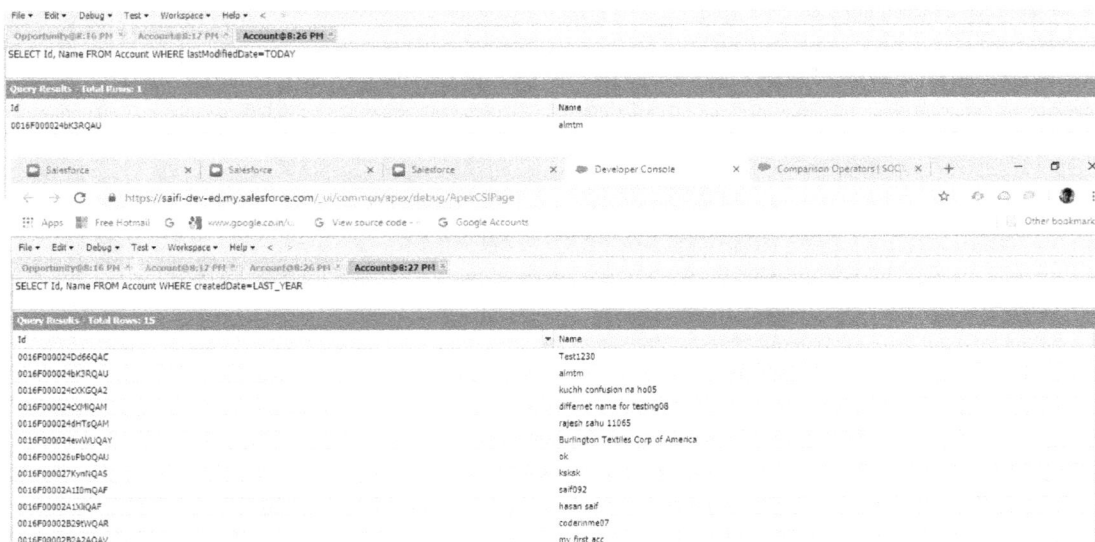

Figure 14.10: Date query

That is the magic; you just think about the date or day, and it is there in SOQL. Following are the keywords that can be used to filter out the records based on **Date** fields:

TODAY, TOMORROW, YESTERDAY, THIS_WEEK, LAST_WEEK, NEXT_WEEK, LAST_MONTH, NEXT_MONTH, THIS_MONTH, THIS_YEAR, LAST_YEAR, NEXT_YEAR

Now you can know the amount of data you want from the query, that is, data for the whole year or a whole month. Not only that, SOQL has **THIS_QUARTER**, **LAST_QUARTER**, **NEXT_QUARTER**, and so on. SOQL has some more **Date**-related reserved words, and they are amazing.

Let us see one example: suppose we want all **Account** that are updated in the last ten days. The query and result will be like this:

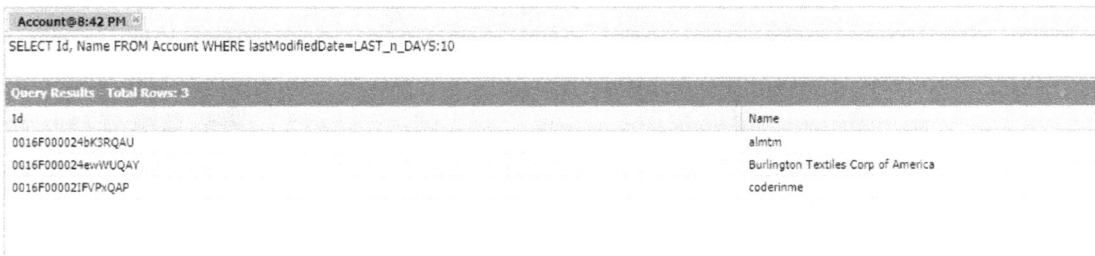

Figure 14.11: Last N days query

Now, we have the following solution for that as well:

LAST_N_DAYS:n, NEXT_N_DAYS:n, LAST_N_MONTHS:n, NEXT_N_MONTHS:n, LAST_N_WEEKS:n, NEXT_N_WEEKS:n, LAST_N_YEARS:n, NEXT_N_YEARS:n

Let us take one more example. Suppose a company wants to know about all the opportunities from the last six weeks:

```
SELECT Name FROM Opportunity WHERE lastModifiedDate = LAST_N_WEEKS:6
```

Now, we can use all the **Date** keywords for SOQL. and it will help us more in our entire Apex life.

SOQL with related objects

If you know SQL foundationally, you would have heard about the foreign key, primary key, JOIN, and nested query. You must wonder why we have not used any of these. This is because Salesforce is not like **Relational Database Management System** (**RDBMS**). It works on the parent-child concept. You have learned the basics of lookup relation and master-detail relationship; Salesforce works on that concept.

Sometimes, we need the data from both **Account** and **Opportunity** or **Contact** and **Opportunity**. In that case, we will need SOQL with a parent or child object. For that purpose, we will understand the relationship of objects at first.

Child to parent relationship

For a standard object, it is very simple. For example, if we want to call an account from a contact, it is like: **Account.Name**:

```
SELECT lastName, Account.Name from Contact
```

For a custom object, we will replace **__c** with **__r** in the parent.

For example, we have a parent object **Employee__c** and a child object **Salary__c**; now, the query will look as follows:

```
SELECT Amount__c, Employee__r.Name From Salary__c
```

So for the parent data, we will just need the name of the parent object if a parent is standard, or we will use **__r** at the end for a custom parent object.

In a single child-to-parent relationship, we can go upto five levels only.

Suppose we want to know the owner's e-mail of account for a particular **Opportunity**; we use the following code:

```
SELECT Account.Owner.email from Contact where id='a0612hhh2fsfs'
```

This was of two levels, **Contact.Account.Owner.FirstName (three levels)**.

Parent-to-child relationship

For a parent to a child relationship, we will use an inner query for child records, and in the standard object, we just have to append s at the end of the child object name. For custom child objects, we will replace __c with __r.

Suppose we want the contact records in **Account** query then:

```
SELECT Name,(SELECT lastName from Contacts) FROM Account
```

In the preceding code, we can see SOQL is on **Account** object, but we want contact details as a child also, so we add that query as an inner query, and add s in the contact object name.

We have a parent object **Employee__c** and child object **Salary__c**. Now, the query will look like the following:

```
SELECT Name ,(SELECT Amount__c From Salaries__r)FROM Employee__c
```

We can go only one level down from parent to child. However, we can call more than one child in an account query.

> **Note: If you are confused with the relationship with the child's name or how it's not saved, just do one thing. Go on that lookup field of child object and check the API name and child relationship name; that is your parent and child name.**

For example, we have a child of **Account** named as **Salary** object. Now, if we want to know the relationship name of the child, we will check the lookup field on the salary object.

Refer to the following figure to understand the child relationship name:

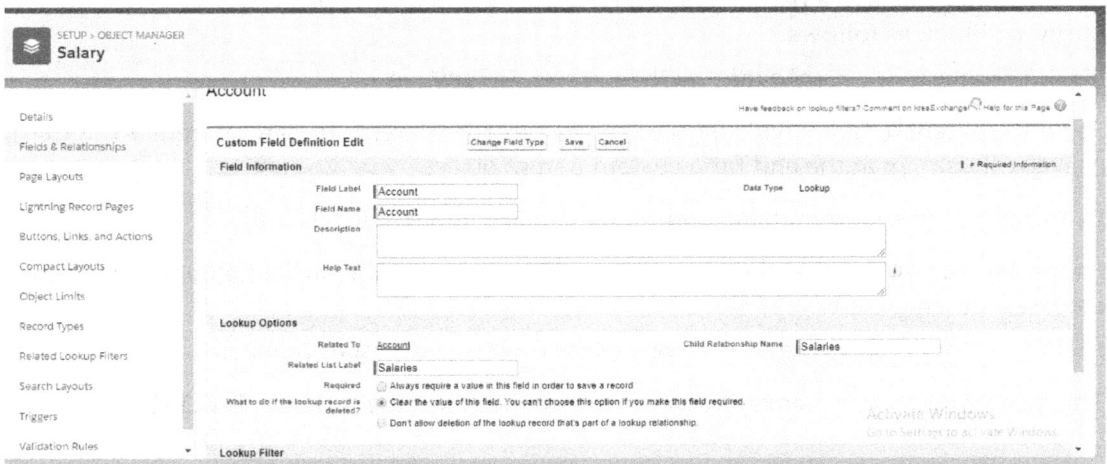

Figure 14.12: Field relationship on salary object

So, from child to parent, we will just use Field Name : **Account__r**.

From parent to child, we will use the field child relationship name: **Salaries__r**

Please be careful with the name of the child relationship because sometimes the label is different from the field API name.

SOQL aggregate functions

We can use aggregate functions in SOQL queries to roll up and summarize your data. Aggregate functions include **AVG()**, **COUNT()**, **MIN()**, **MAX()**, **SUM()**.

We can also use aggregate functions without using a **GROUP BY** clause.

We could use the **AVG()** aggregate function to find the average **Amount** for all your opportunities.

```
SELECT AVG(Amount) FROM Opportunity
```

We could find the average **Amount** for all your opportunities by campaign.

```
SELECT CampaignId, AVG(Amount) FROM Opportunity GROUP BY CampaignId
```

How to use Aggregate SOQL in Apex

```
AggregateResult[] groupedResults
  = [SELECT CampaignId, AVG(Amount) FROM Opportunity GROUP BY CampaignId];
for (AggregateResult ar : groupedResults) {
    System.debug('Campaign ID' + ar.get('CampaignId'));
    System.debug('Average amount' + ar.get('expr0'));
}
```

Salesforce Object Search Language

SOSL is used to construct text-based search queries against the search index. It will help us to search text, e-mail, and phone fields for multiple objects (standard or custom). SOSL has the following features:

- SOSL can be useful for retrieving data for a specific text that exists in a field.
- SOSL searches are faster.
- SOSL uses text-based tokenizer to search fast.
- It can be used to search records from multiple related or unrelated objects.
- We can find records from a particular division in an organization using the division's feature.

SOSL simple syntax*

The first line of code of SOSL will look like the following:

```
FIND {SearchQuery}
[ IN SearchGroup ]
[ RETURNING FieldSpec ]
```

You can check the preceding syntax on *developer.salesforce.com*.

- FIND {saif}

  Using this SOSL, will search all `saif` in the entire system. It will return Id of the record. This is not a case-sensitive search which shown as follows:

- FIND {saif}

  IN Name Fields

  RETURNING Account

  It will search all **saif** in the name field of **Account** and return the record ID.

- FIND {saif}

  IN Name Fields

  RETURNING Account(name, Industry)

It will search all **saif** in the name field of **Account** and will return the name and industry details of that record.

Here is the first example and output of SOSL:

Figure 14.13: SOSL

Here is the query and its output:

```
FIND {saif} IN Name Fields
RETURNING Account(name, Industry), contact(name, phone)
```

This query will return all the account and contact with name saif and will displays industry and phone fields, which is as follows:

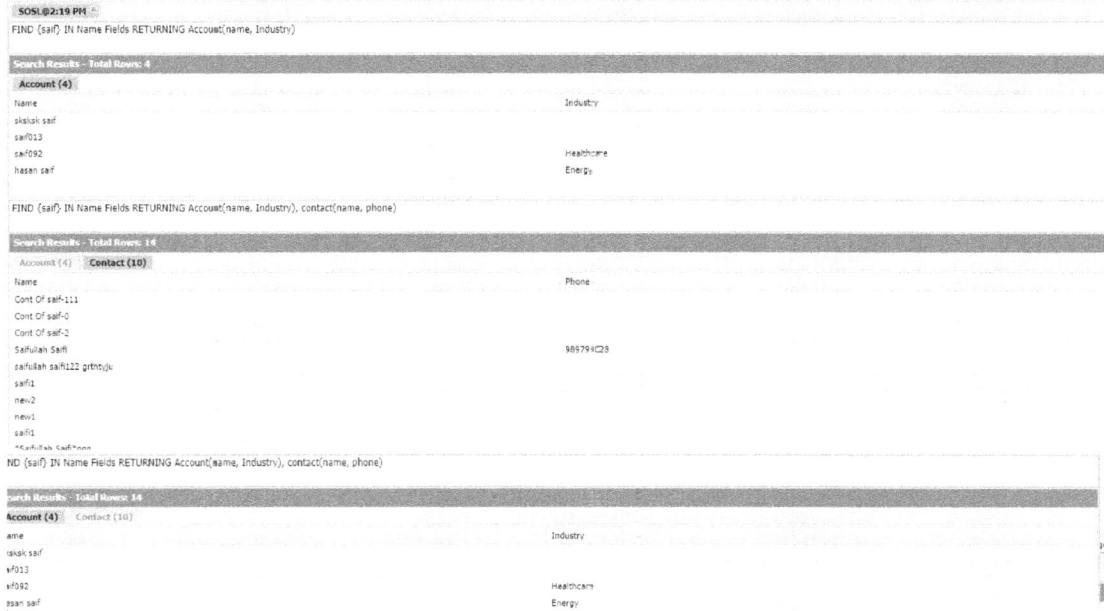

Figure 14.14: SCSL queries

- FIND {saif}

  IN Name Fields

  RETURNING Account (name,incustry where createddate = THIS_YEAR)

You can see that through using SOSL, we can f_ter the data the same as SOQL, as shown in the following query:

FIND {closed} RETURNING Opportunity(id), Contract LIMIT 20

We can use limit the same as SOQL.

SOSL can search for a maximum of 2000 records.

SOSL in Apex

Apex uses SOQL or SOSL data in the list.

In the following query, SOSL gives us the list of **sObject** in which data is from **Account** and **Contact:**

```
List<List<SObject>> searchList = [FIND 'SFDC' IN ALL FIELDS
  RETURNING Account(Name), Contact(FirstName,LastName);
```

Let us take an example. We have written some queries in SOSL. Here is how we will check the account data or opportunity data:

```
List<List <sObject>> searchList = [FIND 'test' IN ALL FIELDS RETURNING Ac-
count (Id,Name,type),Contact(name,email),Opportunity(name,StageName),Lead(-
company,name,status) ];

accList = ((List<Account>)searchList[0]);

conList = ((List<contact>)searchList[1]);

optyList = ((List<Opportunity>)searchList[2]);

leaList = ((List<Lead>)searchList[3]);
```

You can learn more about SOSL on *developers.salesforce.com*.

> **Note:** **You should use SOSL very carefully. If you will search in general, it will take more time.**

If we use the following keywords, it will find the records faster:
- **IN**: Specify the field name or object name.
- **LIMIT**: Records limitations will be good.
- **OFFSET**: Next, n records can be used for pagination.
- **RETURNING**: Limits the objects and fields to return.
- **WITH PricebookId**: Specifies the price book ID to return.

Limitations of Salesforce for SOQL and SOSL

Salesforce is a Cloud-based technology, so it must have some limitations.

In a single transaction, the number of queries we can do or DML operations we can perform are somehow limited, which are as follows:
- Total number of SOQL queries in a single transaction is 100
- Total number of records retrieved by SOQL queries 50,000
- Total number of SOSL queries in a single transaction is 20
- Total number of records retrieved by a single SOSL query 2,000
- Total number of DML statements issued 150

Due to the preceding limitations, Apex programming becomes more interesting and amazing because developers have to find a good way to optimize the code; for example, they cannot use SOQL or SOSL inside a FOR or while loop, or they cannot use DML inside a loop. You can check these in every debug log of the Developer Console as shown in the following figure:

Execution Log

Timestamp	Event	Details
20:01:11:000	LIMIT_USAGE_...	Number of SOQL queries: 0 out of 100
20:01:11:000	LIMIT_USAGE_...	Number of query rows: 0 out of 50000
20:01:11:000	LIMIT_USAGE_...	Number of SOSL queries: 0 out of 20
20:01:11:000	LIMIT_USAGE_...	Number of DML statements: 0 out of 150
20:01:11:000	LIMIT_USAGE_...	Number of DML rows: 0 out of 10000
20:01:11:000	LIMIT_USAGE_...	Maximum CPU time: 0 out of 10000
20:01:11:000	LIMIT_USAGE_...	Maximum heap size: 0 out of 6000000
20:01:11:000	LIMIT_USAGE_...	Number of callouts: 0 out of 100
20:01:11:000	LIMIT_USAGE_...	Number of Email Invocations: 0 out of 10
20:01:11:000	LIMIT_USAGE_...	Number of future calls: 0 out of 50
20:01:11:000	LIMIT_USAGE_...	Number of queueable jobs added to the queue: 0 out of 50
20:01:11:000	LIMIT_USAGE_...	Number of Mobile Apex push calls: 0 out of 10

Figure 14.15: *Governor limit*

Conclusion

In this chapter, we learned about SOQL and SOQL as a Salesforce query and search language, for whenever we want to search or retrieve data from Salesforce; we can use SOQL or SOSL. We also covered how and when to use SOQL and SOSL in Apex. For a single object or parent-child object, we can use SOQL, and for multiple objects and fast searching, we can use SOSL. We discussed what a limitation is and how SOQL and SOSL are useful in Salesforce as Salesforce is a Cloud-based system. So, for every transaction, we have to follow the limits.

In the next chapter, we will discuss the Data Manipulation Language in which we will learn how to insert or delete record(s) from the database.

Questions

1. Find the count of the industry of all accounts (using set/List).
2. Find the account ID of all opportunities.
3. A developer writes a SOQL query to find child records for a specific parent. How many levels can be returned in a single query?
    a. 1
    b. 7
    c. 5
4. Select all accounts whose name ends with ri.
5. Select all opportunities whose probability is between 20 to 75.
6. Income is a custom object; it is a child of a salary object, which is a child of contact.
    a. Write a query from contact to find the name of income.
    b. Write a query from income to find lastName of contact.
7. Write a query for 10 contacts, which is in sorted order of phone, and add 1,2,3,4 at the beginning of the last name of every contact.

8. Write a query for the opportunity close date which is two days more than tomorrow.

9. Income child of salary, salary is a child of contact, contact is a child of account.

   a. Write a query on income and find the owner email of account.

   b. Write a query on salary and find the count of income.

   c. Write a query on income and find the industry of account.

10. We can call all the contacts and opportunities of a particular Account. Try it in your Org.

11. Please see the query: Contact c = [SELECT id, firstname, lastname, email FROM Contact WHERE lastname = 'Smith']; What will be the output of the query if there is no Contact with the last name 'Smith'?

   a. A contact initialized to null.

   b. An error that no rows are found.

   c. An empty list of contacts.

   d. Contact with empty values.

Answers

1. `SELECT COUNT(ID),INDUSTRY FROM Account GROUP BY INDUSTRY`

2. `SELECT Account.Id from Opportunity`

3. a

4. `SELECT name From account where Name LIKE '%ri%'`

5. `SELECT id from opportunity where probablity>=20 and probablity<=75`

6. Parent to child (query on parent) >>>> inner query 1 level

   `SELECt id,(SELECt id from Salaries__r) from Contact`

   a. `string contactid ='…';`

      `[SELECT id,(SELECT Name from Incomes__r) from salary__c where contact__c =:contactid]`

   b. >>> child to parent(query on child) >>> relationship 5 level

      `[SELECT salary__r.AMount__c , salary__r.contact__r.lastName from Income__c];`

7. `List<contact> contList= [SELECT phone,lastname from contact Order by Phone LIMIT 10];`

   `Integer i=1;`

   `for(contact con: contList){`

   `con.lastname = i+'--'+con.lastname;`

```
    //con.firstName = con.firstName.remove('f');
    //i++;
    }
    update contList;
    system.debug(contList);
```
8. `SELECT ID from opportunity WHERE CloseDate=NEXT_N_DAYS:3`
9.
   a. Write a query on income and find the owner of the e-mail account using:

      `SELECT Salary__r.Contact__r.Account.owner.email FROM Income__c`
   b. Write a query on salary and find the count of income:

      `SALARY__c sal= [ SELECT id, (SELECT id from Incomes__r) FROM SALARY__c LIMIT 1];`

      `system.debug(sal.Incomes__r.size());`
   c. Self-attempt.
10. Self-attempt
11. b

Join our Discord space

Join our Discord workspace for latest updates, offers, tech happenings around the world, new releases, and sessions with the authors:

https://discord.bpbonline.com

CHAPTER 15
Data Manipulation Language Essentials

Introduction

In order to manipulate or change data, Salesforce provides **Data Manipulation Language** (**DML**). We can create a record using the DML operations, such as the insert command. Similarly, we can update or delete records using the DML operations. DML operation processes the record to save or remove from the Salesforce Database. Insert, update, delete, upsert, undelete, and merge are the common DML statements that we will use in Apex.

Structure

In this chapter, we will discuss the following topics:
- Data Manipulation Language
- DML syntax
- Limitations of DML

Objectives

After studying this unit, you will learn to use DML in Apex. You will also learn syntax and limitations of DML. Lastly, you will see some example-based approaches with DML.

Data Manipulation Language

Apex gives you a way to insert, update, delete, or restore data in the database using DML. Through DML operations, we can modify the records at one time or in batch. It means we can insert one record of account, or we can make a list of accounts and insert it in a single statement.

It is advisable and is best practice to perform DML operations in such a way that multiple records can be manipulated (inserted or deleted) with a single command since it will help us to avoid the governor limit of 150 in a single transaction.

By default, DML operations work in a system context. This means it often does not depend on the user-based sharing rule. The user may have no access to perform DML operations from the profile. We should always check **Create, Read, Edit, Delete** (**CRUD**) permissions of the current user before performing DML operations.

If a user is executing DML in an anonymous block of the developer console, then all the permissions related to the user will apply to DML.

DML syntax

DML syntax is similar to the DML of other databases like MySQL, and so on. Some common syntax that we will use in Apex are:

- Creation of record: `insert sObject`
- **Updation of an existing record**: `update sObject`
- **Deletion**: `delete sObject`
- **Restoration**: `undelete sObject`
- **Want to insert or update in a single statement**: `upsert sObject`

DML examples

Let us check some examples of DML in Apex:

- **Example one:** If we want to create an account record with name the 'saif', then syntax will be as follows:

```
Account acc= new Account();
acc.Name= 'saif';
insert acc;
```

- **Example two:** If we want to insert multiple records with a single statement then:

```
List<Account> accList= new List<Account>();
Account acc1= new Account();
acc1.Name= 'saif';
```

```
accList.add(acc1);

Account acc2= new Account();
acc2.Name= 'neha';
accList.add(acc2);

insert accList;
```

- **Example three**: Update the existing record using the following code:

```
Account acct = [SELECT Id, BillingCity FROM Account WHERE Name ='saif'
LIMIT 1];
acct.BillingCity = Darbhanga';
update acct;
```

- **Example four:** Delete an account record through performing the following code:

```
Account acct = [SELECT Id FROM Account WHERE Name ='saif' LIMIT 1];
delete acct;
```

- **Example five:** Restore the deleted record from the recycle bin through the following code:

```
Account[] savedAccts = [SELECT Id FROM Account WHERE Name ='saif'  ALL
ROWS];
undelete savedAccts;
```

For undelete, we may have to use **ALL ROWS** so that it can search all the deleted records and archives.

- **Example six:** Sometimes, we need to perform the insert and update operation at once, or we might not want to filter the data that is to be inserted or updated. In that case, we use the Upsert command. Upsert is used when we have an external ID, and we want to manipulate data using that:

```
List<Account> accList = new List<Account>();
// we add some data into it
Account acc = new Account(name='test1', ExtIDField__c='1');
Account acc1 = new Account(name='test2', ExtIDField__c='2');
accList.add(acc);
accList.add(acc1);
upsert accList ExtIDField__c;
```

Here, **ExtIDField__c** is the external ID. Apex will insert or update all the account on the basis of **ExtIDField__c**. If it is already present in the data base, it will update, otherwise insert.

If we have to insert 2 types of **sObject** or update 2 types of **sObject**, we will need 2 DML statements.

Note: **One DML statement will work on one object in one statement, which means we cannot insert account and contact in a single line DML. For this purpose, we will use sObject.**

- **Example seven:** Please check the following code to understand how multiple DML statements are required for different objects:

```
List<Account> accList=[SELECT Name,(SELECT lastName from Contacts)
from Account where Name LIKE '%saif%'];
for(Account acc : accList){
    acc.Name=acc.Name+'-India';
    for(Contact cnt : acc.Contacts){
        cnt.lastName= cnt.lastName+'--Bihar';
    }
}

// Now you can see here, we have changed the name of account and
Lastname of contact
// if we want to update it, we can't update these in a single statemnent
update accList;
// it will only update the accList, not contact of it
// for that, we will need a new conatctlist and update statement
List<Contact> cntList= New List<Contact>();
for(Account acc : accList){
    for(Contact cnt : acc.Contacts){
        cntList.add(cnt);
    }
}
update cntList;
```

Atomicity of Data Manipulation Language operation

You might have heard about the **Atomicity, Consistency, Isolation, and Durability (ACID)** properties of the database transaction. If not, you can learn more about it in any DBMS book by BPB Publications. DML operation is generally atomic; if we have ten records in a list, and we are using the insert command on that list and three records are inserted, but seven have failed due to some validation such as required field issue and custom validation rules, then Apex will abort all the ten records, and the transaction will fail. This means either all ten will be inserted or none of them. That is known as atomicity.

We generally use **Try** and **Catch** to avoid these types of unexpected errors. It means if the **DML** failed, it would go to catch, and if not, it will successfully work in the **try block**. Let us check the following code to understand:

```
Account acct = [SELECT Id, BillingCity FROM Account WHERE Name ='saif' LIMIT
1];
acct.BillingCity = Darbhanga';
try{
update acct;
}Catch(Exception e){
System.debug(e.getLineNumber());
Sytem.debug(e.getMessages());
}
```

However, if we want no atomicity, we can use the database class to perform DML operations.

Database class

The database class contains methods for creating and manipulating data.

It has DML methods, as shown in the following code:

```
Database.insert(sObject records, Boolean allorNone);
Database.upsert(sObject records, Boolean allorNone);
Database.update(sObject records, Boolean allorNone);
Database.delete(sObject records, Boolean allorNone);
```

All of these methods take two parameters that are a list of records or single records of Salesforce object and Boolean value.

The Boolean value will ask you to operate with full success or partial success.

This means you want all data to be manipulated or some of these if some records failed.

For example, consider that we have ten records in a list; we use the insert command on that list and three records are inserted, but seven have failed due to some validation such as required field issue and custom validation rules. If the Boolean value is true, then all the ten records will fail and would not get inserted. This means either all ten records will be inserted or none of these.

However, if the Boolean value is false, then three will be inserted. Let us check the following code:

```
List<Account> accList= new List<Account>();
Account acc1= new Account();
acc1.Name= 'saif';
accList.add(acc1);
Account acc2= new Account();
acc2.Name= 'neha';
accList.add(acc2);
Database.insert(accList ,false);
// partial success , if one fails , other can be inserted
Database.insert(accList ,true);
// ful success , either both or none can be inserted
```

We have a similar method for all DML in database class.

The SaveResult class

Check out the following code:

```
// We are Creating two contacts, one of which is missing a required field
lastName and Phone
Contact[] cnts = new List<Contact>{
    new Contact(LastName='cnt of Atul', Phone='+919897699028'),
    new Contact()};
Database.SaveResult[] srList = Database.insert(cnts, false);
// Iterate through each returned result
for (Database.SaveResult sr : srList) {
    if (sr.isSuccess()) {
        // Operation was successful, so get the ID of the record that was
processed
        System.debug('Successfully inserted Contact. Contact ID: ' +
sr.getId());
    }
    else {
        // Operation failed, so get all errors
        for(Database.Error err : sr.getErrors()) {
            System.debug('The following error has occurred.');
            System.debug(err.getStatusCode() + ': ' + err.getMessage());
```

```
        System.debug('Contact fields that affected this error: ' + err.
getFields());
        }
    }
}
```

The **SaveResult** class will give you the output of a DML operation that fails or succeeded.

Inserting multiple sObjects in single DML

Every object of Salesforce is **sObject**. Which is why if we want to insert **contact** and **Account** in a single DML statement, we use the **sObject**. Take a look at the following:

- We will make the list of sObject.
- We will add account and contact into that list.
- We will insert that list.

Let us see the following syntax:

```
List<sObject> multipleObjRecords= new List<sObject>();
Account acc = new Account(Name = 'Saif');
Contact con = new Contact(lastName='test 1' , email='abc@gmail.com');
multipleObjRecords.add(acc);
multipleObjRecords.add(con);
insert multipleObjRecords;
```

Limitations of DML

Here is the list of drawbacks of DML:

- In a single transaction, only 150 DML operations are allowed.
- We can insert/update/delete the records in bulk, means in a list.
- We should not use DML inside For Loop.
- We should use try and catch if we are not sure that data is fully validated, which means the required field is missing or there is some validation rule issue.
- We should check the data or validate before DML, to avoid DML exception error.
- We should avoid the hardcode value as much as we can.

Take the following example:

```
List<Account> accList=[SELECT Name,(SELECT lastName from Contacts) from
Account where Name LIKE '%saif%'];
for(Account acc : accList){
```

```
    acc.Name=acc.Name+'-India';
    for(Contact cnt : acc.Contacts){
        cnt.lastName= cnt.lastName+'--Bihar';
    }
    update acc.Contacts;
}
update accList;
// if count of update command is less than 150, no issue but when it cross
150, dml exception limit error will be there
// because update command is within the for loop
```

You can check example 7; we used DML outside the loop.

Try the DML on an anonymous window and check the beauty of it. In the following figure, you can see we used DML inside the loop, and DML count is 200 so it is giving an error:

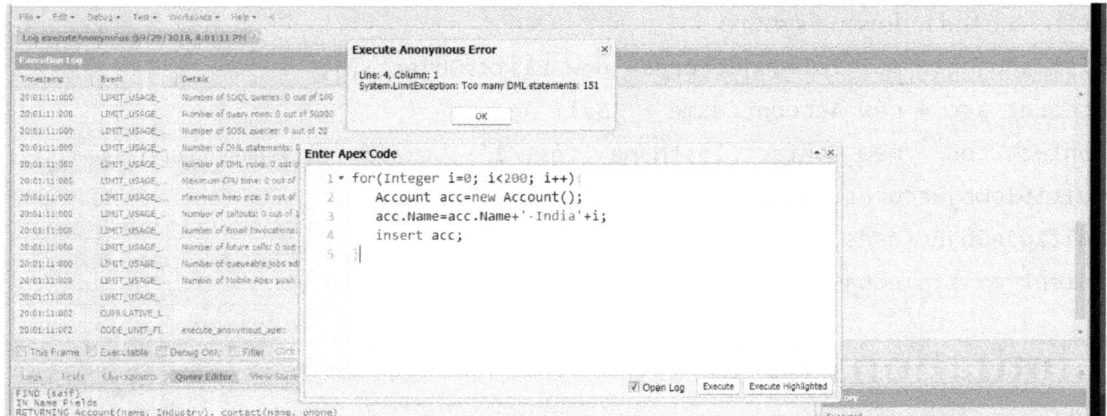

Figure 15.1: DML Limit error

In the following figure, since DML is outside the loop, all 200 records will insert in bulk, and the DML count is only 1:

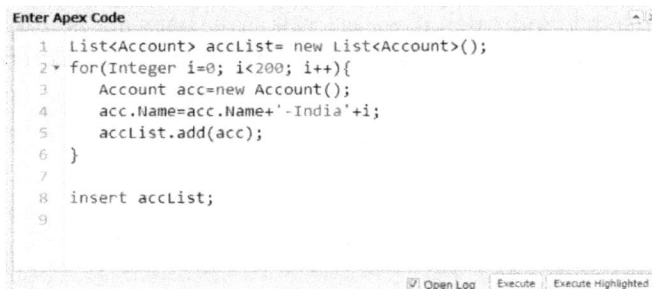

Figure 15.2: Bulk DML

Conclusion

In this chapter, we learned about DML as a data operation language which will be used to save, modify, or delete the data. We learned that we can insert a single record, list of records, and records of multiple objects using a single DML statement. We have covered the uses and limitations of DML and how to handle the database transaction. We also learned that in order to check the DML results, we can use **SaveResult** class, and to control, we can use the **Database** class. In the next chapter, we will discuss the Apex trigger, in which we will learn about all the use cases of the trigger. We will also study about the best practices of writing trigger questions.

Questions

1. What are the number of records in a single DML transaction?
2. Can we insert an account and contact using a single DML.
3. Can we check the result of DML? If so, how?
4. How to rollback from DML?
5. Upsert command syntax.

Answers

1. 10000
2. Yes, through using List<SObject> and we can add both in that List and do DML
3. Using SaveResult class, isSuccess, and getError method we can use.
4. Savepoint and Rollback:
   ```
   Account acc = new Account(Name = 'test1');
   insert acc;
   // Create a savepoint
   Savepoint sp = Database.setSavepoint();
   // Change the account number
   acc.AccountNumber = '1223';
   update acc;
   // Rollback to the previous null value
   Database.rollback(sp);
   //now the account number will be null after rollback
   ```
5. Upsert List<SOject> externalId (optional).

Join our Discord space

Join our Discord workspace for latest updates, offers, tech happenings around the world, new releases, and sessions with the authors:

https://discord.bpbonline.com

Chapter 16
Trigger Essentials

Introduction

If we want something that cannot be customized or done by Salesforce's declarative approach when a record is getting created or updated, then we need an Apex trigger. In this chapter, we will learn about the Salesforce triggers, which are a bunch of code that are executed based on record manipulation, resulting in the updation, insertion, or deletion of record or records. We will learn that if any record is inserted, deleted, or updated, we can write a trigger and work with the code.

Structure

In this chapter, we will discuss the following topics:

- Apex trigger
- Writing triggers
- Bulkifying the trigger
- Best practices for trigger
- Trigger helper

Objectives

After studying this unit, you will understand the Apex trigger. We will also study the use and advantage of triggers along with ways to write triggers that can handle records in bulk using best practices.

Apex trigger

You might be familiar with Lightning Flow. Sometimes, they cannot help with our needs. We know that they can update the related field or work on schedule, but there are various cases where only a trigger can work.

For example, we know that to roll up a summary, only a master-detail relation can be used. However, we want some type of rollup in lookup objects and we cannot use Lightning Flows.

In simple words, if we want something that cannot be customized or done by Salesforce's declarative approach, then we need an Apex trigger.

Before fully going into its use, let us have the basic knowledge of Salesforce triggers, how they can help us, how to operate them, and so on.

Salesforce triggers are units of code that is executed based on record manipulation, resulting in the updation, insertion, or deletion of record or records. Trigger can also help while merging and restoring records.

If any record is inserted, deleted, or updated, we can write a trigger and work with the code.

The syntax of the trigger is as follows:

```
trigger trigger_name on object_name (events){
    —-trigger body—-
}
```

These triggers are worked upon various events, such as:

- **Insert**: This will run on the **Before** and **After** condition.
- **Update**: This will run on the **Before** and **After** condition.
- **Delete**: This will run on the **Before** condition only.
- **Upsert**: This will run on the **Before** and **After** only.
- **Undelete**: This will run on **After** only.

Knowing the Before and After events in trigger

The Before and After is a condition for a trigger that decides when this trigger will execute. If we say **before insert**, this means that we are creating a record, and before it saves to the database, we want this trigger to execute it. If we are using **before insert** trigger, we do not need to do any **Data Manipulation Language (DML)** operation on that record inside the trigger. Before insert trigger will populate the value before actual commit or insertion in database.

If we are saying **after insert**, this means that we are creating a record, and after it saves to the database, that is, we now have a record ID; we want this trigger to execute it.

Suppose we have a trigger that auto-appends −91 as a suffix for every account phone field before the insertion of record. Then, if we create a record and put the phone in the account phone's field, this trigger will work, and we will not need any extra DML, as shown in the following figure:

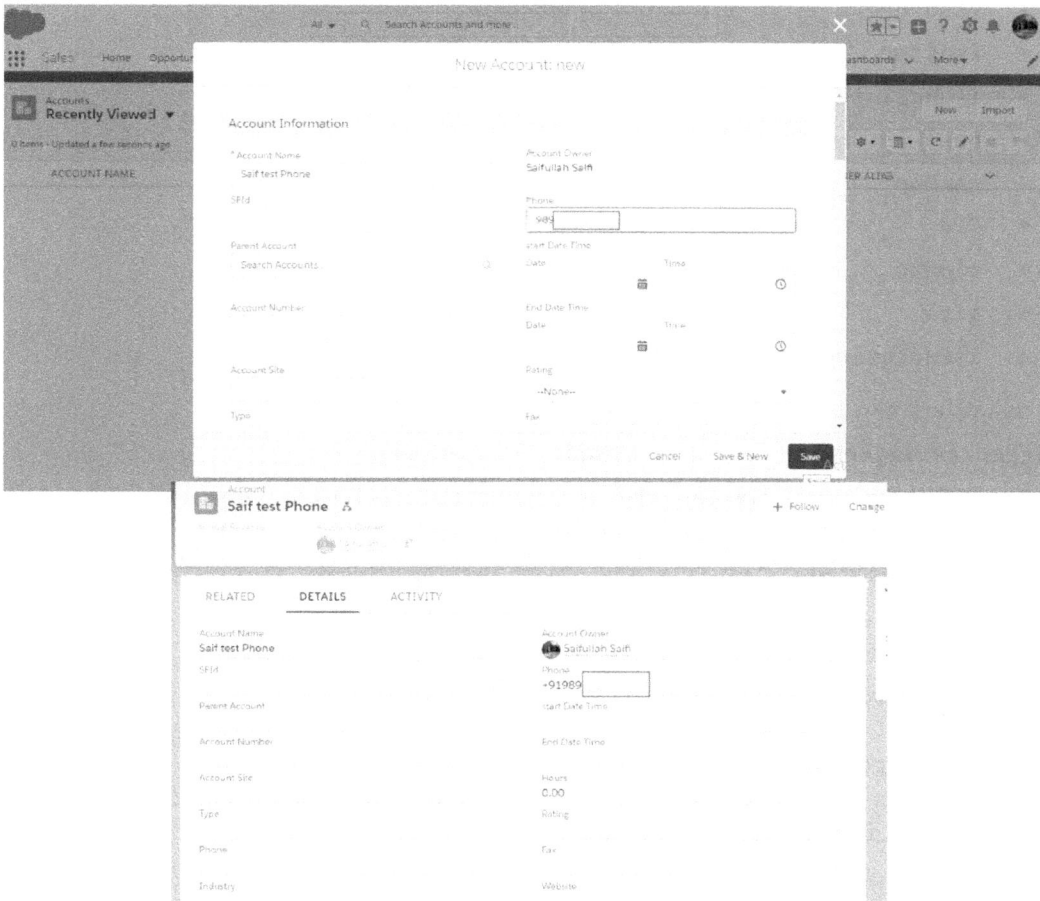

Figure 16.1: Trigger example one

For the preceding figure, the code is as follows:

```
trigger updatePhone on Account (before insert) {
    for(Account acc: Trigger.New){
        if(acc.Phone!=null)
            acc.phone='+91'+acc.Phone;
    }
}
```

The following are the special variables of the trigger used to customize the trigger efficiently:

- **isInsert**
- **isUpdate**
- **isDelete**
- **isBefore**
- **isAfter**
- **isUndelete**
- **new**
- **newMap**
- **Old**
- **oldMap**
- **size**
- **isExecuting**

Let us understand the following syntax and code in order:

Trigger <triggerName> on <ObjectName> (<events>)

- **<triggerName>**: You can write any name, but it is best to name it according to the work it will do, for example, **updatePhoneTrigger**.
- **<ObjectName>**: Any salesforce object on which this trigger will execute.
- **<events>**: On the event you want to execute trigger. For example, **before insert**, **before update, after update, after undelete, before delete**, and so on.
- **Trigger.New**: It always holds the value of a list of **sObject** on which trigger is written. At the time of event, whatever is the data or record there, it is always in **Trigger.New**. In the preceding code, you can see our code was written on **Account**, so **Trigger.new** was holding the records of **Account**, that is, **Trigger. New = List<account>** this time.
- **Trigger.old**: Suppose you are changing the phone number of an account. So, if a trigger is there and the event is update, **Trigger.old** will hold the value of that record before changes, and **Trigger.new** will hold the changed data.

Trigger.old cannot work with insert events, it can only work with update and delete.

We will use **Trigger.NewMap** and **trigger.OldMap** in the as well . These maps contain the ID of the record as a key and that whole record as a value.

- **Trigger.addError**: If we want a custom validation such as validation rule on a record, we can use **trigger.addError** in before trigger.

Trigger always works in batch. It means a **Trigger.New** or **trigger.old** works on 200 records in one execution. So, we should write a trigger in a way that no governor limit should exceed.

Writing triggers

There are multiple ways to write a trigger. Salesforce provides its development environment called the developer console, similarly, we can use the **Visual Studio (VS)** code for writing a trigger.

Let us discuss the same in order.

We can use the developer console to create the Apex trigger through the following steps:

1. Open your developer console.
2. Go to **File** and then **New**.
3. In the dropdown list, click on the second option **Apex Trigger**, as shown in the following figure:

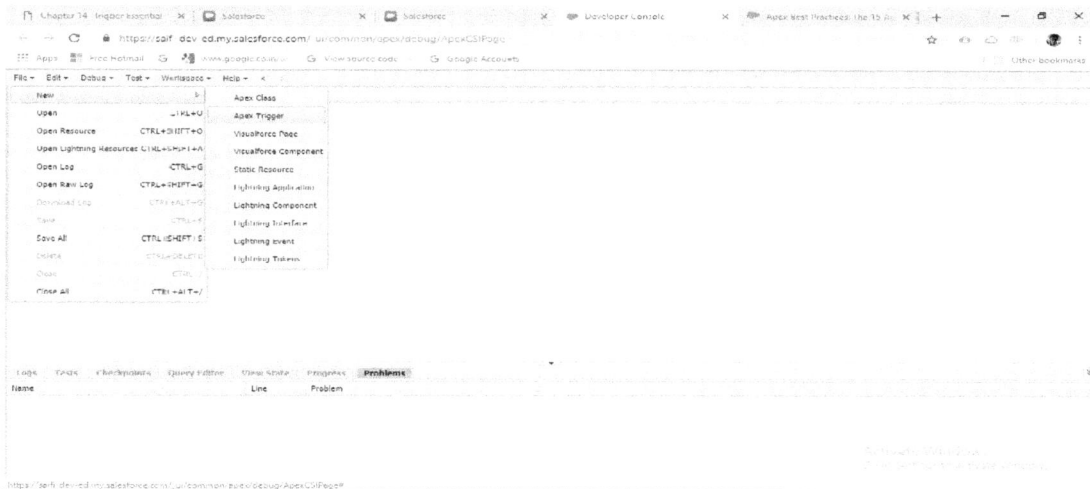

Figure 16.2: Trigger developer console

4. Write the name of the trigger and choose the object from the dropdown. Now, write the logic you want to write:

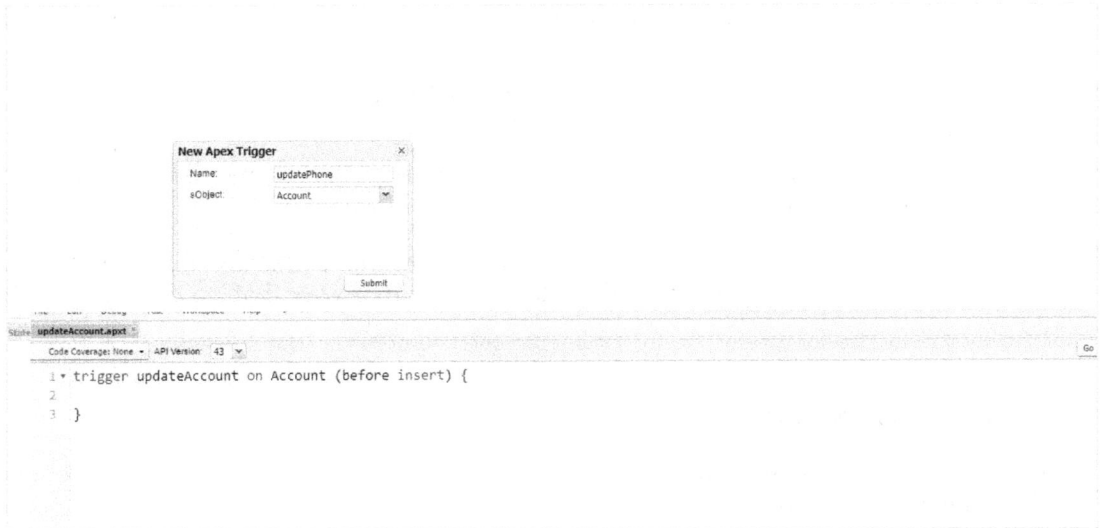

Figure 16.3: Trigger naming convention

In Setup, if you want to create an Apex Trigger, here are the steps as follows:

1. Go to **Setup** in Salesforce.
2. Click on **Object Manager.**
3. Click on the object you want to write trigger on.
4. On the left-hand side, click on **Trigger:**

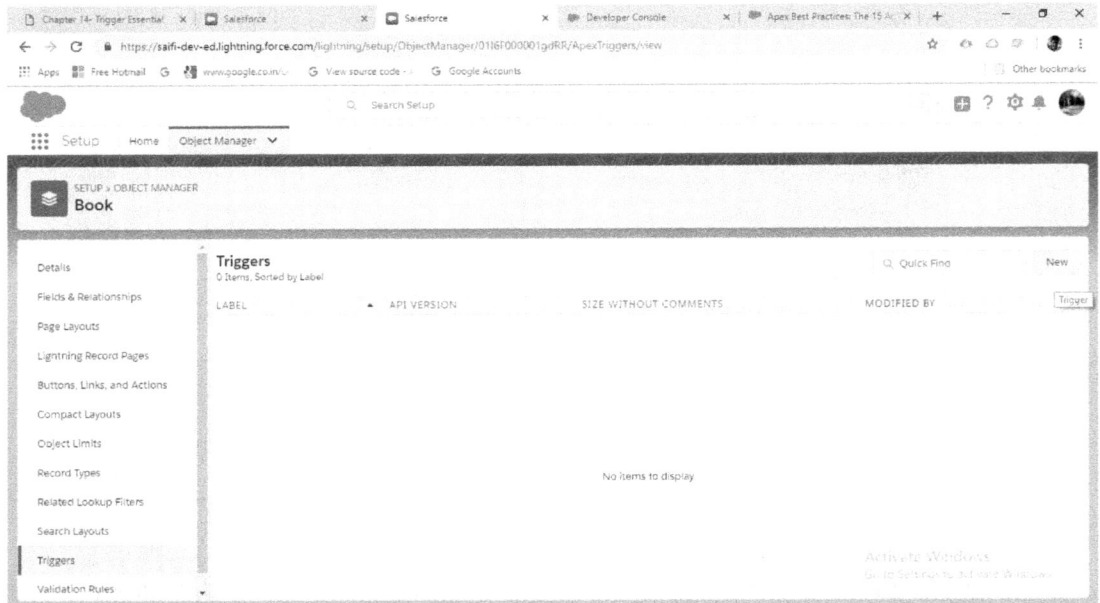

Figure 16.4: Trigger from Setup

5. There is a new button on the right side. Click on that.6. Change the name and events and write the code inside it.

7. Click on **Save**:

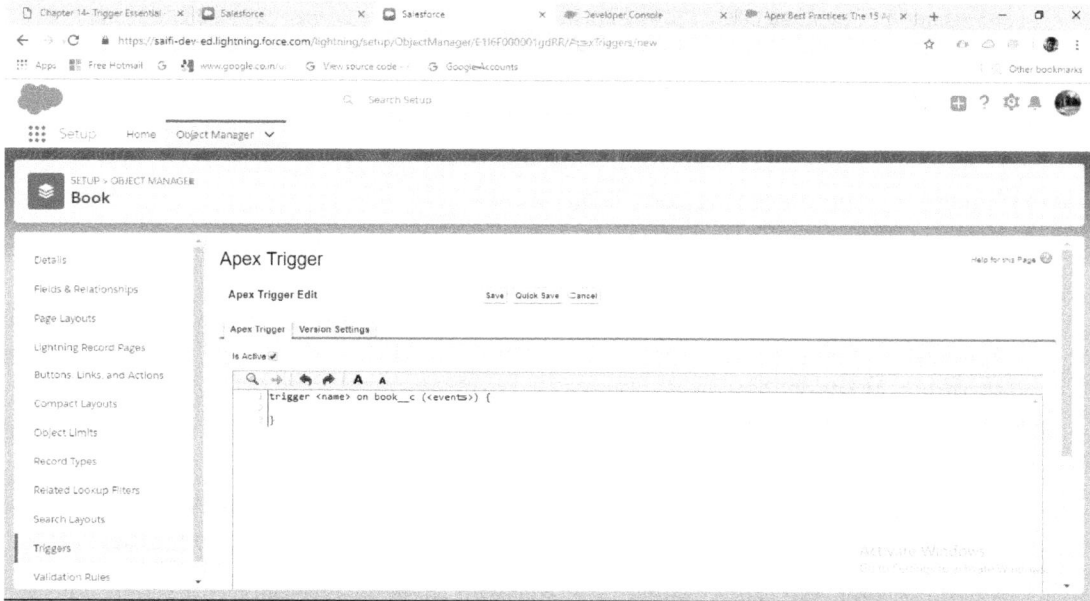

Figure 16.5: Trigger Setup two

In the preceding figure, you can see a **Is Active** check box. If this checkbox is checked, trigger is active.

Remember that, sometimes you have to deactivate the trigger, so you need to uncheck that box.

Use case one

When an account is created or updated, we have to change the status to **Active** or **Inactive** based on the account type. If the account type is a prospect, then the status will be active and the active checkbox will be true; otherwise, it should be inactive. Trigger will update or throw an error if the checkbox is checked wrong. Now, understand the following trigger code:

```
trigger updateType on Account (before insert,before update) {
        for(Account ac:Trigger.new){
             if(ac.Type=='Prospect')
                  ac.Status __c='Active';
             else
```

```
                        ac.Status __c='Inactive';
            if(ac.Status __c=='Active' && ac.Active__c!=true)
                ac.Active__c.addError('Active field should be checked);
            else if(ac.Status __c=='Inactive' && ac.Active__c!=false)
                ac.Active__c.addError('Active field should be Unchecked);
        }
    }
}
```

The explanation of the preceding code is as follows:

- In the first line, the trigger is working on the **Account** object of Salesforce and the event as before insert before the update.
- Then, a **for** loop is running, fetching all the new records from **trigger.New** in **Account** variable **ac**. It means any account record that is creating or updating are stored in **trigger.New**.
- After that, it checks the **if** condition, that is, if the account type is **Prospect**, then this account will become active; otherwise, it is inactive.
- Then in the next **if** condition, it checks if the account status is **Active**. Since the **Active** field is not checked, it throws an error; otherwise, the **else** will work.

Let us test the trigger. We will create a new Account of Type **Prospect** and when we save it, it will throw an error, as shown in the following figure:

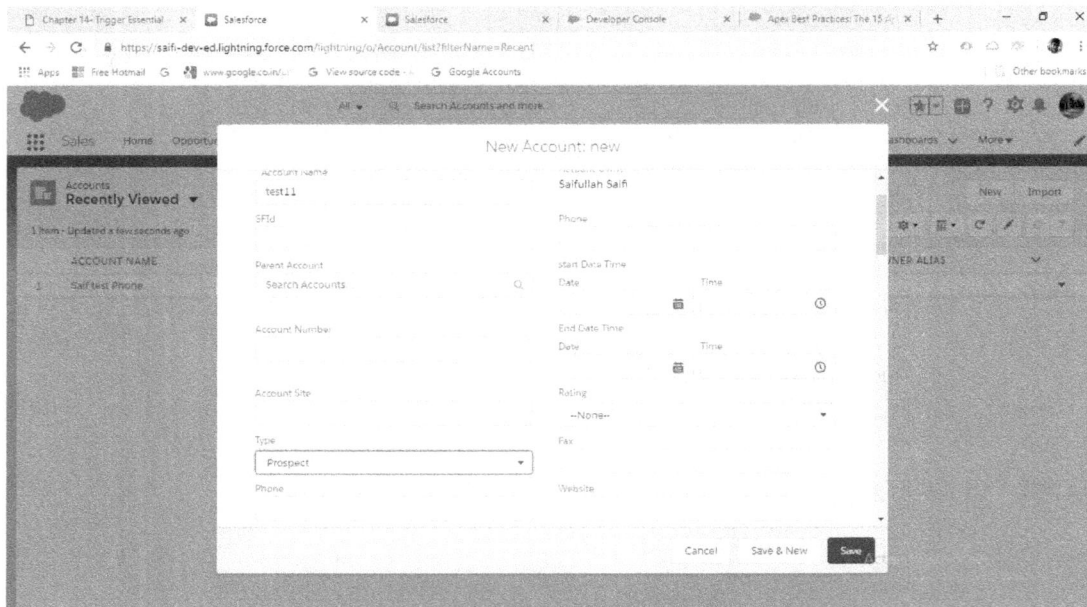

Figure 16.6: Trigger example two

Click on **Save** and an error will appear, as shown in the following figure:

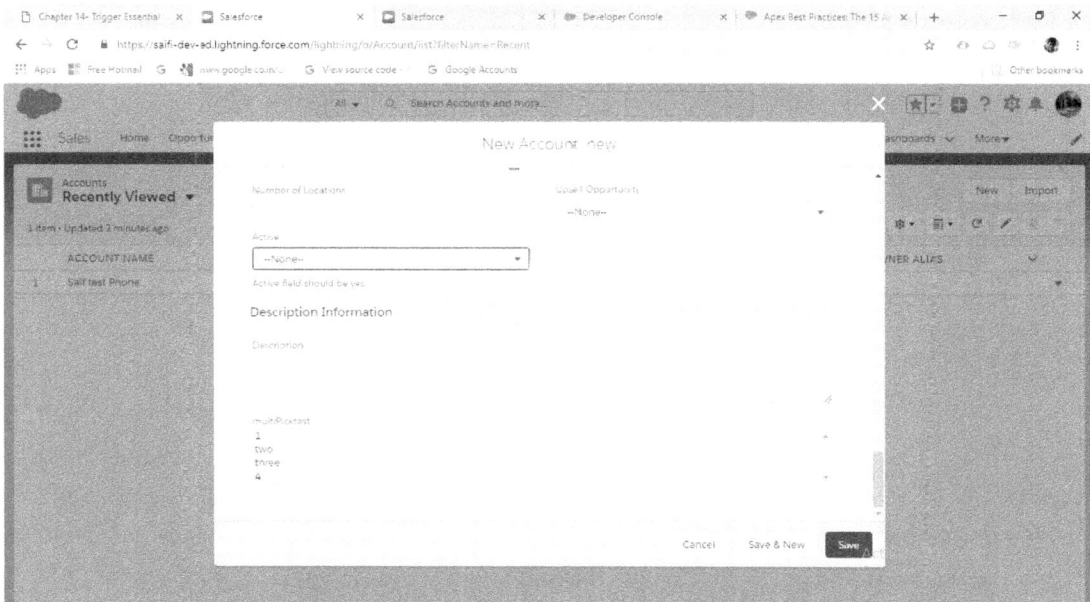

Figure 16.7: Trigger example error case

Use case two

Here we will create related records or contacts of a particular account, based on the value in the **no of contact** field. Let us see the following code:

```
trigger createContact on Account (after insert, after update){
    // we have to insert contacts based on the count on Account's No of
contact field, so we need a list of contacts
    List<contact> contlist=new List<contact>();
    for(Account a:Trigger.new){
        integer i=0;   //contact number
        if(a.No_of_Contact__c!=null){
// based on no of contact field we will create contact
            if((trigger.isUpdate && a.No_of_Contact__c != Trigger.oldMap.
get(a.id).No_of_Contact__c) || trigger.isInsert){
                /* here if account record is being inserted then we will need
to create contact or we are updating no of contact field on the account
    */
                while(i<a.No_of_Contact__c){
```

```
                        contact c=new contact();
                        c.LastName='Cont Of '+a.Name+'-'+i;
                        c.AccountId=a.id;
                        contlist.add(c);
                        i++;
                    }
                }
            }
        }
        if(contlist.size()>0)
            insert contlist;
}
```

In the preceding code, we made a list of contacts that can store more than one record at a time. Then the for loop of **Account**, which fetches the data from **trigger.new**.

In the **for** loop first, we will check whether the account field **No_of_Contact__c** is not null. If **No_of_Contact__c** is not null, it will go inside the loop and check if the **trigger. isUpdate** operation is fired. If the previous value of the field is not as same as the current value, then go for the insertion part. After the validation of the if loop, the contacts will insert or update as per the value given in the field, for example, if it is 2, then two contacts are created.

In the end, it will check whether the contact list is empty, then it will insert all the contact records in the org.

Use case three

Let us solve one problem using map: Write a trigger for every time a lead is created; an account will be created or updated based on an e-mail. If the lead's e-mail is in any existing account's e-mail, then it will update the account name to the lead's last name. If the lead's e-mail does not belong to any account, then the new account should be created with the name as the lead's **lastName** and e-mail as a lead's e-mail.

If we code it using for loop and list, then the update trigger code will be as follows:

```
trigger saveAccountForEmailTrigger on Lead(after insert){
    List<Account> acList = new List<Account>();
    List<String> emailList = new List<String>();

    for(Lead ld : Trigger.New){
```

```
        if(ld.email!=null){
            emailList.add(ld.email);
        }
    }

    if(emailList.size()>0){
        acList = [SELECT name, email__c FROM Account WHERE email__c IN :
emailList];
    }

    if(acList.size()>0){
        for(Lead ld : Trigger.New){
            for(Account acc : acList){
                if(ld.email == acc.email__c){
                    acc.Name = ld.LastName;
                }
            }
        }
    }
    else{
        for(Lead ld : Trigger.New){
            Account acc = new Account();
            acc.Name = ld.LastName;
            acc.email__c = ld.email;
            acList.add(acc);
        }
    }

    if(acList.size()>0){
            upsert acList;
        }
    }
}
```

However, it is not an optimized code due to a nested for loop. In the preceding code, a
simple trigger, which will work on before insert, was written. This means whenever a new

lead will be created, this trigger will execute. We will use a map like the following; then, you will see how the code is well-optimized:

```
trigger emailAcc on Lead (after insert) {
    set <string> emailset=new set <string>();
    for(lead ld: Trigger.New){
        if(ld.email!=null){
            emailset.add(ld.email);
        }
    }


    Map<String,Account> emailmap=new Map<String,Account>();
    if(emailset!=null && emailset.size()>0){
        list<Account> aclist=[Select Id,name,email__c from Account where
email__c in:emailset];
        if(aclist.size()>0){
            for(Account a: aclist)
                emailmap.put(a.email__c,a);
        }
    }

    list<Account> upsertlist=new List<Account>();
    for(lead ld: Trigger.New){
        Account acc = new Account();
        if(emailmap.size()>0 && emailmap.containsKey(ld.email)){
            acc = emailmap.get(ld.email);
            acc.name=ld.LastName;
            upsertlist.add(acc);
        }else{
            acc.Name= ld.LastName;
            acc.email__c = ld.email;
            upsertlist.add(acc);
        }
    }

    if(upsertlist.size()>0){
```

```
        upsert upsertlist;
    }
}
```

Let us understand the preceding code:

We have stored the lead's e-mail into to **emailset** if the email field is not blank in the lead. Then, we queried it on **Account** to find whether there is any account with the same e-mail as any lead. If any account appears, we can put the value in the map with every account e-mail as a key. Finally, we iterated every lead and checked in the map whether was any key that had the same e-mail as a lead. If there is, we update that account name with the help of the map and add it to a list **upsertlist**. If there is no account with the same e-mail, then we create a new one and add it again into the **upsertlist** after the loop. We checked the size of that list and **upsert** it as there may be some new and some existing accounts.

> Note: **Always check the size of the list or set, map before using that list in Salesforce Object Query Language (SOQL) or DML. If you are using map, please use containskey before using get.**

Bulkifying the trigger

Trigger always works on a batch of 200 records in a single transaction. So, the trigger should be **bulkified**. Bulkified simply means that the trigger should work for 200 records, at least without exceeding the governor limit, it means no more than 100 SOQL or 150 DML in a trigger should work. The use of **Map** will give us a way to write code in an optimized and bulkified way. Let us take one more example and the use of **Map** in the trigger.

Use case four

There is a custom object **AREA** with three fields- **Name**, **AreaCode__c**, **AreaCount__c**, and we have created two custom fields **Area_Count__c** (**Number** field) and **Area__c** (Lookup of **AREA**) in the standard object **ACCOUNT**. If we create an account with the existing area, then the number of **Area_Count__c** increases by 1 and displays as "*for Dilshad Garden it would be like DG-001,*" and after the second insertion, it will be *DG-002,* and so on. We can delete the account also, and the count remains accurate. If we again insert an account, it will again increment from the last count value.

The code is as follows:

```
trigger PopulateArea on Account(before insert,after delete){
    if(trigger.isInsert){
        Set<id> strNew = new Set<id>();
        for(Account ac:trigger.new)
```

```
        strNew.add(ac.Area__c);
                Map<id,Area__c> mapArea = new Map<id,Area__c>([Select
Name,AreaCode__c,AreaCount__c,(select id, Area_Count__c from Accounts__r
Order By createdDate DESC LIMIT 1) from Area__c where id IN: strNew]);
        Map<id,Integer> mapCount = new Map<id,Integer>();
/* In the above section, we are operating upon insertion.
```

First, we added the ID of the area of **Account** in the set that we just inserted, then queried it. The above query will get fields like (**Name, AreaCode__c, AreaCount__c**) of the object **Area** and the fields of related **Account** in the inner query. We are only taking recently created account, so that we have the last counter value to increase it.

Now, we are checking in which account the area exists and will increase the count of area related to that account by 1:

```
*/
        for(Account act:trigger.new){
            if(mapArea.containsKey(act.Area__c)){
                Integer count = 0, arCount=0;
                if(mapArea.get(act.Area__c).Accounts__r.size()>0)
                    arCount =Integer.valueOf(mapArea.get(act.Area__c).
Accounts__r[0].Area_Count__c.split('-')[1]);
                if(mapCount.containsKey(act.Area__c)){
                    count =   arCount + 1 + apCount.get(act.Area__c);
                    Integer mpcnt=mapCount.get(act.Area__c)+1;
                    mapCount.put(act.Area__c,mpcnt);
                }
                else{
                count = arCount + 1;
                mapCount.put(act.Area__c,1);
                }
                if(count<10)
                    act.Area_Count__c = mapArea.get(act.Area__c).AreaCode__c
+ '-00' + count;
                else if(count>=10 && count<100)
                    act.Area_Count__c = mapArea.get(act.Area__c).AreaCode__c
+ '-0' + count;
                else if(count>100)
```

```
                    act.Area_Count__c = mapArea.get(act.Area__c).AreaCode__c
+ '-' + count;
            }
        }
/*
```

In the preceding code, we check whether the map contains that area, then increase the **countMap** by 1 to store the count of the **Area**, increment it and put that counter value on the map.

In the next logic, we just checked whether it crosses the limited value to a particular range, then the counter will change:

```
*/
        for(Area__c ar: mapArea.values()){
            if(mapCount.containsKey(ar.id))
                ar.AreaCount__c += mapCount.get(ar.id);
        }
        update mapArea.values();
    }
/*
```

Then, at last, we put the **Area_Count** value in the field from the map and update it:

```
*/
    if(trigger.isDelete){
        Set<id> strOld = new Set<id>();
        Map<id,Area__c> mapDel = new Map<id,Area__c>();
        Map<id,Integer> mapDelCount = new Map<id,Integer>();
        for(Account acct : trigger.old)
            strOld.add(acct.Area__c);
        List<Area__c> arr = [select Name,AreaCode__c,AreaCount__c from Area__c
where id IN: strOld];
        for(Area__c area : arr)
            mapDel.put(area.ic, area);
        for(Account acct : trigger.old){
            if(mapDel.containsKey(acct.Area__c)){
                if(mapDelCount.containsKey(acct.Area__c)){
                    Integer countDel=mapDelCount.get(acct.Area__c)+1;
                    mapDelCount.put(acct.Area__c,countDel);
```

```
            }
            else
                mapDelCount.put(acct.Area__c,1);
        }
    }

    for(Area__c ar: mapDel.values()){
        if(mapDelCount.containsKey(ar.id))
            ar.AreaCount__c -= mapDelCount.get(ar.id);
    }

    update mapDel.values();
    }
}
```

We do the same as we did in the case of delete- we retrieve the values, store it and delete the **Account**.

Use case five

Every **Account** has a child object named leave application with these fields, as shown in the following figure:

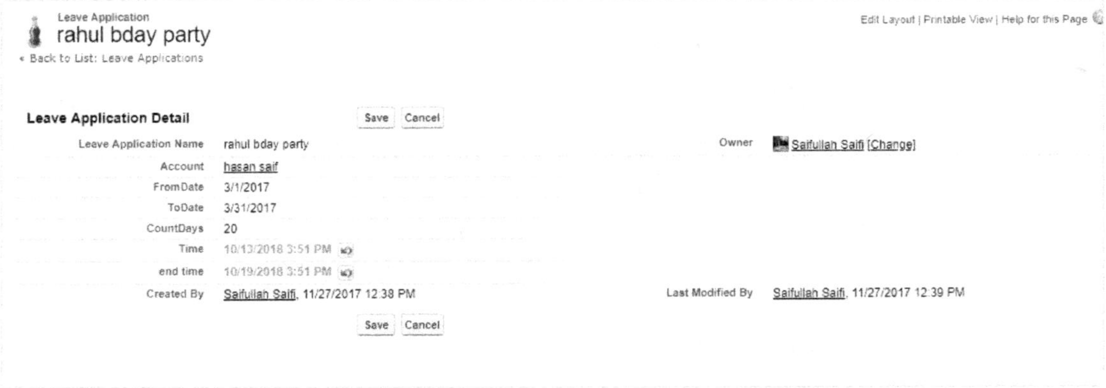

Figure 16.8: Trigger example three

One-holiday object is there to keep the record of Holiday, as shown in the following figure:

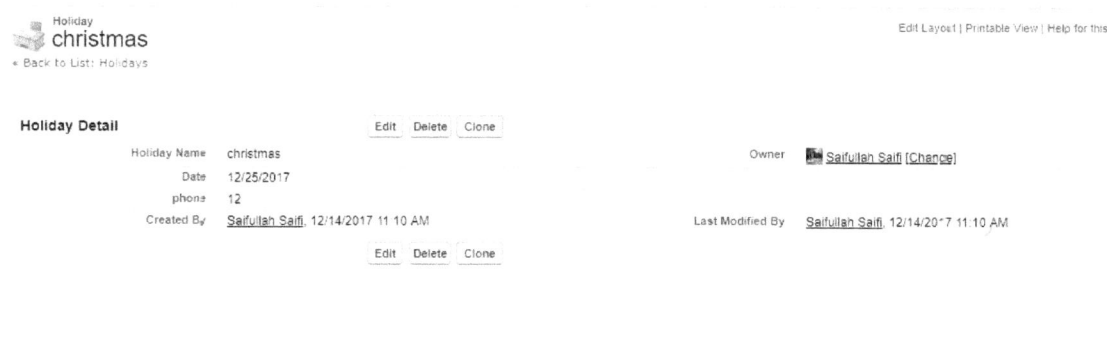

Holiday
christmas
« Back to List: Holidays

Edit Layout | Printable View | Help for this

Holiday Detail   Edit   Delete   Clone

Holiday Name   christmas
Date   12/25/2017
phone   12
Created By   Saifullah Saifi, 12/14/2017 11:10 AM

Owner   Saifullah Saifi [Change]

Last Modified By   Saifullah Saifi, 12/14/2017 11:10 AM

Edit   Delete   Clone

Figure 16.9: Holiday object

Now, anyone who wants to take leave will create a new leave application. They will fill the **FromDate** and **ToDate**. The trigger should update the count of days they want to take the leave. However, **Holiday**, weekends (Saturday, Sunday) should be excluded for the count.

Let us see the following code:

```
trigger LeaveDaysCount on Leave_Application__c (before insert,before update)
{
    Integer count=0;
    set<Date> holidays=new set<date>();
    for(Holiday__c c:[SELECT date__c from Holiday__c]){
        holidays.add(c.date__c);
    }
    For(Leave_Application__c  l:Trigger.New){
        for(Date d=l.FromDate__c; d<=l.ToDate__c; d=d+1){
            Datetime dt=date.newInstance(d.year(), d.month(), d.day());
          if(dt.format('EEEE')!='Sunday' && dt.format('EEEE')!='Saturday' &&
!holidays.contains(d)){
            count++;
        }
        }
      l.CountDays__c=count;
    }
}
```

Before the insertion or updation of the record, we checked the date and compared it with weekends and holidays in the trigger. We took a variable with **count =0**, then stored all the **Holidays** date into a set. Then, for every application, we started a loop, from **startdate** to **endDate (ToDate)**. We check every date with the Holidays set with the weekends and counted it. We put the value in the count days.

Now, take a look at the following figure:

Figure 16.10: Trigger count days

Hasan Saif applied for leave from *14th Dec 2018* to *31st Dec 2018*, and this trigger has updated the **countDays** value to 11. Now, we can see that there are three Saturdays and three Sundays between 14 and 31 December (total 18 days), so we will remove six days from it. From the 18th to the 6th, the leave is for 12 days, but again, we know the *25th of December* is Holiday, so count the days are 12-1 = 11.

Use case six

If we want a trigger to prevent a record creation, for example, we want an account to have only one contact. To throw such type of error, we have to write a trigger which is as follows:

```
trigger preventContact on Contact(before insert) {
  Map<id, Integer> accContCountMap = new Map<id, Integer>();
  for (Contact c : Trigger.new) {
    if (c.AccountId != null)
      accContCountMap.put(c.AccountId, null);
  }
  if (accContCountMap.size() > 0) {
    for (Account acc : [
      SELECT id, (SELECT id FROM Contacts)
      FROM Account
      WHERE Id IN :accContCountMap.keySet()
    ])
      accContCountMap.put(acc.id, acc.Contacts.size());

    for (Contact c : Trigger.new) {
      if (
        c.Account != null &&
        accContCountMap.containsKey(c.AccountId) &&
        accContCountMap.get(c.AccountId) > 0
      )
        c.addError('You can create multiple Contact for 1 account');
    }
  }
}
```

Figure 16.11: Trigger example validation

Best practices for trigger

As the trigger is an automated, custom-coded process, it needs to be highly optimized and well-written. If our trigger fails, the record will not get saved, the calculation will be wrong, or the Salesforce limits can be exceeded. So, the following are some practices we can do to optimize code:

- The code should be bulkified; it should be written in such a way that it can handle 200 records in a single batch without exceeding any limit or time.
- Use the set to avoid any duplicate data.
- Use **Map** to optimize and remove loops.
- Trigger should not be recursive. (Recursion is the process of executing the same Trigger again and again to update the record due to some automation.)
- The event handler should be managed as *"when to run what,"* for example, which part of the code will run before insert or after the update.
- There should be only one trigger for one event on an object. More than one triggers will create confusion in the order of execution.

Trigger helper

You can understand its complexity if we write one trigger per object. So, all codes will be in a single trigger. To make it easy to use, we create **TriggerHelper**. It is a simple Apex class, which can take input from the trigger and perform the operation if possible. Also, using this, you can handle the sequence and categorize it based on the event and the operation.

Let us take an example. Trigger to call helper:

```
trigger SingleTrigger on Lead (after insert, after update, before insert,
before update)
{
    //helper class name
    TriggerHelper helperClass= new TriggerHelper();

    if(trigger.isAfter && trigger.isInsert)
    {
        helperClass.sendData(trigger.New, trigger.newMap);
    }
    if(trigger.isBefore && trigger.isInsert)
    {
//sequence which method 1st
```

```
        helperClass.addTax(trigger.New, trigger.newMap);
        helperClass.updateDate(trigger.New, trigger.newMap);
    }
    if(trigger.isBefore && trigger.isUpdate)
    {
            helperClass.updateValues(trigger.New,  trigger.newMap,trigger.
Old,trigger.oldMap);
    }
    if(trigger.isAfter && trigger.isUpdate)
    {
        helperClass.addChild(trigger.New, trigger.newMap,trigger.Old,trigger.
oldMap);
    }
}
```

The helper class is as follows:

```
public class TriggerHelper {
    public void sendData(list<Lead> triggerNew,map<Id,Lead> triggerNewmap){
        ---
    }

    public void addTax(list<Lead> triggerNew,map<Id,Lead> triggerNewmap){
        ---
    }

    public void updateDate(list<Lead> triggerNew,map<Id,Lead> triggerNewmap)
{
        ---
    }

    public void updateValues(list<Lead> triggerNew,map<Id,Lead> triggerNewmap,
list<Lead> triggerOld,map<Id,Lead> triggerOldmap){
        ---
    }

    public void addChild(list<Lead> triggerNew,map<Id,Lead> triggerNewmap,
list<Lead> triggerOld,map<Id,Lead> triggerOldmap){
```

```
        - - -
    }
}
```

In the preceding code, you can see that we are calling different methods based on the event. Also, in the same event, we can handle the sequence of methods easily. The benefits of this helper class are that the trigger becomes readable and is easy to debug. We also have better control over the event and order of execution.

Conclusion

In this chapter, we learned about trigger and its syntax. We also covered how to write and when to write a trigger using the example of *use cases*. We learned about the best practices to write Apex triggers. We also covered the use of map to bulkify and optimize the code of the Apex trigger. In the next chapter, we will learn about the *Visualforce Page, we will study about how and when to use this VF Page, and we will also learn about some syntax and Tags of VF page*.

Questions

1. **Which trigger event allows a developer to update fields in the Trigger.new list without using an additional DML statement? Choose two answers.**

    a. Before insert

    b. Before update

    c. After update

    d. After insert

2. **A developer wrote a flow e-mail alert on case creation so that an e-mail is sent to the case owner-manager when a case is created. When will the e-mail be sent?**

    a. After committing to the database.

    b. Before trigger execution.

    c. After trigger execution.

    d. Before committing to the database.

3. **In which order does the Salesforce execute events upon saving a record?**

    a. Before Triggers; Validation Rules; After Triggers; Assignment Rules; Workflow Rules; Commit

    b. Validation Rules; Before Triggers; After Triggers; Workflow Rules; Assignment Rules; Commit

  c. Before Triggers; Validation Rules; After Triggers; Workflow Rules; Assignment Rules; Commit

  d. Validation Rules; Before Triggers; After Triggers; Assignment Rules; Workflow Rules; Commit

Answers

 1. a, b

 2. d

 3. a

Join our Discord space

Join our Discord workspace for latest updates, offers, tech happenings around the world, new releases, and sessions with the authors:

https://discord.bpbonline.com

Creating Visualforce Pages

Introduction

Visualforce pages are framework specially designed for Salesforce to create custom UI. They look similar to web pages or any markup language like HTML. Salesforce already has some standard pages, like a detail page, related list page, reports, and Dashboards. Sometimes, we need a custom form or page to take input from the user or populate data dynamically. In those cases, Salesforce has many things: **Lightning component**, **Lightning flow**, **Lightning web component**, **Visual Force (VF) page**, **Lightning Record pages**, **Lightning Home pages**, **Lightning App pages.** The first UI framework for custom UI is the VF page.

Structure

In this chapter, we will discuss the following topics:

- Visualforce page
- Working of the Visualforce page
- Developing the first Visualforce page
- Visualforce page syntax and tags
- Developer mode

- Using Salesforce fields on the Visualforce page
- Designing the Visualforce page

Objectives

After studying this unit, you will learn the basics of Visualforce pages. You will also learn about tags and action related to VF page, lastly you will learn to write some code to play with data and build UI.

Visualforce page

You might have heard about HTML, the hypertext markup language used to build a web page. In Salesforce, whenever we need to design a custom page, we use **VF page**.

Visualforce is the component-based UI framework for the Salesforce platform. It includes a tag-based markup language similar to HTML.

Let us see the sample code for VF page:

```
<apex:page standardController="Account">
    <apex:form >
        <apex:pageBlock title="Edit Account for {!$User.FirstName} {!$User.
LastName}">
            <apex:pageMessages />
            <apex:pageBlockButtons >
                <apex:commandButton value="Save" action="{!save}"/>
            </apex:pageBlockButtons>
            <apex:pageBlockSection >
                <apex:inputField value="{!account.name}"/>
                <apex:inputField value="{!account.Industry}"/>
            </apex:pageBlockSection>
        </apex:pageBlock>
    </apex:form>
</apex:page>
```

The VF page will look like this:

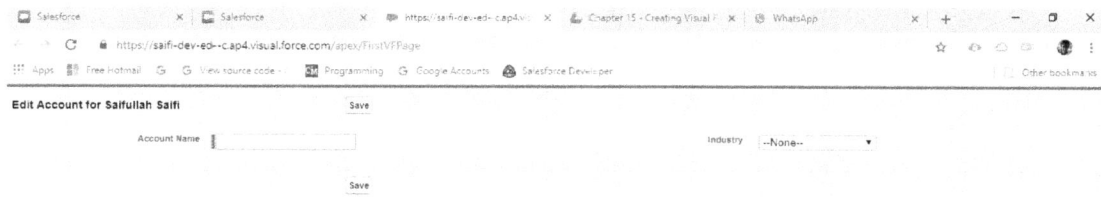

Figure 17.1: VF page sample UI

Working of the Visualforce page

VF pages work on the **Model View Controller** (**MVC**) pattern. We have already read about the MVC structure in *Chapter 13, Programming with APEX)*. An example of a model is any Salesforce object (standard or custom), **StandardController**, controller, or extension is **Controller & View** is a detail page, list view page, or Visualforce page.

We can create a VF page using a standard controller or a custom controller or extension. VF pages provide tight integration with the database; it simply binds the fields directly into pages and binds the data related to it easily. It also provides AJAX components and embeds formula language for any actions. **Asynchronous JavaScript and XML (AJAX)** is a web development method that enables web pages to transmit and receive data in the background by communicating with a web server asynchronously.

We will learn one by one from standard controller pages to extensions in the next chapters.

Developing the first Visualforce page

To develop the first VF page, perform the following steps:

1. Go to the **Developer Console**, click on **File**, and **New** click on **Visualforce Page**:

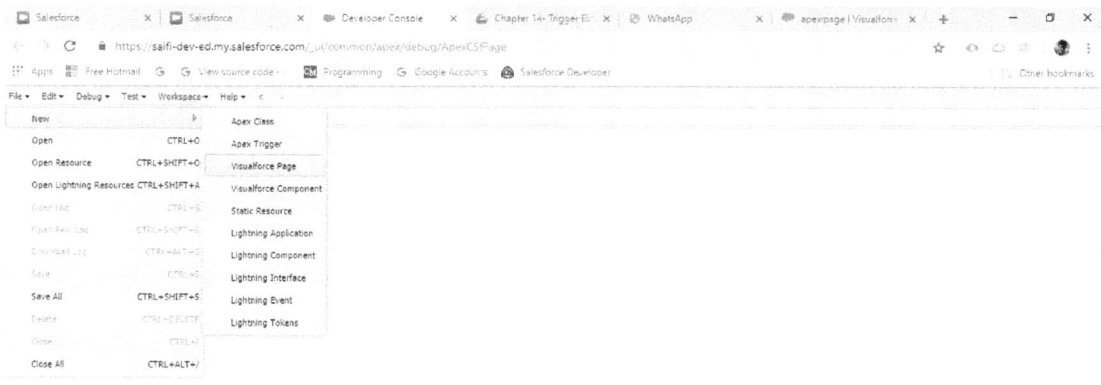

Figure 17.2: VF Page create page

2. Write the name of the page and click on **OK**. Write something in it to check, and click on **Preview**:

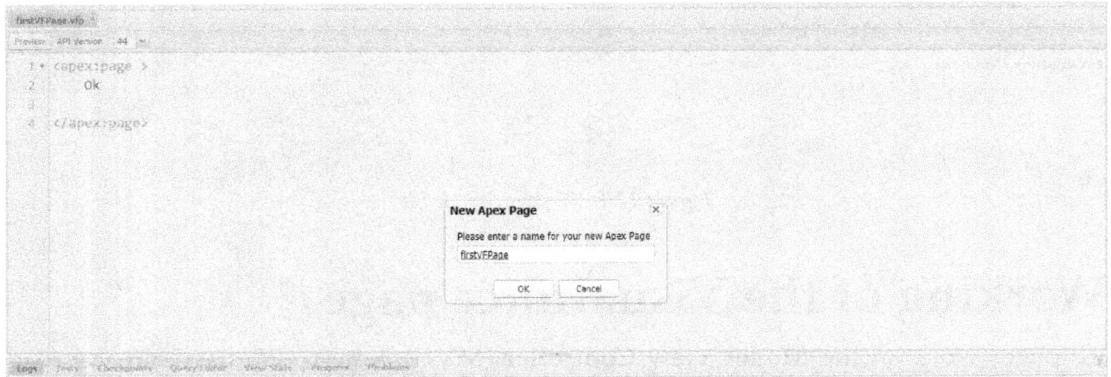

Figure 17.3: VF Page example one

3. Go to **Setup**, type `Visualforce page` in Quick Find Box, click on **Visualforce Page**, and then click on the **New** button:

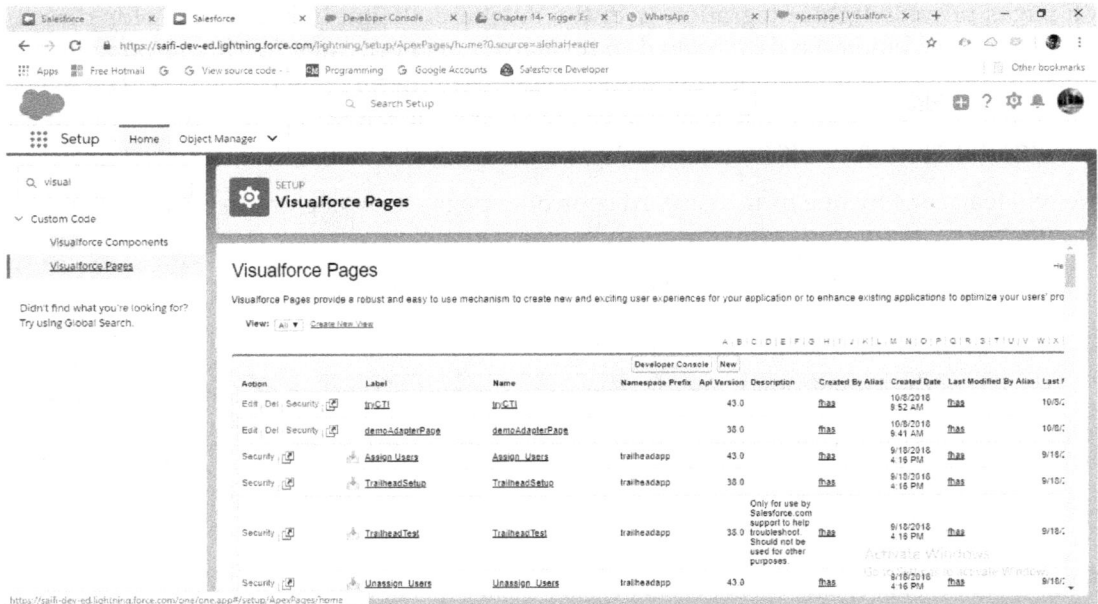

Figure 17.4: VF Page from setup

4. Put the name of the page and copy the code that was at the beginning of the chapter.

5. Please click on **Available for Lightning Experience, Lightning Communities, and the mobile app** checkbox as we are using lightning experience now.

6. Save it and then click on **Preview**. You can see your page, which will look like the following figure:

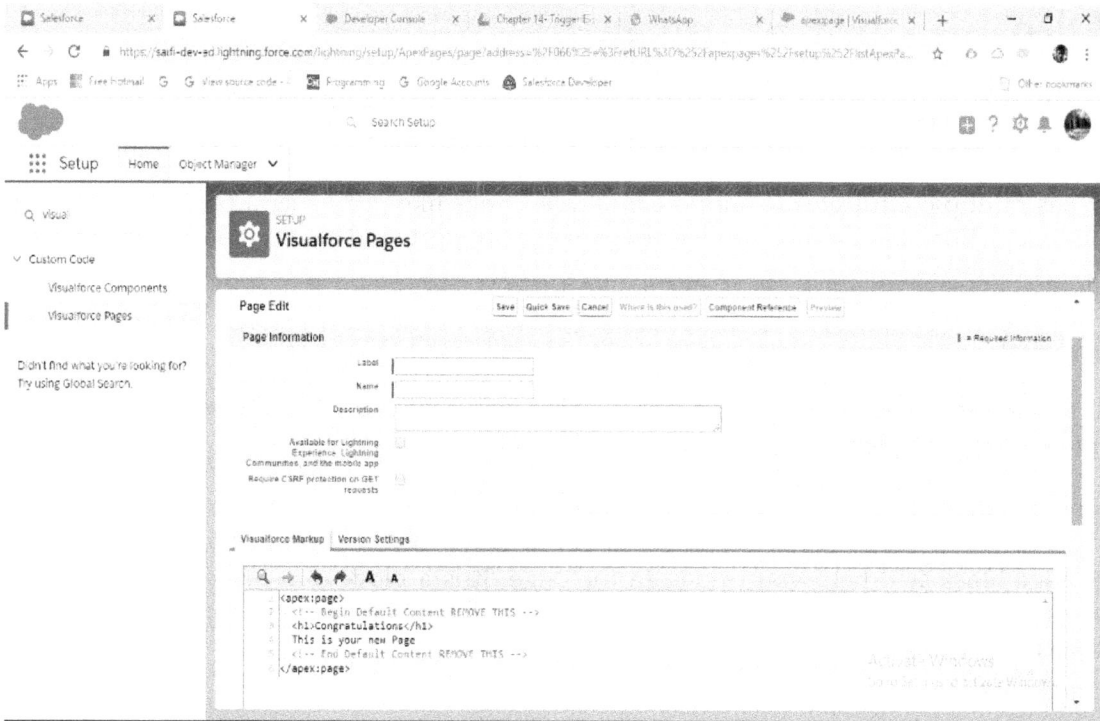

Figure 17.5: VF Page example two

Note: The VF page supports almost all HTML tags, but every beginning tag should have an end tag also.

Visualforce page syntax and tags

Let us start the coding. Following is the sample code of VF page:

```
<apex:page>
<br/>
<table>
<tr>
<td></td>
</tr>
</table>
</apex:page>
```

Let us understand the syntax line by line.

Page

Every VF page should start with **`<apex:page>`** and end with **`</apex:page>`;** whole code will be within the following tags:

`<apex:page> every vf page should start with this tag and end with </apex:page>`

It has multiple attributes to support multiple things like pdf generation, cache support, on-load action, standard controller or controller support, and so on. We will learn it later about attributes.

Form

If you want to take any input on the VF page, you will use **`<apex:form></apex:form>`**, and all the input tags should be between it.

Page block

A page block will help you to design the page. It is a block of a page that will give a similar design as Salesforce detail page. The syntax is like this **`<apex:pageBlock> </apex:pageBlock>`**:

```
<apex:page>
    <apex:pageBlock title="check first page block">
        content inside the first block
    </apex:pageBlock>
</apex:page>
```

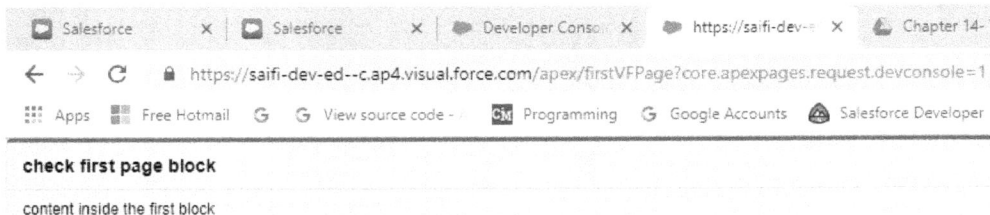

Figure 17.6: VF page UI example

Section

If you want a section on a page similar to the standard detail page, you can use: **`<apex:pageBlockSection>`**.

You can also specify the number of columns inside the section. You can check the following syntax to understand section**<apex:page >**:

```
<apex:pageBlock title="check first page block">
    <apex:pageBlockSection columns="1" title="first section">
     <apex:pageBlockSectionItem> first value</apex:pageBlockSectionItem>
    <apex:pageBlockSectionItem> second value</apex:pageBlockSectionItem>
    </apex:pageBlockSection>
    <apex:pageBlockSection columns= '2' title="second sectior">
      <apex:pageBlockSectionItem> first item</apex:pageBlockSectionItem>
     <apex:pageBlockSectionItem> second item</apex:pageBlockSectionItem>
    </apex:pageBlockSection>
    </apex:pageBlock>
</apex:page>
```

Take a look at the following figure:

Figure 17.7: VF page UI example two

Now, you can see any values inside the section. For this, we will use: **<apex:pageBlockSectionItem>**, and for multiple columns, we can use column attribute of **<apex:pageBlockSection>**.

Output text

<apex:outputText> is used to display text. We can also design it using style or give format for currency or date value. You can check the following syntax to understand **apex:output**:

```
<apex:page>
    <apex:pageBlock>
        <apex:outputText> first text</apex:outputText>
    </apex:pageBlock>
</apex:page>
```

The page will look like the following:

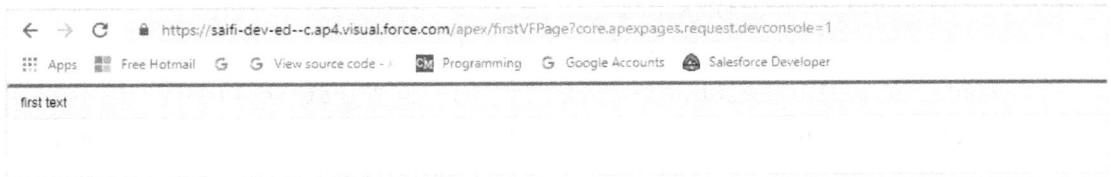

Figure 17.8: VF page UI example three

Param

Inside the output text, we can use the **<apex:param>** and design it accordingly. You can check the following syntax to understand **<apex:param>**:

```
<apex:page>
    <apex:pageBlock>
        <apex:outputText value="check {0}  and then see {1}">
            <apex:param value="I am first"/>
            <apex:param value="You are last or second"/>
        </apex:outputText>
    </apex:pageBlock>
</apex:page>
```

Now, look at the following figure:

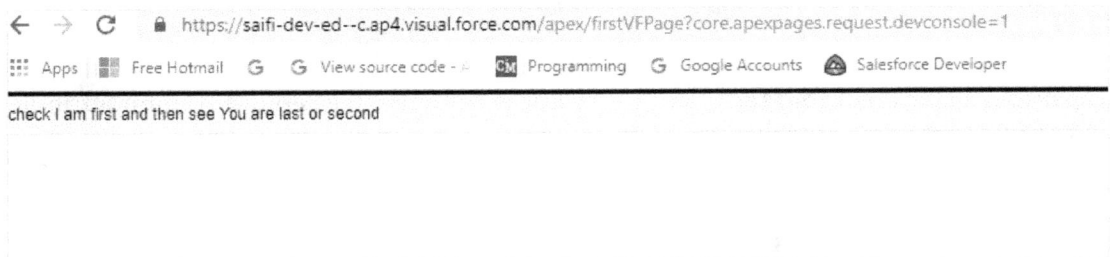

Figure 17.9: VF page UI example four

Another example of **<apex:param>** is as follows:

```
<apex:page>
    <apex:pageBlock>
        <apex:outputText value="{!NOW()}" />
        <br/>
        <apex:outputText value="{0,date,dd/mm/yyyy 'and time is' HH:mm:ss}">
```

```
            <apex:param value="{!NOW()}"/>
        </apex:outputText> <br/> the amount is :
        <apex:outputText value="{0, number, 00,00.00}">
        <apex:param value="{!124343}"/>
        </apex:outputText>
    </apex:pageBlock>
</apex:page>
```

Refer to the following figure :

Figure 17.10: *VF page UI example five*

Variable

<apex:variable> is used to define some local variables to avoid any repetitive things. You can check the following syntax to understand **<apex:variable>**:

```
<apex:page>
    <apex:pageBlock>
        <apex:variable value="{!0}" var="i" />
        {!i}
        <br/>
        <apex:variable value="{!(i+2)}" var="i" />
        {!i}
    </apex:pageBlock>
</apex:page>
```

The page will look like the following figure when you will preview it:

Figure 17.11: *VF page UI example six*

> **Note: VF page uses {} as a formula expression to bind the variable or value on the page; if it is variable, it will use similar to {!varName}.**

Developer mode

Let us see one trick that will help you to code and see in the same window. Go to setup, search advance user details, click on edit, and check the **Development Mode** checkbox. Click on **Save**. Open any VF page and preview it.

In the VF page, you can see your page name at the bottom, click on that, now you can see code and design on the same page:

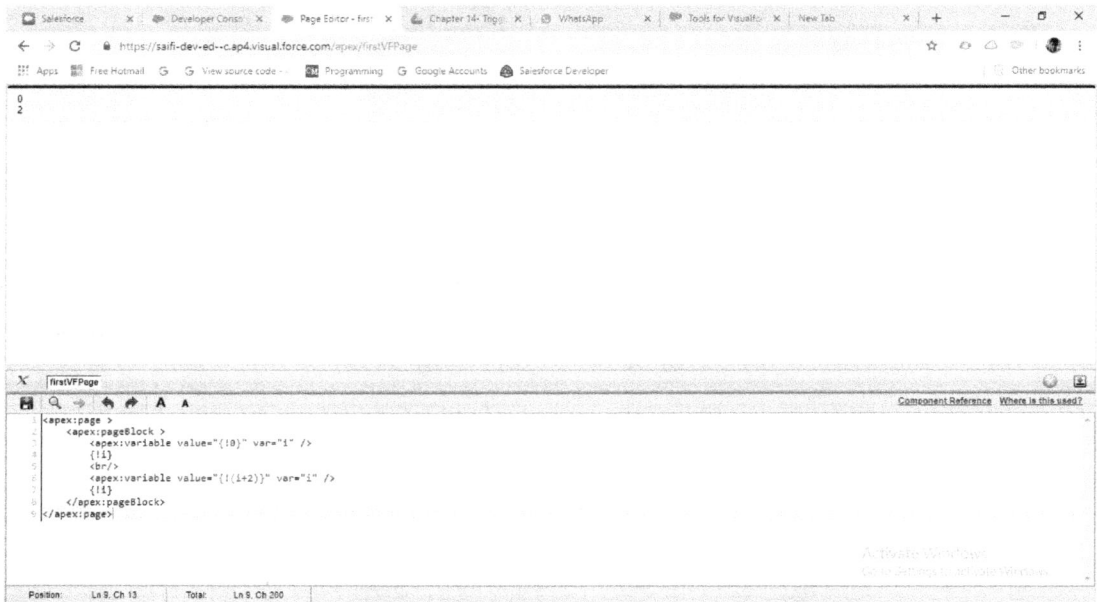

Figure 17.12: VF page Developer log

Using Salesforce fields on the Visualforce page

Visualforce page uses expression language as formulas— {! }. Anything inside it is an expression that will be evaluated in the context of user and records and Salesforce. Like we want to display the current username:

```
<apex:page >
    Hello, you are {!$User.FirstName} {!$User.LastName}
</apex:page>
```

The output will be as follows:

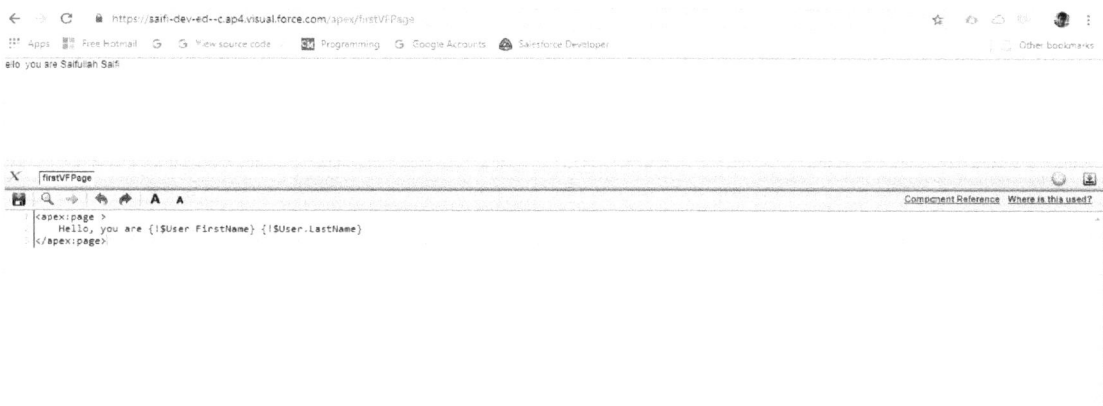

Figure 17.13: VF Page example seven

Records on Visualforce page

Let us do one thing; open an account record, and find the account ID in the URL. Put that ID in the VF page URL.

Suppose the account record URL is **https://saifi-dev-ed.lightning.force.com/lightning/r/Account/0016F00002eYToXQAW/view**. So, the ID is **0016F00002eYToXQAW**. Now, put this ID in the last of the VF page URL like this:

https://saifi-dev-ed--c.ap4.visual.force.com/apex/firstVFPage?id=0016F00002eYToX-QAW

Now, you can display any fields related to that account on this VF page using the following code:

```
<apex:page standardController="Account">
    Hello, you are {!$User.FirstName} {!$User.LastName}
    <br/>
    And you want to check the account detail of {!Account.Name}
```

`</apex:page>` the page will look like the following:

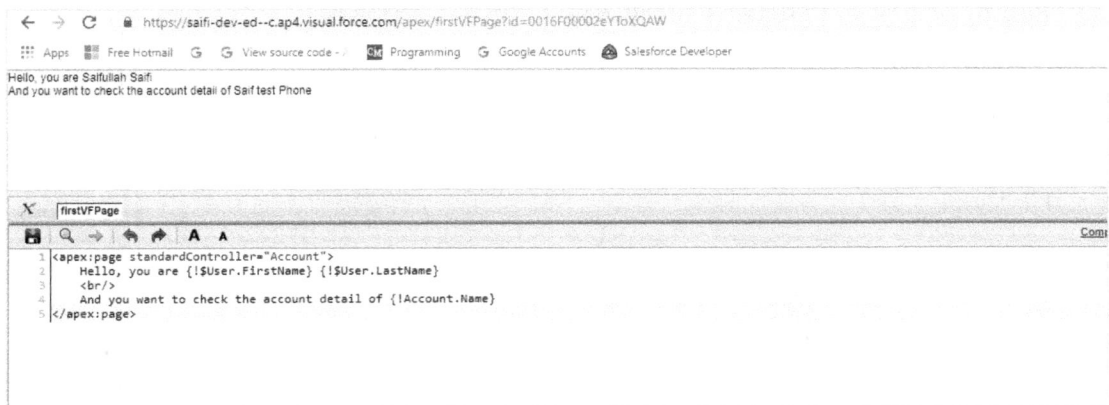

Figure 17.14: VF page UI example eight

Detail page on the Visualforce page

If we want to display the whole Salesforce detail page on the VF Page, we can use the following:

```
<apex:detail />

<apex:page standardController="Account">
    <apex:pageBlock >
        Hello, you are {!$User.FirstName} {!$User.LastName}
        <br/>
        This is the account detail of {!Account.Name}
    </apex:pageBlock>
    <apex:detail />
</apex:page>
```

The page will look like following:

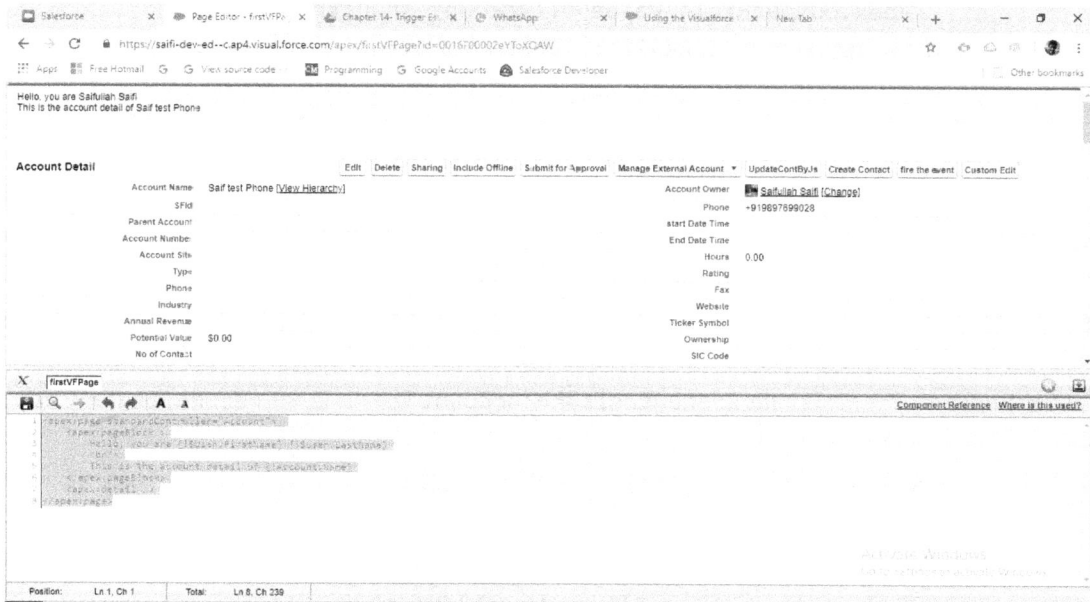

Figure 17.15: VF page detail

All the buttons and related lists related to this account record, are visible if we are using: `<apex:detail />`.

OutputField

If you want to display any fields related to **Account** or any object, you can also use the following:

`<apex:outputField>`

`<apex:outputField value="{!Account.Name}" />`

`<apex:outputField value="{!Account.Industry}" />`

RelatedList on the Visualforce page

If you want to display any related list of **Account**, and know that we are now using Account ID, we can use the following code:

`<apex:relatedList subject="{!account}" list="contacts" />`

`<apex:page standardController="Account">`

   `<apex:pageBlock >`

      `Hello, you are {!$User.FirstName} {!$User.LastName}`   `<br/>`

```
            <apex:outputField value="{!Account.Name}" />          <br/>
            <apex:outputField value="{!Account.Industry}" />
        <apex:relatedList subject="{!account}" list="contacts" />


    </apex:pageBlock>
</apex:page>
```

Save the preceding code of the VF page and click on **Preview**. You will see the related list on the page.

If you remember, in the beginning, it was mentioned that we can make a custom detail page and list view page. Here is the code for custom list view page for Accounts:

```
<apex:page          standardController="Account"          recordSetVar="acc"
lightningStylesheets="true">
    <apex:pageBlock title="Account List">
        <!-- Account List -->
        <apex:pageBlockTable value="{! acc}" var="ct">
            <apex:column value="{! ct.Name}"/>
            <apex:column value="{! ct.Industry}"/>
        </apex:pageBlockTable>
    </apex:pageBlock>
</apex:page>
```

The page will look like following:

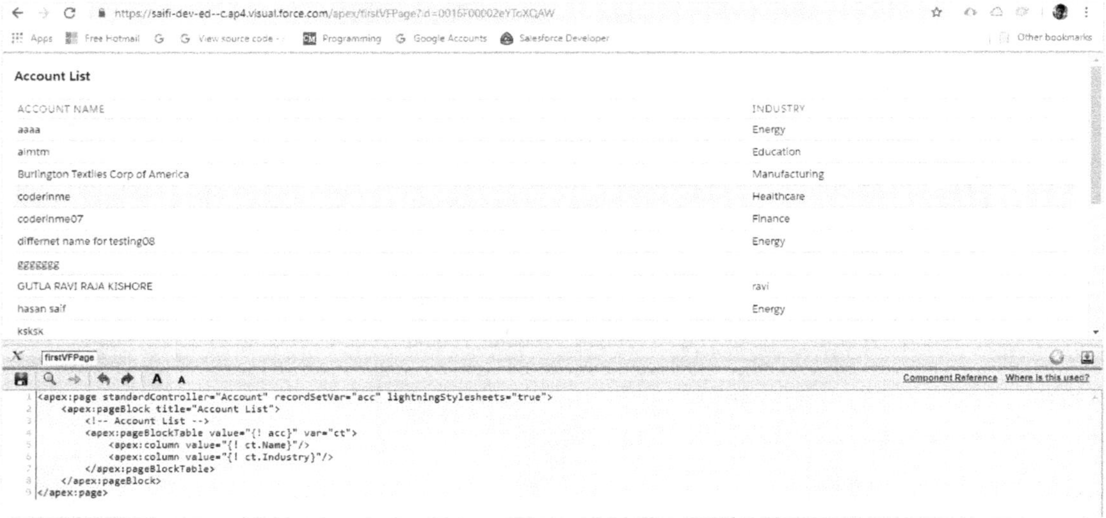

Figure 17.16: VF page list view

Note: VF page can only display 1000 records (maximum) on a single page.

Dynamic table in the Visualforce page

In the preceding code, we used two new attributes in the **<apex:page>**. They are as follows:

- **lightningStylesheets="true"** will give this page a Lightning Experience design. It is a salesforce out-of-the-box design that looks much better and works perfectly with browsers and mobile. **recordSetVar="acc"** is used to define **acc** as a list of accounts, as the standard controller is the account here.

If we want to display a list of **sObjects** like a list of **Account** on a VF page or a list of anything, then you will use **<apex:pageBlockTable>** or **<apex:repeat>**.

Now, you can see that the same variable name in **pageBlockTable**, which was defined in **recordSetVar** can be used.

Now, we have to display some fields of every record of **Account**, so we will use **<apex:column>** for the same.

Use of tab in Visualforce page

Check the following code first:

```
<apex:page id="pg" lightningStylesheets="true">
    <apex:tabPanel selectedTab="tab1" id="frstTabPanel">
        <apex:tab label="First" name="tab1" id="tab1">value content at tab one</apex:tab>
        <apex:tab label="Second" name="tab2" id="tab2">value content at tab two</apex:tab>
    </apex:tabPanel>
</apex:page>
```

The output of the preceding code is as follows, as you can see there are two tabs, **First** and **Second**, and by default the **First** tab is selected as mentioned in the code:

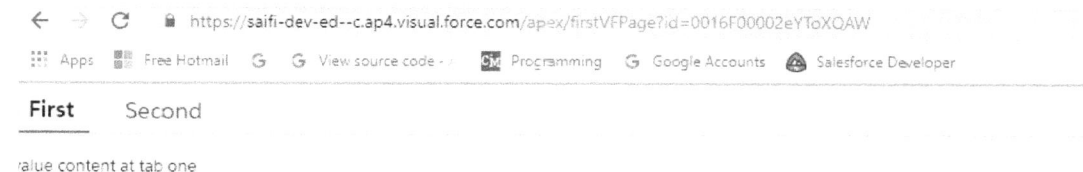

Figure 17.17: VF page tab

Command button

If you have used HTML, you might remember that `<input type="submit" value="submit"/>` , `<apex:commandButton >` is similar to the preceding code, and this is the child of `<apex:form>`, so it should be within the `<apex:form>`. Check the following syntax to understand:

```
<apex:page lightningStylesheets="true">
    <apex:form >
        <apex:commandButton action="{!Save}" value="save" />
    </apex:form>
</apex:page>
```

In this command button, the value is the name/label of the button that you want to show.

Action

The standard action of Visualforce controller or custom action will call any custom controller or extension method. Following are some standard actions:

*   **save**: It will save the record and will redirect to the detail page.
*   **quicksave**: It will save the record but will not redirect to any page.
*   **edit**: It will open the page in editable mode or editing context.
*   **delete**: Similar to the standard delete button.

inputText, input field

`<apex:inputField>` is used to input data or to open the page in editable mode. Suppose we are using this account id **0016F00002eYToXQAW** and the page is this **https://saifi-dev-ed--c.ap4.visual.force.com/apex/firstVFPage?id=0016F00002eYToXQAW**. Now, you can see the following code will open this account record for editing:

```
<apex:page lightningStylesheets="true" standardController="Account">
    <apex:form >
        <apex:inputField value="{!Account.Name}" />
        <apex:commandButton action="{!Save}" value="save" />
    </apex:form>
</apex:page>
```

The page will look like following figure:

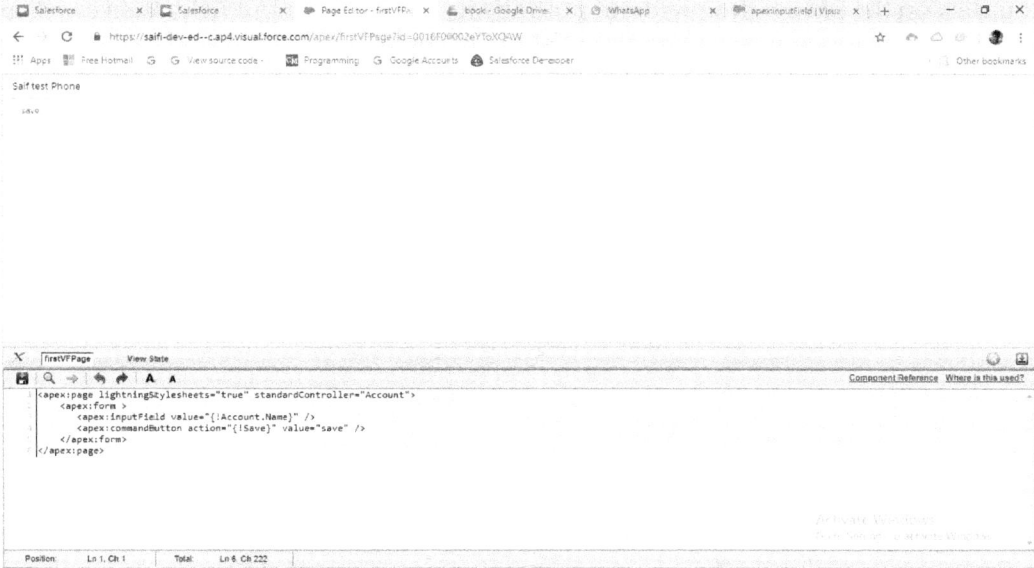

Figure 17.18: VF page button

If we want to save a new account record.

We can remove the ID from the URL, and then we can input new account record, as shown in the following figure:

Note: **inputField will respect all the attributes, validation related to that field.**

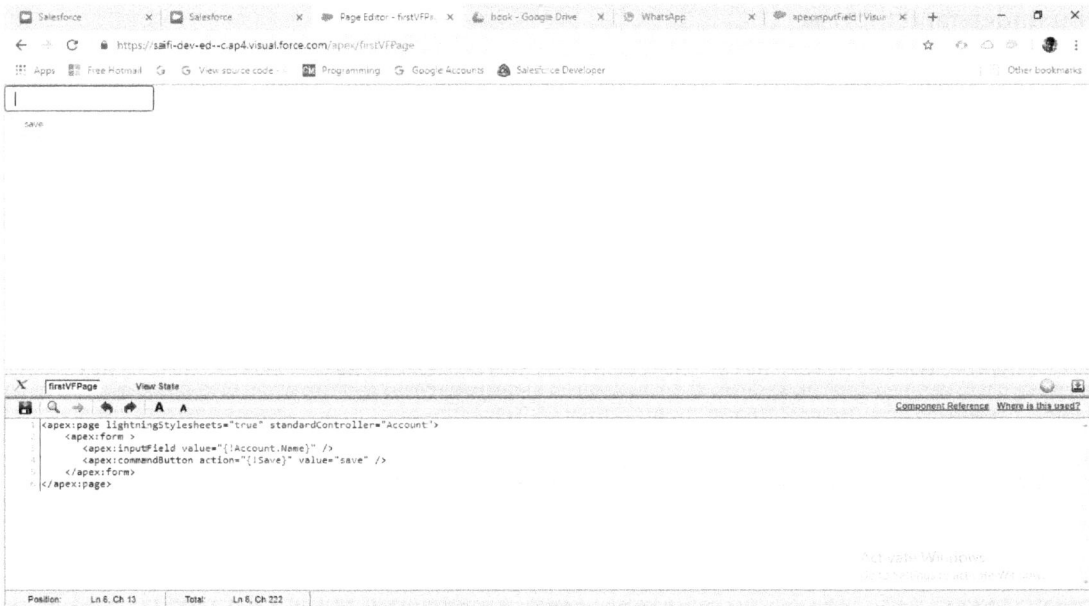

Figure 17.19: VF page input

If you click on the **Save** button without putting any data in the input field, then it will give you an error because name is a required field in **Account**:

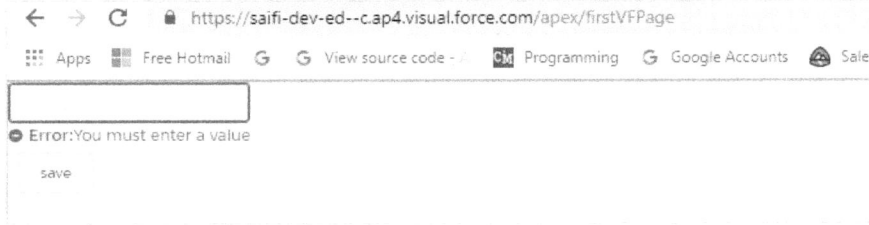

Figure 17.20: VF page validation

Save and quickSave

If you put the value and click on **Save,** then it will save the record.

There are some standard buttons which we can use in any custom page according to need. The **Save** button will save the new or existing record. The **quickSave** button will work similar to **Save** and **New** button.

Edit

The **Edit** button will edit it in the editable mode from the standard detail page, and delete will be used for standard deletion. The **Cancel** button will work similarly to cancel the transaction and will go back to the detail page of that record. The following code will help you understand the use:

```
<apex:page lightningStylesheets="true" standardController="Account">
    <apex:form >
        <apex:pageBlock>
            <apex:outputField  value="{!Account.Name}" />
            <apex:commandButton action="{!Edit}" value="Edit" />
            <apex:commandButton action="{!Cancel}" value="Cancel" />
        </apex:pageBlock>
    </apex:form>
</apex:page>
```

Remember the following image tag in html:

```
<img src="https://coderinme.com/wp-content/uploads/2017/03/1-2.png"/>
```

Similar to that, the VF page has **<apex:image />** tag:

```
<apex:image url="https://coderinme.com/wp-content/uploads/2017/03/1-2.png"/>
```

The page will look like the following figure:

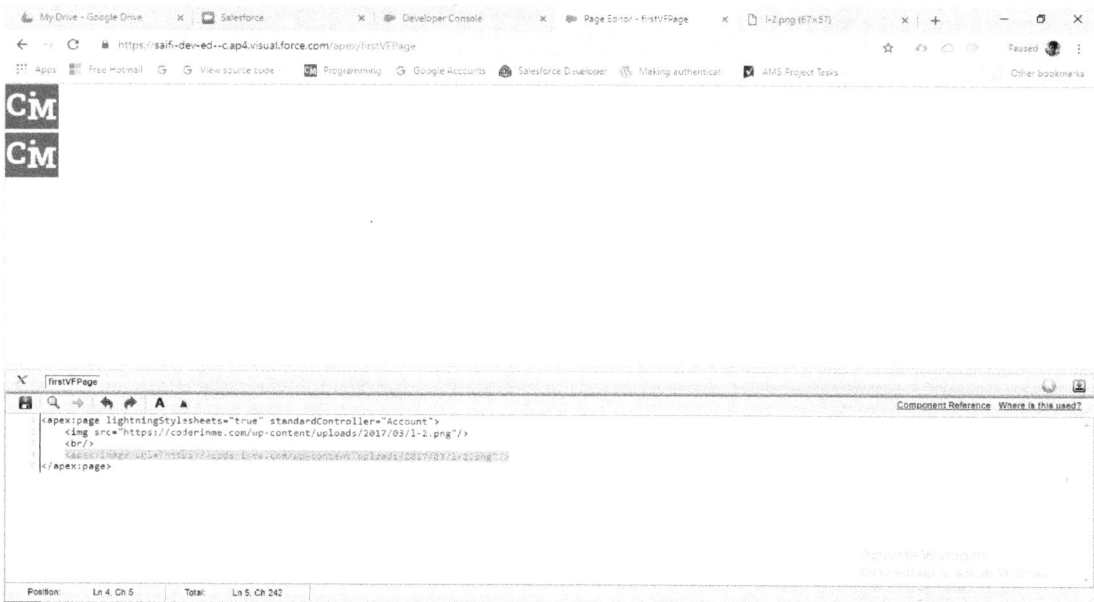

Figure 17.21: *VF page CSS*

Doctype="html-5.0" will give the VF page to use all the HTML5 supported tags, and JavaScript code. Now, we can use any HTML tag if necessary:

```
<apex:page lightningStylesheets="true" docType="html-5.0" ></apex:page>
```

Rendered and reRender

This attribute of Visualforce will be used to make the page dynamic. Rendered tags can take true/false values and will be used to show or hide the panel or section of the page.

reRender will be used to refresh that specific section mentioned without reloading the entire page:

```
<apex:page lightningStylesheets="true" docType="html-5.0" >

    <apex:outputText rendered="true">this is true value</apex:outputText>

     <apex:outputText rendered="false">this is not true value</
apex:outputText>

</apex:page>
```

What will be displayed?

This is the true value.

Suppose we have a checkbox field **VPA__c**, we want to show a section based on that field:

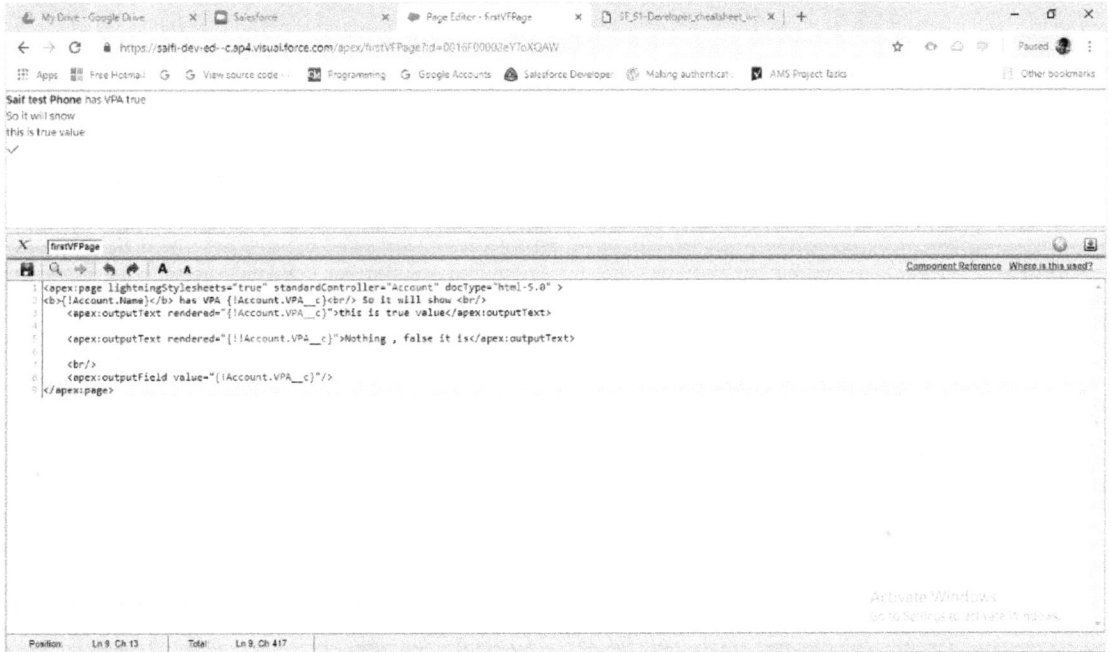

Figure 17.22: VF page rendered

Designing the Visualforce page

VF page is designed in a way that every user (developer or end-user) sees it in an HTML view.

When you, as a developer, design the VF page and save it, the platform server tries to compile it. If there is any error, the save is denied, and the error returns to the page. If there is no issue, then the server saves it to the VF renderer. Now, if you click on the **Preview** button, VF renderer will return it to an HTML view.

Now, if any end-user means the page is calling from any button or tab, then VF renderer will always return it into the HTML format.

Conclusion

In this chapter, we learned about the Visualforce page and its markup tag that is similar to HTML but can easily bind with Salesforce objects and data. We covered how to create the VF page, and how to add it as a tab or test the page. We learned about standard actions, input, and output tags. In the next chapter, we will learn about custom controller and controller extensions.

Questions

1. **A developer needs to provide a Visualforce page that lets users enter product-specific details during a sales cycle. How can this be accomplished? (Choose 2)**

   a. Download a managed package from the AppExhange that provides a custom Visualforce page to modify.

   b. Copy the standard page and then make a new Visualforce page for Ppoduct data entry.

   c. Download an unmanaged package from the AppExchange that provides a custom Visualforce page to modify.

   d. Create a new Visualforce page and an Apex controller to provide product data entry.

2. **A Visualforce page has a standard controller for an object that has a lookup relationship to a parent object. How can a developer display data from the parent record on the page?**

   a. By adding a second standard controller to the page for the parent record.

   b. By using a roll-up formula field on the child record to include data from the parent record.

   c. By using SOQL on the Visualforce page to query for data from the parent record.

   d. By using merge field syntax to retrieve data from the parent record.

3. **What is the tag for a table in the VF page.**

4. **How many columns can we design in a section?**

Answers

1. c, d

2. d

3. <apex:pageBlockTable>

4. maximum two

Join our Discord space

Join our Discord workspace for latest updates, offers, tech happenings around the world, new releases, and sessions with the authors:

https://discord.bpbonline.com

CHAPTER 18
Basics of Lightning Web Components

Introduction

Lightning Web Components (**LWC**) is the new UI framework for Salesforce based on the current standard of the World Wide Web and **European Computer Manufacturers Association** (**ECMA**) Script. LWC only delivers what is required to function properly in Salesforce-supported browsers, according to the fundamental Web Components requirements. LWC can run extremely fast and are lightweight since their code is native to browsers. The majority of the code you write is HTML and regular JavaScript.

Structure

In this chapter, we will discuss the following topics:

- Introduction to JavaScript
- Defining a component
- Components of an LWC
- Decorators
- Rules for naming convention of properties
- Creating your first LWC
- Lifecycle flow

382 Cloud Computing using Salesforce

- Working with Salesforce data
- Composition
- Communicate with events
- Using static resources in Lightning Web components
- Lightning Web Components security

Objectives

After studying this unit, you should be able to learn how to create basic LWC. You should also learn about decorators, how LWC reacts with Salesforce data, and what Salesforce-provided base components are in LWC.

Introduction to JavaScript

JavaScript is a programming language that is used to create interactive and dynamic web pages. It is mostly used as client-side scripting language to show complex and new features on Web browser.

Today, JavaScript has many standard features and framework. It is also being used as API and can be used to create websites and applications.

Let us learn the basics of JavaScript. JavaScript is a case-sensitive language. It is a loosely typed language, so you cannot specifically tell if it is integer or string. Variables are used to store data in JavaScript. Variables are used to store reusable values.

We will use let, var, and const with a variable; if we know the value will be changed, then we use const; otherwise, we will use let. Check the following code on how to use the variable:

```
1.  let c = 5;
2.  let sum = x + y;
3.  let books= ["BPB", "Shine", "TMH"];
4.  // It store object data (objects are
5.  // represented in the below way mainly)
6.  let Student = {
7.      firstName: "John",
8.      lastName: "Doe",
9.      age: 35,
10.     mark: "blueEYE"
11. }
```

Even though var was the oldest way of declaring variables, now after new updates in ECMASCRIPT 6, let is introduced. There are two big differences between them:

- **var** has global scope or full function scope, but let has only block scope (within {}).
- **var** can be updated and redeclared. However, let can only be updated; we cannot redeclare it:

```
let c = 5;
let c = 9; // it will throw an error due to re declaration
var a = "John";
var a = "nm";  // it's possible
```

JavaScript function

Functions are blocks of code which is used to perform an operation. Let us check the following code:

```
1. // Function definition
2. function addNumber() {
3.     // Declare a variable
4.     let a = 4;
5.     let b=5;
6.     return a+b;
7. }
8. // Function call
9. console.log(addNumber());
```

In the preceding code, we are calling a method **addNumber,** and this function is returning the sum of a and b.

JavaScript comparison: if you use == then it will compare the value not the datatype of variable. However, if we use === then it will check datatype and value.

For example, x=5; y='5'; if we will check x==y, then it is true, but if we use x===y, then it is false as x is a number and y is a string.

All other things are almost the same in every programming language. LWC is a standard new JavaScript framework for Salesforce, being used to create customized web pages and applications in Salesforce. So, it is necessary to learn JavaScript for all Salesforce developers who want to learn LWC.

Defining a component

LWC is a new programming technique for creating Lightning components. It works flawlessly with Salesforce's Aura programming; LWC makes use of many of the improvements in web standards over the previous years, and it offers an exceptional experience.

An LWC is a combination of an HTML, JavaScript, metadata configuration, and/or **Cascading Style Sheets** (**CSS**) file. All files should have the same name so that they can be auto-linked, but they will have their specific extensions. For example, if we want to create an LWC with the name **showBook**:

```
showBook
     ├──showBook.html (Required & Auto created)
     ├──showBook.js   (Required & Auto created)
     ├──showBook.js-meta.xml (Required & Auto created)
     ├──showBook.css (Optional)
     ├──showBook.svg (Optional)
     └──__tests__    (Optional & Auto created)
        ├──data
        └──showBook.test.js
```

Component names must follow the following rules:

- The initial letter must be lowercase.
- Only underscore or alphanumeric characters may be used.
- Not allowed to have whitespace or a dash (hyphen)
- Cannot use an underscore in the end or two underscores in a row.

Components of an LWC

Let us understand all the components of an LWC one by one in detail, as we will be creating those in this chapter.

HTML file

The HTML file will always be with the root tag **<template>,** like:

```html
<!-- showBook.html -->

<template>
  <!-- Replace comment with component HTML -->
</template>
```

Component JavaScript file

Every UI component must include a JavaScript file with at least the following code:

```js
import { LightningElement } from "lwc";
export default class MyComponent extends LightningElement {}
```

"lwc" is the main module of LWC. LightningElement is imported from the LWC module using the following import statement:

```
import { LightningElement } from "lwc";
```

LightningElement is a custom wrapper of the standard HTML element. Extend the **LightningElement** to create a JavaScript class for an LWC. You cannot extend any other class to create an LWC:

```
export default class MyComponent extends LightningElement { // Your code here
}
```

A customized version of the common HTML element is called **LightningElement**. A JavaScript class for an LWC can be created by extending **LightningElement**. To develop an LWC, you cannot extend any other class.

Component configuration file

The configuration file defines the metadata values for the component, including supported targets and the design configuration for Lightning App Builder and Experience Builder. The configuration file looks like the following:

```
<?xml version="1.0" encoding="UTF-8"?>
<LightningComponentBundle xmlns="http://soap.sforce.com/2006/04/metadata">
    <apiVersion>45.0</apiVersion>
    <isExposed>false</isExposed>
<targets>
    <target>lightning__RecordPage</target>
    <target>lightning__AppPage</target>
    <target>lightning__HomePage</target>
  </targets>
</LightningComponentBundle>
```

Component CSS

A CSS file may be included in a component. We can use standard CSS syntax for styling LWC.

Make a stylesheet with the same name as the component in the component bundle in order to style it. The style sheet is **showBook.css** if the component is named **showBook**. Then, the above stylesheet is automatically used in.

The largest size allowed for a CSS file for a component is 128 KB.

Importance of JavaScript file in LWC

As mentioned earlier JavaScript file is mandatory for LWC. If we are building a user interface using LWC and we use HTML in that, the JS file will be used to define variables used with HTML elements. If the component is just being used as a utility, then in JS, we will create method and export it.

In the JavaScript file, we will define a variable, also known as a property or attribute. Reactivity is the core feature of Web components architecture as it can observe the change to the value of a variable. This means that if the value is changed, the component will populate the new value everywhere it is being used, like in an HTML file or in a JS file. There are many type of properties like local and public variables. Decorators will be used with properties to add functionalities.

Decorators

Three decorators in the LWC programming model extends the functionality of a property or function. While ECMAScript allows the creation of decorators, LWC is the only tool that offers these three decorators.

@api

To expose a public property, use **@api** decorator with the field. Public properties can be accessed outside of a component and can be used in other components. Public properties define the API for a component, as shown in the following code:

```
@api book = 'Cloud computing'
```

@track

Previously, to make a field reactive, we had to use the **@track** decorator. All fields in a LWC class are reactive now by default. Reactive means that whenever the value changes in **JavaScript (JS)**, the changed value should auto-populate in HTML. You will still need to use the track when:

- Observing changes to the properties of an object.
- Observing changes to the elements of an array.

The syntax will be as follows:

```
@track fullName = { firstName : '', lastName : ''};
this.fullName.firstName = 'John';
```

@wire

Reactive wire services are used by LWC to read Salesforce data. The component renders when the wire service provisions data. To provide a wire adapter or an Apex function, components utilize the **@wire** annotation in their JavaScript classes. The wire syntax will be as follows:

```
import { LightningElement, api, wire } from "lwc";

import { getRecord } from "lightning/uiRecordApi";

import ACCOUNT_NAME_FIELD from "@salesforce/schema/Account.Name";


export default class Record extends LightningElement {
  @api recordId;

  @wire(getRecord, { recordId: "$recordId", fields: [ACCOUNT_NAME_FIELD] })
  record;
}
```

This code imports the **Account.Name** field and uses it in a wire adapter's configuration object.

Rules for naming convention of properties

JavaScript property names use camel case, while HTML attribute names use kebab case to match with HTML conventions. For example, JavaScript property name is **bookName** and HTML attribute will be **book-name**.

The JS file will look like the following:

```
import { LightningElement, api} from "lwc";


export default class Record extends LightningElement {
  @api bookName;
}
```

The HTML file will be as follows:

```
<template>
  <c-branch book-name-name="Salesforce book"></c-branch>
</template>
```

We cannot name the JS properties starting with the following prefix:

on , is , part, data

We cannot use Uppercase in HTML attributes, but we can use lowercase alphabetic character, underscore (_), and the dollar sign ($).

Lightning Web Components first example

Refer to the following code of LWC, which includes html and JS files:

```html
<!-- firstComponent.html -->
<template> Welcome to {greeting}! </template>
```

```js
// firstComponent.js
import { LightningElement } from "lwc";
export default class FirstComponent extends LightningElement {
    greeting = "coding";
}
```

In the preceding code, you see there is a variable defined as **greeting** in JS, and we use that variable in the HTML file as **{greeting}**. Please remember there should not be any space before or after the variable name inside {} so **{ greeting}** or **{greeting }** is invalid.

Lightning Web Components second example

If we have to take a text input in an HTML file and store that value in JS, then check the following example:

```html
<!-- Html file -->
<template>
        <p>Hi, {name}!</p>
        <lightning-input label="Name" value={name} onchange={handleNameChange}>.              </lightning-input>
</template>
```

```js
<!-- JS file -->
import { LightningElement } from "lwc";
export default class SecondComp extends LightningElement {
    name = "World";
    handleNameChange (event) {
```

```
                    this.name = event.target.value;
        }
}
```

As you can see in the preceding code, the input html field uses the **onchange** attribute to detect changes to its value. When the value changes, the **handleChange** function in the JavaScript file executes, and the name property is now assigned the input value.

Creating your first LWC

Unlike Apex and VF Page, we cannot create LWC using the developer console of Salesforce org. As the LWC is based on the web standard, we will be using multiple other tools to create the LWC and those are known as **Salesforce Developer Experience (DX)** or **(SFDX)**.

Some of the tools are Salesforce **Command Line Interface (CLI)**, **Integrated Development Environment (IDE)**, especially **Visual Studio (VS)** code, DevHub, Scratch Org, Package Generation tools, etc.

So, we will install VS Code into our desktop, and then install the Salesforce CLI. These are prerequisites of Creating LWC.

Open the VS Code and go to the extension and install the Salesforce pack:

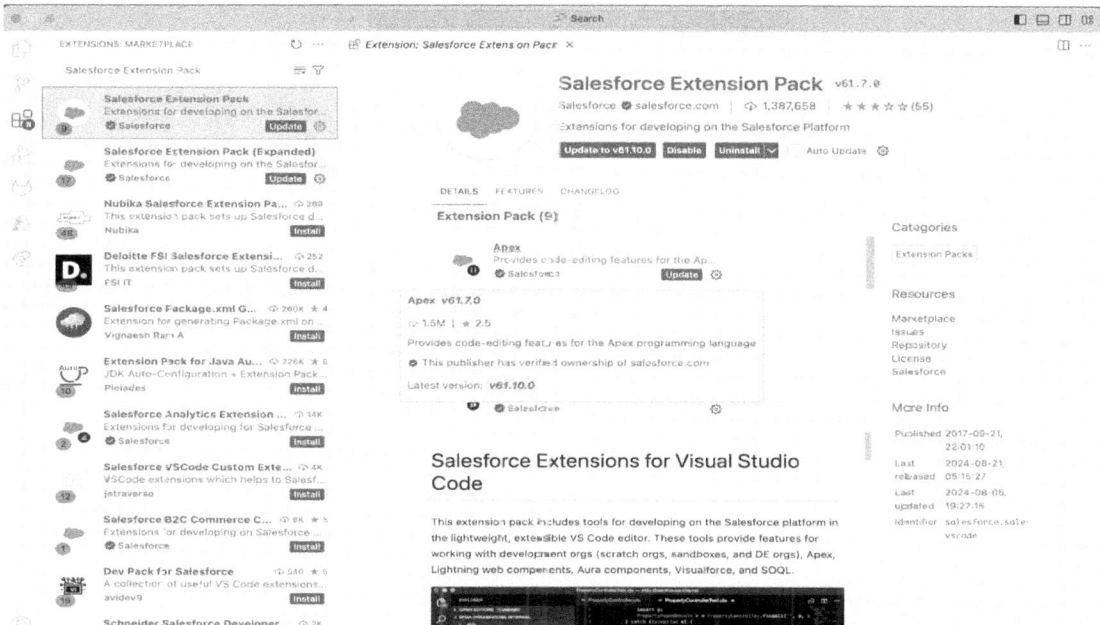

Figure 15.1: VS Code

Now, we need to make sure our VS Code is ready to use for Salesforce and LWC. For that, we will open the command palette on VS Code and write sfdx through the following steps:

1. You can type *Ctrl+Shift+P* (Windows) or *Cmd+Shift+P* (macOS). You can also go to menu view and click command palette.

2. Enter sfdx.

3. If you see some commands there, then good, otherwise all prerequsisite are done.

We can create a project now, and connect the VS Code to Salesforce, and authorize it through the following steps:

1. In the VS Code, open the command pallate by typing *Ctrl+Shift+P* (Windows) or *Cmd+Shift+P* (macOS).

2. Enter **Sfdx:Create** project, and choose standard type the name of project, and choose folder:

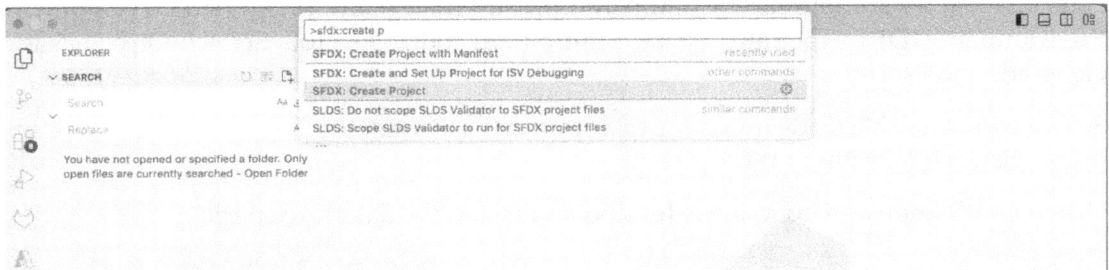

Figure 18.2: Create project

3. Open the command palette again, type SFDX: Authorize an Org.

4. Choose the login URL sandbox or production and put the alias name.

5. Now, you will be redirected to Salesforce login page. You can login and authorize, and you will be connected to Salesforce org.

6. Open the command again and type **sfdx: create lightning web component**:

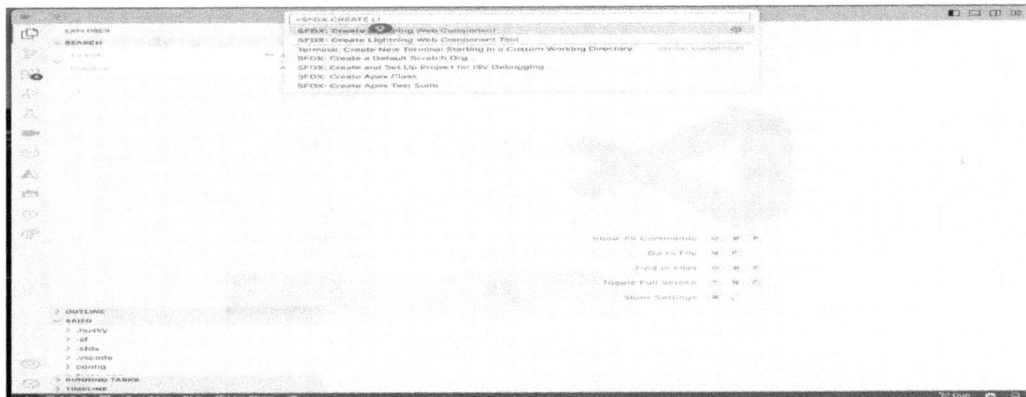

Figure 18.3: Create LWC

7. Enter **firstComponent**, the name of LWC and it will be saved inside **force-app/ main/default/lwc**. Select that, and you will see the component bundle in VS Code:

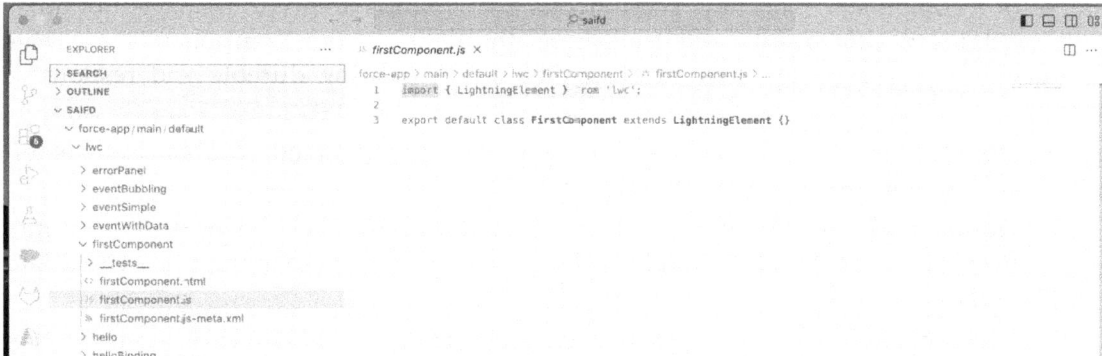

Figure 18.4: *First component*

8. Make the changes in First component html and JS file and save it.

9. Now, we need to deploy this LWC to Salesforce org:

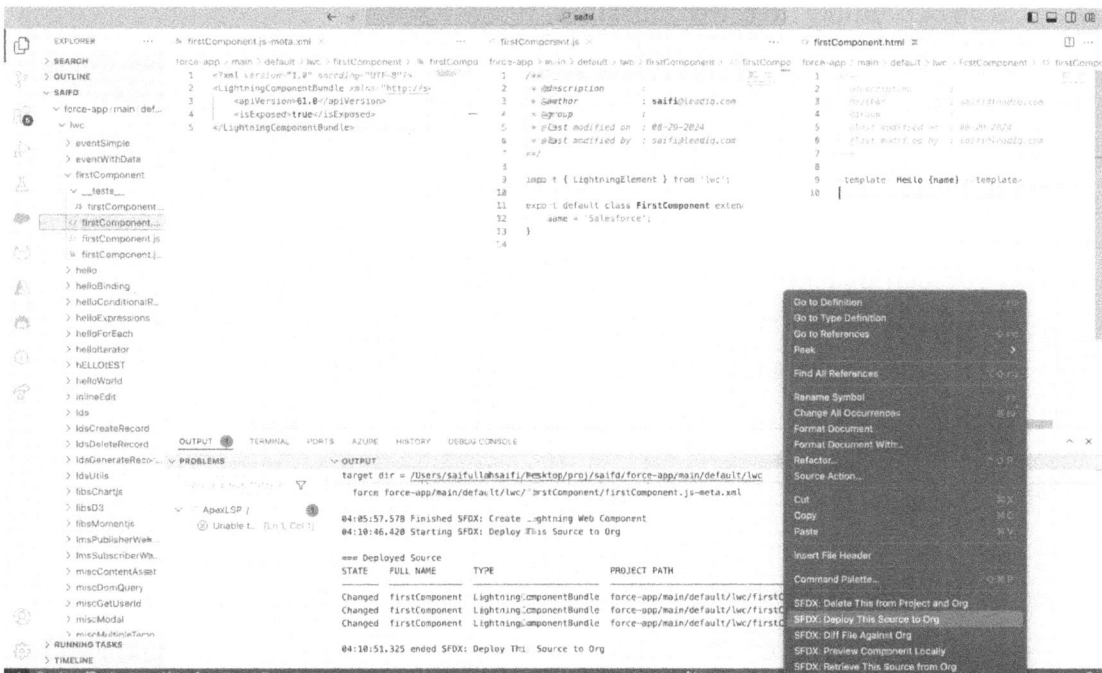

Figure 18.5*: Deploy component*

10. You can see in the preceding figure that the component is deployed.

Lifecycle flow

LWC lifecycle hooks are predefined methods that allow developers to intervene at different stages of a component's journey. These hooks give you the ability to manage, optimize, and react to specific events and transitions throughout your component's lifecycle. Understanding and using them effectively is key to creating durable and responsive components. You can use the following lifecycle hooks with LWC:

- **constructor ():** This is where the component is initialized. You can set default values and customize them at the same time.
- **connectedCallback():** This hook is executed after the component is inserted into the **Document Object Model (DOM)**. It is a great place to manipulate DOM and get data.
- **renderCallback():** This hook is fired after rendering. It is useful for tasks that require understanding the rendered DOM.
- **disconnectedCallback():** This hook is called when the element is removed from the DOM. It is used for cleaning and delivery of material.
- **errorCallback():** This hook is called when an error occurs during rendering. This is an opportunity to correct mistakes.

Let us look at a simple example that illustrates the importance of lifecycle hooks. Consider creating a countdown timer. See how to use lifecycle hooks:

```
<!-- JS file -->
export default class CountdownTimer extends LightningElement {
    timeInSec = 5;
    connectedCallback() {
        this.countDownTimer = setInterval(() => {
            if (this.timeInSec > 0) {
                this.timeInSec--;
            }
        }, 1000);
    }
    renderedCallback() {
        if (this.timeInSec === 0) {
            clearInterval(this.countDownTimer);
        }
    }
    disconnectedCallback() {
```

```
        clearInterval(this.countDownTimer);
    }
}
```

In this example, **connectedCallback** sets the **countDownTimer**, **renderedCallback** updates the UI when the time reaches 0, and **disconnectedCallback** ensures that the **countDownTimer** ends when the component is removed, as shown in the following figure:

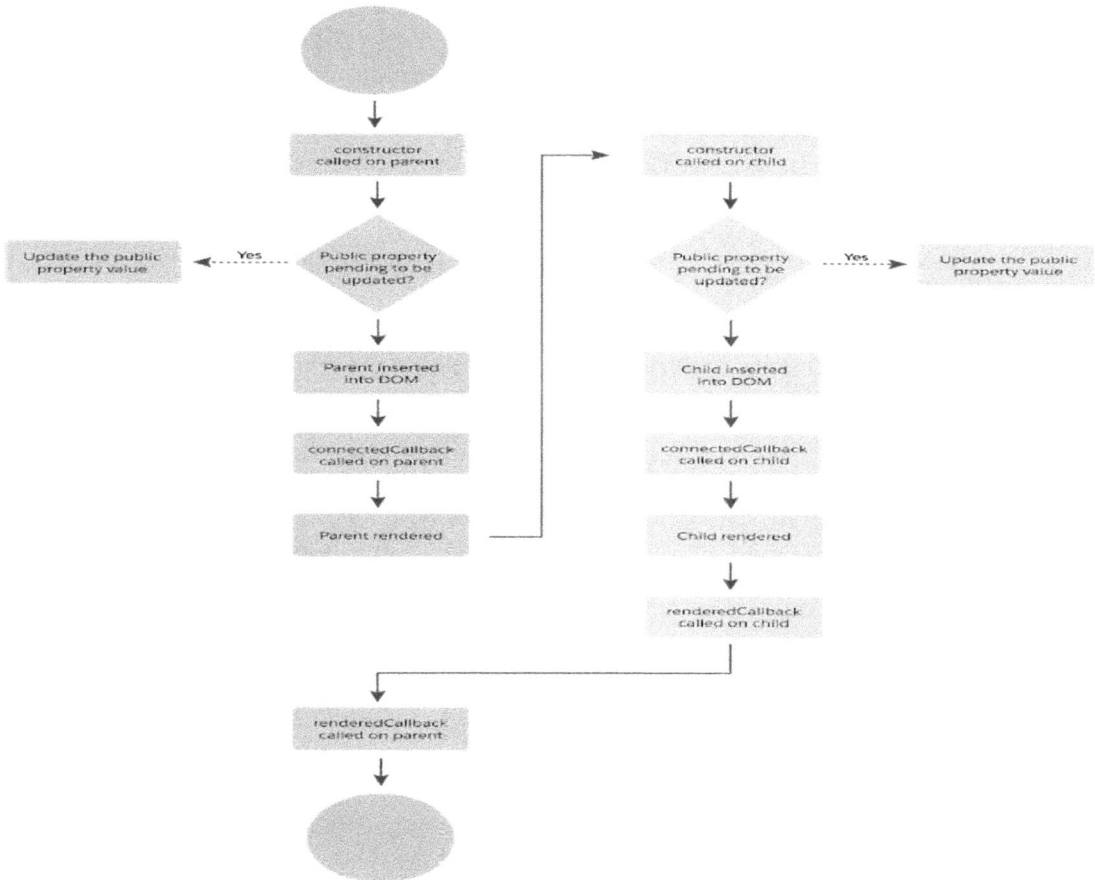

Figure 18.6: LWC lifecycle

Working with Salesforce data

Salesforce has multiple ways to access or save data for LWC. The idea is try to use a simple and easy way and then customize or use more features when needed.

We can use the following features from LWC for Salesforce data interaction:

- Base Lightning components
- Lightning Data Service and wire adapters
- Apex
- GraphQL

We will discuss the preceding features in order. Using the basic Lightning components based on **Lightning Data Service (LDS)** is the simplest method of working with Salesforce data. Use a LDS wire adapter straight if you require greater flexibility. Different data and metadata are provided by each wire adaptor. The information and data are provided to your component by the wire service.

If sending many queries in one operation is what you want to start with, use the GraphQL wire adaptor. Finally, utilize Apex if the flexibility of GraphQL and LDS wire adapters is insufficient.

Base Lightning components

Base Lightning components include Lightning Design System brands and classes to provide better performance and usability in a small footprint.

These core components manage HTML and CSS information for you. Each component contains simple attributes that allow style variations. This means that you usually do not need to use CSS at all. The simplicity of Lightning's core attributes and their clear, consistent definitions make them easy to use, allowing you to focus on business logic.

Some of the examples are:

A `lightning-input` component is a replacement of an HTML `<input>` element. This component supports the following input types: `checkbox, date, datetime, time, email, url, number, text (default)`

The syntax will be as follows:

```
<lightning-input type="text" label="Enter text" onchange={handleInputChange}> </lightning-input>
```

The LWC will look like the following figure:

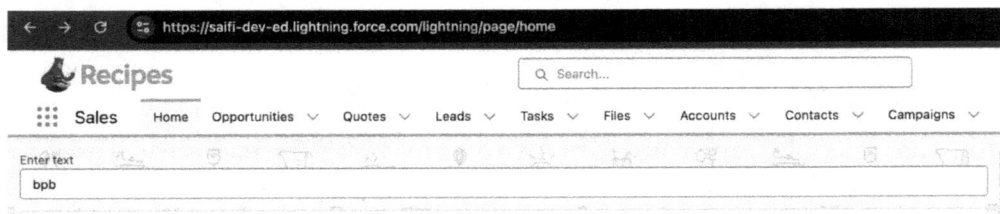

Figure 18.7: LWC text

A **lightning-button** component represents a button element that performs an action. Use the **lightning-button** when users need to submit or reset a form, etc.

The syntax will be as follows:

```
<lightning-button variant="brand" label="Download" title="Download action
with brand variant" icon-name="utility:download" class="slds-m-left_x-
small"></lightning-button>
```

A **lightning-formatted-text** component displays text in a read-only format and can convert or bind URLs and email addresses. It also converts the **\r** and **\n** characters into **
** tags

The syntax will be as follows:

```
<lightning-formatted-text value="Email info@salesforce.com" linkify>  </
lightning-formatted-text>
```

The component, **lightning-layout**, is a flexible grid system for placing containers next to or inside another container. The default layout is mobile-oriented and can be easily configured to work on different devices.

The syntax will be as follows:

```
<lightning-layout>

    <lightning-layout-item padding="around-small">

        <div class="header-column">

        <p class="field-title" title="Field 1">Field 1</p>

            <p>Name</p>

        </div>

    </lightning-layout-item>

    <lightning-layout-item padding="around-small">

        <div class="header-column">

            <p class="field-title" title="Field2 (3)">Field 2 (3)

            <lightning-button-icon icon-name="utility:down" variant="bor-
der-filled" size="small" alternative-text="More Actions"></lightning-but-
ton-icon>

            </p>

            <p>Eligibility</p>

        </div>

    </lightning-layout-item>

</lightning-layout>
```

The LWC will look like the following figure:

Figure 18.8: LWC icon and button

Let us take an example of how variable binding works in LWC. The {greeting} variable is showing the default value, and if you change the value in the first name input box, it will be changed everywhere:

```
<!-- Html file -->
<template>
    <lightning-card title="Saif CoderinMe" icon-name="custom:custom14">
        <div class="slds-m-around_medium">
            <p>Hello, {greeting} {greeting1}!</p>
            <lightning-input label="First Name" value={greeting} placehold-
er="Please enter your first name" onchange={changeHandler}></lightning-in-
put>
            <lightning-input label="Last Name" value={greeting1} on-
change={changeHandler1} placeholder="Please enter your last name"></light-
ning-input>
        </div>
    </lightning-card>
</template>
<!-- JS file -->
import { LightningElement, track} from 'lwc';

export default class HelloWorld extends LightningElement {
    @track greeting = '';
    @track greeting1 = '';
    changeHandler(event) {
        this.greeting = event.target.value;
    }
    changeHandler1(event) {
```

```
        this.greeting1 = event.target.value;
    }
}
```

The LWC will be displayed as shown in the following figure:

Figure 18.9: *LWC variable binding*

Lightning Data Service

LDS is a powerful tool provided by Salesforce that provides access for LWC to interact with Salesforce data without the need for Apex code. Records uploaded to LDS are stored and shared between components. If a page consists of components that display the same record, all components display the same version of the record. The performance of components using the same record is greatly improved because the record is loaded once, regardless of how many components use it.

In an LWC, perform operations on data and access metadata using these technologies built into the LDS.

The base components used for LDS are lightning-record-edit-form, lightning-record-form, and lightning-record-view-form.

Wire adapters and functions for LDS can be found in **lightning/ui*** Api modules

LDS manages the data for you and changes to a specific record will be auto-reflected in all the components built using this LDS. In contrast, Apex data is unmanaged; you must update the information.

When the LDS detects a change in a record or any data or metadata it supports, all components using the appropriate **@wire** adapter will receive the new value. Detection is triggered when a LWC modifies a record.

The LDS cache expires, and then the Lightning network component starts reading @wire. The cache tag and the Lightning Web Part must be in the same browser and application (such as Lightning Experience) for the same user. To improve performance, LDS maintains a client-side cache of record data loaded by the wire adapter. Loading data from this cache is faster than asking the server.

Some benefits of LDS are:

- LDS does a lot of work to make your code work well.
- Load record data incrementally.
- Saves the results to the client application and invalidates cache entries when Salesforce dependency data and metadata changes.
- Optimizes server calls by making them bulkified and through the deduplication of requests.

    It is an underlying service that makes Base Lightning components and LDS metadata aware, resulting in significant productivity gains.

The **lightning/uiRecordApi** module includes wire adapters to record data and default values to create records. It also includes JavaScript APIs to create, delete, update, and refresh records.

The wire adapters are:

- getRecord
- getRecordCreateDefaults

Some of the JavaScript methods are:

- createRecord(recordInput)
- deleteRecord(recordId)
- getFieldValue(record, field)

Let us use some of these method in the LWC code:

```
<!-- HTML file -->
<template>
    <lightning-card title="WireGetRecordDynamicContact" icon-name="standard:contact">
        <template if:true={contact.data}>
            <div class="slds-var-m-around_medium">
                <p>{name}</p>
                <p>{title}</p>
                <p>
                    <lightning-formatted-phone value={phone}></lightning-formatted-phone>
                </p>
                <p>
```

```
                    <lightning-formatted-email value={email}></light-
ning-formatted-email>
                </p>
            </div>
        </template>
        <template if:true={contact.error}>
            <c-error-panel errors={contact.error}></c-error-panel>
        </template>
        <c-view-source source="lwc/wireGetRecordDynamicContact" slot="foot-
er">
            Create an ad-hoc UI for a specific record. This recipe uses a
dynamic schema definition (fields are
            specified as string).
        </c-view-source>
    </lightning-card>
</template>
<!-- JS file -->
import { LightningElement, api, wire } from 'lwc';
import { getRecord } from 'lightning/uiRecordApi';
const fields = ['Contact.Name', 'Contact.Title', 'Contact.Phone', 'Contact.
Email'];

export default class WireGetRecordDyramicContact extends LightningElement {
    @api recordId;
    @wire(getRecord, { recordId: '$recordId', fields })
    contact;
    get name() {
        return this.contact.data.fields.Name.value;
    }
    get title() {
        return this.contact.data.fields.Title.value;
    }
    get phone() {
        return this.contact.data.fields.Phone.value;
```

```
    }
    get email() {
        return this.contact.data.fields.Email.value;
    }
}
```

Using Apex in Lightning Web components

If you cannot use the core component or the LDS wire adapters or features, then use Apex.

You can use Apex in the following situations:

- You can work with objects not supported by the UI API, such as task and event.
- Work with functions not supported by the UI API, such as conditionally loading a list of records (for example, loading the first 200 accounts with an amount > $1 million).
- To execute the transaction. For example, creating an account and creating a new account-related opportunity. If each fails to create, the entire transaction is aborted. Perform a mandatory method call, not via thread service. You can choose to call the method strictly in response to a button click or delay loading outside the critical path.

If you call an Apex method absolutely, restart the Apex method to refresh the data.

Apex does not share data caches or store data with LDS. Information obtained with Apex may conflict with information obtained with LDS wire adapters, both online and offline. For example, your component might behave unexpectedly, and if it retrieves data through Apex, it then executes a search query on the same data using the GraphQL wire adapter.

If you are using **Salesforce Object Query Language** (**SOQL**) to retrieve data, use the GraphQL wire adapter when performing the search query. By consistently using the GraphQL wire adapter for both retrieval and retrieval, you can avoid problems such as retrieving Apex data when the corresponding null value is retrieved by the GraphQL wire adapter.

Calling Apex method from Lightning Web components

This is the first example of how to call Apex from LWC JavaScript. Let us have a look at the code:

leadDataFromApex.js will look as follows:

```
import { LightningElement } from 'lwc';
```

```
import getLeadList from '@salesforce/apex/LeadController.getLeadList;

export default class LeadDataFromApex extends LightningElement {
    leadList;
    error;

    async handleShowLeads() {
        try {
            this.leadList = await getLeadList();
            this.error = undefined;
        } catch (error) {
            this.leadList = undefined;
            this.error = error;
        }
    }
}
```

The Apex class **LeadController.cls** will look like this:

```
public with sharing class LeadController {
    @AuraEnabled(cacheable=true)
    public static List<Lead> getLeadList() {
        return [
            SELECT Id, FirstName,Email,Company
            FROM Lead
            WHERE Email != NULL
            WITH SECURITY_ENFORCED
            LIMIT 5
        ];
    }
}
```

HTML file **leadDataFromApex.html** will be written as follows:

```
  <template>
<lightning-card title="LeadDataFromApex" icon-name="custom:custom66">
    <div class="slds-m-around_medium">
```

```
        <p class="slds-m-bottom_small">
            <lightning-button label="Show Contacts" onclick="{handle-
ShowLeads}"></lightning-button>
        </p>
        <template lwc:if="{leadList}">
            <template for:each="{leadList}" for:item="lead">
                <p key="{lead.Id}">{lead.firstName}</p>
            </template>
        </template>
        <template lwc:elseif="{error}">
          {error}
        </template>
      </div>
  </lightning-card>
</template>
```

Composition

You can add a component to the body of another component. Composition allows you to create complex pieces from simple building blocks. With a set of smaller components to make the code more reusable and maintainable.

The parent component HTML is as follows:

```
<!-- todoComp.html -->

<template>
    <div class="listing">
        <c-todo-item item-name="Milk"></c-todo-item>
        <c-todo-item item-name="Bread"></c-todo-item>
    </div>
</template>
```

As you can see, the child component is **todoItem**. We are passing values as milk and bread in the **itemName** variable:

```
// todoItem.js
import { LightningElement, api } from "lwc";
export default class TodoItem extends LightningElement {
```

```
  @api itemName = "New Item";
}
```

This is the child component JS, where **itemName** is a public variable that will get the data from the parent component:

```
<!-- todoItem.html -->
<template>
  <div class="view">
    <label>{itemName}</label>
  </div>
</template>
```

This child HTML displays the values.

If we have to send data from child component to the parent components then we have to use Events.

Communicate with events

LWC dispatches standard DOM events, and it may create and dispatch custom events.

Create and dispatch events in a component's JavaScript class. To create an event, use the **CustomEvent()** constructor. To dispatch an event, we will call the **dispatchEvent()** method.

Let us check the following code to understand events:

```
<!--pageLwc.html -->
<lightning-input
    onchange={handleChangeMethod}
    type="number"
    name="input1"
    label="Enter a number">
</lightning-input>


// pageLwc.js
import { LightningElement } from "lwc";
export default class PageLwc extends LightningElement {
  handleChangeMethod() {
    let num = event.target.value;
```

```
    // Creates the event with the data.
    const sendEvnt = new CustomEvent("sendnum", {
    detail: num
    });

    // Dispatches the event.
    this.dispatchEvent(sendEvnt);
  }
}
```

We can use **Bubbles** and **Composed** to handle events propagation, for example, which component can read or subscribe to that event or where it is published.

Now, in the parent component, we will use this event in the following way:

```
<template>
  <lightning-card title="Getting num From Child Comp">
      <lightning-progress-bar
        value={index}
      ></lightning-progress-bar>
      <c-page-lwc
        onsendnum={handleEvent}
      ></c-page-lwc>
  </lightning-card>
</template>
```

In the preceding code, you can see the child component page in LWC is being used, and the **on** prefix is added on the event name **sendnum** that was dispatched from child LWC JS:

```
import { LightningElement } from "lwc";

export default class ParentLwc extends LightningElement {
  index = 0;
  handleEvent(event) {
    this.index = event.detail;
  }
}
```

Common JavaScript method

Sometimes you want to do same thing but on different screen or different components, for that, we can create multiple components and one JavaScript web component, in which we will export all the functions that we want to use at multiple places.

Let us take an example. We have two components, comp1 and comp2, and we have multiple things, but we want to create a custom URL link in both components.

Component comp1 has 3 files, **comp1.html conp1.js, comp1.js-meta.xml**

Component comp2 has 3 files, **comp2.html comp2.js, comp2.js-meta.xml**

Now, we will create the utility component. It will have two files **Utility.js, Utility. js-meta.xml**:

- **Utility.js:** Let us check the following common code:

```
1. import timezone from "@salesforce/i18n/timeZone";
2. export function makeUserLink(sid,pos) {
3.     return 'https://in.bpbonline.com/products/Cloud-computing-us-
   ing-salesforce?_pos='+pos+'&_sid='+sid+'&tz='+timezone;
4. }
```

- **Comp1.js:** Let us implement the following component code:

```
1. import { makeUserLink } from 'c/iQ_Utility';
2. export default class comp1 extends LightningElement {
3.     url;
4.     connectedCallback() {
5.       this.url = makeUserLink('12teg',1);
6.     }
7. }
```

- **Comp2.js:** Let us implement the following component code:

```
import { makeUserLink } from 'c/iQ_Utility';
export default class comp1 extends LightningElement {
    valuCode;
    connectedCallback() {
this.valuCode = 'https://www.amazon.in?redirectul=' makeUser-
Link('12teg',1);
    }
}
```

In the preceding code, you see **Utility.js** has an export function **makeUserLink** which will return the url with certain parameters.

Comp1 and comp2 is using that method by importing it and using it for their own purpose.

Using static resources in Lightning Web components

First, upload the static resource in Salesforce like any JS file. You can go to **setup** and search **Static resource**, and click **new static resources** and upload the zip file named as img folder. In this folder, we have stored **bpb.png**.

Now, we will use that in LWC:

```
<!-- JS file -->
import { LightningElement } from 'lwc';
import BPB_Resource from '@salesforce/resourceUrl/myResource';
export default class ResourceExample extends LightningElement {
    bpbLogo = BPB_Resource + '/img/bpb.jpg';
}
<!-- HTML file -->
<template>
    <lightning-card title="Resoucre example" icon-name="custom:custom19">
        <div class="slds-m-around_medium">
            <img src={bpbLogo}>
        </div>
    </lightning-card>
</template>
```

GraphQL wire adapter

With GraphQL wire adpater, we can query the Salesforce data like SOQL and do the filter, etc. Retrieve specific records, fields, and object information in a single server call using the GraphQL wire adapter. With built-in shared caching, LDS manages your data, and you do not need different wire adapters for each GraphQL query you define.

Let us check an example of how GraphQL is being used in LWC:

```
import { LightningElement, wire } from "lwc";
import { gql, graphql } from "lightning/uiGraphQLApi";

export default class MyGQLQuery extends LightningElement {
  @wire(graphql, {
```

```
query: gql`
  query LeadInfo {
    uiapi {
      query {
        Account(first:5, where: { LastName: { like: "Lead1" } }) {
          edges {
            node {
              Name {
                value
                displayValue
              }
            }
          }
        }
      }
    }
  }`,
  })
  propertyOrFunction;
}
```

Lightning Web components recipe

Salesforce has created an opensource code on GitHub and on Trailhead, in which most of the LWC examples are there. We can use those in our app and can learn all about LWC. It provides basic examples from hello World, variable binding, parent to child component uses, data access from Salesforce and third party library.

You can find the link here: **https://github.com/trailheadapps/lwc-recipes**

Lightning Web components security

Lightning Locker provides component isolation and security, allowing code from many sources to run and communicate through secure, standard APIs and event mechanisms. Lightning Locker was the default security architecture for Lightning components.

Lightning Web Security (LWS), designed to facilitate secure coding of components, replacing Lightning Locker.

LWS takes a radically different approach to Locker to achieve its security goals. Virtualization is the cornerstone of LWS, transforming how security is managed within the browser by acting as a virtualization engine. It is a client-side (meaning they run within an end user's browser) security architecture designed to isolate components from different developers (for example, Salesforce, AppExchange packages, and your own code). It is to prevent them from performing actions (potentially malicious) on components they are not supposed to (such as a managed package reading data from a local component) and to enforce safe and secure best practices.

Conclusion

In this chapter, we learned about the basic introduction of LWC. We also checked how and when to use the decorators. We got an idea about the LWC lifecycle, base component, and LDS. At last, we saw an example of calling the Apex method from LWC.

In the next chapter, we will see when to avoid coding and use flow in Salesforce.

Questions

1. Does LWC support Web Standard?
2. Can we use LWC without JS code?
3. Can we access the data from LWC.

Answers

1. Yes
2. No
3. Yes, we can access data imperative or using wire or LDS.

Join our Discord space

Join our Discord workspace for latest updates, offers, tech happenings around the world, new releases, and sessions with the authors:

https://discord.bpbonline.com

More Customization and Less Coding

Introduction

Salesforce always works as **Software as a Service (SaaS)**; hence, it promotes less coding, as we can use Salesforce inbuilt tools to complete the automation. In this chapter, we will compare three important automated tools (Lightning Flow, trigger) of Salesforce and understand their uses in multiple scenarios.

Structure

In this chapter, we will discuss the following topics:

- Learning about the Salesforce automated tools
- Order of execution
- Advantages and limitations of trigger
- Advantages and limitations of Lightning Flow
- Choosing tools

Objectives

After studying this chapter, you will be able to decide on the best automation tool for different scenarios and problems. You will also learn to solve a problem with the best solution. You will study the advantages and limitations of the Salesforce automated tool and Apex.

Learning about the Salesforce automated tools

Salesforce has a custom automated tool, in which we require less knowledge of code with click or drag-and-drop options known as Lightning Flow. Salesforce also has a trigger that requires Apex coding, but it helps to solve increasingly complex problems. We will discuss the pros and cons of every tool. First, let us understand the whole journey of a Record Transaction as what happens when the data saved to databases.

Order of execution

Whenever a record is inserted or updated, all the events and rules in that transaction will run in a certain specific order, and it is known as order of execution.

We have the following order of execution if a record is created:

1. New records are loaded from the database, and then Salesforce runs system validation if the record is created from UI.
2. It will run the record-triggered flow that is designed for before saving.
3. Salesforce runs all before insert trigger.
4. Salesforce will run system validations (Like null, datatype, to name a few) and custom validation rule.
5. Now, it is time for the execution of duplicate rules.
6. The record is saved in the database, but it is not committed into the database so it can rollbacked if needed.
7. Now the system will execute triggers with after events, such as after insert and after update.
8. Now, there are some standard assignment rules used to assign leads or cases based on load or assigning the queue.
9. The next order is for workflow rule if there is one available. If in workflow action, any field is updated, it can start the execution of before or after trigger again. (Optional as workflow is deprecated mostly)
10. In the last process, record-triggered flows that are configured to run after the record, is saved.
11. Data will be committed to Salesforce.

Advantages and disadvantages of trigger

When Salesforce extends the salesforce for the developer to use it as **Platform as a Service (PaaS)**, then the trigger is introduced as code-based business logic automation using Apex.

Here are the pros and cons for trigger:

- **Pros:**
  - We can control the process and order of the flow. For example, which field should be updated first and which will be second in order.
  - In workflow or process builder, if we need to update more than one field, we use multiple workflow actions. However, in the case of the trigger, we can write all update logic for fields in a single trigger.

- **Cons:**
  - You will need an Apex developer to write the code.
  - Development cycle is not as fast as other tools because its development will be done in Sandbox, after that, we will write the test class, and then we can deploy it to a live environment.
  - It is not easy to enable/disable the Apex Trigger like Lightning Flow.
  - It requires a test class and code coverage of 75 or more, although it gives a robust, tested automation in the org that can be validated before it hits production.

Here are the points we know about trigger:

- It can work on multi-level objects, such as from parent to child or child to parent object, etc.
- Trigger works when any DML happens, but we need to make sure which syntax we can used as per need, like before insert or after insertion.
- In the master-detail relationship, we know the roll-up summary field always works to calculate the count, the average, or the total of the child. If we need a similar thing in common lookup child-parent objects, we use a trigger.
- We need to consider all the Salesforce limitations, like the governor limit, before writing a trigger or building a flow. In a single transaction, the following are the limits:
  - DML statement: up to 150
  - **Salesforce Object Query Language (SOQL)** statement: up to 100
  - Number of records from a SOQL query: 50,000
  - Number of records can be used in DML: 10000

    o   Number of **Salesforce Object Search Language (SOSL)**: 20

    o   Number of characters allowed in a trigger: 1 Million.

Advantages and disadvantages of Lightning Flow

Lightning Flow (New version) came out recently in 2019, which looks like an updated version of the process builder and with multiple new features, like the creation of post into Chatter, DML on related objects, invoking the Apex class, and building a good screen for inputting data. It also provides an option to choose before save and after save events and delete event.

The following figure from *salesforceben.com* can give you an idea of what we can do or cannot do using flow:

Low Code ——————————————————————————————————→ Pro Code

	Before-Save Flow Trigger	After-Save Flow Trigger	After-Save FLow Trigger+Apex	Apex Triggers
Same-Record Field Updates	Available	Not Ideal	Not Ideal	Available
High-Performance Batch Processing	Not Ideal	Not Ideal	Not Ideal	Available
Cross-Object CRUD	Not Available	Available	Available	Available
Asynchronous Processing	Not Available	Available	Available	Available
Complex List Processing	Not Available	Not Ideal	Available	Available
Custom Validation Errors	Not Available	Not Available	Not Available	Available

Figure 19.1: Flow and trigger comparison

There are two important things when it comes to the order of execution. Which are as follows:

- Before save Flows will run earlier than before Apex triggers.
- Apex triggers can also run multiple times in a single transaction.

Let us explore a use case:

In a company, Sam (Developer) was working on a framework where a customer number on a custom object is expected to populate from the parent account. Thus, Sam created a workflow that would populate the customer number from the record when the record was created or when the account lookup field was changed. Our customer, likewise, needed to implement that the customer number of objects should not be blank, so we made a validation rule. Generally, it worked until somebody found an account that did not have a customer number. We can move this object from one account to this account. We can easily update the field from the parent and validate the field. However, the issue was the order of execution.

Tracking with the request for execution, you can see that the record gets refreshed, changing the account ID, and afterward, the workflow runs. The system, at that point, runs the validation rules and sees that the customer number still has value since it has not changed in the workflow. At that point, the workflow fires to refresh the field, which, in this situation, is blanked out since the new record does not have a customer number. The system will re-run standard validation once more, yet the custom validation rule only runs once.

Both the workflow and the validation rule were composed effectively. Both are executing, yet they were executing at an inappropriate time. At last, Sam would end up re-doing this usefulness as a trigger, where Sam could more readily control when things would occur and realize that the field has its last value from the get-go all the while.

Through this use case, we do not just learn that workflow is tedious, and triggers are acceptable. It is more that you must be aware of the numerous things occurring in Salesforce. A workflow may be flawless in certain situations; however, not incredible in others. At the point when you can bear the cost of the time and have the appropriately prepared assets, a trigger can quite often give you the control you need.

Let us explore the second use case:

Whenever an account changes its status we must create all contacts in an external system:

Hundreds of accounts might update with thousands of contacts in this case. We must update the external ID field for synchronization, including retry logic and error handling, based on the response. This business logic will be so complex that it would not work well in a flow where comments and splitting the logic up into several classes and methods are not practical. Flows may fail for several reasons, such as timeouts when contacting external systems, if we are updating thousands of contacts in a single transaction. However, triggers have the ability to address this through future (asynchronous) approaches. Thus, in this case, using a trigger is the most sensible and progressive course of action.

We will discuss the following scenarios in which we will try to find out possible options from the three automated tools:

Scenarios	Option	Reason
Scenario one: We want to populate lookup field.	Flow	A long time ago, the trigger was the answer, but now a flow can populate lookup.
Scenario two: Populate a Lead Owner based on criteria based on record.	Flow	Flow can run on the related object.
Scenario three: Post into Chatter when a record, records	Flow	The Chatter option is not in workflow but now Flow has everything needed.
Scenario four: Submit a quote for approval when opportunity stage= proposal	Flow	We already know about flow features.
Scenario five: Launch a Lightning Flow	Flow	We can invoke Lightning Flow from a flow.
Scenario six: Clone a Lead and change the field values	Flow	We know we can use a process builder to create a new record, but it cannot reference any of the values from the cloned Lead directly.
Scenario seven: Clone a Lead and change the field values	Flow	With new features, we can clone the record and populate a record variable with the values from the existing record. For example, look up the record with a Get Records element. Obtain the record from a Flows action in a process.

Table 19.1: Use case to decide tools:

Let us take examples:

- **Example one:** We want to update the shop category as finance, whenever a user with a finance profile updates the amount field on an object. We also we have to divide this amount among his child-related records according to start date and end date only for the finance category.

  The category field update is easy with a specific condition so that we can use workflow. Still, the amount distribution in the child object is a complex calculation logic that can only be developed using the trigger. Still, we need the category as finance in the trigger so that the trigger can work, but workflow runs after trigger execution. However, it is possible to use workflow and trigger, but the trigger needs it before, so that we can put all things in the trigger.

- **Example two:** We want to add some validation, or we want to show an error if one field is blank or data is incorrect, please check that it is possible using validation rule or not. If it's not possible, then only we can use trigger and trigger.addError to show validation.

- **Example three**: You want to send an e-mail to contacts on every birthday. It is possible use the scheduler (Apex code) and workflow/process builder as well. It is advised to use a time-based Lightning Flow in those cases.

Choosing tools

When you are confused about what to do, the golden rule of Salesforce: Keep it simple. Use the simplest tool that will get the job done! Let us look at some of the following use cases:

- **Use case one**: If we need to update the fields on same record we can use both Before-Save Flow Trigger or Apex Triggers as we do not need to do extra DML as data is already loaded in memory. We can update the fields according to business logic and before event will take care of it.
- **Use case two:** If we need to handle large data volume and process it in Batch, we can only use Apex Triggers and not Flow as:
  - Trigger is good at defining and evaluating complicated logical expressions or formulas.
  - In trigger, we can use all the collections that require map-like or set-like functionalities.
  - Trigger has transaction save points so we can roll back or control the transaction with better error handling.
  - Scheduled flows can currently do batch operations on up to 250 000 records per day only.
  - Batch size limit more than 200 (up to 2000).
- **Use case three**: If we need to do DML operation on cross objects, we can create update or delete multiple objects in the same transaction. For this case, we can use Apex Triggers or after save Flow, but we need to keep the following things in mind:
  - Apex runtime requires less time to prepare and perform any specific database operation than the flow runtime.
  - If you want to work with Flows, you should reduce the number of DML statements against the same record as much as possible.
- **Use case four:** If we need to do an asynchronous process, we can use Apex Triggers or after save Flow, but with large data, Apex is better. Both Flow and Apex can execute logic asynchronously when:
  - Separate transactions are required.
  - External callouts are needed.

- o **For Apex:** we will implement asynchronous logic inside of a queueable class.

- o **For Flow:** we will run an asynchronously path.

- **Use case five:** If we need to process a complex list of data, we will use Apex, as Before Flow has no way to reference and is hard to debug with flow and large data set. We can use after save flow and Invoke apex from flow.

- **Use case six:** If we need to show custom validation errors: Until now, it was not possible to show a custom error on UI with the help of flow, but from the Winter'24 release, it will be possible. Apex trigger can always add Error to show the custom issue.

Conclusion

In this chapter, we learned about the advantages and disadvantages of all three tools. We also covered the differences between these tools to understand when to use which and studied multiple scenarios to understand the limitations of Salesforce and its tools.

In the next chapter, we will learn about testing in Salesforce, especially Apex testing. We will also learn how to write Apex Test class and why it is important.

Questions

1. **The intern cannot view opportunities but needs to see the most recent closed date of all child opportunities when viewing an account record. What can a developer do to achieve this requirement? Choose any 2**

   a. Create a trigger on the account object that queries the close date of the most recent Opportunities.

   b. Create a workflow rule on the opportunity object that updates a field on the parent account.

   c. Create a formula field on the account object that performs a MAX on the opportunity close date field.

   d. Create a roll-up summary field on the account object that performs a MAX on the opportunity close date field.

2. **What should you consider when developing in a multi-tenant environment? Choose any 2.**

   a. Governor limits prevent tenants from impacting performance in multiple organizations in the same instance.

   b. Unique domain names take the place of namespaces for the code developed for multiple organizations on multiple instances.

   c. Polyglot persistence provides support for a global, multilingual user base in multiple organisations on multiple instances.

   d. Organisation-wide data security determines whether other tenants can see data in multiple organizations in the same instance.

3. **What can we do by using the Developer Console?**

   a. Execute Anonymous Apex code, Create/Edit code, view Debug Logs.

   b. Execute Anonymous Apex code, Run REST API, create/Edit code.

   c. Execute Anonymous Apex code, Create/Edit code, Deploy code changes.

   d. Execute Anonymous Apex code, Run REST API, Deploy code changes.

4. **A reviewer should enter a reason in the comments field only when a candidate is recommended to be hired. How can this validation be implemented?**

   a. Required Visualforce component.

   b. Formula field.

   c. Required comments field.

   d. Validation rule.

Answers

1. d, a (developer can write trigger also if needed.)

2. c a

3. a

4. d

Join our Discord space

Join our Discord workspace for latest updates, offers, tech happenings around the world, new releases, and sessions with the authors:

https://discord.bpbonline.com

CHAPTER 20
Testing Essentials

Introduction

Salesforce always fulfills customer and developer needs, so when it comes up with Apex, it also provides a testing framework to write test classes for Apex class and Apex trigger. Salesforce is a Cloud-based system, so it should ensure quality and trust. For that purpose, the test class will help us check the quality of our Apex code.

It gives the developer confidence and provides customers with quality code and reliability. We write a test class for Apex code (Trigger class) and check the code coverage of at least 75%; we also compare the expected result of the code and the actual result using test class.

Structure

In this chapter, we will discuss the following topics:

- Apex testing framework
- Knowing code coverage
- Use of test class
- Running a test class
- Key points of the test class
- Test class for Apex class, controllers and extensions

- Test class for integration
- Best practices

Objectives

After studying this unit, you should be able to learn why we need a test class and what is test class in Apex. We will also learn how to achieve quality code using test class.

Apex testing framework

As the name suggests, we will create a test class to test something. Still, in Salesforce, we always write a trigger and controller, or an Apex class that can be a custom controller, batch class, email class, helper class, a utility class or controller extension. For any class or trigger, we need a test class that will inspect and test its functionality and logic.

You may ask what does it mean that you have to inspect the functionality? This means that if we have written some code, the code will work in the exact manner as it is written. We will test the same thing in the test class and that will give you an answer that your code is working or not. Let us understand the definition and use of test class.

If we know that this trigger is for the **account record with contact** creation, we can test it using the **new button** on the account, and then we will enter the data. After hitting the **Save** button, it will automatically create the contact. Now that you can see that it is working, let us look at the need for a test class.

Salesforce has a vision for improving the approach for a developer and the reliability of a customer, so we cannot deploy any class and trigger written in the Salesforce sandbox organization until we have not written the test class with a code coverage of 75%. So, the first test class is needed for any Salesforce classes and trigger for any trigger. Classes and trigger will be deployed into production only if their test class has a minimum code coverage.

Knowing code coverage

Code coverage is the quality analysis or output of the test class section. Suppose there are three methods in the Apex class and we tested only two using the test class; so, the code coverage will be 2/3 or nearly 66%. Similarly, the following figure illustrates the code coverage in the developer console:

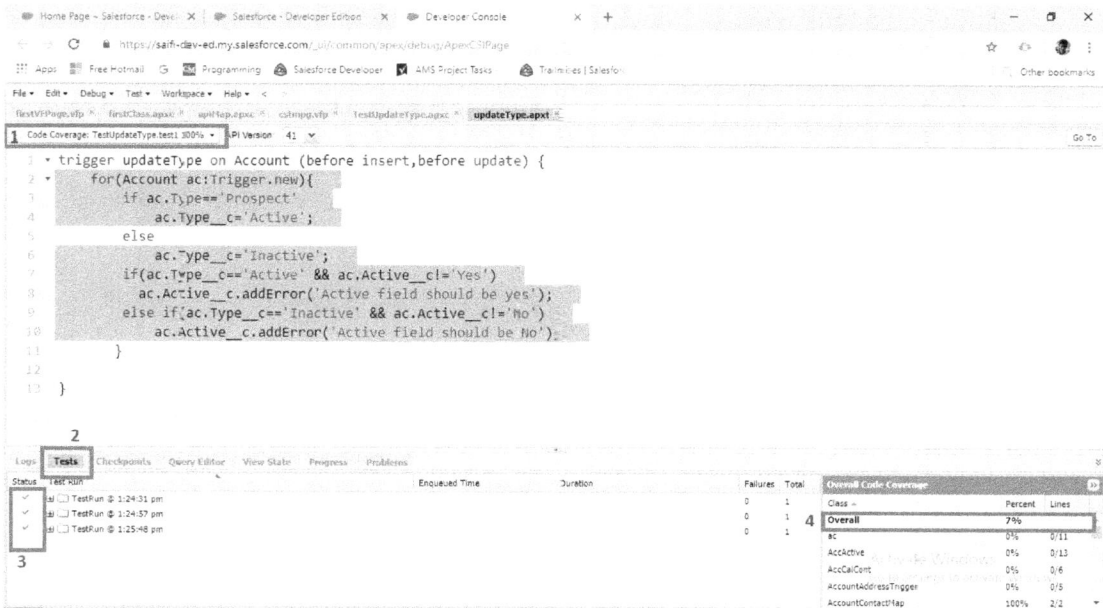

Figure 20.1: Code coverage

The preceding figure shows which test class and test method the coverage is from and the percentage covered:

- The **Tests** tab will show you the result when you run a test, as it fails or passes.
- On the right side, you can see the overall organization %.
- In the preceding example, the updateType Apex coverage is 100% by test class, and the overall org coverage is 7%.

The benefit of the test class is that the test class gives you high-quality code, and is trustworthy since you can easily believe the controller or trigger because we have tested it with different true and false conditions with every logic. This test class shows when the code fails, passes, or does not fail when it should. Every condition is there in the test class and has been tested for that class or trigger, which is the best benefit of the test class in Salesforce.

Note: **Test class data is temporary in the database.**

Using test class

A test class checks the code to test its quality, functionality, and output.

Here are some examples:

- A class/trigger working on a single record.

- Working on bulk records, like 200 records in a batch for trigger.
- Positive behavior, like the code, will pass.
- Negative behavior, like the code will fail or throw an error when it should fail.
- Restricted users for which use it will show or hide.

For the test class, we have to follow certain rules for the first time. We always use a notation with the name, and we will discuss that further as we move ahead.

Test class syntax:

```
@isTest private class testClassName {
    @isTest static void testmethod1 (){

    }
}
```

Every test class will start with **@isTest** notation; the class scope can be private or public. You can write the class name yourself, but it is best to keep the name of a test class similar to the name of the class and trigger on which we want to write, with the prefix or suffix as Test. For example, if we have a trigger named **UpdateTypeTrigger**, the test class name should be **UpdateTypeTriggerTest** or **TestUpdateTypeTrigger**.

Every method of the test class is known as an Apex unit test that checks whether each piece of code is working perfectly. It also starts with **@isTest** notation and is of a static data type with the void return type.

To provide and manage the development of robust, error-free code, Apex supports the creation and execution of unit tests. Unit tests are Apex Class methods that verify whether a specifix piece of code is working or not. Unit test methods take no parameters, commit no data to the database, and send no emails. Such methods are started with the **@IsTest** annotation in the method definition. Unit test methods must be defined in test classes, that is, classes annotated with **@IsTest**.Types of test data

For the test class, if it is working on an object-like account, we will insert an account that will not commit to the database. Suppose we insert an account to test that trigger, and that trigger inserted a record of contact, it will be inserted as temporary just to work with test class. So, record that is inserted in test class is never saved into database.

Trigger sample

Let us understand the trigger and write the test class:

```
trigger updateType on Account(before insert, before update) {
    for (Account ac : Trigger.new) {
        if (ac.Type == 'Prospect')
            ac.Type__c = 'Active';
```

```
            else
                ac.Type__c = 'Inactive';
        }
}
```

In the preceding trigger, we are checking whether any account type is "prospecting." If so, the **Type__c** field will be active, and it will be inactive for other conditions.

In the second part, we are putting the validation that if the type is active and if the Active field is not Yes, then it will prompt an error, and vice versa.

Now, if we write the test class, remember that for any trigger, we will just insert a record for that object. The trigger will work on insert and update, so if we create a record for account or update it, the test class will fulfill the criteria.

As there are certain conditions in the trigger, we will assign the account type as a prospect in the test class:

```
@isTest private class TestUpdateType {
@isTest static void test1(){
Account ac=new Account();
ac.Name='saif test';
ac.type='Prospect';
        insert ac;
}
}
```

If we write and execute this test class, it will cover the first criteria only, so we will create two records of an account with different types to fulfill the second criteria:

```
@isTest private class TestUpdateType {
    @isTest static void test1(){
        List<Account>acl=new List<Account>();
        Account ac=new Account();
        ac.Name='saif test';
        ac.type='Prospect';
        acl.add(ac);
        Account ac1=new Account();
        ac1.Name='saif test';
        acl.add(ac1);
        insert acl;
```

```
        }
}
```

Now, it will cover the first two parts, and the coverage will be 100%. Now, let us add this section in the trigger:

```
        if(ac.Type__c=='Active' &&ac.Active__c!='Yes')
          ac.Active__c.addError('Active field should be yes');
        else if(ac.Type__c=='Inactive' &&ac.Active__c!='No')
            ac.Active__c.addError('Active field should be No');
        }
```

Test class example two

The test class will fail because, in the last section, as you can see, there was a validation rule that if **type__c** is active, the active field should be yes. Otherwise, it will go through a validation error. For that type of code, we will use it to try and catch to pass the test class:

```
@isTest private class TestUpdateType {
    @isTest static void test1(){
        List<Account>acl=new List<Account>();
Account ac=new Account();
ac.Name='saif test';
ac.type='Prospect';
acl.add(ac);

        Account ac1=new Account();
ac1.Name='saif test';
acl.add(ac1);

        try{
            insert acl;
        }
        catch(Exception e){
system.assertEquals(e.getMessage(), e.getMessage());
        }
    }
}
```

Trigger sample

This trigger will create the contacts based on the **No_of_Contact** field. We will first write the trigger and then the test class:

```
trigger createContact on Account(after insert, after update) {
    // we have to insert conatcts based on the count on Account's No of
contact field, so we need a list of contacts

    List<contact> contlist = new List<contact>();

    for (Account a : Trigger.new) {
        //contact number
        integer i = 0;
        if (a.No_of_Contact__c != null) {
            // based on no of contact field we will create contact

            if ((Trigger.isUpdate && a.No_of_Contact__c != Trigger.oldMap.
get(a.id).No_of_Contact__c) || Trigger.isInsert) {
                /* here if account record is being inserted then we will
need to create contact or

                //we are updating no of contact field on the account  */
                while (i < a.No_of_Cortact__c) {
                    contact c = new ccntact();
                    c.LastName = 'Cont Of ' + a.Name + '-' + i;
                    c.AccountId = a.ir;
                    contlist.add(c);
                    i++;
                }
            }
        }
    }
    if (contlist.size() > 0)
        insert contlist;
}
```

Test class

For the preceding trigger, we can just insert the account with the **No_of_contact** field to provide coverage for the trigger:

```
@isTest private class testCreateCont {
    @isTest static void test1(){
        List<Account>acl=new List<Account>();
        Account ac=new Account();
ac.Name='saif test';
ac.No_of_Contact__c=2;
acl.add(ac);
        Account ac1=new Account();
ac1.name='yeye';
acl.add(ac1);
        insert acl;
    }
}
```

Running a test class

There are two ways to run a test that is through using the setup and the developer console. Let us see both these methods in detail.

The Salesforce setup

Go to the Quick Find box, type **Test**, and click on **Apex Test Execution**.

You will see something like the following figure:

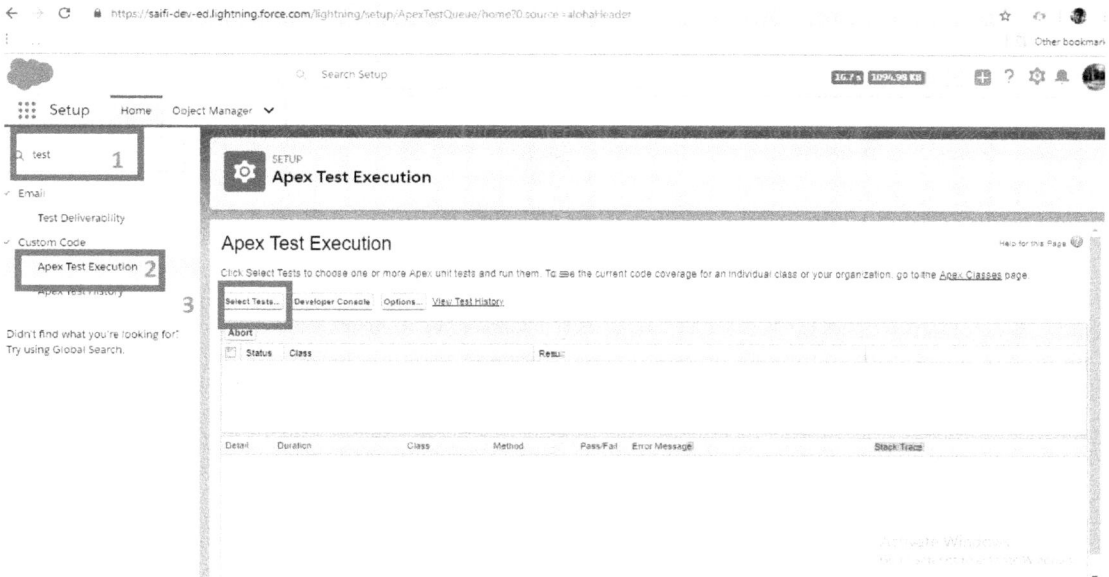

Figure 20.2: *Test class from setup*

Click on **Select Tests** and choose the test class you want to run, as shown in the following figure:

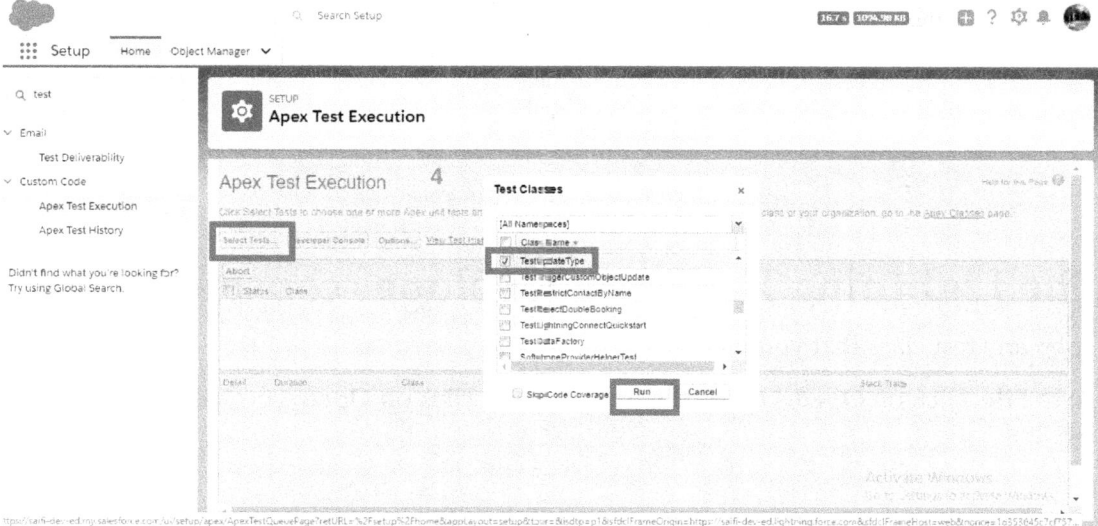

Figure 20.3: *Test class run*

When you click on **Run**, you will see the status of test class running:

SETUP
Apex Test Execution

Apex Test Execution

Click Select Tests to choose one or more Apex unit tests and run them. To see the current code coverage for an individual class or your organization,

Select Tests... Developer Console Options... View Test History

Abort

	Status	Class		Result				
Test Run: 2018-12-17 23:51:38, admin@coderinm1.com, (1 test class run)								
	⊙	[View] TestUpdateType						

Detail	Duration	Class	Method	Pass/Fail	Error Message		Stac

Apex Test Execution

Click Select Tests to choose one or more Apex unit tests and run them. To see the current code coverage for an individual class or your organization, go to the A

Select Tests... Developer Console Options... View Test History

Abort

	Status	Class		Result	
Test Run: 2018-12-17 23:51:38, admin@coderinm1.com, (1 test class run)					
	✓	[View] TestUpdateType		(1/1) Test Methods Passed	

Detail	Duration	Class	Method	Pass/Fail	Error Message	Stack Trace

Figure 20.4: Test class coverage

The Lightning Platform developer console

Open any test class that you want to run.

Go to **File**, click on **Open,** choose the test class and click on **Open**; you will see something like this:

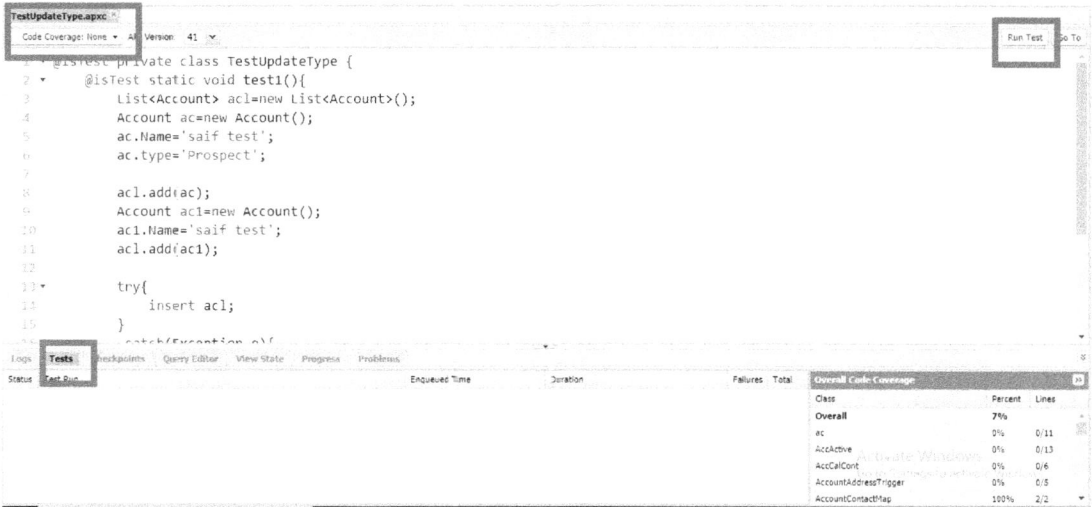

Figure 20.5: Code coverage check

Click on **Run Test** (top-right button):

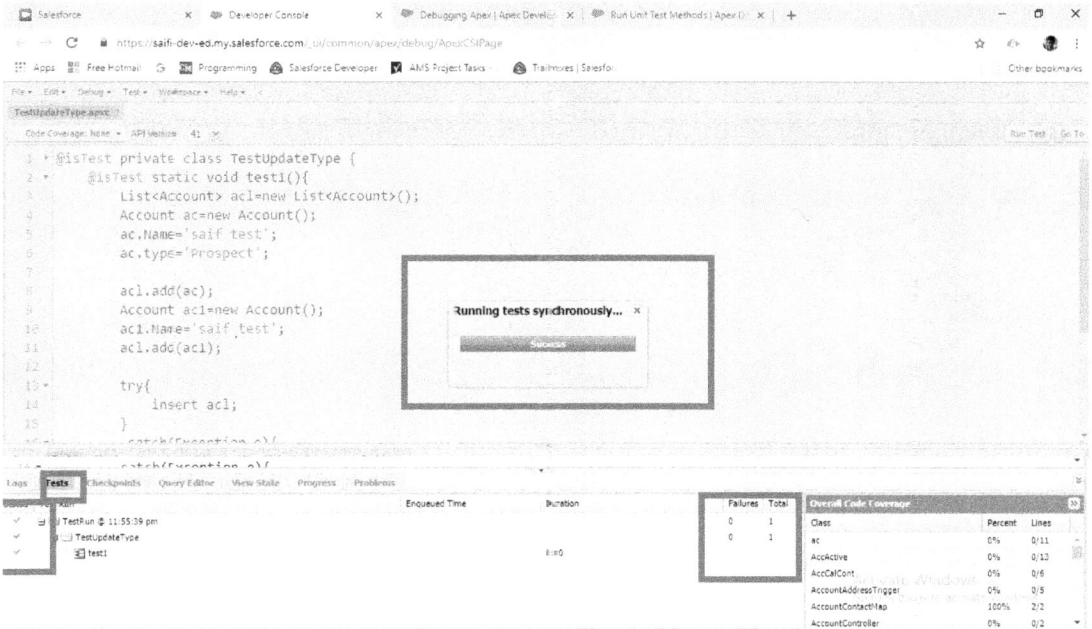

Figure 20.6: Test class status

Check the following section. A complete test run will look like the preceding figure; click on **Test Result**. You will see that the Apex class/trigger for which you wrote the test class also shows you the coverage of that code:

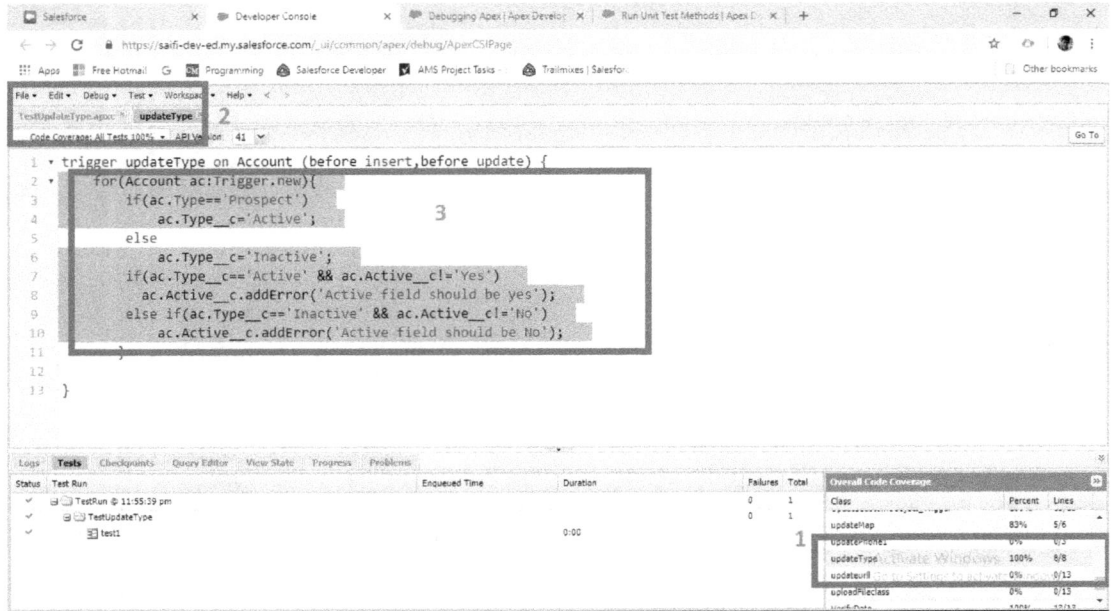

Figure 20.7: Class line coverage

When the test class runs successfully, you will see the green tick; if the test class fails, you will see a red cross, as in the following screenshot. It will also give you the number of methods in which the test class failed:

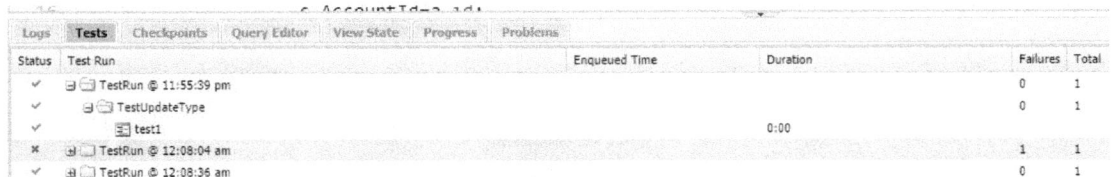

Figure 20.8: Test run report

We can also test or run the test class using the **integrated development environment (IDE)** like *The Force.com IDE* vs. Code and the **Simple Object Access Protocol (SOAP)** API.

Using Asserts

It is used to affirm various conditions with test methods, such as whether two values are the same, a condition is true, or a variable is null.

Assert.areEqual is used to check or test the expected value and actual value:

Syntax: **Assert.areEqual(expected, actual, msg);**

Suppose an Apex code is taking the temperature in degrees Fahrenheit, and the result is in degrees Celsius:

```
public class TempratureClass {
    Public Double fahrenToCelsius( Double f){
        return  ((f-32)/1.8);
    }
    Public Double fahrenToCelsiusWrongMethod( Double f){
        return  ((f-30)/1.8);
    }
}
```

When one of the methods of a class is wrong, so when we run the test class, it will fail. To test the preceding code, we will use **Assert.areEqual** to give us true or false:

```
@isTest
public class TestTempratureClass {
    @isTest
    static void testmthd1() {
        TempratureClasstc = new TempratureClass();
        Double c = tc.fahrenToCelsius(212);
        Assert.areEqual(100, c, 'Answer is correct');
    }
    @isTest
    static void testmthd2() {
        TempratureClasstc = new TempratureClass();
        Double c1 = tc.fahrenToCelsiusWrongMethod(212);
        Assert.areEqual(100, c1, 'Answer is correct');
    }
}
```

If you copy the preceding code and run it into the developer console, you will see the test results. When you run it:

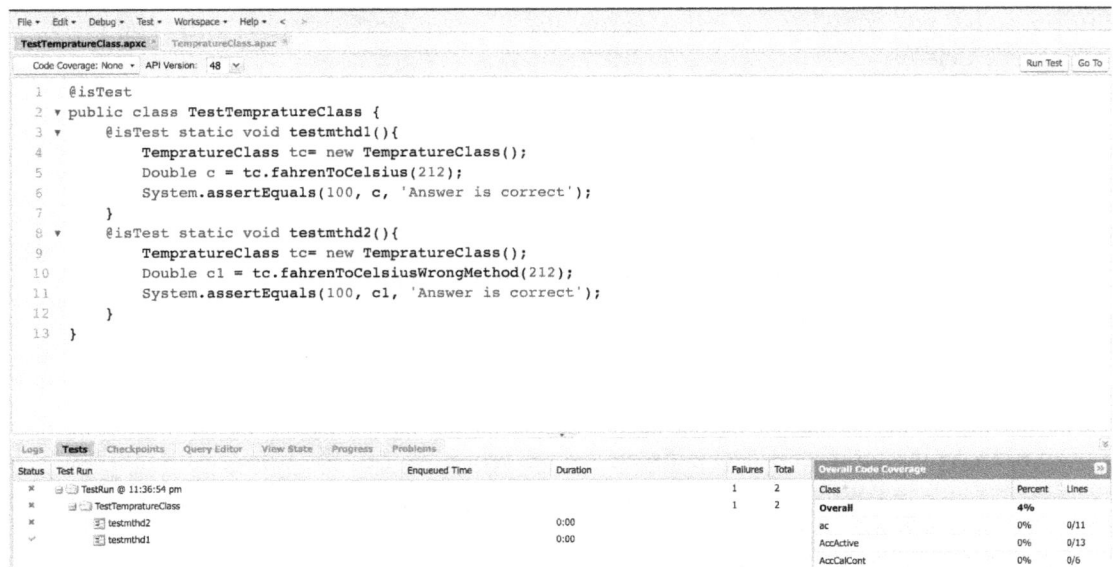

```
File ▾  Edit ▾  Debug ▾  Test ▾  Workspace ▾  Help ▾   <   >
TestTempratureClass.apxc *   TempratureClass.apxc *
Code Coverage: None ▾   API Version:  48 ▾                                              Run Test   Go To
 1    @isTest
 2 ▾  public class TestTempratureClass {
 3 ▾      @isTest static void testmthd1(){
 4            TempratureClass tc= new TempratureClass();
 5            Double c = tc.fahrenToCelsius(212);
 6            System.assertEquals(100, c, 'Answer is correct');
 7        }
 8 ▾      @isTest static void testmthd2(){
 9            TempratureClass tc= new TempratureClass();
10            Double c1 = tc.fahrenToCelsiusWrongMethod(212);
11            System.assertEquals(100, c1, 'Answer is correct');
12        }
13  }
```

Logs	**Tests**	Checkpoints	Query Editor	View State	Progress	Problems						
Status	Test Run			Enqueued Time		Duration	Failures	Total	Overall Code Coverage		
✗	TestRun @ 11:36:54 pm						1	2	Class	Percent	Lines
✗	TestTempratureClass						1	2	Overall	4%	
✗	testmthd2					0:00			ac	0%	0/11
✓	testmthd1					0:00			AccActive	0%	0/13
									AccCalCont	0%	0/6

Figure 20.9: Test assertion

Key points of the test class

We have to follow certain guidelines while writing a test class:

- We can only write a test class in Sandbox or the Developer Environment. It cannot be developed in production, but we can deploy the test class to production.
- Test class gives us a base for quality codes, best-quality application, and customer trust as we can test every aspect of our code.
- It is unit testing of Apex class, and it will help common human error.
- Test class should not fail for any class.
- Any **Data Manipulation Language** (DML) operation we perform in the test class will be temporary; there will be no effects on our original database.

If there are more than two conditions, we will write two test methods in the test class for each.

Sometimes, we need four or five methods to cover the trigger or class. Remember that any record used in one method cannot be used in another, so we need to create or update records in each method.

In that case, we may not need to insert the record again. We can use the same record in the whole class if we use the **testSetup** method in the test class.

The @testSetup method

The method is the same, the only difference is that it will use **@testSetup** before it:

```
@isTest private class testCreateCont {
    @testSetup static void testFill(){
        // record creation
        Account acc= new Account(Name='saif');
        Insert acc;
    }
    @isTest static void test1(){
        acc.Name= 'saif changed';
        update acc;
    }
    @isTest static void test2(){
        System.debug(acc.Name);
        acc.Name= 'saif changed 2';
        update acc;
    }

}
```

The **testFill** method is the **TestSetup** method, so we can use record account in both **test1** and **test2** methods, but any changes done in **test1** will not be seen or used in **test2**:

```
@isTest (SeeAllData=true)
```

If we want to use the original org data, we will use **@isTest (SeeAllData=true)** in the test class.

Test class for Apex class, controllers and extensions

The test class for the controller is easy. In the test class, we will initialize the controller and then call each method.

Suppose the following is the controller or Apex class:

```
public class Mycontroller{
    public Integer addMethod(Ineteger a, Integer b){
```

```
        return a+b;
    }
    public Decimal FarenhietMethod(Decimal cel){
        return ((9 * cel )/ 5 +32);
    }
}
```

Then the test class will look like the following:

```
@isTest private class MycontrollerTest{
    @isTest static void test1(){
  Mycontrollermcnt = new Mycontroller();
        Integer sum = mcnt.addMethod(5,6);
        Integer far = mcnt.FarenhietMethod(-40);
    }
}
```

Let us test whether the formula in the method is correct. We can use the **system.assert** to check the result:

```
@isTest private class MycontrollerTest{
    @isTest static void test1(){
  Mycontrollermcnt = new Mycontroller();
        Integer sum =mcnt.addMethod(5,6);
  System.assertEquals(11, sum);
        Integer far = mcnt.FarenhietMethod(-40);
  System.assertEquals(-40, far);
    }
}
```

If we have used a standard controller in the Visualforce page, we will not need any test class, but we will need a test class if there is a controller extension.

Let us take an example of this type of extension and test class.

Visualforce page

The following is a **Visualforce (VF)** page with accCheck name which is using an extension, and we are passing one parameter in URL:

```
<apex:pagestandardController="Account" extensions="accControllerExtension">
<!----- some line of code-->
```

```
<!------>
</apex:page>
```

Controller

This is the extension for the preceding VF page where we are getting the value of ID from the URL parameter:

```
public class accControllerExtension{
    public Account acc;
    public accControllerExtension(ApexPages.StandardController controller) {
  acc = (Account)controller.getrecord();
        string accId= ApexPages.currentPage().getParameters().get('Id');
        }
    // some other method
    public void methd1(){
        //…   ……..
    }
}
```

Test class

The test class for the preceding extension will be as follows:

```
@isTest
public class accControllerExtensionTest{
    @isTest
    public static void testmethd1(){

    Account acc= new Account(name='saif');
    insert acc;
        // suppose page name is accCheck
PageReferencepageRef = Page.accCheck;
Test.setCurrentPage(pageRef);
// parameter passing for page
pageRef.getParameters().put('Id', String.valueOf(acc.Id));

 // standard controller
```

```
ApexPages.StandardControllersc = new ApexPages.StandardController(acc);
 // calling extension with standardcontroller
accControllerExtensionaccExt = new accControllerExtension(sc);
      // calling method of extension
accExt.methd1();
    }


}
```

Here, you can see that if we want to write a test class for an extension, we must first initialize the standard controller with the proper object, and we can then use it in extension instance.

Test class for integration

When we call third-party API in an intergration, the response comes from the other software. However, we cannot afford to call an API in testing, and it is not a good thing either. So, we make a fake response and check it using **HttpCalloutMock**. This interface can be used for any REST-based API.

Let us see the following API class:

```
public class CalloutapiMap {
    public static void chckMap() {
        Http h = new Http();
        HttpRequest req = new HttpRequest();
        String url = 'https://maps.googleapis.com/maps/api/geocode/json?
                          key=AIzaSyDCJfSJhXuKJlffbFfB57yOO_iQK4kA-
mio&latlng=28.5810215,77.3152004&sensor=true';
        req.setEndpoint(url);
        req.setMethod('GET');
        HttpResponse res = h.send(req);
        if (res.getStatusCode() == 200) {
            string str = res.getBody().split('"formatted_address" : "')[1].
split('",')[0];
            system.debug('This is the address' + str);
        }
```

```
    }
}
```

In the preceding code, we call Google API to find the address. So, we will first write a mock class that will give us a fake response:

```
global class MockApiResponseAPI implements HttpCalloutMock {
    protected integer statuscode;
    protected String body;
    public MockApiResponseAPI(integer code, String body) {
        this.statuscode = code;
        this.body = body;
    }
    global HTTPResponse respond(HTTPRequest req) {
        HttpResponse res = new HttpResponse();
        res.setHeader('Content-Type', 'application/json');
        res.setBody(body);
        res.setStatusCode(statuscode);
        return res;
    }
}
```

HttpCalloutMock is an interface provided by Salesforce to use in Apex to enable sending fake response while testing Http Callout. In real life, when you do a callout, you will get a response and accordingly your class methods will process. However, to test that Apex method salesforce has multiple ways. One of the way is **HttpCalloutMock**. In this method, we are creating a fake response and when Apex method will be called, this response will be returned.

In the preceding code, the respond method will return a fake response, and a constructor will give us an option to make the response dynamic. Now, we can set the mock in our test class and run the test class:

```
@isTest
public class CalloutapiMapTest {
    public static testMethod void testCallout() {
        string responseBody = '{"formatted_address" :"vyapar market sector-2noida",jjj"}';
```

```
        MockApiResponseAPI fakeResponse = new MockApiResponseAPI(200, re-
sponseBody);
        //using constructor we can decide what body/status code should come
in      //fake response
        Test.setMock(HttpCalloutMock.class, fakeResponse);
        CalloutapiMap.chckMap();
    }
}
```

Best practices

The best practices for writing a test class are:
- We should put the data for every condition.
- Test data for all valid and invalid conditions.
- Use the **System.assert** methods to check the actual and the expected outcome.
- Use the **runAs** method to test for another user context.
- For the trigger, try to insert data in bulk, for example, 10-20 records, to test whether the trigger is bulkified.
- Write comments in the test class to see the assumption and logic.

Conclusion

In this chapter, we learned the testing concept in Salesforce. We also studied how to write a test class for trigger or Apex class, along with the best practices. We also looked at the syntax and understood how to run a test class. In the next chapter, we will learn about the Apex Handler, where we will cover batch class, API, email service, etc.

Questions

1. **What should be the test coverage for the Apex class?**
2. **How we can pass the URL parameter in the Apex class using the test class?**
3. **What can we do for API callout?**
4. **What is the use of Test.isRunningTest()?**
5. **Can we write the test class in production?**
6. **Which scenario is invalid for execution by unit tests?**
   a. Executing methods for negative test scenarios.
   b. Loading the standard Pricebook ID using a system method.

  c. Loading test data in place of user input for Flows.

  d. Executing methods as different users.

7. **If you create an Apex class that includes private methods, is there any way to ensure that the private methods can be accessed by the test class?**

  a. Add the TestVisible attribute to the Apex class.

  b. Add the SeeAllData attribute to the test methods.

  c. Add the TestVisible attribute to the Apex methods.

  d. Add the SeeAllData attribute to the test class.

8. **Choose the correct process for an Apex Unit Test.**

  a. Query for test data using SeeAllData = true. Call the method being tested. Verify that the results are correct.

  b. Query for test data using SeeAllData = true. Execute runAllTests(). Verify that the results are correct.

  c. Create data for testing. Execute runAllTests(). Verify that the results are correct.

  d. Create data for testing. Call the method being tested. Verify that the results are correct.

9. **Which feature can we use to check whether all tests currently pass in a Salesforce environment? (Choose 2 answers)**

  a. ANT migration tool.

  b. Workbench metadata retrieval.

  c. Salesforce UI Apex test execution.

  d. Developer console

Answers

1. At least 75% per class or trigger or Org wise.
2. pageRef.getParameters().put('Id',value);
3. We write the mock class for it.
4. Anything we write under it will work only for the test class
5. If(Test.isRunningTest()){
6. c
7. c
8. c
9. c, d

Join our Discord space

Join our Discord workspace for latest updates, offers, tech happenings around the world, new releases, and sessions with the authors:

https://discord.bpbonline.com

Apex Handler and Using Apex Class

Introduction

Salesforce has some good features that we can use as a tool, or we can write some code to use some features. Web-to-lead form will be used as a lead form to take input for lead. Email service is used to create a record when we receive an email. Batch class and scheduler is used to update records or send some mails at a specific time with a bunch of records. Webservices and callout will be used to communicate with other APIs that can be used to send or receive data.

Structure

In this chapter, we will discuss the following topics:

- Web-to-lead form
- Email service
- Batch class
- Batch class and scheduled Apex
- Integration
- Integration with Simple Object Access Protocol
- Asynchronus Apex

- Using Apex class as custom controller
- Controller extension
- Custom controller to build Visualforce page
- Wrapper class and junction object

Objectives

After studying this unit, you should be able to learn how to publish a web-to-lead form. You would also study email services, scheduler Apex, batch class, and the use of Aura enabled. We would also learn about API using Apex.

Web-to-lead form

Salesforce always comes with good features like a web-to-lead form, as a lead is the basic pillar of the Salesforce Sales Lifecycle. Every company that needs to capture lead from a website or campaign form will need this type of form, as Salesforce provided.

The steps to find the web-to-lead form are:

1. Go to set up, search the **web to lead**:

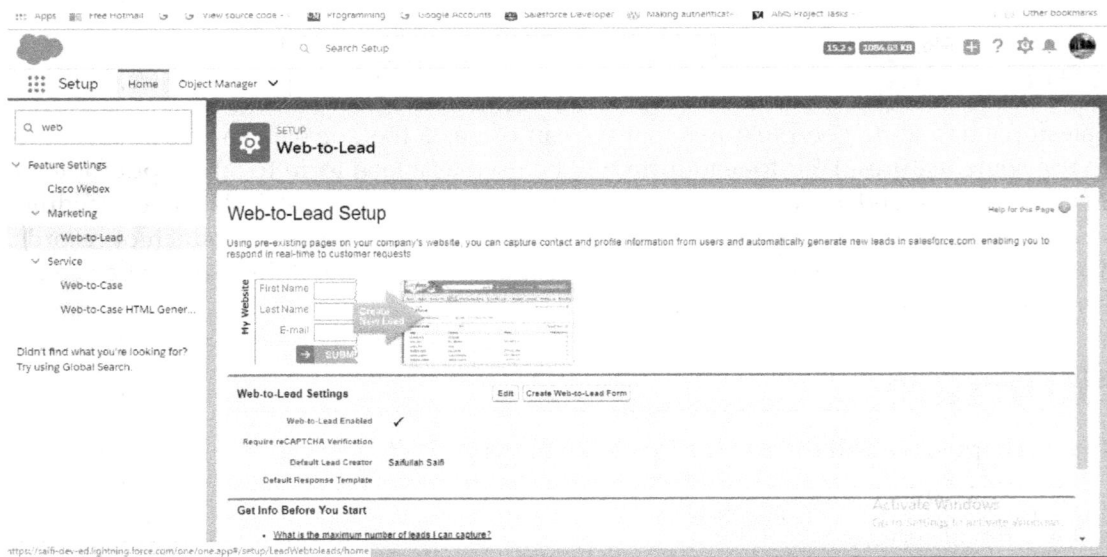

Figure 21.1: Web to lead setup

2. First of all, we need to make **Web-to-Lead Enabled** as checked. There is also an option to put Google Captcha in the form; then we can check that as well. Click on create **Web to Lead** form. You will see the following type of window:

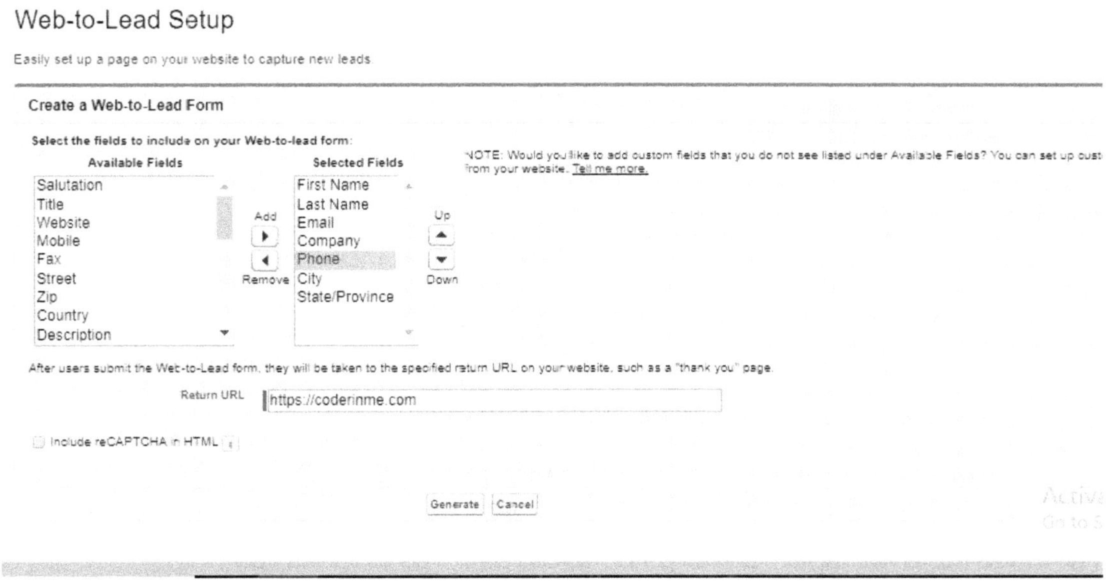

Web-to-Lead Setup

Easily set up a page on your website to capture new leads.

Create a Web-to-Lead Form

Select the fields to include on your Web-to-lead form:

Available Fields | Selected Fields

Available Fields:
- Salutation
- Title
- Website
- Mobile
- Fax
- Street
- Zip
- Country
- Description

Add ▶
Remove ◀

Selected Fields:
- First Name
- Last Name
- Email
- Company
- Phone
- City
- State/Province

Up ▲
Down ▼

NOTE: Would you like to add custom fields that you do not see listed under Available Fields? You can set up cust... from your website. Tell me more.

After users submit the Web-to-Lead form, they will be taken to the specified return URL on your website, such as a "thank you" page.

Return URL | https://coderinme.com

☐ Include reCAPTCHA in HTML

Generate | Cancel

Figure 21.2: Web to lead field choice

3. You can choose all the fields that you want to put on the form. You will see a field return URL; that is, after submitting the form, the user will be redirected back to see which site or what page.

4. Click on **Generate**; you will see an HTML tag in the box, as shown in the following figure:

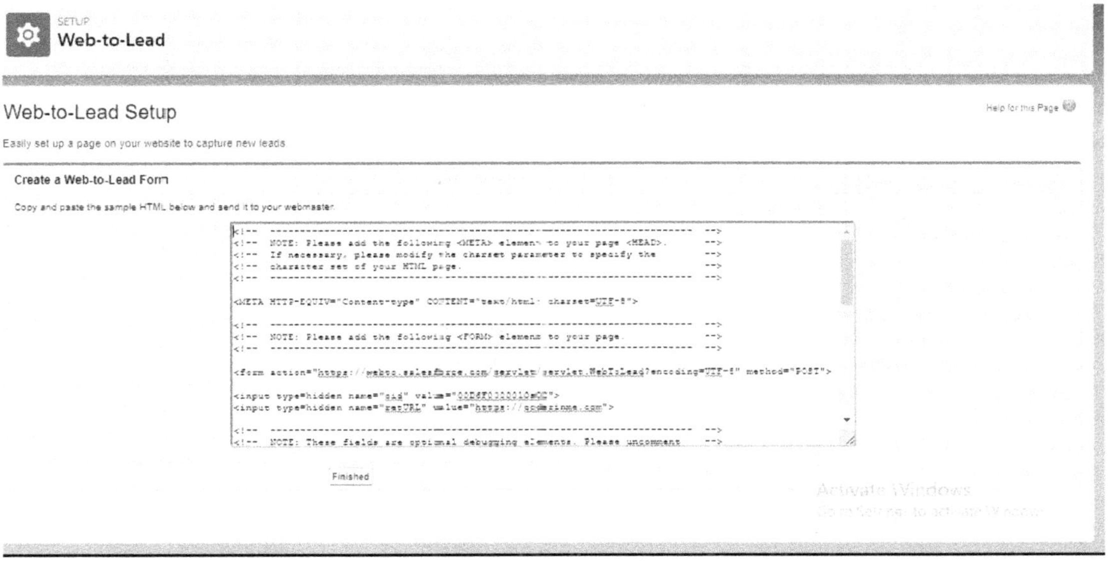

SETUP
Web-to-Lead

Web-to-Lead Setup

Easily set up a page on your website to capture new leads.

Create a Web-to-Lead Form

Copy and paste the sample HTML below and send it to your webmaster.

```
<!-- ----------------------------------------------------------- -->
<!-- NOTE: Please add the following <META> element to your page <HEAD>. -->
<!-- If necessary, please modify the charset parameter to specify the -->
<!-- character set of your HTML page. -->
<!-- ----------------------------------------------------------- -->

<META HTTP-EQUIV="Content-Type" CONTENT="text/html; charset=UTF-8">

<!-- ----------------------------------------------------------- -->
<!-- NOTE: Please add the following <FORM> elements to your page. -->
<!-- ----------------------------------------------------------- -->

<form action="https://webto.salesforce.com/servlet/servlet.WebToLead?encoding=UTF-8" method="POST">

<input type=hidden name="oid" value="00D6F000010s0C">
<input type=hidden name="retURL" value="https://coderinme.com">

<!-- ----------------------------------------------------------- -->
<!-- NOTE: These fields are optional debugging elements. Please uncomment -->
```

Finished

Figure 21.3: Web to Lead code

5.   Copy the code and save it in an HTML file. If you open this HTML file on the web browser, you will see the following type of form:

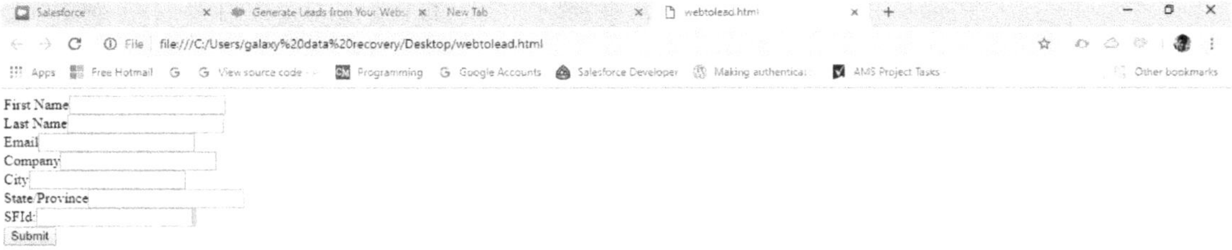

Figure 21.4: HTML preview

6.   Now, we can design this HTML form according to any company needs, but remember that you cannot change the name of any input field.

The following is a sample generated HTML code for web to lead form:

```
<!-- NOTE: Please add the following <META> element to your page <HEAD>. -->
<!-- If necessary, please modify the charset parameter to specify the
 -->
<!-- character set of your HTML page. -->
<meta http-equiv="Content-type" content="text/html; charset=UTF-8"
<!-- NOTE: Please add the following <FORM> element to your page.
  -->
<!-- ------------------------------------------------------------------->
<form                  action="https://webto.salesforce.com/servlet/servlet.
WebToLead?encoding=UTF-8" method="POST">
 <input type="hidden" name="oid" value="00D6F000001OsOC" />
 <input type="hidden" name="retURL" value="https://coderinme.com" />
 <!-- ----------------------------------------------------------------->
 <!-- NOTE: These fields are optional debugging elements. Please uncomment-->
 <!-- these lines if you wish to test in debug mode. -->
 <!- <input type="hidden" name="debug" value=1>
 -->
 <!-- <input type="hidden" name="debugEmail" value="help@coderinme.com"> >
 <!-- ----------------------------------------------------->
 <label for="first_name"> First Name </label>
```

```
<input id="first_name" maxlength="40" name="first_name" size="20" type="text"
/>
<br />
<label for="last_name"> Last Name </label>
<input id="last_name" maxlength="80" name="last_name" size="20" type="text"
/>
<br />
<label for="email"> Email </label>
<input id="email" maxlength="80" name="email" size="20" type="text" />
<br />
<label for="company"> Company </label>
<input id="company" maxlength="40" name="company" size="20" type="text" /
<br />
<label for="city"> City </label>
<input id="city" maxlength="40" name="city" size="20" type="text" />
<br />
<label for="state"> State/Province </label>
<input id="state" maxlength="20" name="state" size="20" type="text" />
<br />
SFId:
<input id="00N6F00000HqnP2" maxlength="20" name="00N6F00000HqnP2" size="20"
type="text" />
<br />
<input type="submit" name="submit" />
</form>
```

As you can see, there are some hidden fields like "**oid**" as Salesforce org ID and **returnURL**, as discussed earlier.

Other than that, all fields are input fields with a name and label, so do not change any input field name. Do not change the following line in the generated code:

```
<input  id="state" maxlength="20" name="state" size="20" type="text" />
<input  id="00N6F00000HqnP2" maxlength="20" name="00N6F00000HqnP2" size="20"
type="text" />
```

Whenever any user fills out the form, one new lead will be created in your Salesforce. You can test it.

Note: Only 500 web-to-lead is possible per day.

Email service

Email service is a tool that helps us use inbound email to create records automatically. We can set an email to create a record based on mail content.

Suppose someone sends an email regarding any product to a company email, that the person is interested in this product. The company will then need to work on it. Now, the solution for this is as follows:

- The company person opens every email and checks who the person is and what they are interested in.
- They are using Salesforce; hence a lead will automatically be created when anyone sends a mail to the company's mail.

For that purpose, we write an email service.

To use an email service in Salesforce, go to **Setup**, search **Email Services**, and click on it:

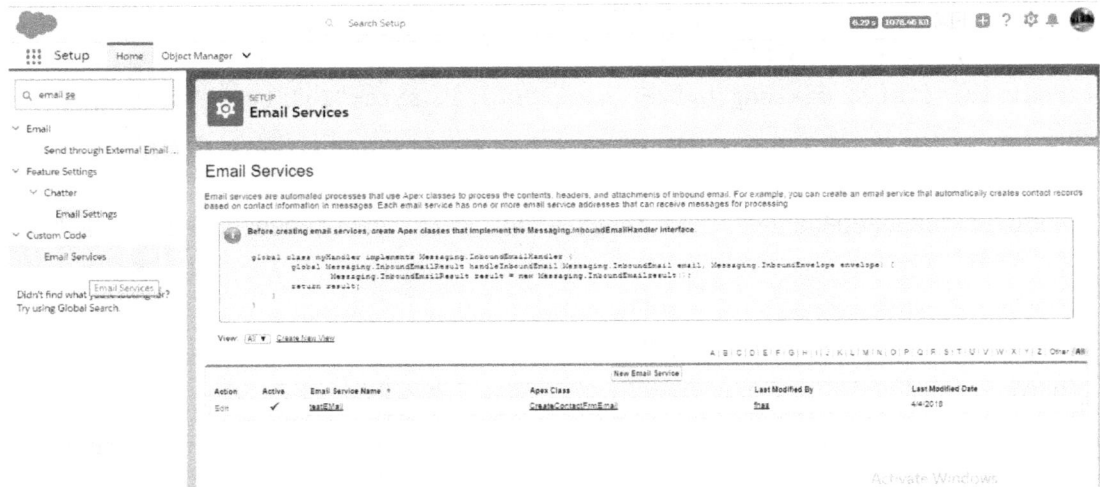

Figure 21.5: EMail service setup

Click on the new email service; you can edit the existing one, activate or deactivate it.

For that purpose, we will also need an Apex class (Email service).

The Apex class will be similar to the following code:

```
global class myHandler implements Messaging.InboundEmailHandler {
    global    Messaging.InboundEmailResult    handleInboundEmail(Messaging.
InboundEmail email, Messaging.InboundEnvelope envelope) {
  Messaging.InboundEmailResult result = new Messaging.InboundEmailresult();
return result;
    }
}
```

Add one class and update it. Now, when you save the above form, you have to add an email address:

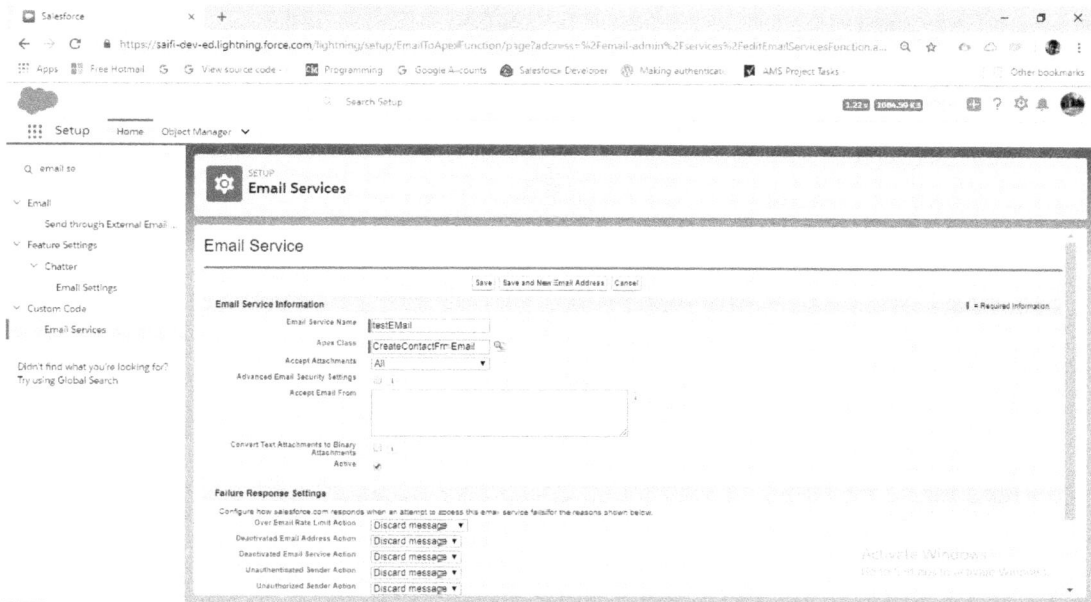

Figure 21.6: Email service class

Let us take an example. Any time someone is sending an email, we will create a case under that contact from the sender's email:

```
global class myHandler implements Messaging.InboundEmailHandler {
  global Messaging.InboundEmailResult handleInboundEmail(
      Messaging.InboundEmail email, Messaging.InboundEnvelope envelope) {
    // Create an InboundEmailResult object for returning the result of the
    // Apex Email Service
    Messaging.InboundEmailResult result = new Messaging.InboundEmailRe-
sult();
```

```
String emailBody = '';

// Add the email plain text into the local variable
emailBody = email.plainTextBody;

// New Case object to be created
Case cs = new Case();

// Try to look up any contacts based on the email from address
// If there is more than one contact with the same email address,
// an exception will be thrown and the catch statement will be called.
try {
    Contact Con = [
        SELECT Id, Name,
        Email FROM Contact WHERE Email = : email.fromAddress WITH USER_MODE
                                        LIMIT 1
    ];

    // Add a new case to the contact record we just found above.
    cs.ContactId = con.id;
    cs.Reason = 'Other';
    cs.priority = 'Medium';
    cs.description = emailBody;
    cs.Origin = 'Web';
    cs.Type = 'IT Support';
    cs.status = 'New';
    cs.Other_Reason__c = email.subject;

    // Insert the new Task
    insert as user cs;
```
1.
```
        System.debug('New Task Object: ' + cs);
}
    // If an exception occurs when the query accesses
    // the contact record, a QueryException is called.
```

```
    // The exception is written to the Apex debug log.
    catch (QueryException e) {
        System.debug('Query Issue: ' + e);
    }

    // Set the result to true. No need to send an email back to the user
    // with an error message
    result.success = true;

    // Return the result for the Apex Email Service
    return result;
  }
}
```

You can see that in the preceding code, we are first searching for contact based on **email. fromAddress**.

If it is not available, it will be go to catch exception. If we find it, then we will create a case using the email subject and email body:

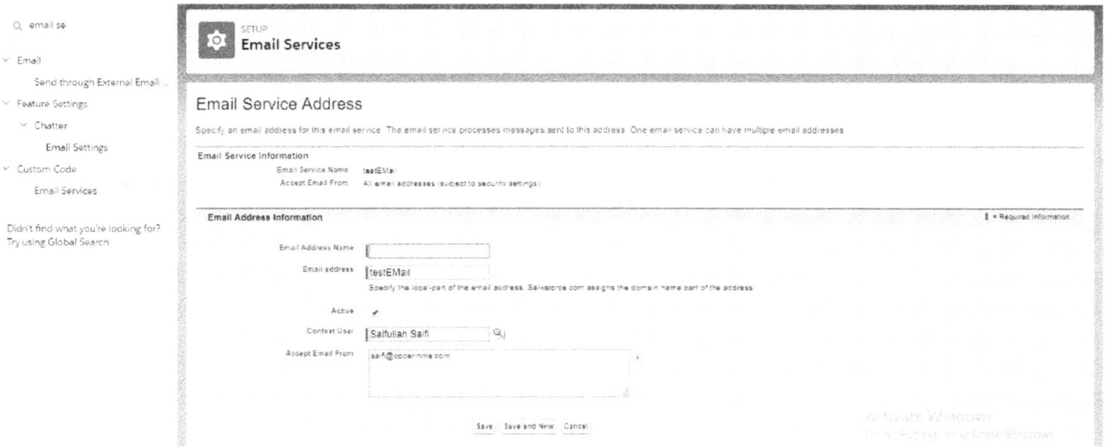

Figure 21.7: Email service setup

This is the email service address added by us to inform which emails are forwarding mail.

We will also add the emails in **Accept Email From**, from which we want to use email as a record.

Email service is very useful if you want to automate the process for inbound email. As discussed, and shown with code, the email service can process the header body or attachments.

Batch class

Sometimes, we need a long process on thousands of records in the lightning environment. For example, if we want to send mail or send some data into other systems every night. For all these tasks, Salesforce provides out of the box feature of Apex known as batch. It will break a large number of records into smaller chunks and process them step-by-step. We will need to implement a batch interface for this purpose. We can schedule this batch at a particular time using the scheduler class.

The format of the batch is as follows:

```
global class batchFormatClass implements Database.Batchable {
    global Database.QueryLocator start(Database.BatchableContext BC) {
        string query = '';
        return Database.getQueryLocator(query);
    }
    global void execute(Database.BatchableContext BC, List < sObject > scope)
{
        for (sobject s: scope) {
            // operation or process
        }
        update scope;
    }
    global void finish(Database.BatchableContext BC) {
    }
}
```

From the preceding code, you can see we have added **Implements Database.Batchable<sObject>** in Apex Class. It is the interface that we use to create batch class. Every Batch class consists of three methods: **start()**, **execute()**, and **finish()**.

In the **start()** method, we will write the query on the object we need to work on.

These query records will be used in **execute()** method, and we will write all statements and processes. When we want to send an email, after finishing the batch, we will use **finish()** method.

One of the most common examples for batch is the following: From your company, you want to send an email to your sales team every morning, or you want to check the attendance of all your employees in the company. You can use the batch using the Apex class in Salesforce.

Apex batch will be useful for long-running large data records and to be performed in chunks. It is also helpful when you need to query a large number of records as basic SOQL will return a maximum of 50,000 records, but with batch Apex query in **Database. QueryLocator** you can query 50 million records. In the next topic we will use batch with Apex scheduler.

Batch class and scheduled Apex

The scheduler is used to schedule a class or bunch of tasks at a specific time for once or at regular intervals. The batch class is the class that will be scheduled; it is a special type of class for bulk records. It will help us to overcome the following:

- CPU time limit
- Heap size issue
- Governor limit
- Schedule at a particular time
- Where Salesforce workflow or process builder fails

First, let us take a look at the sample code of the batch class:

```
global class batchAccountUpdate implements Database.Batchable<sObject> {
    //start
    global Database.QueryLocator start(Database.BatchableContext BC){
        // query from an object for records
        String query='SELECT Id, Name FROM Account';
        return Database.QueryLocator(query);
    }
    //execute
    global void execute(Database.BatchableContext BC,List<Account > Scope){
        // here we will write logic for that what we want to do
        integer i=1;
        for(Account a: Scope){
            a.name=a.name+i;
            i++;
        }
        update ac;
        system.debug('mine'+ac);
    }
    //finish
```

```
global void finish(Database.BatchableContext BC){
    /* after the completion of batch anything we want to do like a
confirmation of              batch execution/*
    }
}
```

Now, we will see what the scheduler class will look like for the preceding batch class:

```
global class scheduledBatchable implements Schedulable {
    global void execute(SchedulableContext sc) {
        // batch class name do you want to call
        batchAccountUpdate b = new batchAccountUpdate();
        // size of batch how much record in single batch
        database.executebatch(b,200);
    }
}
```

Let us see how we will schedule it, through the following steps:

1. Go to Apex class. Find the following, and click on it:

pex Classes

ex Code is an object oriented programming language that allows developers to develop on-demand business applications on the Lightning Platform.

✔ **Percent of Apex Used: 21.3%**
You are currently using 639,031 characters of Apex Code (excluding comments and @isTest annotated classes) in your organization, out of an allowed limit of 3,000,000 characters. Note that the includes both Apex Classes and Triggers defined in your organization.

stimate your organization's code coverage i
ompile all classes i
ew: All ▼ Create New View

‹Prev

A B C D E F G H I J K L M N O P Q R S T U V W

Action	Unmanaged	Name ↑		Namespace Prefix	Api Version	Status	Size Without Comments	Last Modified By	Last Modified
	✔	Search	Developer Console | New | Generate from WSDL | Run All Tests | Schedule Apex		▼	▼	▼		▼	Search
Edit | Del | Security		ContactsTodayController			33.0	Active	2,660	Saifullah Saifi	2018-12-01 12:18 pm
Edit | Del | Security		ContactsTodayController_test			33.0	Active	555	Saifullah Saifi	2018-12-01 12:18 pm
Edit | Del | Security		AddMultipleOpportunities			41.0	Active	1,865	Saifullah Saifi	2018-08-02 11.05 am

Figure 21.8: Apex scheduler

Choose the scheduler class, schedule it accordingly, and save it, as shown in the following figure:

Schedule Apex

Schedule an Apex class that implements the Schedulable interface to be automatically executed on a specified interval.

Help for this Page ?

Save   Cancel

Job Name   [   ]

Apex Class   [   ] 🔍

Schedule Using   ⦿ Schedule Builder   ○ Cron Expression

Schedule Apex Execution

Frequency   ⦿ Weekly   Recurs every week on
                ○ Monthly
                               ☐ Sunday
                               ☐ Monday
                               ☐ Tuesday
                               ☐ Wednesday
                               ☐ Thursday
                               ☐ Friday
                               ☑ Saturday

Start   [10/5/2024]   [10/5/2024]
End   [11/5/2024]   [10/5/2024]
Preferred Start Time [--None-- ⌄]

Exact start time will depend on job queue activity.

Figure 21.9(a): Scheduler setup

If you want to run a batch only once, then go to the developer console and open an anonymous window. Write the batch class name like the following:

```
batchAccountUpdate b = new batchAccountUpdate();

    // size of batch how much record in single batch

database.executebatch(b,200);
```

The code will take all accounts and will rename the name of an account with name + number. For example, consider five accounts with the following names:

```
saif, luqs, prabhu, sam, harry.
```

When the batch class executes, it will update it as the following:

```
saif1, luqs2, prabu3, sam4, harry5
```

Now, since Salesforce has many features, you have the option to schedule a class, delete the job, or you can manage the means to update the job. You can pause the job also.

As you can see in the following figure, there is an option to also put the cron expression as well:

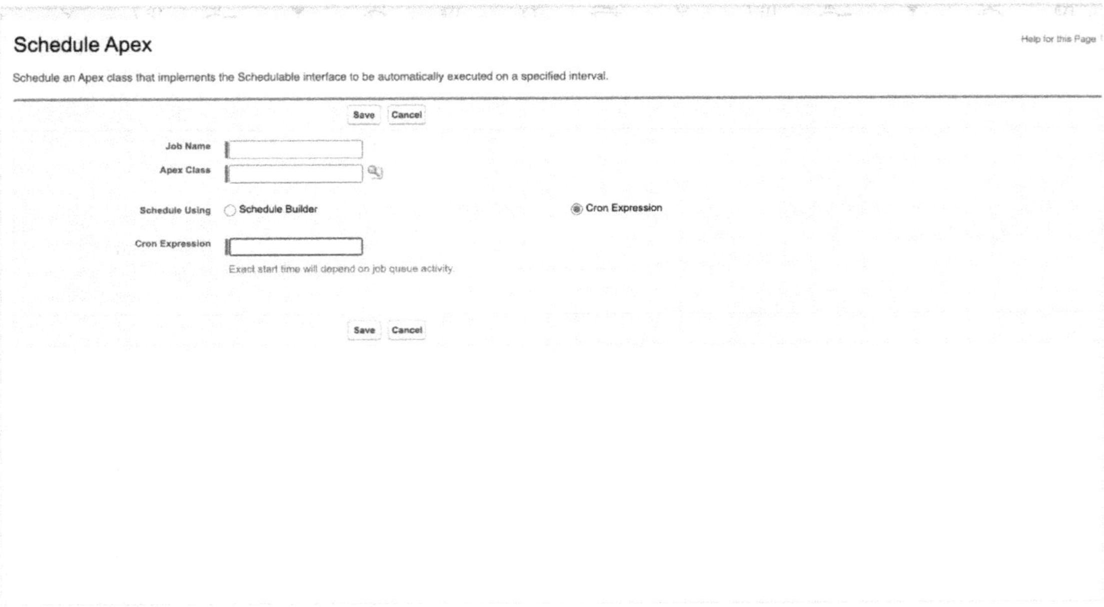

Schedule Apex

Schedule an Apex class that implements the Schedulable interface to be automatically executed on a specified interval.

Help for this Page

Save   Cancel

Job Name

Apex Class

Schedule Using   ○ Schedule Builder   ⦿ Cron Expression

Cron Expression

Exact start time will depend on job queue activity.

Save   Cancel

Figure 21.9(b): Scheduler cron expression

We can schedule the job from the Apex class also. We will create a scheduler class first. It will look like following code:

```
global class ScheduledBatchJobClass implements Schedulable {
        global void execute(SchedulableContext SC) {
 batchAccountUpdate M = new  batchAccountUpdate ();
                // size of batch how much record in single batch
database.executebatch(b,200);
 }
}
```

This scheduler class has the schedulable interface. You can save this class, and then you can schedule it using the following code or from setup schedule Apex class:

```
ScheduledBatchJobClass scb = new ScheduledBatchJobClass();
String sch = '20 30 8 10 2 ?';
String jobID = System.schedule('Merge Job', sch, scb);
```

You can see the preceding code, the **System.schedule** method has three arguments: job Name, schedule job time expression, also know as cron expression, and the name of the class. This expression has the following syntax:

Seconds Minutes Hours Day_of_month Month Day_of_week Optional_year

Let us take an example:

```
0 0 15 * * ? Job will run at 3pm every day
0 0 10 ? * MON-WED Job will run at 10 am from monday to wednesday
0 0 * * * ? Job will run ever hour
```

Salesforce has provided multiple options to choose these values, like:

Name	Value	Special Value
Seconds	0–59	None
Minutes	0–59	None
Hours	0–23	, - * /
Day_of_month	1–31	, - * ? / L W
Month	1–12 or the following: JAN FEB MAR APR MAY JUN JUL AUG SEP OCT NOV DEC	, - * /
Day_of_week	1–7 or the following: SUN MON TUE WED THU FRI SAT	

Table 21.1: Cron expression table

Integration

If you want to connect two devices or software over a network (World Wide Web), then you will need some web service that will help you to connect them.

Let us look at what a web service is:

- A web service is a software system designed to support interoperable machine-to-machine interaction over a network (According to *w3.org*)
- Web services are a standardized way or medium to propagate communication between the client and server applications on the World Wide Web. (*guru99*)

Web service describes a standardized way of integrating web-based applications using XML, Async JS, and JSON.

Extensible Markup Language (XML) is a simple, and flexible text format used to exchange data between two systems, websites, and databases. It provides flexible self-description. You can create your own tags. For example:

```
<note>

<to>BPB</to>

<from>Saif</from>

<heading>Reminder</heading>

<body>Don't forget me this weekend!</body>

</note>
```

JavaScript Object Notation (JSON) is a text-based format used for storing and sharing data, and is both human-readable and computer-understandable. So, JSON is easy to learn and to troubleshoot. For example:

```
{
    "note": {
        "to": "BPB",
        "from": "Saif",
        "heading": "Reminder",
        "body": "Don't forget me this weekend!"
    }
}
```

Two popular services are used for for Web service and callout. They are:

- Simple Object Access Protocol (SOAP)
- Representational State Transition (REST)

Representational State Transfer

REST is an architectural style that defines a set of constraints and properties based on HTTP. **REST**-compliant web services allow the requesting systems to access and manipulate textual representations of web resources by using a uniform and predefined set of stateless operations.

Simple Object Access Protocol

SOAP is a messaging protocol specification for exchanging structured information during the implementation of web services in computer networks:

- Apex code supports the ability to expose Apex methods as a Web service.
- Apex also supports the ability to invoke external web services known as callouts.
- Webservice and callout.

Let us look at REST API versus SOAP API in the following table:

SOAP	REST
It transfers data in xml format	It can transfer data in XML, JSON formats
It follows standard set of rules and is Stateful	There is no standard format and it's stateless
Well structure used for legacy and large data system.	Less structured and used for fast and convenience
It works with WSDL	It works with GET PUT POST DELETE, etc.

Table 21.2: SOAP vs.REST

Every API has the same structure, which looks like the following:

REST API URL: Where the API is exposed.

Any one or multiple of the following in the header:

- Access token/token
- username,
- password
- certificate
- content-type

- **Method type**: GET/POST/PUT/DELETE
- **Body**: It may be (json/xml/ app-form-data) or blank in case of GET

If we want to connect some app or software with Salesforce, like we want to send some data from Salesforce to SAP technology, then we will write a web service (API) for that. For this, we will create a new remote site setting, in which we will enter the details of the URL which we want to hit through API, make sure if there is any port number in API, make sure to put that also:

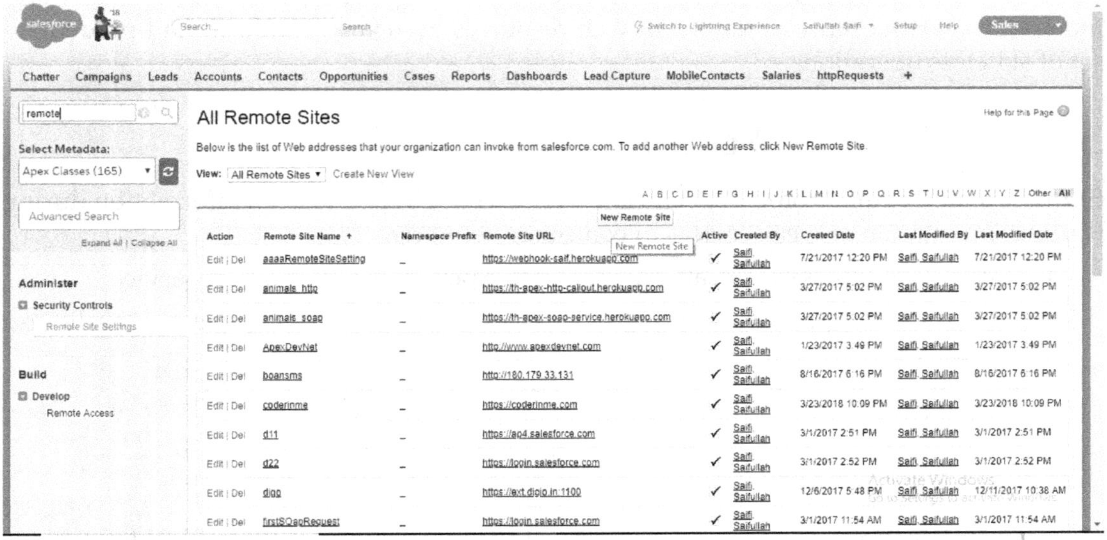

Figure 21.10: Remote site

If someone's app/software wants to connect, then we will give them the access token, URL, and login credentials. We will also write a service callout that will redirect that URL and give them what they want.

Go to setup, search **Apps,** and click on it. You will see the connected Apps List, as shown in the following figure:

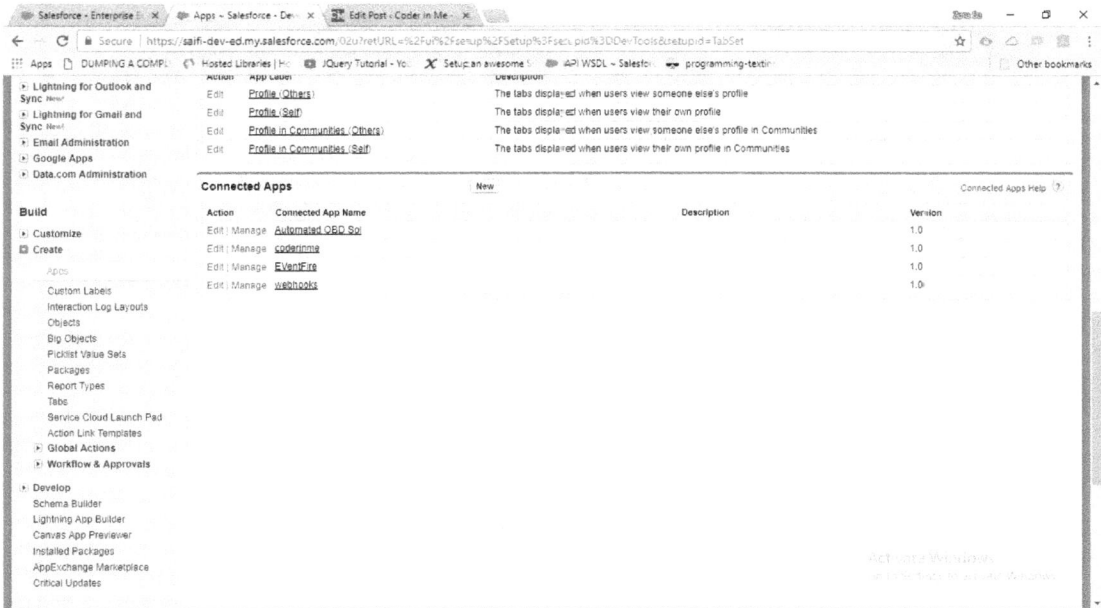

Figure 21.11: Connected app

To create connected apps, we will do the following steps in Salesforce.

1. We will create a new connected App, give that a name, email ID, and a site URL for callout URL.

2. Enable OAUTH.

3. Give them access data API.

4. We will save it using **Continue**.

Connected app will look like the following figure:

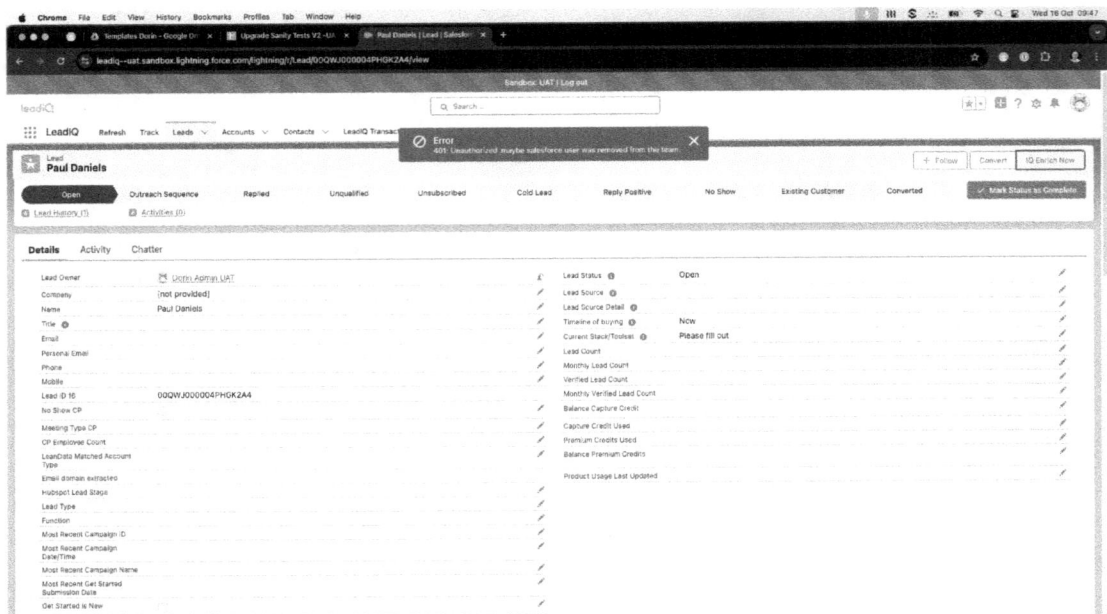

Figure 21.12: Connected app setup

Now, you can see client ID, and client secret; you will provide it to that app developer. This was the basic idea behind API introduction, and we will understand the coding part in the next topic.

API testing tools and code

You can use curl or Postman or **Advance Rest Client** (**ARC**), a chrome extension:

The response code is as follows:

```
200 OK connecting
400 bad request, your data, or password or something is wrong the data or
format
500 - internal server error: that's error of that software that you are using
403 : no access // forbidden
404 : wrong url /not found
```

First example of REST API

First, we will learn how to get an address from the Google API if we pass the latitude and longitude using an APEX callout. You can check the following code that you can execute in your anonymous org window of the developer console:

```
Http ht = new Http();
```

```
HttpRequest  req = new HttpRequest ();
String key =´'; // you can get the google api key from google services
String          url          ='https://maps.googleapis.com/maps/api/geocode/
json?key='+key+'&latlng=28.5810215,77.3152004&sensor=true';
req.setEndpoint(url);
req.setMethod('GRT');
//req.setBody('body');
HttpResponse res = ht.send(req);
if(res.getStatusCode()==200){
          string str= res.getBody().split('"formatted_address" : "')[1].
split('",')[0];
          system.debug(str);
}
```

Before that, add the following URL to your remote site setting:

https://maps.googleapis.com/

If, in execution, it says API key or exceeds the limit of API, then get the API key and paste the new key in the code. You can get the key from here:

Open the debug log. You will see the following in the log:

Vyapar Marg, D Block, Sector 2, Noida, Uttar Pradesh 201301, India

Figure 21.13: Debug log

Code explanation

From the preceding code, we will try to understand how it works:

- **Class call, Http, HttpRequest, HttpResponse**: You can see that we created an instance of **Http, HttpRequest, HttpResponse**. Then, we have **setEndpoint** URL, where we want to communicate, or share/access data. We set the method **GET/ POST/PUT/ DELETE**, and requested it via the send method. Then, we fetch the status code of the response and body, as you can see in the following code:

```
{         "formatted_address" : "Vyapar Marg, D Block, Sector 2, Noida,
Uttar Pradesh 201301, India" }
```

We have used the split method of string to split it and get the address part only from the response. In the first split, we get two strings because, when we use split (**'"formatted_address" : ""'**), we will find **"formatted_address" : "Vyapar Marg, D Block, Sector 2, Noida, Uttar Pradesh 201301, India" }** in the preceding response, then split it again for the address.

- **Store into contact location and address**: Now, if we want to add three fields in contact, let us say: Longitude, latitude, and address; after the insertion or updation of contact, if we will input latitude and longitude, a trigger will hit the Google API and update the address of the contact:

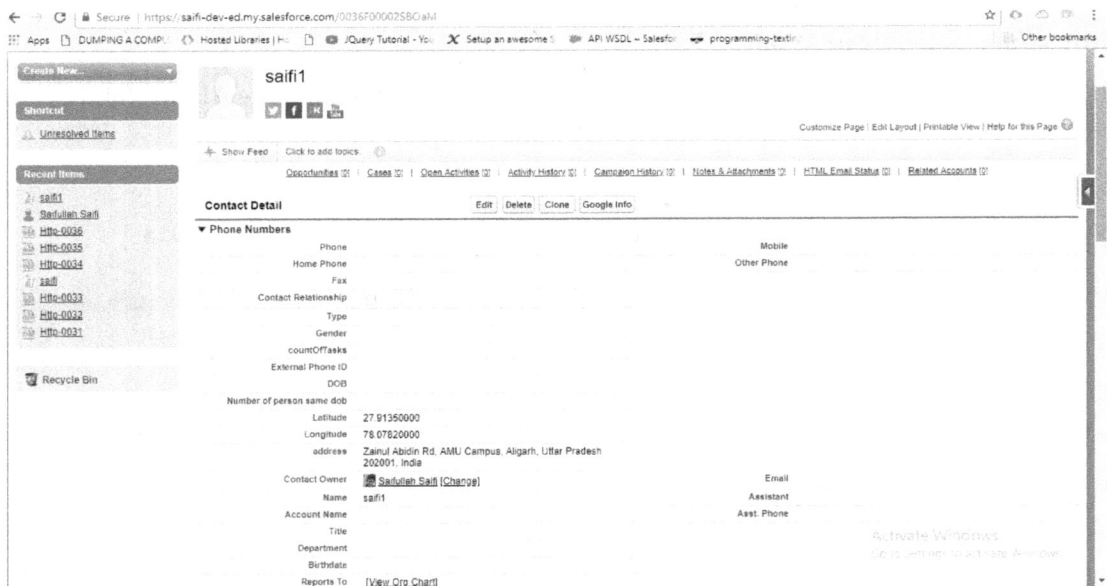

Figure 21.14: Record example

We created a trigger and API class used using future method. Refer to the following code:

```
trigger updateMap on Contact(after insert, after update) {
  for (Contact c : Trigger.new) {
    if (trigger.isUpdate) {
      // for update if location change we will call apiMap Class
```

```
    if (c.Latitude__c != Trigger.oldMap.get(c.id).Latitude__c
        || c.Longitude__c != Trigger.oldMap.get(c.id).Longitude__c)
      apiMap.chckMap(String.valueOf(c.Latitude__c),
          string.valueOf(c.Longitude__c), c.id);
    }
    if (trigger.isInsert)
      apiMap.chckMap(
          String.valueOf(c.Latitude__c), string.valueOf(c.Longitude__c),
c.id);
      // we are passing three args Longitude, Latitude and contact Id.
  }
}
public class apiMap {
  /* if we are using api call we will use future callout then trigger will
   * support API Callout */
  @future(callout = true)
  public static void chckMap(string lat, string lon, string conId) {
    // we will use these lat and lon on api url
    Http h = new Http();
    // 28.5810215,77.3152004
    HttpRequest req = new HttpRequest();
    String url =
        'https://maps.googleapis.com/maps/api/geocode/json?key=AIzaSyDCJfS-
JhXuKJlffbFfB57yOO_iQK4kAmio&latlng='
        + lat + ',' + lon + '&sensor=true';
    req.setEndpoint(url);
    req.setMethod('GET');
    HttpResponse res = h.send(req);
    if (res.getStatusCode() == 200) {
      string str =
          res.getBody().split('"formatted_address" : "')[1].split('",')[0];
      system.debug(str);
      // update contact with address from API response
```

```
  contact c = new Contact();
  c.id = conId;
  c.address__c = str;
  update c;
}
// making a log for every API Hit for best practice
httpRequest__c log1 = new httpRequest__c();
log1.Request__c = 'MapAPI';
log1.response__c = str;
log1.status__c = String.valueOf(res.getStatusCode());
insert log1;
}
```

- **Code to receive data from API**: If any other software connects our URL and sends data, for that purpose, we will use the following code to receive and process the request:

```
RestRequest req = RestContext.request;

RestResponse res = RestContext.response;

ApplicantDetails appDetails = (ApplicantDetails)JSON.deserialize(req.
requestBody.toString(),ApplicantDetails.class);


public class ApplicantDetails {
        public String Session_Key;
        public String Method_Type;
        public String Application_Id;
        public String Applicant_Id;
}
```

- **Code to call any API**: If we want to send the request to any other software, then our code will be as follows:

```
htttp hreq = new Http();
HttpRequest req = new HttpRequest();
//req.setHeader('userid','mukeshlms');
req.setHeader('Content-type', 'application/json');
req.setEndpoint(url);
```

```
req.setMethod('POST');
req.setBody(body);
HttpResponse res = hreq.send(req);
System.debug('>>>'+req.getbody())
```

Integration with Simple Object Access Protocol

Similar to REST, Apex can also make a callout using SOAP. SOAP Integration is a bit complex but useful. Salesforce has a tool known as **Web Services Description Language (WSDL)** to Apex, which can be used to generate the Apex class from the **SOAP** WSDL file. The WSDL file stores all the information for SOAP-based integration.

The WSDL file will look like the following figure:

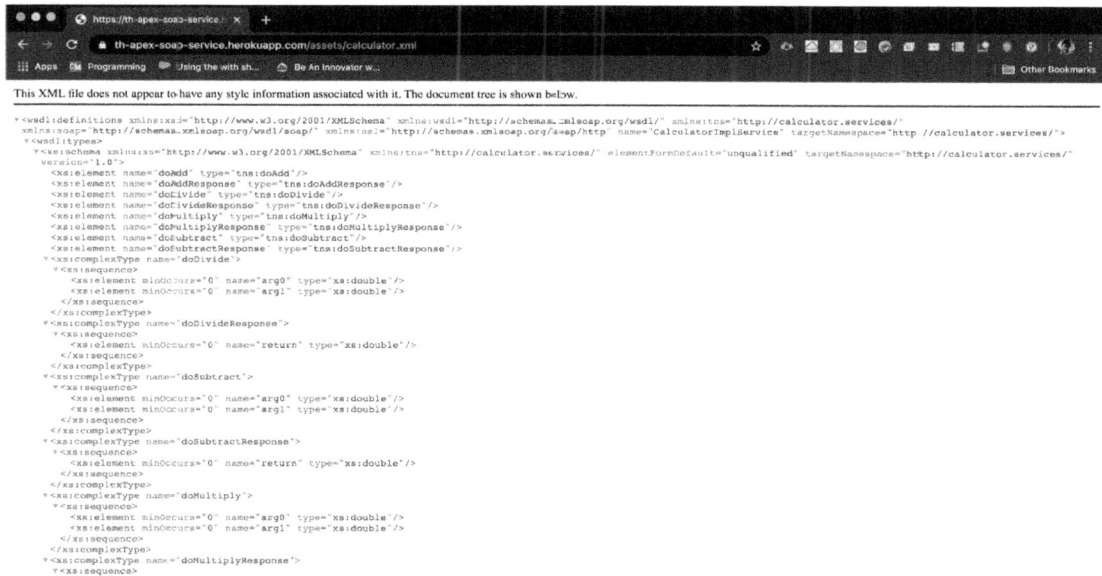

Figure 21.15: XML SOAP

You can visit to the following link provided by Salesforce, to check one example of WSDL:

https://th-apex-soap-service.herokuapp.com/assets/calculator.xml

If you are making a callout, you will receive a WSDL file that you will use to generate the Apex class. Download the preceding WSDL file on your desktop and go to Salesforce Setup. Search the Apex class; you will see a button **Generate from WSDL**:

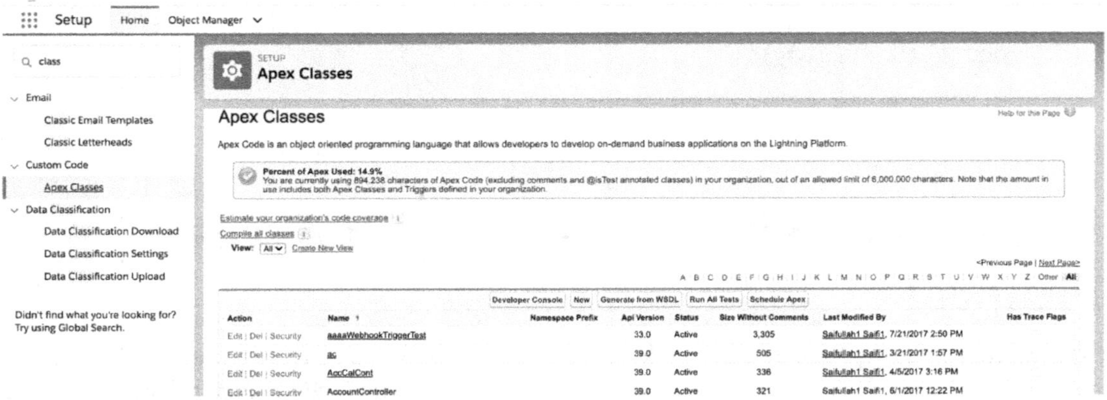

Figure 21.16: WSDL generate setup

Click on this button and choose the file that you saved on your desktop. Click on **Parse WSDL**:

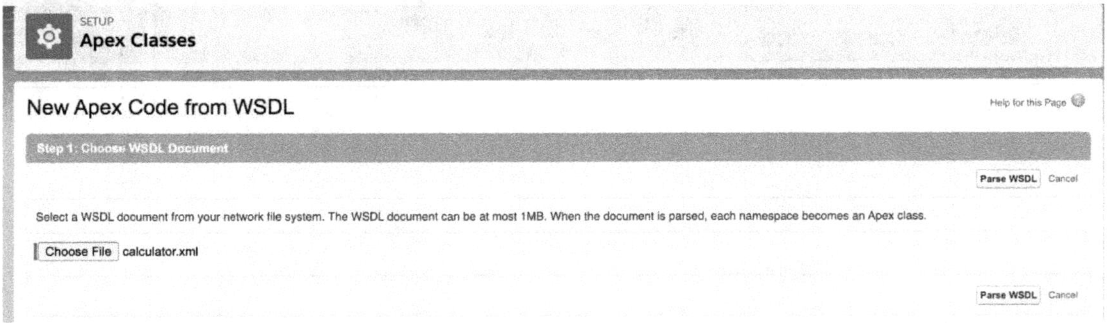

Figure 21.17: WSDL setup

If the WSDL file is correct, it will give you the option to generate the Apex class:

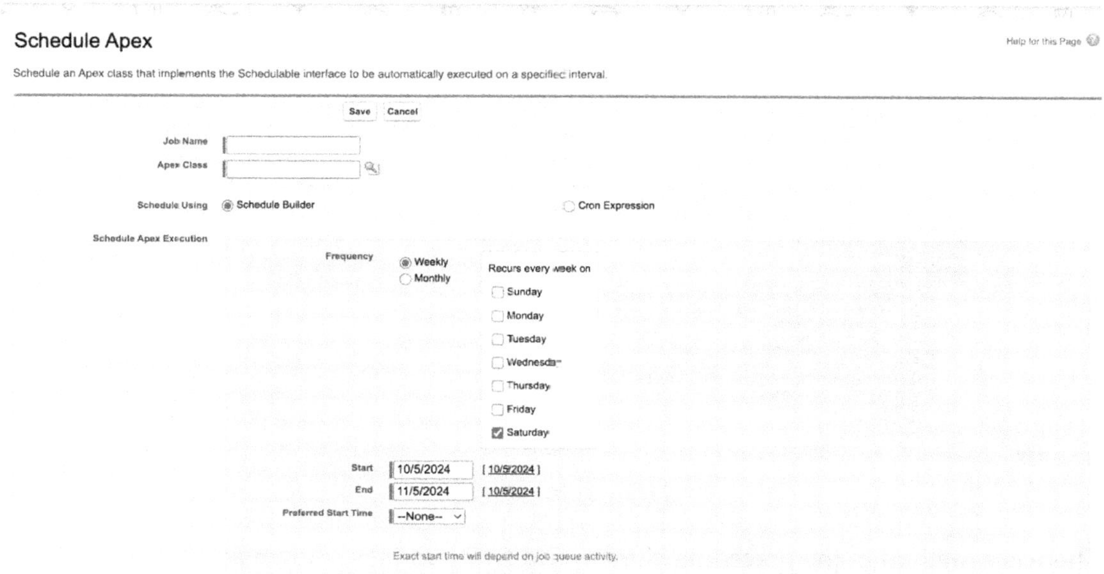

Figure 21.18: WSDL setup

From that Apex class, we can use it to call the SOAP API:

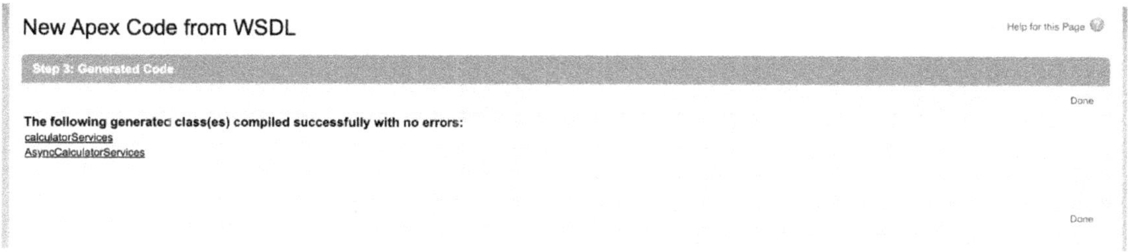

Figure 21.19: Apex code from WSDL

The Apex class will look something like the following figure:

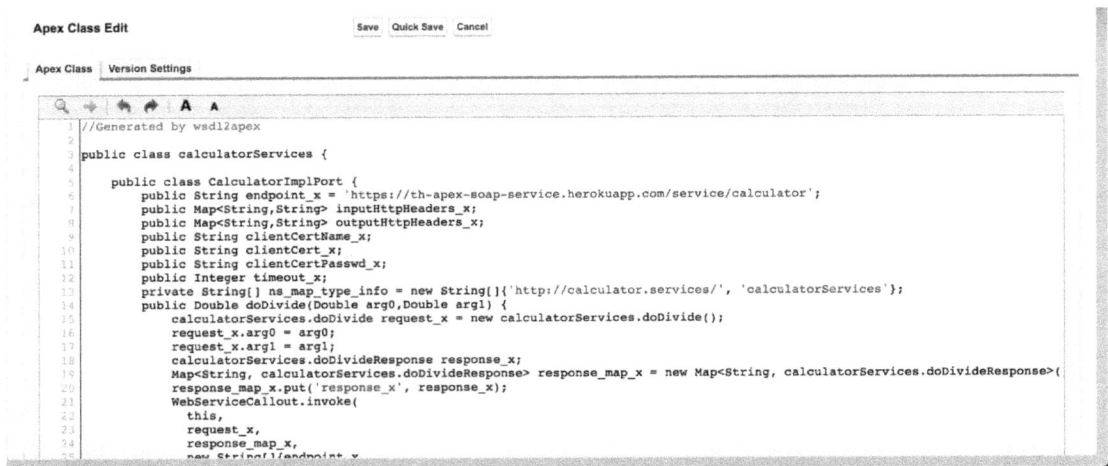

Figure 21.20: Apex class

There is a method in the preceding class to add two numbers, shown as follows:

```
public Double doAdd(Double arg0,Double arg1){
//code
        }
```

Now, we can use this class to call the API and add method:

```
Integer x=12;

Integer y = 19.0

calculatorServices.CalculatorImplPort calculator = new calculatorServices.
CalculatorImplPort();

Double sum =. calculator.doAdd(x,y);
```

Webservice using SOAP

If we want to generate the Webservice using SOAP, we need to generate WSDL from Salesforce. There are two types of WSDL for Salesforce, which are as follows:

- **Enterprise WSDL:** This file is generated for a Single Salesforce org, so it is strongly related to one specific Salesforce Org and their configuration. Two Enterprise WSDL files from two orgs can never be the same.

- **Partner WSDL**: This file is general-purpose or loosely typed. It will work for multiple Org.

If you want to generate a WSDL file, go to **Salesforce Setup**, and search API. You will see the options to download WSDLs, as shown in the following figure:

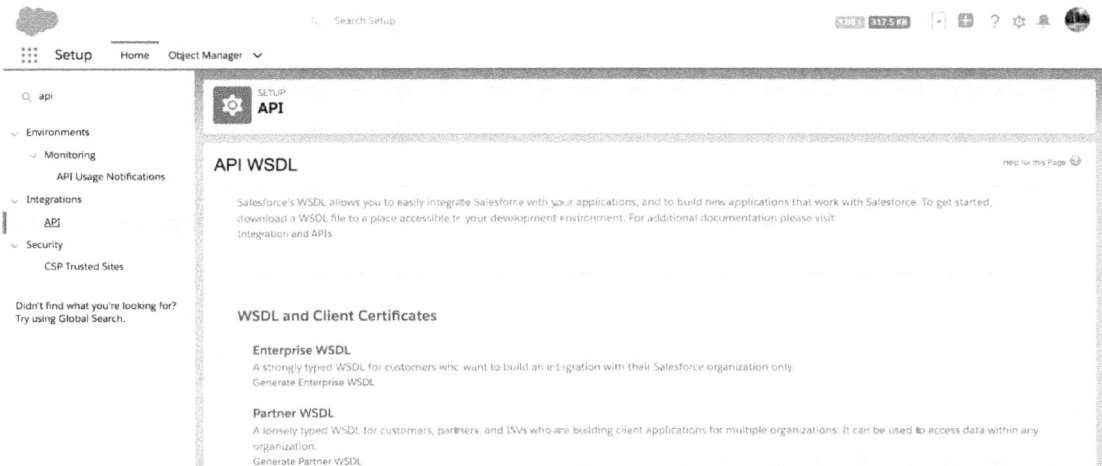

Figure 21.21: API WSDL

Send this WSDL to your integration partner. They can call or retrieve data from your org using SOAP now.

Asynchronous Apex

Apex offers multiple ways for running your Apex code asynchronously. You will learn some of the ways in this section. You will also learn some annotation used in Apex for various use.

Future method

Future is an asynchronous method which will help in the following situations:

- When you want to avoid postponing an Apex transaction because you have a long-running process going on
- Whenever you invoke external Web services
- To avoid the mixed save DML issue, separate DML operations

In the event that a transaction rolls back, all future jobs in queues will be rolled back. The sample code of the **future** method is as follows:

```
global class FutureClass
{
    @future
    public static void myFutureMethod()
    {
```

```
        // Perform some operations
    }
}
```

You can call future methods like any other method. However, a future method cannot call another future method.

Queueable

The **Queueable** class is used for the following purpose:

- To start a long-running operation and get an ID for it
- To pass complex types to a job
- To chain jobs

This example implements the Queueable interface. The execute method in this example adds a new account. The **System.enqueueJob(queueable)** method is used to enqueue a job. Sample code for Queueable is as follows:

```
public class AsyncExecutionExample implements Queueable {
    public void execute(QueueableContext context) {
        Account a = new Account(Name='Acme',Phone='(415) 555-1212');
        insert a;
    }
}
```

To enqueue this class as a job, call the following method:

```
ID jobID = System.enqueueJob(new AsyncExecutionExample());
```

AuraEnabled

An Apex controller method can be accessed from both the client and the server side using the **@AuraEnabled** annotation. Your Lightning components can access your methods by providing this annotation.

A Lightning web component can only access static Apex methods that are either global or public. Put **@AuraEnabled** in the method's annotation:

```
public with sharing class AccountController {
    @AuraEnabled(cacheable=true)
    public static List<Contact> getContactList() {
        return [
            SELECT Id, Name, Industry,Phone
```

```
FROM Account
        WHERE Industry != null
        WITH SECURITY_ENFORCED
        LIMIT 10
    ];
  }
}
```

Annotate the Apex method with **@AuraEnabled(cacheable = true)**, which caches the method results on the client to increase runtime speed:

- A method that has cacheable=true configured must only retrieve data. It cannot alter or modify data. By allowing a method to be marked as cacheable, you can increase the speed of your component by displaying data from client-side storage instantly rather than waiting for a server trip.

- The framework obtains the most recent data from the server, if the data that is cached is outdated. Customers with erratic, slow, or high latency connections can benefit most from caching.

- Use cacheable techniques whenever you can because they work better.

- You need to set cacheable=true i to use **@wire** to call an Apex method.

- You can choose to set cacheable=true, to force an Apex method to be called immediately.

Using Apex class as a custom controller

A custom controller is an Apex class for any Visualforce page, like a standard controller. This is an Apex class in which we will write all the logic for **Visual Force (VF)** pages without using the standard controller.

The standard controller works in a user mode, as it will always follow all the sharing rules and permission access for every user. However, the custom controller works in system mode; it does not respect the user context. Sometimes, we need that type of VF Page, so we need a custom controller.

A controller extension is a helper class (Apex class) that extends the functionality of a standard or custom controller.

Custom controller is a simple Apex class with the following good features:

- The controller has a default constructor with no parameter.

- We can define any variable that is needed for VF pages, and we can also create any methods in the class that will be called from VF pages.

Let us check some of the examples of Apex controller:

- **Controller sample one:** This is a sample controller in which we are accessing one account and assigning it into a variable account:

```
public class myFirstAccountController{
    public Account acc{get;set;}
    public myFirstAccountController(){
        acc =[SELECT id, Name FROM Account LIMIT 1];
    }
}
```

- **Related VF page**: This VF page is using the preceding controller to display account details:

```
<apex:page controller="myFirstAccountController">
    <apex:pageBlock title="Hi {!$User.LastName}">
        this is your first custom controller data
        <br/>
        Account Name: <apex:outputField value="{!acc.name}"/>
    </apex:pageBlock>
</apex:page>
```

When we preview it, it will look like the following figure:

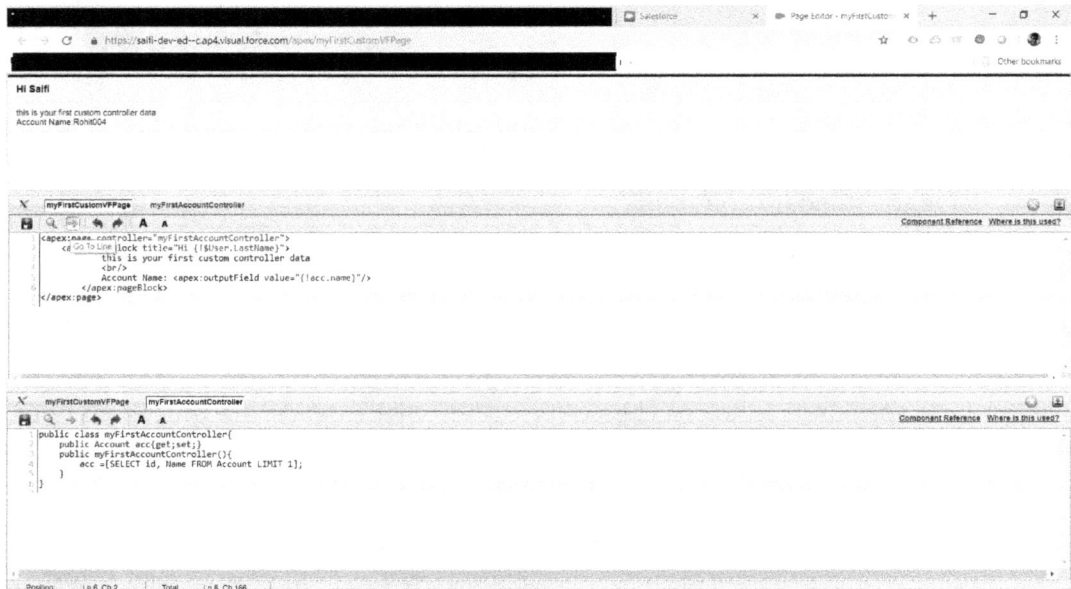

Figure 21.22: VF page setup

Now, let us understand the same line-by-line:

```
public class myFirstAccountController{
      public Account acc{get;set;}
      public myFirstAccountController(){
            acc =[SELECT id, Name FROM Account LIMIT 1];
      }
}
```

The controller is a simple class; the first line is the controller's name with public access.

The second line is a definition a variable **acc** of type Account. You also see use of get and set with it. You will learn about get and set in this chapter in the section *Use of get and set*.

The third line is the constructor of this controller; hence, you can see that the name is the same as the class. In the constructor, there is a query on account for only one account, and we are assigning it into the **acc** variable. So now we know in this controller, we have an **acc** variable in which we have assigned one account record. This variable is public so that we can access it outside the class; now we will come to the VF page:

```
<apex:page controller="myFirstAccountController">
      <apex:pageBlock title="Hi {!$User.LastName}">
        this is your first custom controller data
        <br/>
        Account Name: <apex:outputField value="{!acc.name}"/>
    </apex:pageBlock>
</apex:page>
```

The page is calling the preceding controller that we have discussed. Now, we can use any public variable of that controller in the VF page because we have called the controller. As you can see in the fifth line, we have the account Name, and we are using **acc** because **acc** is an account. So, we can display or use **Name** field of account for which we have used **{!acc.name}**, the expression is used to bind the apex variable on a VF page. In the *Figure 21.22*, you can see, an account name is displayed.

Use of get and set

Visualforce page always requires a *getter* and *setter* also known as (get, set) to reference/ use a variable in the controller or extension. Without a getter or setter, even public or global variables cannot be used in Visualforce expressions.

The get methods are used to initialize a variable in a class so that the VF page can call or use it. For that purpose, we use the get method to pass data from the Apex code to the Visualforce page. The get method is public, so it will look like the following:

```
public getVarName(){
        integer varName=2;
        return varName;
}
```

In the VF page, it will be: **{!VarName}**

The set methods are used to assign a value to the variable.

The set method is used to pass values in the variable from your Visualforce page to the controller.

The get method is public so it will look like the following:

```
public void setVarName(integer value) { varName = value; }
```

Getter and setter also known as the get accessor method and the set accessor method. The syntax can be as follows:

```
public integer var1 {
      get { return var1; }
      set { var1 = value; }
  }
```

We can also do in one line like the following:

```
public integer var1{get;set;}
```

Now we know, we can use any variable in the VF page using getter setter in the controller.

Let us take the following example to make it simpler:

```
public Class customController{
      public Account acc{get;set;}
      public customController(){
            acc = new Account();
      }
      public void save(){
            system.debug(acc);
      }
}
```

The Visual Force page code will look like the following:

```
<apex:page controller="customController" sidebar="false">
    <apex:form>
```

```
        <apex:pageBlock>
            <apex:pageblocksection title="Account Form">
                <apex:inputField value="{!acc.Name}" />
                <apex:inputField value="{!acc.Industry}"/>
                <apex:commandButton value="Save" action="{!save}"/>
            </apex:pageblocksection>
        </apex:pageBlock>
    </apex:form>
</apex:page>
```

Let us create this class and VF page and preview it:

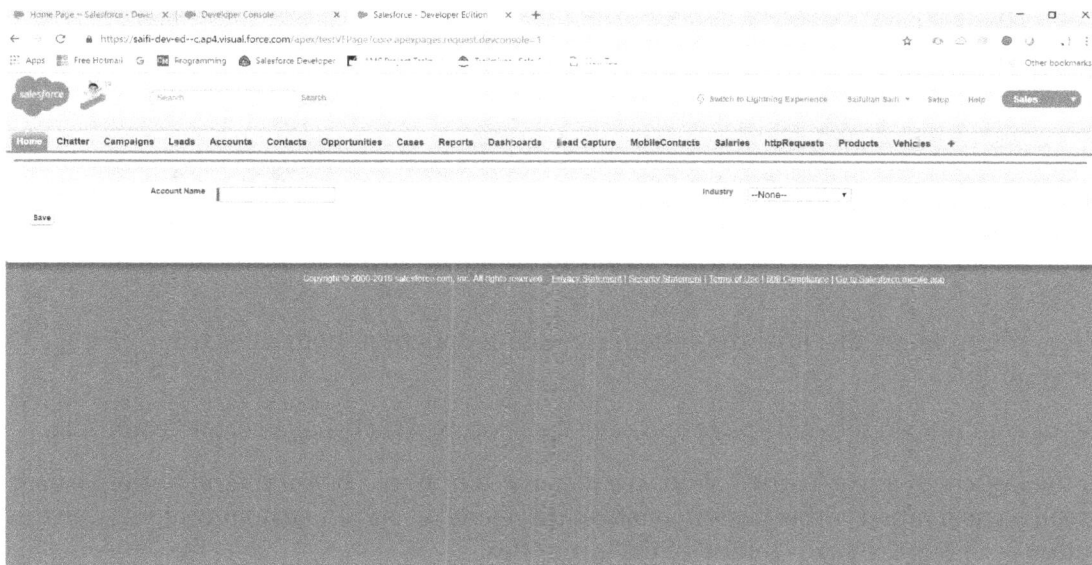

Figure 21.23: VF page preview

On this page, as we can see, we have input form for an account, and we have used **acc** as an Account variable for it. In the constructor, you can see we have just initialized the account, but there is no value assigned to it. Now, if you will fill the form, in the Account variable, the value will be set due to setter. The **system.debug** was used in the class, so we can see the value when we open the page. We can see the debug, as shown in the following figure:

testVFPage.vfp	customController.apxc	Log executeAnonymous @2/3/2019, 4:08:43 PM

Execution Log

Timestamp	Event	Details
16:08:43:006	USER_DEBUG	[5]|DEBUG|Account:{}

Figure 21.24: Debug log

Now, we have filled the form and saved it so we can see the debug now:

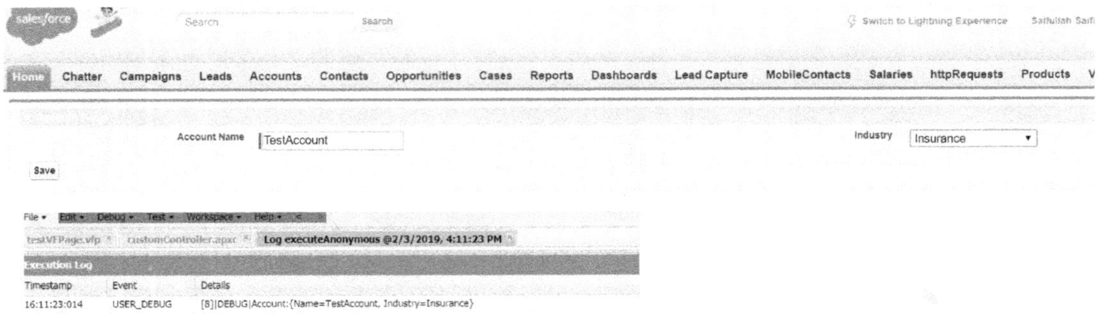

Figure 21.25: VF page preview

Now, you have an idea how the system is binding data from both sides from VF page to the controller.

Let us continue on the same page and save the account data using a custom controller.

In the last chapter, we learned about the command button. The command button is used to call some method, either custom or standard. Here, we have a custom controller, so this button is calling the save method of this controller:

```
<apex:commandButton value="Save" action="{!save}"/>
```

So, as you can see in the debug log, when we hit the button, form value is updated in account **acc**, and now we can insert it:

```
public Class customController{
        public Account acc{get;set;}
        public customController(){
                acc = new Account();
          system.debug(acc);
        }
        public pageReference save(){
```

```
        system.debug(acc);
    insert acc;
    return new PageReference('/'+acc.Id);
    }
}
```

The UI will look like the following figure:

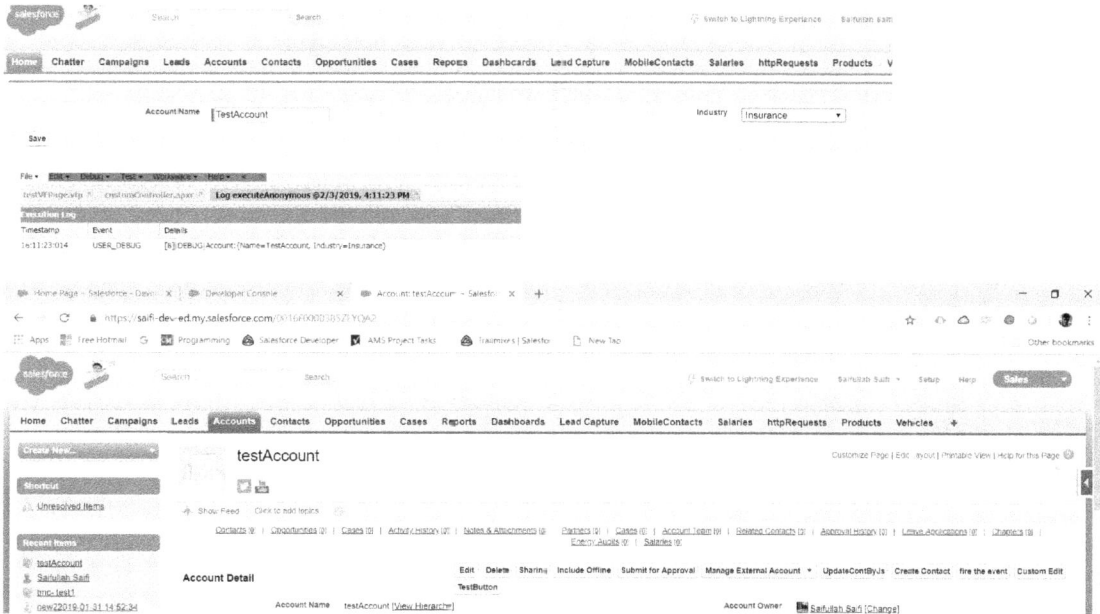

Figure 21.26: Page layout

In the save method, we have used **pageReference** as return type as we need to open that account or redirect the page. So, if you want to redirect the page, you can use the page reference:

```
public pageReference save(){
    insert acc;
    return new PageReference('/'+acc.Id);
}
```

You can check this method. We have inserted the account, and now, we are redirecting the page with / and account ID.

We will now see the following example, in which we will create an account and contact record from 1 page:

```
<apex:page controller="customController" sidebar="false">
```

```
<apex:form>
    <apex:pageBlock>
        <apex:pageblocksection title="Account Form">
            <apex:inputField value="{!acc.Name}" />
            <apex:inputField value="{!acc.Industry}"/>

        </apex:pageblocksection>
        <apex:pageblocksection title="contact Form">
            <apex:inputField value="{!cont.lastName}" />
            <apex:inputField value="{!cont.email}"/>
            <apex:inputField value="{!cont.phone}"/>
        </apex:pageblocksection>
            <apex:commandButton value="Save" action="{!save}"/>
    </apex:pageBlock>
</apex:form>
</apex:page>


public Class customController{
    public Account acc{get;set;}
    public Contact cont{get;set;}
    public customController(){
        acc = new Account();
            cont= new Contact();
    }
    public pageReference save(){
            insert acc;
        cont.AccountId= acc.id;
        insert cont;
        return new PageReference('/'+acc.Id);
    }
}
```

The new UI will look like following figure:

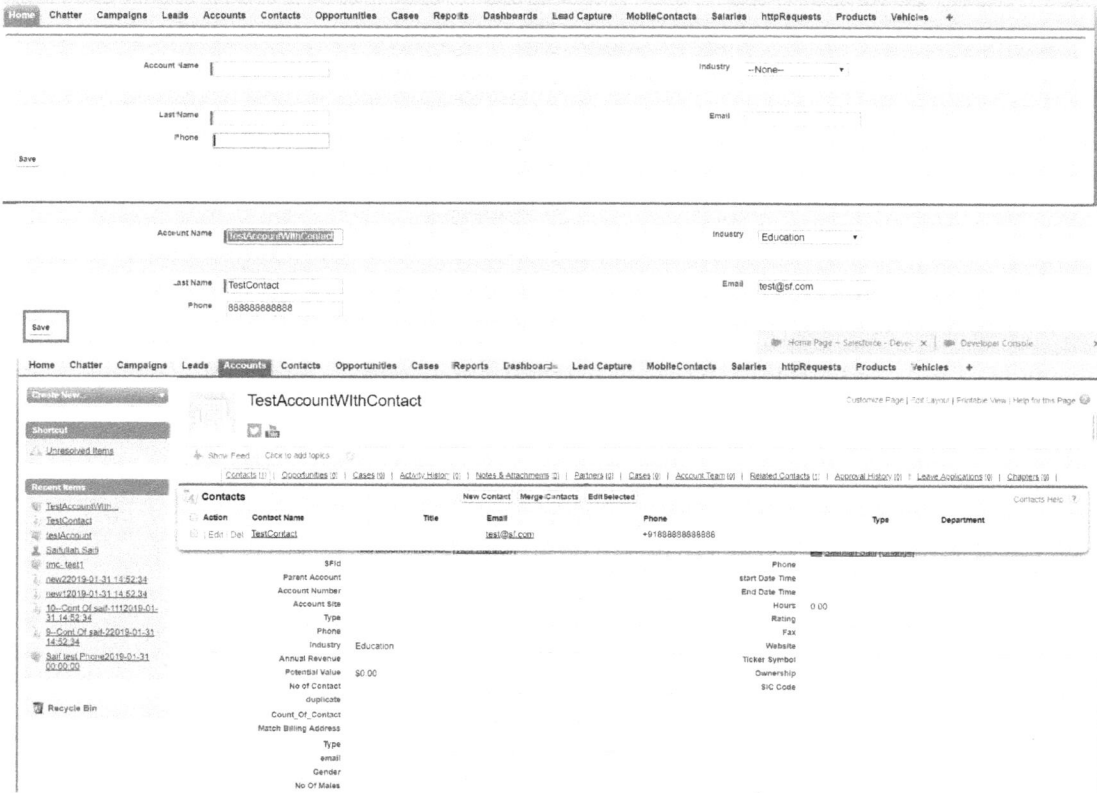

Figure 21.27: *Layout*

Everything is the same; now, we have two variables **acc** and **cont**. In the VF page, there are two sections, one for the account input form and second for the contact input form. In the save method, we have inserted the account, then we assigned the **accountId** into contact **accountId** as we are relating contact and account, after that, we are inserting the contact and redirecting it to the account record now we can see, we have contact in the related list.

This was all about a simple input form, now we will show the details of a particular account record and related contact, we will also edit it from there. You can refer to the following code to understand it better:

```
public Class customControllerRecord{
     public Account acc{get;set;}
     public customControllerRecord(){
          Id recId = ApexPages.currentPage().getParameters().get('Id');
          acc = [SELECT Name,Industry from Account WHERE ID=:recId];
```

```
                system.debug(acc);
        }
}


<apex:page controller="customControllerRecord" sidebar="false">
    <apex:form>
        <apex:pageBlock>
            <apex:pageblocksection title="Account Detail">
                <apex:outputField value="{!acc.Name}" />
                <apex:outputField value="{!acc.Industry}"/>
            </apex:pageblocksection>
            </apex:pageBlock>
    </apex:form>
</apex:page>
```

The output will look like the following figure:

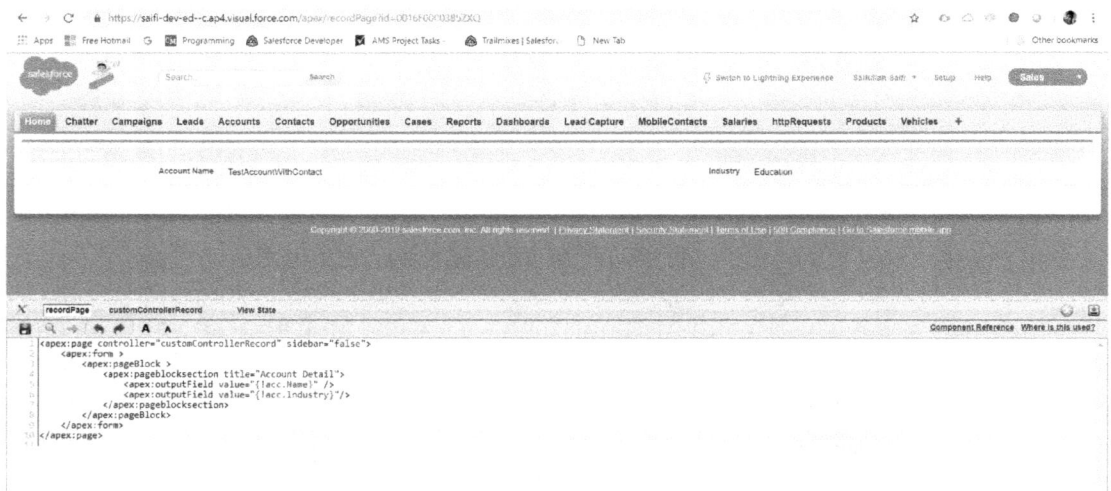

Figure 21.28: VF page review

Check the preceding figure, you can see in the URL we have **/apex/ recordPage?id=0016F0000385ZXQ**

We have used this ID in our controller, and we found the account of that particular ID.

Let us have a look at the controller:

```
public Class customControllerRecord{
    public Account acc{get;set;}
    public customControllerRecord(){
        Id recId = ApexPages.currentPage().getParameters().get('Id');
        acc = [SELECT Name,Industry from Account WHERE ID=:recId];
        system.debug(acc);
    }
}
```

In this controller, we have defined a variable **acc** for an account with getter and setter, now in the constructor, we need the Id from the URL, so we used **getParameters()**, the method you can see we used **get('Id')** this is same from URL id=0016F0000385ZXQ

So now in **recId**, the value is **0016F0000385ZXQ**. Then, we do SOQL in Account to find the account, and in the query, we have selected Name and Industry. Now, on the page, we have just used the **acc** variable in the **<Apex:outputField>**.

Controller extension

According to the Salesforce developer guide, a controller extension is an Apex class that extends the functionality of a standard or custom controller.

We can use a controller extension when:

- We want to enhance or extend some new logic with an inbuild standard controller.
- If we want to add custom new actions for any new logic.
- We know the standard controller works in user mode, but sometimes we need to run it in system mode for that purpose. We can create an extension and write the logic in it.

Format of controller extensions

This is a controller extension of account, any record of account will be assigned in **acc**:

```
public class accControllerExtension {
    private final Account acc;
// The extension constructor initializes the private member
    public accControllerExtension(ApexPages.StandardController sc){
        this.acc = (Account)sc.getRecord();
    }
}
```

The Visualforce page will look like following. We will add standard controller as **Account** and **Extension**:

```
<apex:page   standardController="Account"   extensions="accControllerExten-
sion">
    Hi, <p/>
    <apex:form>
        <apex:inputField value="{!account.name}"/> <p/>
        <apex:commandButton value="Save" action="{!save}"/>
    </apex:form>
</apex:page>
```

We can add more than one extension for a VF page separate by ",". You can check the following code on how to use multiple extensions:

```
<apex:page standardController="Account" extensions="ext1,ext2">

</apex:page>
```

Custom controller to build Visualforce page

Most of the time when we need a custom controller to build a VF page, we will need this type of controller when we want to extract data from multiple related or unrelated objects and want to perform some complex calculation or logical operation. We can also generate Excel, or PDF using VF page. We can call any API from the custom controller.

Visualforce page as PDF

If we want to create a pdf using VF Page, we will add this **renderAs="pdf"** in Apex Page, and we will get the result:

```
<apex:page standardController="Account" renderAs="pdf" recordSetVar="acc">

-----

</apex:page>
```

For Excel generation, we will add **contentType** tag in **<Apex:page>**:

```
<apex:page standardController="Account" contentType="application/vnd.ms-ex-
cel#filename.xls"   language="en-US" cache="True">

</apex:page>
```

Wrapper class and junction object

We are going to start with the junction object:

- **Junction object:** They are used to create many-to-many relationships between objects. If you take the recruiting application example, you can see that a position can be linked to many candidates, and a candidate can apply for different positions. To create this data model, you need a third object, **Job Application**, that links the two.

  So, you will create a lookup field for both the position and candidate object on the "Job Application object. This will establish many-to-many relationships between position and candidate via the **Job Application** object, known as the junction object.

- **Wrapper class:** A wrapper class is a class whose object wraps or contains primitive data types. When we create an object to a wrapper class, it contains a field, and in this field, we can store primitive data types. In other words, we can wrap a primitive value into a wrapper class object.

  Example of wrapper class:

```
public class wrapperExample{
        public Account acc{ get; set; }
        public Integer no_of_Contacts{ get; set; }
        public String remaining_tech { get; set; }
}
```

If we use this wrapper or initiate this in Apex, we will use it like:

```
WrapperExample wr1 = new wrapperExample();
Wr1.acc = new Account(name='saif');
Wr1.no_of_Contacts=5;
Wr1.remaining_tech = 'Labgue';
```

Now, let us understand both the topics with examples. We will be using the following objects and fields to understand the concepts:

- **Objects**: Student, course, registration, fee fields are as follows:
  - **Student__c**: Name , **City__c,Date_Of_Birth__c**
  - **Course__c: Duration__c, Fees__c,Name, Rollup summary field named as Total_Student__c**
  - **Registration__c: Master detail with Course__c Object, Master detail with Student__c , Date_of_Registration___c**

> ○ **Fees__c: Amount__c, Date_of_Deposit__c, Master detail with Course__c Object, Master detail with Student__c**

The code to find out the fees of students for different courses who register for it, is as follows:

```
public class RegisteredStudentList {
    // wrapper List
    public list<stdWrapper> stdListWrapper { get; set; }
    //constructor
    public RegisteredStudentList() {
        // query for student ( inner query for registration(course) and Fee
        list<student__c> stdList = [
            SELECT
                id,name,City__c,Date_Of_Birth__c,
        (SELECT id, course__r.Fees__c, course__r.Name FROM Registrations__r),
        (SELECT id, Amount__c FROM Fees__r)
            FROM student__c
            WHERE Total_Course__c > 0
        ];
        // wrapper all value
        stdListWrapper = new List<stdWrapper>();
        double pd = 0, payb = 0, rem = 0;
        // courses string
        String courseDet = '[ ';
        for (student__c std : stdList) {
            stdWrapper stw = new stdWrapper();
            for (Registration__c reg : std.Registrations__r) {
                //payable amount
                payb += reg.course__r.Fees__c;
                // courses string
                courseDet += reg.course__r.Name + '--> Rs.' + reg.
course__r.Fees__c + ', ';
            }
            courseDet = courseDet.removeEnd(', ');
```

```
            courseDet += ' ]';
            //paid fees
            for (Fees__c fe : std.Fees__r)
                pd += fe.Amount__c;
            // // remaining
            rem = payb - pd;
            stw.stud = std;
            stw.payable = payb;
            stw.paid = pd;
            stw.remain = rem;
            stw.crsDet = courseDet;
            //adding this wrapper into list
            stdListWrapper.add(stw);
        }
    }
    // wrapper class
    public class stdWrapper {
        public student__c stud { get; set; }
        public string crsDet { get; set; }
        public double payable { get; set; }
        public double paid { get; set; }
        public double remain { get; set; }
    }
    // code s'f
}
```

Explanation: In this code, two nested/inner queries for registration and fee is applied with the query of the student where the Total Course of Student is greater than 0 and then, a for loop for the student, in which the wrapper class reference is created. Again, a for loop of registration to calculate the payable amount is created. In the next line, the calculation for the course is done, and then in the // Remaining comment, we fetch out the data from the wrapper of all the object that needs to be visible on the VF page. At the end, the wrapper class is created for few fields to be visible on the VF page like paid, payable, and remaining mainly.

There is also an alternate way to code this with the aggregate query:

```
public class RegStuList {
    // wrapper list
    public list<stdWrapper> stdListWrapper { get; set; }
    //constructor
    public RegStuList() {
        // query for student ( inner query for registration(course) and Fee
        list<student__c> stdList = [
            SELECT id, name, City__c, Date_Of_Birth__c, (SELECT id,
course__r.Fees__c, course__r.Name FROM Registrations__r)
            FROM student__c
            WHERE Total_Course__c > 0
        ];
        set<id> stdSet = new Set<id>();
        Map<id, double> stdPaidMap = new Map<id, double>();
        for (student__c std : stdList)
            stdSet.add(std.id);
        for (AggregateResult agR : [
            SELECT student__c, sum(Amount__c) totalfee
            FROM Fees__c
            WHERE student__c IN :stdSet
            GROUP BY student__c
        ])
            stdPaidMap.put(string.valueOf(agR.get('student__c')), Double.
valueOf(agR.get('totalfee')));
        // wrapper all value
        stdListWrapper = new List<stdWrapper>();
        for (student__c std : stdList) {
            double pd = 0, payb = 0, rem = 0;
            stdWrapper stw = new stdWrapper();
            // courses string
            string courseDet = '[ ';
            for (Registration__c reg : std.Registrations__r) {
```

```
                    //payable amount
                    payb += reg.course__r.Fees__c;
                    // courses string
                    courseDet += reg.course__r.Name + ' --> ' + reg.course__r.
Fees__c + ', ';
                }
                courseDet = courseDet.removeEnd(', ');
                courseDet += ' ]';
                if (stdPaidMap.containsKey(std.id))
                    pd = stdPaidMap.get(std.id);
                // remaining
                rem = payb - pd;
                stw.stud = std;
                stw.payable = payb;
                stw.paid = pd;
                stw.remain = rem;
                stw.crsdt = courseDet;
                // adding this wrapper into list
                stdListWrapper.add(stw);
            }
        }
        // wrapper class
        public class stdWrapper {
            public student__c stud { get; set; }
            // public string crsDet{get;set;}
            public string crsdt { get; set; }
            public double payable { get; set; }
            public double paid { get; set; }
            public double remain { get; set; }
        }
}
```

For both the preceding controller, we have a VF page which can apply to both:

```
<apex:page controller="RegisteredStudentList" sidebar="false">
   <apex:pageBlock title="Student Panel">
      <apex:pageBlockTable value="{!stdListWrapper}" var="stw">
         <apex:column headerValue="Id">
            <apex:outputField value="{!stw.stud.id}"/>
         </apex:column>
         <apex:column headerValue="Name">
            <apex:outputField value="{!stw.stud.Name}"/>
         </apex:column>
         <apex:column headerValue="City">
            <apex:outputField value="{!stw.stud.City__c}"/>
         </apex:column>
         <apex:column headerValue="Date of Birth">
            <apex:outputField
               value="{!stw.stud.Date_Of_Birth__c}"/>
         </apex:column>
         <apex:column headerValue="Courses">
            <apex:outputText
               value="{!stw.crsDet}"/>
         </apex:column>
         <apex:column headerValue="Payable amount">
            <apex:outputText value="{!stw.payable}"/>
         </apex:column>
         <apex:column headerValue="Paid Amount"><apex:outputTextval-
ue="{!stw.paid}"/>
         </apex:column>
         <apex:column headerValue="Remainimg Balance">
            <apex:outputText
               value="{!stw.remain}"/>
         </apex:column>
      </apex:pageBlockTable>
   </apex:pageBlock>
```

```
</apex:page>
```

The VF page looks like the following figure:

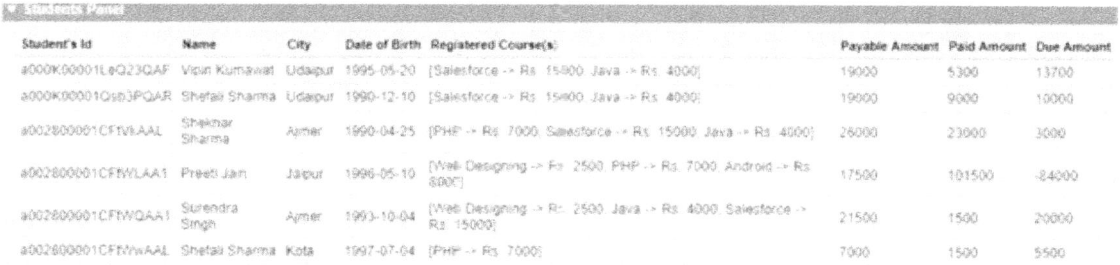

Student's Id	Name	City	Date of Birth	Registered Course(s)	Payable Amount	Paid Amount	Due Amount
a000K00001LeQ23QAF	Vipin Kumawat	Udaipur	1995-05-20	[Salesforce -> Rs. 15900 Java -> Rs. 4000]	19000	5300	13700
a000K00001Qsb3PQAR	Shefali Sharma	Udaipur	1990-12-10	[Salesforce -> Rs. 15900 Java -> Rs. 4000]	19000	9000	10000
a002800001CFtVLAAL	Shekhar Sharma	Ajmer	1990-04-25	[PHP -> Rs. 7000, Salesforce -> Rs. 15000 Java -> Rs. 4000]	26000	23000	3000
a002800001CFtWLAA1	Preeti Jain	Jaipur	1996-05-10	[Web Designing -> Rs. 2500, PHP -> Rs. 7000, Android -> Rs. 8000]	17500	101500	-84000
a002800001CFtWQAA1	Surendra Singh	Ajmer	1993-10-04	[Web Designing -> Rs. 2500 Java -> Rs. 4000, Salesforce -> Rs. 15000]	21500	1500	20000
a002800001CFtWwAAL	Shefali Sharma	Kota	1997-07-04	[PHP -> Rs. 7000]	7000	1500	5500

Figure 21.29: *Visualforce page using wrapper*

Starting with **SelectList**, it is a list of multi-select options from which the user can choose the most suitable one. This component supports HTML pass-through attributes using the HTML-prefix. Pass-through attributes are attached to the generated **<select>** tag.

Syntax:
```
<apex:selectList value="{!AttributeName}" multiselect="true">
        <apex:selectOptions value="{!items}"/>
</apex:selectList>
```

Moving forward to the next thing, that is, **SelectOptions.** It is the collection of possible values that can be used in **<apex:selectCheckBoxes>**, **<apex:selectRadio>**, or **<apex:selectList>** component. Basically, **<apex:SelectOptions>** is the child of the component discussed earlier.

Syntax:
```
<apex:selectCheckboxes value='{!attribute}" title="TitleName">
    <apex:selectOptions value="{!items}"/>
</apex:selectCheckboxes>
```

Lasly, **ActionFunction** is a component that provides support for invoking controller action methods directly from JavaScript code using an AJAX request. An **<apex:actionFunction>** component must be a child of an **<apex:form>** component. Since binding between the caller and **<apex:actionFunction>** is done based on the parameter order, ensure that the order of **<apex:param>** is matched by the caller's argument list.

Unlike **<apex:actionSupport>**, which only provides support for invoking controller action methods from other Visualforce components, **<apex:actionFunction>** defines a new JavaScript function which can then be called from within a block of JavaScript code.

This is all basic knowledge. Now, let us go further and look for an example of code to learn how to use it.

Visualforce page:

```
<apex:page Controller="StudentVfComponentController" tabStyle="Account"
   sidebar="false" id="pg">
  <apex:form id="frm">
    <apex:pageBlock id="pb">
      <apex:actionstatus id="status">
        <apex:facet name="start"> <div class="waitingSearchDiv"
          id="el_loading" style="background-color: #fbfbfb;height:
          100%;opacity:0.6;width:100%;"> </div>
          <div class="waitingHolder"
          style="position:center;top:50px;left:50%; opacity:0.9;z-in-
dex:50; width:
          20px;">
          title="Please Wait..." />
          <img class="waitingImage" src="/img/loading.gif"
          <span class="waitingDescription">Loading...</span> </div>
        </apex:facet>
      </apex:actionstatus>
      <apex:actionFunction action="{!selectCourse}" name="fun"
        rerender="frm" status="status">
        <apex:param name="s" assignTo="{!selectStudent}" value="" />
      </apex:actionFunction>
      <apex:pageBlockSection title="Student Panel" id="pbs">
        <apex:selectList multiselect="false" size="1"onchange="-
fun(this.value);">
          <apex:selectOptions value="{!Student_List}" />
        </apex:selectList>
        <apex:selectList multiselect="false" size="1"
          rendered="{!Course_List.size >
          0}" >
          <apex:selectOptions value="{!Course_List}" />
        </apex:selectList>
        <apex:outputPanel rendered="{!flag}" id="">
```

```
            <span style="color:red; '>Not Registered with any
            Course</span>
        </apex:outputPanel>
      </apex:pageBlockSection>
    </apex:pageBlock>
  </apex:form>
</apex:page>
```

Controller:

```
public class StudentVfComponentController {
    public List<SelectOption> Student_List { get; set; }
    public List<SelectOption> Course_List { get; set; }
    public String selectStudent { get; set; }
    public boolean flag { get; set; }
```

1.

```
    //Constructor
    public StudentVfComponentController() {
        Student_List = new List<SelectOption>();
        Course_List = new List<SelectOption>();
        list<Student__c> Stu_List = [SELECT id, Name FROM Student__c];
        Student_List.add(new SelectOption('', '--Select a Student--'));
        for (Student__c stu : Stu_List)
            Student_List.add(new SelectOption(stu.Id, stu.Name));
        Course_List.add(new SelectOption('', '--Select course--'));
        flag = false;
    }
    public void selectCourse() {
        List<Registration__c> regList = [
            SELECT id, Course__r.id, Course__r.Name
            FROM Registration__c
            WHERE Student__c = :selectStudent
        ];
        Course_List.clear();
```

```
        if (regList.size() > 0) {
            Course_List.add(new SelectOption('', '--Select course--'));
            for (Registration__c reg : regList)
                Course_List.add(new SelectOption(reg.Course__r.Id, reg.
Course__r.Name));
            flag = false;
        } else
            flag = true;
    }
}
```

Explanation: In the VF page, you can see the use of an action function tag in which action = *selectCourse* is the method of the controller written below the VF, which lets the code do the task according to the steps written in the controller. Then, in the **pageBlock** section, we created a select-option drop-down, where one can select any student name (**Student_ List**), which is retrieved from the list as coded in the controller. Similarly, we are fetching the details of the course through **Course_List** in the controller.

We are checking for the student if they are enrolled in any course or not; if not, then it will throw an error message in the **<apex:outputPanel>**. All the conditions are verified and checked in the controller, as querying for the student name or course name to be shown in the dropdown as:

```
Course_List=new List<SelectOption>();
list<Student__c> Stu_List = [SELECT id,Name FROM Student__c];
Student_List.add(new SelectOption('','--Select a Student--'));
for( Student__c stu: Stu_List){
    Student_List.add(new SelectOption(stu.Id,stu.Name));
}
Course_List.add(new SelectOption('','--Select course--'));
```

Then, check for the student, and if they are registered for the course or not, in the following code:

```
List<Registration__c> regList=[select id,Course__r.id, Course__r.Name from
Registration__c where Student__c=:selectStudent];
Course_List.clear();
if(regList.size()>0){
    Course_List.add(new SelectOption('','--Select course--'));
    for( Registration__c reg: regList)
```

```
      Course_List.add(new SelectOption(reg.Course__r.Id,reg.Course__r.
Name));

    flag=false;

}

else

    flag=true;
```

Try this page and controller and preview this page and try to check how it will work.

Conclusion

In this chapter, we learned about the web-to-lead form. We have also covered email services. We learned about Batch class, Apex controller and Scheduler and how to use it. We have also studied API to connect with other software to receive or send data. We have also used some of the annotations like future, Aura Enabled.

In the next chapter, we will learn debugging and deployment in Salesforce. We will study about debug log, multiple deployment tools and Appexchange.

Questions

1. Can we call API from the trigger directly?
2. Can we call API from batch?
3. What is the batch maximum record size
4. What is stateful?
5. What is 404?

Answers

1. No, using a future method (callout=true)
2. Yes
3. 200
4. If you specify database. Stateful in the batch class definition, you can maintain state across these transactions. Store value until the finish method.
5. Status code that api url is wrong and not found.

Join our Discord space

Join our Discord workspace for latest updates, offers, tech happenings around the world, new releases, and sessions with the authors:

https://discord.bpbonline.com

CHAPTER 22
Debugging and Deployment

Introduction

To check the quality and output of the code, every language uses some checkpoints and debug statements. Similarly, Apex Salesforce has debugging tools and generates a debug log for developers which we will learn about in this chapter. Salesforce has an inbuilt IDE called developer console; we can check the debug log and set checkpoints for that. We also learned that Salesforce uses tools like *Changeset* and *DevOps Centre* to deploy changes from the testing environment (Sandbox) to production (Live). Salesforce has its own marketplace for custom apps known as *AppExchange*.

Structure

In this chapter, we will discuss the following topics:

- Debugging Apex
- Developer console
- Deployment
- Changeset
- DevOps Center
- AppExchange

Objectives

After studying this unit, you should be able to set the debug log for Apex. would also learn to deploy code from a testing environment to a live organization. At last, you should be able to install app from AppExchange.

Debugging Apex

Apex provides debugging support. What is debugging? This is a method of detecting the error and correcting the code.

You might remember **system.debug**. It is the statement to check or debug your code so that we can debug Apex code using the developer console and debug logs, as shown in the following figure:

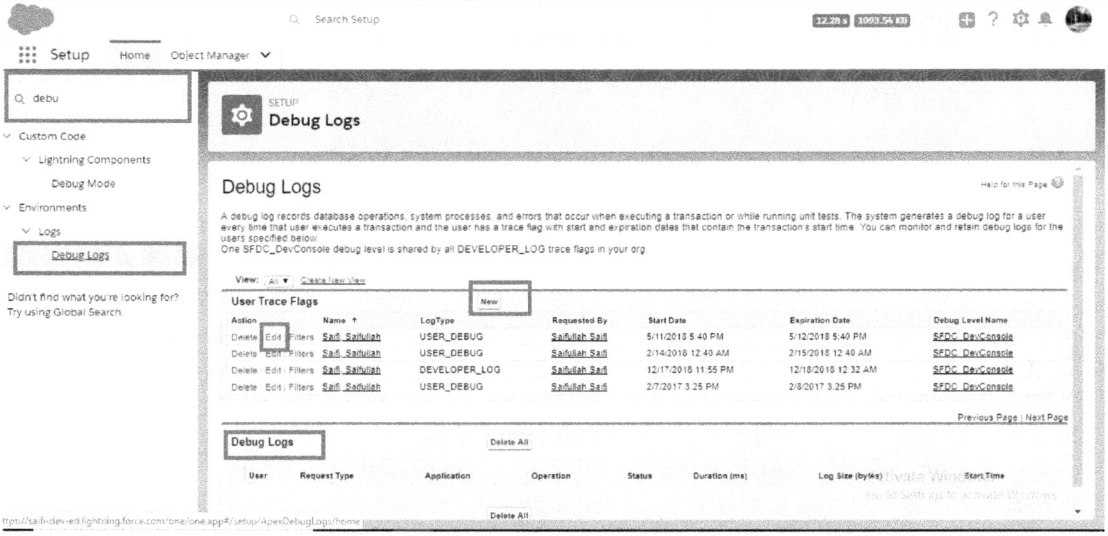

Figure 22.1: Debug log page

You will create New Trace Flag first:

Figure 22.2: New log creation

We can set the debug log for the user to 24 hours, and then we can view the debug:

Figure 22.3: Log detail

Click on view to open any debug log; you will see the full log:

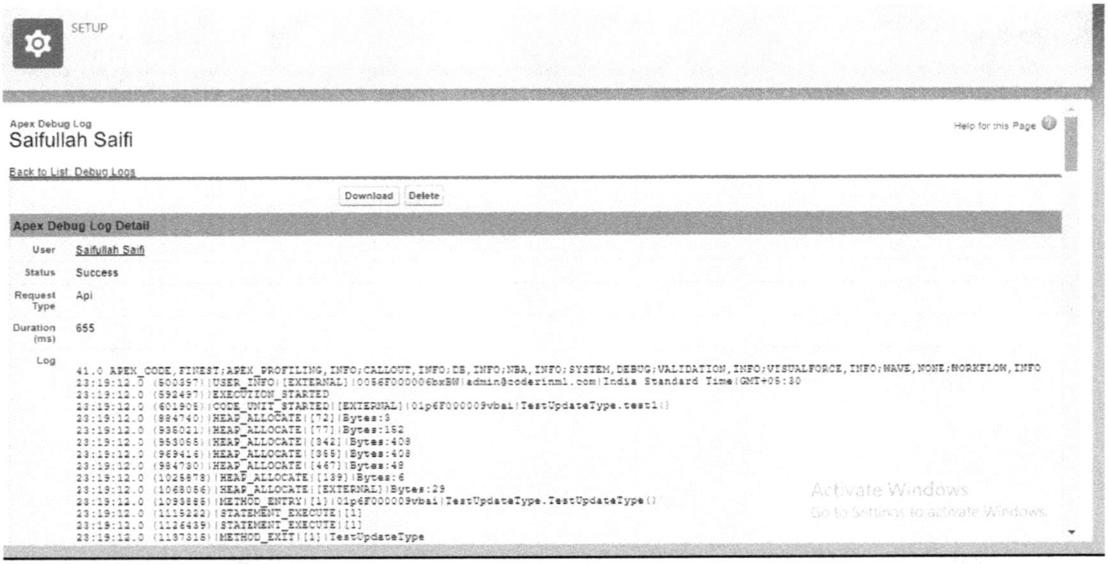

Figure 22.4: Log detail page

We can see the log in the developer console, as shown in the following figure:

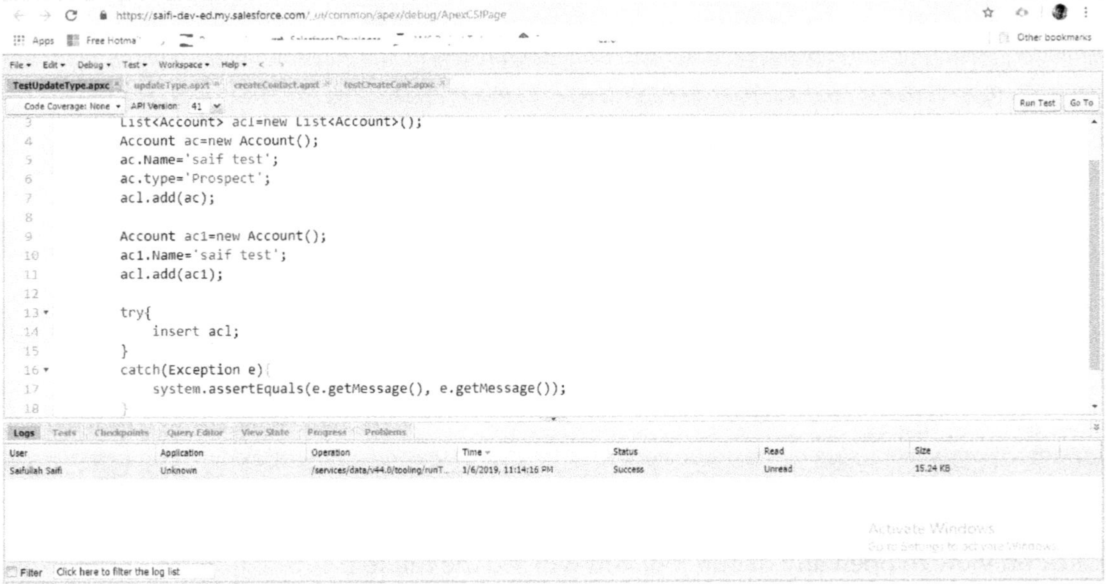

Figure 22.5: Developer consoler debug log

Apex also supports exception statements and custom exceptions. Also, Apex sends emails to developers for unhandled exceptions. Let us understand how debug log can help understand apex:

- A debug log can store all database operations, processes, and errors that occur during transactions or running unit tests.
- It will contain the following information:
  - o Database changes
  - o HTTP callouts
  - o Apex errors
  - o Resources used by Apex
  - o Automated workflow processes, such as the following:
    - ▪ Workflow rules
    - ▪ Assignment rules
    - ▪ Approval processes
    - ▪ Validation rules

  However, it will not store time-based workflow action.
- The debug log size should be less than 5MB, and it should be available for 24 hours.
- All the errors can be checked using a debug log.

We can use try-catch to help us find the error and line number of code using exceptions:

```
public class sampleClass {
1.    public void mthd() {
2.        Account acc = new Account();
3.        /*
4.         some line of code
5.         */
6.        try {
7.            insert acc;
8.        }
9.        catch (Exception e) {
10.           system.debug('error in line>> ' + e.getLineNumber() + ' and er-
    ror is: ' +
11.                            e.getMessage());
12.       }
13.    }
14. }
```

As you can see, if something fails while inserting an account, it will automatically go to catch and debug the line number and issue.

Debug log category

Salesforce can create a log on the following. We can set the following categories as we want, to see in the log by choosing each category and its level:

- **Database**: Info regarding **Data Manipulation Language (DML)**, **Salesforce Object Search Language (SOSL)**, **Salesforce Object Query Language (SOQL)**.
- Workflow
- **Validation**: All validation rule and result true or false.
- **Callout**: API call
- **Apex Code**: Execution of Apex code
- **Visualforce (VF)**: VF page detail from view state and render/serializing
- **System**: Like `sytem.debug`

Debug log level

Each log includes one of the following levels for each category. Each level decides what we want to see in the log (none means nothing will be debugged) and so on:

- NONE
- ERROR
- WARN
- INFO
- DEBUG
- FINE
- FINER
- FINEST

The preceding levels are listed as lowest to highest; mostly, a log starts with the INFO level.

Levels are cumulative, so if we select FINER, it will include DEBUG, INFO, WARN, and FINE.

Example of debug log line

Every debug log line looks like the following:

```
16:52:21.071 (55856000)|DML_BEGIN|[5]|Op:Insert|Type:Account|Rows:1
Time stamp   15:51:01.071
and then event identifier
DML_BEGIN : event Name
```

`[15]: line number of Apex`

Similarly, it is an insert operation on the Account object, and 1 row is being inserted:

a. `16:52:21.071 (55856000)| USER_DEBUG | [6]| DEBUG| debug testing`

Now, you can see that if we used **system.debug('debug testing');** in line no 6, the preceding log will be recorded.

Apex uses exceptions to record errors and other events that disrupt the normal flow of code execution. Throw statements can be used to generate exceptions, try, catch, and finally to recover from an exception.

Types of exceptions

Salesforce Apex supports several inbuilt exceptions, including the following:

- **ListException**: Any problem with a list like an index out of the bounding.
- **DmlException:** Any problem with DML, like error before insert.
- **NullPointerException:** Problem with dereferencing a null variable.
- **QueryException**: Problem with a query, like an assignment with no record or more than one record when using a single record assignment.
- **SObjectException:** Related to sObject, like trying to update a formula field by update statement or query a record without a field in SOQL

Consider the following example:

```
1. public void mthd() {
2.     Account acc = new Account().
3.     try {
4.         insertacc;
5.     } catch (DMLException e) {
6.         system.debug('error in line>> ' + e.getLineNumber() + ' and
   error is: ' + e.getMessage());
7.     }
8. }
```

We can create our custom exception; the following is a sample:

```
1. public class CustomException1 extends Exception {}
```

The extends exception is necessary here.

An example of the custom exception will be as follows:

```
1.  // Define two custom exceptions
1. public class CustomException1 extends Exception {}
2. public class CustomException2 extends Exception {}
```

```
3. try {
4.     Integer y;
5.     // Your code here
6.     if (y > 5) throw new CustomException1('This is greater');
7. } catch (CustomException2 e) {
8.     // This catches the other
9. }
```

Developer console

According to trailhead developer, the console is like an **Integrated Development Environment** (**IDE**) where you can create, debug, and test apps in your org. According to Salesforce, the developer console can be defined as follows:

- It is your one-stop solution for a variety of development tasks.
- Navigate, open, create, and edit Apex classes and triggers, Aura components, and VF pages and components.
- Browse packages that you have created or installed in your org.
- Generate logs for debugging and analyze them using different perspectives.
- Write and execute SOQL and SOSL queries to find, create, and update the records in your org.
- Test your Apex code to ensure that it is error free.
- Identify and resolve errors by setting checkpoints in your Apex code.

The structure of developer console looks like it has two sections: Main, where we code, and Tabs, where we see the log, query or test class results, etc.

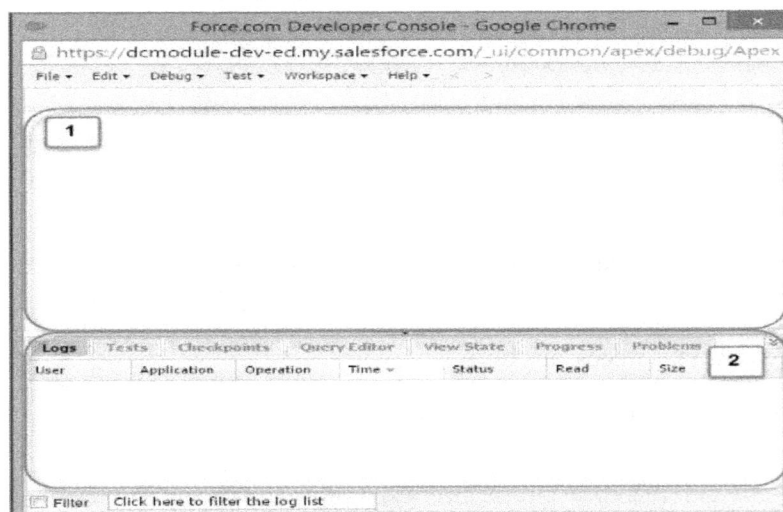

Figure 22.6: Developer console pane

The *main pane (1)* is the source code editor, where you can write, view, and modify your code. The *tabs pane (2)* is where you can view logs, errors, and other information and write queries to interact with the records in your org.

Log analyzer

Go to Debug and View log panel for any log. You will see all seven panels:

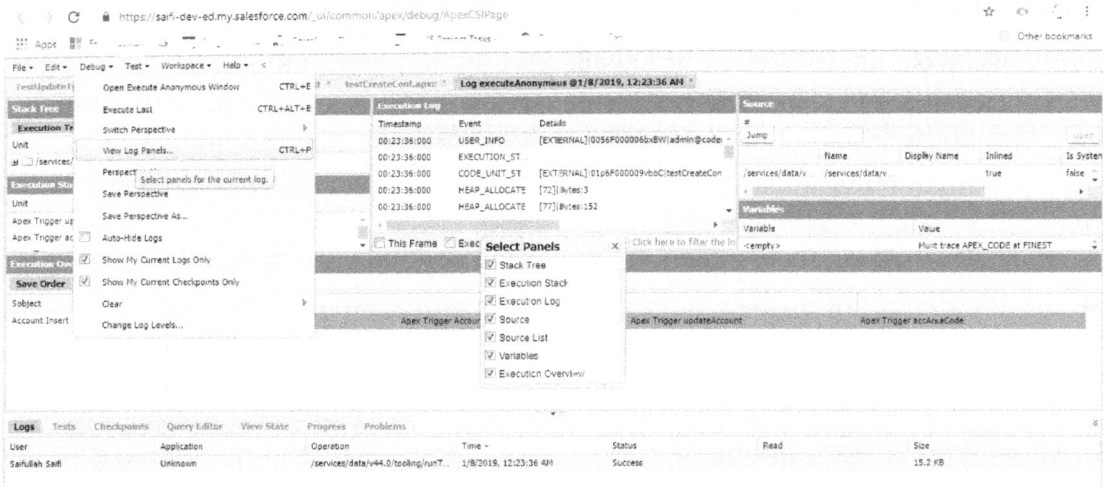

Figure 22.7: Developer console panel

According to Salesforce log, the inspector panels are as follows:

- **Stack Tree:** Displays log entries within the hierarchy of their objects and their execution using a top-down tree view. For instance, if one class calls a second class, the second class is shown as the child of the first.

- **Execution Stack:** Displays a bottom-up view of the selected item. It displays the log entry, followed by the operation that called it.

- **Execution Log:** Displays every action that occurred during the execution of your code.

- **Source:** Displays the contents of the source file, indicating the line of code being run when the selected log entry was generated.

- **Source List:** Displays the context of the code being executed when the event was logged. For example, if you select the log entry generated when the faulty email address value was entered, the Source List shows **execute_anonymous_apex**.

- **Variables**: Displays the variables and their assigned values that were in scope when the code that generated the selected log entry was run.

- **Execution Overview**: Displays statistics for the code being executed, including the execution time and heap size.

Sandbox

Sandbox is a development environment where we can write logic and code, customize it, and deploy it to live production org once testing is complete. It is available in Salesforce Professional, Enterprise, Performance, Unlimited, and Database.com editions.

There are four types of sandboxes, which are as follows:

- **Developer sandbox**: This sandbox is best suitable for development and testing; it will copy no data from production except metadata like code, workflows, object, etc. It has limited storage of 200MB.

- **Developer Pro sandbox**: It is a copy of production configuration data with large data sets.

- **Partial sandbox**: Using this sandbox, we can copy some records and templates of production with all metadata.

- **Full sandbox:** This sandbox is just a clone or a full copy of production used for real-time testing.

The details of the size and when we can refresh these sandboxes are as follows:

SANDBOX TYPE	REFRESH INTERVAL	STORAGE LIMIT
Developer Sandbox	1 day	Data storage: 200 MB
		File storage: 200 MB
Developer Pro Sandbox	1 day	Data storage: 1 GB
		File storage: 1 GB
Partial Copy Sandbox	5 days	Data storage: 5 GB
		File storage: 5 GB
Full Sandbox	29 days	Same as your production org

SANDBOX TYPE	PROFESSIONAL EDITION	PERFORMANCE EDITION	UNLIMITED EDITION	ENTERPRISE EDITION
Developer Sandbox	10	100	100	25
Developer Pro Sandbox		5	5	
Partial Copy Sandbox		1	1	1
Full Sandbox		1	1	

Figure 22.8: Sandbox type

Deployment

As we know, we cannot develop Apex in Salesforce production org, so it is done in a sandbox or a Developer Edition org.

We can deploy Apex in production using:

- Changesets
- DevOps CentrerSOAP API
- Third-party tools that use Metadata API or Tooling API
- VS Code with Salesforce DX plug-ins

In your developer org, you cannot do the exact deployment, because this org is only for learning purposes. Here, we will learn the basic concepts and its processes.

Changeset

The changeset is only available in Performance, Unlimited, and Enterprise orgs of Salesforce, where we have the sandbox and Production. So, we will first complete the deployment settings. There are two types of changeset, as shown in the following figure:

- **Outbound**: When we send an Apex code/component from this org to other.
- **Inbound**: When we receive an Apex code/component from another connected org to this org:

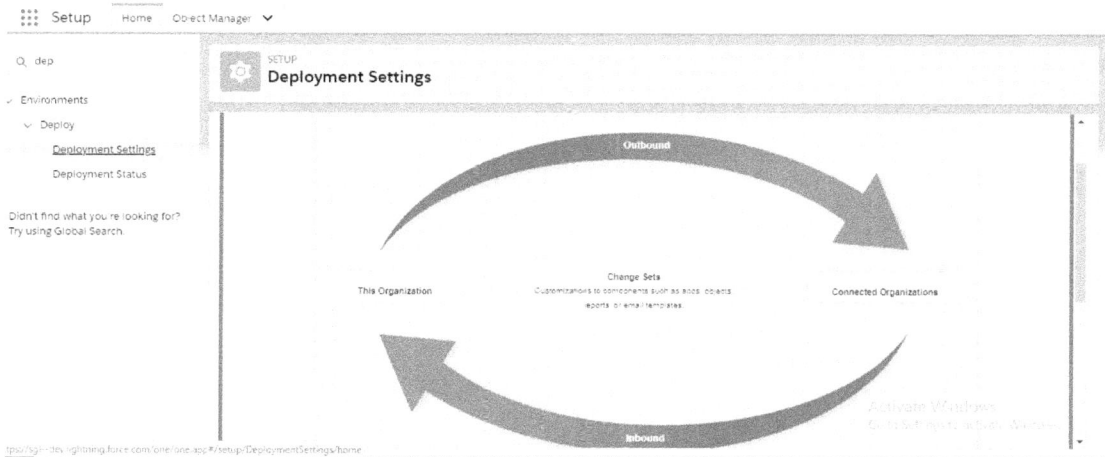

Figure 22.9: Deployments Setting landing page

When you see the **Deployment Setting**, you will see all connected org, like all sandbox and Production:

Figure 22.10: Deployment Setting page

Here, two org are connected with dev org, and the first line shows a green, two-way arrow, which means we can make outbound changeset and accept inbound from production org. However, the second one is red and broken, which means no changeset allowed; we can edit it and click on the checkbox from both org.

In the changeset, we can add components like profile, objects, fields, workflow, approval process, etc., and Apex code (Apex class, Apex trigger, with their respective test classes), VF page, and lightning component. Go to Outbound Changeset and click on New:

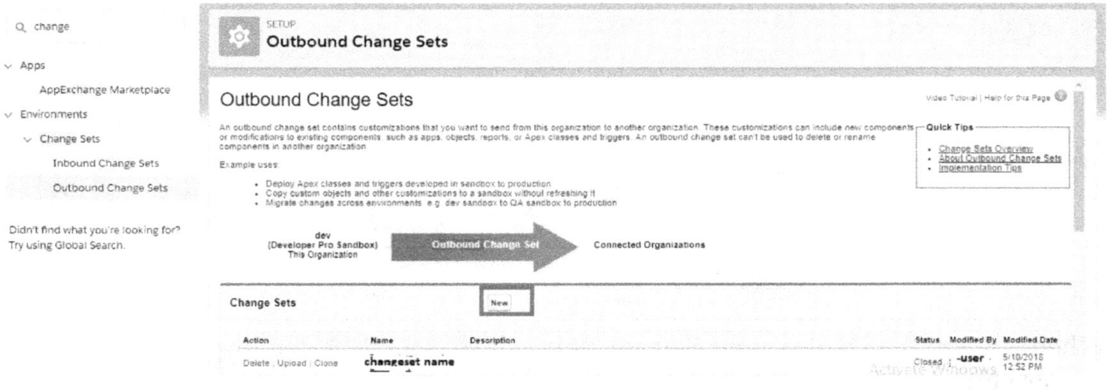

Figure 22.11: Outbound changeset

Type the changeset name and the description of what you want to deploy and add:

Change Set
test
« Back to List: Outbound Change Sets

A change set contains customizations to components such as apps, objects, reports or email templates. You can use change sets to move customizations from one organization to anothe

After a change set has been uploaded, its components aren't refreshed and you can't add or remove components. To refresh the source of components and modify the component list, clo

Change Set Detail		Edit	Delete	Upload	Clone			

	Change Set Name	test				Status	Open
	Description						
	Created By	SFDC App Devs, 02/04/2025, 8:55 am				Modified By	SFDC App Devs, 02/04/2025, 8:55 am

Edit   Delete   Upload   Clone

Change Set Components   Add   View/Add Dependencies

Action	Name	Parent Object	Type	API Name
Remove	IQ_AccountTriggerTest		Apex Class	IQ_AccountTriggerTest
Remove	IQ_Analytics		Apex Class	IQ_Analytics

Figure 22.12 (c): Deployment changeset creation

We can create a new changeset and give the name and description of what we are deploying:

Choose components to add to your change set.

Add To Change Set   Cancel

Component Type: Apex Class

	Name ↑
☐	ChangePasswordController
☐	ChangePasswordControllerTest
☐	ForgotPasswordController
☐	ForgotPasswordControllerTest
☐	IQ_AccountTriggerHandler
☐	IQ_AccountTriggerTest
☐	IQ_Analytics
☐	IQ_AnalyticsEvent
☐	IQ_AnalyticsTest
☐	IQ_BatchDeleteJob
☐	IQ_Constant
☐	IQ_ContactJobChangedQueryBatch
☐	IQ_ContactJobChangedQueryBatchTest
☐	IQ_ContactJobChangeQuerySchedule

Figure 22.12 (b): Deployment changeset page

After saving, we will add the component we want to deploy. When we click on add component, we will see all types of components, like Apex class, App, trigger, etc.; we will choose and add accordingly. Remember that every field and object related to any Apex code or workflow/approval process should be included, and the test class is necessary for an Apex code. After adding it, we can upload it to Production.

In the Production, open inbound changeset; you will see the same name that you uploaded in the outbound changeset of sandboxes. It will appear in approximately 5-30 minutes. You can now deploy it after validating. If you are deploying the Apex class or Apex Trigger, you need to put the test class name while validating, Now, choose how to validate, and wait for the validation changeset status. Then, you can deploy it:

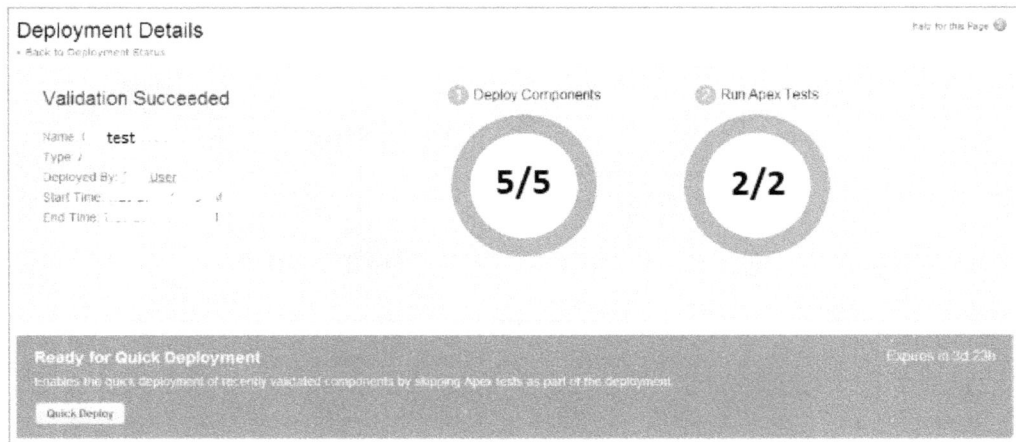

Figure 22.13: Deployment Status page

DevOps Center

DevOps Center is a salesforce tool provided for admin and developer to release the product in a seamless manner with low code/no code approach. For now, GitHub is the only current source control system supported for DevOps Center.

The following terms will be useful on how to use it:

- **Releases**: Any set of changes will be added into a release. We can divide a release into one or more user stories.
- **User stories**: With the discussion between the team the same set of work can be added here. A user story can relate to one or more work items.
- **Work items**: It will only add a list of metadata items that are being changed. The item will send through the pipeline stages from dev orgs through to production.
- **Pipelines and stages**: These are the steps in sequential order for orgs (stages) that the work item is pushed (promoted) through from dev to prod.

- **Source control**: Behind the scenes, the DevOps Center manages all GitHub branches, including moving metadata between branches, and the Salesforce orgs.

With DevOps Center:

- Changes are tracked automatically.
- Everyone can work independently, and the GitHub repository is the source of truth.
- Everyone has the visibility of everyone's work.

You have already learnt how to use Visual studio code and deploy the code using VS Code in *Chapter 18, Basic of Lightning Web Components*.

There are multiple 3rd Party tools that can be used for deployment as it helps developers streamline the deployment with less effort and it is useful for big projects. Some of the popular tools are *Copado, Gearset, AutoRABIT, Flosum, Blue Canvas, Prodiy*, and *Opsera*. Some of the useful features they provide are the following:

- Responsive UI
- Code Scan tool
- Impact analysis
- Review Reports

AppExchange

AppExchange is the marketplace for all things Salesforce, including apps, Lightning components, and Flow solutions.

AppExchange provides us with a ready-to-use application, a small module, or help.

AppExchange gives two things: solution and consultant. The solution is an add on for a Salesforce product, like survey tool for Service Cloud, Lightning Component, or other modules. Consultants are Salesforce professionals who provide solutions or design the system.

On AppExchange, some solutions are free, like the Salesforcelab products, and some have pricing as well.

According to Salesforce, there is an app that meets your needs if you are short on time and do not want to build a solution from scratch. That third-party service your users have been asking you to integrate? It is available on AppExchange! Since it is the official Salesforce store, everything you expect, like security and trust, carries over to the listings.

 is the link of AppExchange where we can see 4000 plus solution with more than 7 million installations, as shown in the following figure:

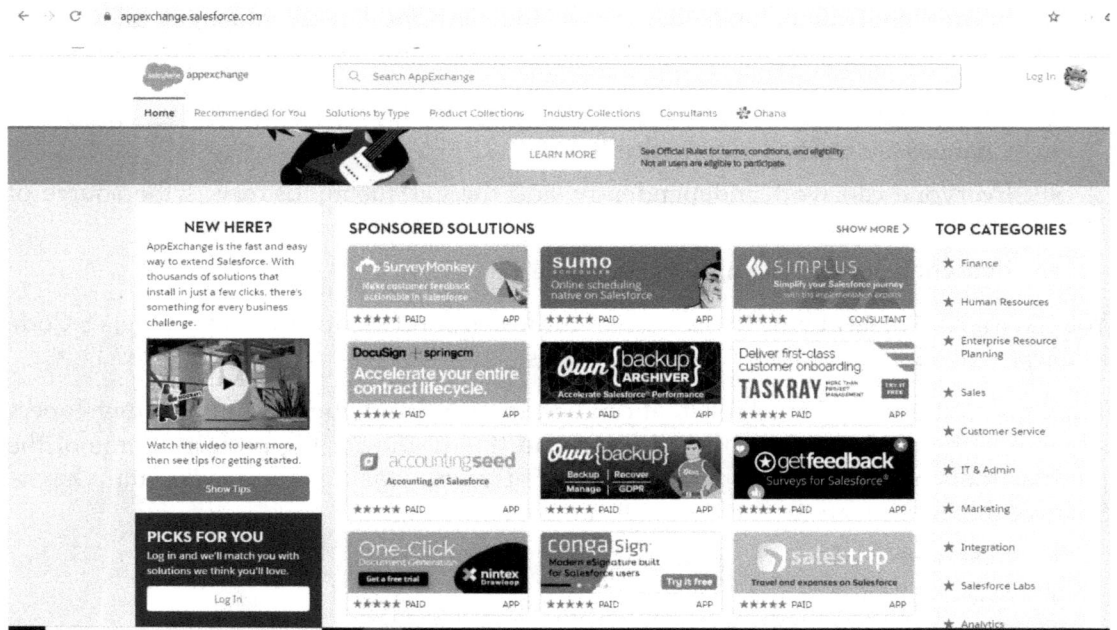

Figure 22.14: *AppExchange homepage*

Now, how can we use AppExchange more efficiently? It looks like Trailhead has answers:

Criterion	Requirements
Solution type	Solution or consultant? You have limited resources for this project, so you really prefer something that works out of the box. That probably means a solution, such as an app.
Functionality	You need user adoption data, such as who's logging in most often. It'd also be nice to know which features they're using, but that's not essential.
Budget	Free, if possible.
Stakeholder needs	You definitely want to share the data that you gather with Ursa Major's managers. They love visuals, so it would be great to show that data in a chart or graph.
Testing	You have a Developer Edition org that you use for trying out new features and completing Trailhead challenges.
Technical considerations	Compatible with Lightning Experience.

Perfect, you've got a strategy. Off to AppExchange.

Figure 22.15: *AppExchange Use case*

Now, we will install an app from AppExchange named *Project and Task Management*. We will search for it on AppExchange:

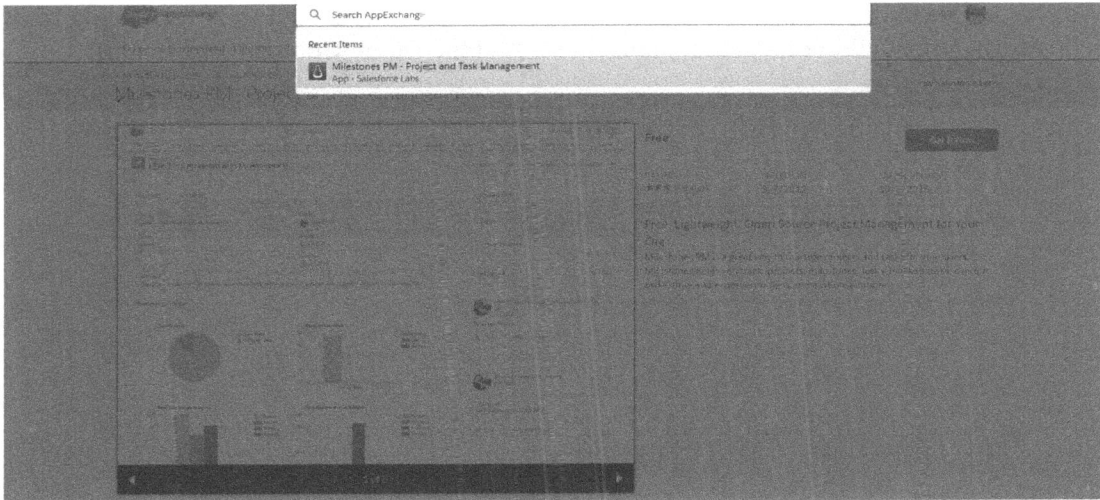

Figure 22.16: AppExchange

We can read reviews and descriptions before installing it. Then, we will click on **Get it now**:

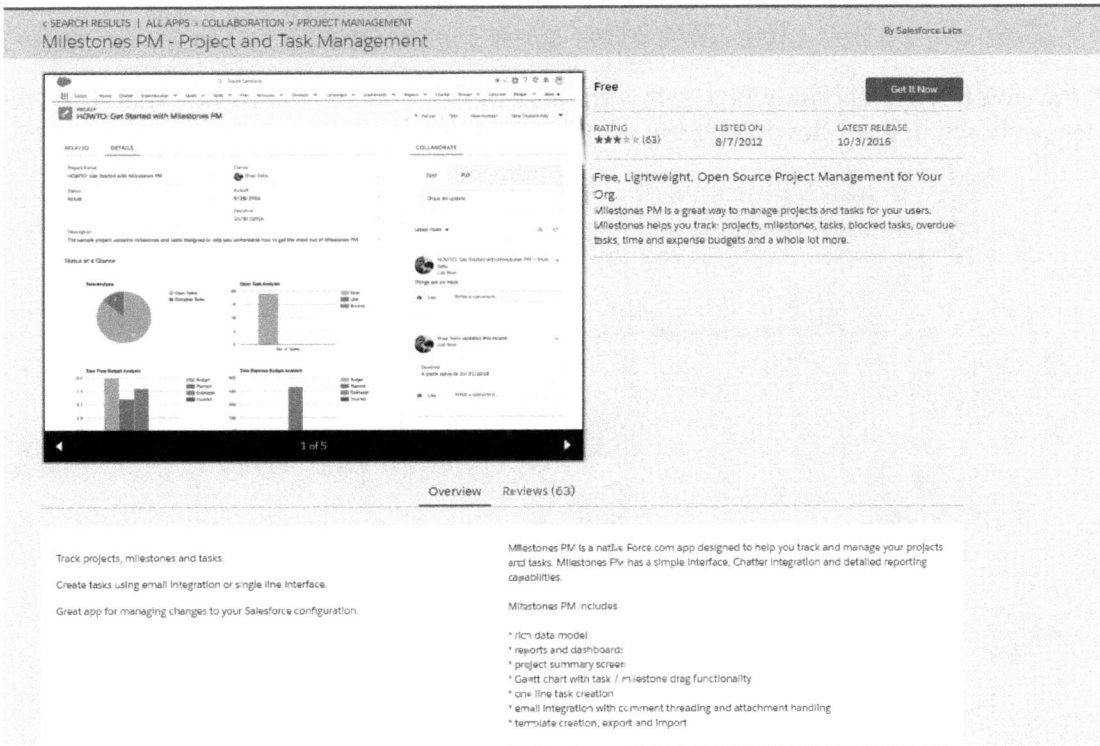

Figure 22.17: AppExchange package

We will log in to our Salesforce developer or sandbox org to install it. After we log in, it will ask the production or sandbox, and then we will click on **Confirm and install**:

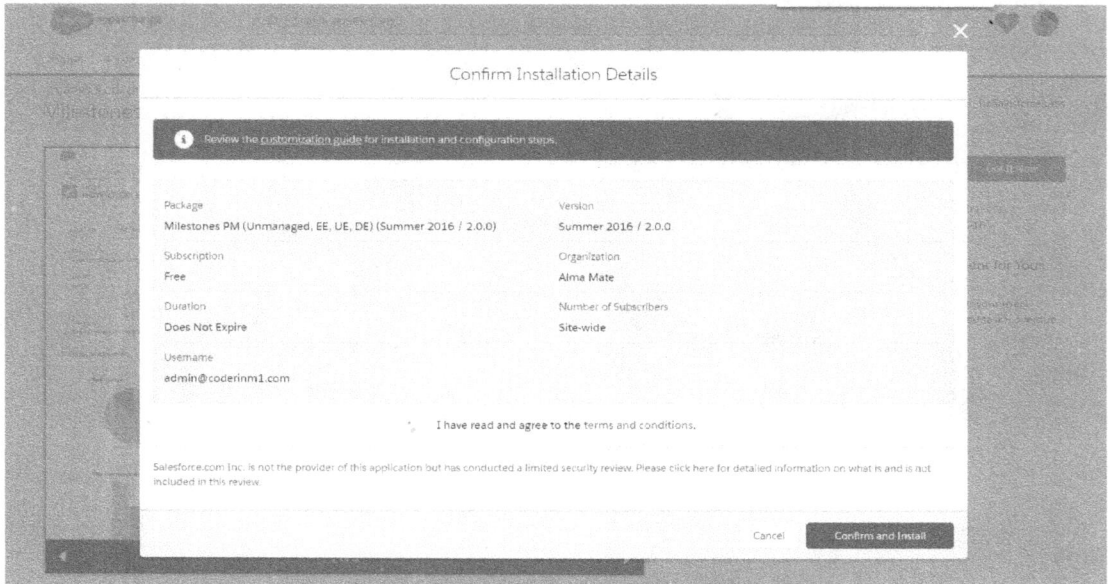

Figure 22.18: Package installation AppExchange

Now, you have to choose whether it is for all users or only for the admin, then click on Install shown in the following figure:

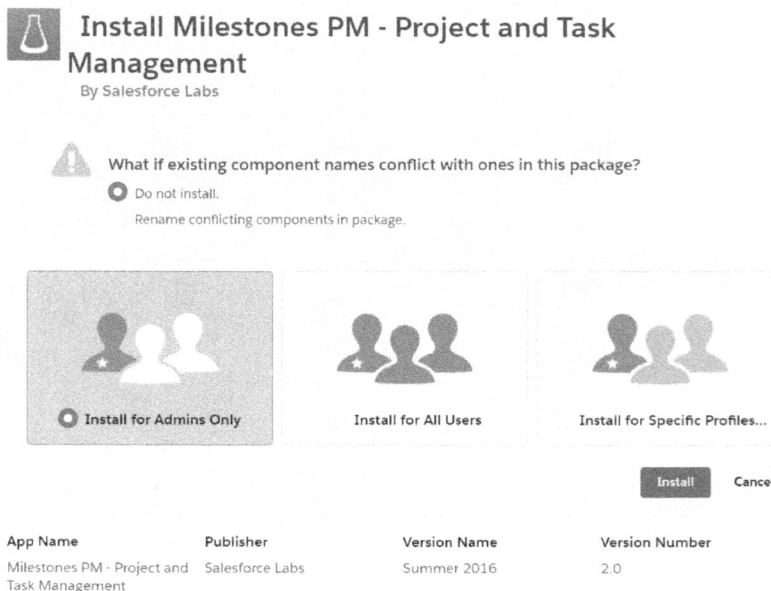

Figure 22.19: Package installation Setup

You will see the next window showing the message Installing; sometimes, it takes up to 30 minutes to install:

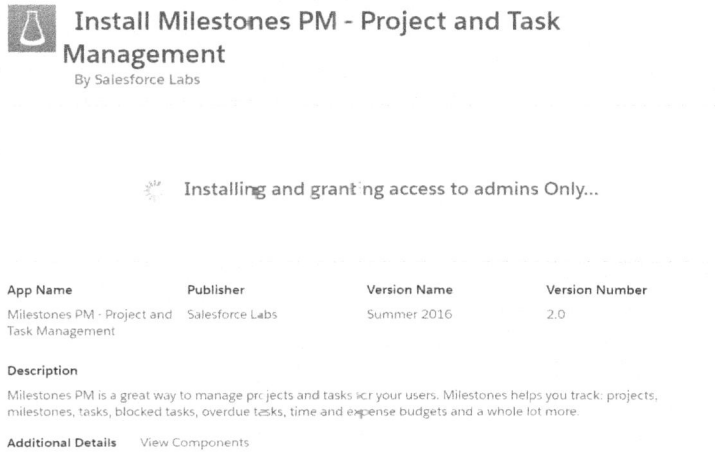

Install Milestones PM - Project and Task Management
By Salesforce Labs

Installing and granting access to admins Only...

App Name	Publisher	Version Name	Version Number
Milestones PM - Project and Task Management	Salesforce Labs	Summer 2016	2.0

Description

Milestones PM is a great way to manage projects and tasks for your users. Milestones helps you track: projects, milestones, tasks, blocked tasks, overdue tasks, time and expense budgets and a whole lot more.

Additional Details   View Components

Figure 22.20: Package installation status

After this, the app will be shown in your Salesforce org, and you can use it directly.

The apps on AppExchange are of the following two types:

- **Managed Package**: Publisher can update them.
- **Unmanaged Package**: Publishers cannot update them.

The following can publish applications on AppExchange:

- Third-party developers.
- Force.com labs.
- **Independent Software Vendors (ISV)**

You can publish your idea/solution on AppExchange in the following ways:

- Join the Salesforce community and be an ISV (Salesforce Partners).
- Build your app in developer org. Make two developer org to build solutions.
- In one org, perform development and build the package in the other one; the package is collection of your development, class, object, field, trigger, component, etc.

Making a package

Go to Setup, search for **Package Manager**, and click on **New**:

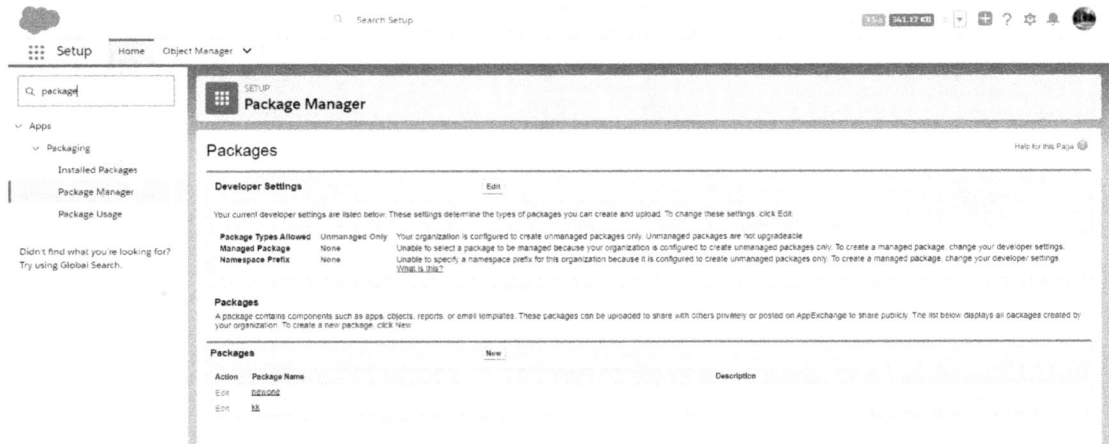

Figure 22.21: Package setup page

Type the name of the package add language and description; then, click on **Save**:

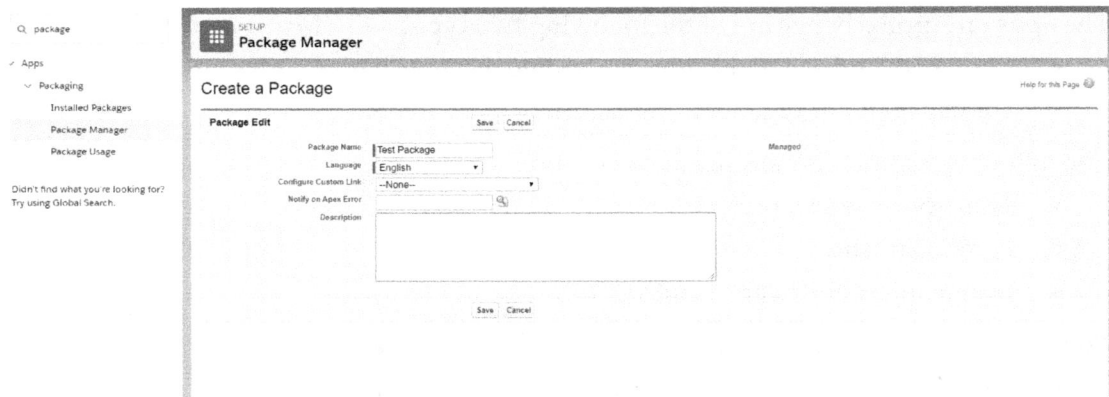

Figure 22.22: Create Package setup

Now, you can add any field object or class in the package:

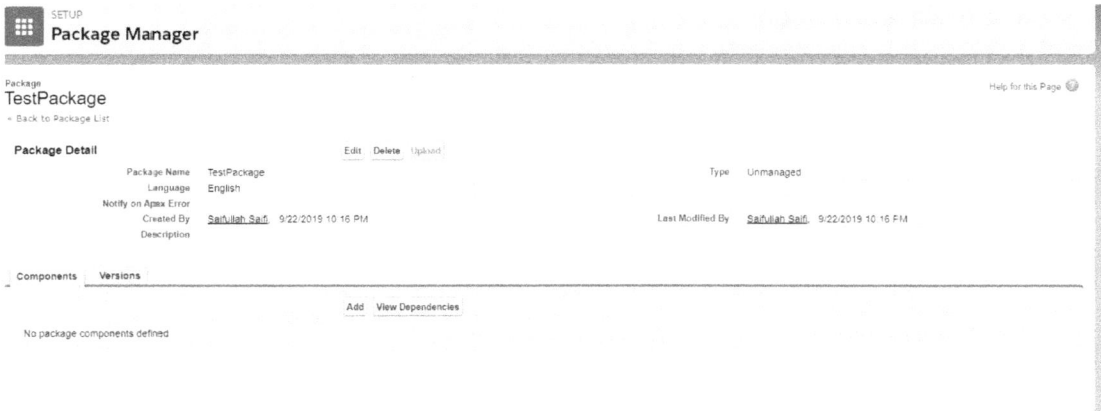

Figure 22.23: Package detail

Now that you have developed something and packaged it, test it thoroughly.

- Design the page on AppExchange by putting the demo, screenshots, and description for users.
- You can search the ISV guide to publish your package; you can connect your org and upload your app.
- Then, you have to wait. The Salesforce security review will check your application because every app on the AppExchange must go through a mandatory review, which assesses the app's security posture.
- You will pass the review, after which you can publish. It will be available on the AppExchange list.

Conclusion

In this chapter, we learned how to debug our code and deploy it from testing to a live environment. We also covered the developer console and looked at its features.

We explored multiple deployment tools, like Changeset and ANT Tool, and we also studied how AppExchange is useful for Salesforce and us.

Questions

1. **What possible source and destination pair can send or receive changesets? (Choose 2 answers).**

   a. Developer Edition to Sandbox

   b. Sandbox to Production

c. Sandbox to sandbox

d. Developer Edition to Production

2. **Which of these statements about changeset deployments are accurate? (Choose 3 answers)**

a. They use an all or none deployment model.

b. They require a deployment connection.

c. They can be used to transfer contact records.

d. They can be used to deploy custom settings data.

e. They can be used only between related organizations.

3. **Does developer sandbox has all the code from Production?**

4. **Can you run the SOQL query using the developer console?**

Answers

1. b,c
2. a, b, e
3. Yes, code will be copied, but not data.
4. Yes, there is a query editor in Tabs pane below.

Join our Discord space

Join our Discord workspace for latest updates, offers, tech happenings around the world, new releases, and sessions with the authors:

https://discord.bpbonline.com

Certification Exam Guide Paper 1

Certification mapping with the chapters

Here, we will show chapter wise mapping for every certificate. Take a look into this table:

#	Module	Admin	App Builder	Dev I
1	Introduction to Cloud Computing		☒	
2	Introduction to Salesforce	☒	☒	☒
3	Introducing Salesforce Lightning and Salesforce Data Modeling		☒	
4	Introducing Salesforce Customer Relationship Management	☒	☒	☒
5	Organizational Set up	☒		
6	Designing Applications on Force.com	☒	☒	
7	Implementing Business Processes	☒		☒
8	Data Management	☒	☒	☒

#	Module	Admin	App Builder	Dev I
9	Data Analytics - Reports & Dashboards	☒	☒	
10	SECURITY AND ACCESS	☒	☒	
11	Introduction to Chatter	☒		
12	Mobile Administration	☒		
13	Programming with Apex		☒	☒
14	Use SOQL & SOSL		☒	☒
15	DML Essentials		☒	☒
16	Trigger Essential		☒	☒
17	Creating Visualforce Pages			☒
18	Basic of Lightning Web Component			☒
19	More Customization Less Programming		☒	☒
20	Testing Essentials			☒
21	Apex Handler and Use of Apex class		☒	☒
22	Debugging & Deployment		☒	☒

Table 24.1: Certificate and chapter classification

Salesforce Certified Administrator

The Salesforce Certified Administrator program is designed for individuals who have experience as a Salesforce administrator. The program encompasses the breadth of applications, the features and functions available to an end user, and the configuration and management options available to an administrator across the Sales, Service, and Collaboration Clouds.

The first credential in the program is the Salesforce Certified Administrator. This credential focuses on the features and functionality used to maintain a Salesforce implementation. The second level in the program is the Salesforce Certified Advanced Administrator. This credential is targeted toward the Salesforce Certified Administrator who has mastered Salesforce configuration maintenance, can demonstrate an understanding of administration best practices, and can use the advanced features and functionality to solve a variety of business problems.

Examination outline

The Salesforce Administrator exam measures a candidate's knowledge and skills related to the following objectives. A candidate should have hands-on experience as a Salesforce Administrator and have demonstrated the application of each of the features/functions mentioned in the following table:

#	Topic	Exam Weight %
1	Organization Setup	3
2	User Setup	7
3	Security and access	13
4	Standard and custom objects	14
5	Sales and marketing applications	14
6	Service and support applications	13
7	Activity management and collaboration	3
8	Data management	10
9	Analytics - reports and Dashboards	10
10	workflow/process automation	8
11	Desltop and mobile administration	3
12	appexchange	2

Table 24.2: Admin exam weightage

The weightage can also be seen in the following figure:

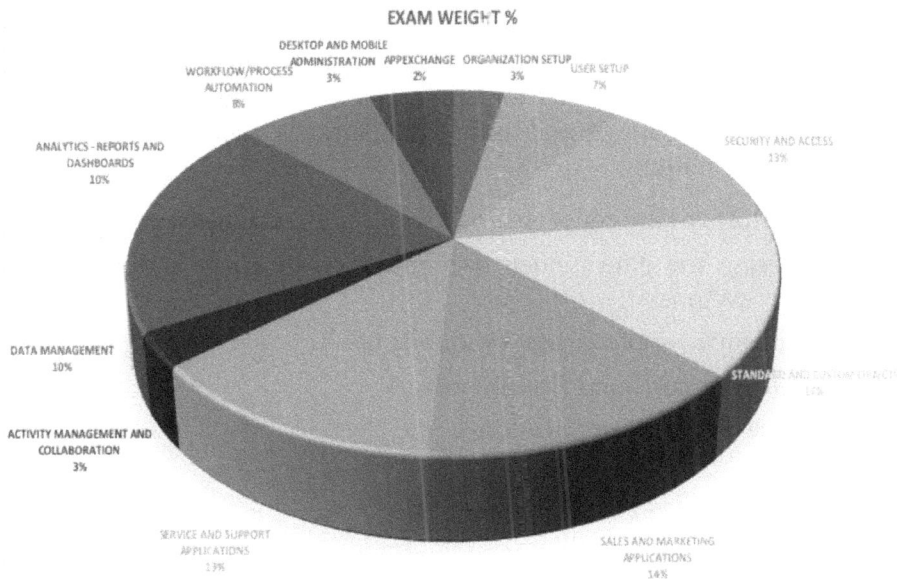

Figure 24.1: Admin chart Weightage

About the exam

Read on for details about the Salesforce Administrator exam.

- **Content**: 60 multiple-choice/multiple-select questions
- **Time allotted to complete the exam**: 105 minutes
- **Passing score**: 65%
- **Registration fee**: USD 200 plus applicable taxes as required per local law.
- **Retake fee**: USD 100 plus applicable taxes as required per local law.
- **Delivery options**: Proctored exam delivered onsite at a testing center or in an online proctored environment. Click here for information on scheduling an exam.
- **References**: No hard-copy or online materials may be referenced during the exam.
- **Prerequisite**: None required; course attendance highly recommended.

Note: **The certification guidelines may vary from time to time. For updated information, please visit below link:**

https://trailhead.salesforce.com/help?article=Salesforce-Certified-Administrator-Exam-Guide

Salesforce Platform App Builder

The Salesforce Platform App Builder credential is designed for individuals who would like to demonstrate their skills and knowledge in designing, building, and deploying custom applications using the declarative customization capabilities of the Lightning Platform. The candidate can create, manage, and update data models, application security, business logic, and process automation.

Here are some examples of the concepts you should understand to pass the exam:

- How to design the data model, user interface, business logic, and security for custom applications.
- How to customize applications for mobile use.
- How to design reports and Dashboards.
- How to deploy custom applications.

Examination outline

The Salesforce Platform App Builder exam measures a candidate's knowledge and skills related to the following objectives. A candidate should have hands-on experience developing custom applications on the Lightning Platform and have demonstrated the application of each of the following features/functions:

#	Topic	Exam weight%
1	Salesforce fundamentals	8
2	Data modeling and management	20
3	Security	10
4	Buisness Logic and process automation	27
5	Social	3
6	User interface	14
7	Reporting	5
8	Mobile	5
9	App Development	8

Table A.3: App builder exam weightage

The weightage can also be seen in the following figure:

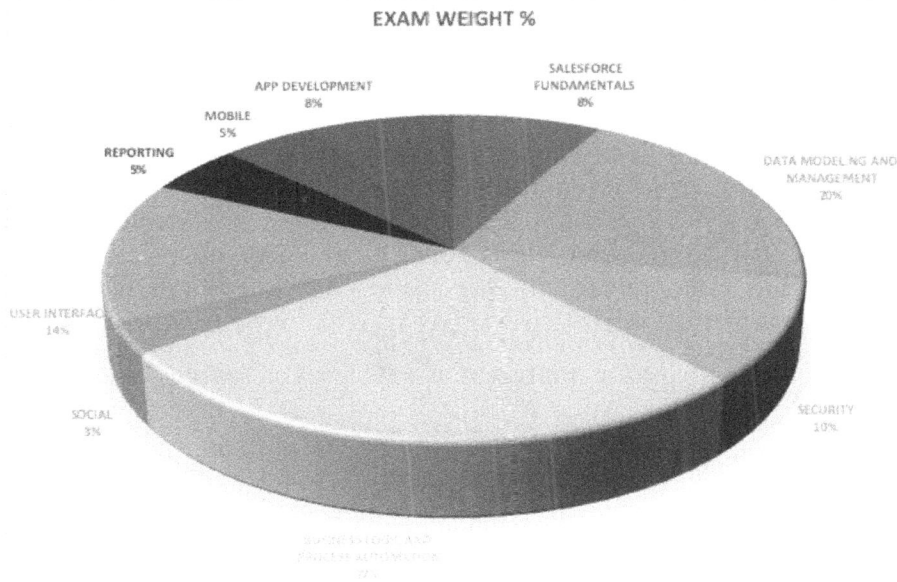

Figure 24.2: App builder chart weightage

About the exam

Read on for details about the Salesforce Platform App Builder exam:

- **Content**: 60 multiple-choice/multiple-select questions

- **Time allotted to complete the exam**: 105 minutes
- **Passing score**: 63%
- **Registration fee**: USD 200, plus applicable taxes as required per local law.
- **Retake fee**: USD 100, plus applicable taxes as required per local law.
- **Delivery options**: Proctored exam delivered onsite at a testing center or in an online proctored environment.
- **References**: No hard-copy or online materials may be referenced during the exam.
- **Prerequisite**: None

Note: **The certification guidelines may vary from time to time. For updated information, please visit below link:**

https://trailhead.salesforce.com/help?article=Salesforce-Certified-Platform-App-Builder-Exam-Guide

Salesforce Certified Platform Developer I

The Salesforce Platform Developer I credential is intended for individuals who have the knowledge, skills, and experience in building custom applications on the Lightning Platform.

This credential encompasses the fundamental programmatic capabilities of the Lightning Platform to develop custom business logic and interfaces to extend Salesforce using Apex and Visualforce. To achieve this credential, a candidate must successfully pass the Salesforce Platform Developer I exam. This exam is also a prerequisite to the Salesforce Platform Developer II Multiple Choice exam.

This exam guide provides information about the Salesforce Platform Developer I exam.

Examination outline

The Salesforce Platform Developer I exam measures a candidate's knowledge and skills related to the following objectives. A candidate should have hands-on experience developing custom applications on the Lightning Platform and have demonstrated the application of each of the following features/functions:

#	Topic	Exam Weight %
1	Salesforce fundamentals	10
2	Data Modeling and Management	12
3	Logic and process automation	46
4	User interface	10

#	Topic	Exam Weight %
5	Testing	12
6	Debug and deployment tools	1C

Table A.4: Dev I Weightage

The weightage can also be seen in the following figure:

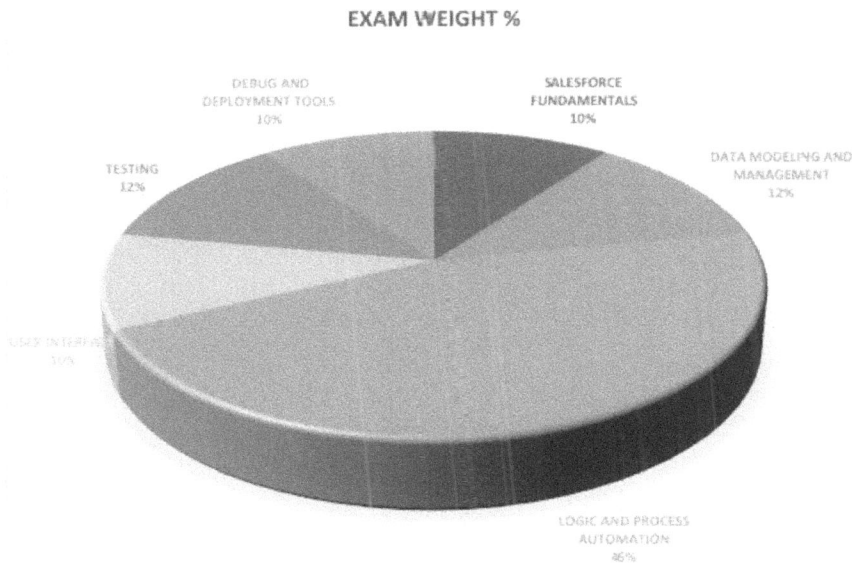

Figure 24.3: Dev I Weightage chart

About the exam

Read on for details about the Salesforce Platform Developer I exam:

- **Content**: 60 multiple-choice/multiple-select questions
- **Time allotted to complete the exam**: 110 minutes
- **Passing score**: 65%
- **Registration fee**: USD 200, plus applicable taxes as required per local law.
- **Retake fee**: USD 100, plus applicable taxes as required per local law.
- **Delivery options**: Proctored exam delivered onsite at a testing center or in an online proctored environment.
- **References**: No hard-copy or online materials may be referenced during the exam.
- **Prerequisite**: None.

Note: The certification guidelines may vary from time to time. For updated information, please visit below link:

https://trailhead.salesforce.com/help?article=Salesforce-Certified-Platform-Developer-I-Exam-Guide

Join our Discord space

Join our Discord workspace for latest updates, offers, tech happenings around the world, new releases, and sessions with the authors:

https://discord.bpbonline.com

Certification Exam Sample Paper 2

Salesforce Certified Administrator Sample Paper

1. **How many User records can be imported via Import Wizard?**
   a. 500
   b. 5,000
   c. 50,000
   d. User Records cannot be imported via Import Wizard

2. **Which of the following is true about Page layouts?**
   a. Control the layout and organization of detail and edit pages.
   b. Control which fields, related lists, and custom links users see, on detail and edit pages only.
   c. Control which standard and custom buttons display on detail pages and related lists.
   d. Determine whether fields are visible, read only, or required on detail and edit pages only.
   e. All of the above.

3. **When a field is deleted from the page layout, does it is also deleted from the Object?**

    a. Yes

    b. No

4. **If a Report is run that returns 20,000 records, then what happens?**

    a. All 20K records are displayed in the UI.

    b. First 2K records are displayed in the UI.

    c. 10 Reports each having 2K records are created.

    d. Report Fails and an error is reported.

5. **Which of the following statements is True?**

    a. Tasks allow you to track the specific actions you plan to perform or have performed; Email Alerts.

    b. Cannot track specific actions.

    c. Email Alerts allow you to track the specific actions you plan to perform or have performed, Tasks.

    d. Cannot track specific actions.

    e. Email Alerts and Tasks allow you to track the specific actions you plan to perform or have performed.

    f. Email Alerts and Tasks cannot track the specific actions you plan to perform or have performed.

6. **Which of the following is used for automatically opening records by an administrator when they meet**

    a. A data Trigger point?

    b. Manual sharing

    c. Criteria-based sharing Rules

    d. OWD

    e. None of the Above

7. **Which combination of objects is available when creating a custom report type for Chatter reports?**

    a. Choose 2 Opportunities, Followers, User Feed.

    b. Accounts, User Feed, Comments.

    c. Users, User Feed, Comments.

    d. Chatter Groups, Members.

8. **Which of the following statements are true about Data Validation?**
   a. Validation rules apply to all new and updated records for an object.
   b. Validation rules can update fields which are not included in a page layout.
   c. Validation rules can reference fields which are not included in a page layout.
   d. If an error message is not set, a default message will be prompted instead.
   e. All of the above.
   f. None of the Above

9. **The number of formulas in a Custom summary formula is limited to how many?**
   a. 5000
   b. 3900
   c. 4000
   d. 3000

10. **The list view can (Choose all that apply).**
    a. Show up to 2000 records in the record count display.
    b. Print up to 1000 records in print view.
    c. Be enabled and disabled by individual users.
    d. Print list can be exported to excel.

11. **Which of the following are Customizable Related Lists? Choose 3 answers.**
    a. Open Activities
    b. Notes & Attachments
    c. Activity History.
    d. HTML Email Status.

12. **The Sharing Setting for Contacts is "Controlled by Parent". John has a profile that has Create Permission on contacts. Which of the following is true?**
    a. If John has Read and Edit permissions only on Accounts he can only Read and Edit Contacts.
    b. John will not be able to see contacts on an Account to which is not visible to him.
    c. John can still create contacts under those accounts which are visible to him.
    d. John can still create contacts to any account.

13. **Which is a correct statement about the Console?**
    a. The Console is composed of the list view, the detail view, the mini view and the search bar.

    b. Administrators customize what displays on the console's list view, detail view, and mini view by

    c. Configuring console layouts, related objects, and mini page layouts.

    d. Users can create list views on Objects within the Console.

    e. The Console tab is just like other tabs in Salesforce except that the console can display records from

    f. Several different Salesforce Orgs all on one Console tab.

14. **Choose the correct statements about Roles and Role Hierarchy. Choose 2 answers**.

    a. Every user must be assigned to a role, or their data will not display in opportunity reports, forecast.

    b. Roll-ups, and other displays based on roles.

    c. It is always necessary to create individual roles for each title at your company, rather than define a

    d. Hierarchy of roles to control access of information entered by users in lower-level roles.

    e. When an account owner is not assigned a role, the sharing access for related contacts is Read/Write,

    f. Provided the organization-wide default for Contacts is not Controlled by Parent.

    g. To simplify user management in organizations with large numbers of users, you can enable delegated

    h. Administrators. Delegated Administrators are automatically assigned a Cloned System Administrator

    i. Profile giving them virtually all privileges of a System Administrator over the entire organization

15. **What page do you access to uninstall an app**?

    a. Critical Updates

    b. Sandbox

    c. Installed Packages

    d. Storage Usages

    e. Monitor Deployments

16. **What are good practices when creating Validation Rules? Choose 2 answers**.

    a. Creating two validation rules with contradicting criteria.

    b. Write helpful error messages. Include instructions when necessary.

    c. Activate a new validation rule upon completion of its formula and error messages so that users can.

    d. Provide feedback immediately.

    e. Since validation rules run on the Self-Service portal, make sure your validation rules do not prevent

    f. Self-Service users from creating cases

17. **Permissions are organized by Assigned Apps, Object and Tabs, App Permissions, Apex Class Access, VisualForce Page Access, System Permissions, Desktop Client Access, Login Hours, Login IP Ranges and Service Providers. Where will you go if you want to hide the Accounts from a certain User Profile and then enable Content Users assigned to the same profile to Deliver Uploaded Files and Personal Content? Choose 2 answers.**

    a. Assigned Apps

    b. Object and Tabs

    c. System Permissions

    d. App Permissions

18. **What happens when you convert a Lead? Choose 2 answers.**

    a. Leads that are members of multiple campaigns will display all associated campaigns in the Campaign Influence related list of the opportunity.

    b. The last campaign that a Lead became a member of will be listed as the Primary Campaign Source.

    c. Regardless if the lead is a member of a campaign or not, you have to manually add influential campaigns to the Campaign Influence related list.

    d. If you convert the lead from the Campaign Member Detail page of a certain campaign, that campaign will be listed as the Primary Campaign Source in the Campaign Influence Related list.

19. **Bob set up a Library to store all his team files. He added all of his direct reports as Members of that Library, including John. He then started to upload team files. All the other team members except John can view the uploaded files. What could be the problem?**

    a. Bob's User Role is not above that of John's in the Role Hierarchy.

    b. John has no Read permission to Documents.

    c. John access to the Files Tab.

    d. John is not a Salesforce CRM Content user

20. **What are the ways to create a new User Record?Choose 2 answers.**

    a. Using Insert in Dataloader.

    b. Clone Existing User Record from the detail page.

    c. Add Multiple Users option at the Users page.

    d. User Import Wizard

21. **Choose the correct statements about Holidays in Salesforce CRM: Choose 2 answers.**

    a. Holidays that are not associated with any business hours will apply to the whole Organization.

    b. Holidays enable you to specify the dates and times at which your customer support team is

    c. Unavailable.

    d. You can only delete a holiday that is not associated with any business hours.

    e. During holidays, access to Salesforce CRM is restricted.

22. **Who can create a new Campaign in Salesforce CRM?**

    a. Penny, who has a Marketing User profile although their System Administrator unchecked the Marketing User checkbox in her user record.

    b. Sheldon, who is a Marketing Executive. She has a Create permission on Campaigns and is set to be a Marketing User.

    c. Leonard, a System Administrator who is not a Marketing User.

    d. Raj has a Solution Manager profile and is set to be a Marketing User.

23. **Which of the following scenario will trigger Case Auto-Response Rules? Choose 2 answers.**

    a. Customer replied to a support representative's email.

    b. A Case is created from a web-to-case form.

    c. A customer submitted a case from the Self-Service Portal.

    d. A Case is created by the support representative during a customer call.

24. **How is access granted through the Role Hierarchy?**

    a. If the Organizational Default permits the view of a certain record to all users, a Role Hierarchy can be set up to restrict view to some users or group of users.

    b. If the Organizational Default restricts the view of a certain record to some users, a Role Hierarchy can be set up to open access to them.

c. If a Field is hidden to a Manager Profile using **Field Level Security (FLS)**, a Role Hierarchy can be set up to open visibility of the said Field to the Users with Manager Profile.

d. If a Field is hidden in the Page Layout of the Manager Profile, a Role Hierarchy can be used to open visibility of the said Field to the Users with Manager Profile.

25. **Which counts against File Storage in Salesforce CRM?**

a. Files in attachments, the Documents tab and the Files tab.

b. User Profiles, Photos and Chatter Files.

c. Google Docs, Chatter: Feed posts and tracked changes, and Quotes

26. **What are the differences between Sales and Account teams?**

a. Roles assigned to members in Account teams are based on the Account team Roles list, while that for the Sales teams are based on the Sales team Roles list. You can manage these lists of Roles separately for each team.

b. A Sales team is a group of users that typically work together on opportunities while an Account team is a team of users that work together on an account.

c. A Sales team is a group of users that typically work together on Opportunities and Leads while an account team is a team of users that work together on an account.

d. A Sales team is a subset of an Account team. The latter may be composed of one or more of the former.

e. An Account team is a subset of a Sales team. The latter may be composed of one or more of the former

27. **When using Knowledge, when can Articles be created?**

a. Upon initial post of the customer in the Answers community.

b. Upon reply to a customer's email.

c. When closing a Case.

d. Upon reply from the customer.

28. **When do you use the Import Wizard? Choose 2 answers.**

a. When updating 150 Leads records, so that a custom field in the updated records will contain a null value.

b. When updating 900 Accounts records so that the email field in the updated records will have the Marketing User's Email address.

c. When importing 1900 new records to a custom field.

d. When Mass Deleting more than 250 records at a time.

29. **What may not be specified when creating a Web Tab?**
    a. Tab Label and Tab Name.
    b. URL of a web page/site.
    c. Tab Style
    d. Content Frame Height (pixels)

30. **How does Folder access differ from Record access?**
    a. Folder Access is controlled by permissions, while Record Access is controlled by Role Hierarchy and Org-Wide Defaults.
    b. Folder Access is controlled by permissions, while Record Access is controlled by Role Hierarchy, Field Level Security and Org-Wide Defaults
    c. Folder Access is controlled by permissions, while Record Access is controlled by Field Level Security and Org-Wide Defaults.
    d. Folder Access is controlled by permissions, while Record Access is controlled by Role Hierarchy and Field Level Security.

31. **What is true if a record is "locked"? Choose 2 answers.**
    a. Salesforce prevents the record owner from editing or deleting the record.
    b. Users must have the "Modify All" object-level permission for the given object or the "Modify All Data" permission to edit the locked record.
    c. If the record is a Campaign, you cannot add campaign members to it prior to approval.
    d. You can still edit the default action for initial submission and recall actions.

32. **Which objects use Folders? Choose 3 answers.**
    a. Emails
    b. Documents
    c. Dashboards
    d. Reports

33. **Which statement is true about Fiscal Year settings in Salesforce?**
    a. When you change the Fiscal Year Start Month of a Standard Fiscal Year, you come up with a Custom Fiscal Year.
    b. When you enable Custom Fiscal Year, a default Custom Fiscal Year Template will be assigned to your Organization.
    c. Standard fiscal years can start on the first day of any month.

34. A telecom company is implementing Salesforce in its service and support department. They want to receive emails in Salesforce so that a Case will be created for new incoming emails. They also want to set it so that if an email contains words such as "frustrated", "aggravated" and the likes will automatically be routed to the Tier 2 support. What Case management features will have to be used in order to satisfy the above requirements? Choose 2 answers.

    a. Case Escalation Rules.

    b. Email to Salesforce

    c. Email to Case.

    d. Case Assignment Rules.

35. Which extra step has to be done when you invite a user to an event in Salesforce CRM if that user has a different time zone?

    a. There is no extra step because Salesforce automatically converts the users available and busy times into your time zone.

    b. You have to convert the time zone in a drop in the timezone picklist to match that of yours.

    c. If you are inviting multiple users from many different time zones you need to set the default time zone first.

    d. You can't invite a user from a different time zone. You must set all users to have similar time zone before you can send an invite.

36. Salesforce allows me to add a reporting hierarchy (or organization chart) to my contacts. This way I can better understand the structural dynamics within the businesses I am selling to and remember who to contact for certain aspects of a sale.

    a. True

    b. False

37. What type of relationship should be built for a one-to-one?

    a. Master-Detail Relationship

    b. Look-up Relationship

    c. Master-Detail Field

    d. Look-up Field

38. Which action must be taken to view contacts associated with a case in the console?

    a. The related lists of the case page layout must be modified.

    b. The custom links of the case page layout must be modified.

c. The related object of the case page layout must be modified.

d. The mini page layout of the case page layout must be modified.

39. **When configuring Customizable Forecasting, you can set which of the following Forecast Dates for determining which opportunities contribute to the forecast?**

a. Opportunity Close Date Only

b. Product Date Only

c. Schedule Date Only

d. Commit Date

e. Opportunity Close Date, Product Date, Schedule Date

40. **The difference between an opportunity record type and a sales process is:**

a. The sales process controls the stage field, and the record type controls all other picklist fields.

b. The record type controls the stage field, and the sales process controls all other picklist fields,

c. The record type controls the picklist fields.

d. The sales process controls all picklist fields.

41. **What happens when you delete an object that is related to a junction object by a lookup relationship?**

a. The junction object is deleted.

b. The related field in the junction object is deleted.

c. The master records are deleted.

d. The intersection object is deleted.

42. **Which statements are true for the integrated campaign builder**

a. Cannot filter views by more than one campaign at a time.

b. The maximum number of Leads/Contacts that can be added from a report at one time is 50,000.

c. The maximum number of Leads/Contacts that can be added from the wizard at one time is 250.

d. Can add converted leads to a campaign.

e. Integrated campaign builder views are not exposed through the Force.com API.

43. Multiple Approvers have received your request for approving a discount that was invoked by the approval process? Approver A rejects your request. Approver B accepts your request after Approver A rejects it. Is your request approved or denied? (Assume you need only one person to approve out of all the approvers)

    a. Approved

    b. Denied

    c. Approval process is revoked.

    d. Approval changes to pending stage due to conflict within approvers.

44. Which of the following cannot be done by a user to records owned by others when the organization-wide default is set to Read / Write to an object?

    a. Add related records

    b. Search Records

    c. Delete records

    d. Change ownership

    e. Report on records

    f. Edit details on records

45. Org-wide default is set to private. Kathy is assigned a US Sales Director role with access rights to view opportunities owned by other users associated to her accounts. Jennifer is assigned EMEA Representative Role and Phil to US representative role. Which business opportunities can Kathy VIEW and EDIT? 3 answers

    a. KAthy can edit and view her own oppurtunities

    b. Kathy can EDIT and VIEW her jennifers oppurtunities

    c. Kathy can edit and view Phils oppurturities

    d. Kathy can view but cannot EDIT phils oppurtunities

    e. Kathy can View but cannot edit Jennifers oppurtunities

46. How would you allow collaborative access to accounts, contacts, contracts, oppurtunities, and cases of a US Sales representative, and Asia sales representative, and an EMEA sales representative?

    a. By Creating three sharing rules between them

    b. By creating a public group with all three Sales Representatives

    c. By changing the Org wide defaults

47. **The org wide default is set to private. Phil smith the owner of ABC account is a US Sales Representative reporting to the US Sales Director. The users in the US sales representative role can edit ALL opportunities associated with the accounts they own. Tim, an EMEA sales representative, owns an opportunity associated with the ABC account. Identify the correct role access. There are two correct answers.**

   a. Phil can view but cannot edit Tims ABC opportunity.

   b. TIM cannot VIEW/EDIT phils account.

   c. Phil can EDIT and VIEW Tims ABC opportunity.

   d. Tim can VIEW and EDIT Phils account.

   e. Tim can VIEW but cannot EDIT phils account.

48. **AW Computing has a discount workflow that requires approval from the Sales director when the discount is over 15% and from the VP of Global sales if the discount is over 30%. The sales representative has created a discount for 10% on a new opportunity. What happens when the sales Representative submits the request for approval?**

   a. Discount will be automatically approved.

   b. Request will be sent to the Sales director for approval.

   c. Request will be sent to Sales director and VP of Global Sales for approval.

   d. Request will be sent to VP of Global Sales for approval.

49. **Which of the following statements are true about trusted ranges?**

   a. They enable end users to activate additional IP addresses for accessing salesforce.

   b. They are used to identify regular Salesforce users

   c. They include IP addresses that are used in conjunction with a browser cookie

   d. They approve login requests from unknown browsers and IP addresses.

50. **Which step is required when configuring the new Salesforce for outlook?**

   a. Select sync direction and conflict behaviour.

   b. Select the appropriate config template.

   c. Assign users and profiles to a configuration.

   d. Enable the Chatter feed sync with Outlook.

51. **What can users do when Chatter feed tracking is enable for Dashboards? Choose 2 answers.**

   a. Follow files and links for a dashboard.

   b. Follow posts and comments for a dashboard.

c. Follow posts and comments for the dashboard source reports.

d. Auto-follow Dashboards created by the user.

52. **A sales manager would like to view a dashboard from the perspective of different users and switch between users without editing the dashboard. How would an administrator enable this?**

a. Grant the sales manager the "Drag-and-Drop Dashboard Builder" permission.

b. Create the dashboard as dynamic dashboard.

c. Grant the sale manager the "Manage Dynamic Dashboards" permission.

d. Grant the sales manager the "View My Teams Dashboards" permission.

53. **The Mass Mail Contacts option does not appear under the Tools section in the Contacts tab, what could have caused this?**

a. The user Role is insufficient to view this tool.

b. Email is unchecked for that profile in FLS.

c. This is a bug and must be escalated.

d. Mass mail is not enabled for the profile.

e. Mass mail is not checked in FLS.

54. **When you transfer ownership of an account, the new owner will also gain Ownership of the following records related to the transferred account automatically: Choose 3 answers.**

a. Any notes that belong to the existing owner.

b. All contacts that belong to the existing owner.

c. All opportunities - open and closed.

d. All open activities assigned to the existing owner. Note that completed activities will not be transferred.

55. **Which is a capability of the new service Cloud console? Choose 3 answers.**

a. It provides data visibility by combining a list view and related records on one screen.

b. It allows agents to view key record information in the highlights panel.

c. It preserves the context of calls using primary tabs and subtabs.

d. It allows access to data by opening each record in a new window.

e. It allows agents to take notes in an interaction log while on a call.

56. **Sales management wants to stay informed when big opportunities are close. They have requested that they receive notifications when opportunities with large amounts are close. How can a system administrator accomplish this? Choose 2 answers.**

    a. Opportunity update reminders

    b. Validation rule

    c. Big deal alerts

    d. Workflow field updates

57. **If a user selects the manage members button on a campaign, they will be able to select what? Choose 4 answers.**

    a. Add members | search

    b. Add members | import file

    c. Edit members | search

    d. Add member | profile

    e. Update & add members | import file

58. **Which of the following cannot be used as a source report for the analytical snap shot?**

    a. Tabular reports

    b. Summary reports

    c. Matrix reports

    d. All can be used

59. **How many ranges can be defined in the case of conditional highlighting?**

    a. 2

    b. 3

    c. 4

    d. 5

60. **How many solution records can be imported via the import wizard?**

    a. 500

    b. 5000

    c. 50000

    d. Solution records cannot be imported via the import wizard

Answers

1.	d	31.	c
2.	b.	32.	c, d
3.	a	33.	a
4.	b	34.	a
5.	c, ,d	35.	b
6.	a, c	36.	d
7.	b	37.	a
8.	a, b	38.	a
9.	a, c, d	39.	b
10.	b, c	40.	a, b, c, e
11.	b	41.	b
12.	a, c	42.	c, d
13.	c	43.	a, c, e
14.	b, d	44.	b
15.	b, d	45.	c, e
16.	b, d	46.	a
17.	d	47.	b, c
18.	a, c	48.	a, c
19.	b, c	49.	b, c
20.	b	50.	b, d
21.	b, c	51.	b, d
22.	b	52.	a, b, d
23.	a	53.	b, c, e
24.	b	54.	c, d
25.	c	55.	a, b, c, e
26.	b, d	56.	c
27.	b	57.	b
28.	a	58.	c
29.	a b	59.	d
30.	b, c, d	60.	c

Salesforce Platform App Builder Sample Paper

1. **Which rule can be configured for the Opportunity object? Choose 2 answers**

   a. Escalation Rule

   b. Workflow Rule

   c. Validation Rule

   d. Assignment Rule

2. **Universal Containers wants to standardize their business logic. They want to ensure that the workflow order is guaranteed to be the same each time. Which feature can be used to accomplish this? Choose 2 answers.**

   a. Lightning Process Builder

   b. Workflow

   c. Chatter Actions

   d. Visual Workflow

3. **What is a true statement regarding managing access to reports and Dashboards? Choose 2 answers.**

   a. Users with the "Manage Public Reports" permission can organize reports by creating custom report folders and sending invitations to users to access them.

   b. Users must have certain permissions to access public, hidden, or shared folder.

   c. Users with the "Manage Public Reports" and "Create and Customize Reports" permissions can create custom reports that all users can view.

   d. Users that want to grant access to personal folders can manually share a personal folder with a user or public group.

4. **Universal Containers would like to embed a chart of all related Opportunities, by stage, on the Account detail page. Which type of report should the App Builder create to add to the Account page layout?**

   a. A summary report on the Opportunity object.

   b. A summary report on the Account object.

   c. A tabular report on the Account object.

   d. A tabular report on the Opportunity object.

5. **What is recommended to refresh a full sandbox?**

   a. After a UAT sign-off.

   b. Whenever a new production user is added.

    c. After a major production release.

    d. Within three hours of when it is needed.

6. **When a user creates an Account report, the user does not see Industry as an available field in the report builder. However, this same user is able to see it in the Account page layout. What scenario would cause this?**

    a. The user uses a custom report type that does not include the Industry field.

    b. The Industry field has no record values in the Account.

    c. The Industry field is not enabled for the particular record type

    d. The user does not have Industry field visibility in the field l level security

7. **A divisional manager wants to add a chart into a page layout. Which report format can be used as the source report to accomplish this? Choose 2 answers.**

    a. Matrix format with a chart.

    b. Joined format with a chart.

    c. Tabular format with a chart.

    d. Summary format with a chart.

8. **What is the capability of a schema builder? Choose 2 answers.**

    a. To update description of standard and custom objects.

    b. To modify custom field help text on standard objects

    c. To create new look-up or master-detail object relationship

    d. To enable field history tracking on standard objects.

9. **Which statement is true for embedding a Visualforce page in a page Layout. Choose 2 answers.**

    a. Visualforce Pages on a field set have attributes for width and height.

    b. Visualforce Pages can be placed anywhere in the page layout.

    c. Visualforce Pages on a page layout have attributes for width and height

    d. Visualforce Pages can only be place in the Visualforce section in a page layout.

10. **Universal container has a custom object for shipping information. They have to ship to both businesses and consumers. They need to show additional values in the custom field called insurance type for business shipping records. How can this be set up?**

    a. Use Record type with single page layout.

    b. Create multiple picklist fields on the object

    c. Use Record Types with multiple page layout

    d. Create a multi-select pick-list field.

11. **What metadata changes can be made directly in a production environment without deploying from sandbox? Choose 2 answers.**

    a. Apex Triggers

    b. Visualforce Pages

    c. Validation Rules

    d. Apex Classes

12. **Universal Containers would like to automatically assign a specific permission set to new users. How can this requirement be met? Choose 2 answers.**

    a. Create an approval process on the User object to assign a permission set

    b. Create a flow on the user object to assign a permission set.

    c. Create a lightning process on the user object to launch a flow.

    d. Create a workflow rule on the User object to assign a permission set.

13. **Universal Containers has two teams: Sales and Services. Both teams interact with the same records. Sales users use ten fields on the Account record. Services users use three of the same fields as the Sales team, but also have five of their own, which the sales team does not use. What is the minimum configuration necessary to meet this requirement?**

    a. One profile, two Record Types, one page layout

    b. Two profiles, two Record Types, two page layouts

    c. One profile, one record type, one page layout.

    d. Two profiles, one record type, two page layouts

14. **Universal Containers has a custom assessment object used by three divisions. Each division wants to track different information on the assessments, including different values for the status picklist. Division managers do not want their teams to be able to create another division's assessment. How can this be accomplished?**

    a. Create additional custom assessment objects, one for each division, to track their assessments so information can be tracked separately. Use profiles to restrict access to the three custom objects.

    b. Create separate assessment Record Types for each division and use them to limit picklist values.

    c. Create separate page layouts for each record type and use profiles to restrict record type access.

    d. Create three page layouts to determine the fields and picklist values for each user based on the division indicated on their user record. Use field-level security to restrict access to each division's fields.

    e. Create a separate page layout for each division and assign them profiles. Use the profile setting to configure each division's custom field list and picklist values for assessments

15. **An App Builder creates an Account validation rule on the Industry field that will throw an error if the length of the field is longer than six characters. Another App Builder creates a workflow rule with a field update that sets the Industry field to Technology whenever the Billing City field is set to San Francisco. What will happen the next time a sales person saves an Account with a Billing City of San Francisco?**

    a. The record will save and the Industry field will change to Technology.

    b. The record will not save and the validation rule's error message will be displayed.

    c. The record will not save and no error message will be displayed.

    d. The record will save but the Industry field will not change to Technology.

16. **Universal Containers needs the ability to generate contract documents. All the data required for a contract resides in a custom object. What is the recommended solutions?**

    a. Enable the contract feature and create a custom Contract template based on the Standard template.

    b. Store a template in the static resources and configure the Action Link Template to use it.

    c. Create the HTML template for contracts and store it in the Public Folder.

    d. Select and install an AppExchange product to meet the contract generation needs.

17. **What should be done to provide managers access to records of which they are not the owner in a private sharing model?**

    a. Create a Manager Permission set and select the "View All Data" option.

    b. Create a Manager profile and select the "View My Teams Data" option.

    c. Define a Role Hierarchy and use the Grant Access Using Hierarchies option.

    d. Set the Manger field for each User Record on the Manager's team.

18. **Sales representatives want to capture custom Feedback record details related to each Account. The sales representatives want to accomplish this with minimal clicks on the Salesforce1 mobile application. What is the recommended solution to meet this requirement? Choose 2 answers**

    a. Create predefined values for most of the fields.

    b. Create a global action on Account.

    c. Create a feedback object as a parent of Account.

    d. Create an object-specific action on Account.

19. **Universal Containers sales representatives can modify fields on an opportunity until it is closed. Only the sales operation team can modify the post closed follow-up dates and post closed follow-up comments fields. How can these requirements be met?**

    a. Use Record Types with field sets and restrict editing fields using field-level security.

    b. Use field-level security on page layouts to restrict editing fields

    c. Use multiple Record Types, page layouts and profiles.

    d. Use field level security to mark fields as read only on the sales profile

20. **A sales manager would like to look at an account record and view charts of all of the related open opportunities. Closed/won opportunities, and open cases. How many report charts can be added to the account page layout to meet this requirement?**

    a. 3

    b. 2

    c. 1

    d. 4

21. **In order to delete the Opportunities, Universal Containers would like sales representatives to submit requests for approval from their sales manager. What can be used to meet these requirements?**

    a. Approval Process with Time-Dependent workflow action.

    b. Approval Process with Apex Trigger.

    c. Two-step Approval process.

    d. Process Builder with Submit for Approval action

22. **What is a feature that can extend record access beyond the organization-wide defaults? Choose 2 Answers**

    a. Public or private groups.

    b. Criteria-based sharing rules.

    c. Owner-based sharing rules.

    d. Dynamic role hierarchy.

23. An App Builder is loading the data into salesforce. To link the new records back to the legacy system, a field will be used to track the legacy ID on the account object. For future data loads this ID will be used when upserting records. Which field attribute should be selected? Choose 2 answers.

    a. Unique

    b. Required

    c. External ID

    d. Text(encrypted)

24. Universal containers would like to use a Chatter group for their mergers and acquisition team to collaborate on potential new projects. This group should not be visible for non-members to see or join, and can be accessed by invite only. Which Chatter Group type should the App Builder recommend?

    a. Member Group

    b. Unlisted Group

    c. Public Group

    d. Private Group

25. At Universal Containers, the VP of Service has requested a visual indicator flag on each case, based on the case priority. High-priority cases should be flagged red, medium-priority should be flagged yellow, and low-priority cases should be flagged green. Which formula would accomplish this requirement? Choose 2 answers

    a. CASE(Priority, "Low", "img/samples/flag_green.gif", "Medium", "img/samples/flag_yellow.gif","High", "img/samples/flag_red.gif", "/s.gif")

    b. IMAGE(IF(ISPICKVAL(Priority, "Low"), "img/samples/flag_green.gif", IF(ISPICKVAL(Priority,"Medium"), "img/samples/flag_yellow.gif", IF(ISPICKVAL(Priority, "High"), "img/samples/flag_red.gif"))), "Priority Flag")

    c. IF(ISPICKVAL(Priority, "Low"), "img/samples/flag_green.gif", IF(ISPICKVAL(Priority, "Medium"),"img/samples/flag_yellow.gif", IF(ISPICKVAL(Priority, "High"), "img/samples/flag_red.gif", "/s.gif")))

    d. IMAGE(CASE(Priority,"Low","img/samples/flag_green.gif","Medium","img/samples/flag_yellow.gif", "High", "img/samples/flag_red.gif", "Priority Flag")

26. An App Builder has been asked to provide users a way to identify a contact's "preferred contact method" directly on the contact record. Users need to be able to identify whether a phone number or an email, is the contact's preferred communication method. Which field type will allow the App Builder to accomplish this with the fewest fields possible?

    a. Formula

   b. Checkboxes

   c. Picklist

   d. Email

27. **To Synchronize Accounts, orders and shipments in real time, a developer has built a custom interface between an external system and salesforce, prior to deployment, the developer needs to confirm that the interface can sustain the syncing of thousands of records at a time. Which sandbox environment is recommended to complete performance and load testing?**

   a. Partial Sandbox

   b. Developer Sandbox

   c. Developer Pro Sandbox

   d. Full Sandbox

28. **Universal containers is importing 1000 records into Salesforce. They want to avoid any duplicate records from being created during the import. How can these requirements be met?**

   a. Include a column in the import file that has either record names, Salesforce IDs, or external IDs that can be used to match records.

   b. When importing the file, select the "Prevent Duplicates" option on the last step of the Import Wizard and import the file.

   c. After importing all of the custom objects, run a duplicate check report, export the record to a CSV File, and run a mass delete to purge any duplicates.

   d. After importing all of the custom objects, review all records created and manually merge or delete and duplicate record

29. **The director of marketing has asked the App Builder to create a formula field that tracks how many days have elapsed since a contact was sent a marketing communication. The director is only interested in whole units. Which function should be used to calculate the difference?**

   a. Datevalue()

   b. Now()

   c. Date()

   d. Today()

30. **Universal Containers has a requirement that an Opportunity should have a field showing the value of its associated account's billing state. This value should not change after the Opportunity has been created. What is the recommended solution to configure this automation behaviour?**

   a. Formula Field

b. Workflow

c. Roll-up-summary field

d. Apex

31. **What is a true statement regarding roll-up summary fields? Choose 2 answers**.

a. Roll-up summary fields can only be created on the master of a master-detail relationship.

b. The roll-up summary field inherits the field l level security of the child object.

c. Changes to the value of a roll-up summary field column of roll-up summary filters.

d. Multi-select picklist fields can be used in the field column of roll-up summary filters.

32. **The Director of Customer Service wants to know when agents are overwhelmed with high-priority items in the support queue. The Director wants to receive a notification when a new case is open with the status of "New" for more than four business hours. Which automation process could be used to accomplish this? Choose 2 answers**.

a. Escalation rules

b. Visual workflow

c. Lightning Process Builder

d. Scheduled Apex

33. **Universal Containers provide access to Salesforce for their sales, service and marketing teams. Management wants to ensure that when user login, their home tab provides access to links and documentation that are specifically relevant to their job function. How can this requirement be met?**

a. Create separate home page custom components and layouts; assign to user by role.

b. Expose specific elements within a home page custom component determined by profile.

c. Create separate home page custom components and layouts; assign to user by profile.

d. Expose specific elements within a home page custom component determined by role.

34. **Where can a custom button be placed? Choose 3 answers**.

a. On the User Object.

b. On the Custom List View.

    c. On a Person Account.

    d. On a related list.

    e. On a Web-to-Case form.

35. **What is a key consideration when using unmanaged packages? Choose 2 answers**

    a. A namespace is not required to create an unmanaged package.

    b. The person who created the unmanaged package can change or update installed components.

    c. The person who created the unmanaged package has no control over the installed components.

    d. A namespace is required to create an unmanaged package.

36. **What type of field can be referenced by a Roll-up Summary field using SUM? Choose 3 answers.**

    a. Formula

    b. Currency

    c. Number

    d. Percent

    e. Date

37. **Universal Containers has deployed custom tabs through change sets, without including the profiles, to production (enterprise edition). Which statement is true in regards to the visibility of custom tabs?**

    a. Custom tabs are exposed for all users

    b. Custom tabs are hidden for all users

    c. Custom tabs are default off for all users

    d. Custom tabs are default on for all users

38. **A custom object has a public reads-only sharing setting that does not grant access using hierarchies. A dynamic sharing rule provides write access to the object to the global marketing public group if the record is marked as global. A user creates a new record and marks it as global. Who will have write access to the record?**

    a. The global marketing public group and anyone above the owner in the role hierarchy.

    b. The record owner and the global marketing public group.

    c. The global marketing public group, the record owner, and anyone above the owner in the role hierarchy.

    d. The record owner and anyone above the owner in the role hierarchy.

39. **Representatives at Universal Containers use Salesforce to record information for leads. When new prospects are added, an outbound message is sent to SAP with lead's information. Which automation process will accomplish this without writing any code?**

    a. Create a process using Lightning Process Builder to send the outbound message.

    b. Create a Workflow Rule with an outbound message as the action.

    c. Use Visual Workflow to create a wizard that will send an outbound message.

    d. Design an Approval Process that sends an outbound message upon arrival.

40. **What salesforce functionality is ignored when processing field updates in workflow rules and approval processes? Choose 3 answers.**

    a. Validation Rules

    b. Decimal Places and Character Limits

    c. Record Type Picklist Value Assignments

    d. Multiple Currencies

    e. Field Level Security

41. **When an opportunity close date is delayed by more than 60 days, the manager and the VP sales must approve the change. How can this requirement be met? Choose 2 answers.**

    a. Build an approval process that requires unanimous approval from the manager and VP of sales.

    b. Create a workflow rule that checks for close date less that 60 days and add an email alert.

    c. Create a Lightning Process Builder flow that submits the record for an approval process

    d. Build a validation rule that does not allow a user to save the opportunity record.

42. **Universal Containers uses a custom object to track Site Visits. When the status of a Site Visit is changed from "In Progress" to "On Hold", the business wants the Site visit owner to be automatically assigned to an "On Hold" queue. Which capability can be used to accomplish this?**

    a. Apex Trigger

    b. Action

    c. Assignment Rule

    d. Visual Workflow

43. **Universal Containers needs a field on the Account to track how many Opportunities are closing within the next 30 days. What can be used to accomplish this goal?**

    a. Process Builder

    b. Apex Code

    c. Roll-up Summary Field

    d. Workflow Rule

44. **Universal container needs to update a field on an account when an opportunity stage is changed to close lost. What can be used to accomplish this requirement? Choose 2 answers.**

    a. Lightning Process Builder

    b. Approval Process

    c. Assignment Rules

    d. Workflow Rule

45. **Which statement is true about field update actions from workflow rules and approval processes? Choose 2 answers**

    a. Field update with "re-evaluate workflow rules" selected can cause a recursive loop if the updated field is included in a workflow.

    b. Field update are not available on currency field if the organization uses multi-currency.

    c. Field updates to records based on workflow rules and approval processes do not trigger validation rules

    d. Field updates are tracked in the history related list of a record regardless of whether or not History tracking is set for those fields.

46. **What the true statement is in regards to converting a tabular, summary, or matrix report to a joined report? Choose 3 answers.**

    a. Joined report blocks are formatted as matrix reports.

    b. Bucket fields are not supported in joined reports.

    c. Cross filters are not supported in joined reports.

    d. The rows to display filter is not supported in Joined reports.

    e. Report formula fields are nor supported in Joined reports.

47. **Which statement is true when defining a Create custom action for the Contact object? Choose 2 answers**

    a. The create action will ignore field requirements.

    b. The create action can pre-define Contact field values.

c. The create action allows a user to select a record type.

d. The create action will respect validation rules.

48. **Universal Containers has a junction object called Invoices with a primary Master-Detail relationship with Accounts and a secondary Master-Detail relationship with Contacts. The App Builder has a requirement to change the primary Master-Detail relationship to Lookup. What happens to the Master- Detail relationship with Contacts?**

    a. The Contacts Master-Detail values are cleared from invoices.

    b. The Contacts Master-Detail also converts to Lookup.

    c. The Contacts Master-Detail field is deleted from the object

    d. The Contacts Master-Detail becomes the primary.

49. **Universal Containers would like to show different picklist values to different groups of user in a custom picklist field. What should be configured?**

    a. Permission sets

    b. Field-level security

    c. Record Types

    d. Page Layouts

50. **What is the capability of schema Builder? Choose 2 answers.**

    a. Showing selected objects on the page.

    b. Editing custom settings.

    c. Viewing page layout in a new window

    d. Creating a new record type.

51. **Universal container manages internal projects by department using a custom object called projects. Only employees in the project's respective department should have view access to all of the department's project records. If an employee changes job roles and moves to another department, the employee should no longer have access to the projects within their former department. How can these requirements be met, assuming the organization-wide default for projects is set to private? Choose 2 answers.**

    a. Create a criteria based sharing rule using the projects department that grants access to users by permission set.

    b. Create a criteria based sharing rule using the projects department that grants access to users by roles.

    c. Create a criteria based sharing rule using the projects department that grants access to users by public groups.

d. Create a criteria based sharing rule using the projects department that grants access to users by profiles

52. **Universal Containers has created the custom objects Candidate and Interview in Salesforce to track candidates and interviews respectively. The company wants to track the total number of interviews a candidate has gone through on the candidate record without writing any code. How can App Builder accomplish this requirements? Choose two answers.**

    a. Use a roll-up summary field on the candidate record to show the total number of interviews.
    b. Use a master-detail relationship between the Candidate and the Interview objects.
    c. Use a lookup relationship between the Candidate and Interview objects.
    d. Use a formula field on the candidate record to show the total number of interviews.

53. **When configuring a record type, an App Builder can configure the available value of a picklist field for the page layout. Which opportunity standard field is available to be configured directly in the Opportunity record type? Choose 2 answers**

    a. Forecast Category
    b. Lead Source
    c. Type
    d. Stage

54. **What is a use case for approval processes? Choose 2 answers.**

    a. Approve expense reports automatically when less than $50.
    b. Update the PTO record field with the user's manager.
    c. Require the CFO to review the salary range for all job offers.
    d. Ensure an opportunity that has at least one product added.

55. **Universal Containers conduct evaluations of their sales representatives using a custom object consisting of numerical scores and executive comments. The company wants to ensure that only the sales representatives, and their manager's executive can view the representative's evaluation record but the representatives should not be able to view the executive comment field on their review. How can these requirement be met?**

    a. Use a private sharing model granting record access using hierarchy; manage field access with Record Types and field-level security
    b. Use a private sharing model granting record access using custom setting; manage field access with page layouts and field level security
    c. Use a private sharing model granting record access using hierarchy; manage field access with field-level security

d. Use a private sharing model granting record access using custom setting; manage field access with Record Types and page layouts

56. **A custom field contains a feedback score which is on a scale of one to five. End users would like a visual indicator of one to five stars based on the number found in the feedback score custom field. How can this visual indicator be displayed?**

   a. Use a custom formula field.

   b. Use a custom image field.

   c. Use a custom number field.

   d. Use a custom text field

57. **What option is available to an App Builder when defining an object-specific Create Record custom action? Choose 2 answers.**

   a. Pre-Defining field values on the target object.

   b. Redirecting the end user to the detail page of the target object.

   c. Specifying the fields and layout of the action.

   d. Allowing the end user to choose the record type.

58. **A customer service representative at a call center would like to be able to collect information from customers using a series of question prompts. What could be used to accomplish this?**

   a. Lightning process builder

   b. Workflow Rules

   c. Lightning Connect

   d. Visual workflow

59. **The CRM Manager at Universal Containers has requested that a custom text field be converted to a picklist in order to promote better data hygiene. What needs to be considered before changing the field type? Choose 2 answers.**

   a. Existing list views that reference the field may be deleted.

   b. Field references will be removed in Visualforce pages.

   c. All data should be backed up before converting a text field.

   d. Changing a field type will remove existing field history.

60. **A junction object has two Master-Detail relationships. What happens to a junction object record when either associated master record is deleted?**

   a. The record is deleted and placed in the recycle bin.

   b. The master record cannot be deleted if it has a child record.

c. The look-up field on the junction object record is cleared.

d. The record is permanently deleted and cannot be restored.

Answers

1.	b, c	**31.**	a, b
2.	a, d	**32.**	a, c
3.	a, c	**33.**	c
4.	a	**34.**	b, c ,d
5.	c	**35.**	a, c
6.	a	**36.**	b, c, d
7.	a, d	**37.**	b
8.	b, c	**38.**	b
9.	b, c	**39.**	b
10.	d	**40.**	a, c, e
11.	b, c	**41.**	a, c
12.	b, c	**42.**	a
13.	b	**43.**	c
14.	b	**44.**	c
15.	a	**45.**	a, d
16.	d	**46.**	a, c
17.	a	**47.**	b, c , d
18.	a, d	**48.**	c, d
19.	b	**49.**	d
20.	b	**50.**	c
21.	c	**51.**	a, c
22.	b, c	**52.**	b, c
23.	a, c	**53.**	a, b
24.	b	**54.**	b, c
25.	a, d	**55.**	a
26.	c	**56.**	c
27.	d	**57.**	a
28.	a	**58.**	c, d
29.	d	**59.**	d
30.	b	**60.**	a, c

Salesforce Certified Platform Developer I Sample Paper

1. **An Org has a single account named 'NoContacts' that has no related contacts. Given the query: List accounts = [Select ID, (Select ID, Name from contacts) from Account where Name= 'NoContacts'];**
   a. Accounts[0] is Null.
   b. Accounts[0].contacts is invalid Apex.
   c. Accounts[0].contacts is an empty list.
   d. A QueryException is thrown

2. **Which three declarative fields are correctly mapped to variable types in Apex? Choose 3 answers.**
   a. Number maps to integer.
   b. Textarea maps to list of type String.
   c. Checkbox maps to Boolean.
   d. Date/Time maps to Datetime.
   e. Number maps to Decimal.

3. **Which set of roll-up types are available when creating a roll up summary field?**
   a. COUNT, SUM, MIN, MAX
   b. AVERAGE, COUNT, SUM, MIN, MAX
   c. AVERAGE, SUM, MIN, MAX
   d. SUM, MIN, MAX

4. **Which approach should be used to provide test data for a test class?**
   a. Use a test data factory class to create test data.
   b. Query for existing records in the database.
   c. Access data in @TestVisible class variables.
   d. Execute anonymous code blocks that create date.

5. **What are three ways for a developer to execute tests in an org? choose 3 answers**
   a. Bulk API
   b. MetaData API
   c. Tooling API
   d. Developer console
   e. Setup menu

6. **Using the schema builder, a developer tries to change the API name of a field that is referenced in an Apex Test Class. What is the end results?**

   a. The API name of the field is changed, and a warning is issued to update the class

   b. The API name of the field and the reference in the test class is updated

   c. The API name of the field and the reference in the test class is changed

   d. The API name is not changed and there are no other impacts.

7. **Why would a developer consider using a custom controller over a controller extension?**

   a. When a Visualforce page needs to replace the functionality of a standard controller.

   b. When a Visualforce page does not reference a single primary object.

   c. When a Visualforce page should not enforce permissions or field-level security.

   d. When a Visualforce page needs to add new actions to a standard controller.

8. **What are the two testing consideration when deploying code from a sandbox to production? Choose 2 answers.**

   a. 75% of test must execute without failure.

   b. 100% of test must execute without failure.

   c. Apex code requires 75% coverage.

   d. Apex code requires 100% coverage.

9. **A developer writes the following code:**

   List<Account> acc = [SELECT Id FROM Account LIMIT 10]; Delete acc; Database. emptyRecycleBin(acc); system.debug(Limits.getDMLStatements() +', '+ Limits. getLimitDMLStatements());

   What is the result of the debug statement?

   a. 1,150

   b. 2,200

   c. 1,100

   d. 2,150

10. **A developer created a visualforce page and a custom controller with methods to handle different buttons and events that can occur on the page. What should the developer do to deploy to production?**

    a. Create a test page that provides coverage of the custom controller.

    b. Create a test class that provides coverage of the visualforce page.

c. Create a test class that provides coverage of the custom controller.

d. Create a test page that provides coverage of the visualforce page.

11. **A developer needs to create a visualforce page that displays case data. The page will be used by both support representatives and support managers. The support representative profile does not allow visibility of the customer_Satisfaction_c Field, but the support manager profile does. How can the developer create the page to enforce field level security and keep future maintenance to a minimum?**

a. Create one visualforce page for use by both profiles

b. Use a new support manager permission sets

c. Create a separate visualforce page for each profile

d. Use a custom controller that has the with sharing keywords

12. **A developer executes the following query in Apex to retrieve a list of contacts for each account: List<account> accounts = [Select ID, Name, (Select ID, Name from Contacts) from Account] ; Which two exceptions may occur when it executes? Choose 2 answers.**

a. SOQL query limit exception due to the number of queries.

b. CPU limit exception due to the complexity of the query.

c. SOQL query limit exception due to the number of contacts.

d. SOQL query limit exception due to the number of accounts.

13. **Which three options allow a developer to use stylesheets?**

a. A static resource

b. Apex:stylesheet>tag

c. Tag

d. Inline CSS

e. Tag

14. **A platform developer needs to write an apex method that will only perform an action if a record is assigned to a specific Record Type. Which two options allows the developer to dynamically determine the ID of the required Record Type by its name? Choose 2 answers.**

a. Hardcode the ID as a constant in an Apex class

b. Execute a SOQL query on the RecordType Object

c. Use the getRecordTypeInfosByName()method in the DescribeSObjectResult Class

d. Make an outbound web service call to the SOAP API.

15. **Which SOQL query successfully returns the Accounts grouped by name?**

    a. Select type, Max(CreatedDate) FROM Account GROUP BY Name

    b. Select Name, Max(CreatedDate) FROM Account GROUP BY Name

    c. Select Id, type, Max(CreatedDate) FROM Account GROUP BY Name

    d. Select type, Name Max(CreatedDate) FROM Account GROUP BY Name LIM

16. **Which approach should a developer use to add pagination to a visualforce page?**

    a. The extension attribute for a page

    b. StandardController

    c. The action attribute for a page

    d. StandardSetController

17. **A Developer needs to test an invoicing system integration. After reviewing the numbers of transaction required for the test, the developer estimates that the test data will total about 2GB of data storage. Production data is not required for integration testing. Which two environments meet the requirements for testing? Choose 2 answers.**

    a. Full sandbox

    b. Developer sandbox

    c. Developer Pro Sandbox

    d. Developer Edition

    e. Partial Sandbox

18. **How should a developer prevent a recursive trigger?**

    a. Use a private Boolean variable.

    b. Use a "one trigger per object" pattern.

    c. Use a trigger handler.

    d. Use a static Boolean variable.

19. **What is the capability of the <ltng:require> Tag that is used for loading external javascript libraries in lightning components? Choose 3 answers.**

    a. Loading scripts in parallel

    b. One-time loading from duplicate scripts

    c. Loading files from documents

    d. Specifying loading order

    e. Loading externally hosted scripts

20. **What is a requirement for a class to be used as a custom visualforce controller?**

    a. Any top-level Apex class that has a constructor that returns a PageReference

    b. Any top-level Apex class that implements the controller interface

    c. Any top-level Apex class that has a default, no-argument constructor

    d. Any top-level Apex class that extends a PageReference

21. **The operation manager at a construction company uses a custom object called Machinery to manage the usage and maintenance of its cranes and other machinery. The manager wants to be able to assign machinery to different construction jobs, and track the dates and cost associated with each job. More than one piece of machinery can be assigned to one construction job. What should a developer do to meet these requirements?**

    a. Create a lookup field on the machinery object to the construction job object

    b. Create a junction object with Master-Detail Relationship to both the machinery object and the construction job object.

    c. Create a lookup field on the construction job object to the machinery object

    d. Create a Master-Detail lookup field on the machinery object to the construction job object

22. **Which three tools can deploy metadata to productions? Choose 3 answers.**

    a. Data Loader

    b. Change set from sandbox

    c. Change set from developer org

    d. Force.com IDE

    e. Metadata API

23. **How should a developer create a new custom exception class?**

    a. Public class CustomException extends Exception{}

    b. CustomException ex = new (CustomException) Exception();

    c. (Exception) CustomException ex = new Exception();

    d. Public class CustomException implements Exception{}

24. **Which two number expression evaluate correctly? Choose 2 answers.**

    a. Integer I = 3.14159;

    b. Decimal D = 3.14159;

    c. Long I = 3.14159;

    d. Double D =3.14159;

Given the code block:

```
Integer x;
For(x=0;x<10; x+=2) {
If(x==8)
   break;
 If(x==10)
  break;
 }
System.debug(x);
```

25. **Which value will the system debug statement display?**

    a. 2

    b. 10

    c. 8

    d. 4

26. **A developer wrote a unit test to confirm that a custom exception works properly in a custom controller, but the test failed due to an exception being thrown. What steps should the developer take to resolve the issue and properly test the exception?**

    a. Use the finally block within the unit test to populate the exception.

    b. Use database methods with all or none set to False.

    c. Use try/catch within the unit test to catch the exception.

    d. Use Test.isRunningTest() within the custom Controller.

27. **A developer has the following controller class:**

    ```
    Public with sharing class myFooController {
        Public integer prop { get; private set;}
    }
    ```

    Which code block will run successfully in an execute anonymous window?

    a. myFooController m = new myFooController();

       ```
       System.assert(m.prop != null);
       ```

    b. myFooController m = new myFooController();

       ```
       System.assert(m.prop == 1);
       ```

    c. myFooController m = new myFooController();

       ```
       System.assert(m.prop == null);
       ```

```
d. myFooController m = rew myFcoController();
   System.assert(m.prop == 0);
```

28. **What is the benefit of using an after insert trigger over using a before insert trigger?**

    a. An after insert trigger allows a developer to bypass validation rules when updating fields on the new records.

    b. An after insert trigger allows a developer to make a callout to an external service.

    c. An after insert trigger allows a developer to insert other objects that reference the new records.

    d. An after insert trigger allows a developer to modify fields in the new record without a query.

29. **While writing a test class that covers an OpportunityLineItem trigger, a Developer is unable to create a standard Pricebook since one already exist in the org. how should the developer overcome this problem?**

    a. Use @IsTest(SeeAllData=true) and delete the existing standard Pricebook.

    b. Use @TestVisible to allow the test method to see the standard Pricebook.

    c. Use Test.getStandardPricebbokId()to get the standard Pricebook I

    d. Use Test.loaddata() and a Static Resource to load a standard Pricebook.

30. **When should an apex Trigger be required instead of a process builder process?**

    a. When an action needs to be taken on delete or undelete, or before a DML operation is executed.

    b. When a record needs to be created.

    c. When a post to Chatter needs to be created.

    d. When multiple records related to the triggering record need to be updated.

31. **A user selects a value from a multi-select picklist. How is this selected value represented in Apex?**

    a. As a string ending with a comma

    b. As a string

    c. As a list with one element

    d. As a set with one element

32. **When an Account's custom picklist field called Customer Sentiment is changed to a value of "Confused," a new related Cases should automatically be created. Which two methods should a developer use to create this case? Choose two answers.**

    a. Process Builder

    b. Custom Button

    c. Apex Trigger

    d. Workflow Rule

33. **How can a developer set up a debug log on a specific user?**

    a. Ask the user for access to their account credentials, log in as the user and debug the issue

    b. Create an Apex code that logs code actions into a custom object.

    c. It is not possible to setup debug lots for users other than yourself.

    d. Set up a trace flag for the user, and define a logging level and time period for the trace.

34. **A developer is asked to set a Picklist field to 'Monitor' on any new Leads owned by a subset of Users. How should the developer implement this request?**

    a. Create a lead Workflow Rule Field Update

    b. Create an after insert Lead trigger

    c. Create a Lead formula field

    d. Create a before insert lead Trigger

35. **When viewing a Quote, the sales representative wants to easily see how many discounted items are included in the Quote Line Items. What should a developer do to meet this requirement?**

    a. Create a workflow rule on the Quote Line Item Object that updates a field on the parent Quote when the item is discounted.

    b. Create a roll-up summary field on the Quote Object that performs a SUM on the Quote Line Item Quantity field, filtered for only discounted Quote Line Items.

    c. Create a Trigger on the Quote Object that queries the Quantity filed on discounted Quote Line Items.

    d. Create a formulat field on the Quote Object that performs a SUM on the Quote Line Item Quantity field, filtered for only discounted Quote Line Items.

36. **A visualforce interface is created for Case Management that includes both standard and custom functionality defined in an Apex class called myControllerExtension. The visualforce page should include which attribute(s) to correctly implement controller functionality?**

    a. StandardController = "case" and extensions =" myControllerExtension"

    b. Extensions=" myControllerExtension"

    c. Controller=" myControllerExtension"

    d. Controller = "case" and extensions =" myControllerExtension"

37. **Which two strategies should a developer use to avoid hitting governor limits when developing in a multi-tenant environment? Choose two answers.**

    a. Use variables within Apex classes to store large amounts of data.

    b. Use collections to store NOT all fields from a related object ,just minimally required fields.

    c. Use methods from the "LIMITS" class to monitor governor limits.

    d. Use SOQL for loops to iterate data retrieved from queries that return a high number of rows.

38. **Which statement results in an Apex compiler error?**

    a. Map<Id,Leas> lmap = new Map<Id,Lead>([Select ID from Lead Limit 8]);

    b. Date d1 = Date.Today(), d2 = Date.ValueOf('2018-01-01');

    c. Integer a=5, b=6, c, d = 7;

    d. List<string> s = List<string>{'a','b','c'};

39. **How should a developer avoid hitting the governor limits in test methods?**

    a. Use Test.startTest() to reset governor limits

    b. Use @TestVisible on methods that creates records

    c. Use @IsTest (SeeAllData=true) to use existing data

    d. Use Test.loadData() to load data from a static resource.

40. **A newly hired developer discovers that there are multiple triggers on the case object. What should the developer consider when working with triggers?**

    a. Trigger execution order is not guaranteed for the same sObject.

    b. Trigger execution order is based on creation date and time.

    c. Unit test must specify the trigger being tested.

    d. Developers must dictate the order of the trigger execution.

41. **What are three characteristics of static methods? Choose 3 answers.**

    a. Initialized only when a class is loaded.

    b. A static variable is available outside of the cope of an Apex transaction.

    c. Allowed only in outer classes.

    d. Allowed only in inner classes..

    e. Are not transmitted as part of the view state for a Visualforce page

42. **A developer is asked to create a PDF quote document formatted using the company's branding guidelines, and automatically save it to the Opportunity record. Which two ways should a developer create this functionality? Choose two answers.**

    a. Create a visualforce page with custom styling.

    b. Create a visual flow that implements the company's formatting.

    c. Install an application from the AppExchange to generate documents.

    d. Create an email template and use it in Process builder.

43. **A method is passed a list of generic sObjects as a parameter. What should the developer do to determine which object type(Account, Lead, Or Contact, for example) to cast each sObject?**

    a. Use the getSObjectName method on the sObject class to get the sObject name

    b. Use a try-catch construct to cast the sObject into one of three sObject Types

    c. Use the getSObjectType method on each generic sObject to retrieve the sObject Token

    d. Use the first three characters of the sObject ID to determine the sObject Type.

44. **A developer has created a visualforce page and apex controller that uses the with sharing keyword. The page will be used by sales managers and should only display account owned by sales representative who report to the running sales manager. The organisation wide sharing for account is set to private. Which additional set of steps should the developer take?**

    a. Create one profile, one permission set, and one role.

    b. Create two profile, one permission set, and one role.

    c. Create one profile, one permission set, and two role.

    d. Create one profile, two permission set, and one role.

45. **What are two benefits of the lightning component framework? Choose 2 answers.**

    a. It allows faster PDF generation with lightning components.

    b. It simplifies complexity when building pages, but not applications.

    c. It provides an event-driven architecture for better decoupling between components.

    d. It promotes faster development using out-of-the-box components that are suitable for desktop and mobile devices.

46. **What should a developer use to implement an automatic Approval Process Submission for Cases?**

    a. A workflow rule

b. Process builder

c. Scheduled Apex

d. An Assignment rule

e. Force.com IDE REST Explorer Tab

47. **Which tool allows a developer to send requests to the salesforce REST APIs ad view the responses?**

a. Developer Console REST tab

b. REST resource Path URL

c. Workbench Rest Explorer

d. Force.com IDE REST Explorer Tab

48. **A developer working on a time management application wants to make total hours for each timecard available to the application user. A timecard entry has a Master- Detail relationship to a timecard. Which approach should the developer use to accomplish this declaratively?**

a. A roll-up Summary field on the Timecard Object that calculates the total hours from timecard entries for that timecard.

b. A process builder process that updates a field on the timecard when a timecard entry is created.

c. An Apex trigger that sues an aggregate query to calculate the hours for a given timecard and stores it in a custom field.

d. A visualforce page that calculates the total number of hours for a timecard and displays it on the page.

49. **A developer encounters APEX heap limit errors in a trigger. Which two methods should the developer use to avoid this error? Choose 2 answers.**

a. Use SOQL for loops, instead of assigning large queries results to a single collection and looping through the collection.

b. Query and store fields from related object in a collection when updating related objects.

c. Remove or set collection to null after use.

d. Use the transient keyword when declaring variables.

50. **Where can a developer identify the time taken by each process in request using Developer console log inspector.**

a. Save order tab under Execution Overview panel.

b. Performance Tree tab under Stack Tree Pane.

    c. Timeline tab under Execution Overview panel.

    d. Execution tree tab under Stack Tree Panel.

51. **What are two features of Heroku Connect?**

    a. Real time sync between salesforce and Postgres.

    b. Bidirectional sync, allowing data to be written into SFDC.

    c. Near Real Time Sync between Heroku Postgres and Salesforce.

    d. Displaying data from an external data store via External Objects.

52. **A developer needs to display all of the available fields for an object. In which two ways can the developer retrieve the available fields if the variable myObject represents the name of the object? Choose 2 answers.**

    a. Use getGlobalDescribe().get(myObject).getDescribe().fields.getmap () to return a map of fields

    b. Use schemdescribeSObjects(new String[] {myObject}[0].fields.getMap() to return a map of fields

    c. Use SObjectType.myObejct.fields.getMap() to return a map of fields.

    d. Use myObejct.sObjectType.getDescribe().fieldSet() to return a set of fields.

53. **In a single record, a user selects multiple values from a multi-select picklist. How are the selected values represented in Apex?**

    a. As a set with each value as an element in the set.

    b. As a list with each value as an element in the list.

    c. As a string with each value separated by a semi colon.

    d. As a string with each value separated by a semi comma.

54. **Which approach should a developer take to automatically add a" Maintenance Plan" to each opportunity that includes an "Annual Subscription" when an opportunity is closed?**

    a. Build an OpportunityLineItem trigger that adds a PriceBookEntry Record.

    b. Build an Opportunity trigger that to add OpportunityLineItem Record.

    c. Build an Opportunity trigger that adds PriceBookEntry Record.

    d. Build an OpportunityLineItem trigger to add OpportunityLineItem Record.

55. **What are two uses of External IDS? Choose 2 answers**

    a. To prevent an import from creating duplicate records using Upsert.

    b. To identify the sObject type in Salesforce.

    c. To create a record in a development environment with the same salesforce ID as in another environment.

d. To create relationships between records imported from an external system.

56. **What are two valid options for iterating through each Account in the collection List named AccountList? Choose 2 answers.**

    a. For (Integer i=0; i<AccountList.Size(); i++){.}

    b. For (List L : AccountList) {…}

    c. For(AccountList){…}

    d. For (Account theAccount : AccountList){…}

57. **Which three options can be accomplished with formula fields?**

    a. Generate a link using the HIPERLINK function to a specific record in a legacy system.

    b. Determine if a datetime field has passed using the NOW function.

    c. Determine which of three different images to display using IF function.

    d. Return and display a field value from another object using the VLOOKUP function.

    e. Display the previous value for a field using the PRIORVALUE function.

58. **Which two platform features align to the controller portion of MVC architecture**

    a. Standard Objects

    b. Workflow Rules

    c. Apex Rules

    d. Field updates

59. **A Developer wants to override a button using visualforce on an object. What is the requirement?**

    a. The object record must be instantiated in a controller or extension.

    b. The standardController attribute must be set to the object.

    c. The controller or extension must have a PagerReference Method.

    d. The Action attribute must be set to a controller method.

60. **Which two Apex data types can be used to reference a Salesforce record ID Dynamically? Choose two answers.**

    a. ENUM

    b. External ID

    c. SObject

    d. ID & String

Answers

1.	c	**31.**	b
2.	c, d, e	**32.**	a, c
3.	a	**33.**	d
4.	a	**34.**	a
5.	c, d, e	**35.**	b
6.	a	**36.**	a
7.	a, c	**37.**	b, d
8.	a, c	**38.**	d
9.	d	**39.**	a
10.	c	**40.**	a
11.	d	**41.**	a, b, e
12.	c, d	**42.**	a, c
13.	a, b, d	**43.**	c
14.	b, c	**44.**	c
15.	b	**45.**	c, d
16.	d	**46.**	b
17.	a, e	**47.**	c
18.	d	**48.**	a
19.	a, b, d	**49.**	a, c
20.	b	**50.**	c
21.	c	**51.**	b, d
22.	b, d, e	**52.**	b, c
23.	a	**53.**	c
24.	b, d	**54.**	b
25.	c	**55.**	a, d
26.	c	**56.**	a, d
27.	c	**57.**	a, b, c
28.	c	**58.**	b, c
29.	c	**59.**	b
30.	a	**60.**	b, d

Index

www.ingramcontent.com/pod-product-compliance
Lightning Source LLC
Chambersburg PA
CBHW061737210326
41599CB00034B/6707